The Making of the
American Creative Class

The Making of the American Creative Class

*New York's Culture Workers
and Twentieth-Century
Consumer Capitalism*

———◈———

SHANNAN CLARK

OXFORD
UNIVERSITY PRESS

OXFORD

UNIVERSITY PRESS

Oxford University Press is a department of the University of Oxford. It furthers
the University's objective of excellence in research, scholarship, and education
by publishing worldwide. Oxford is a registered trade mark of Oxford University
Press in the UK and certain other countries.

Published in the United States of America by Oxford University Press
198 Madison Avenue, New York, NY 10016, United States of America.

Library of Congress Cataloging-in-Publication Data
Names: Clark, Shannan, author.
Title: The making of the American creative class : New York's culture
workers and twentieth-century consumer capitalism / Shannan Clark.
Description: New York, NY : Oxford University Press, [2021] |
Includes bibliographical references and index.
Identifiers: LCCN 2020016657 (print) | LCCN 2020016658 (ebook) |
ISBN 9780199731626 (hardback) | ISBN 9780199912643 (epub) |
ISBN 9780190941451
Subjects: LCSH: Labor unions—New York (State)—New York—History—
20th century. | Cultural industries—New York (State)—
New York—History—20th century.
Classification: LCC HD6517.N7 C53 2021 (print) | LCC HD6517.N7 (ebook) |
DDC 331.88/36097471—dc23
LC record available at https://lccn.loc.gov/2020016657
LC ebook record available at https://lccn.loc.gov/2020016658

1 3 5 7 9 8 6 4 2

Printed by Sheridan Books, Inc., United States of America

For Jess

Contents

Acknowledgments

THE RESEARCH, WRITING, and publication of *The Making of the American Creative Class* would not have been possible without the invaluable contributions and support of so many people. I am deeply honored and humbled by everything that others have done to make this book a reality. All I can hope to do is to try to pay forward the debts that I have incurred over the long course of its production in the way that I live my life as a teacher and mentor, as a scholar and citizen, and as a friend and neighbor.

I am tremendously grateful to Susan Ferber of Oxford University Press for her central role in making possible the completion of this book. She saw the potential of this project in its early stages, and she continued to believe in it during a difficult period when my progress slowed. I cannot thank her enough for the time and energy that she put into her developmental editing of the manuscript, which greatly sharpened the book's historical analysis and enhanced its readability. She deserves much of the credit for the final result. In addition, I want to thank Anne Sanow for her meticulous copyediting of the final manuscript and Jeremy Toynbee for patiently guiding the book through the production process. I very much appreciate their indispensable creative labor as exemplary publishing professionals.

I am also indebted to the many archivists and librarians whose efforts and guidance enabled the research that furnishes the book's empirical foundation. The largest share of the archival research was completed at the Tamiment Library and Robert F. Wagner Labor Archives at New York University over a span of roughly fifteen years. Gail Malmgreen kindly provided me with an orientation on Tamiment's rich collections documenting the history of white-collar unionism in twentieth-century New York, while Peter Filardo introduced me to resources that proved essential for reconstructing key aspects of the Popular Front. In more recent years, K. Kevyne Baar, Rachel Yood, Kate Donovan, Sarah Moazeni, and Michael Koncewicz have generously assisted me as I completed the latter phases of my research there. This book would be inconceivable without Tamiment's collections, and the experts and staff who preserve them and keep them accessible.

It is also hard to imagine writing this book without access to the resources of the New York Public Library's Research Division, including the general research library on Fifth Avenue at 42nd Street, the Science, Industry, and Business Library, and the Performing Arts Library. These research libraries were especially important for their holdings of twentieth-century periodicals, ranging from newspapers and general interest magazines to trade journals and union publications. Some of these are exceedingly rare, and regrettably in desperate need of preservation measures if they are to survive for future researchers. Despite budget constraints and other challenges, the librarians and staff do a phenomenal job of making the vast collections available to a diverse clientele. They are why the New York Public Library's Research Division remains for me such an inspiring monument to the idea of public institutions of culture.

Numerous other archivists and librarians at institutions in New York City and around the country also facilitated my research in crucial ways. I am very appreciative of the assistance provided by Steven Van Dyk, Elizabeth Broman, and Emily Orr of the Cooper Hewitt National Design Museum in accessing and utilizing its collections and materials, and by Joy Weiner of the New York branch repository of the Archives of American Art. Lynn Eaton of Duke University's Rare Books and Manuscripts Library kindly expedited my archival research there, which was generously supported by a travel grant from its John W. Hartman Center for Sales, Advertising, and Marketing. I would also like to thank William LeFevre of the Archives of Labor and Urban Affairs at Wayne State University, Jane Stoeffler of the American Catholic History Research Center at Catholic University of America, Laurie Ellis of the Schlesinger Manuscript Library at Harvard University's Radcliffe Institute, Mary Huelsbeck of the Wisconsin Center for Film and Theater Research, and David Kuzma and Caryn Radick of Special Collections and University Archives Division of Rutgers University Libraries for their help in locating and accessing archival materials. Riche Sorenson of the Smithsonian American Art Museum, Christiana Newton of Getty Images, and Gary Bono of the *People's World* were all very helpful in granting permissions to reproduce images in this book.

In the process of writing *The Making of the American Creative Class*, and in the intertwined process of my own development as an historian, I have incurred many other debts as well. I am deeply grateful to Casey Blake for supervising the doctoral dissertation that was the seed from which this book eventually grew, and also to Elizabeth Blackmar, Howard Brick, Jean-Christophe Agnew, and Ellen Baker for agreeing to serve as readers on the dissertation committee. Their comments and criticisms guided me through the subsequent cycles of research and writing that produced this book, and I remain greatly appreciative of the support that they have provided for my career. Nelson Lichtenstein and an anonymous referee for Oxford University Press very generously read a preliminary draft of the book manuscript, and their detailed reviews were immensely helpful as I moved forward with its development. Their referee's reports set the bar against which I measure my own efforts when I am performing peer review. Daniel Horowitz kindly read drafts of several chapters during the intermediate stage of the writing process, and I am thankful for his advice as well. Also, I have an extraordinary debt of gratitude to J. T. Way and Jennifer Fronc—two of the greatest friends a person could possibly have in this world as well as two of the most gifted historians I know—who read multiple draft chapters from every iteration of the manuscript and furnished detailed commentary and criticism. Carl Bon Tempo and Kristin Celello—also both wonderful friends and talented historians—deserve special thanks for pushing me forward with the writing process during periods when I had lost momentum and for always furnishing such wise advice on professional matters.

Since I began work on this book, I have been honored to have had many opportunities to present portions of my research at conferences and symposia. Many individuals have commented on or criticized these presentations in ways that have been invaluably beneficial, and that led me to clarify my analysis or pointed my efforts in new directions. In particular, I would like to thank Regina Bittner, Donna Cartwright, Elizabeth Faue, Dana Frank, Gregory Geddes, Erik Gellman, Roger Horowitz, Lisa Jacobson, Jeremy Kargon, Mark Leier, Julia Ott, Kim Phillips-Fein, Paula Rabinowitz, Adolph Reed, Ellen Schrecker, David Suisman, Heather Ann Thompson, and Mark Wilson for sharing their thoughts on my work.

Institutional support for *The Making of the American Creative Class* was provided by Columbia University, which through its award of the Bancroft Dissertation Prize furnished a greatly appreciated subvention for the publication of this book. Montclair State University, where I have been a member of the faculty since the Fall 2008 semester, has also contributed to its completion through the award of a competitive sabbatical leave at reduced salary during the 2015–2016 academic year as well as through continual participation in the university's Faculty Scholarship Program. I would like to give special thanks to former Deans of the College of Humanities of Social Sciences Marissa Morrissey and Luis Montecinos, and former History Department chairs Michael Whelan, Robert Cray, and Esperanza Brizuela-Garcia for their assistance in making these forms of scholarly support available. Thanks also to my colleague Jeff Strickland for helping me get started using SPSS.

In addition, I am especially grateful for the other friends and family members who have helped to sustain me through the years of research and writing. Julie Lehrman and Mark Sage have been dear friends since we were teenagers in St. Louis, and more than three decades later I am still fortunate to enjoy their companionship and camaraderie. Michael Lewis and Amy Verdon have been exceptional friends for the two decades that I have called Brooklyn my home, and it is difficult for me to contemplate how I could have finished the book without their contributions. I am also thankful for the wonderful friendship of Dermot Ryan, Alexandra Neel, Maggie M. Williams, Eden Schulz, Tom Finkenhofer, Suzanne Weller, Theresa Ventura, Ted McCormick, Alexandra MacWade, and Chris Prince.

My parents, Sharon and Steven Clark, instilled in me from an early age a strong sense of curiosity about the world and the people it, and their hard work created the opportunities that I am fortunate to have had. For better or worse, they never questioned my decision to pursue a career as an historian. I am incredibly grateful for their generous love and support. Also, I am thankful for the encouragement from other members of my family: Sara Clark, David Meyer, Pamela Dickson, Don Dickson, Dan Dickson, and Sarajane Dickson.

No one has been more essential to the completion of this book than Jessica Dickson. Jess learned that I was writing this book on our first date, and living with me has meant living with it as well. She has contributed immensely to it through her exemplary copyediting, her tolerance of the time that I have had to commit to research and writing over the years, and her patience with me during the periods when I have struggled to make progress. Her love amazes me, and I am blessed that we are sharing our lives together. It is why this book is dedicated to her.

Abbreviations

AAAA	American Association of Advertising Agencies (4As)
ABC	American Broadcasting Company
ACLU	American Civil Liberties Union
ADA	Americans for Democratic Action
AFL	American Federation of Labor
AFM	American Federation of Musicians
AFRA	American Federation of Radio Artists
AFTRA	American Federation of Television and Radio Artists
ALA	Artists' League of America
AMC	Advertising Mobilization Committee
ANA	Association of National Advertisers
ANG	American Newspaper Guild
AP	Associated Press
AT&T	American Telephone and Telegraph Company
BBDO	Batten, Barton, Durstine, and Osborne
BMG	Book and Magazine Guild (UOPWA Local 18)
BS&AU	Bookkeepers, Stenographers, and Accountants Union
CAB	Consumers' Advisory Board (within the NRA)
CAW	Congress of American Women
CBS	Columbia Broadcasting System
CIO	Congress of Industrial Organizations (Committee for Industrial Organization 1935–1938)
CIO-PAC	Congress of Industrial Organizations Political Action Committee
CLUW	Coalition of Labor Union Women
CP(USA)	Communist Party (of the United States of America)
CPM	Cost Per Thousand Impressions (readers/listeners/viewers)
CR	Consumers' Research
CU	Consumers Union
DDB	Doyle Dane Bernbach
DPOWA	Distributive, Processing, and Office Workers of America
EEOC	Equal Employment Opportunity Commission

FAECT	Federation of Architects, Engineers, Chemists, and Technicians
FAP	Federal Art Project
FBI	Federal Bureau of Investigation
FCC	Federal Communications Commission
FDA	Food and Drug Administration
FMP	Federal Music Project
FTC	Federal Trade Commission
FTP	Federal Theater Project
FWP	Federal Writers Project
GE	General Electric Corporation
GM	General Motors Corporation
HUAC	House Committee on Un-American Activities
IATSE	International Alliance of Theatrical and Stage Employees
IBM	International Business Machines Corporation
ICCASP	Independent Citizens' Committee of the Arts, Sciences, and Professions
IPO	Initial Public Offering
ITU	International Typographical Union
IUC	Industrial Union Council
JWT	J. Walter Thompson Company
LHC	Lois Holland Calloway
MBA	Minimum Basic Agreement
NAB	National Association of Broadcasters
NABET	National Association of Broadcast Engineers and Technicians
NAM	National Association of Manufacturers
NBC	National Broadcasting Company
NCASP	National Council of the Arts, Sciences, and Professions
NCPAC	National Citizens' Political Action Committee
NEA	National Endowment for the Arts
NIRA	National Industrial Recovery Act
NLRA	National Labor Relations Act
NLRB	National Labor Relations Board
NOW	National Organization for Women
NRA	National Recovery Administration
NWLB	National War Labor Board
NYRF	New York Radical Feminists
OEIU	Office Employees International Union
OPA	Office of Price Administration
OWI	Office of War Information
OWU	Office Workers' Union
PBS	Public Broadcasting System
PCA	Progressive Citizens of America
PKL	Paepert, Koenig, and Lois

PRF	People's Radio Foundation
RCA	Radio Corporation of America
RWDSU	Retail, Wholesale, and Department Store Union
RWG	Radio Writers' Guild
SISS	Senate Internal Security Subcommittee (of the Judiciary Committee)
SOM	Skidmore, Owings and Merrill
SOPEG	Screen Office and Professional Employees' Guild (UOPWA Local 114)
SPG	Screen Publicists' Guild (UOPWA Local 109)
SWG	Screen Writers Guild
TAC	Television Action Committee
TUUL	Trade Union Unity League
TVA	Tennessee Valley Authority
TWA	Television Writers of America
UAA	United American Artists (UOPWA Local 60)
UAW	United Auto Workers
UE	United Electrical, Radio, and Machine Workers of America
UFT	United Federation of Teachers
UOPWA	United Office and Professional Workers of America
UPW	United Public Workers
VOF	Voice of Freedom Committee
WGA	Writers Guild of America
WPA	Works Progress Administration (Works Projects Administration 1939–1943)
WPP	Wire and Plastic Products Company
WRG	Wells Rich Greene

The Making of the
American Creative Class

Introduction

THE LABOR OF CULTURE

ON CLEAR MORNINGS, shafts of sunlight streaked through the eastern windows of the main hall of New York City's Grand Central Terminal. First-class travelers arriving from Chicago on the *Twentieth Century Limited* mingled with suburban commuters from Rye and Scarsdale as they stepped briskly through the alternating patches of light and shadow on the hall's floor. A few hundred of the disembarking passengers who were bound for the offices of the J. Walter Thompson Company, the world's largest advertising agency in the 1940s, headed straight to the elevators that carried them up to the agency's floors in the Graybar Building adjacent to the terminal. Nearly everyone else filed out onto the surrounding streets, joining the swelling throngs of city residents who poured out of the subways as they made their way to their jobs in midtown Manhattan. Thousands converged on Madison Avenue, just one block west of the terminal, where other top advertising agencies and the headquarters of the CBS broadcasting network were located. Trekking a little further to the west, thousands more reached Rockefeller Center, which housed the NBC network and the offices of *Life* magazine, which in the years following the Second World War earned more advertising revenue than any other publication. Dozens of additional skyscrapers and more modest buildings throughout the area contained the offices of other leading national magazines, major book publishers, and many of the city's daily newspapers, as well as the smaller operations of the industrial design firms that styled the goods advertised in the print and broadcast media. In the middle decades of the twentieth century, the blocks surrounding Grand Central encompassed an unrivaled concentration of writers, editors, photographers, artists, designers, and performers, along with larger numbers of clerical, technical, and other supporting workers, who labored to create a substantial portion of the printed words that Americans read, the broadcast programming that they listened to or watched, the images they saw, and the shape and appearance of the objects they used.

Both celebrants and critics of modern American culture have often portrayed this center of creativity as a smoothly running machine. But those who worked in New York's culture industries, and even ordinary people on the city streets, episodically experienced the tensions that existed within the offices of the advertising agencies, broadcast networks, and major publishers. During October 1946, for instance, crowds in the vicinity of Rockefeller Center on weekday mornings or during lunch hours might have encountered picketing in front of NBC headquarters by members of the Radio Guild, a white-collar union then organizing throughout New York broadcasting. Parodying a Pepsi-Cola radio jingle from the period, pro-union employees of NBC and other broadcasters derided their meager weekly salaries, chanting, "glamour doesn't hit the spot, when thirty bucks is all you've got," and carrying signs that asked, "who can afford white collars on our pay?" In addition to highlighting their inadequate earnings, the picketers also hoped to dissuade NBC management from interfering in the Radio Guild's negotiations with CBS, where the union had already won a certification election supervised by the National Labor Relations Board. Myra Jordan, a secretary in the news division of CBS who headed the fledgling union, declared during the protests that her employer had repeatedly refused to "give us our demands because they don't want to be too far out in front of the rest of the industry with regards to salary and conditions of work." Management's recalcitrance only increased the unionists' determination, she continued, to set "a pattern for the radio industry" with "the kind of contract that will not only benefit us, but that will help other radio white-collar workers."[1]

Like millions of white-collar workers across the United States during the Second World War and its aftermath, Jordan had struggled to make ends meet. Wartime regulations strictly limited pay increases at the same time that inflation eroded purchasing power, despite measures to promote price stability. Those who worked in offices, moreover, lacked the opportunities that many manufacturing workers had to boost their pay with overtime. In the summer of 1945, Jordan and three of her coworkers wrote a leaflet calling on CBS employees to join a new "salary increase committee" backed by the Congress of Industrial Organizations (CIO) to press for raises within the wartime system of wage controls. Before and after work, and during lunch hours, they began handing out leaflets in front of network headquarters.

FIGURE I.I Supporters of the United Office and Professional Workers of America's Radio Guild demonstrating at Rockefeller Center in October 1946. From the *Daily Worker* Photo Archive held at the Tamiment Library, New York University by permission of the Communist Party USA.

Gradually the committee grew. Encouraged, Jordan's group embarked upon a full-fledged unionization drive as the newly formed Radio Guild, receiving a local charter from the CIO-affiliated United Office and Professional Workers of America (UOPWA).[2]

Jordan and her fellow unionists at CBS were hardly anomalous. Rather, they were at the forefront of a movement for white-collar unionism that brought the militancy of the CIO into the heart of New York's culture industries. After months of dedicated organizing, in June 1946 the UOPWA

Radio Guild overcame the opposition of CBS management and emerged victorious in their certification election, as a majority of the more than 700 eligible white-collar workers at the network, including many in its fledgling television operations, voted to make the union their collective bargaining representative.[3] As the breakthrough spurred organizing throughout the city's broadcasting industry, executives of other firms leaned on CBS management to resist coming to terms with the union. The pressure from the Radio Guild's public campaign, and a strike authorization by its supporters among the CBS workforce, finally compelled the network to relent in November. The two-year contract settlement provided 25 percent raises for employees ranging from billing clerks to publicity copywriters and production assistants. It also instituted a procedure for reclassifying positions based on their actual work content, which primarily benefitted women at the network who had experienced systemic sex-based employment discrimination.[4]

The Making of the American Creative Class examines the history of people like Myra Jordan, her coworkers, and their supporters throughout New York's culture industries during the middle decades of the twentieth century. It investigates two important and interrelated developments in the modern United States: the expanding production and circulation of a pervasive culture of consumer capitalism, and the transformation of the middle class from a social grouping of proprietors and independent professionals to one comprised primarily of salaried employees. White-collar workers in the print and broadcast media, in advertising, and in the field of industrial design found themselves at the nexus of these two historical processes. With the rise of new systems for the mass production of consumer goods during the late nineteenth and early twentieth centuries, manufacturers searched for ways to boost profits by differentiating their wares from those of their competitors. As these enterprises increasingly relied on marketing strategies such as advertising, branding, and product styling, they opened up jobs for an array of creative, professional, technical, sales, and clerical workers. Rising employment in publishing, advertising, commercial art and design, and, eventually, broadcasting contributed significantly to the overall growth across all white-collar occupational sectors, which were already expanding at a faster rate than blue-collar occupations. Through their labors, white-collar workers in the culture industries cultivated the values, consumption habits, and social practices that defined the emergent new middle class.[5]

Not only did these white-collar workers create cultural representations of the new middle class and its supposed affluence, their own circumstances were often taken as indicative of the working conditions and standard of living of this growing segment of the population. Advertising agencies and the advertising-supported media furnished employment for thousands of people who found writing, editing, illustrating, laying out text and images on a page, improving the appearance of objects, acting, directing, or engaging in other creative activities to be a fulfilling and remunerative means of earning a living. Thousands more who toiled in clerical, paraprofessional, and other supporting occupations in the culture industries aspired to advance into professional and creative roles. Over time, employers' impulses toward efficiency and rationalization in cultural production came into conflict with these workers' expectations of middle-class social status and creative autonomy. In their daily routines in the offices of newspapers, magazines, book publishers, advertising agencies, commercial art and design firms, and broadcasters, many white-collar workers encountered an intensification of labor processes, or a spreading division of labor, in which creative endeavors were broken down into simpler tasks, as employers pushed for greater productivity. White-collar earnings, which had increased at an impressive rate during the early years of the twentieth century, grew at a slower pace after the First World War. As the supply of educated workers expanded relative to demand, the economic premium for many white-collar skills diminished. Although the differential between clerical workers' salaries and manufacturing workers' wages narrowed most significantly, many professional and technical occupations were still affected by the trend.[6] Consequently, many of those employed in the production of America's culture of consumer capitalism struggled to partake in the standard of living promoted through advertising and the media, or to experience the personal autonomy that was portrayed as a prerogative of middle-class status.[7]

America's culture industries were also rife with discrimination on the basis of sex, race, and ethnicity, reflecting deeply rooted historical patterns of social inequality. Women comprised a majority of workers in many clerical occupations by the 1920s, but they were badly underrepresented in technical, professional, and creative positions in advertising and the media. Within enterprises that routinely propagated sexist norms and attitudes to sell goods and services, women like Myra Jordan were systematically deprived of opportunities for career advancement; in the instances when they were able to move into creative roles, they were often writing society columns for the women's pages of local newspapers, or advertising copy for toiletries or household cleaning products.[8] African Americans and other minorities, who were either absent from the depictions of consumerism offered by the mainstream media or represented as humiliating racist caricatures, found themselves excluded from most employment within the culture industries. Only in media enterprises with minority ownership and orientation could they find white-collar jobs.[9] To the extent that the culture industries did offer some people a chance to earn a living through creative pursuits, the career lottery operated on a rigged basis.

The economic catastrophe of the Great Depression further disrupted the already unstable class and status identities of white-collar workers in America's culture industries. Total expenditures by national advertisers plummeted by 35 percent between 1929 and 1933, leading to waves of layoffs throughout all enterprises that depended upon the promotion of consumer demand. The J. Walter Thompson Company reduced the staff at its New York headquarters from 470 employees in 1930 to 335 by 1934, while other agencies made even deeper cuts.[10] Newspapers and magazines also slashed employment, as some high-profile publications, such as the Pulitzer Company's *New York World*, went out of business. Even in the booming new media of radio, in which advertising expenditures continued to grow during the leanest years of the early 1930s, layoffs were not unusual. As in other sectors of the American economy, workers who were fortunate enough to keep their jobs were nonetheless subjected to reductions in pay. Top copywriters and art directors in advertising agencies who might have earned the princely sums of $150 or $200 per week in the late 1920s were working in some cases for as little as $40 weekly by 1933, while secretaries at the leading advertising agencies or the more exclusive magazines, who might have been earning $35 weekly before the crash, often saw their pay slashed in half. In the newspapers' city rooms and the offices of the pulp magazines, where standards had always been lower, the pay cuts drove many workers into dire poverty. Retrenchment also resulted in increased workloads or productivity demands, only adding to the remaining employees' frustration and discontent.

White-collar Americans responded to the crisis in a variety of ways. Some redoubled their allegiance either to corporate hegemony or to the fading individualistic economic and social order associated with the traditional middle class of proprietors and independent professionals.[11] Others were radicalized by their circumstances. Thousands of white-collar workers throughout the culture industries organized new unions to improve their terms and conditions of employment through collective action. Many utilized their creative talents to develop a variety of initiatives, typically sponsored by cooperative, labor, or public patronage, to provide alternatives to America's culture of consumer capitalism. Through these endeavors, they connected to wider movements for social justice and progressive political change. These white-collar activists enthusiastically backed the relief, reform, and recovery measures of the New Deal, which they hoped would form the basis of a more expansive social-democratic order, with a "mixed" economy that included substantial public provisioning of goods and services. They supported the protection of labor rights, and most also favored progress toward racial and gender equality, and international solidarity against fascism. Quite a few of them identified at some point during the 1930s or 1940s with a broad social movement, a "Popular Front," that aspired to unite procommunists along with noncommunist liberals, progressives, and radicals to press for the realization of these objectives.

Because *The Making of the American Creative Class* argues that the emergence of modern consumer capitalism in the United States was intertwined with the emergence of the social formations that furnished the nation's culture industries with their artistic, professional, technical, sales, and clerical workforce, the chronological scope of this book is defined by the epoch of modern political economy often described as "Fordism." From the 1910s through the 1970s, the Fordist mode of capitalism was predicated upon substantial fixed investment in technologies for the mass production of durable consumer goods and the maintenance of adequate consumer demand to keep these investments profitable.[12] Chapter 1 surveys the growth of the white-collar workforce during the first three decades of the twentieth century, and the related development of the culture industries centered in New York. The fundamental relationships that linked advertisers to the media took shape during these years, as manufacturers' need to reach potential consumers fueled the expansion of existing newspapers and magazines, quickly dominated the new technology of radio, and pushed firms to become more attentive to the design and appearance of products. Even as the culture industries swelled to meet the imperatives of consumer capitalism, economic inequality constrained consumer demand, contributing to the onset of the Great Depression. Although business interests attempted to defend capitalist principles and to maintain their control over the advertising and media enterprises, the severity and duration of the Depression incited radical critiques of both the working conditions within the culture industries and the content that they produced.

Chapter 2 explores the development of white-collar unionism in New York's culture industries during the 1930s.[13] The economic downturn hit employees throughout the city's advertising agencies, newspapers, magazines, book publishers, radio broadcasters, and design studios in differing ways. The most militant minority of those who were impacted by layoffs, pay cuts, intensification of labor, and division of labor during the worst years of the

Depression came to understand white-collar work as subsumed within an expanding proletariat with revolutionary potential. A larger contingent of white-collar workers identified with some notion of an emerging new class that, although allied with manufacturing workers and the liberal segment of the traditional middle class in support of the New Deal and progressive social change, was nonetheless distinct from any prior class formations. For other office workers, narrower conceptions of solidarity within their industry, occupation, or profession furnished a suitable basis for collective action within certain bounds of social propriety. In many cases, white-collar workers formed strident professional advocacy associations that only gradually evolved into unions seeking formalized collective bargaining. During the second half of the decade, a majority of these organizing initiatives in New York's culture industries gravitated into the orbit of the CIO. Larger bodies with jurisdictions that were dispersed across the country, like the American Newspaper Guild (ANG) and the Federation of Architects, Engineers, Chemists, and Technicians (FAECT), received charters from the CIO as affiliated international unions, although the New York locals contained a large share of the total membership. Workers in cultural fields that were more concentrated in the metropolitan area, like the Book and Magazine Guild, the Artists' Union, and the American Advertising Guild, became local unions within the UOPWA, which was the CIO affiliate with a general jurisdiction over white-collar workers in the private sector.

These efforts to cultivate a culture of solidarity in the midst of the culture industries' competitive ethos, and to form new organizations through which workers collectively bargained with their employers, unfolded within a complex and contingent process of workplace interactions involving pro-union workers, adversarial supervisors, and other workers who might be apathetic or even hostile to the social and political ramifications of unionization. Under the terms of the National Labor Relations Act (NLRA) of 1935, representations of these office disputes before labor boards and the courts defined the parameters of the rights that white-collar workers might enjoy. This chapter devotes special attention to the organization of a unit of the Newspaper Guild of New York by employees of Time Inc. Henry Luce and his partner Brit Hadden had invented the newsmagazine genre when they launched *Time* in 1923, and by 1937 the firm had expanded to include the iconic business magazine *Fortune, Life,* the *March of Time* newsreels screened in thousands of cinemas, and the identically branded docudrama radio programs on current events. Time Inc. attracted an intellectually and artistically talented staff of people who were integral to the success of the cutting-edge media conglomerate, and many of them were well-compensated relative to employees of other cultural enterprises. Nonetheless, a majority of the employees in its editorial departments still favored unionism, and through their organizing, the writers, researchers, editors, artists, photographers, film technicians, graphic designers, and other employees challenged Luce and his executives' managerial prerogatives. At Time Inc., and throughout the culture industries, white-collar unionists constituted an adversarial subculture within the means of production.

Women frequently took a leading role in white-collar organizing. Because of the systemic sex discrimination that they encountered in the workplace, unionism appealed to many women as a way to confront sexist employers, open up opportunities for advancement, and elevate pay standards to enable more independent lifestyles. The women who became involved in unions like the Book and Magazine Guild, which had a female president by 1941, shaped the course of most of the struggles throughout the culture industries during the 1930s and 1940s.[14]

Additionally, the chapter addresses the complex role of procommunists within the white-collar unions of the CIO. The Popular Front birthed these unions and sustained them through their early development, linking progressives in the culture industries with other Americans who shared their values and provided support during strikes or other confrontations with employers. Yet the association of some union leaders with the Communist Party, or with organizations that it sponsored to support progressive causes, also exposed the unions to attack, furnishing executives and other opponents with effective ammunition. This became increasingly evident at the end of the decade, when the Nazi–Soviet pact shattered international antifascist solidarity and led many noncommunist liberals to distance themselves from the Popular Front. Even though the Popular Front revived during the Second World War, the presence of procommunists in the white-collar unions, and in various progressive cultural initiatives, made both vulnerable to future assaults.[15]

Chapter 3 shifts to the white-collar insurgents' efforts to create viable alternatives to the culture of consumer capitalism. Throughout the early twentieth century, critics had condemned aspects of consumerism that they perceived as manipulative or wasteful. With the onset of the Depression, the more radical among them began assailing the basic function of branding and advertising in buttressing the entire political economy of American capitalism.[16] These analyses found expression in new media ventures based in New York, including Consumers Union (CU), a product testing and ratings institute that published its findings in its monthly *Reports* as well as in other formats; the advertising-free daily tabloid newspaper *PM*; the weekly news-letter *In Fact*; and the weekly photo-journalistic magazine *Friday*. Founded in 1936, CU had a central role in propagating the Popular Front's vision of social consumerism, as the institute's publications and syndicated content for labor and leftist periodicals encouraged Americans to purchase union-made goods, participate in consumer cooperatives, harbor deep skepticism toward adver-tising claims, use graded or generic goods instead of typical branded goods when possible, and demand an increase in the public provisioning of goods and services. Its ideological orientation influenced the launching in 1940 of *In Fact* and *PM*, which eschewed advertising on the grounds that commer-cial sponsorship compromised journalistic integrity, as well as *Friday*, which solicited conventional advertising as it tried to adapt the techniques of slick picture magazines to promote a Popular Front view of the world.

The men and women behind these four media ventures grounded their critiques of America's culture of consumer capitalism in their pre-vious experiences working for advertising agencies or the newspapers and magazines that subsisted on their clients' largesse. As they produced material that contravened the messaging of mainstream consumerism and legitimated a range of social-democratic values and practices, they also enjoyed a de-gree of creative autonomy that had been missing in their previous work. Yet these publications still had to support themselves financially as cultural commodities in a capitalist media marketplace. In addition, advertisers and conventional media enterprises made ferocious counterattacks, enlisting their political allies to level accusations of subversion against their critics, as Congressman Martin Dies' Special Committee to Investigate Un-American Activities did in 1939 when it alleged that CU was a Communist front.

Chapter 4 turns to efforts to transform the material and visual cultures of consumer capitalism. It explores the attempts by those with a creative interest in the design of goods, graphics, and the built environment to de-vise a distinct modernist aesthetic and to obtain adequate public, labor, or other nonprofit patronage to enable the realization of their vision. The Design Laboratory, which opened in 1935 in New York City as the country's first comprehensive school of modernist design open to general enroll-ment, was a model for the kinds of alternative cultural institutions that the white-collar insurgents strove to establish. Initiated under the auspices of the Federal Art Project (FAP) of the Works Progress Administration (WPA), the Laboratory attracted left-leaning faculty and students who disapproved of the streamlined style of modernism propagated by early industrial de-sign entrepreneurs like Raymond Loewy, Norman Bel Geddes, and Henry

Dreyfuss.[17] In contrast, the Laboratory's designers developed a functionalist modernism that reflected their social-democratic ideals of utility, integrity, and sustainability.[18] These aesthetic and social values informed various other educational endeavors undertaken by many of the white-collar unions in New York's culture industries as well. CU also consistently favored the functionalist modernism promoted by the Laboratory, as the institute's writers condemned the expressive streamlined styling deployed by manufacturers of durable consumer goods as wasteful product-differentiation measures that were used to justify inflated prices, but that added little or no utility for the purchaser, or might even conceal basic defects.

While they could promote a functionalist aesthetic in the Design Laboratory's classrooms and studios or in the pages of *Consumers Union Reports*, these Popular Front modernists nonetheless struggled to translate their advocacy into influence over the production of actual objects, visual media, or physical spaces and structures. The New Deal made the government both a patron of culture and a provider of an expanding range of public goods, and the social-democratic proponents of functionalist modernism looked to its public housing and community development programs to procure appliances and to construct buildings that suited their aesthetic sensibilities. Yet the future of these programs seemed uncertain as the New Deal lost its political momentum and war loomed abroad. Labor and cooperative sponsorship, while ideologically attractive, proved to be even more unreliable options as the CIO and other progressive organizations battled to establish their institutional permanence, as the disbanding of the Design Laboratory in 1940 due to lack of funds clearly showed. The government's enlistment of the American home front to fight the Second World War seemed to revive the possibility of public patronage, but Popular Front activists attempting to secure public backing for initiatives like the Advertising Mobilization Committee (AMC) that promoted social consumerism were largely thwarted, as federal agencies instead turned to advertising and media executives, rather than their pro-union employees, to direct the production of wartime information and propaganda.

As Popular Front modernists strove to establish functionalist modernism's cultural significance as a social-democratic aesthetic, they competed with individuals and institutions that sought instead to make it an indicator of elite sophistication and status. Since its founding in 1929, the Museum of Modern Art (MoMA) had showcased the austere functionalist design produced by European modernists, particularly those associated with the Bauhaus, which the Nazis had shuttered in 1933. Throughout the 1930s and 1940s, proponents of social democracy and white-collar unionism mingled and collaborated with representatives of elite cultural patronage, with each group seeking legitimacy through these alliances even as they hoped to establish the hegemonic power of their particular version of modernism. Sometimes key figures, such as the Bauhaus émigré Herbert Bayer, who taught courses for UOPWA educational programs in addition to curating a definitive MoMA retrospective exhibition on the Bauhaus, considered themselves aligned with both groups. Over time, the proponents of high modernism gradually became increasingly successful at defining functionalist aesthetics as a mark of elite taste, with Popular Fronters finding that their efforts to aestheticize the provisioning of social goods were subverted to reinforce the refinement afforded by capitalist affluence. Still, even in the first few years after the war, social consumerism, including goods and buildings with a functionalist modern look, remained a possibility for the American people.

Chapter 5 refocuses the narrative on the experiences of white-collar workers employed within the mainstream of New York's commercially oriented culture industries between 1941 and 1947. As economic conditions improved rapidly with the mobilization for war, the chronic underemployment and precariousness of work during the Depression gave way to the tightest labor market of the twentieth century. Wartime conditions facilitated union organizing even as they restricted unionists' range of permissible collective action. In 1941, the Newspaper Guild completed its organization of nearly the entire core of daily newspaper publishing in the city. The UOPWA made new inroads within other media enterprises, including its expansion into the New York offices of the major motion picture studios and the broadcast networks. Moreover, the Radio Writers Guild (RWG), which remained outside of either the American Federation of Labor (AFL) or the CIO, evolved during these years from a professional advocacy association into an organization that assertively pursued collective bargaining.[19] By the mid-1940s, the RWG was on its way to becoming an influential force within broadcasting, as was the AFL-affiliated American Federation of Radio Artists (AFRA).

The resurgence of unionism within the city's culture industries occurred within the context of a seismic shift toward a more equal distribution of income and wealth in the United States.[20] During the war, average weekly wages for many blue-collar occupations suddenly surpassed average weekly salaries for a range of white-collar occupations that had previously enjoyed greater relative earnings.[21] The impact of this compression and inversion of prevailing pay patterns was most pronounced for clerical, sales, technical, and professional workers within the middle two statistical quartiles of the prewar income distribution, which only deepened the class and status contradictions inherent within most types of white-collar work that had been exposed during the Great Depression.

Wartime conditions only intensified the political polarization of white-collar workers. Between 1941 and 1947, the UOPWA enjoyed considerable organizational growth, with its greatest surge occurring in the period following V-J Day. White-collar progressives beyond the reach of union drives in their workplaces were mobilized by the National Citizens' Political Action Committee (NCPAC), which served as the main CIO auxiliary for middle-class supporters of its social-democratic program, and the Independent Citizens Committee for the Arts, Sciences, and Professions (ICCASP). Through these organizations, white-collar progressives advocated the continuation on a peacetime basis of the unprecedented consumer regulations that had been introduced by the Office of Price Administration (OPA) to police the marketplace. They also pushed for the expansion of Social Security to include nationalized coverage for healthcare and the public provisioning of affordable housing and other goods and services, along with the continued spread of unionization within the salaried middle class.[22]

Simultaneously, many white-collar workers who resented their decline in relative earnings and status flocked to the Republican Party. They dismissed the idea of the global struggle against fascist tyranny as a "People's War," bristled at the imposition of restrictions on their liberty within the consumer marketplace, embraced an ethos of competitive individualism that remained intractably opposed to unionism, and objected vehemently to the increased purchasing power and concomitant rise in social status of minorities and women. Republicans gained House and Senate seats in the 1942 midterm elections, and while Roosevelt won reelection to an unprecedented fourth term two years later, his death shortly afterward thrust the untested Harry Truman into the presidency during an exceptionally volatile moment in modern American politics. Strong turnout by white-collar Republicans combined with exhaustion from the colossal wave of strike activity that followed V-J Day, apathetic abstention by some workers, and the outright disenfranchisement of many others, whether migrants caught up in the tremendous demographic churn that followed the war or minority voters in the South, to generate a Republican landslide in the low-turnout midterms of 1946.

This chapter also highlights the continued vibrancy of Popular Front labor feminism during the 1940s and its profound influence on the surge in white-collar union organizing. The number of women employed in the

United States nearly doubled between 1940 and 1945, and as women came to hold a growing share of white-collar jobs, they also comprised a growing proportion of the activist cadre in the UOPWA and the Newspaper Guild. Increasingly, they insisted on incorporating demands for equal employment opportunity into their unions' collective bargaining agendas. Furthermore, the labor feminists' drive for workplace equity melded with the more comprehensive program put forth by the Popular Front-oriented Congress of American Women (CAW) during the second half of the 1940s.

Chapter 6 examines the impact of the domestic Cold War on white-collar progressives in the culture industries and their unions. As relations between the United States and the Soviet Union rapidly deteriorated during the second half of the 1940s, the attacks on the Popular Fronters within the culture industries became more intense and more effective. In 1947 congressional Republicans, allied with reactionary southern Democrats, passed the Taft-Hartley Act, which drastically curtailed the rights extended to unions under the NLRA. One of the new law's provisions required union officials to sign affidavits swearing that they had no links to the Communist Party in order for their unions to access the services of the NLRB. Also, that year the Republican-led House Committee on Un-American Activities (HUAC) launched a series of sensationalistic investigations into alleged Communist subversion within the culture industries, commencing with a probe into radical influence in Hollywood. Soon, the federal government's official security and surveillance apparatus grew to encompass not just HUAC, the Federal Bureau of Investigation (FBI), and the attorney general's office, but the Senate Internal Security Subcommittee (SISS) and the Senate Permanent Subcommittee on Investigations chaired by Joseph McCarthy of Wisconsin. Outside of government, anticommunist activists mobilized popular opposition to those individuals and organizations associated with the Popular Front.[23]

New York's culture industry workers and their unions were affected in varying degrees by the anticommunist onslaught mounted by employers, conservative activists, and their political allies. For the UOPWA, with its dispersed membership scattered among book and magazine publishing, motion pictures, radio and television broadcasting, popular music, architecture and design, and the graphic arts, the determination of its procommunist leaders to reject Taft-Hartley compliance and to back former Vice President Henry Wallace's ill-fated 1948 presidential campaign on the Progressive Party ticket had devastating consequences. By 1951, most of the local unions that had been built up under the UOPWA banner had disintegrated under the intense repression of the early Cold War. Within the Newspaper Guild of New York, anticommunists gained control by 1948, but continued internecine political strife between the declining remnants of the Popular Front and the new leadership enervated the union. These tensions hindered the union's expansion into broadcasting and into unorganized segments of magazine publishing, and stymied any effort for a unified front to defend those who were targeted by the new inquisition, which included a wide-ranging SISS investigation of New York-based journalists in 1955 and 1956. For the RWG and the other talent guilds in broadcasting, the wave of domestic anticommunism coincided with the transition from radio to television as the principal medium for distributing programming to a mass audience of consumers, undermining the bargaining position of writers, artists, performers, and technicians who earned a living in the industry.

The effects of the domestic Cold War were felt most acutely by those outspoken radicals and progressives who found themselves denied employment within the entertainment, media, and educational sectors—blacklisted—on account of their support for unions like the UOPWA, their endorsement of Wallace's presidential bid, or their involvement with Popular Front organizations. A larger circle of writers, artists, educators, performers, and other creative talent and support personnel with progressive inclinations curtailed their political activities or renounced their pasts in order to keep their jobs. The Cold War purge ensured that conservative values—manifest in both a zealous enthusiasm for consumer capitalism as well as the reinforcement of longstanding social hierarchies of sex, race, and ethnicity—predominated within mainstream American culture during the 1950s, while the progressive social and political values embodied in the Popular Front receded from public consciousness. Advancement toward equality for women or for African Americans and other minorities was blocked, both within the culture industries and in the advertising, news, and entertainment that they produced and circulated.

Furthermore, the attacks on unionism in New York's culture industries represented the leading edge of a much broader management counteroffensive against white-collar organizing throughout the private sector. By the 1950s, significant gains in earnings for white men in professional, technical, and sales occupations, along with new legal and political impediments to white-collar organizing, had combined to stymie the spread of unions throughout the growing social strata of the new middle class. The thwarting of the union impulse marginalized commonplace understandings of white-collar work that acknowledged the persistent reality of alienated labor, or that posited collective means for achieving career fulfillment as alternatives to individualized competition. As the years of postwar prosperity progressed, intellectuals such as the sociologists C. Wright Mills and Daniel Bell, and economist John Kenneth Galbraith contended that the contemporary white-collar condition indicated not just the latest stage in the evolution of capitalist labor relations, but also a coming transcendence of capitalist relations of production in a new epoch of unprecedented abundance.[24]

Chapter 7 explores how the ideal of creativity evolved within the postwar culture industries, with a particular focus on developments in advertising and industrial design. Following the defeat of the Popular Front, many in the advertising and design fields embraced the assertions made by Galbraith and Bell that the substantial increase in earnings for those employed in professional, technical, and creative occupations indicated that a large and growing segment of the population enjoyed a level of affluence that set them in a new realm of freedom beyond necessity. The notion of creative autonomy underwritten by affluence enticed progressive designers who had once identified with the Popular Front as they adapted to the practical impossibility of securing public, labor, or cooperative patronage in Cold War America. As exemplary members of what Galbraith termed the "New Class," these designers created a refined modernism for affluent consumers who shunned the crass styling of many durable goods for the mass market. For a younger group of writers and artists in advertising who were active in the industry's "creative revolution" of the 1960s, the supposition that abundance was diminishing the significance of conventional market impulses legitimated not only greater artistic autonomy and nonconformist workplace practices, but also the idea of advertisements as works of popular art and not merely sales pitches. Yet while their faith in creativity liberated from material constraint facilitated the absorption of countercultural styles and attitudes into the previously staid world of Madison Avenue, ultimately it could not bring about a transcendence of capitalist relations of production and exchange within an industry that remained the nerve center of America's culture of consumer capitalism. The conditions of postwar affluence made it possible for a relatively small number of creative professionals in advertising and design to achieve artistic freedom and independence from supervisory discipline by becoming entrepreneurs or successful freelancers. For the majority of those employed in these fields, however, the 1950s and 1960s brought rising incomes, but the autonomy associated with the creative ideal still proved elusive.

In Chapter 8, the narrative returns to New York's publishing and broadcasting sectors, which experienced significant deindustrialization during the postwar period. Even as intellectuals and social commentators heralded the rising tide of affluence, supposedly epitomized by white-collar workers engaged in cultural production, in fact tens of thousands employed in the city's culture industries experienced considerable economic insecurity and inequality. Network television was born in New York, but by 1953 the completion of transcontinental cable connections enabled programming to originate from studios anywhere in the country. Furthermore, as the networks and advertisers came to prefer filmed rather than live programming for the primetime evening hours, Hollywood quickly emerged as the leading center for television production. ABC, CBS, and NBC kept their corporate headquarters in New York along with their news divisions, and the production of many lower-budget daytime serials remained in the city as well. Most production for primetime, however, relocated to Southern California by the end of the 1950s, taking thousands of jobs, ranging from performers, writers, and directors to a wide array of craft, technical, and professional positions.[25] Although there were sporadic efforts to revitalize the production of filmed television programming in New York during the 1960s, by the end of the decade these initiatives had largely ceased, forcing those who wished to continue working in primetime television, or young people hoping to enter the field, to follow the westward migration.

At the same time that television's geographical division of labor drastically curtailed employment opportunities for one segment of the city's creative class, another confronted the structural crisis of New York's print media, which struggled with declining readership and rising costs. Between 1963 and 1967, four of the city's seven major daily newspapers—the *Daily Mirror*, the *Herald Tribune*, the *World-Telegram and Sun*, and the *Journal-American*—ceased publication. Leading national magazines with editorial offices in the city also fell victim to the turmoil in print, with the *Saturday Evening Post*, *Look*, and *Life* all folding between 1969 and 1972. These closings, along with retrenchments by other publishing enterprises, not only eliminated thousands of jobs, but also restrained salary growth and stymied improvements in conditions for other white-collar workers in the city's media. Even though New York remained the nation's dominant site for the production and circulation of the written and printed word, workers in the publishing sector were adversely affected by deindustrialization during these years.

These economic dislocations in New York's broadcasting and publishing industries coincided with a resurgence of movements for equal employment opportunity during the late 1960s and 1970s. Deprived of their fair share of creative, professional, or managerial positions during the peak years of the postwar boom, women and minorities only started to overcome the barriers of discrimination in white-collar workplaces just as the underpinnings of Fordism began to crumble. Chapter 8 focuses in particular on the impact of second-wave feminism on the city's media, as women organized to combat systemic pay inequities and sexual harassment, and to open new paths for career advancement. Frequently, women fighting for equal employment opportunity backed feminist campaigns against the egregious sexism that pervaded media content, linking the conditions of cultural production to prevailing modes of cultural representation. Efforts to fight sex-based discrimination also exposed class divisions, as some highly educated professional women saw feminist activism primarily as a means of boosting their own individual careers with little concern for the structural inequalities affecting larger numbers of women employed in clerical, paraprofessional, and other support roles.[26]

As the last two chapters of *The Making of the American Creative Class* show, the dismantling of the Popular Front bequeathed legacies that limited the ways in which white-collar workers in New York's culture industries could respond to the pressures of the 1960s and 1970s. The destruction of the UOPWA and the weakening of the Newspaper Guild made it harder for workers to engage in effective collective action to resist the city's cultural deindustrialization and maintain employment levels. Despite important initiatives like the development of public broadcasting and the establishment of the National Endowment for the Arts (NEA) during the heyday of Great Society liberalism, on the whole the possibilities for public, labor, or other noncommercial patronage for cultural production grew more circumscribed over the postwar years.[27] The dearth of new endeavors comparable to the Design Laboratory or *Friday* that explicitly connected advocacy for organized labor and other progressive social movements with the need to challenge America's dominant culture of consumer capitalism deprived writers, artists, and other creative professionals, even those who were high earners, of alternative employment options that might have provided a greater degree of creative autonomy. While a new generation of activists involved with the New Left, African American empowerment, feminist, and gay liberation movements founded numerous alternative cultural projects, they struggled to avoid cooptation by mainstream advertisers, publishers, and broadcasters, which quickly grew adept at appropriating the countercultural symbols of rebellion.[28] The new social movements centered racial, gender, and sexual identities in necessary and vital ways that the Popular Front had not, but these movements, and their supporters throughout New York's culture industries, often had difficulty forging a united progressive front that might have more successfully promoted the cause of equality.

The disintegration of Fordism during the 1970s precipitated substantial long-term changes for both America's culture of consumer capitalism and for those who labored to produce it. After nearly four decades during which income inequality in the United States had slowly but steadily decreased, the trend reversed as inflation and unemployment hobbled the economy, heralding a new age of rising inequality.[29] This crisis in mass purchasing power coincided with the fracturing of the mass market for standardized consumer goods that advertisers and the media had conjured into existence. As early as 1969, some marketing consultants began touting the concept of "narrowcasting" to niche segments of consumers instead of attempting to cast the widest net possible.[30] Technological and regulatory constraints initially limited the application of this strategy to magazines, as titles geared toward specific demographics and lifestyles flourished even as many mass-market publications faltered, and to decidedly down-market media segments like local radio and direct mail. By the 1980s, the expansion of cable television sparked the proliferation of countless new outlets for programming, commencing a gradual erosion in the legacy networks' ratings share and cultural reach. The internet accelerated the dispersal of viewers, listeners, and readers, with the emergence of digital media also generating a wide array of entirely new creative, technical, professional, and support occupations engaged in the production of culture. Yet while all of the transformations in social and cultural practices, political economy, and technology since the 1970s set the formative decades of the creative class apart from the era that followed, the history of white-collar workers in America's culture industries during the mid-twentieth century still shapes nearly every aspect of our contemporary media as well as contemporary experiences of nearly all forms of mental labor.

This book highlights the achievements of white-collar insurgents like Myra Jordan, particularly their successes in improving their pay and working conditions, and their experimentation with a range of alternative models for cultural production that called into question the prevailing modes of American consumer capitalism. Yet it is also by necessity a catalog of missed opportunities, unintended consequences, gross miscalculations, and abject failures. Its purpose is not to romanticize the Popular Front of the 1930s and 1940s, nor to cultivate nostalgia for a bygone era when the unions in New York's culture industries were first ascendant. Rather, by taking stock of the advances and reversals experienced by these earlier generations of activists in the fields of advertising, publishing, broadcasting, and design, this study is intended to offer a fresh perspective on the forms of labor and culture that have come to define modern American life, as well as useful lessons for those who will write the next chapter in the story of the creative class.

I

White-Collar Work, the Culture Industries, and the Origins of the Creative Class

"THE WHITE COLLAR people slipped quietly into modern society," wrote sociologist C. Wright Mills in 1951. "Whatever history they have had is a history without events; whatever common interests they have do not lead to unity; whatever future they have will not be of their own making." To the extent that they had any aspirations, Mills continued, it was "to a middle course, at a time when no middle course is available, and hence to an illusory course in an imaginary society." He declared that "internally, they are split, fragmented; externally, they are dependent on larger forces. Even if they gained the will to act, their actions, being unorganized, would be less a movement than a tangle of unconnected contests." Nonetheless, it was to this "white-collar world that one must look for much that is characteristic of twentieth-century existence," including many of the root causes of the "malaise of our time." According to Mills, the white-collar man had "no culture to lean upon except the contents of a mass society that has shaped him and seeks to manipulate him," while his "isolated position" made him "excellent material for synthetic molding at the hands of popular culture—print, film, radio, and television."[1]

While few of Mills's intellectual contemporaries matched his pessimistic tone in *White Collar*, many of them shared his preoccupations with the political, social, and cultural consequences of the emergence of a "new middle class" of salaried clerical, technical, professional, and managerial employees. Sociologist David Riesman, for instance, argued in *The Lonely Crowd* (1950) that the "inner-directed" social character common in the nineteenth-century United States, which he associated with an "'old' middle class" of independent proprietors and professionals, had given way by the postwar era to an "other-directed" social character that he identified with the "'new' middle class" of "the bureaucrat" and "the salaried employee in business." Through their work habits, their leisure activities, and their approach to public life, Riesman contended, the swelling ranks of white-collar men and women were advancing a profound transformation in which the country was coming to be defined by constant adjustment to the norms of mass culture and an obsessive quest for peer approval.[2] Journalist William H. Whyte Jr. offered a similar portrayal of the new middle class in *The Organization Man* (1956). In place of the traditional "Protestant Ethic" that stressed "the pursuit of individual salvation through hard work, thrift, and competitive struggle," Whyte found that those who staffed the corporate hierarchies and other institutional bureaucracies of postwar America had adopted a "Social Ethic" that made "morally legitimate the pressures of the society against the individual," and posited "the group as the source of creativity."[3] Likewise, sociologist Daniel Bell, in *Work and Its Discontents* (1956), asserted that as economic changes created "a new *salariat* instead of a *proletariat*," the increasing technological complexity of production would guarantee that "the team, not the individual worker, will assume a new importance."[4]

These seismic shifts in ideology and occupational structure received an influential historical elaboration in Richard Hofstadter's *The Age of Reform* (1955), which traced a narrative arc that stretched from the Populist and Progressive ferment of the late nineteenth and early twentieth centuries through the New Deal. Both the agrarian Populists and the Progressives of the burgeoning cities and towns, he suggested, had been motivated by a desire "to restore a type of economic individualism and political democracy that was widely believed to have existed earlier in America and to have been destroyed by the great corporation and the corrupt political machine." Among the Progressive reformers, Hofstadter granted pride of place to independent professionals and proprietors who had not suffered "economic deprivation," but who were "victims of an upheaval in status." Even as anxiety over their status amidst the expansion of large-scale organizations and institutions led them toward a "moralistic" rhetorical style, he noted that "object though they might to the many sacrifices of traditional values that the new society demanded," activists from the old middle class "did not seriously propose to dismantle this society, forsake its material advantages, and return to a more primitive technology." The strength of support for Progressivism demonstrated that it "also appealed—as all the rhetoric about the trusts and the consumer made abundantly clear—to the new middle class of technicians and salaried professionals, clerical workers, salespeople, and public-service personnel that multiplied along with the great corporations," he acknowledged, but members of these groups tended to be followers rather than leaders of the crusades for reform.[5]

By the time of the Great Depression, Hofstadter found that the ironic tension inherent in Progressivism had largely dissolved, as the proponents of an individualistic sensibility utilized the tools of organization to counter the threat that economic and political consolidation posed to their social status. The New Deal had been "a product of that overorganized world which had so much troubled the Progressives," since "the trend toward management, toward bureaucracy, toward bigness everywhere had gone so far that even the efforts of reform itself had to be consistent with it." A cool pragmatism characterized the experimentation of Franklin D. Roosevelt's first two terms as president that had little of the moralistic fervor that Hofstadter associated with Progressivism, and instead focused on the development of new mechanisms for balancing the interests of competing groups. The New Deal had produced a more democratic society, he believed, even if civic engagement had declined among certain segments of the public, most notably the "white-collar class," which had become "more apathetic and more self-indulgent" as it hoped "chiefly for security, leisure, and comfort and for the enjoyment of mass entertainment."[6]

Within postwar social thought, these analyses of the new middle class that emphasized its members' purported tendencies toward alienation, complacency, or conformity coexisted with a second tendency that offered intimations of new varieties of liberation and transcendence. Riesman, for instance, devoted the concluding chapters of *The Lonely Crowd* to the "autonomous" personality type that he hoped would soon become prevalent in the United States. Autonomous people were, in his interpretation, "those who on the whole are *capable* of conforming to the behavioral norms of the society," but "who are free to choose whether to conform or not."[7] In a similar vein, Whyte maintained that it would be necessary to "fight the organization" on occasion. To "recognize the dilemmas of organization society," he explained, was not "inconsistent with the hopeful premise that organization society can be as compatible for the individual as any previous society."[8]

Belief in the potential for white-collar autonomy despite the stultifying aspects of middle-class existence was linked to a series of related assumptions about the unprecedented material prosperity of the postwar years, the changing composition of the American workforce, and the impending impact of technological change. Many commentators hoped that the apparent consumer abundance of the 1950s and 1960s, along with the declining share of Americans engaged in agriculture or manufacturing, heralded an era of productivity increases so dramatic as to render superfluous any social conflict over the distribution of goods and services. Unfulfilling toil would be gradually eliminated, while people pursuing creative activities would feel less and less motivation to maximize their earnings as the marginal utility of additional consumption diminished. Educated professionals—and the young men and women who swelled enrollment in America's colleges and universities in the hopes of joining their ranks—were generally cast as the vanguard in this process of social transformation. Economist John Kenneth Galbraith designated them in *The Affluent Society* (1958) as a "New Class," whose labor fundamentally differed from that of the traditional working class in that it was done for fulfillment and not solely for a wage. From just "a handful of educators and clerics" and "a trifling number of writers, journalists, and artists," who in the mid-nineteenth century United States "could not have numbered more than a few thousand individuals," he contended that the New Class of people "whose primary identification is with their job, rather than the income it returns" had grown exponentially, so that the tally of its members was "undoubtedly in the millions." The "further and rapid expansion" of the New Class, Galbraith concluded, "should be a major, and perhaps next to peaceful survival itself, *the* major social goal."[9]

Supporters of popular struggles for social equality, economic security, and democratic politics had long assumed that the working class, through its unions, labor-oriented parties, and other associations, would be at the forefront of progress. Yet as the postwar period unfolded, many intellectuals began to note what Bell described as the "exhaustion of the left." Wherever the means of production had been collectivized in the name of the worker—whether through the revolutionary expropriation of capital in Soviet Russia or through the compensated nationalizations of the coal and railroad industries carried out by Britain's Labour government—it had failed to empower workers on the job or to inspire their loyalty, Bell argued, because the managers of state enterprises, along with the leaders of communist, socialist, and laborite political parties, continued to push for ever greater efficiency and productivity the same way any capitalist might.[10] By the end of the 1950s, Mills proclaimed that "the 'historic agency' of the working class" had, at least in the United States and other advanced nations, "either collapsed or become most ambiguous." In place of an obsolete "labor metaphysic," Mills asserted that in one country after another, coherent movements of university students and younger educated professionals were already emerging as the clear driving force for change.[11]

Bell eventually gave this vision of transcendence perhaps its most sophisticated exposition in *The Coming of Post-Industrial Society* (1973). In his estimation, "post-industrial society" had five principal attributes: (1) a shift "from a goods-producing to a service economy," (2) the "preeminence of the professional and technical class," (3) the "centrality of theoretical knowledge as the source of innovation and of policy formulation," (4) a "future orientation" that required "the planning and control of technological growth," and, lastly, (5) the "rise of a new intellectual technology" for "the management of organized complexity" that featured cybernetics, systems analysis, and computerized data processing. In sum, these developments heralded a fundamental shift away from the "economizing" logic that characterized industrial society. Thus, while industrial society was "defined by the quantity of goods as marking a standard of living," Bell claimed that postindustrial society was coming to be "defined by the quality of life as measured by the services and amenities— health, education, recreation, and the arts—which are now deemed desirable and possible for everyone." The ascendancy of professional, scientific, and technical occupations pointed beyond conventional class conflict between labor and capital precisely because knowledge was supplanting fixed industrial plant as the critical means of production. As a result, Bell asserted, "the major class of the emerging new society is primarily a professional class, based on knowledge rather than property."[12] While he postulated that the rise of this professional and technical class was driving the transition away from the industrial epoch's economic rationality of individual utility maximization toward a new, postindustrial "sociologizing mode," Bell insisted that this development differed from conventional notions of socialism in which the working class acted as the agent of social transformation. At the same time, he explicitly dismissed the possibility that the bulk of white-collar personnel, including professionals and technicians, comprised a "new working class." "The crucial fact," Bell declared, "is that the 'labor issue' *qua* labor is no longer central, nor does it have the sociological and cultural weight to polarize all other issues along that axis."[13]

The lasting power of these classic assessments of the white-collar condition by Mills, Riesman, Bell, Whyte, Hofstadter, and Galbraith is perhaps more indicative of their prescriptive appeal than their descriptive accuracy. While these thinkers provided invaluable insights into the new middle class, they tended to discount or overlook the actual workplace activism of clerical, sales, technical, artistic, and professional employees. Their analyses largely ignored the militancy demonstrated by white-collar unionists, even though these collective efforts to obtain a higher standard of living and enhanced workplace autonomy undercut any facile assumptions about either middle-class complacency or the impending irrelevance of organized labor. Mills, for one, offered mostly dismissive speculation regarding the attitudes of office workers toward organizing. At the end of the 1950s, as he implored those who toiled in what he termed the "cultural apparatus" to reassert their agency, he gave no hint that this might involve forms of collective action that were grounded in their shared experience of employment.[14]

Furthermore, these commentators' disregard for white-collar unionism or other manifestations of progressive activism within the new middle class was all the more significant given that so many of them had personal experiences with the tumult that roiled America's culture industries during the middle decades of the twentieth century. Bell, Whyte, and Galbraith all worked for *Fortune* magazine during a period of repeated confrontations between the Time Inc. unit of the Newspaper Guild of New York and the media empire's management. While Bell was labor editor for the magazine in the late 1940s and early 1950s, he also filled in on occasion as the acting chair of the Guild unit at Time Inc. in addition to serving on several city-wide committees for the union. Whyte, who had been involved with the Guild since he was hired as a writer for *Fortune*, resigned reluctantly from the union when he was promoted in 1950 to a managerial position with the magazine. Galbraith, who joined *Fortune* after he was sacked from his job with the wartime Office of Price Administration to mollify the agency's conservative opponents, was among the scores of higher-paid writers, artists, editors, and other creative professionals at Time Inc. who challenged management's efforts to exclude them from a general salary increase negotiated by the Guild. Even intellectuals who spent their careers primarily within academia often had indirect familiarity with the Guild's struggles against Luce and his top executives; Hofstadter's first wife, Felice Swados, was a leader in the early development of the Guild unit at the media giant when she was a researcher for *Time* during the late 1930s and early 1940s.[15]

To take in the full measure of the history of labor activism within Time Inc. and throughout the culture industries requires us to look beyond the frameworks and tropes that these postwar thinkers developed, and that have continued to shape popular conceptions of the creative class in the early twenty-first century.[16] We must turn back to the early decades of the twentieth century, to investigate the emergence of the white-collar workforce as well as the genesis of the enterprises that employed white-collar workers to produce America's culture of consumer capitalism. Doing so provides a basis for reestablishing the historical agency of white-collar workers in publishing, advertising, broadcasting, and industrial design as more than either apolitical bureaucratic drones or the privileged beneficiaries of deterministic sociological and technological processes inexorably bringing about the end of labor. It enables us to see and appreciate in their entirety and complexity the struggles of white-collar unionists as well as the efforts of writers, artists, and other creative workers to found alternative means of cultural production. Moreover, it ultimately guides us toward an understanding of why and how these collective and cooperative endeavors came to be marginalized within our popular memory of the white-collar occupational strata, or erased altogether.

The Occupational Structure of the New Middle Class

Mills organized *White Collar* around an evocative occupational taxonomy that included such classifications as "The Enormous File," "The Giant Salesroom," and "Brains, Incorporated." Yet even as he disaggregated the vague but powerful social category of the "middle class" in order to subject it to more rigorous analysis, he was nonetheless unwilling to dispense with it altogether. Mills conceded that clerical workers accounted for fully 40 percent of the new middle class in postwar America, which indicated that it did "not make up one single compact stratum" but rather "a new pyramid within the old pyramid of society at large." Nonetheless, he maintained that this statistical agglomeration shared enough quantifiable attributes and lived experiences to constitute a coherent subject for sociological study.

Within Mills's ken, ownership of property was no longer a meaningful way of establishing class identity, since "bookkeepers and coal miners, insurance agents and farm laborers, doctors in a clinic and crane operators in an open pit" all earned their livelihood principally through the sale of their labor. Although he acknowledged that the gap between the average weekly earnings of manufacturing workers and members of his white-collar middle class had narrowed during the second quarter of the twentieth century, so that by the late 1940s many clerical employees took home less than many craftsmen and even less than some assembly-line operatives, Mills still pointed to the differential between average blue-collar earnings and the average of all white-collar earnings as a mark of distinction. He also emphasized what he characterized as the "psychological" differences between those who toiled in factories and those who toiled in offices. Most white-collar employees, he asserted, exercised "a derived authority in the course of their work." The advantages of "youth, education, and American birth" were magnified at the "wide base" of the white-collar pyramid, and the "white-collar masses" were "managed by people who are more like the old middle class, having many of the social characteristics, if not the independence, of free enterprise."[17]

Labor statistics alone shed little light on the consciousness of class, occupation, rank, or status that workers might have had in a particular place at a particular point in time. Yet even a cursory examination of the composition of the American labor force in the late nineteenth and early twentieth centuries suggests a variety of possible ways in which people might have understood long-term shifts in occupational opportunities. Employment in white-collar occupations in the United States expanded tremendously between 1880 and 1940, with rates of growth far surpassing those for blue-collar jobs. Professional occupations, broadly defined, swelled by 481 percent, and the number of managers jumped 568 percent. Clerical employment surged ahead at the fastest clip, gaining 1,767 percent over the sixty-year interval. Demand for white-collar workers induced an increase in the supply of people with the requisite training and skills. The expansion of the new middle class of salaried white-collar employees was inextricably bound to the transformation of public schooling and the concomitant advance in Americans' average level of educational attainment. The proportion of the population earning four-year college degrees crept steadily upward, although it remained in the single digits prior to the Second World War. Levels of high school enrollment and completion posted more substantial gains. While fewer than 10 percent of Americans aged eighteen to twenty-nine were high school graduates in 1900, more than 40 percent were by 1940.[18]

For relatively affluent families already comfortably ensconced in the old middle class, the decision to take advantage of expanded educational opportunities was an easy one. The choice to keep adolescent children in school was more fraught for families headed by farmers, small-scale proprietors, skilled craftworkers, operatives, and laborers, in addition to lower-level clerical and sales employees. In poorer families, economic necessity dictated that most children entered the workforce as soon as feasible to help sustain the household. Even in many families that were not as hard pressed, the decision to keep teenage children in school was driven as much by the calculation of immediate versus deferred earnings as by intimations of the shifting frontiers of class and status in American society. Allowing children to complete even a portion of high school reflected populist aspirations for self-improvement as well as more anxious determinations to avoid downward social mobility, as technological changes in manufacturing rendered many traditional craft skills obsolete, and the rise of large-scale corporate enterprise pushed many independent proprietors to the economic fringes.[19] As the supply of workers able to fill white-collar jobs increased, the earnings premium enjoyed by employees in many clerical, sales, and technical occupations, and even in some professions, during the first years of the twentieth century declined by the 1920s. While average weekly earnings for male clerical workers in 1909–1914 were 67 percent more than the average for male production workers in manufacturing, by 1923–1929 the premium had contracted to a barely discernable 11 percent.[20]

Systemic sex discrimination in white-collar employment resulted in a gendered division of labor that shaped the entire occupational structure. Although women still participated in the paid labor force at much lower rates than men during the early twentieth century, they comprised a steadily growing share of the white-collar workforce. Yet they tended to be concentrated in occupations with relatively meager pay, very little autonomy, and few avenues for career advancement. As the number of typists, stenographers, and secretaries increased more than ten-fold between 1900 and 1940, the percentage of these positions held by women soared to 95 percent. Within the ostensibly more affluent professions that represented the new middle class ideal, roughly 40 percent of the total growth in the occupational sector during this period was due to the proliferation of teachers and nurses, two fields staffed principally by women. Women consistently accounted for no less than three-quarters of the expanding teaching workforce, but they faced inadequate pay—often less than $1,200 per year in the 1920s—as well as invasive employer scrutiny of their personal conduct away from the classroom, leading many to abandon the profession for clerical employment.[21] In effect the nation's expansion of education access depended on the undervalued labor of educated women whose own employment options were terribly circumscribed. Even with the exploitation and inequities evident in the typical office, for most women in the labor force the conditions were preferable to most of the available alternatives. Furthermore, women in clerical occupations enjoyed a substantial earnings premium over women in factory work; in 1909–1914, average weekly earnings for female office workers were fully double that for women employed in manufacturing, and while the differential narrowed over time, as it did for men, it remained at 48 percent in 1923–1929.[22]

Employers' efforts to increase labor productivity had nearly as great an effect on the evolution of the white-collar occupational structure. Firms introduced new office machinery, ranging from typewriters and letterpresses to keypunch and tabulation machines, which represented a quantum leap forward in the storage and manipulation of information and prefigured the advent of computerized data processing after the Second World War. Yet the average value of office equipment per white-collar worker remained relatively low, especially compared to manufacturing. As late as the middle of the twentieth century, the average fixed capital investment per worker in even a low-wage, labor-intensive manufacturing sector like textiles was well more than double the figure for the typical office.[23] Limited mechanization coincided with schemes to rationalize office work, usually through some combination of measures designed to break down tasks into their component operations, reduce the level of skill required, and intensify the labor process. The implementation of these techniques tended to reinforce the gendered division of labor in many offices, as clerical occupations staffed by women were most likely to be subjected to the most thorough rationalization.[24] These attempts at increasing labor productivity slowed the rate of growth in white-collar employment, but not as much as employers hoped. Lagging productivity growth and modest ratios of fixed capital per worker also characterized many technical, professional, and creative occupations. In many fields, a considerable part of the labor process still involved tedious or repetitive tasks that could not yet be eliminated or substantially reduced by the application of available technology. In research laboratories, for instance, scientists often expended valuable time and mental effort making routine computations or collecting data. In design and engineering offices, many draftsmen spent their days tracing copies of plans and blueprints in the absence of automated means of reproduction. As with clerical work, the limited possibilities for raising labor productivity through technological advancement led managers to look for ways to rationalize mental labor. Furthermore, managers' concerns with productivity pushed them to focus on controlling labor costs, thus reinforcing the drag on white-collar earnings that resulted from the increasing supply of educated workers by the 1920s.

The movement toward professionalization, which was vital to the development of the individualist values and political outlook typical of the upper reaches of the new middle class, was as much a response to these real economic pressures as it was an expression of status anxiety. The associational ethos of professionalization was most pervasive in occupations that required some education beyond high school, but it was also evident among upper-level employees and the self-employed in management and sales fields in which college was not yet deemed essential. The gamut of professional organizations stretched from the American Medical Association and the American Bar Association, which held sway in the traditional core of the old middle class, to a proliferation of newer groups like the American Society for Mechanical Engineers, the American Institute for Certified Public Accountants, and the National Association of Real Estate Boards. To assert that one belonged to a profession was to claim certain forms of expertise that commanded a high salary and that could not be easily rationalized or replaced. Ideally, professional associations established licensing requirements or minimum educational credentials that maintained quality standards while limiting entry into the field. In addition, many professional associations discriminated against women and racial and ethnic minorities well into the middle decades of the twentieth century, reserving the overwhelming share of the most economically and socially privileged positions in the occupational structure for white men.[25] Advertising reified the affluence enjoyed by the top tiers of professionals and managers as a middle-class standard of living that the mass of consumers should aspire to emulate. In reality, these prosperous professionals and managers only constituted a fraction of the white-collar population that they were so often used to represent.

Although the demand for various kinds of white-collar labor, the supply of sufficiently educated workers, the gendered segmentation of the white-collar occupational structure, and employers' fitful efforts to increase productivity all defined the social experiences of the new middle class, the relative impact of these forces varied significantly. Office staffing levels in some sectors or industries grew consistently regardless of the business cycle, while in others employment became noticeably less secure during periods of slackened economic activity. Some personnel managers placed a higher value on formal schooling than their counterparts at other firms. The intensity of sex-based discrimination and the ways in which it was practiced also varied; although employers in some sectors restricted women exclusively to certain clerical occupations or fired women when they married, in other sectors limited numbers of women were able to rise into certain types of midlevel professional and managerial roles. Finally, the long-term economic outlook for a firm or sector influenced managers' interest in prodding the office staff to work harder, or experimenting with labor-saving machinery, or holding the line on salaries.

To the extent that the millions of Americans employed in clerical, sales, technical, professional, creative, or managerial positions during the first half of the twentieth century shared anything, it was their social ambiguity. Even as Mills glossed over many of the complexities and contradictions inherent in the white-collar condition, the limited degree of occupational and social diversity that he did acknowledge in the early 1950s seemed to him just additional sources of apathy and disengagement; the supposed alienation of the new middle class and its inability to move the levers of political power in the modern United States, he concluded in *White Collar*, were the commonalities that unified it. Yet while the forces that shaped the development of the expanding white-collar occupations may not have fused the new middling strata of American society into a coherent whole, they generated neither the indifference nor the impotence that Mills depicted. When confronted with the crises and upheavals of the 1930s and 1940s, many within this broad swath of the population demonstrated that they were entirely capable of robust social, political, and cultural activism.

The Economic Logic of Consumer Capitalism

The creative class of the early twentieth century had much in common with the larger pool of white-collar workers, but its specific development was driven by the economic logic of consumer capitalism. Advances in the scale and scope of manufacturing enabled firms to turn out previously unimaginable volumes of goods. The dazzling increase in manufacturing capacity held out the possibility of a rising standard of living, but it frequently resulted in fierce competition that jeopardized firms' investments in plant and equipment. Assiduously controlling costs offered executives one path toward maintaining profitability. For many, however, measures that permitted price increases proved to be a more promising path toward increased profits. Outright collusion between firms furnished one way to raise prices above the competitive market equilibrium, as did the concentration of market share that accompanied the corporate mergers of the late 1800s and early 1900s.[26] For most manufacturers of consumer goods, however, product differentiation—usually first through branding and advertising and later through the styling of the packaging or the product itself—furnished the most important basis for competition on terms other than price. Implementation of these product differentiation strategies generated employment for several hundred thousand people within the nation's culture industries, who accounted for slightly more than 4 percent of the white-collar workforce in 1920 and about 5.5 percent by 1940.[27]

Branding furnished the initial means for product differentiation. As late as 1870 there were fewer than two hundred registered trademarks in the United States, but over the next few decades the number of trademarked brands surged into the thousands.[28] Successful branding required not only a unique identifier for a product, but also persistent promotion of the brand's positive attributes to justify a higher price to consumers. While much retail and wholesale advertising remained focused on price competition, the growing volume of advertising on behalf of the manufacturers of branded goods instead aimed to diminish competition on the basis of price by cultivating consumers' perceptions of brand quality. By the 1920s, account executives and creative professionals at the more prestigious advertising agencies frequently asserted that overt price appeals in advertising for national branded goods were undignified, but in practice any reversion to price competition generally reflected a manufacturer's inability to establish a strong brand identity in the minds of consumers.[29]

Advertisers utilized a variety of means of reaching the consuming public, including billboards, posters, and myriad promotional items like calendars and playing cards, but the most important were the mass-circulation print media. The enormous growth in advertising expenditures between the 1880s and the 1920s precipitated a revolution in newspaper and magazine publishing, giving rise to the modern print culture of consumer capitalism. Newspapers received the largest share of advertisers' largess. Retail and classified advertising continued to account for two-thirds or more of their total advertising revenue during the early twentieth century, but manufacturers of nationally branded consumer goods also found it worthwhile to advertise heavily in newspapers. The surge in advertising expenditures coincided with innovations in typesetting and printing technologies that dramatically increased the quantity of papers that a publisher could print each day. The most ambitious publishing entrepreneurs of the late nineteenth and early twentieth century, such as Joseph Pulitzer and William Randolph Hearst, took advantage of these developments to establish vast media empires.[30] As circulations climbed into the hundreds of thousands, the major urban newspapers became even more attractive venues for advertising. In the turn-of-the-twentieth century circulation wars between Pulitzer's *New York World* and Hearst's *New York Journal*, as in similarly bruising battles in other American cities, the real prize was the increased advertising revenues that followed readership gains. Publishers and managing editors used advertising dollars to enhance and expand the content of their papers—thereby boosting their employment of reporters, writers, copywriters, illustrators, and photographers along with advertising salesmen, bookkeepers, secretaries, file clerks, and telephone operators—while simultaneously decreasing the share of total costs covered by circulation. Sunday editions, including rotogravure sections with color and heavily laden with advertising, were especially lucrative. In 1880, advertising still accounted for only 44 percent of newspaper revenues, but by 1909 the $149 million that advertisers spent that year on newspaper advertising accounted for 63 percent of publishers' total annual revenues. By 1929, yearly advertising expenditures in newspapers had more than quintupled to $797 million and represented nearly three of every four dollars of income for the daily press in the United States.[31]

Major urban newspapers provided access to the broadest mass market, but the leading weekly and monthly magazines enabled advertisers to target their appeals to the more affluent segments of the buying public with more discretionary income to spend on branded goods that sold at a premium. Most of the top magazines, like the Curtis Publishing Company's *Ladies Home Journal* and *Saturday Evening Post*, or Hearst's *Cosmopolitan* and *Good Housekeeping*, had much higher production standards than the newspapers. By permitting extensive use of color, high-quality illustration and photography, and a virtually unlimited range of typography, these magazines provided the best available canvass for art directors and copywriters in the burgeoning advertising agencies. In addition, magazines served as an ideal medium for the growing field of institutional advertising, which sought to burnish the image of the corporation itself rather than the goods it produced.[32] For these reasons, advertisers paid far more per reader (or "impression") to run similarly sized ads in leading national magazines than in major daily newspapers. Following the newspapers' lead, magazine publishers boosted circulation further by giving readers more media for their money, which in turn enabled them to raise their rates for advertisers. American magazines earned $54 million from advertising in 1909, which was slightly more than half of their total revenues for that year. Two decades later, in 1929, magazines' annual advertising income had jumped almost six-fold to $320 million which constituted 63 percent of their net revenues. The most commercially successful magazine that year, the *Saturday Evening Post*, had a weekly circulation of 2,780,000 and alone carried $52 million worth of advertising.[33]

Most conspicuously, American periodicals of the early twentieth century contained a growing volume of advertisements that represented consumer goods as idealized commodities, often by situating branded products within an aspirational social context. Readers were not just treated to a spectacle of commodities available for consumption, but were rendered into a new kind of commodity—the media market segment—for enterprising publishers to sell to advertisers. Of course, the papers and magazines were also commodities, providing whatever assortment of news, features, stories, and artwork publishers and managing editors believed would appeal to particular reading publics at a particular price. These relations of production and exchange involving the manufacturers and merchants who furnished the bulk of advertising revenue, the owners of the media enterprises that conveyed advertisers' messages, and the consumers of the advertising-supported media formed the sinews of a new American culture. They also furnished the basis for a new model of capitalist development in which manufacturers and merchants were able to sell goods at premium prices above the competitive equilibrium, and the production and sale of culture became big business in its own right.

Advertising agencies came into their own during the early twentieth century as entities especially adept at mediating the relationships between manufacturers and merchants, publishers, and consumers. The earliest agencies founded following the Civil War operated primarily as wholesalers of space in newspapers and magazines. Over time, agencies gradually began to produce advertising, first by writing copy and providing special typesetting, and then by incorporating illustration and art direction into the process. Some agencies even began to offer rudimentary market research services to their major clients, which became more sophisticated by the 1920s as some of the top agencies, like J. Walter Thompson, Young and Rubicam, and Barton, Durstine, and Osborne, added professional psychologists, sociologists, and statisticians to their staffs.[34] As emissaries of many of the nation's leading industrial concerns, agency executives carefully crafted an image of respectability and tried to squelch any lingering associations of advertising with the disreputable claims of carnival barkers and patent-medicine peddlers.[35] Yet to attain the rational objectives of consumer capitalism, the creators of advertising frequently resorted to the suggestive power of irrationality. Selling propositions and their visual accompaniments evoked desires for approval, success, romance, or fame—along with fears of failure and ostracism—to mold consumer preferences and motivate purchases. While the occupational basis of the new middle class remained vague, Americans with enough discretionary income to afford the *Saturday Evening Post, Liberty, Ladies Home Journal,* or *Cosmopolitan* were keenly aware of advertisers' efforts to define their values and aspirations.

Over the first three decades of the twentieth century a substantial proportion of Americans came to accept this new system of consumer capitalism as an apparently viable model for steady economic growth. The costs of advertising and the advertising-supported media added to the cost of producing and distributing goods and services, but as long as the additional revenue gained exceeded the additional costs, companies had every incentive to intensify their use of advertising. Consumer capitalism's economic logic was so pervasive that it shaped the development of even those culture industries, like motion pictures, live theater, the music business, and book publishing, which did not rely directly on advertising revenue.[36] Motion picture studios, for instance, earned their revenues through ticket sales, but few products depended as heavily as the movies on advertising and promotion; these activities were so important to the motion picture firms that they incorporated them into their vertically integrated structures instead of entrusting them to independent advertising agencies and publicists. Movie reviews and coverage of the lives of movie stars became staple features in much of the print media, attracting readers as well as advertisers, and entirely new publications appeared, like the magazine *Photoplay*, to sell the glamorous fantasy of Hollywood to a mass audience. The attention helped to boost motion picture attendance, while celebrity actors became their own personal brands within the industry.[37] Even in the comparatively staid realm of book publishing, advertising and promotional costs accounted for a growing share of total business expenses at most presses. Moreover, the increase in the number of book authors largely resulted from their ability to support themselves by also writing for mass-circulation newspapers and magazines. As the twentieth century progressed, few forms of cultural endeavor in the United States remained untouched by the spread of consumer capitalism.

New Media and New Aesthetics

The tendency for new communications technologies, new enterprises, new groups of workers, and new cultural paradigms to be incorporated into the already established patterns of consumer capitalism in the United States was demonstrated in the 1920s by two developments in particular. One was the rapid spread of the new medium of radio broadcasting, which within a little more than a decade of the first regularly scheduled broadcasting over the AM frequency band had become a rival to the established print media. The other was merchants' quest to devise new design strategies for visually representing modernity to consumers. While the spectacular growth of radio may have been more dramatic in its impact than the diffuse germination of variants of modernism suitable for application to advertising, packaging, and products, the emergence of both broadcasting and industrial design had significant ramifications for the culture industries and the burgeoning creative class. The ascent of these two fields completed the core group of culture industries most closely linked to the propagation of twentieth-century American consumer capitalism. Subsequently, the assimilation of broadcasting and industrial design into the existing systems of advertising-supported cultural production also determined the range of possible employment opportunities and work experiences for the majority of writers, artists, performers, and others engaged in creative pursuits.

Despite how entrenched the advertising-supported model of commercial broadcasting became, first with radio and later with television, at the outset Americans had varying ideas about how the new communications technology should be controlled and used. The first stations commenced regularly scheduled broadcasting in 1920, and by the middle of the decade the number of stations had already grown into the hundreds. With no established formats for programming, early radio broadcasters improvised a wide assortment of entertainment and information. Many newspaper publishers launched stations in the hopes that the programming they offered, which sometimes included free reporting from the papers, would serve to promote their print sales.[38] Department store owners also initiated many of the early stations in the hopes that programming offered as a public service would boost their sales. Universities and colleges began experiments with educational broadcasting. Organized labor founded several stations, including WCFL, operated by the Chicago Federation of Labor, and WEVD of New York City, which took its call letters from the initials of Socialist Party leader Eugene Victor Debs. New York City pioneered the concept of public broadcasting with its municipally owned station WNYC. Additionally, the relatively low initial cost of getting on the air led many small businessmen, as well as a colorful assortment of eccentrics, to set up stations as public platforms for their own political, social, religious, and lifestyle views. Until the late 1920s, the one commonality most of these stations shared, despite the diversity of their owners, was that they did not generate much revenue, since most stations did not yet operate on the model of regularly selling advertising time.[39] The position that radio should remain a public service unfettered by advertising had significant support in the federal government through the middle of the decade, most conspicuously from Secretary of Commerce Herbert Hoover. Even executives at the leading advertising agencies were wary of radio initially, fearing that listeners would find the broadcasting of overt advertising appeals as a crass intrusion into the intimacy of the domestic sphere.[40]

Nonetheless, powerful interests were already promoting the commodification and centralization of the new medium. By 1919, as radio technology advanced toward standards of fidelity and reliability that would make regular broadcasting feasible, the principal corporate owners of the key patents—General Electric, American Telephone and Telegraph (AT&T), and Westinghouse—pooled their intellectual properties by forming the Radio Corporation of America (RCA) to mass-produce receiving equipment for consumers as well as to foster the development of broadcasting capacity. As programming became more widely available and its quality improved, demand for radio sets skyrocketed. Americans bought $60 million worth of radio equipment in 1922, increasing to $350 million in 1924 and $850 million in 1929.[41] While RCA profited handsomely from this boom, the company also began to experiment with ways to generate revenue from broadcasting. During 1924 and 1925, the AT&T station in New York City, WEAF, pioneered the sale of airtime to commercial sponsors of entertainment programming. At the same time, AT&T engineers devised heavy-duty coaxial transmission cables to link multiple stations, so that programs originating in one location could be broadcast live to audiences from a station hundreds or thousands of miles away. To capitalize on these developments, in 1926 RCA founded the National Broadcasting Company (NBC) as the first radio network in the United States, consisting of a handful of owned-and-operated stations that the new entity inherited from RCA, AT&T, GE, and Westinghouse along with a much larger number of independently owned affiliates. By 1928, NBC offered two streams of programming, Red and Blue, both of which originated from flagship stations (WEAF and WJZ) in New York City. The Columbia Broadcasting System (CBS), which competed against NBC as a nationwide network, originated shows in New York as well, while numerous regional networks coalesced during the late 1920s and early 1930s. While fewer than 20 percent of stations belonged to a network, they tended to be the broadcasters that reached the largest audiences; by 1935, all but four of the sixty-eight stations that transmitted with 5,000 or more watts of power were network affiliates.[42]

Additionally, shifts in federal regulatory policy abetted the commodification of the airwaves. By the middle of the 1920s, the proliferation of broadcasters had resulted in radio cacophony, as station operators proved unwilling to share the limited number of frequencies allocated by the Department of Commerce. Listeners in more populated areas attempting to tune in to a particular station often encountered interference or found it drowned out entirely by another broadcaster with a stronger transmitter. To address the problem, in 1927 Congress authorized a new Federal Radio Commission—forerunner of the Federal Communication Commission (FCC)—with regulatory and licensing powers as well as a mandate to reallocate stations across a broader swath of the electromagnetic spectrum for the purpose of terrestrial broadcasting. As the new agency went about imposing order, it moved away from the noncommercial idealism evident in the federal government's earlier radio policy. Major stations in the incipient networks and stations with influential backers—such as WGN in Chicago, which took its call letters from the "World's Greatest Newspaper" slogan of its owner, the *Chicago Tribune*—received licenses to broadcast as "clear-channel" stations. Enabled to use transmitters as powerful as 50 kilowatts, these stations dominated their assigned frequencies for hundreds of miles. At the same time, educational, religious, labor, and other nonprofit stations had to justify why they should remain on the air at all; those stations that did not have their licenses revoked were usually reassigned to marginal frequencies, forced to share frequencies with other stations, limited in their hours of operation, and restricted to low-wattage transmission. Not surprisingly, many of these stations eventually discontinued operations.[43] By effectively privatizing radio frequencies within certain geographical bounds, federal policy secured the value of broadcasters' investments, and guaranteed that the continued commodification of broadcasting would become even more lucrative.

As stations began to sell airtime on a regular basis, and as the rise of the networks gave manufacturers and merchants another means of addressing consumers on a mass basis, advertising agencies began to move into radio. Those agencies that most actively pursued radio opportunities during the crucial years of the late 1920s and the early 1930s—including J. Walter Thompson, Young and Rubicam, and Batten, Barton, Durstine, and Osborne (BBDO)—leapt ahead of their rivals. Low initial rates from the networks elicited the agencies' interest, as an hour of coast-to-coast network time on NBC Red for a sponsored program in 1929 was roughly equivalent in cost to a full-page, four-color ad in the *Saturday Evening Post*. Sponsors' expenditures for network radio time equaled just $18,700,000 that year, but climbed to $39,100,000 in 1932, and $56,200,000 by 1937.[44] While these agencies adhered to the established logic of branding, there were fundamental differences in its application to broadcasting. Most significantly, advertising agencies quickly assumed direct responsibility for the production of sponsored programming—whether the format was music, variety, comedy, or melodrama—whereas newspaper and magazine editors still supervised the production of content.[45] Agencies, or independent "package" producers working on behalf of agencies or sponsors, often rented studios and other facilities owned by the networks or by major stations, but exercised complete supervisory control over the directors, writers, actors, and other performers on a program. Yet agencies also carefully insisted on the casualization of most of these culture workers: contractually, they were simply expediters of talent for sponsors, although not technically employers of the men and women whose creativity actually made the shows possible.

The transformative advent of radio exemplified the technological and cultural modernity that manufacturers and merchants were increasingly trying to convey visually through design. On the most elementary level, imbuing products with an aura of novelty or innovation was a logical way to distinguish them from competing goods. For the nondurable goods like groceries, drugs, toiletries, and household products that had always depended most on branding, this could be accomplished through advertising graphics and layout, labeling, and packaging. The redesign of durable goods, whether furniture and housewares, or newer home appliances, was more complicated, but it likewise reflected manufacturers' desire to use modern styling as a product differentiation strategy for coping with increasingly saturated markets. Ultimately, most firms would gravitate toward a streamlined visual idiom for representing the modernity of consumer capitalism.

From the outset the connotations of modernist aesthetics in the United States were contested, as radicals and progressives hoped to use the new artistic techniques to provoke a fundamental reimagining of life in the machine age and to galvanize support for socialist and social-democratic movements. The 1913 Armory Show in New York City, which constituted the major debut in America for the first wave of European modernist innovators as well as their domestic counterparts, was organized by a group that included the painter John Sloan, who also designed the set for the Industrial Workers of the World's Paterson Strike Pageant at Madison Square Garden that same year and created numerous cover illustrations for the radical journal *The Masses*.[46] Photographer Lewis Hine, another important member of America's founding generation of modernist artists, used his talents to promote labor reform, creating a series of stunning photomontages for a poster campaign by the National Child Labor Committee. With radical groups like the Socialist Party and the Wobblies pummeled by official repression during the First World War, and progressive reform organizations losing momentum in the early 1920s, the commercial artists employed to propagate consumer capitalism had an opening to appropriate modernist visual culture. Some magazine advertisements of the 1920s utilized cubist or constructivist graphic elements, but these tended to be relatively rare, as most art directors and clients worried that ordinary consumers might find them freakish rather than forward-looking. More common during the second half of the decade was the lavish expressionism inspired by the Exposition Internationale des Arts Décoratifs et Industriels Modernes held in Paris in 1925. The Art Deco style provided advertisers with a vivid means for enticing consumers to aspire to a luxurious conception of modernity, but perhaps the most pervasive influence discernable in advertising art was a subtler aesthetic modernization, as illustrations evolved from heavily detailed oil paintings to simpler wash drawings or photographs.[47]

The incorporation of modern design elements into durable goods proved more challenging. Well into the early twentieth century, many manufacturers of existing lines of consumer goods relied on the eclectic styles that had gained popularity during the Gilded Age. Makers of durable goods like living-room furniture, sewing machines, and cast-iron stoves had found that a variety of familiar decorative forms—such as cabriole legs, rococo handles, and elaborate scrollwork—were compatible with serial production methods. These design elements harkened back to historical notions of aristocratic leisure, bourgeois proprietorship, or artisan craft labor, as numerous critics noted, instead of signifying modernity.[48] Moreover, no customary typeform existed to dictate the shape or appearance of new consumer goods. The invention of reliable nickel-chromium electric heating elements, for example, made possible a range of new household electrical appliances, from toasters and waffle irons to electric kitchen ranges and electric heaters. Advances in alternating-current motors likewise facilitated the development of other new appliances, including electric washing machines, vacuum cleaners, and refrigerators. As manufacturers struggled at first simply to mass-produce electrical goods that functioned properly, appearance remained a secondary concern and these appliances exhibited a starkly utilitarian aesthetic.[49]

The automobile—the single most important mass-produced durable consumer good—illustrated most clearly the drawbacks of both historicist eclecticism and utilitarianism that modernist designers hoped to overcome. As the Ford Motor Company revolutionized auto manufacturing by introducing the inexpensive Model T and developing a gargantuan assembly line system to mass-produce the cars, Ford engineers and die-makers designed visible body and chassis components to be as cheap as possible, regardless of the consequences for the appearance of the assembled vehicle. Every Model T received a quick-drying black enamel finish. Although nominally a branded good, Model T advertising stressed its price—cut by 70 percent between 1913 and 1923—and in the early 1920s Ford suspended all advertising for more than a year. Nonetheless, millions of Americans chose it as their first car, and by 1921 the Model T accounted for half of all new car sales in the United States.[50]

Ford's competitors, particularly General Motors (GM), deployed product differentiation strategies to undermine its dominant position. Beginning in the early 1920s, GM made heavy use of advertising to cultivate a refined image of aspiration and advancement, which was reinforced by a marketing plan in which the company's five automotive brands—Chevrolet, Pontiac, Oldsmobile, Buick, and Cadillac—constituted a status hierarchy that allowed successful consumers to graduate from one GM product to another. The company's effective branding program also relied upon actual changes in product styling and design. GM took advantage of manufacturing innovations, such as the advent of quick-drying Duco color paints and the development of more powerful metal presses that could stamp curved fender and body panels, to emulate some of the visual elements of craft-made vehicles in its mass-production brands. Ford initially responded by cutting the price of its coupe to $290 in 1924, but made no changes to the car's design. Two years later, as GM and other automakers cut more deeply into sales, Ford began offering the Model T in colors other than black. Finally, in 1927, when Ford's domestic market share had shrunk to 15 percent and GM's share had grown to 40 percent, the company discontinued Model T production and furloughed tens of thousands of workers while it spent $18 million retooling its rigidly specialized production lines for the new Model A.[51]

Commentators throughout the culture industries took note of what one wag quipped was the "most expensive art lesson in history," although many durable goods manufacturers looked beyond GM's vaguely historicist designs of the 1920s toward a distinctively modern look. The applied ornamentation and angular shapes and motifs associated with Art Deco offered one option that many makers of furnishings and housewares dabbled with in the second half of the decade, although many of these design elements remained ill-suited for mass-produced appliances. By the late 1920s and early 1930s, a group of commercial artists who began describing themselves as "industrial designers" started to address the shortcomings in the typeforms and styling of numerous durable goods, developing in the process the expressionistic streamlined variant of modernism that pervaded much of American material culture at mid-century. Many of them, like Raymond Loewy and Walter Dorwin Teague, had worked for years as illustrators and graphic designers in advertising before reinventing themselves as practitioners of a new profession. Others, such as Norman Bel Geddes and Henry Dreyfuss, had started out as theatrical set designers and had moved into product redesign by way of their window displays for prominent New York retailers. Typically, these artistic entrepreneurs portrayed themselves as celebrity craftsmen capable of encompassing all of the disparate skills involved in the creation of mass-produced consumer goods, highlighted in some cases by designers' "signatures" on models of washing machines, refrigerators, and kitchen stoves. For their clients, streamlining provided a superficial gloss of organic unity that evoked technological progress and social order under corporate auspices. While these designers enhanced the actual functionality of some goods, manufacturers were usually most impressed by the impact of product redesign on sales, and they often engaged designers for routine model makeovers that promoted artificial style obsolescence as a way of stimulating consumer demand.[52]

Much as the rise of radio brought aspects of audio culture and habits of listening into the ambit of business, the emergence of industrial design integrated material culture and the sensations of seeing and touching objects into the system of consumer capitalism. Radio and industrial design both amplified the influence that manufacturers and merchants had over the lived experiences of ordinary people. Advertising jingles and the routines of popular broadcast entertainers, along with streamlined appliances and stores, became embedded within the American vernacular, and demonstrated an increasing centralization in the production of American culture.[53]

New York's Culture Industries and Their Workers

One of the consequences of this centralization was that an increasing number of the nation's leading advertising, publishing, broadcasting, and design firms came to be based in New York City. By 1930, the metropolitan area's 56,000 white-collar employees in publishing accounted for 19 percent of the nationwide total for the sector, while the area's 16,000 white-collar advertising employees constituted 25 percent of that industry's national total. Even in the nascent field of broadcasting, with a small but growing workforce, the New York region's 3,000 white-collar workers accounted for 25 percent of the total for the industry.[54] As New York solidified its position as the nation's financial capital and became a location of choice for corporate headquarters, advertising agencies, mass-circulation magazines, radio producers, and design consultants all benefitted from proximity to their patrons. The phenomenal population growth in the city and its surroundings during the early twentieth century made the New York metropolitan area the largest media market in the United States; the top-circulating daily newspapers in the city were among the nation's circulation leaders, and the New York region accounted for a significant share of the readership base for key magazines. Additionally, the city became a magnet for young writers and artists from across the country. Whether they were drawn by New York's flourishing bohemia, its opportunities for remunerative employment, or both, by the 1910s and 1920s access to its expanding pool of creative people provided another compelling incentive for cultural enterprises to do business in the city. Only motion pictures bucked the trend, as production migrated from its original home in New York to southern California to take advantage of the open spaces and mild weather. Nonetheless, even the major movie studios elected to keep their corporate headquarters located in Manhattan.

Newspaper and magazine publishing accounted for the largest share of advertising expenditures as well as the greatest number of white-collar employees during this period. The print media was also a highly dynamic sector, with established periodicals enjoying steady growth even as a range of new publications quickly established themselves as circulation leaders. In the local news market, the biggest event was the launching of the *Daily News* as the city's first tabloid in 1919. Touting itself as "the Picture Newspaper," the *News* made far more extensive use of photography than its rivals, with stories often reported entirely through images and pithy captions.[55] Its success incited the Hearst chain to start its own morning tabloid, the *Daily Mirror*, in 1924, and by the late 1920s the weekday circulation of the *News* passed the 750,000 mark, making it the city's top-circulating paper. The *News* pitched itself to potential advertisers as a means to "tell it to Sweeney," the archetypical ethnic worker who had recently become a reliable consumer of nationally branded goods. In the magazine field, a comparable broadening of the consumer market was evident in *True Story* magazine, founded in New York in 1919 by health enthusiast and *Physical Culture* publisher Bernarr Macfadden. *True Story* pioneered confessional-style pulp fiction that had acquired a circulation of more than 2,000,000 copies by 1927. Macfadden billed the publication to advertisers as a way to reach a vast nationwide market of working-class women, and while space buyers still had reservations about their value as potential customers, these apprehensions began to ease as the circulation figures—generated entirely from newsstand sales—continued to climb. By the end of the 1920s, *True Story* ranked among the top ten American monthly magazines in terms of number of pages of advertising carried, and in 1930 a *True Story* radio serial made its debut on CBS.[56]

New York also presented opportunities for cultural entrepreneurs interested in founding new publications oriented toward more sophisticated readers. Of these upscale magazines that came on the scene during the 1920s, the two most successful were *Time* and the *New Yorker*. Recent Yale graduates Henry Luce and Brit Hadden started *Time* in 1923 as a current affairs journal and in the process virtually invented the modern news magazine. Although the magazine covered a mix of domestic politics, international relations, business news, profiles of powerful people, and cultural affairs intended to appeal to the affluent and educated, its terse, snappy style and capsule approach to reporting shared a penchant for brevity with the *Daily News*. Although Luce and Hadden moved most of the editorial operations to Cleveland in 1926, within several years they returned to New York to be closer to advertisers as well as to creative talent. By 1930, *Time* had a weekly circulation of only 350,000, but its readership was so desirable to advertisers that it ranked third among weekly magazines in the total number of pages of advertising carried.[57] Harold Ross targeted a similarly affluent and educated readership when he launched the *New Yorker* in 1925. While the magazine's format, with its combination of literary fiction and journalism, was hardly new, the *New Yorker* offered its thoroughly modern cultural sensibilities and an erudite tone, due to talented writers such as E. B. White, James Thurber, and Dorothy Parker. Like *Time*, it had a circulation that was modest in size compared to that of many other national magazines, but flush with discretionary income; consequently, the *New Yorker* carried the second most pages of advertising of any weekly magazine by 1930.[58]

Although the concentration of publishing and corporate headquarters in New York had long made the city the leading center of American advertising, it was during the 1920s that Madison Avenue clearly asserted its national dominance. Agencies based in New York accounted for the largest share of total national billings to clients, but as late as 1926 the agency with the second highest billings, the venerable N. W. Ayer and Company, was based in Philadelphia, while the agency with the third highest billings, Lord and Thomas, had its home office in Chicago. Yet the growth of lucrative new publications like the *Daily News, True Story, Time,* and the *New Yorker,* along with the establishment of New York as the hub of operations for NBC and CBS, induced major agencies based elsewhere to conduct a greater proportion of their business through their branch offices in Manhattan. The creation, sale, and placement of a substantial quantity of the advertising for nationally branded goods became increasingly concentrated in a handful of skyscrapers in the vicinity of Grand Central Terminal. Moreover, the ascendency of New York advertising in the late 1920s coincided with a spike in compensation levels for the top account executives and copywriters, many of whom earned in excess of $12,000 annually. The tendency toward upper-class settings and elements in so much of the advertising produced by Madison Avenue in these years reflected not just an aspirational ethos, but also the difficulties that some advertising professionals had in imagining an ideal consumer beyond their own realm of privilege.[59]

The salaries and lifestyles of those at the pinnacle of advertising were barely more representative of the bulk of workers in New York's culture industries than they were of the mass of American consumers. While some of the corporate largess did trickle down, making many clerical and other low-level support jobs in advertising agencies more lucrative than comparable positions in other sectors, only a handful of city's advertising employees enjoyed the affluence of the top personnel working on the leading national accounts at agencies like J. Walter Thompson or BBDO. In the print media, the income gap between the highest paid employees and the majority of workers was even more glaring. The publishers and managing editors of the most successful newspapers and magazines, along with the star authors and columnists, earned salaries on a par with those of the most handsomely compensated advertising executives. Producing the editorial matter between the ads, however, required a sizeable pool of writers, editors, and layout staff with fairly modest salaries on average, along with substantial numbers of clerical workers who made up more than half of the white-collar workforce at many of the city's publications. This disparity was particularly evident for the relatively few women who did obtain jobs as editors, writers, artists, designers, publicists, marketing consultants, and other creative professionals. According to a survey conducted by the American Woman's Association (AWA), successful professional women in New York's culture industries had a median annual salary in 1929 of roughly $3500, far greater than the $900 citywide median salary for clerks that year and the $1300 citywide median salary for bookkeepers.[60] Yet this figure was only a fraction of the salaries paid to most male professionals in the culture industries with comparable experience and talent. Even within the culture industries devoted to promoting the notion of a "New Era" of mass consumption to which all Americans might aspire, the reality of economic inequality was too blatant to be indefinitely ignored.

The Crisis of Consumer Capitalism and the Crisis of the Creative Class

By the end of the 1920s, the unequal distribution of purchasing power in the United States imposed a drag on consumer demand that was too weighty a burden for advertisers' constant enticements to overcome. While corporations and investors had used profits to expand productive capacity, lagging incomes for most workers made it difficult for them to buy the surfeit of goods. The American auto industry, for example, set a sales record of five million new cars in 1929—a figure that would not be surpassed until after the Second World War—although manufacturers had installed plant capacity for eight million units annually.[61] Easier access to consumer credit enabled many people to live beyond their means, obscuring the full impact of income inequality. During the second half of the decade, speculative bubbles in real estate and in securities also artificially boosted the economy. The stock market collapse that commenced with the October 1929 crash was not a cause of the protracted period of deep retrenchment that followed so much as a symptom of the structural imbalances of an economy that was predicated on mass consumption but that did not provide the conditions necessary to sustain adequate demand. The Great Depression was a crisis of consumer capitalism as a model for economic growth, and subsequently a crisis for the creative class as well.

In the first few months after the crash, many manufacturers and merchants maintained their promotional expenditures, dampening the immediate impact on the advertising agencies and the media. During the first half of 1930, the *Saturday Evening Post* carried only 1.5 percent fewer pages of advertising than the previous year, while the number of advertising pages in the *New Yorker* was off 3.8 percent. A few lucky titles bucked the trend entirely. *Time* posted a stunning 43.5 percent increase in its advertising pages in the first six months of 1930 over 1929, while *True Story* posted a gain of 10 percent.[62] As unemployment soared and consumer spending evaporated, however, most purveyors of consumer goods and services slashed their advertising appropriations. Many firms reverted to cutthroat price competition in a desperate attempt to attract customers, which only fueled the destructive deflationary spiral. The advertising that was produced during the early 1930s became increasingly shrill in an attempt to grab the attention of those people who still had money in their purses and wallets. Crass appeals that borrowed from the comic strips and tabloids played on the fears and anxieties of Americans.[63]

Periodicals also resorted to intensified price competition as they fought over advertisers' rapidly shrinking budgets, repeatedly reducing their rate per thousand reader impressions (CPM) as well as their circulation guarantees. The Curtis Publishing Company, for instance, whose *Saturday Evening Post* remained the nation's leading advertising medium, had its advertising revenue for 1931 plummet 24 percent from the previous year. By 1932, one index showed a 43 percent decline in national advertisers' expenditures in magazines from the peak attained in 1929. Even titles like *True Story* and *Time* suffered contractions of 30 percent in their advertising lineage between March 1932 and March 1933. America's newspapers endured similar losses, with total advertising revenue for the nation's daily papers falling from $797 million in 1929 to $429 million in 1932. For the agencies, these precipitous declines in advertising outlays for print media translated directly into equally deep cuts in the commissions that sustained them.[64]

The emerging fields of radio and industrial design fared somewhat better during the crisis. In broadcasting, improvements in production and transmission facilities, the honing of formulas for sponsored programs, and the inauguration of the first rating services to give sponsors a metric for valuing airtime all made the new media more attractive for advertisers. Total advertising expenditures for radio, including national sponsored programs on NBC and CBS, sponsored programs on regional networks or unaffiliated stations, and local spot advertising, increased continuously; by 1937 they had reached $150 million although that was, by comparison, still only a quarter of national newspaper advertising expenditures that year. Even as the commercial exploitation of the ether intensified, the persistence of depressed economic conditions nonetheless limited broadcasters' revenue potential. As late as 1934, the national networks were only able to sell about a third of their total combined airtime to sponsors, and not until 1937 did NBC succeed in selling its entire primetime schedule, with the exception of Saturday evenings, on its top-rated Red Network.[65] During the unsold periods, NBC and CBS offered their affiliates "sustaining" programs that lacked commercial sponsorship, including news, educational programs, classical music concerts, and serious drama. Network executives pointed to these programs as evidence that broadcasters were fulfilling the public service obligations stipulated by the FCC in exchange for their licenses. This opened some genuine opportunities for experimentation with the possibilities of radio as an art form; Orson Welles's adaptation of H. G. Wells's *War of the Worlds* in October 1938, for example, was broadcast by CBS during a Sunday evening slot that it could not sell because of the dominance of the *Jack Benny Show* and the *Edgar Bergen—Charlie McCarthy Show* on NBC Red.[66] While such broadcasts garnered prestige for the networks, they emerged from tepid interest on the part of sponsors.

Industrial design was often described as a "Depression baby," but it was nearly stillborn due to the fierce price competition of the early 1930s. Manufacturers of durable consumer goods like automobiles and home appliances that were the principal prospective clients for the designers' services were among the most frantic price cutters. Leading manufacturers of electric refrigerators such as Frigidaire, for instance, slashed prices by more than 40 percent between 1929 and 1932.[67] As prices tumbled with no apparent bottom in sight, some of the more forward-looking manufacturers and retailers began to take a greater interest in design as a means of product differentiation. For most firms, however, the shift came only after the passage in June 1933 of federal legislation establishing the National Recovery

Administration (NRA) as the cornerstone of President Franklin Delano Roosevelt's initial New Deal program. The NRA effectively suspended existing antitrust measures and instead encouraged price fixing among firms as a way of halting deflation and stabilizing the economy. This major economic intervention gave manufacturers a compelling inducement to recommit to non–price competition and allocate scarce funds for the restyling of their goods. Even after the Supreme Court ruled the NRA unconstitutional in May 1935, most of these firms continued to employ the services of industrial designers. The successful early entrepreneurs of the new field established their agencies as viable concerns that offered an expanding range of design services to clients, so that even large corporations with their own in-house product styling departments frequently contracted with them as consultants.[68]

While broadcasting and industrial design experienced uneven growth, the hiring gains in these sectors hardly offset the layoffs and salary reductions throughout the rest of the culture industries. In the print media, many firms opted for pay cuts and short hours as a way of preserving jobs, so that total newspaper and magazine employment in the United States contracted by 16.3 percent between 1929 and 1932, while total payrolls fell 35.5 percent between the precrash peak and the trough reached in 1933. White-collar workers in publishing disproportionately bore the brunt, as unionized typographers, pressmen, and other craft workers in the printing trades were better able to defend their wage standards.[69] The capacity of some of the larger publishing enterprises to endure losses likely mitigated unemployment in the print media, but even major firms could not sustain money-losing operations indefinitely. When the Pulitzer Company decided to close its flagship *New York World* in February 1931 after it failed to find a suitable buyer, 2,000 people lost their jobs. A few of the defunct paper's stars quickly found new positions, most notably columnist Walter Lippmann, who even in the nadir of the crisis joined the *Herald Tribune* at a salary of more than $30,000 a year, but the overwhelming majority of those left without work faced very grim prospects. Hearst's New York papers, which had been Pulitzer's principal rivals, hemorrhaged red ink until 1937 when the publishing empire, which was on the brink of insolvency, folded its morning *American* into its afternoon *Journal*, eliminating hundreds more jobs.[70]

Fields in which employment was directly contingent on the maintenance of client patronage—with the conspicuous exception of industrial design—tended to be hit even harder than the print media. Although work at the leading advertising agencies had been highly lucrative before the crash, it had always been somewhat insecure, as the loss of an account usually led to layoffs. During the early 1930s, not only did commission payments from clients plummet, but nearly every account also became "hot" or "loose," as anxious merchants and retailers looked to switch agencies in the hopes that a fresh team and a new campaign might resuscitate sales. Furthermore, both current and prospective clients increasingly expected agencies to produce speculative work prior to any outlays for commissioned advertising and began demanding other services for free.[71] Agencies responded to the pressures with waves of salary reductions and layoffs that reduced employment by more than a third between 1929 and 1933, at which point an uptick in advertising expenditures following implementation of the NRA stabilized the situation. Freelance writers and artists found themselves in even more dire straits, as assignments and commissions became increasingly infrequent, and clients slashed what they were willing to pay. Architecture was likely the most adversely affected creative field. As construction ground to a halt, unemployment among architects approached 90 percent by the early months of 1933 before various New Deal public works programs and housing initiatives slowly began to provide a lifeline for the profession.[72]

Culture workers endured greater hardship and dislocation than white-collar workers in many other sectors of the economy. Although no group within American society was unscathed by the Great Depression, generally people employed in clerical, professional, and managerial occupations, and even in many sales positions, fared better than those with blue-collar occupations. Confronted with the sharp business contraction of the early 1930s followed by an anemic recovery in the middle of the decade, most employers found that their demand for various kinds of office personnel was less elastic than their demand for manufacturing workers. Average unemployment rates were substantially lower for most white-collar workers than for craftsmen, operatives, or laborers, and the differential between average incomes for clerical workers and average incomes for manufacturing workers, which had narrowed considerably from 1914 through 1929, began to widen again in the early 1930s.[73] Still, for the bulk of white-collar workers, the layoffs, pay cuts, and general economic insecurity of the Depression years rudely contradicted the aspirational middle-class attitudes of the previous years.

In response to the economic collapse, some members of the creative class began to propose radical new understandings of the white-collar condition that were quite at odds with the middle-class ideologies prevalent before the crash. An early and influential expression of this impulse to devise a revolutionary role for those engaged in cultural, educational, and intellectual pursuits was the *Culture and the Crisis* manifesto issued in October 1932 by the League of Professional Groups for Foster and Ford. Written in support of the Communist Party's presidential and vice presidential candidates, the tract, which was signed by fifty-two members of the League, including Lewis Corey, Malcolm Cowley, John Dos Passos, Waldo Frank, Sidney Hook, Langston Hughes, and James Rorty, declared that the "unprecedented severity and duration of the depression" demonstrated that the economic disaster was not just another downturn in the business cycle but rather indicative of the "break-down of capitalist society." Only socialist revolution, it asserted, could alleviate the misery that the crisis had visited upon professionals as well as those who toiled in the nation's factories and on its farms. "Why should intellectual workers," it asked, "be loyal to the ruling class which frustrates them, stultifies them, patronizes them, makes their work ridiculous, and now starves them?" Since they did not "constitute an independent economic class," they faced a stark choice of "serving either as the cultural lieutenants of the capitalist class or as allies and fellow travelers of the working class." By casting ballots for the Communists, they would hasten the transformation of society so that "professional workers, whom capitalism either exploits or forces to become exploiters," would be "liberated to perform freely and creatively their particular craft function." The alternative course of supporting capitalism as it degenerated would only serve to accelerate "the pauperization of the most highly creative groups in society."[74]

Even in the depths of American capitalism's worst crisis, few voters heeded the League's call. William Z. Foster and James Ford received a paltry 103,307 votes, compared to 884,885 votes for their Socialist rival Norman Thomas, 15,761,254 for Hoover, despite his record of economic failure, and 22,821,277 for FDR. Yet the critique that *Culture and the Crisis* articulated had a tremendous effect on the creative class. Over the subsequent two decades, numerous men and women in advertising, the print media, broadcasting, and design engaged in the kind of critical reevaluation of their economic and social position that the manifesto's signers had hoped to provoke. This was most readily apparent in their organization of vibrant white-collar unions throughout New York City's culture industries. It was also evident in the tendency of many of those who labored to produce culture, or who aspired to creative occupations, to challenge the principles of consumer capitalism that heavily determined the terms under which they could earn a living. And although only a minority of the participants ever joined the Communist Party or openly supported it, enough did at one point or another to furnish the defenders of consumer capitalism with plenty of ammunition to use against their adversaries.

The varieties of white-collar consciousness that informed *Culture and the Crisis*, as well as most of the progressive and radical activism in the creative class of the 1930s and 1940s, contrasted sharply with most of the enduring depictions of middle-class life subsequently promulgated during the 1950s and early 1960s. While postwar scholarship and journalism was generally predicated on the assumption that individuals employed in white-collar occupations naturally enjoyed middle-class affluence and comfort, *Culture and the Crisis* portrayed the lot of professionals, let alone clerical workers, under unfettered capitalism as one of exploitation, insecurity, and degradation. The insurgent writers, artists, intellectuals, and organizers examined in the chapters that follow not only cast white-collar workers as agents of transformative social change, but also set forth a politics and culture of labor solidarity that, in their minds, furnished a practical means of actually exercising that agency. Their conception of white-collar consciousness diverged sharply from pessimistic postwar representations of the middle class as politically disengaged, apathetic, or complacent. It also differed, moreover, from the more utopian postwar claims about the latent potential for autonomy and liberation inherent in privileged elements of the middle class.

The power that these radicals and progressives imputed to the growing ranks of white-collar workers also entailed momentous responsibility. Proponents of the alliance between white-collar and blue-collar workers that was limned in *Culture and the Crisis*, and elaborated or revised in various iterations in the years that followed, emphasized the seriousness of the choice facing those employed in clerical, sales, technical, professional, and creative occupations. They could embrace the cause of workers' collective empowerment, a more egalitarian distribution of income and wealth, enhanced economic security, an equitable provisioning of goods and services through public or other nonprofit means, and the intensified regulation of business. Or, conversely, they could recommit their allegiance to conservative middle-class ideology, with its emphasis on individual merit and status distinction, and to the business interests that promoted it. Those among the cultural radicals who took the crisis of America's middling strata as their subject, like the printmaker Elizabeth Olds, represented the gravity of the choice in stark terms.[75] While working for the Graphic Arts Division of the Federal Art Project in New York City during the late 1930s, Olds produced a number of drawings and prints intended to illuminate the Depression's impact on white-collar workers, including her allegorical lithograph *The*

Middle Class (1938), which grotesquely aestheticizes the analysis presented in *Culture and the Crisis*. Penned in by a flimsy barrier that obscures the rest of the social landscape, many within Olds's middle class direct their attention to a homegrown fascist demagogue who addresses them from his perch on a pedestal just beyond the right-hand wall. While he distracts his rapt listeners, rich old men sneak their loot out of the pen into an ominous terrain littered with the remnants of a lynching as well as stockpiles of armaments and munitions. To the left, away from the demagogue's crowd, however, more and more of the people in the pen reject fascist propaganda and discover ways to escape. As these fugitives gain a clear view of their surroundings, they flock to a large mass of people rallying under the banners of organized labor.

Whether it was conveyed through Olds's symbolism or the polemics of *Culture and the Crisis*, the cultural insurgents imagined white-collar workers in general, and the creative class more specifically, in ways that repudiated entrenched notions about the nature of the middle class that were common before the Depression, and that seem almost like a dystopian inversion of the placid conceptions of middle-class life that would become hegemonic during

FIGURE 1.1 Elizabeth Olds, *The Middle Class*, 1938, lithograph on paper, 10 x 14 in. From the Smithsonian American Art Museum, transfer from the Archives of American Art, Smithsonian Institution.

the long era of postwar prosperity. However shocking Olds's portrayal may appear, it furnishes illuminating insights into the consciousness of the men and women who, during the 1930s and 1940s, organized unions in the culture industries, demonstrated for public sponsorship for the arts, and launched media enterprises that called into question key tenets of consumer capitalism.

2

The Emergence of White-Collar Unionism in New York's Culture Industries

THE LABOR INSURGENCY of the 1930s and 1940s transformed the United States like few other social movements in the nation's history. Total union membership swelled from three million American workers in 1932 to sixteen million by 1947.[1] The labor movement's growth propelled a major political realignment, as working-class voters became a core constituency of the New Deal Coalition that enabled Democratic candidates to win seven out of nine presidential elections between 1932 and 1964. Organized labor provided key political support for a variety of lasting legislative achievements, including the old-age income and unemployment benefits provided through the Social Security Act of 1935 and the minimum-wage and overtime pay mandated by the Fair Labor Standards Act of 1938. The spread of collective bargaining throughout wide swaths of the American economy, facilitated by the 1935 passage of the National Labor Relations Act, elevated millions of workers' living standards, resulting in a more equitable distribution of income and establishing the basis for postwar prosperity. Collective bargaining also brought greater dignity on the job through negotiated work rules, improved safety procedures, restraints on managerial discipline, and grievance procedures to furnish the rudiments of due process in the workplace. Furthermore, the growth of the labor movement during the 1930s and 1940s, particularly of the new industrial unions, facilitated the incorporation of Eastern- and Southern-European workers into the mainstream of American politics and culture. While the labor movement's overall record with respect to the inclusion of women and African Americans was much more uneven during these years, progressive unions were at the forefront of the struggle for social equality, and activists in these unions planted the seeds for empowerment movements that flourished in the 1960s and 1970s.

Numerous white-collar workers also participated in the labor upheaval of the Depression years. The proliferation of grassroots organizing efforts and outbursts of labor militancy among these workers, in large cities as well as small towns, suggests their willingness to experiment with collective action rooted in class or occupational solidarity. Often, their efforts received little coordination or institutional support from the wider labor movement, which partly explains why many of them were fleeting. Thus, while clerks in the mine office and company store of the Consolidated Coal Company in Van Lear, Kentucky, for instance, petitioned the fledgling Committee on Industrial Organization (Congress of Industrial Organizations after 1938) for a local union charter in the summer of 1937, little trace exists of why their activities petered out over the next several years.[2] In cities with a vibrant labor movement, white-collar workers' interest could still be ephemeral, as with the bank employees in San Francisco who attempted to organize under the CIO umbrella.[3] Even when white-collar workers staged contentious strikes that divided communities, like the nation's first major walkout by department store clerks and sales staff in Milwaukee in November 1934, their actions might fail to produce a lasting local union.[4]

Despite the obstacles that caused many incipient organizing efforts by white-collar workers to wither away, several hundred thousand clerical, sales, technical, professional, and creative workers across the United States succeeded in establishing unions during the "Age of the CIO." The greatest advances were made in and around New York City. Within the metropolitan area, for example, roughly 35,000 public school teachers, 8,000 social-service workers, and 15,000 insurance agents belonged to CIO affiliates by 1947. The city's culture workers proved particularly receptive to unionism, and their activism had a disproportionate influence on the labor movement as a whole. Precisely because their jobs involved representing the world through the newspapers, magazines, books, advertising, graphic arts, design, and broadcast programming that they created, their organizing endeavors tended to be highly visible. Inside the offices, studios, drafting rooms, and other workplaces where they organized, these unionists comprised an adversarial subculture that not only fought for improved pay and conditions, but that also sought to transform America's culture of consumer capitalism. Many of them utilized their creative talents as writers and artists to build and sustain a variety of progressive groups committed to labor rights, social equality for

women and African Americans, international antifascist solidarity, and socially conscious consumerism.

During the 1930s, they founded an array of new unions throughout
New York's culture industries. Although these unions had a range of origins
and followed differing paths, by the end of the decade most of them had affiliated not with the more established, craft-oriented American Federation
of Labor, but with the upstart CIO. Some, like the American Newspaper
Guild (ANG) and the Federation of Architects, Engineers, Chemists, and
Technicians (FAECT), were active throughout the United States and secured
charters from the CIO as national affiliates. Others that were only active in
a select number of cities, like United American Artists (UAA), or that were
active primarily in New York, like the Book and Magazine Guild (BMG)
and the American Advertising Guild, were structured as locals within the
United Office and Professional Workers of America (UOPWA), which was
the national union chartered by the CIO with primary jurisdiction for white-
collar workers in the private sector. Only in broadcasting was a clear preference lacking: the American Federation of Radio Artists (AFRA) received a
charter from the AFL soon after its founding in 1937, while the Radio Writers
Guild (RWG) opted not to join either of the major labor federations, and
the National Association of Broadcast Engineers and Technicians (NABET)
eventually affiliated with the CIO in 1951.

Although proponents of white-collar organizing demonstrated considerable enthusiasm and initiative, their unions experienced varying degrees of
success. The Newspaper Guild of New York, for example, had by 1941 secured
recognition from all but one of the city's major daily papers as well as from
the publishers of the newsmagazines *Time* and *Newsweek*. Conversely, the Ad
Guild was only able to negotiate contracts covering a tiny fraction of the city's
advertising workforce employed by a handful of small agencies and ancillary
firms. Like unionists in the core manufacturing sectors in which the labor
movement scored its most impressive gains during the period, organizers in
New York's offices confronted antipathy from most executives and managers
as well as antiunion sentiments or apathy from a significant portion of the
workforce. The spatial configuration of many offices, with employees frequently compartmentalized into separate departments, along with the residential dispersal of white-collar workers throughout the metropolitan area,
presented additional organizing challenges. Firm size and market structure
also influenced organizing efforts. While newspaper publishing and network broadcasting were oligopolies characterized by vertical integration and
high capital requirements, other fields of cultural production—including

advertising, book and magazine publishing, and commercial art and design—tended to be highly competitive, with limited fixed capital requirements and comparatively low barriers to entry. In addition, unionists in New York's culture industries were often constrained by the lack of institutional support for white-collar organizing in general. Despite the long-term growth trends in clerical, sales, technical, and professional employment, both the AFL and the CIO often ignored white-collar unionists' pleas for assistance. The National Labor Relations Board (NLRB), the federal agency empowered to adjudicate labor disputes and to certify unions for collective bargaining, was, in many instances, relatively indifferent to the organizing efforts of white-collar workers. Finally, the issue of Communist influence became increasingly divisive in many of the unions in publishing, advertising, design, and broadcasting by the end of the 1930s. Still, even in the face of all of these obstacles, the unions in just a few years managed to ensconce themselves in the culture industries. Whether they would thrive in the long term or fundamentally transform America's culture of consumer capitalism, however, still remained to be seen as the Great Depression drew to a close and the Second World War loomed on the horizon.

Craftsmen, Proletarians, and Guild Members: Modes of White-Collar Organizing

When white-collar unionists considered their workplace grievances and the possible organizational responses, they drew upon three general currents of thinking about modern mental labor. One, based on the craft traditions long espoused by the AFL, put a premium on the maintenance of exclusive jurisdictions defined by discrete sets of skills. A more radical tendency, articulated in *Culture and the Crisis*, emphasized the proletarianization of white-collar workers and stressed the common exploitation of blue-collar and white-collar workers. A third, somewhat ambiguous, way of thinking evolved around the notion that salaried white-collar workers belonged to an emerging social category that was distinct from other existing classes and strata, but whose interests were still best served through a social-democratic alliance with blue-collar workers. In reality, most proponents of unionism for clerical, sales, technical, professional, and creative workers pragmatically combined aspects of these approaches in their understanding of their own careers, their activism, or the general position of white-collar workers in American society. Although few of them were doctrinaire adherents to any one of these currents of thinking, an explication of the three tendencies nonetheless provides a useful starting point for examining the development of white-collar militancy during the Great Depression.

The ideology and practice of craft unionism furnished the oldest of these conceptual frameworks. In the late nineteenth and early twentieth centuries, the mainstream adherents of the AFL idealized the possession of specialized craft skills and knowledge. Usually acquired through rigorous apprenticeships that guaranteed the quality of training while simultaneously restricting access to employment, craft skills functioned as a moral equivalent of property that could legitimate claims to workplace autonomy and republican citizenship. Driven by their veneration of skilled labor and their perception of the threats to their organizing paradigm in America's dynamic economy, most AFL-affiliated unions jealously guarded the craft prerogatives of their members as they excluded the unskilled laborers and semiskilled operatives who comprised a growing majority of the nation's industrial workforce.[5] Within New York City, a number of AFL-affiliated unions organized workers employed in the mechanical production (or reproduction) of culture, including Local One of the International Alliance of Theatrical Stage Employees (IATSE) for the stagehands in Broadway theater, IATSE Local 306 for the city's motion picture projectionists, United Scenic Artists (International Brotherhood of Painters Local 829) for theater set designers, and the "Big Six" local of the International Typographical Union (ITU) for the linotype operators and other typesetters in the city's printing industry. A few other craft unions, such as American Federation of Musicians (AFM) Local 802 and the Actors' Equity Association, organized performing talent in the city's entertainment industry.[6] Although the majority of white-collar workers in publishing, advertising, design, or broadcasting lacked the requisite craft skills to join these organizations, the nature of their work periodically brought them into contact with their members. The long-term success of these AFL affiliates in maintaining the living standards of the circumscribed groups of tradesmen and performers they represented, however, guaranteed that craft unionism would continue to be a compelling model for some white-collar workers.

During the early twentieth century, the AFL did take some groups of office workers under its wing, such as New York City's Bookkeepers, Stenographers, and Accountants' Union (BS&AU) Local 12646. The initial impetus to form the BS&AU came in 1907 from the socialist feminist Helen Marot, and through the 1910s it promoted an understanding of white-collar work that was explicitly class-conscious. Prior to America's entry into the First World War, the local was part of the roughly one-third of AFL unions led by members

of the Socialist Party and their allies, and in 1919 and 1920 it backed the unsuccessful efforts of five Socialist Assemblymen to fight their expulsion from
the New York state legislature on account of their political views. Although
the BS&AU asked the AFL in 1918 to charter a new affiliated international
union to organize office workers, AFL president Samuel Gompers feared
strengthening the restive left wing and denied the request. Consequently,
the BS&AU and other clerical locals around the country continued on with
"federal" charters issued directly from the AFL.[7] In 1922, Gompers temporarily suspended the local's charter as part of a wholesale purge of radicals,
including supporters of the recently established Communist Party. The union
attempted several organizing drives among clerical workers in some of the
city's major banking and insurance firms during the mid-1920s, but these
were unsuccessful. Often, the local's new AFL-imposed leadership appeared
to care more about expelling suspected Communists than expanding its scope
of collective bargaining. Confined primarily to its original membership base
among the office staffs of other AFL affiliates, various progressive and pro-
labor institutions, and a handful of marginal firms, BS&AU Local 12646 had
fewer than 1,000 members through most of the second half of the decade.[8]

Much of the local leadership's hostility to the alleged procommunist
presence was based on fundamental disagreements about both the nature of
the white-collar condition and the ideal mode of organizing. Radicals who
gravitated toward a procommunist political orientation frequently eschewed
craft unionism, with its increasingly conservative connotations, and instead
espoused a conception of white-collar work as a new kind of industrial
labor; tellingly, when the AFL reorganized the local in 1922, its functionaries
found that one of the procommunists' gravest sins was their proposal to re-
name the local as simply an "office workers'" union without any reference
to specific clerical crafts. Despite the Federation's insistence on the exclusive
primacy of craft, its fierce anticommunism, and its increasing willingness to
pursue nonadversarial relations with employers, the struggling Communist
Party of the United States continued to encourage its adherents to join AFL
unions through the middle years of the decade. In 1928, as part of Josef Stalin's
consolidation of his dictatorial rule in the Soviet Union, the Communist
International proclaimed that the revolutionary struggle had entered a
"Third Period" that necessitated an ultra-radical stance in opposition to existing liberal and social-democratic organizations. In response to directives
from Moscow, American Communists abandoned the AFL and inaugurated
a new labor center, the Trade Union Unity League (TUUL). While some of
the Communists' new organizing entities, such as the National Miners Union

and the National Union of Textile Workers, were clearly "dual unions" intended to compete with established AFL affiliates, others were chartered in fields where the AFL presence was either moribund or nonexistent.[9]

As part of this new initiative, the Communist Party sponsored the formation of several militant unions for clerical, sales, technical, professional, and creative workers during the late 1920s and early 1930s. The first and largest of these was the Office Workers Union (OWU), launched shortly after the establishment of the TUUL. In November 1928, the OWU declared its intention "to hammer home the truth that the office worker is a WORKER, toiling for wages and subjected to wretched conditions like his fellow worker in shop, mill, mine or factory." By exposing how white-collar workers were "subjected to abuses of all kinds, such as espionage, petty tyranny, low wages, long hours, unpaid overtime, the speed-up system, groundless dismissals and long spells of unemployment," the new union hoped to disabuse them of the notion that they comprised a "privileged caste" and lead them "to carry on a successful struggle for their rights." As part of its efforts, the OWU pledged itself "to secure equal pay for equal work, regardless of sex, age, or race," and more generally "to combat race, color or creed discrimination."[10] The severity of the Great Depression made the union's analysis seem plausible to a growing number of white-collar workers. As the number of jobless surged in the early 1930s, the OWU began to coordinate its activities with the Communist Party's Unemployed Councils, spurring the eventual formation of a New York Committee of Unemployed Office, Store, and Professional Workers. The union demanded that the federal government furnish jobs for the millions of people who were out of work and implement a permanent system of unemployment insurance. In response to the drastic pay cuts, which reduced the salaries of some clerks in the city to as little as $10 per week, and the overall deterioration in working conditions, the OWU kicked off new organizing drives that targeted employees of department stores, book publishers, and newspaper offices.[11]

Even as the Communist Party remained highly critical of the Roosevelt administration during its first two years, the partial enactment of some of its demands, such as the creation of public relief employment and the stimulus to unionization provided by Section 7(a) of the National Industrial Recovery Act, prompted additional radical organizing among white-collar workers. In 1933, procommunists founded the Federation of Architects, Engineers, Chemists, and Technicians as a TUUL affiliate, which soon established its initial membership base among technical and professional personnel on New Deal public works projects. Shortly thereafter, radical painters, illustrators, muralists, and sculptors formed the Artists' Union, which lobbied for the extension of relief employment to include those engaged in cultural production.[12] In June 1934, the OWU led the first strike in New York book publishing when the employees of Macaulay Press walked off the job to win the reinstatement of a colleague who was discharged for his union organizing plus the introduction of paid sick leave and vacation time. Continued recalcitrance by the publisher precipitated a second strike a few months later, in which the unionists were again victorious.[13] Between November 1934 and February 1935, several hundred workers organized by the OWU staged a highly public series of demonstrations and strikes to win improved conditions at Klein's and Ohrbach's discount department stores on Union Square.[14] In addition, in April 1935, the discharge of two OWU activists from the *American Mercury* magazine precipitated a strike by its office employees, who also demanded a new minimum salary of $21 a week. As part of the effort to mobilize broader support and show solidarity for these early strikes, leftist intellectual and literary figures—including Malcolm Cowley, Matthew Josephson, Tess Slesinger, Nathaniel West, and Louis Kronenberger—participated in picketing and were arrested by the police.[15]

In *The Crisis of the Middle Class* (1935), radical intellectual Lewis Corey furnished the most lucid exposition of the theory of white-collar proletarianization that underpinned the organizing approach of the OWU. An avowed revolutionary during the 1910s, the Italian-born Corey had helped to found the American Communist Party in 1919 but dropped out after a few years. By 1926, he had started his second career as a writer, contributing articles to progressive magazines like the *New Republic* while working on several book manuscripts. The onset of the Depression induced Corey to move to the left again. While he did not officially rejoin the Communist Party he was one of the principal authors of *Culture and the Crisis*, and he elaborated its analysis in *The Crisis of the Middle Class*. Corey contended that by the 1930s the "middle class" had become "composed overwhelmingly of propertyless elements whose interests are identified with the abolition of capitalist property." Under these circumstances, the traditional conception of a middle class obfuscated the growing economic divergence between a shrinking remnant of entrepreneurs, *rentiers*, and well-paid managers, and the growing majority of white-collar workers. He feared that many white-collar workers, motivated by a desperate desire to cling to the psychological benefits of middle-class status, would turn toward fascism and "state capitalism." The challenge for radical activists was to convince "the masses of lower salaried employees, including the intellectuals" that they "must break away from the middle class" and "recognize their identity with labor." Corey predicted that the "lower salaried employees and professionals" would "adopt proletarian forms of action," including "unions, strikes, mass demonstrations" and a "labor party" to advance "the communist struggle for power and socialism."[16]

While the OWU and FAECT tried to cultivate Corey's support and capitalize on the buzz generated by publication of *The Crisis of the Middle Class*, a shift in Communist policy spelled the end for the Party's "revolutionary" unions.[17] Following the official adoption of the Popular Front program—emphasizing cooperation with non-Communist radicals, progressives, and liberals—by the upper echelons of Communist Party, the TUUL voted to disband in May 1935, and to instruct its constitutive unions, including the OWU and the FAECT, to seek entry into the AFL. Members of the OWU Department Store Section in New York City joined the corrupt and ineffectual AFL Retail Clerks Local 1250, quickly taking it over and using it as a base for widespread organizing during the late 1930s and early 1940s. Members of the Newspaper Office Section and some members of the Literary Trades Section received new federal charters from the AFL. The remaining members of the OWU in New York joined BS&AU Local 12646, and after almost a year of factional infighting succeeded in electing a procommunist leadership slate.[18]

A third approach to white-collar organizing in New York's culture industries, which was neither centered around a notion of white-collar workers as craftsmen nor grounded in an idea of a revolutionary office proletariat, was evident in the formation of a number of militant professional organizations, of which the Newspaper Guild was the first and most important. Discontent among journalists grew throughout the early 1930s as conditions in the print media deteriorated, but it was Heywood Broun of the *New York World-Telegram* who took the lead in his syndicated column on August 7, 1933. Conceding his own comfortable situation, Broun nonetheless confessed that he hated "to see other newspaper men working too hard," while it embarrassed him "even more to think of newspaper men who are not working at all." He admitted his own ambivalence about construing the relationship between journalists and management as inherently adversarial, but still concluded that "the fact that newspaper editors and owners are genial folk should hardly stand in the way of the organization of a newspaper writers' union." In October, a group of 150 New York journalists convened to draft a provisional constitution for the "Guild of New York Newspaper Men and Women," but remained divided over the extent to which the new organization should adopt the structure or objectives of a conventional labor union. By December, they joined other like-minded groups scattered around the country in establishing the American Newspaper Guild.[19]

Over the next two years, the Newspaper Guild drifted as members continued to disagree about the new organization's goals and tactics. Many

FIGURE 2.1 Newspaper Guild leader Heywood Broun demonstrating against the unfair labor practices of the *Staten Island Advance* newspaper during the mid-1930s. From the *Daily Worker* Photo Archive held at the Tamiment Library, New York University by permission of the Communist Party USA.

wanted to pursue collective bargaining with employers, while others, who were still apprehensive about the loss of flexibility they feared would result from binding contracts and the loss of status they worried would come with acknowledgment of their position as "labor," thought the Guild should function solely in an advocacy role. Some believed the Guild must retain its independence; others insisted that it would remain weak outside of a larger organizational structure. Some, who sought to emulate the gains secured by the ITU and the other craft unions in printing, wanted the ANG to request a charter from the AFL. Proponents of affiliation who were more financially successful or more status-conscious, however, tended to be amenable to the overtures of the Authors' League of America, which focused primarily on copyright enforcement and ensuring the proper payment of residuals and royalties. Additionally, the question of whether or not the Newspaper Guild should expand its jurisdiction to include all white-collar workers in the print media led to further dissension. The Guild's continuing weakness, which was painfully exposed in its strike against the *Newark Ledger* and other early disputes, gradually convinced the bulk of the membership to support unionization. In June 1935 the Guild's national convention adopted a resolution favoring the "vertical" organization of all white-collar newspaper employees and authorized a member referendum on AFL affiliation. The balloting narrowly missed the required two-thirds supermajority, but bitter strikes against Hearst papers in Milwaukee and Seattle during 1936 fortified members' resolve. That August the ANG received its charter from the AFL as an affiliated international union.[20]

The ambivalence that many early Newspaper Guild advocates exhibited about adopting a union structure revealed not just a reluctance to jettison the supposed prerogatives of middle-class status, but a sense that they represented the emergence of a new social type whose condition could not be easily explained by the existing theories of wage labor under capitalism. One of the most influential and coherent efforts at articulating these sentiments came from Alfred Bingham. Raised in a conservative and privileged New England family, he was radicalized by the coming of the Depression. In 1932, Bingham and Selden Rodman launched *Common Sense*, a magazine dedicated to the encouragement of "production for use and not for profit." Bingham endorsed white-collar unionism as well as the cooperatives proposed by Upton Sinclair in his End Poverty in California (EPIC) gubernatorial campaign of 1934. In *Insurgent America: Revolt of the Middle Class* (1935) Bingham offered a social analysis that was at once anticapitalist and anti-Marxist. Most significantly, he rejected Corey's contention in *Crisis of the Middle Class* that the middle class was disintegrating and the long historical phase in which it had acted as an agent for progress had ended. Instead, Bingham asserted that the multiple middle classes remained the principal agents for bringing about a "cooperative commonwealth" in the United States, and that the expanding ranks of salaried white-collar workers—including those involved in the production of culture and knowledge—constituted the most potentially radical element.[21]

The idea that the new white-collar groups transcended the conventional divisions between capital and labor, along with the Newspaper Guild's steady advance, inspired the formation of other militant professional organizations that chose the "guild" appellation. In the spring of 1935, activists in book publishing formed a Book and Magazine Guild for "men and women engaged as executive and professional workers." James Gilman, who worked as a chief of the manufacturing department for book publisher F. S. Crofts, Viking Press editor David Zablodowsky, and renowned book designer and typography expert Robert Josephy led the BMG during its first several years. Although the BMG did not initially pursue collective bargaining, it did mobilize in support of the strike by the employees of Consumers' Research in September 1935, and Gilman served on the initial board of directors of rival Consumers Union when it was established the following year.[22] By the fall of 1936, copywriters, illustrators, art directors, and publicists had set up the American Advertising Guild along similar lines. As with the BMG, Ad Guild activists at first directed their efforts toward consciousness-raising, although during 1937 both of these guilds began to transition to trade unionism.[23] In addition, the Author's League of America chartered a new division, the Radio Writers Guild, in July 1937. While the leadership of the Authors' League hoped that its prestige would attract those who earned a living writing for radio, the RWG struggled in its first few years to gain a following. The organizing tactics that had proven effective for novelists, playwrights, and screenwriters turned out to be less effective for writers dependent on the patronage of the advertising-supported radio networks or the advertising agencies that sponsored and produced much of the programming for broadcast. After three years, the RWG only had 211 members in the New York area, less than one-third the number of eligible writers it estimated were working in the region.[24]

White-Collar Workers and the Industrial Union Project

The quickening pace of white-collar organizing in New York's culture industries by the middle of the 1930s occurred against the backdrop of a contentious struggle over the issue of industrial unionism that split the American labor movement. Unlike most AFL craft unions, industrial unions sought to organize all workers regardless of their occupation or skill level. Despite the substantial increase in the employment of unskilled laborers and semi-skilled assembly-line operatives and the marginalization of a variety of traditional crafts during the first three decades of the twentieth century, the AFL had resisted organizing on an industrial basis.[25] As workers in the mass-production industries instigated a new wave of militant labor activism in the early 1930s, some rallied under the banner of the Communists' TUUL, but most preferred to enter the long-established AFL. Yet even with several million workers clamoring to join its ranks, the Federation's leadership still refused to facilitate their organization by endorsing industrial unionism. A minority within the AFL executive council, led by United Mine Workers president John L. Lewis, saw this as squandering a once-in-a-generation opportunity, but their attempts to promote industrial unionism were thwarted by the construction trades and their conservative allies. The disagreement precipitated an outright schism at the September 1935 AFL convention, after which Lewis and like-minded unionists formed their Committee on Industrial Organization. During the first half of 1936, they launched a Steel Workers Organizing Committee, which disregarded the jurisdictional claims of existing AFL craft unions in the metal trades, and they embraced union militants in the auto, rubber, and electrical goods industries who wanted to organize entire factories and firms without regard for skill. When Lewis's Mine Workers and most of the other affiliates that backed the Committee refused to desist, the AFL proceeded to expel unions that accounted for roughly 30 percent of its total membership. By the spring of 1937, the CIO was operating as a de facto independent rival to the AFL and chartering its own array of new industrial unions.[26]

For many white-collar unionists, the CIO represented a blank screen onto which they could project their aspirations for political, social, and cultural change. They saw the CIO as not simply a movement to improve working conditions for millions of Americans, but also as a means of bringing about a social-democratic realignment of the polity to support a massive expansion of New Deal programs and the development of a mixed economy with significant productive capacity in the public sector. Many also hoped that the CIO might someday sustain a robust system of consumer cooperatives, or become a patron for writers, artists, designers, filmmakers, and performers to create a pro-labor popular culture. Furthermore, these white-collar unionists saw CIO affiliation as an opportunity to jettison the conservative legacies of the AFL that frequently seemed ill suited to the constantly evolving tasks of the modern office. Existing AFL affiliates often alienated these unionists by attempting to preserve claims to jurisdictions in which they were not active; even though the United Scenic Artists, for example, had done nothing to organize either cartoon animators or advertising illustrators, it objected strenuously to an AFL representative's decision to issue a new federal charter to a group that contained both kinds of artists, thus ultimately driving these unionists into the CIO.[27] Additionally, white-collar procommunists and their allies were attracted by the prospects of exercising a far greater influence in the nascent CIO than they might hope to attain in the AFL.

Following the dissolution of the TUUL, the FAECT attempted to enter the AFL in 1936 by merging with its feeble affiliate in the engineering and drafting fields, but it was rebuffed on account of its Communist lineage.[28] Subsequently, the FAECT immediately applied for a charter from the CIO, which it saw as a license to absorb other independent groups of designers, engineers, and technicians. As one FAECT organizer wrote in the union's monthly magazine, the "average technical man" was "a long way from being trade union conscious" and still harbored "snobbish" attitudes, but the CIO was disabusing white-collar workers of the conception that unions were "crooked dictatorships." In contrast to "the old idea of unionism with the business agent and his proverbial cigar," he continued, professional and technical workers were learning that "C.I.O. unions are democratic and that members conduct their own affairs through their own elected officers."[29] The FAECT strategy of being the first in its field to affiliate with the CIO soon generated growth, as the Society of Designing Engineers (SDE), a vibrant union of engineers, draftsmen, designers, and stylists in Detroit's auto industry that had several thousand members, voted in 1938 to merge with the FAECT as a means of coming under the CIO umbrella.[30]

The advent of the CIO also attracted the interest of the American Newspaper Guild. The ANG had already committed itself to including all white-collar workers in its field, including those in newspapers' advertising, business, and circulation departments. Although entry into the CIO complicated future joint actions with the AFL craft unions in the printing trades and risked isolating small Guild units on local papers in towns where the CIO had no significant presence, Broun and other ANG leaders were ideologically aligned with the industrial union project and bolted the AFL for the CIO in the spring of 1937.[31] Within a few months, locals like the Newspaper Guild of New York (ANG Local 3) that were based in major metropolitan areas with multiple large-circulation daily papers began a sustained period of growth along industrial lines, absorbing various groups of clerical workers while also signing up a larger proportion of the reporters, writers, and editors on the top dailies. By 1940, the nationwide membership of the ANG had reached 19,000, with the Newspaper Guild of New York accounting for 25 percent of the total.[32]

The greatest potential for organizing large swaths of the white-collar occupational strata came withthe formation of the United Office and Professional Workers of America. The new international union had its origins in a group led by Lewis Merrill, Peter Hawley, and Norma Aronson, who in 1936 gained control of New York's BS&AU Local 12646. Merrill contacted John L. Lewis late that year to propose the creation of a nationwide organization under the sponsorship of the CIO, and by early 1937 he took the lead in bringing together AFL federal locals of office workers from around the country. In June, a convention of twenty-three locals received a CIO charter granting a sweeping jurisdiction that included potentially millions of white-collar workers, and elected Merrill to serve as president.[33] Within the next few months, many of the independent unions operating in New York's culture industries amalgamated and reorganized as UOPWA locals. The Book and Magazine Guild absorbed the literary trades section of BS&AU Local 12646 and Technical, Editorial, and Office Assistants Local 20055 to become UOPWA Local 18, while the American Advertising Guild became UOPWA Local 20. Seven artists' locals from around the United States also became UOPWA locals, with the largest group, the New York Artists' Union, combining with Commercial Artists and Designers Local 20329 to become United American Artists Local 60.[34] To coordinate the efforts of Local 18, Local 20, Local 60, and its other New York locals for general clerical workers, insurance employees, financial services employees, and social service employees, the UOPWA set up a citywide joint council in 1938. The union's presence in New York's culture industries expanded further in the 1940s, with the affiliation of the independent Screen Office and Professional Employees' Guild (as UOPWA Local 109) and Screen Publicists' Guild (as Local 114) early in the decade, as well as the formation of the Radio Guild (Local 50) following the Second World War.[35]

Proponents of industrial unionism in the culture industries often explained their advocacy in terms of the transformations of clerical, technical, professional, and creative labor that had resulted from the rise of large-scale corporate enterprise and the protracted economic crisis of the 1930s. Architect and designer George Nelson, an active member of the Newspaper Guild in his position as an editor of *Architectural Forum*, wrote in the FAECT journal in 1938 that "it was no accident that the golden period of architecture in America—speaking professionally, not esthetically—coincided with the heyday of industrial capitalism." In the Gilded Age, Nelson noted, "free competition, a strong, prosperous middle class, [and] above all an expanding economy provided the basis for the comfortable existence of the private architect." Since then, however, the "increasing control of industry by a small financial oligarchy" and "a shift in the middle class from substantial, property-owning citizens to a salaried group" had an effect on architectural practice that was "anything but abstract." Large-scale entities in regular need of architectural services, like the major retail chains, hired their own in-house design staff, while even "those merchants who survive in the face of chain competition can get architectural services from bureaus maintained by fixtures manufacturers." Anticipating the continued standardization of commercial as well as residential design, Nelson contended that unionization held out the promise of making creative labor in the emerging regime of "agency architecture" preferable to the older model of independent practice.[36]

Sometimes the logic of industrial unionism was articulated with an acerbic edge, as the radical journalist George Seldes did in his *Lords of the Press* (1938). Long inclined to believe that they were "too good to join in any organization or movement," according to Seldes, journalists had faced exploitation and insecurity. Only the recent formation of the Newspaper Guild, Seldes maintained, had "led the American newspaper workers out of the red-light district of journalism," making the creation of the news again into "a profession, and one no longer akin to the oldest—and worst paid." Under the protections of a Guild contract, "reporters, assured for the first time in their lives of economic security so long as they are efficient, begin telling the real facts, the truth behind the news, and stop slanting the news—consciously or unconsciously—to please the First National or the Peoples Light, or the other pecuniary forces with which the owner is allied in some way." The Guild, he boasted, was "not a union in the old A.F. of L. sense, and is even miles ahead of the C.I.O.," in realizing that "labor unions whose whole objective is better working conditions and better money for its membership, are only a small step forward in American progress." It was precisely because American newspaper publishers were "either unaware of the social issues, or, worse yet, insistent that the public be kept in ignorance," that they had "united all their forces and venom to fight the intelligent leadership of the socially conscious Newspaper Guild."[37]

The white-collar unions that affiliated with the CIO adopted the industrial model to varying degrees. In the Newspaper Guild of New York's largest single unit at the *New York Times*, with 1,400 workers under contract at the paper in 1941, and at other papers like the *Daily Mirror*, the union represented not only all of the reporters, writers, photographers, artists, and nonsupervisory editors who created the news content, but also all of the clerical workers in the editorial departments, plus the clerical and sales staff in the advertising, business, and circulation departments, plus the building custodial staff, plus semiskilled operatives in the composing room who were ineligible for membership in the Big Six typographical union. In contrast, the Newspaper Guild units at Time Inc. and at *Newsweek* only included employees in the editorial departments.[38] In the BMG's early burst of growth in 1937 and 1938, activists at book publishers Knopf, Modern Age, Random House, and Viking organized units that included most nonexecutive editors along with the clerical staff, as was also the case at the smaller magazines like *American Scholar*, *Saturday Review of Literature*, and *New Republic* where the union won contracts. By the start of the 1940s, the BMG moved into distribution, organizing workers at the Doubleday and Walden bookstore chains in New York City along with several units of book publishers' shipping employees, and also absorbing a large local of newsstand employees in the city's subways and railroad terminals.[39] Commercial artists drawn into the orbit of the Artists' Union or the short-lived Commercial Artists and Designers' Union that merged to form UAA Local 60 originally established groups defined by craft, but were subsequently integrated into larger organizations along industrial lines. Advertising artists on the staff of Hearst's *New York American* and *Evening Journal* obtained their own separate contract in 1937 before joining the larger Newspaper Guild unit at the newly combined *Journal-American*, while in 1939 the UOPWA transferred the remaining members of the UAA commercial artists' section to the Ad Guild.[40]

The growth of these unions during the late 1930s and early 1940s helped to give the CIO in New York City a distinctive white-collar inflection, one that was reinforced by the leftist orientation of the Greater New York Industrial Union Council. Industrial Union Councils (IUCs) functioned as the CIO analogue of the traditional AFL Central Labor Councils, bringing together all affiliated local unions in a metropolitan area. Despite the absence of some important CIO locals that initially refused to participate to protest the conspicuous influence of procommunists in its affairs, the Greater New York IUC still represented 350,000 union members at its inception in the summer of 1940; by 1945, with nearly all of the city's CIO locals, including those of Sidney Hillman's Amalgamated Clothing Workers, finally in the fold it led half a million workers. The Newspaper Guild of New York, the UOPWA locals, the department store employees, the city's public-school teachers (who had seceded from the AFL-affiliated American Federation of Teachers to join the CIO), and other groups of white-collar unionists together accounted for one-fifth of the Council's membership. No other IUC in the United States had such a large share of white-collar members.[41] Throughout the 1940s, members from the unions in the culture industries played a crucial role in the activities of the Greater New York IUC to bring together workers across industrial lines, with writers, artists, and performers contributing their creative talents to promote the Council's community-based organizing.

Although the industrial organizing strategies adopted by many white-collar unionists in New York had numerous advantages, their overall efficacy was affected in part by the economic structure of the city's various sectors of cultural production. In oligopolistic, vertically integrated, capital-intensive manufacturing sectors such as auto, steel, and electrical goods, CIO unionists obtained recognition early on from a dominant market leader—whether General Motors, US Steel, or General Electric—and then used these breakthroughs with top firms to bring smaller competitors gradually into line. In the culture industries, by contrast, only the motion picture industry, nation-wide network broadcasting, and newspaper publishing were characterized by comparable barriers to entry, firm integration, and market concentration. In magazine publishing, mass-appeal titles like *Life* and *Saturday Evening Post* each had weekly sales in excess of 4 million copies by the early 1940s, which put them at the top in terms of circulation, but they still only accounted for a fraction of total magazine sales. Despite the fact that metropolitan New York accounted for more than 60 percent of book publishing in the United States by the late 1930s, this field was similarly fragmented; consequently, it was difficult for the BMG to use its base in midsized presses like Knopf or Viking, each with 60 to 70 employees, to take on the organization of larger firms like Macmillan, which had nearly 500 employees.[42] Within some segments of the culture industries, the possibilities for collective action were undercut not just by a proliferation of competitors, but also by the market power exercised by buyers, especially the corporate clients of the advertising agencies. Many jobs in the agencies were linked to specific accounts, which contributed to the culture of insecurity that stymied the Ad Guild; when, for example, the New York-based Benton and Bowles Agency lost the lucrative Colgate-Palmolive account in 1940 to a new firm launched by one its own former executives, Ted Bates, it laid off 80 of its 300 employees.[43] In addition, some white-collar unionists whose employers had little in the way of fixed capital investment to tie them down confronted the problem of "runaway shops." Although the animators at Fleischer Studios who made the firm's popular

Betty Boop and *Popeye* cartoons struck successfully in 1937, winning union recognition and significant pay raises, the owners moved their operations to Florida the following year. Although UAA Local 60 was able to win severance payments for its members at the studio, it could not prevent the flight of 250 jobs.[44]

Also, while the logic of industrial organization fit many segments of New York's culture industries, it actually complicated the efforts of the UOPWA and the FAECT to establish themselves as robust national organizations. Both unions had received charters from the CIO designating vast white-collar jurisdictions, but by 1938 the CIO affiliates in auto, steel, and electrical goods began invoking the principle of industrial unionism in some cases to claim office and technical personnel in the factories where they had contracts covering manufacturing workers. The situation for the FAECT became acute in 1939, when the NLRB determined that the UAW could negotiate on behalf of FAECT members in auto plants as part of its own regular collective bargaining.[45] Yet there were many cases in which clerical and technical workers supported the CIO and wanted to cooperate with blue-collar workers on the assembly lines but still wanted separate unions. In Detroit, for example, the design and technical staff who belonged to the Society of Designing Engineers had chosen amalgamation with the FAECT largely to enter the CIO without having to join the UAW. Similarly, office and technical employees of Westinghouse formed the Federation of Westinghouse Independent Salaried Workers, which coordinated its negotiations and its strike activities with the CIO union that represented the corporation's blue-collar employees.[46] In some instances, the CIO manufacturing affiliates exercised their jurisdictional privileges in plants in which they were not actually making any effort to represent office personnel. The UOPWA was sometimes granted permission to organize clerical and technical employees in facilities in which a CIO manufacturing affiliate had lost a representation election among the blue-collar workforce to an AFL rival, and in some of these cases it successfully unionized large groups of hundreds, or even several thousands, of white-collar workers. Although these jurisdictional quarrels were remote from the struggles in advertising, publishing, design, and broadcasting, they had a direct financial impact. By depriving the FAECT and the UOPWA of some of their easiest opportunities for early growth, the CIO stunted the development of these key white-collar affiliates and left them without additional resources for organizing in the cultural fields.

White-collar progressives' lofty hopes for the CIO as a social movement, cultural patron, or political force did not necessarily lead to a reciprocal

commitment of resources for the organization of clerical, technical, professional, and creative workers. John L. Lewis and his associates, many brought
from the Mine Workers to jumpstart the CIO, likely saw white-collar unionism as a luxury they could ill afford at the time. After a rapid advance in
the closing months of 1936 and the early months of 1937, the upstart industrial
labor center's expansion had stagnated by 1938, as it faced deteriorating economic conditions with the onset of the "Roosevelt Recession," fierce resistance from many second-tier manufacturers, debilitating factionalism, and the
incessant sniping of the AFL. Besieged, Lewis's team concentrated on shoring
up its organizational core, giving particular attention to the steelworkers'
drive. The CIO contributed well over $1 million between 1936 and 1940 to
the Steel Workers Organizing Committee to help it organize a primary jurisdiction of roughly 750,000 workers, even though major firms like Bethlehem
and Republic still remained nonunion until 1941. By contrast, as of April 1940
the UOPWA, with a potential jurisdiction well into the millions, had received
a meager $56,000 in financial assistance. Early on, in the summer of 1937, the
CIO was paying the salaries of 17 of the 37 national organizers for the nascent
white-collar union, but it had been forced to withdraw this support after a
few months as the economy worsened. In response to Merrill's request for an
emergency loan of $6,000 in 1939 to defray the legal expenses related to an
NLRB case that paved the way for the eventual unionization of more than
20,000 insurance agents, Lewis's brother Dennis, an advisor to the CIO president, recommended that Merrill needed "to get his feet on the ground and
to put into effect some economy moves." One can only speculate how the reallocation to white-collar organizing of the hundreds of thousands of dollars
that Lewis wasted on a futile effort to raid the AFL construction trades might
have helped the CIO to capitalize on an unprecedented opportunity to expand the social frontiers of the American labor movement. Draconian austerity certainly hampered all UOPWA organizing drives, particularly in the
culture industries. After BMG members conducted a comprehensive survey
of wages and salaries in book publishing in 1940 as a prelude for a new membership drive, for instance, the UOPWA executive board determined that it
could contribute only $320 toward the hiring of an additional part-time or-
ganizer for the local.[47]

The Social and Legal Spaces of White-Collar Organizing

The inability of the CIO leadership to furnish an adequate stream of financial assistance for organizing in New York's culture industries only amplified

the importance of the unionists' own activism. Walking a picket line during a strike was only one of the most conspicuous actions by which clerks, secretaries, writers, editors, designers, and artists could demonstrate their commitment to making a more just and egalitarian workplace. Far more mundane acts were significant in their cumulative impact, such as staying late after work to attend a meeting of the negotiating committee, making decorations for the local's fundraising dance, distributing leaflets outside of an unorganized office during lunch hour, viewing an exhibition of artwork by members of the local, or bringing up the subject of the union with a newly hired coworker around the water cooler. These myriad acts of commitment gave the unions their presence within the offices of publishers, advertising agencies, architecture and design firms, and broadcasters. Through their minute manifestations of solidarity, the unionists constituted an adversarial subculture of like-minded men and women who believed that they had the collective capacity to bring about greater autonomy for the creative class. At the same time, the micropolitics of workplace organizing came to be mediated by the new administrative apparatus established to interpret and implement the National Labor Relations Act of 1935. Highly particular and personal interactions between union supporters and the firms that employed them, their direct supervisors in the office, and their coworkers became rendered, through the decisions of distant NLRB officials, as legalistic abstractions. This dynamic interplay between the immediate social experiences of union activists in the workplace and the procedures of the NLRB effectively defined the scope of white-collar organizing.

During the second half of the 1930s, union supporters did whatever they could to draw attention to their organizations and create positive public perceptions of white-collar unionism. The most elementary opportunities for publicity came when they spoke at professional or business conclaves, or at government hearings. Establishing institutions that could represent the unions and their principles on a consistent basis required a greater investment of organizational resources. Among the most influential of these were the series of schools and courses sponsored by the unions where students could receive advanced training in editing, layout, illustration, graphic design, typography, and art direction from union supporters who were respected creative professionals in their fields. These educational programs boosted the prestige of the unions. Unionists also found opportunities for modernist expression in social events, such as the annual "mAD Arts Ball" held annually from 1936 through 1941 at major venues like Webster Hall in Manhattan. First started by Commercial Artists and Designers Local 20329 and continued by the UAA and the Ad Guild, the mAD Arts Ball raised money for organizing while providing supporters a chance to create elaborate decorations and costumes that lampooned contemporary advertising campaigns.[48] The unions also provided supplemental welfare benefits, such as the pioneering healthcare program established by the UOPWA New York Joint Council in 1939. Structured as an early type of cooperative group medical practice, the plan initially covered about 16,000 members who, in exchange for a low monthly premium, gained access to a panel of physicians who had agreed to accept a retainer from the union in lieu of fee-for-service payment from patients enrolled in the plan. In an era prior to the widespread availability of employer-provided health insurance, this perk was significant.[49]

These educational, social, and welfare activities raised general awareness of white-collar unionism, as did rallies and picketing, but a significant portion of the painstaking, day-to-day work of union building was largely invisible. In order to win improvements such as increased pay, paid sick leave and vacation time, more satisfactory work rules, heightened job security, and protections against supervisory discipline, most unionists sought to establish collective bargaining with employers under the provisions of the NLRA. To reach a point where collective bargaining could commence required a period of organizing, sometimes quite protracted, to gain union recognition, which almost invariably required pro-union employees to defy traditional managerial prerogatives, confront bosses with their demands, convince wary coworkers to support the union, and risk employer retaliation, including denial of promotion, demotion, or outright discharge for union firebrands.

While employers in New York's culture industries never resorted to the kind of violence deployed by Republic Steel or Ford Motor Company, they did go to considerable lengths to intimidate or coerce workers who might be supportive of unionism. Some firms, including the publishers Macmillan and McGraw-Hill, used the services of private detective agencies like Pinkerton and Burns to spy on their workers and identify union activists.[50] More commonly, managers relied on less formal means of surveillance, including information shared by employees who were ideologically anti-union or simply seeking to curry favor with the boss. Often, when managers learned of an incipient organizing drive, they subjected employees to mandatory meetings in which supervisors or outside consultants condemned unions. In many cases, managers used both carrots and sticks, offering surprise raises for some workers while the most vocal unionists received pink slips. The persistent economic insecurity of the 1930s only enhanced the effectiveness of these tactics. For example, designer Irving Harper, who worked for Gilbert Rohde's agency in 1938 and 1939 creating exhibits for the New York World's Fair, recalled becoming a member of the FAECT because "everyone else there joined up." Despite their overwhelming support for the union, Harper and his colleagues were reluctant to push for formal recognition, reflecting their realization that design agencies such as Rohde's remained workplaces that were "guided by fear." Nonetheless, when Rohde fired Harper for his unionism, the pleading of the other designers helped lead to Harper's reinstatement. Even unionists' efforts to satirize managerial tyranny could not necessarily transcend this atmosphere of intimidation. When the Ad Guild, as part of its ongoing membership drive, held a contest in 1938 in which agency employees were invited to fill in the blank dialogue balloons of a comic strip in which bosses imposed onerous work demands upon harried secretaries, copywriters, and art directors, it had to reassure entrants that their names and contact information would remain confidential.[51]

The difficulties encountered by white-collar unionists exposed many of the congenital defects of the NLRA. The legislation granted unprecedented legal privileges to unions and their supporters, but it failed to define and protect the right to organize as a substantive civil right; American unionism, from a legal standpoint, would always remain constrained by the imperatives of economic rationality and social harmony invoked to justify the federal government's intervention into labor relations.[52] The NLRA also instituted a bureaucratic apparatus for adjudication and enforcement that was a cumbersome, and sometimes ineffective, means for realizing organizational and collective bargaining objectives. The NLRB certification process, usually involving secret-ballot representation elections, could be delayed for weeks or even months by hearings to determine which workers belonged in the official bargaining unit or address other administrative issues. Because many technical, creative, and professional employees, and even some clerical staff exercised a significant degree of discretion in their jobs, attempts to impose standards developed for mass-production manufacturing proved problematic. Procedural delays demoralized union supporters and gave employers time to campaign against unionization. Although the NLRA prohibited a range of coercive employer tactics—such as firing union supporters, threatening pro-union workers, or refusing to negotiate with a certified union—that were defined as "unfair labor practices," unions could only attain redress by bringing charges before the Labor Board, with resolution easily taking months or, in some cases, years. Pending resolution, unfair labor practice charges could delay representation elections or contract negotiations, and even when the NLRB ruled against employers the punishments were often little more than a slap on the wrist.

Scarce financial resources created further disadvantages. Although the white-collar unionists did enjoy the services of a dedicated cadre of labor attorneys, the costs of filing legal motions and briefs, or engaging in lengthy hearings, were still substantial. Since most employers had deeper pockets, their recalcitrance could force unions to drop promising cases. The inadequate funding and staffing of the NLRB also created obstacles, as the Board could decline to consider cases that directly involved only dozens of employees in a particular office, but that might establish important precedents affecting exponentially larger numbers of white-collar workers.

Despite the Board's limitations, media executives vehemently opposed its encroachment into the managerial domain and took a leading role in challenging the constitutionality of the NLRA. By 1935, reporters, writers, and non–managing editors employed at the New York headquarters of the Associated Press (AP) had formed a unit of the Newspaper Guild, and as their membership grew into a majority of the editorial staff they began to demand union recognition and the negotiation of a contract. Determined to crush the organizing drive, in October of that year AP executives fired reporter Morris Watson, one of the most prominent unionists among its editorial employees. Watson's firing was only the culmination of a typical course of managerial coercion. His periodic performance evaluations from his supervisors at the AP had been highly favorable after he joined the firm in 1928, but once Watson became an organizer for the Guild in the fall of 1933, his evaluations turned negative, he was demoted, he was transferred from the daytime shift to the midnight shift, and finally his employment was terminated. The Guild filed unfair labor practice charges with the NLRB in December, which certified the Guild's complaint and scheduled investigative hearings on Watson's dismissal to determine if it had been carried out as retaliation for legally protected activities. In the meantime, the AP, with the backing of the American Newspaper Publishers' Association, initiated a lawsuit in federal court challenging the authority of the NLRB. Throughout the first months of 1936, the AP litigation wended its way through the courts on a path parallel to the NLRB investigation of the wire service's unfair labor practices. Watson in the meantime was hired by the WPA Federal Theater Project to direct its "Living Newspaper" series that dramatized current events through experimental stage productions that included the projection of images and text, audience participation, and radical political critique. Watson joined the WPA cultural projects at an early phase when they could still hire a significant fraction of nonrelief personnel, though his $200 monthly salary was still a cut from the $295 he had been earning at AP.[53]

In his initial arguments in district court in January 1936, AP attorney John W. Davis attacked the validity of the NLRA using language that echoed other business litigators who were fighting the new law, following the logic and constitutional interpretation that businesses had utilized since the Gilded Age to thwart various forms of regulation. "The act is unconstitutional," he contended, "because it is not a bona-fide regulation of interstate commerce. Morris Watson was an editorial employe [*sic*], and the courts have held repeatedly that the relation between employer and employe [*sic*] is not commerce and does not directly affect commerce. The fact that The Associated Press itself transmits news to all parts of the country," he continued, "was immaterial." Furthermore, Davis maintained that "the act impairs the right of contract and violates the due-process clause of the Fifth Amendment. The right of the employer to engage at his pleasure and the right of the employe [*sic*] to engage at his pleasure are property rights with which Congress cannot interfere." Following the federal district court's rejection of the wire service's request for an injunction, the NLRB proceeded to review the complaint. Yale Law School Dean Charles E. Clark, who served as trial examiner for the Labor Board, determined that the AP had engaged in unfair labor practices and directed it to reinstate Watson and to commence collective bargaining with the Guild for a contract covering the 157 editorial employees in its New York office. Significantly, as Clark's decision indicated, the AP had started to pivot from an original argument that rested upon a narrow construction of due process and the constitution's commerce clause to one that also placed increasing emphasis on the First Amendment protections of press liberties. Noting that the wire service's challenge was based "upon its claim that there are factors peculiar to its business, requiring accuracy in news gathering and freedom of the press, which make the act clearly inapplicable or invalid to it," Clark instead concluded that "freedom of the press would be facilitated by a freedom of organization." Watson praised the decision as a "bill of rights for editorial workers," but the AP stubbornly refused to comply with the NLRB directives that attempted to put Clark's findings into effect, forcing the Board to request an order of enforcement from the Second Circuit Court of Appeals.[54]

Although the AP lost again at the appellate level, its lawsuit became one of the five challenges to the constitutionality of the NLRA that the United States Supreme Court considered during its 1936–1937 term. The wire service reiterated all of the major points advanced by the other four employers seeking to overturn the law, but as the AP refined its position it amplified its insistence that the First Amendment exempted it from the Labor Board's purview. "Can freedom and independence of the press be maintained," AP counsel Davis queried in his brief to the Supreme Court, "if a Federal bureau may dictate to the American newspapers the persons they employ to prepare their news reports? How can impartiality and independence of reporting be maintained under such a system of administrative supervision?" If the AP prevailed, it could easily establish a precedent by which workers who created media content would be deprived of coverage by the NLRA. Furthermore, the AP made its claims at a critical juncture in American jurisprudence. With the Supreme Court in the process of drastically undercutting the legal reasoning that had long allowed business to limit government regulation, the stance taken by the AP pointed toward other possible invocations of First Amendment liberties as part of a broader strategy for reconstructing the power of corporate personhood. When the Supreme Court issued its decisions in the Labor Board Cases on April 12, 1937, it upheld the validity of the NLRA and rejected an exemption for the media. Writing for the majority, Justice Owen Roberts ruled that the "business of the Associated Press is not immune from regulation because it is an agency of the press. The publisher of a newspaper has no special immunity from the application of general laws. He has no special privilege to invade the rights and liberties of others."[55]

The Supreme Court's unequivocal inclusion of writers, artists, and other creative professionals under the coverage of the NLRA expedited the spread of the Newspaper Guild and other white-collar unions in the culture industries. The AP was required to enter into negotiations with the Guild, which the Labor Board had certified as collective bargaining representative for the wire service's New York employees while its lawsuit was on appeal. The pace of organizing quickened at its other offices as well, and in September 1937 the Guild petitioned the NLRB for elections covering 180 editorial employees in the AP bureaus in Boston, Philadelphia, and Washington, DC. The court decision also intensified public debate about the purpose and scope of the First Amendment and, more fundamentally, the proper function of mass communications in modern society. Owners of media enterprises tended to construe the constitutional freedom of the press as a negative liberty that only assured their exemption from governmental regulation in their operations. By contrast, most white-collar unionists and their progressive allies, like civil libertarian Morris Ernst, who served as counsel for the Newspaper Guild in its legal battle against the AP, understood the freedom of the press as a positive liberty enjoyed not just by the owners of media enterprises but by all citizens. In their conception, it was a guarantee of the public's fundamental right to access a diverse flow of information and media content. For trial examiner Clark and the federal attorneys and officials who followed his lead in arguing for the

FIGURE 2.2 Newspaper Guild activist Morris Watson (left) shaking hands with his attorney, Morris Ernst of the American Civil Liberties Union, following the April 1937 US Supreme Court ruling that denied media enterprises an exemption from the National Labor Relations Act. From the *Daily Worker* Photo Archive held at the Tamiment Library, New York University by permission of the Communist Party USA.

application of the NLRA to editorial employees, this understanding of press freedom as a positive liberty reconciled the militancy of Guild activists like Watson with the legislation's official goals of promoting commerce and social harmony. For many progressives within the creative class, their more expansive conception of the freedom of expression as a positive liberty also justified the substantive changes in the culture of consumer capitalism that they hoped might result from unionization. For Watson, the legal challenge completely altered his life trajectory. He returned to his job at the AP New York office the day after the Supreme Court ordered his reinstatement—almost eighteen months after his firing—although he resigned within weeks. After a second brief stint directing the Federal Theater's Living Newspaper, Watson became a labor journalist, editing the newspaper of the left-led International Longshore and Warehouse Union (ILWU) from 1942 until his retirement in 1965.[56]

Unfortunately for the proponents of white-collar unionism, the Supreme Court's vindication of Watson and the Newspaper Guild only defined what was legally possible under the NLRA; it did not guarantee that other groups of employees would have similar success in protecting their organizing activities. Consequently, many fledgling drives in New York's culture industries were still frustrated by employers who flouted the law. The attempt by employees of the Gussow-Kahn advertising agency to organize under the auspices of the UOPWA Ad Guild in the late 1930s, for instance, followed an all too common course. Workers at the small agency, which primarily produced newspaper display advertising for department stores and other retailers in the metropolitan area, began to join the union in 1938 in an attempt to improve their pay and conditions. In early 1939, when a majority of the firm's forty-five employees had joined the Ad Guild, the unionists requested that Gussow-Kahn management recognize the union and commence negotiations. Agency executives instead insisted upon formal NLRB certification, with an election coming only after hearings to determine the appropriate bargaining unit. While hearings were pending, Gussow-Kahn fired four union activists and coerced a fifth into resigning from the Ad Guild, leading the union to file unfair practice charges with the NLRB in March. To publicize their dispute and pressure management, Ad Guild supporters picketed important agency clients like the upscale Lord and Taylor department store. The Ad Guild's adherents deployed their creative talents as part of their struggle, with copywriters and illustrators devising witty signs and placards that parodied well-known advertising slogans of the day, including a send-up of the Ivory Soap motto which proclaimed that Gussow-Kahn employees were "99 $^{44}/_{100}$% poor." Humor did nothing about the delays at the Labor Board or the opportunities that they provided for management to campaign against the union. Over the summer, Gussow-Kahn raised the salaries of its lowest-paid employees by approximately 25 percent and agreed to a truce in exchange for the union withdrawing its unfair labor practice charges. After the advertising agency fired three more pro-union employees in October the organizing drive fizzled.[57]

The experiences of the Gussow-Kahn employees, who were ultimately dissuaded from unionization by their bosses' aggressive anti-union stance, or the cartoonists at Fleischer studios, who won a contract after a long strike only to have their employer leave the city, showed the continuing impediments to white-collar organizing despite the protections of the NLRA. Securing recognition from an employer and successfully negotiating a first contract hardly meant the end to workplace organizing. Labor turnover constantly brought new people into the office, many of whom had no previous union experience or harbored anti-union sentiments, while the allegiance of some union supporters could waver over time. To preserve improvements already achieved and to make further gains required continuous organizing and new activists to take the place of union stalwarts who moved on to other jobs or life opportunities.

Inside the Culture of Consumer Capitalism: The Newspaper Guild at Time Inc.

In few workplaces were the ongoing efforts required not just to start unions but to sustain them more evident than at Time Inc., where editorial employees established a unit of the Newspaper Guild of New York. As one of the most dynamic media enterprises of the mid-century decades, Time Inc. exerted a significant influence on the evolution of America's culture of consumer capitalism. While competitors faltered during the Depression, the company expanded its operations and attracted an impressive roster of literary and artistic talent, including writers Dwight Macdonald, Archibald MacLeish, and James Agee, and photographers Margaret Bourke-White and Walker Evans. In addition to its flagship weekly newsmagazine *Time*, by 1937 the company also published *Architectural Forum*, the business magazine *Fortune*, and the recently launched *Life*. The firm had also expanded its reach into other media, producing the *March of Time* motion-picture newsreels and network radio programming.[58]

Nonetheless, enough employees were dissatisfied with conditions at Time Inc. to begin organizing with the Newspaper Guild toward the end of 1936. Although star writers and artists were well compensated, many others, as well as the large number of assistant editors, technicians, researchers, and clerical staff whose labor produced the company's prodigious media output, earned salaries that were equal to or less than those for comparable jobs at less profitable publications. The firm's growing pains only exacerbated many employees' discontent. Executives misgauged the popularity of *Life* and offered advertisers a circulation guarantee that grossly underestimated the actual demand for the magazine. Initial advertising rates were far too low, so that until the rates could be adjusted in late 1937, the company actually lost money on each additional copy of *Life* it printed and sold. While it took advantage of the opportunity to build market share for its pioneering experiment in photojournalism, its net profits plunged from $2,747,232 in 1936 to just $168,430 in 1937, largely on account of *Life's* early losses. The financial strain led the company to withhold raises and increase workloads; on the *March of Time* newsreels, some film technicians were averaging 15 to 20 hours a week of overtime without any additional pay above their base salary. As some midlevel managers caught wind of the organizing that was taking place in the editorial departments during the spring of 1937 and began to threaten union members, *Fortune* writer Cameron Mackenzie, then chairman of the Newspaper Guild's unit committee at Time, asked the union's leadership to intercede with the company's top executives in order to protect Guild supporters from retaliation and open discussions about the possibility of negotiations.[59]

Time Inc. executives, including publisher-in-chief Henry Luce, vice president Roy Larsen, and general managing editor Ralph Ingersoll, sought to reach an accommodation with the unionists that would maintain managerial prerogatives. Unlike firms that aggressively fought unionization, the company recognized the Newspaper Guild without requiring NLRB certification and commenced negotiations on a first contract in the fall of 1937. But the stance taken by Time's executives during negotiations revealed a paternalism which would shape relations between the Guild and the company for years to come. From their perspective, the union was merely a voluntary association of employees, potentially one among many, and not the employees' exclusive bargaining representative with particular legal prerogatives. "What individuals who work for this company," Ingersoll declared in a memo distributed to all staff, "do with their own time is their own business. What organizations they join—whether it be the Republican Party or the New York Newspaper Guild—is likewise a matter for their own conscience." Consequently, executives adamantly rejected Guild negotiators' demands for a union shop provision, under which management would retain control over hiring in the editorial departments but employees would subsequently be required to join the Guild. Luce shared his objections to the "Guild Shop" with Time's employees in an October 1937 memo. Management objected, he maintained, out of "respect for the rights of minorities" as well as its concern that "the idea of collective bargaining in journalistic enterprise should have further testing," even though the *New York Post* had accepted a union shop provision in its Guild contract since 1935.[60]

As negotiations dragged on into 1938, it became clear that management was determined to ensure that employees saw them, rather than the union, as responsible for the positive aspects of working for the company. Some union supporters, Ingersoll admonished in April, had "gone off track" by assuming that "pleasant conditions in TIME Inc. were the creation of the N.Y. Newspaper Guild." Rather, he insisted, the relatively generous terms of employment stemmed from the fact that "as a group of people we have been able to create something which is useful to those who live on this continent," for which management was "intelligent enough" to "collect sufficient monies to make these conditions possible." The company readily agreed to stipulate minimum salaries for various job classifications, but it was reluctant to accede to the Guild's desire for incremental increases in the minimums to reward experience and rejected outright the idea of an across-the-board percentage raise for employees earning salaries above the minimums. Ultimately, the contract agreed to in July 1938 provided starting minimum salaries for each classification with step increases for each of the first two years in the position. Typists and file clerks in the editorial departments started at salaries of at least $25 per week, while secretaries, researchers, writers, proofreaders, assistant editors, art directors, and photographers began at no less than $30. Layout designers, photo printers, and motion-picture film handlers started at no less than $45 weekly, and newsreel film editors began at no less than $60. Over time the differences in the minimum salaries became much more pronounced. After two years, secretaries earned a weekly minimum of $35, while researchers earned at least $50 and writers no less than $75. The new minimums resulted in raises for about half of the roughly 300 employees covered by the contract, with some receiving pay hikes of as much as $20 per week. In addition, the deal provided overtime pay, enhanced severance compensation, and three weeks of paid vacation for all editorial department employees with at least three years of service. After all parties had signed, Ingersoll announced that the company was extending the contract minimums for clerical positions to the commercial departments based in New York, a move that executives hoped would thwart any expansion of the Guild at Time and show editorial employees that they had gained nothing by unionization that they might not otherwise have received from management.[61]

In organizing a unit of the Newspaper Guild at Time Inc., the company's editorial employees were responding not just to dissatisfaction over pay and hours, but also to the concerns that many of them harbored about issues of creative autonomy within the expanding media empire. The willingness of Time executives during the 1930s to hire talented people with views substantially to the left of their own periodically resulted in conflict over content, including in 1936 when *Fortune* refused to publish an article by Dwight Macdonald on US Steel that criticized the industrial behemoth's labor practices. After quitting his $200 per week position at the magazine in protest, he subsequently denounced the "Lucepapers" as corporate propaganda. While many in the Guild saw the protections of a union contract as basic prerequisites for journalistic objectivity, Luce and his team of executives recapitulated many of the same arguments wielded by the Associated Press

in its unsuccessful attempt to secure exemption from the NLRA. At a prestigious media outlet like Time, where many creative staff saw themselves as
superior to their counterparts elsewhere, these arguments had particular res-
onance, leading Guild activists to rebut claims that a strong union would result in slanted coverage. As they observed in their shop newsletter, during
the 1936 presidential campaign "many a Hearst reporter faithfully typed out
anti-New Deal stories for his boss and then went off to vote for Roosevelt."
Fortune editor Archibald MacLeish complained at an open Guild meeting
in October 1937 that he was "very tired" of writers who used the principle of
"freedom of the press" as an excuse for not joining the union. He ridiculed
the idea that Guild membership would preclude unbiased reporting by
pointing to the example of the increasingly anti-labor *World-Telegram* columnist Westbrook Pegler, whose fulminations were syndicated nationwide by
the Scripps-Howard chain. Although Pegler still belonged to the Newspaper
Guild during the late 1930s, his writing, MacLeish observed, assailed nearly
every aspect of the union's official policy.[62]

The position taken by MacLeish and other Guild supporters may seem
defensive in light of the executives' firm grasp of the editorial reins, but Luce
and his top deputies increasingly viewed the union as a threat to their control. In response to the Guild grievance committee's diligent contract enforcement, Luce asserted in early 1939 that if " 'labor' (for us) were a commodity,
if labor could be bought by standard weight and measure and price, the job
of management would be no more difficult than a rather simple cross-word
puzzle." The Guild, he suggested, failed to appreciate the executives' need for
flexibility. "Sometimes we want experience and sometimes experience is an
obstruction and we want 'new blood,'" Luce insisted. "Endless are the varieties
of consideration which enter into our estimates of the usefulness of various
people." *Editor and Publisher*, reflecting the press magnates' interests, quoted
his memo at length and added that "Mr. Luce's problem is that of every editorial room," since "people who write stuff for public print cannot be weighed
on the same scales with those who put written words into slugs and plates or
turn them out on cylinder presses." Guild activists at Time Inc. responded in
their shop newsletter that the argument that the "ability to do editorial work,
unlike other kinds of ability, is intangible and cannot be objectively measured" and that "the only persons who are capable of judging or have the right
to judge such ability are publishers," was merely a variation on the rhetoric
used by anti-union employers throughout the culture industries. "It is not the
Guild that looks upon labor as a commodity," they contended, but management. "Treating labor as a commodity means changing the brand every week

if it seems desirable. You can do that with paper or ink, but not with human beings."[63]

As negotiations on a second contract began in the summer of 1939, Newspaper Guild activists sought a wide range of improvements, many of which they had failed to attain in their first round of collective bargaining. They proposed increases in minimum salaries, the introduction of an additional third-year step-up in the minimums for most categories, enhancements in vacation and maternity leave, nine paid holidays, an expansion of the bargaining unit to include stockroom employees on the commercial side of the operation, and the addition of a union shop clause. Management's representatives agreed only to more generous maternity and vacation policies. Guild members responded with a petition to Luce in September expressing their disapproval of the company's counteroffers, which unit chair Anna Goldsborough, an assistant head of the letters department at *Life*, followed up with a stinging personal rebuke to him for his intransigence. As it became clear that there was inadequate support among the membership for stronger action, the union had little choice but to accept in December a second contract that was just marginally better than the first one, with the only significant hikes in minimum salaries accruing to writers, photographers, art directors, and assistant editors.[64]

Nonetheless, the Guild had established itself as a lasting organizational entity at Time Inc., an accomplishment made possible by the dedication of a core group of perhaps thirty to forty union activists. A survey of the rosters of the organizing, negotiating, grievance, and dues-collection committees during the late 1930s and early 1940s provides some measure of their career trajectories. In general, they tended not to be the highly paid star writers or photographers, nor the lower-level clerical workers whose employment tenure with the company might be relatively brief, but rather the skilled midlevel professionals and paraprofessionals whose contributions were absolutely essential to the company's mass production of words and images. Some, like Joseph Kastner, who was a writer for *Life* when he was elected unit chairman in December 1939, had years of experience with the firm. Originally hired to write for *Time* back in 1924, Kastner left the company after a year to begin a stint at the *New York World* before returning in 1930 to write for *Fortune*. Many more had been hired in the mid-1930s as part of the firm's ongoing expansion. Helen Sweeney, elected vice chair along with Kastner, had started with the company in 1934 and worked her way up to the position of assistant librarian in the "morgue," which was several rooms filled with cabinets of indexed notecards, memos, and newspaper and magazine clippings that served as Time Inc.'s reference database in an age before computers. While Kastner and Sweeney had taken part in the earliest Guild organizing at the company in 1936, some key activists were more recent hires; researcher Anna Goldsborough, for one, had only become an employee in 1937 but had quickly taken a leading role in Guild affairs. In 1939 the unit's executive committee included film technician John Bradford, *Life* researcher Ruth Berrien, *Time* researcher Carolyn Marx, researcher Maria de Blasio, and John McManus, a *Time* writer who was eventually elected president of the New York Newspaper Guild in 1943. Through these activists' tireless efforts, the Time unit weathered the political storms of 1939 and 1940, and emerged in a stronger position when it again faced Luce's representatives at the bargaining table in 1941.[65]

Labor Feminism in the White-Collar Unions

The Newspaper Guild's organizing efforts at Time Inc. provided just one example of women's vital role in the development of the white-collar unions in New York's culture industries. Their labor activism directly confronted the structural inequality and discrimination they experienced on a daily basis in the workplace, and represented one of the most important manifestations of American feminism between the suffrage struggles of the early twentieth century and the emergence of "second-wave" feminism during the 1960s and 1970s.[66] Explicating the experiences and contributions of these white-collar labor feminists requires not only accounting for the obfuscation of working women's struggles in general, but also the effects of the repression directed against the Popular Front political and social movements with which they identified.[67]

Beginning in the early 1930s, a vanguard of radical women had propelled the development of the Office Workers' Union and its successor organizations. In recognition of the preponderance of female employees in many lines of white-collar work, women held key leadership positions in the fledgling OWU, including Laura Carmon, who served as the union's general secretary, and Clarina Michelson, who headed the union's department store section and led the walkouts at Klein's and Ohrbach's. Susan Jenkins, a Communist activist who worked intermittently for the *Daily Worker*, led both the 1934 strike by OWU members against book publisher Macaulay and the highly publicized 1935 strike by the editorial and technical staff of Consumers' Research. After the Communist Party officially adopted the Popular Front strategy and dissolved the OWU, these radical women led their followers briefly into AFL locals and then ultimately into the CIO. Members of the

OWU Department Store Section followed Michelson into AFL Retail Clerks Local 1250, which eventually became the hub of a cluster of CIO locals that organized thousands of sales and clerical workers, including staff at Macy's, Bloomingdale's, Saks, and Gimbel's. Norma Aronson headed the group from the OWU that entered the BS&AU in early 1936 and made possible the election of Lewis Merrill's procommunist slate in the local elections later that year. Throughout the entire history of the UOPWA, Aronson continued to be one of the most important organizers in the New York area, helping to bring many new shops into the union while also serving on the union's international executive board. Anne Berenholz, another Communist stalwart with roots in the OWU, became the first executive secretary of the UOPWA New York Joint Council in 1938, and served as a Midwest regional director for the international union during the 1940s.[68]

Although their experiences as women workers profoundly shaped these activists' understanding and practice of labor feminism, as Communists they were also influenced by a particular radical discourse about gender. During the first half of the 1930s, the Communist Party addressed gender issues most explicitly in its monthly magazine *Working Woman*, which was directed at "working women, farm women, and working-class housewives." Like most doctrinaire Marxist thinking about the condition of women, the magazine's analysis was grounded in the propositions advanced by Friedrich Engels in *The Origin of the Family, Private Property, and the State* (1884). It attributed nearly all aspects of women's continuing oppression to capitalist class relations, while pitching revolutionary socialism as the only means to women's liberation. *Working Woman* excoriated Rose Schneiderman and the Women's Trade Union League as collaborators with capital, but still concurred with the League's calls for the expansion of "protective" workplace legislation for women—such as laws stipulating maximum hours or minimum wages for female employees—and, consequently, its opposition to the Equal Rights Amendment.[69] The magazine highlighted the roles of procommunist women in the "revolutionary" unions of the TUUL and in organizing boycotts and demonstrations by working-class consumers and tenants.[70] It repeatedly condemned most female-oriented mass-circulation periodicals, and it also included frank discussions of abortion and forcefully advocated for greater access to birth control.[71] The procommunist *New Masses* also ran some essays that addressed themes central to *Working Woman*, including one by Rebecca Pitts in the February 1935 issue in which she asserted that in the discriminatory conditions of their wage labor, women found themselves "exploited as workers and doubly exploited as *women.*" Class equality, Pitts insisted, offered the potential not only for economic justice in the workplace but also redress for grievances in women's personal lives. "Only when exploitation, therefore, is destroyed—and the psychology of power and profit—can women be free," she concluded. "We all need to see this: the oppressed industrial worker, to be sure; but also the professional woman, the ambitious college girl, the wife who has stifled her native talents in domestic slavery."[72]

Following the shift to the Popular Front position in the spring of 1935, the Communist Party backed away from the overtly proletarian feminism of the early part of the decade and discontinued *Working Woman*. It continued to endorse a "Women's Charter" of comprehensive federal legislation that would extend protective regulations and create new social programs for working women and their children, but it also focused on initiatives geared toward middle-class women, such as the League of Women Shoppers, a group that organized demonstrations and boycotts against retailers that exploited their employees or sold goods made by anti-union firms or imported from fascist nations.[73] More significantly, the shift abetted the development of a labor feminism with broader appeal that could accommodate the varying class ambiguities of professional, technical, and clerical work. In the fall of 1938, the UOPWA New York Joint Council initiated an "Us Women" discussion forum that, according to the BMG newsletter, was focused on "women labor leaders, birth control, women's role in peace movements and trade unionism," in addition to "more frivolous topics like make-up, dress, and personality." Even sessions on seemingly tame topics like "Charm" could be expected to have a critical bite when led by radical figures like clothing designer and author Elizabeth Hawes, and journalist and humorist Ruth McKenney. In some cases, women activists specifically gendered class solidarity as a feminine trait in contrast with the masculine attributes of selfish and disloyal individualism that they saw as inimical to the success of white-collar unionism. This was the moral of Shirley Jackson's short story, "One of the Boys," which chronicles the experiences of an obsequious male scab in a publishing house who deserts his mostly female coworkers during their strike for union recognition only to find that he is cast aside once the boss capitulates.[74]

The organizational networks of the Popular Front cultivated a second cohort of women activists such as Jane Benedict, who had envisioned becoming an author when she graduated from Cornell University in 1933. Instead, she found herself toiling in the bookshop at Macy's Herald Square department store for a starting full-time salary of $15 a week. Benedict had no previous experience with either leftist politics or the labor movement, and her first contact with the BMG came through its educational program. Enticed

initially by the chance to take an inexpensive class on editing, Benedict became increasingly interested in the unionization of the publishing field. "The
compensation of working in publishing was supposed to be the glamour of
the industry," she later recalled, "and the creative aspect" was "supposed to
satisfy your inner soul," when in fact workers "didn't get enough money to
live decently." At her new job as an editorial assistant at Macmillan she became active in the BMG, which led to her firing in 1937 several weeks after
she began distributing union leaflets to her colleagues on the way from the
subway to the office. She subsequently joined the staff of the union, and in
1942 she succeeded book designer Robert Josephy as president of the local.
Less visible than Benedict but no less important were the cadre of women
who volunteered to chair unit committees or serve as stewards. Women
like Esther Temple, a billing clerk at Random House who chaired the unit
committee there and had been fired from a previous job for her union activism, maintained morale among supporters in the workplace, confronted
supervisors with members' grievances, and helped to negotiate contracts.[75]

Within the Popular Front social movements, the issues that women
faced as women *per se* were often superseded by a primary focus on labor
and class, as well as by concerns over matters pertaining to race, ethnicity,
international antifascist solidarity, and even the specific issues of consumers
and tenants. "I am really ashamed to say," Benedict confessed decades later,
"that I was not terribly conscious of myself as a woman" who was "a pioneer."
When UOPWA president Lewis Merrill once referred to her as "being 'the
woman leader,'" it "suddenly dawned on me: Oh, well, how many women
are there that are presidents of locals?" For women like Benedict, union activism seemed the most practical response to the heavily gendered division
of labor they encountered in the office. It allowed them to step out of def-
erential roles expected by their male supervisors and to confront the sexist
ideology that suffused most workplaces. Their dual empowerment as women
and workers rested on their resistance to the discrimination and harassment
they encountered on the job and on their agitation for salaries that could adequately support an independent lifestyle. While Benedict acknowledged that
"in publishing, there was discrimination in terms of women being promoted,"
the unionists' "main fight was on wage standards, because they were so bad."
When BMG members surveyed salaries in book publishing in 1940, they
found that fully one-third of the employees in book publishing still earned
less than $22.93 a week, which was the amount that the State Department
of Labor estimated as the minimum needed for a single woman to live on
her own in New York City. For the underpaid women in publishing and in

FIGURE 2.3 Jane Benedict in 1940 shortly before becoming the first woman president of the UOPWA Book and Magazine Guild. From the *Daily Worker* Photo Archive held at the Tamiment Library, New York University by permission of the Communist Party USA.

New York's other culture industries, to attain a salary that could make personal autonomy possible furnished as important a measure as any of what was at stake in the organization of the creative class.[76]

Popular Front Unionism in a Turbulent World

By the close of the 1930s, the white-collar unions in the culture industries began to face mounting attacks from opponents due to the significant influence of procommunists within their ranks. Communists had always been viewed with deep suspicion if not outright hostility by large segments of the American public. Early members of the Communist Party had encountered intense persecution, and while the repression eased somewhat in the late 1920s and the early 1930s, dogmatism often isolated American Communists and hindered effective cooperation with other groups. The advent of the Popular Front brought the Communist movement closer to the mainstream of American political life than it had ever been before or would be again. Communists joined much larger numbers of non-Communist radicals, progressives, and liberals in an array of organizations dedicated to championing the rights of labor, combating racism, building international antifascist solidarity, strengthening civil liberties, and mobilizing consumers. At its peak in the late 1930s between 80,000 and 100,000 Americans belonged to the Party, although membership turnover remained high. The pool of former members—including those who remained sympathetic "fellow travelers" and others who became indefatigable foes—was much larger. Still, the relative success of the Communists' efforts at promoting left-leaning social democracy—neatly captured in their Popular Front slogan "Communism is Twentieth-Century Americanism"—gave them influence significantly beyond their modest membership figures.[77]

Even during the heyday of the Popular Front, anticommunism remained a potent force. The perfidy of Communists' defense of the Soviet regime spurred a principled opposition among many Americans. In addition, some non-Communist participants in the Popular Front came to object to the manipulative tactics that procommunists sometimes used to influence or control various organizations. Most of the corporations and conservatives that bankrolled the anticommunist campaign and spread its message, however, reacted to the Popular Front's domestic political program, particularly its empowerment of workers, its withering critiques of consumer capitalism, its advocacy for an expanded public sector, and its support for gender and racial equality. The CIO was a prime target. Many activists who had been involved with the Communists' own unions before 1935 had moved into the CIO, gaining influence in many affiliates. For media moguls and advertisers seeking to check labor's advance, raising the specter of the "Red Menace" emerged as a consistent tactic. Furthermore, Congressional anticommunists appropriated the form of the crusading investigative committees that had been used so effectively in the 1930s by liberals and redeployed it to serve their political aims by establishing in 1938 a new House Special Committee Investigating Un-American Activities chaired by Texas Democratic Representative Martin

Dies. This committee performed a crucial function in legitimating the anticommunist crusade by enabling allegations raised in hearings testimony to be recycled as official findings, which could then be used as additional ammunition by private groups opposed to the progressive agenda.

To a considerable extent, the corporate and conservative opponents of the CIO depended on AFL officials or jaded former radicals for the details of their narratives of subversion. John Frey, the head of the AFL Metal Trades Department, provided the Dies Committee with extensive testimony about the history of Communist labor agitation and named scores of organizers and officials throughout the entire CIO—including Merrill of the UOPWA—as Communist stalwarts.[78] Journalist Benjamin Stolberg, an ex-Communist, relentlessly redbaited the CIO, beginning with several articles in the *New York World-Telegram* in 1938, followed the next year by additional attacks in the *Saturday Evening Post* and other magazines. Stolberg repeatedly accused Merrill and his UOPWA associates of ineffectual organizing, providing misleading information about union membership and finances, and provoking internal dissention.[79] Perhaps the most prolific of these experts on the Communist threat was J. B. Matthews, a self-described former fellow traveler who earlier in the 1930s had once been a leader of the League Against War and Fascism and a director of Consumers' Research, but whose political inclinations veered sharply to the right after the acrimonious strike by the product testing institute's employees in 1935. By 1938, he had become the chief researcher for the Dies Committee while simultaneously working as a research consultant for Hearst Publications, which faced both the internal challenge of the Newspaper Guild within its newspaper and magazine offices and the external challenge to its integrity by Popular Front consumer activists and the Federal Trade Commission. In his dual capacity, Matthews was uniquely positioned to apply pressure on the white-collar unions, Popular Front organizations like Consumers Union, and progressive government officials like Consumers' Counsel Donald Montgomery by tarring them all as agents of Communist infiltration.[80]

White-collar unionists did what they could to deflect the accusations of Communist influence, which they asserted were unfounded attempts by antilabor employers to discredit their organizing efforts. The UOPWA pointed to the AFL pedigrees of the local unions that had founded it in 1937 and went so far as to threaten legal action against Stolberg and his publishers for his articles.[81] Even though many members and potential members found these defenses credible, for others the accusations planted the seeds of doubt. In a few cases, ideological tensions resulted in wholesale defections of established bargaining units to the AFL.[82] A more common response, more troubling for the long-term viability of the young white-collar unions, was the individual disaffection that the allegations engendered in many workers. At a meeting of the Newspaper Guild of New York's extended executive committee in June 1939 to discuss perceptions of malaise in the local and possible solutions, one organizer at the *Herald Tribune* opined that workers in the papers' commercial departments were "dominated by fear," believing that Guild membership would cost them "the $1.50 raise they hope to get," and that "CIO affiliation is equivalent to Communism."[83]

The signing of the Nazi–Soviet pact in August 1939 and the subsequent outbreak of the Second World War in Europe only exacerbated the situation. Following the pact, procommunists in the United States abruptly shifted their position on world affairs; instead of rallying all liberals, progressives, and radicals to contain fascist aggression as they had for years, procommunists suddenly insisted that the armed conflict was simply a squabble among imperialist powers. Nazi conquests in Western Europe during the spring and summer of 1940 only rendered the procommunists' stance even more controversial, as many liberals and progressives began to see assistance to Britain and the other remaining Allies as vital. Throughout the CIO, anticommunist unionists introduced resolutions at unit and local meetings that condemned both Nazism and Communism and equated the two in what amounted to an early formulation of the concept of totalitarianism. Where members were especially attuned to the international situation, such as the Newspaper Guild unit at Time Inc., arguments over Communism threatened to scuttle any discussion of regular union affairs. At one membership meeting in June 1940, for instance, Whittaker Chambers, the ex-Communist writer and editor who had recently joined the staff of *Time*, charged that CIO counsel Lee Pressman was a Soviet agent and also introduced a motion, subsequently tabled, praising Westbrook Pegler for his latest column attacking the Guild for its supposed Communist sympathies.[84]

Chambers subsequently offered a narrative frame for the Popular Front that typified anticommunists' efforts to discredit the white-collar militancy that had emerged in the culture industries. In his sensationalistic memoir *Witness*, published in 1952, he looked back on the radical ferment of the Depression era, depicting it as the time of "the big undergrounds, the infiltration of the Government, science, education and all branches of communications, but especially radio, motion pictures, book, magazine and newspaper publishing." Over the course of the 1930s, he alleged, "simply by pursuing the careers that ordinarily lay open to them," white-collar radicals and progressives "would carry the weak and stumbling American Communist Party directly into the highest councils of the nation." While the Popular Front was, in Chambers's account, just a ruse for subversion and treason, the supporters of left-led unions like the UOPWA and the Newspaper Guild were nearly beneath contempt. "The *Time* unit of the Guild," he maintained, "was made up of a proletariat of file clerks, office boys, and other unskilled intellectuals whose interests the Communists were peculiarly solicitous of, for their numbers gave them control." It also included "a sizable group of responsible writers and researchers, most of them college graduates, and, in the case of the writers, men who helped to shape the opinions of a million people every week," but who, in union meetings, were "time and again dutifully voting what was wanted by the Communists whom most of them were completely incapable of recognizing for what they were. To them the Communists just looked like more impassioned liberals."[85]

Excepting a small handful of the thousands of men and women who participated in the white-collar insurgency, Chambers's claims in *Witness* constituted a form of collective libel. In depicting the overwhelming majority of the people who risked their livelihoods or simply committed their free time and energy to organize for collective bargaining, improved pay and conditions, a greater degree of workplace autonomy, and equal employment opportunity as nothing more than an assemblage of con artists, stooges, and dupes, he propagated an egregious slur. And yet the exceptional handful existed; the subversion was not only in the imagination of anticommunist zealots like Dies, Matthews, and Chambers. Even as Chambers filibustered about Communists during meetings of the Time Inc. unit of the Newspaper Guild in early 1940, a procommunist official of the New York local, Nat Einhorn, was exploiting his position to recruit several journalists into Soviet espionage. Einhorn generally spent 50 or 60 hours a week performing the mundane and largely thankless organizational and administrative tasks that helped to solidify the Guild's presence within the city's print media; the time he spent abetting Soviet intelligence was a tiny fraction of the time he spent building white-collar trade unionism, but his activities as a foreign agent would cast a pall over his work for the Guild. Perhaps the most notorious American convicted of espionage during the early Cold War, Julius Rosenberg, was most likely recruited through his membership in the FAECT.[86] However rare these actual instances of subversion were, given the number of clerical, technical, professional, or creative workers who supported the left-led unions during the 1930s and 1940s, they nonetheless furnished the unions' adversaries with a crucial line of attack.

In the uneasy interlude that followed the outbreak of war in Europe, Communists were far from the only Americans who favored a noninterventionist course for the United States. Large numbers of conservative isolationists, and initially some liberals as well, backed the America First Committee, which campaigned to keep the country out of the escalating global conflict.[87] Within the CIO itself, support for nonintervention transcended the boundaries of the procommunist caucus. CIO president John L. Lewis not only expressed skepticism regarding intervention on behalf of Britain and the Allies, but also endorsed the Republicans' 1940 presidential candidate, Wendell Willkie, while most within the CIO supported FDR as well as his program for defense mobilization. Interpreting the election results, particularly in working-class districts that went heavily for Roosevelt, as a repudiation of his leadership, Lewis resigned as president of the CIO despite pleas from procommunists, including many in the UOPWA, that he remain in the top post.[88]

The lingering effects of the recession of the late 1930s combined with the rising tide of anticommunism and the general disarray within the CIO to produce a lull in the organizational development of the white-collar unions in New York's culture industries. Most of the unions—with the notable exception of United American Artists—continued to add members and to win recognition in new shops during 1939 and 1940, although the rate of growth was more modest than it had been during much of the heady period from 1933 through 1938. Member interest also waned during these slack years. In the Newspaper Guild of New York, for example, only about half of its roughly 5,000 members during the first half of 1940 were sufficiently current in their payment of dues and assessments to be "in good standing," and thus eligible to vote on union matters.[89] By early 1941, however, the quickening economic tempo brought about by the defense buildup and the restoration of stability within the CIO under the leadership of its new president, Philip Murray, created a more promising environment for expansion for all of the industrial unions, including those that organized white-collar workers. It remained to be seen, however, which groups of white-collar workers in New York's culture industries would make the most of the new opportunities.

3

Challenging the Culture
of Consumer Capitalism

IN THE FALL of 1935, during the weeks that followed the tumultuous AFL convention and the first tentative announcement of a Committee on Industrial Organization, labor activists from across the country inundated John L. Lewis's office with inquiries. Proponents of industrial unionism, many with political positions far to the left of Lewis's own views, wrote seeking guidance and support for their efforts. While the bulk of this correspondence came from unionists in the manufacturing sector, a significant portion of it came from white-collar activists like Susan Jenkins, a Communist organizer with the AFL-affiliated Technical, Editorial and Office Assistants Union Local 20055. She wrote several times soliciting Lewis's assistance for her local's strike against Consumers' Research (CR), a product testing and rating institute based in rural Washington, New Jersey. Reminding him that she had been "one of a committee of seven which drew up the resolution in favor of industrial unionism" at the AFL convention, she attempted to leverage that connection into not just a donation of relief funds for the weary strikers, but a commitment from the nascent CIO to sponsor a new consumer organization. "It is highly important," Jenkins insisted, "that a close relationship be maintained between the consumer movement and the labor movement, since a split in interest and in purpose between these two movements has potentialities of great danger." Were the consumer movement to become "captured by individuals or groups who are opposed to the interests of organized labor and the working class," she concluded, "there is the possibility of its [*sic*] taking a decidedly fascist turn."[1]

Lewis was unable to assist her proposed initiative, but Jenkins and the other strikers were undeterred. Along with a group of former CR subscribers led by Book and Magazine Guild President James Gilman, they went ahead with their plans for a new consumer organization aligned with the Popular Front. Despite several favorable NLRB rulings in early 1936, none of the striking technicians, writers, and clerical workers returned to their jobs at CR. Instead, they established Consumers Union (CU) in New York City as a leftist rival to CR, and they produced the first issue of their monthly *Reports* for the institute's member-subscribers that April.[2] By 1940, *Consumers Union Reports* was just one of a number of publications—including the New York daily tabloid newspaper *PM*, the weekly national newsletter *In Fact*, and the weekly magazine *Friday*—that challenged the culture of consumer capitalism. *PM* founder Ralph Ingersoll and *In Fact* publisher George Seldes demonstrated their aversion to the influence of consumer capitalism over the media by eschewing advertising entirely, with the expectation that readers would provide the sole source of revenue. In contrast, *Friday* publisher Daniel Gillmor and his associates implemented a different discursive and aesthetic strategy by appropriating the form and style of commercially oriented magazines, borrowing elements from both slicks like *Life* and pulps like *True Story* and reinterpreting them to propagate the Popular Front political agenda. Despite the differences in their formats and their means of support, *Consumers Union Reports*, *PM*, *In Fact*, and *Friday* all promoted a social consumerism defined by a deep skepticism—if not outright hostility—toward advertising, a desire for an increased supply of public goods and services, a preference for increased regulation of markets, and a fundamental belief that the purchase and use of goods were participatory political acts as well as a form of work on the part of the consumer. Furthermore, as Jenkins had called for in her letter to Lewis, all four of these publications linked their progressive consumer advocacy directly to their staunch support for organized labor, particularly the CIO.

Although radio was the dynamic new media of the 1930s and 1940s, the print media generally proved more conducive to progressives and radicals in the creative class who wished to criticize the prevailing culture of consumer capitalism. Their lack of access to the airwaves stemmed in large part from the regulatory regime of American broadcasting. In its licensing and allocation of the AM spectrum, the FCC consistently favored stations with network affiliations or other formidable commercial backing, particularly newspaper ownership. The few existing nonprofit stations, like labor-sponsored WEVD in New York and WCFL in Chicago, or municipally owned WNYC, that objected to the federal government's role in enabling the commercial domination of the airwaves found themselves subject to various forms of official harassment, including limitations on their signal strength, restrictions on the hours they were allowed to broadcast, and threats of license revocation until they desisted from their protests.[3] Applications by unions and progressive groups to the FCC for new AM station licenses were rejected due to a lack of suitable frequencies or, revealingly, on the grounds that the applicant represented a special interest, unlike privately owned, profit-driven broadcasting enterprises that supposedly provided a public service by virtue of their need to appeal to the wide audiences craved by advertisers. The National Association of Broadcasters (NAB) impeded radio-minded progressives even further with its code of conduct for member stations. The code banned programming on controversial topics, which was taken by most stations to include advocacy of either militant industrial unionism or progressive consumer activism. Denials of requests by unions and consumer groups to obtain airtime were rationalized in terms of respecting community standards of decency, but essentially the NAB code provided cover for stations to keep from transmitting political viewpoints that advertisers found objectionable. Even those stations that periodically carried speeches by labor leaders or consumer activists for their news value were reluctant to commit to regularly scheduled series of progressive programs. Although sustaining airtime did furnish some important opportunities for artistic experimentation to reach a national audience, it did not provide a comparable opening to Popular Front labor and consumer activists.[4]

Publishing, by contrast, allowed progressives and radicals nearly complete control over content without the obstacles that they encountered in radio, but it offered other practical advantages as well. Magazines, newsletters, and weekly or monthly newspapers could be launched with a significantly smaller initial investment. Publishers could then subsequently add pages, increase their frequency, or expand distribution as growth in circulation and revenues warranted. Of the alternative print media projects considered in this chapter, only *PM* required a multimillion dollar outlay at the outset. Because these publications provided opportunities to write, edit, photograph, or illustrate free from most of the creative and political constraints that resulted from the influence of advertisers, they attracted staffs comprised of men and women who sought a respite, if not a refuge, from the mainstream culture industries. When writers for these publications criticized consumer capitalism and the cultural products it sustained, they rooted their analyses directly in their own personal work experiences. Also, as Jenkins and the other CR strikers demonstrated, the people who joined the staffs of CU, *PM*, *In Fact*, or *Friday*, had a passionate commitment to the labor movement, and to the unionization of the creative class especially, that was similarly grounded in their many years of work in the culture industries.

While the publications examined here promoted social consumerism, they all had to build circulation within a media environment that was thoroughly structured by consumer capitalism. Newspapers and magazines that aspired, in part, to provoke a rethinking of the ways in which the media served as conduits for idealized representations of commodities were nonetheless still commodities themselves, and their survival as publishing endeavors depended on their ability to cultivate a following of readers who were willing to purchase them. The progressive media experiments of the 1930s and 1940s could not easily transcend long-established patterns of periodical distribution and sales, or reading habits, or popular tastes in journalistic genre and style. To the extent that these initiatives succeeded, they helped to make Popular Front social movements visible within American culture, and they validated leftist positions on consumer and labor issues within public discourse. Yet the writers, artists, and editors for these publications hewed a fine line between engaging with the conventions of the existing consumer culture and inadvertently reinforcing them. Did the objective technical data that CU distributed to its members, for instance, encourage them to become more ardent foes of advertising and proponents of social democracy, or did it simply help them maximize the utility of their personal consumption choices? Did *Friday* mark a significant step forward in the representation of the Popular Front social movements in the media, or did the magazine potentially facilitate their exploitation by advertisers as just another market segment? For the people who produced these alternative periodicals, and for the advocates of social-democratic consumer activism generally, the constant struggle was to shift fundamentally the parameters of public discourses on political economy, mass consumption, and the media without becoming incorporated into these discourses in ways that buttressed capitalist hegemony.

Critiques of Consumerism from the New Era to the New Deal

The people who produced *Consumers Union Reports*, *PM*, *In Fact*, and *Friday* built upon critiques of American consumer capitalism that had evolved over the first third of the twentieth century. Perhaps no intellectual figure had a greater influence on consumer activists' thinking than sociologist Thorstein Veblen, whose *The Theory of the Leisure Class* (1899) skewered the social pretensions of Gilded Age elites and their habits of "conspicuous consumption." He soon turned his attention more directly to the ways in which manufacturers and merchants exploited new consumer practices. "The captain of industry," Veblen declared in *The Theory of Business Enterprise* (1904), "works against, as well as for, a new and more efficient organization." Firms, through their use of advertising, attained "a monopoly of custom and prestige" which they sold as "good-will, trademarks, brands, etc." Businessmen's complaints about "excessive competition" amounted in actuality to "an excess of goods, or of the means of producing them, above what is expedient on pecuniary grounds—above what there is an effective demand for at prices that will repay the cost of production and leave something appreciable left over for profit." Veblen's assessment thus linked three principal indictments of the culture of consumer capitalism that would resonate with several generations of activists: first, the notion that businesses' chosen methods were technically inadequate, as evident by their inefficiency, waste, and fraud; second, the sense that their methods were socially maladaptive, in that advertising and the commercial media did not effectively guide people's adjustment to the complex conditions of modernity; and finally, the conviction that they were economically unsound, as they underpinned a system of capital accumulation that could not be sustained in its existing form.[5]

As consumer capitalism flourished in the United States during the early twentieth century, Veblen refined his critique. After helping to establish the New School for Social Research in New York City in 1919, he embarked on what would be his last comprehensive examination of American business, *Absentee Ownership and Business Enterprise in Recent Times* (1923). The intensification of extant marketing and promotional methods with all of their resultant inefficiencies, Veblen conceded, did not point toward the dissolution of private ownership, but in fact assured the viability of corporate control for the indefinite future. The growing primacy of "salesmanship" reflected the development of a new type of mental labor, apparent in the employment of "a formidable number of artists and 'copy writers' as well as of itinerant spokesmen, demonstrators, [and] interpreters," that rivaled that of the industrial engineers he venerated. Furthermore, Veblen noted, the economic imperatives that increased employment in promotional activities, broadly construed, also rationalized the new types of mental labor, so that "sales-publicity has with good effect been reduced to mechanical units of space, speed, number, frequency and the like." To facilitate "the fabrication of customers" with "the same degree of assurance as regards the quality, rate and volume" of manufacturing output necessitated supervision by "technically trained persons who might fairly be called publicity engineers." In advertising generally, Veblen concluded that rapid expansion had led to "an extensive standardization and specialization, by which the work has come to be effectually subdivided and apportioned among the personnel within each concern."[6]

Veblen's idiosyncratic thinking on social, economic, and cultural matters facilitated the appropriation of his ideas by people from across the political spectrum. Among those consumer activists of the 1920s who drew their inspiration from Veblen, none wielded more influence than economist Stuart Chase and engineer F. J. Schlink. In *The Tragedy of Waste* (1925), Chase expounded upon the gross inefficiencies of American industry, which through a combination of deliberate restriction and insufficient planning deprived Americans of the full bounty that could be produced in a more rational system. While products were often shoddy or unsafe, customers lacked the ability to properly evaluate them. "If all consumers were reasonably well educated, if all had roughly equal purchasing power in the market, if the goods and services offered for sale were free from adulteration and defect," Chase stipulated, "it might be impertinent to make inquiry at all into human wants." Barring such ideal conditions, however, it was impossible to "accept what the consumer demanded as the real criterion."[7] Chase amplified his criticisms in his subsequent collaboration with Schlink, *Your Money's Worth* (1927), in which they provided a litany of marketing practices they found fraudulent or misleading, including brand-name processed foods, toiletries, or household products sold for prices astronomically higher than the sum of their ingredients; advertisements, like celebrity endorsements, that offered false or unsubstantiated assertions of product quality; and numerous goods that, despite regulatory agencies like the Food and Drug Administration (FDA) and the Federal Trade Commission (FTC), contained mislabeled or harmful ingredients. The solution, they concluded, was the creation of an independent "laboratory and information bureau," supervised by a "group of public trustees, chosen mainly from the professions" and staffed by experts who "could afford to tell the truth and nothing but the truth," to establish standards, test goods, and make the results available so that consumers could regain their agency in the market.[8] In 1929, Chase and Schlink implemented their proposal by founding Consumers' Research as the nation's first independent institute dedicated to the testing and rating of branded goods, with Schlink serving as its director and editing the bulletin that disseminated its findings to a pool of vetted subscribers.

Other critics, like sociologists Robert and Helen Lynd, focused on the social and cultural ramifications of consumer capitalism. In *Middletown* (1929) they explored how the accelerated pace of modernization had affected the social structure of the supposedly typical town of Muncie, Indiana since the late nineteenth century. The Lynds were particularly troubled by what they perceived to be the decline of the traditional identities and practices grounded in the "intrinsic satisfactions" of craft labor, including trade unionism, as "more and more of the activities of living are coming to be strained through the bars of the dollar sign." Yet while the "rise of large-scale advertising, popular magazines, movies, radio, and other channels of cultural diffusion from without are rapidly changing habits of thought as to what things are essential for living and multiplying optional occasions for spending money," these new patterns of consumption had yet to cohere into a set of norms to which the town's residents could adjust, resulting in what their mentor, William Ogburn, had termed "cultural lag." Consequently, the Lynds found that "Middletown's life exhibits at almost every point either some change or some stress arising from some failure to change." While "a new tool or material device" was "fairly certain to be fitted somehow into Middletown's accepted scheme of things," cultural factors "such as tradition and sentiment" would only "slowly open up to make room for it."[9] Unlike Schlink of CR, who emphasized the importance of using standards and test results to police the market, activists who took their cue principally from the Lynds were motivated by their concern over the social and cultural repercussions of consumerism to seek new regulations on advertising and marketing practices, as well as to mold the abstract aggregation of consumers into a real movement with political clout.

The crisis of the "New Era" of mass consumerism and the onset of the Depression only fanned the flames of discontent with prevailing advertising and marketing methods. Many Americans blamed empty advertising hype for artificially stimulating a false sense of prosperity, and Madison Avenue was subjected to unprecedented public scrutiny and widespread scorn. One revealing measure of this sentiment was the meteoric ascent of the humor magazine *Ballyhoo*. Launched in New York in June 1931 by editor Norman Anthony, the inaugural issue contained no actual paid advertising but instead, as its advance publicity materials had promised, nine slick, four-color mock advertisements that acerbically parodied familiar campaigns. The 150,000 copies flew off the newsstands, with quite a few of them, according to the advertising trade publication *Tide*, finding their way into the agencies' back offices where copywriters and art directors pored over ads for fake products like "Old Cold Cigarettes" and "Lox Soap." By its third issue, *Ballyhoo* had a press run of 650,000 and still sold out. The rapid growth in circulation, at fifteen cents a copy, was all the more impressive given the steep circulation losses endured by most magazines as disposable incomes shrank. In October, the publisher, George Delacorte Jr., determined to sell space in *Ballyhoo* for regular advertising, prepared with a tongue-and-cheek tone to fit in with the satirical theme. He offered an initial circulation guarantee of 750,000 copies and ad rates of $3,750 per page, which yielded a cost per thousand readers that was substantially higher than that of many general-interest titles. Not content simply to commodify the popular antipathy over advertising, Delacorte exploited his readership by delivering them to willing advertisers for a tidy sum. His crass attempt to cash in squelched the enthusiasm that the magazine briefly elicited; after circulation peaked at over 1,500,000 copies in 1932 it declined steadily over the next several years, and *Ballyhoo* disappeared at the end of the decade.[10]

The rising prominence of CR and its attacks on consumer capitalism during the early 1930s was of greater concern to advertising executives than satiric jabs. After several years of furnishing test results and commentary to just a limited band of recipients for its "confidential" memoranda, the institute began to distribute a "general" version of its *Consumers' Research Bulletin* in September 1931 in the hopes of reaching a wider public. According to its introductory statement, the *Bulletin's* purpose was to "help ultimate consumers find their way through the market maze to an intelligent selection of purchases" as well as to "present news and comment on business practices affecting or explaining the consumer's deject position at the lower depths of the economic order." CR espoused a starkly utilitarian understanding of consumption, in which the data that it produced furnished the only objective measure of value and the key to restoring consumers' liberty in the market. "The kind of work on goods that profits the consumer is not done with words," one editorial asserted, "but with tools and instruments, and by the aid of calculations, reference books, and other dull, routine devices not at all likely to delight the mind that fashions unrealities into 'sales thrusts,' 'creative merchandising,' and drug-store romance at $1.98 a bottle."[11] Not only did such statements rebuke advertisers' claims that brands indicated quality, but they also suggested the extent to which Schlink and his acolytes questioned the legitimacy of any social uses of consumption, whether as an escape into the playful or aspirational fantasies spun by advertisers, or as a potential source of progressive community norms as advocated by the Lynds.

Despite the libertarian strain that ran through the *Bulletin*, its forceful blasts at advertising garnered favorable coverage for its testing and rating activities in liberal magazines like *The New Republic* and *The Nation* as well as the procommunist *New Masses*.[12] In addition, Schlink and his associates drew attention to CR by penning a series of sensationalistic exposés, including *100,000,000 Guinea Pigs: Dangers in Everyday Food, Drugs and Cosmetics* (1932), which Schlink coauthored with CR engineer Arthur Kallet; *Skin Deep: The Truth about Beauty Aids* (1934) by Schlink's wife, CR business manager M. C. Phillips; *Partners in Plunder: The Cost of Business Dictatorship* (1935) by J. B. Matthews, who had assumed supervision of the institute's editorial departments, and his wife Ruth Shallcross; Schlink's *Eat, Drink, and Be Wary* (1935); and Kallet's *Counterfeit: Not Your Money But What It Buys* (1935). CR membership swelled to 42,000 in 1932, largely due to the buzz generated by *100,000,000 Guinea Pigs*, and by the summer of 1935 it had grown to 58,000 members.[13] Even if relatively few American consumers heeded the advice from CR on how to prepare a homemade toothpaste or breakfast cereal for a fraction of the cost of advertised brands, or to apply the technical data in its *Bulletin* on the longevity of electric motors when buying a washing machine, advertising and media executives felt that they could not ignore the institute's efforts. In one speech, for instance, Roy Durstine, a founding partner of BBDO, lashed out at CR as a "fantastically disingenuous group" of self-righteous cranks who exploited what he insisted were a handful of offending instances of deceptive practices in order to profit from muckraking. Within the agencies, management was vigilant in its opposition. A newsletter for junior staff at J. Walter Thompson in 1935 included reviews of *Skin Deep* and *Partners in Plunder* that rebutted the books' claims, since "friends" would "want to know" about the accusations leveled by the institute's authors against some of the agency's clients.[14]

The prospect of increased state intervention under the New Deal also roiled the advertising industry. The NRA clearly stimulated advertising by halting the deflationary spiral of the 1930s and providing new incentives for manufacturers and merchants to spend money on product differentiation, but it also opened the possibility for far more rigorous regulatory scrutiny than the lax oversight provided by the FTC during the 1920s. Largely to placate consumer activists for the price hikes that resulted from the drafting and implementation of NRA codes, which were intended to stabilize the economy as a precondition to recovery, the federal government created a Consumer Advisory Board (CAB) within the NRA as well as a Consumers' Counsel within the Agricultural Adjustment Administration. Because the powers and prerogatives of both the CAB and the Consumers' Counsel were poorly defined, these federal initiatives only generated more rancor within the ranks of the consumer movement; CR criticized New Deal policy as inadequate and eventually dismissed the CAB as just another fraudulent promotional gimmick, while progressive experts like Robert Lynd attempted to make the most of the CAB as a venue for representing a consumers' interest in public discourse and policy making.[15]

On the whole, the early New Deal of 1933 and 1934 proved disappointing for consumer activists: in addition to rendering the CAB ineffective, business succeeded in killing legislative proposals to strengthen the FDA, expand the purview of the FTC, empower the Department of Agriculture to mandate the grade-labeling of most canned or processed foods, and preserve access to the airwaves for non–commercial broadcasters in the Communications Act. The handful of government officials who staked out progressive positions on consumer matters, like Undersecretary of Agriculture Rexford Tugwell, were pilloried by the advertising press and marginalized within the administration. Yet progressive activists still took encouragement from the federal government's limited experiments with the public provisioning of housing and electricity, and its efforts to induce appliance makers like GE and Westinghouse to develop un-styled, generic models of electric ranges and refrigerators for its projects.[16] Although they were frustrated by their defeats, progressives continued their efforts to use state power to reshape consumption practices, assuring continued political conflict between advertisers and their detractors.

Of all of the American critics of consumer capitalism during this period, none was more thoroughly radical in his analysis than former advertising copywriter James Rorty, who fully explicated the critical role of advertising in buttressing the entire system of profit-driven enterprise. Rorty obtained his first copywriting job fresh out of college in 1913 with H. K. McCann and Company in New York City. While he appeared to be on a promising career trajectory, he harbored radical political and artistic impulses that grew more intense after his military service during World War I. Following his discharge, he stayed for a few months in the same Greenwich Village rooming house as Veblen, where the two men met and shared ideas. By the middle of the 1920s, Rorty led two parallel lives: one toiling as a copywriter for Barton, Durstine, and Osborne, which hired him in 1924, and the other as a poet and original editorial board member of *New Masses* magazine when it launched in 1926. With the onset of the Depression, he was one of many admen to lose his job, which only pushed him farther to the left. In 1932, he joined the League of Professional Groups for Foster and Ford, and along with Lewis Corey took an active role in drafting *Culture and the Crisis.*[17]

Rorty became secretary of the League of Professional Groups and attempted to build it into a permanent organization. In early 1933, the League convened a series of public symposia on "Culture and Capitalism" which included Rorty himself as well as Corey, Joseph Freeman, Michael Gold, John Dos Passos, Malcolm Cowley, Sidney Hook, Meyer Schapiro, Percival Goodman, and Robert Cantwell. Rorty also proposed that the League launch its own magazine in order to provide an outlet for its band of cultural radicals. Through these efforts, the League sought to mobilize what it described as "the professional groupings in the middle class—the engineers and technicians, architects, medical workers, teachers, social and cultural workers" and to win "their active sympathy and support for the revolutionary movement." Within a few months, however, Rorty could no longer abide what he considered the Communist Party's clumsy attempts to impose its doctrinal discipline on the organization; while the Party, he claimed, had failed, despite "the huge opportunities created by the existing economic and social situation," to "exercise the type of leadership which would result in an effective expansion and strengthening of the movement on both the labor and cultural fronts," it nonetheless asserted "the claim of leadership very jealously and suspiciously." In June he resigned from the League, concluding that he would have "contributed more to the revolutionary movement" if he had dedicated himself during the past year "simply to writing as an individual." The League soon withered, as Rorty poured his energies into a comprehensive study of advertising, which he published the next year as *Our Master's Voice*.[18]

Dedicated to "the memory of Thorstein Veblen, and to those technicians of the word whose 'conscientious withdrawal of efficiency' may yet accomplish that burial of the ad-man's pseudoculture which this book contemplates with equanimity," *Our Master's Voice* presented a damning indictment of the culture of consumer capitalism as it had developed in the United States. Unlike many contemporary commentators on advertising, Rorty defined the "advertising business" broadly as "the total apparatus of newspaper and magazine publishing in America, plus radio broadcasting, and with important qualifications the movies; plus the advertising agency structure, car card, poster, and direct-by-mail companies, plus the services of supply printing, lithography, engraving, etc." Synthesizing Veblenian and Marxist insights, he argued that while branding, advertising, styling, and the other methods of product differentiation used by business resulted in higher prices for consumers, their centrality to capital accumulation in an era of mass production and distribution had guaranteed their entrenchment and growth. More pernicious than the resulting economic inefficiencies was the harnessing of "our major instruments of social communication, whose free and disinterested functioning is embodied in the concept of a democracy, to serve the profit interests of the advertisers." Rorty derided "liberal social critics, economists and sociologists" who "wasted much time complaining that advertising has 'elevated mendacity to the status of a profession.'" Such "invidious moral value judgments" between "good" and "bad" advertising simply obscured its real function, which was to shape "the economic, social, moral and ethical patterns of the community into serviceable conformity" with the imperatives of consumer capitalism. He confessed that he saw little use in "reforming" advertising, and he frankly saw the attack on advertising as the opening wedge of an assault on the entire capitalist order. "The American apparatus of advertising" was like a "grotesque, smirking gargoyle set at the very top of America's sky-scraping adventure in acquisition *ad infinitum*," in whose "mouth is a loud speaker, powered by the vested interest of a two-billion-dollar industry, and back of that the vested interests of business as a whole."[19]

More than just a jeremiad, *Our Master's Voice* sought to explain the workings of mass culture structured by advertising. In the book's middle chapters, Rorty offered an innovative investigation of the ways in which readers interacted with popular magazines. Using the subscriber demographic and income data that marketing researcher Daniel Starch had recently started to develop for publishers and for space buyers in the advertising agencies, Rorty attempted to correlate the marketing profiles of a representative sample of leading magazines—including the *American Weekly* supplement inserted into the Sunday editions of Hearst newspapers, *Saturday Evening Post*, *Liberty*, *Photoplay*, and *True Story*—with an analysis of their feature articles, short fiction, and other editorial content. "Examination of this magazine literature reveals clearly," Rorty asserted, "that the democratic dogma is dying if not already dead; that the emulative culture is not accessible to the poor and to the lower-middle class; that the poor are oriented toward crime, and potentially at least, toward revolution; [and] that the middle classes are oriented toward fascism." While he believed the existing system was unsustainable, he did not underestimate the difficulty of constructive change, given that capitalists had rendered the "instruments of social communication" into "instruments of rule."[20]

Soon after the book's publication, Rorty set out on a seven-month, 15,000-mile sojourn through all regions of the United States to report on social and economic conditions and to contribute to the organizing efforts of the short-lived American Workers Party. Upon his return to New York City, he taught a semester-long survey course for the New School for Social Research, "A Functional Critique of Advertising," that attracted a full enrollment of approximately forty students, and also took up the editorship of the *Consumers' Defender* newsletter published by Cooperative Distributors (CD).[21] In his free time, Rorty began compiling a lyrical travelogue of his time on the road, which he published in 1936 as *Where Life Is Better*. As he recollected in his narrative, while driving from Toledo to Detroit he had stopped to pick up a loquacious young hitchhiker who, Rorty quickly learned, was a traveling salesman for "McGladden" magazines, a thinly veiled allusion to publisher Bernarr Macfadden's pulp empire. At first Rorty was intrigued. Was it true, he asked, that masses of blue-collar "Sweeneys" formed the core of the magazines' readerships, as the publisher's trade ads maintained? Did the success of McGladden titles really prove the rise of working-class purchasing power in the United States? The hitchhiker replied that actually white-collar workers comprised the bulk of his customers, so cities that were administrative centers of government relief and recovery programs presented the most lucrative sales targets. "What you steered clear of," Rorty's passenger advised, were "the broke industrial towns, and especially the slum districts of these towns. The real poor didn't read McGladden publications. They didn't read anything except an occasional newspaper." As they drove, and the conversation turned toward the young man's enthusiasm for the magazines he sold—"Yowzir, I'll tell the world I read them"—as well as his crass lifestyle and his reactionary politics, Rorty's curiosity gradually turned to disgust. After the hitchhiker declared that only "another first-class war" would solve the problems of the Depression, Rorty finally had enough. He stopped the car on a deserted stretch of highway and ordered the young man to get out. When he hesitated, Rorty brandished a wrench to make his point, leaving him "standing by the side of the road, his face contorted with bewilderment and indignation."[22]

Rorty's parable neatly captured the thorny dilemma facing progressive and radical activists who aspired to invent a social-democratic consumer culture during the 1930s and 1940s. As they labored on *Consumers Union Reports*, *PM*, *In Fact*, *Friday*, or other alternative media projects, they would constantly struggle for ways to advocate their views effectively using the means of communication that had developed to propagate the culture of consumer capitalism. In doing so they, like Rorty on the road to Detroit, would have to grapple with the question of whether or not America's existing mass culture could or should be redeemed.

Making Consumers Union

By the middle of the 1930s, as consumer activists from across the ideological spectrum invoked CR's technical findings in support of their campaigns, the tensions between the various strains of consumerist thinking became manifested within the institute itself. Schlink aimed to keep the institute's distance from many of the emerging organizations that sought to make common cause with CR. When, for instance, a National Religion and Labor Foundation was proposed to inform consumers of the working conditions under which goods were made, the *Bulletin* noted that although it "has frequently been suggested that Consumer's Research should carry on this service," it was sure that "subscribers' interests will be best served" by keeping the institute's "concern basically with those questions which have to do with the technical and economic qualities of the goods themselves." The *Bulletin* provided minimal coverage of the swelling wave of grassroots boycotts, demonstrations, rent strikes, and civil disobedience staged by militant working-class consumers, many of whom were also participants in the radical labor upsurge of 1933 and 1934. Furthermore, the relocation of the institute from New York City to rural New Jersey in 1933 and the low salaries paid to CR staff—averaging a little more than $13 a week in 1935—sparked dissention in the ranks as well as high employee turnover.[23]

Among the leading personalities at CR, the most significant ideological fissures opened between Schlink and Kallet. While Schlink adhered to his libertarian conception of consumerism, Kallet began to espouse a sharper critique of consumer capitalism that echoed Rorty's analysis. In a 1934 debate against G. D. Crain, publisher of *Advertising Age*, Kallet charged that "the remedy" was not "to try to control advertising at all," but to "take the food, drug and cosmetic industries away from those who are concerned only with profits, whatever the consequences to consumers, and to have those industries operated by the public." Kallet only moved further to the left after Schlink had him removed from the CR Board of Directors. In *Counterfeit*, Kallet railed not just against "false" advertising, but a slew of common marketing strategies he argued were forms of consumer exploitation inherent to modern capitalism. "The remedy must be sought not in legislation," he concluded, "but in a fundamental change in our economic system." Politicians who made "a rapidly decaying economy" look as if it were "worth saving" through "such counterfeit remedies as the 'New Deal' and the N.R.A., 'helping' the consumer by raising prices and increasing the profits of corporations," might, he warned, "finally offer the supreme counterfeit—fascism." Additionally, Kallet began to contribute articles under a pseudonym to the Communist Party publication *Health and Hygiene*.[24]

As Schlink and Matthews were undoubtedly aware, the influence of Communism at the institute was not limited to Kallet. Beginning in late 1934, CR management hired several new employees whose procommunist tendencies were hardly a secret. Jenkins, for example, had been employed by the *Daily Worker* and organized with the OWU before joining CR as a proofreader. Alexander Crosby had been a procommunist activist in the Newspaper Guild until he was fired from his job as a reporter for the *Staten Island Advance* on account of his union militancy. Chemist John Heasty, who joined the staff in the testing laboratory, had been terminated at his previous job due to his involvement with the FAECT. During the summer of 1935, the radicals helped turn the simmering discontent into organizing momentum, and Jenkins used her connections to get the AFL to issue the CR workers their own federal charter as a local union. Union supporters elected Heasty as local president and Jenkins as vice president, and subsequently requested recognition from management along with job security and a minimum salary of $15 a week. Schlink and Matthews rejected the demands, while Kallet and CR Board member Dewey Palmer supported the workers' cause. CR fired Heasty and two other CR employees on August 23, prompting the other union members on the staff to strike on September 4. Kallet and Palmer found themselves forced out shortly thereafter as a result of their disagreement with Schlink and Matthews on the matter of union recognition.[25]

For a relatively small labor dispute involving about fifty strikers out of a staff of roughly eighty employees, the conflict elicited considerable public attention. The five-and-a-half-month strike, which included repeated incidents of violence on the picket line, shocked liberals who had naively considered CR an ally. Both *The New Republic* and *The Nation* denounced the institute, and the strikers convinced thousands of CR members to cancel their subscriptions as an act of solidarity. For the advertising and business press, meanwhile, Schlink and Matthews's discomfiture furnished considerable amusement.[26] The strike's greatest significance, however, was as a key event in the crystallization of white-collar militancy within the culture industries. More than merely revealing the difficulties inherent in cobbling together a unified consumers' interest, the strike demonstrated how white-collar workers could boldly put into practice a radical consciousness of the creative labor involved in cultural production. In addition, both blue-collar and white-collar unionists provided essential support for the strikers. Hosiery workers, dyers, and silk workers from nearby mill towns in northwestern New Jersey joined the strikers on their picket lines, and many were arrested. Although they had farther to travel, militants with the fledgling white-collar unions in New York City, especially the BS&AU, the BMG, and the Newspaper Guild, also maintained a ubiquitous presence. Not only did these white-collar activists take a leading role in fundraising for the strikers, they also organized the subscribers' committee that became the nucleus for a new product-testing institute with an unequivocal pro-labor orientation.[27]

In early 1936, the strikers and the subscribers' committee determined to open their own institute, which they named Consumers Union, as a membership organization based in New York City. They selected consumer activist and Amherst College economics professor Colston Warne to serve as president, while Kallet assumed the position of director, giving him primary supervision over daily operations. Jenkins became the new institute's field secretary, functioning as a liaison between CU and organized labor as well as other left-led consumer and tenant organizations in the Popular Front orbit. In keeping with both the CU charter as well as the institute's contract with Local 20055, Heasty sat on the CU Board of Directors as a staff delegate. Progressive labor was heavily represented on the initial CU Board, which included BMG president Gilman, Newspaper Guild president Heywood Broun, Brotherhood of Sleeping Car Porters president A. Philip Randolph, and Rose Schneiderman of the Women's Trade Union League. A mission statement in the first issue of *Consumers Union Reports*, which appeared in May, declared that "decent living standards for ultimate consumers" would "never be maintained simply by reporting on the quality and the price of products. All the technical information in the world will not give enough food or enough clothes to the textile worker's family living on $11 a week." They, "like the college professor and the skilled mechanic," shared a common relationship to the means of consumption that mirrored their relationship to the means of production. "By reporting on the labor conditions under which consumer goods are produced," CU hoped to organize "consumer buying power" to bring "what pressure it can to the fight for higher wages and for the unionization and the collective bargaining which are labor's bulwark against declining standards of living."[28]

In its monthly magazine, CU combined traditional forms of labor-based advocacy with new modes of consumer activism more attuned to the struggles of white-collar workers within the culture industries. From the outset, *Reports* endorsed the union label and boycott campaigns that from the 1880s up into the 1930s were crucial tactics for AFL affiliates; the first issue simply duplicated the Federation's master list of firms deemed "unfair to labor."[29] Reviews of product tests published in the *Reports* routinely incorporated information about labor conditions, including which manufacturers were unionized. The ultimate rating of tested products as "Best Buys," "Also Recommended," or "Not Recommended" was based exclusively on technical data, but CU, unlike CR, still intended for its subscribers to consider labor matters seriously when making their purchasing decisions. Readers of the first CU review of automobiles in June 1936, for example, learned not only that the Ford V-8 Standard and the Plymouth De Luxe 6 were rated "Best Buys" among low- and medium-priced cars, but also that autoworkers "don't last long, thanks to the speed-up system. They are considered old at forty, and if they get work after reaching that age, they regard it as borrowed time." In addition, the article continued, thousands of them "will never again punch a time-clock in any factory because they have been blacklisted for union activity." Similarly, a review of refrigerators the following month evaluated these appliances as both the idealized commodities presented by advertisers and industrial designers and as products of a ruthless piecework labor regime. "If exceptional skill, superior stamina and complete disregard for health enable one worker to make a decent wage, the piece-work rate may be 'readjusted,' penalizing also the employees who can work at only a moderate pace." Over the course of the late 1930s, CU cheered the CIO manufacturing unions' breakthrough victories, and its reviews tracked the brand-by-brand advance of organized labor. By March 1938, the magazine could inform its readers that "with the exception of three cars—Ford, Lincoln Zephyr, and Hupmobile," all of the models reviewed were "manufactured under agreements with the United Automobile Workers of America."[30]

CU also linked consumer activism with the unionization of white-collar workers in the media, insinuating that a less manipulative consumer culture would follow from improved conditions for the people who made it. They cast themselves as an example of the dedication that, they hoped, could make a new kind of consumer culture possible. To create a "new consumer technical service which is democratically controlled and pro-labor," they had been "willing to work on a semi-voluntary basis to make possible the difficult task of getting such an organization under way almost without funds." In pointed contrast to CR, where Schlink's $70 weekly salary was triple that of the next highest paid employee, at CU all members of the staff, including the director and the technical supervisor, earned $12.50 weekly in May 1936, less than the minimum the union had demanded at CR. In July, the *Reports* ran an article on the Newspaper Guild's pivotal strike against the Hearst-owned *Wisconsin News*. "Consumers have good reason to join hands with workers against Hearst," CU contended. "Willing to do anything which will serve his ends and bring in profits, Hearst has filled up a large part of his papers with advertisements for worthless and dangerous products," while "with his *Good Housekeeping* magazine and its fraudulent Good Housekeeping Institute he has helped advertisers exploit consumers."[31]

The declaration of support for the Newspaper Guild and direct attack on Hearst opened a long and bitter feud between CU and the advertising-backed media. With its "Seal of Approval" which supposedly guaranteed the quality claims made by duly certified advertisers, the Good Housekeeping Institute, CU reiterated, was "one of the greatest frauds now being perpetrated on American consumers." As evidence, it noted that the seal had been bestowed upon a toxic laxative containing phenolphthalein, Fleishman's Yeast, which made completely unsubstantiated assertions in its advertisements regarding its purported health benefits, and four brands of refrigerators rated "Not Acceptable" by CU. Even as CU made these attacks, it counted on using mainstream newspapers and magazines to solicit members; since the *Reports* contained no commercial advertising, only growth in the institute's membership would provide the revenues needed to raise staff salaries and improve testing facilities. During late 1936, for example, CU advertised in the Sunday edition of the *New York Times* on several occasions, but beginning in February 1937 the newspaper declined to sell additional space to CU. The stance taken by the *Times* was hardly unique; by the end of the decade, over sixty major publications had refused to sell promotional space to CU out of deference to their principal advertisers.[32]

The blacklisting of CU advertising created a practical problem for the institute, but it also illuminated its difficulties in constituting a movement of social-democratic consumers. Direct mail solicitation offered a partial solution, and CU still advertised wherever it could obtain space, including liberal weeklies like *The New Republic* and *The Nation*, and Communist Party propaganda vehicles like the *Daily Worker* and the magazine *Soviet Russia Today*. In addition, it continued to seek the sponsorship of organized labor. In May 1937, Jenkins wrote to UAW organizer Wyndham Mortimer to inquire if the union's locals would be interested in a special arrangement where they would take block subscriptions for 500 or more autoworkers, who would become CU members for $1 annually instead of the regular $3. In November 1938, Kallet appealed directly to CIO president Lewis, asserting that "it has been estimated that families save up to $300 a year" through the use of CU services, and also emphasizing how the institute "reports on the labor conditions under which consumers' goods are manufactured" for the purpose of "educating its middle-class members in the need for supporting labor in its struggle."[33]

Despite these efforts at soliciting labor patronage, the institute struggled to build a mass subscription base for *Consumers Union Reports* among blue-collar workers. Although individual union activists joined CU or contributed information to its reporting on labor conditions, most manufacturing workers remained too poor during the Depression to purchase many cultural commodities of any kind, even if it was consumer guidance that might be useful to a family subsisting on less than $25 a week. Many blue-collar union members did have access to CU reporting on consumer issues through the "Your Dollar" features that by late 1938 were included in eighty-five union newspapers reaching an estimated 2,500,000 readers. Significantly, these capsules of consumer information focused on relatively inexpensive foods, drugs, toiletries, household cleaners, clothing, or other nondurable goods, rather than the automobiles, refrigerators, washing machines, and other major appliances reviewed in *Reports*. A 1939 survey by CU showed that more than two-thirds of its members were employed in clerical, professional, and managerial occupations, and that their average annual household income was roughly $2,600, a modest sum but still well above the national average. Like much of Popular Front culture, *Reports* was primarily consumed by white-collar progressives with jobs that provided enough disposable income to support an organization like CU.[34]

In addition to the institute's product ratings, its information on labor conditions in manufacturing, and its blasts at the advertising-supported media, CU in its formative years also promoted consumer cooperatives. In July 1936, it reported on Cooperative Distributors, which through its mail-order service and dozens of affiliated local cooperatives offered inexpensive products in generic form "for which consumers must ordinarily pay excessive prices to cover advertising ballyhoo and the enormous profits extorted through the use of highly puffed trade-marks." CD also insisted that its suppliers prove decent labor conditions, since "the maintenance of adequate standards of living for its members and for all consumers depends first of all upon the high standards of wages and working conditions." Two months later, *Reports* included an article on the Consumers Cooperative Services of Chicago that furnished detailed practical guidance on the basics of running a local food co-op. Yet when CU began to evaluate cooperative products, it showed them no favoritism. Some appliances, such as the B-44 radio by CD, the Co-Op DeLuxe electric iron, and the Co-Op DeLuxe vacuum cleaner, were rated as "Best Buys," while a few, like the Co-Op Model 80 refrigerator of 1939, were classified as "Not Acceptable." In a few cases, CU even reported the results of tests conducted independently by the members of consumer cooperatives such as the one in Greenbelt, Maryland. Moreover, CU reported favorably on cooperative schemes for providing healthcare, including group-practice programs like the Ross-Loos Clinic in California, and it criticized the cozy relationship between the American Medical Association and business interests when the medical lobby began to attack group-practice healthcare and defend the fee-for-service model.[35]

In keeping with its commitment to improving workers' living standards, CU strongly advocated the labor-Keynesian approach to macroeconomic policy favored by progressives in the CIO to foster full employment and rising incomes. The institute staunchly backed the National Labor Relations Act, not just because it introduced a potentially democratic element into the workplace, but also because collective bargaining transferred purchasing power to working-class consumers. CU also gave favorable coverage to the public provisioning of goods and services, including housing, surplus agricultural commodities through the first "food stamp" program, and, by the 1940s, proposals for national healthcare.[36] In addition to these measures, CU lobbied for new regulatory initiatives, the most important of which was the Food, Drug, and Cosmetics Act of 1938, which expanded the powers of the FDA to oversee the production and labeling of products covered by the new law, and enhanced FTC powers to monitor their advertising. Although political compromises kept the final legislation from being as robust as CU stalwarts wanted, passage of the new law marked a huge advance for consumer activists.[37]

Although Warne and Kallet held the top two positions in the institute, responsibility for the editorial content, the design of the magazine, and other CU informational materials came to be exercised by Dexter Masters, who drew upon his previous experience in advertising and the print media. Hired as a writer for *Time* in the late 1920s, Masters was transferred to Britt Hadden's pet project *Tide*, where he rose to managing editor under the magazine's new owner, advertising executive Raymond Rubicam. Although it had initially been a vehicle for flattering agencies and clients that was intended to boost ad sales for *Time*, in the early 1930s *Tide* gained a reputation under Masters for offering incisive, and sometimes critical, analysis of the advertising industry. It also became a small haven for leftists, as Masters hired such writers as Mildred Edie and David Munro, who in 1937 would begin his own radical advertising newsletter dubbed *Space and Time*. Masters and Edie began associating with Jenkins and Kallet in the prelude to the CR strike, and in 1936 they both left *Tide* to join CU. Masters's success in writing effective direct-mail copy for the institute, along with his prior experience as a magazine editor, allowed him to advance into the position of Publications Director in 1938. Edie contributed regularly to *Consumers Union Reports*, helped codirect a short-lived West Coast branch of CU, and in 1941 became editor of CU's new weekly news-letter, *Bread and Butter*. Together, Masters and Edie had a vital role in the development of CU not only as critics of consumer capitalism, but as people with the creative skills needed to make the institute's products attractive to those who desired to consume information about consuming.[38]

Within a little more than three years after the appearance of the first issue of the *Reports*, CU had grown to 85,000 members, making the institute larger than CR and more influential among consumer activists. But the determina-tion with which CU spread its vision of consumer activism made it a target for attacks. Schlink and Matthews remained fiercely hostile to CU, and they continued their denunciations of Communist influence in an attempt to dis-credit their pro-labor rival. In the late 1930s, they allied with advertisers and publishers to fight CU. The Hearst Corporation was especially sensitive to CU's criticisms of *Good Housekeeping*, since it depended on the magazine, which led its category in total advertising lineage and had a monthly circula-tion of two million copies, to help offset the company's staggering losses from its newspaper operations; in 1938, the title accounted for more than 75 per-cent of the $3.35 million in profits earned by the nine magazines published by Hearst. Although CR had itself attacked *Good Housekeeping* as recently as 1934, the chief executive of Hearst's magazine division, Richard Berlin, hired Matthews in 1937 as a researcher. The following year, Berlin arranged for Matthews to join the staff of Congressman Martin Dies's newly formed committee to investigate domestic subversion, a position that he held until 1944 while continuing his employment by Hearst.[39]

The brawl between CU and the Hearst Corporation escalated after the FTC issued a complaint against *Good Housekeeping* in August 1939 that charged the magazine with engaging in "misleading and deceptive acts and practices" through the use and promotion of its famed Seal of Approval. Berlin and Matthews were convinced that CU was responsible for feeding information to the FTC and applying political pressure. During October and November, they plotted their retaliation along with National Association of Manufacturers (NAM) publicist and conservative newspaper colum-nist George Sokolsky, representatives from the Association of National Advertisers, and the executives of several food and drug manufacturers that relied heavily on advertising. The group prepared an investigative report that hit hard at the Communist ties of CU—with particular focus on Jenkins and Kallet—along with other progressive consumer advocacy organizations like the League of Women Shoppers. On a Sunday evening in early December, Matthews met alone with Dies, who, acting as an executive committee of one, accepted the report as evidence and entered it into the legislative record. Within twenty-four hours, Berlin's office distributed copies of the report to hundreds of newspaper and magazine editors, advertising executives, and publicists across the country as a press release, with the implicit understanding that since the report enjoyed the privileges and immunities of Congressional testimony, it could be quoted without fear of libel.[40]

In his report, Matthews contended that following the official promulgation of the Popular Front strategy by the Comintern in 1934–1935, activists in the CPUSA had initiated numerous "Trojan Horse" organizations, including CU, to serve as "transmission belts" for Communist propaganda. These groups, he continued, were especially dangerous because of their ability "to secure adherents from the middle-class," as procommunists proclaimed "concern over consumers for the purpose of tearing down the institutions of capitalist society and erecting in their place the institutions of proletarian dictatorship." In particular, Matthews noted, "Communists understand that advertising performs an indispensable function in a mass-production economy," so they consequently believed that "to sabotage and destroy advertising, and through its destruction to undermine and help destroy the capitalist system of free enterprise is a revolutionary tactic worthy of a great deal of attention."[41]

In blurring the lines between corporate propaganda and legislative authority, Berlin, Matthews, and their confederates overplayed their hand. Liberal legislators questioned the way the report was created and entered into the record, which limited the extent to which some editors and publicists were willing to use its findings as ammunition against CU. As the FTC hearings dragged on into 1940, the Hearst Corporation's retaliation against its detractors became additional grist for the investigation into *Good Housekeeping*. Nonetheless, the anticommunist campaign took a toll. Educators who had incorporated CU materials into home economics curricula reversed course as it was cast as controversial. In April 1940 the Committee on Cultural Freedom, chaired by liberal philosopher John Dewey, declared CU to be "Communist-controlled," thus furnishing a respectable academic front for the redbaiting of the institute. The quarrel had far-reaching consequences beyond the immediate impact on CU, as it brought together a new alignment of anticommunist enterprises, institutions, and personalities that would spend the next two decades committed to eliminating the influence of progressives and radicals from the culture industries.[42]

News Without Advertising: The New York Tabloid PM

The belief that advertising had a corrupting influence on the media and on democracy had been a core value at CU, but it found expression on a much more ambitious scale in June 1940 when the tabloid newspaper *PM* began publication in New York City. As a major daily newspaper that contained no paid advertising, *PM* presented a bold alternative to the culture of consumer capitalism. Free from the influence of the merchants, manufacturers, and commercial purveyors of services whose outlays for promotional space provided most American newspapers with 65 percent or more of their average total income during the 1930s, *PM* reported heavily on the American labor movement, offering coverage that was not only favorable but also quite incisive, and it also publicized various social-democratic consumer initiatives. Yet to survive on circulation revenues alone, the new tabloid's progressive mix of news, editorials, and features would have to attract a sizeable following of readers within the city's highly competitive media marketplace.

PM originated in the imagination of Ralph Ingersoll, one of the more innovative editors of his generation. Raised in an affluent family in New York City and educated at Yale, Ingersoll made his first splash in journalism in 1925 when *New Yorker* publisher Harold Ross hired him for the magazine, which was then on the verge of folding after just a few months. While its early promotional copy haughtily declared that it was "not for the old lady from Dubuque," it seemed that the *New Yorker* might not be for anybody at all, as sales after the first few months averaged under 10,000 copies per issue. Ingersoll proved instrumental in giving the magazine editorial direction, lining up compelling material that attracted readers, and, in the process, making the *New Yorker* a magnet for high-end advertising. In 1930, Henry Luce poached him to edit his new business magazine *Fortune*. Over the next half decade, Ingersoll presided over a stable of brilliant writers that included Archibald MacLeish, Dwight Macdonald, and James Agee. He became increasingly interested in the possibilities of photojournalism, and he took a leading role in the planning and development of Time Inc.'s new picture magazine *Life*, which launched in November 1936. Ingersoll had become arguably the most important figure in the company after Luce himself, and his salary of $45,000 a year made him one of the country's highest-paid media executives. Disagreements between Ingersoll and Luce over the direction of *Life*, however, led to a falling out between the two men. Although Ingersoll was bullish about the potential circulation for the new title, Luce cautiously insisted on an initial guaranteed circulation for advertisers of only 250,000 copies per issue; when *Life* sales immediately took off, its success resulted in initial losses for the company until it could recalibrate its advertising rates. Determined to assume greater control over what was rapidly becoming a cultural phenomenon, Luce reassigned Ingersoll to overhaul *Time*—the oldest, least intellectually dynamic, and most politically conservative of the company's magazines—with orders to make it generate the revenues required to sustain the new venture. In addition, the friction over *Life* coincided with the rise of the Newspaper Guild at Time Inc., and it seems that Ingersoll's reluctance to take a harder line with the unionists only exacerbated his estrangement from Luce. In March 1939, Ingersoll left the company.[43]

Beginning in 1937, as he grew increasingly disillusioned with Time Inc., Ingersoll drafted a series of proposals for a new kind of tabloid newspaper. Ingersoll wanted to introduce to daily newspapers the visually striking photojournalism that had made *Life* a success, even though doing so would require costly production standards. Early plans called for a paper that resembled a magazine in many respects, with four-color printing throughout, and pages of higher-quality paper than conventional newsprint that were stapled together. By January 1940, Ingersoll had raised $1.5 million—the bare minimum for initiating the project—from a band of wealthy investors including Marshall Field III and John Hay Whitney. As he began concrete preparations for publication, he had to strategize how his new enterprise would fit into a crowded market in which a few daily papers, most notably the *Herald*, the *World*, and the *American*, had already gone out of business, and eight major dailies still published in Manhattan. Ingersoll wisely opted against launching his new paper in the morning, when it would have faced brutal head-to-head competition with the two existing tabloids, the *Daily News* and *Daily Mirror*, while the sophisticated coverage of national politics and international relations that he hoped to offer would have been pitted against the quality reporting of the *Times* and the *Herald Tribune*. Afternoon seemed more promising, as Ingersoll's project would stand in contrast to the *Journal-American* and the *World-Telegram*, which both espoused a conservative line. The most direct competition for the new paper would be the feeble *Post*, which at the time was the city's most consistently liberal paper.[44]

Despite the uncertainties of the project, which by the spring of 1940 became known as *PM*, it attracted large numbers of idealistic writers, editors, photographers, and artists who desired to work on a paper founded on progressive principles. Ingersoll hired a starting staff that included a mixture of seasoned newspaper veterans like assistant editor John P. Lewis and copy chief Rae Weimer, ambitious young journalists such as James Wechsler and

Penn Kimball, and innovative graphic artists like Ad Reinhardt. Some had experience working in Luce's media empire, including acclaimed photographer Margaret Bourke-White and *PM* movie, theater, and radio critic John McManus. Ingersoll also brought on board various cultural and intellectual figures associated with the Popular Front, like clothing designer and author Elizabeth Hawes and playwright Lillian Hellman. In keeping with the pro-labor orientation of the new publication as well as the staff Ingersoll selected, *PM* entered into a model contract with the Newspaper Guild of New York that contrasted significantly with the agreement that the Guild had settled for in its negotiations with Time Inc. Not only did the *PM* contract include a union shop clause, but it also included a much stronger grievance procedure than existed at Time, as well as preferential hiring through the Guild's placement service. While Ingersoll's financing arrangements precluded the widespread use of color in the tabloid, he was able to retain an accent of red for the logo and index on the upper-left corner of the front page, a cold-set ink and high-grade paper that gave sharper definition and contrast to photographs, and stapling when it officially rolled out on June 18.[45]

Hawes's "News for Living" section exemplified not just the new paper's commitment to social consumerism, but its experimental approach to newspaper journalism in general. The section's staff included League of Women Shoppers activist Leane Zugsmith, progressive consumer advocate Sidney Margolius, and FAECT organizer Jules Korchien on the housing beat. News for Living featured articles on many topics that concerned CU, leading on the very first day with an update on the FTC investigation into the fraudulent practices of Hearst's *Good Housekeeping*. In its second week, Hawes wrote a column that promoted CU but also mocked its zeal: "CU Reports Can Stretch Your Money—They Can Also Drive You Crazy." Although impressed with the institute's advice, she contended that many people believed that CU "makes no allowance for human nature, acts as if anyone who doesn't use CU reports is a fool, and as if it were immoral to spend money getting a 'lift.'" She recommended taking CU guidance "with a grain of salt." Despite the knocks, CU took her article as an endorsement, asserting in the next issue of the *Reports* that *PM* had "already set journalistic history by carrying a whole story on CU, naming our name, telling more or less what we do, and everything." Over the first several months, other articles promoted militant community-based tenant and consumer groups, exposed the disruptive effects of city planner Robert Moses's expressway construction program on working-class residents in Brooklyn, and condemned the flourishing of informal street-corner markets in the Bronx for African American women seeking casual employment as domestic workers. In addition, the section included a terse synopsis of the advertising copy that department stores, grocers, and other retailers had placed in the city's other papers that day so that *PM* readers would know the availability and prices of goods.[46]

Already by its launch date, however, ominous developments threatened the new paper's survival. In an attempt to stymie Ingersoll's tabloid, *News* publisher Joseph Medill Patterson informed vendors that he would not allow them to sell his paper if they provided space on their stands to *PM*, which forced *PM* to spend additional money for special display racks. Prelaunch expenditures had burned through more than half of the capitalization, driving home the inadequacy of Ingersoll's financing. Initial sales of *PM* were impressive, with curious readers mobbing the delivery trucks as they left the printing plant on the first few days, but circulation department blunders resulted in tens of thousands of advance subscribers not receiving their copies. The paper's problems were not just logistical. *PM* sections like News for Living that represented the tabloid's innovative potential also revealed the shortcomings of the staff that Ingersoll had assembled. Although Hawes and the other members of her section's staff had an abundance of talent and enthusiasm, they lacked basic familiarity with the rhythms and routines of daily newspaper publication. This accounted in large part for the unevenness of the quality of the copy; while some articles were inspired, others read like nondescript filler, and others still—like a September 1940 series on "chicken ghouls" who peddled diseased poultry in the city's markets— seemingly replicated in their style the tawdry sensationalism of the *News* and *Mirror.* The widespread interest sparked by the paper's debut quickly fizzled. After selling 370,000 copies on its first day, by early July daily circulation had slipped below 200,000 copies, which was the level Ingersoll estimated as the breakeven point for the paper, and by the end of the month it was in free-fall. Less than three months after it commenced publication, *PM* was bankrupt. Field saved the paper from closing by buying out the other investors at 20 percent of the original value of their shares, creating a new holding company for the paper, and providing it with a subvention until it could become profitable. Ingersoll retained responsibility for the everyday operations of *PM*, but he did so as an employee of Field Publications and not as a media entrepreneur.[47]

Internal strife added to the tabloid's troubles. Sharp disagreements between the procommunists and anticommunists on the staff, primarily over international affairs, roiled the newsroom through the fall of 1940—punctuated by the firing of the procommunist labor reporter Leo Huberman—and continued into 1941. Ingersoll unequivocally committed *PM* to support for

Britain and the Allies and called for the United States to furnish material assistance, which irked those on the paper who had hoped to steer its editorial line toward the noninterventionism espoused by the Communist Party during the Nazi–Soviet pact. The Communist *Daily Worker* and *New Masses*, which had warmly anticipated the arrival of the progressive mass-circulation daily newspaper, began to lash out at *PM* over its muscular foreign policy positions. Meanwhile, conservative columnists for the Hearst and Scripps-Howard chains attacked *PM* over the continued presence of so many staffers with Communist associations, as did anti-Stalinist leftist periodicals like the *New Leader*. The paper's financial crisis, which necessitated several rounds of emergency layoffs, further exacerbated the political controversy since both sides alleged that their partisans were unduly targeted by the cuts. The tensions subsided somewhat after the Nazi invasion of the Soviet Union and the renewal of the Popular Front, although ideological rivalries continued to rankle the paper, most notably the one between I. F. Stone, who often supported cooperation with procommunists, and the fiercely anticommunist Wechsler.[48]

The economic retrenchment also strained relations between *PM* management and the Newspaper Guild. Although many of the key figures at *PM* earned less than they could have elsewhere, overall salaries for creative professionals aligned with other city papers. In January 1941, the fifty-three employees in the Guild's top contract classification at *PM*, which included the bulk of the journalists and non–managing editors, had an average weekly salary of $102.51. Clerical workers in the lowest classification averaged only $20.52. The union resisted the reductions in force sought by management, but by April approximately eighty-five employees in the Guild's jurisdiction had been laid off. In order to maintain morale and to stifle ongoing speculation about the paper's survival, Field Publications agreed to modest improvements in salaries as well as enhancements to the severance plan. Because of salaries and severance obligations, the Guild contract's contribution to total production costs per page swelled from $56.70 at the beginning of 1941 to $83.33 by September 1944, which was higher than that of any other unionized paper in the New York metropolitan area. Although the company appeared to patch things up with the Guild after the early wave of job cuts, and thus restore the kind of relatively congenial labor relations that were consistent with the paper's progressive advocacy on behalf of working people, its contracts with the Guild hardly helped to put the paper's long-term finances on more secure footing.[49]

As *PM* approached its second anniversary, its staff had accomplished much that they could take pride in, above all continuing to publish a major daily newspaper with no advertising. Nonetheless, the paper was far from what Ingersoll had envisioned. It never became an essential source for breaking national and international news as he had hoped. Rival publishers blocked *PM* from accessing the services of the Associated Press during its early years, and the paper's chronic financial woes precluded the development of a comprehensive newsgathering network. *PM* did manage to maintain a vibrant Washington bureau, and its reporting and commentary on national affairs by Stone, Wechsler, columnist Max Lerner, and others made it a vocal proponent for a social-democratic expansion of the New Deal. *PM* combined this with its liberal internationalism, evident in its insistence on a peace predicated on the total defeat of fascism in the Second World War, support for democratic decolonization, and a leading role for the United States in the economic and political reconstruction of the postwar world. The paper attracted a significant readership beyond the New York metropolitan area and became a crucial media outlet for rallying progressives across the nation. On May 10, 1942, *PM* ran the complete text of a speech that Vice President Henry A. Wallace had given in New York two days earlier, prefaced by the paper's assertion that "he told us plainly and eloquently what we are fighting for and why we must and will win this war." In his address, which was largely ignored by the city's other papers, Wallace questioned the vision of an "American Century," in which the United States exercised a self-interested global hegemony, that Luce had proclaimed the previous year in an editorial in *Life* magazine. Instead, Wallace posited, "the century we are entering—the century which will come into being after this war—can be and must be the century of the common man," in which "America will have the opportunity to support the freedoms and duties by which the common man must live."[50]

The paper's circulation figures steadily improved, from an atrocious average paid daily circulation of not quite 90,000 copies in 1941, to 128,000 copies in 1942, when Ingersoll took leave to enlist in the army, and up to 146,000 in 1943. Of course, this was nowhere near the readership that Ingersoll had once projected. *PM* may have been required reading for the cadres of organizers and activists in New York's progressive unions, but most working-class newspaper readers stuck with the *News*—which pushed its weekday circulation past two million during the war—or the *Mirror*. Sometimes *PM* reporters and editors were stunned by the lack of support from the readers who they thought should be the paper's natural constituency. When Kimball, for instance, went to interview picketing workers during a 1941 strike by the Transport Workers Union, he informed them that *PM* was the only major paper in the city that backed them; they thanked him, he recalled, but much to his dismay they continued reading anti-labor tabloids. For many it was a practical decision: the *News* and *Mirror* sold for two cents while *PM* cost a nickel, and the McCormick-Patterson and Hearst tabloids were published in the morning while *PM* came out in the afternoon. It was also a matter of taste; on the whole the paper was long on edification and short on entertainment. The "Sweeneys" who read the *News* would have had to relinquish the comic strips, sportswriters, and gossip columnists that they followed if they had switched to *PM*.[51]

With circulation remaining below the breakeven point, only Field's periodic infusions of funds kept the presses rolling. No one knew when his patience might run out, a prospect that loomed larger after he started another daily newspaper, the *Chicago Sun*, in October 1941 as a liberal counterweight to the conservative *Chicago Tribune*. Unlike *PM*, Field Publications' *Sun* carried advertising, and it established itself as a profitable enterprise within two years. By the end of the war, however, there was reason for hope at the offices of *PM* too; in 1945, *PM* finally eked out a profit for the year of roughly $100,000. It was a pittance compared to the $4 million Field had invested in the paper thus far, but perhaps Ingersoll's model for news without advertising might prove sustainable after all.[52]

Journalism Without Newspapers: George Seldes's In Fact

A month before the first issue of *PM* appeared, another news publication made its debut that shared the tabloid's aversion to advertising, but that in style and format represented a very different response to progressive critiques of America's culture of consumer capitalism. Whereas Ingersoll set out to produce a journalistically and aesthetically innovative periodical with costly production standards, radical journalist George Seldes conceived of *In Fact* as a purely functional vehicle for delivering information that was generally unavailable or underreported in the mainstream media. *In Fact* was a simple four-page newsletter (occasionally expanded to six pages) with no illustrations that Seldes published with a skeletal office staff in New York City and mailed to subscribers across the country. Started at first on a biweekly schedule in May 1940, Seldes increased the frequency to weekly in February 1941 as its readership grew. It was a far less ambitious enterprise than Ingersoll's, but partly that reflected Seldes's own years toiling for the press barons. To a considerable extent *In Fact* was intended to demonstrate that a journalist could still engage readers directly, even in a media landscape dominated by capital-intensive, vertically integrated enterprises.

Seldes was born in 1890 in the struggling cooperative farming community of Alliance, New Jersey, that his father had helped to establish as a haven for Jewish refugees from Czarist Russia. After the cooperative collapsed, his family moved first to Philadelphia and later to Pittsburgh, where Seldes, fresh out of high school, was hired in 1909 by the *Pittsburgh Leader* as a cub reporter on the city beat. Unlike his younger brother Gilbert, who graduated from Harvard and became a distinguished cultural critic, George was an autodidact whose education came largely through his work as a journalist. When the United States entered the First World War, he traveled to France as a member of the Press Section of the American Expeditionary Force, and after the armistice he remained based in Europe as a foreign correspondent. As the lead European correspondent for the *Chicago Tribune*, Seldes reported scoops that included an interview with Lenin and coverage of the rise of Mussolini. Seldes ironically benefitted from his employer's conservative isolationism, enjoying a considerable degree of autonomy in his journalism during this period. An assignment to Mexico in 1927, however, led to clashes with *Tribune* management after he filed dispatches that criticized American mining and petroleum firms and supported the efforts of the Mexican government to secure more of the benefits of the nation's natural resources. A subsequent transfer back to the United States only exacerbated tensions, and soon afterward Seldes left the paper.[53]

For the next dozen years, he worked mainly as a freelance journalist and book author. Some of his books, like his scathing profile of Mussolini, *Sawdust Caesar* (1935), drew upon his experience covering international affairs, while many, including *You Can't Print That* (1929), *Freedom of the Press* (1935), and *Lords of the Press* (1938), targeted the shortcomings of the print media.[54] While *You Can't Print That* and *Freedom of the Press* cataloged flagrant incidents of editorial bias or outright suppression of news by American newspapers over the preceding half century to demonstrate that the deliberate misinformation of the public was in fact the norm rather than the exception, Seldes moved in *Lords of the Press* to offering a solution. Like Rorty, he emphasized the ways in which newspapers' dependence on advertising revenue assured that certain events would receive slanted coverage while other events received no coverage at all, although Seldes also stressed publishers' own struggles against labor militancy as well as the influence of conservative and religious pressure groups as factors thwarting the free flow of information. To back his assertion that "the newspaper business is a business and nothing more," Seldes furnished twenty-one case studies of the commercial, editorial, and labor practices of leading publishers, revealing the material linkages that made the print media a tool of capitalist power. He deemed his former employer, Robert M. McCormick's *Chicago Tribune*, one of the worst offenders. "I know of no newspaper," Seldes wrote, "which is so vicious and stupid in its attack on labor, no paper so consistent in its Red-baiting, and no paper in my opinion is such a great enemy of the American people." The remedies, Seldes continued, were to be found in a series of structural changes necessary to increase the autonomy exercised by journalists and to establish conditions in which it would be possible for them to report the news as disinterested professionals. Seldes viewed unionization as a tremendous advance, although he regretted that the Newspaper Guild often responded defensively to publishers' accusations that the organization of journalists violated the First Amendment. He found it particularly unfortunate that Guild leaders claimed that the union "was not interested in editorial control of newspapers, or in editing and publishing them." Ultimately, he believed, a truly free press could only be provided by the establishment of independent papers supported by public subsidy or papers backed by the labor movement, which "would be for journalism what the TVA yardstick is for electricity."[55]

Seldes's experiences working for ostensibly liberal employers during the late 1930s only deepened his radicalism. Following the outbreak of the Spanish Civil War, publisher J. David Stern hired him to report on the conflict for his *New York Post* and *Philadelphia Record*. When he arrived in Loyalist Spain, Seldes was profoundly moved by the solidarity and sacrifice of those who had come together to defend the republic, and also outraged by the duplicity of the American, British, and French governments for failing to aid the Loyalists and prevent a fascist takeover. His dispatches clearly conveyed his belief in the justice of the Loyalist cause, which led Catholic organizations and conservative groups in the United States to complain to Stern, and to his papers' advertisers, about Seldes's coverage. Stern caved to the pressure during the summer of 1937; the *Post* and the *Record* shifted their editorial positions on the civil war and carried no more of Seldes's reporting. The next year, *Esquire* magazine publisher David Smart asked Seldes if he would edit a new current affairs magazine called *Ken*. After Smart assured him that *Ken* would have a liberal orientation and that Seldes would enjoy complete autonomy, Seldes accepted the job. He immediately clashed with Smart, however, over a series of articles that alienated advertisers, including an exposé of the American Legion's corporate connections. When Smart canned the articles, Seldes resigned and the magazine folded not long afterward.[56]

Frustrated by these experiences, Seldes began to conclude that the only solution might be his own no-frills publication. In late 1939 and early

1940, Richard Bransten (who wrote in *New Masses* and elsewhere under the pseudonym Bruce Minton) and his wife Ruth McKenney, who were Seldes's neighbors and friends, convinced him that it would be possible to scrape together the few thousand dollars needed to inaugurate his newsletter. Although Seldes had been critical of the Soviet regime in the 1920s, its willingness to aid Loyalist Spain impressed him greatly, and unlike many antifascists he remained willing to cooperate with Communists and their allies even after the Nazi–Soviet pact. Bransten took responsibility for securing most of the $6,000 in start-up financing, including a substantial portion from procommunists, and also for hiring the office staff, which included Rose Euler, the sister-in-law of Communist Party leader Earl Browder, as the new publication's business manager. Under their initial arrangement, Seldes and Bransten took turns editing the fortnightly issues of *In Fact*, but within the first several months they disagreed sharply over what constituted news and how closely the newsletter should adhere to the Communist line. Seldes objected to Bransten's long expositions on international affairs, which he thought gratuitously propagated the Communists' official position without being driven by breaking military or diplomatic developments, or conveying important information unavailable elsewhere. Moreover, Bransten had included his editorials at the expense of material by Seldes and his contacts that publicized actual events and revelations. In October, Seldes gave Bransten an ultimatum: either Seldes would become sole editor of *In Fact* or he would resign. Bransten opted to withdraw and return to *New Masses*. Seldes was forced to be more involved in the everyday operations of *In Fact* than he had anticipated but without Bransten he was free to make the newsletter reflect his sense of what was lacking in the advertising-supported press.[57]

Although circulation had grown steadily since the first issue, *In Fact* began to make greater gains in the fall of 1940 as Seldes refocused it squarely on covering what he defined as "suppressed" news. Published with the motto, "for the millions who want a free press," a significant portion of the articles simply reported information conveyed in Congressional hearings or speeches, or in the deliberations and decisions of government regulatory agencies like the FTC, FCC, and NLRB that were often ignored by most newspapers and magazines. Through his relentless muckraking, Seldes proceeded to expose conservative business groups' efforts at political and economic manipulation. The NAM was a prime target, and he devoted copious ink to revealing its lobbying of legislators and appointed officials, its publicity campaigns that placed pro-business propaganda in the nation's newspapers and magazines and on its airwaves, its programs to have pro-business content incorporated into school curricula, its coordination and encouragement of violations of labor's right to organize, its links to Congressman Dies, and the connections of many of its top executives with American fascist sympathizers. Newspaper magnate Frank Gannett's Committee for Constitutional Government—which called, among other things, for repeal of the Sixteenth Amendment authorizing federal income tax—and Fight for Free Enterprise also came under fire in the pages of *In Fact*. Seldes repeatedly excoriated the American Legion as well, highlighting its founding by a circle of wealthy elites and its past antiunion vigilantism while condemning its continuing hostility to the labor movement and to the political and social agenda of the CIO. Additionally, Seldes reported on pro-fascist organizations that cultivated popular followings, including Father Charles Coughlin's National Union for Social Justice and Gerald L. K. Smith's America First Party, and disclosed the support that these ostensibly grassroots groups received from businessmen.[58] In effect, Seldes's newsletter exposed the conservative front that mobilized in opposition to the Popular Front, explicating the linkages that bound it together so that progressives might improve their odds of overcoming the forces arrayed against them.

In addition to highlighting the conservative and anti-labor political activism of business interests, *In Fact* constantly criticized the culture of consumer capitalism for creating an environment in which a wealthy and powerful minority could exert such influence over public discourse. Seldes had been a charter member of CU, and like the institute's publications, *In Fact* publicized information about fraudulent advertising or dangerous products that other media outlets simply ignored. Most notably, *In Fact* was one of the first news periodicals to report extensively on the early medical research linking cigarette smoking and lung cancer, which most publishers and broadcasters avoided on account of the tobacco companies' massive advertising expenditures. It also documented how *Reader's Digest* planted articles that fit publisher DeWitt Wallace's conservative agenda in other magazines for the purpose of reprinting or excerpting them. Additionally, *In Fact* drew attention to instances in which media enterprises collaborated with firms that were prominent advertisers or had other financial leverage in order to distort coverage of labor activism, as when several New York City newspapers smeared the CIO retail and distributive union during its 1941 strike against Gimbels department store, or when the *Detroit Free Press* colluded with GM during the epic 1945–1946 strike by the UAW.[59]

From the outset, Seldes insisted that *In Fact* would need to sustain itself entirely from subscription revenues and that he would not accept subventions.

He estimated that at the original rate of fifty cents per year, *In Fact* would require roughly 100,000 subscribers to pay its own way; fortunately for Seldes,
the newsletter surpassed the threshold prior to its first anniversary. Its costs
were kept down by relying on unpaid contributions by journalists who ea-
gerly volunteered news that their employers would not print. In some cases—
such as an article by long-time Newspaper Guild activist Morris Watson
and his wife—these contributors wrote under a byline, but frequently they
remained anonymous. The *Guild Reporter* had in the late 1930s included a
regular section devoted to suppressed news, but union officials were nonetheless concerned by Seldes extolling that "several hundred fellow newspaper
men (Guildsmen) throughout the United States contribute the material for
In Fact." As the Guild contract covering the office staff came up for renewal in
1943, the ANG research director reminded local organizers that the union's
policy "has always been opposed to free work performed for any publication."
Despite concerns that Seldes might be inadvertently compromising labor
standards and setting a poor precedent, the practice continued unabated.[60]

With labor costs limited to the salaries of ten or fewer clerical workers, the
principal factor impinging on Seldes's objective of distributing his brand of
progressive reporting as inexpensively as possible was the cost of paper, ink,
and printing. Significant inflation during 1941 made it impossible to maintain
its original subscription terms, and effective January 1942 the price increased
to one dollar per year. Even though inflation continued during the war and
rationing forced Seldes to replace the newsletter's bonded stock with conventional newsprint, he succeeded in staving off another price hike until 1947.
While its combative tone and concise reporting certainly appealed to many
of its subscribers, it was the low price of *In Fact* that helped it to reach such
a wide readership, including what Seldes once labeled the "five-buck-liberals
of *The Nation* and *New Republic*," along with many working-class readers. By
the middle of the decade, more than 1,000 union locals across the country
had block subscriptions for *In Fact*, accounting for one-third of its total
circulation.[61]

Seldes's conviction that *In Fact* could foster progressive victories in the
political realm found some validation in 1944, when subscribers helped to
drive from office one of the Popular Front's most treacherous adversaries,
Congressman Martin Dies of Texas. Dies's political career epitomized the
most reprehensible aspects of the Jim Crow electoral regime in the American
South. Due to the state's poll tax as well as other disenfranchising measures,
including an explicit racial bar that limited participation in Texas Democratic
Party primaries to whites only, Dies was repeatedly elected throughout the

bleakest years of the Great Depression by fewer than 10 percent of the adults in his district. Unaccountable to the majority of his constituents, he became a political mercenary for business interests in their fight against the expanded regulation and social programs of the New Deal. By 1944, however, the CIO Oil and Chemical Workers Union had organized numerous refineries in Dies's East Texas district, increased wages provided many workers with the discretionary income to pay poll taxes, and pending litigation was poised to render the whites-only Texas Democratic primary unconstitutional. *In Fact*'s incessant attacks on Dies reached the 3,000 members of the Oil and Chemical Workers in the district who subscribed to the newsletter, with the CIO Political Action Committee (CIO-PAC) reinforcing the message by reissuing some of *In Fact*'s most damning material on the reactionary congressman. Facing the likelihood of a humiliating primary defeat, Dies aborted his quest for an eighth consecutive House term.[62]

By the middle of the 1940s, *In Fact* had established itself as one of the nation's most important media ventures for progressives. To be sure, key elements of its appeal to its subscriber base—its elementary format and its tight focus on certain strains of political news and media criticism—probably precluded the possibility of reaching the "millions" Seldes alluded to in the newsletter's motto. Yet with 135,000 subscribers in 1944 it had by far the largest circulation of any independent weekly progressive publication in the country. Furthermore, it was one of the few to operate consistently in the black, sustaining itself within the culture of consumer capitalism that it so vociferously railed against.[63]

The Popular Front as a Market Segment: Friday *Magazine*

Roughly a year before Seldes began *In Fact*, he was visited by an earnest young radical journalist named Daniel Gillmor, who claimed that he had recently inherited a fortune of approximately one million dollars and wanted the veteran reporter and media critic's advice about founding his own periodical. Initially, Seldes recalled, Gillmor had floated the idea of launching a major metropolitan daily newspaper with a leftist political orientation. Seldes replied that in his judgment it would take a minimum of $5 million, and possibly as much as $10 million, to establish such a paper in a city like New York or Chicago. Instead, he recommended that Gillmor follow the approach that he would use himself by starting small, with possibly just a four-page newsletter circulated nationally, and potentially expanding over time.

Around the same time, Gillmor also approached Ingersoll about investing in the newspaper project that became *PM*, but even though Ingersoll was fervently seeking funds to realize his vision, he deemed unacceptable Gillmor's apparent insistence that the paper adopt a procommunist position. Instead of following Seldes's advice, Gillmor put his personal wealth into creating *Friday* magazine, which commenced publication in March 1940. Rather than eschew advertising as part of a frontal assault on the culture of consumer capitalism, *Friday* emulated the form, style, and appearance of slick general-interest picture magazines, notably *Life* and its imitator *Look*, although more plebian titles like *True Story* and *Photoplay* were also clearly influences. By fusing lucrative forms of consumer capitalist media with leftist politics, *Friday's* creators aspired to create a new Popular Front genre.[64]

"Most magazines exist because their publishers want to make money, a good old American custom," Gillmor wrote in an introductory editorial. "We want to make money, too. But we believe, unlike some of our contemporaries, that we can make money by telling the truth to our readers." The "truth," as Gillmor presented it, included unswerving support for organized labor, staunch defense of civil liberties, and skepticism toward calls for American intervention in Europe. Yet he reassured readers that "*Friday* has no professional long face. We like to look at a pretty girl all dressed up in a brand-new bathing suit, and we laugh with Fred Allen, and so you'll find plenty about Fred Allen and the pretty girls in our magazine every week." He hoped the magazine would appeal, in the end, to those Americans, who "want to read a little sense, and a little truth, in between digesting the latest news from Hollywood" and who saw no reason why they should "have to pay for a magazine that provides a pleasant evening's entertainment interlarded with the opinions of Wall Street."[65]

To fulfill this goal of balancing amusement and agitprop in a compelling weekly package, *Friday* depended on an experienced staff with staunch Popular Front commitments. Former *Fortune* journalist Cameron Mackenzie, who had been a key organizer for the Newspaper Guild at Time Inc. in the late 1930s, served as executive editor for the new magazine for its first dozen issues before being succeeded by Mildred Edie, who took leave from CU from June through December 1940. Business manager Leverett Gleason brought a knack for cultivating popular tastes as well as an activist bent. In addition to establishing his own successful comic-book publishing venture, which put out titles like *Daredevil Battles Hitler* (1941), he served for many years on the executive board of the Joint Anti-Fascist Refugee Committee. Important *Friday* staff writers included Ruth McKenney and Richard Boyer, both of whom paid the bills writing for magazines like the *New Yorker* while contributing to *New Masses* on the side. From the outset, all employees in the editorial and commercial departments were covered by a model contract with the Newspaper Guild of New York. *Friday* also featured guest articles by eminent intellectual and cultural figures with longstanding progressive allegiances, including historian Charles Beard's caustic August 1940 critique of Librarian of Congress Archibald MacLeish's liberal calls for intervention in the European war, a plea from renowned anthropologist Franz Boas for enhanced funding for public education, and an interview with Harry Bridges, the leftist leader of the CIO-affiliated International Longshore and Warehouse Union, conducted by novelist Theodore Dreiser.[66]

The magazine's strategy of appropriating and reinterpreting key thematic and stylistic elements of the culture of consumer capitalism was perhaps most evident in its complex treatment of celebrity. *Friday* played on common conceptions of fame and glamour that were cultivated by the mass media and familiar to the magazine's intended readers. An article in the first issue, titled "Hollywood Fights Back," featured a photo gallery of motion-picture actors, performers, writers, and directors with Popular Front sympathies. In its retort to accusations of Communist subversion that had been leveled by Congressman Dies against various Hollywood celebrities, the article encouraged readers to identify directly with prominent culture workers who were conspicuous in their support for pro-labor, antifascist, and antiracist causes. "Now is the time for every good American to come to the aid of his favorite movie star," the article declared, as Dies's "smear" targeted "entertainment favorites such as James Cagney, Joan Crawford, Irving Berlin, Bette Davis, Clark Gable, Miriam Hopkins, Gypsy Rose Lee, Lewis Milestone, Frederic March, John Steinbeck, and Franchot Tone." Having "distinguished themselves by joining unions or contributing talent and money to other progressive activities," they "were singled out for a kick-in-the-shins from Dies because they had been so un-American as to fight for the rights of those less fortunate than themselves."[67]

Friday regularly covered films in which Popular Front supporters performed or had a creative role, often with numerous stills as illustrations, with features on the stars of the handful of Hollywood films that explicitly addressed pro-labor or antifascist themes, including Charlie Chaplin, for his parody *The Great Dictator* (1940), and Jean Arthur, who played the title heroine in *The Devil and Miss Jones* (1941), a screwball comedy about white-collar union organizing in a department store.[68] No film received more attention in the magazine than Orson Welles's *Citizen Kane* (1941). A September 1940 preview highlighted the parallels between the plot of the film and William Randolph Hearst's own biography and noted that Dorothy Comingore, who performed the role of Kane's second wife, was "a ringer for Marion Davies," Hearst's longtime mistress. By February 1941, as Hearst tried to pressure RKO Studios into suppressing the film, *Friday* did Welles the favor of running a second article in which he disingenuously denied that the film was based on the media mogul and blamed the magazine for its earlier statements to the contrary.[69]

Even as the writers and editors of *Friday* contested the meanings of America's twentieth-century culture of celebrity, recoding some of its personalities as embodiments of Popular Front social solidarities rather than avatars of individualistic aspirations for luxury consumption and glamorized status, they also deployed a parallel representational strategy that diminished the aura of celebrity by focusing on the ranks of largely anonymous and exploited workers who produced culture. The fourth issue, for example, featured a behind-the-scenes look at the audition process for Billy Rose's Aquacade, a glitzy dancing and synchronized-swimming spectacle, as it hired talent for its second season as an attraction at the New York World's Fair. Focusing on the capricious nature of the selection process, the grueling work schedule for the women who made the cut as Aquacade performers, and the meager pay, *Friday* completely stripped away the attraction's veneer of glamour and attributed the huge turnout for the auditions to the termination of the Federal Theater Project (FTP) in June 1939. "A few years ago Billy Rose could have staged his chorus call in any Broadway theater, since jobs in the Aquacade show are notoriously tough, with low pay and long hours," it observed. In 1940, however, only Madison Square Garden could accommodate the 10,000 applicants for the 600 openings in the show, which paid just $35 weekly in exchange for four daily performances, seven days a week. Although the life of chorus dancers was often portrayed as one of "champagne, orchids, and little gifts from Tiffany's" that led invariably to becoming "the wife of Mr. John Astorglotz, with a villa in Newport and too many diamonds to count," the article assured its readers that in fact, "looking for a job in the Aquacade isn't much different from looking for a job at the factory." Moreover, the Aquacade hopefuls were hardly alone in their plight. According to the Theater Arts Committee, 50 percent of the stagehands, 60 percent of the actors, and nearly two-thirds of the dancers and singers in New York were unemployed. The article concluded by echoing the committee's calls for resurrecting the FTP, extolling not just the opportunity the project provided for thousands of cast and crewmembers to earn a living creating performances that were artistically innovative and politically progressive, but also the way it served "hundreds of thousands of men and women who had never seen any living actors before," giving "theater back to the people who want it but who can't afford to pay $3.30 a ticket for a single night's entertainment."[70]

Friday remained fixated on analyzing the means of cultural production and exchange throughout its existence. Articles on baseball, for example, addressed the rough conditions endured by minor-league players in the farm system, dubbed "baseball's migratory workers," and railed against the persistence of Jim Crow in the national pastime. Asked about standout players like catcher Josh Gibson and pitcher Satchell Paige, Dodgers Manager Leo Durocher replied, "I would certainly use those great Negro stars on the Brooklyn Dodgers. If the big bosses said okay, I would not hesitate for a single minute." An April 1941 photo-essay on the rise of pinball as a popular amusement examined the labor conditions in the Bally Manufacturing factory in Chicago, illustrating every step in the assembly process, as well as the work of the people who ran arcades and maintained the machines. In July, *Friday* covered a strike by the cartoonists at Walt Disney Studios. Other articles emphasized opportunities for ordinary people to create culture themselves. One reported on a film made by UAW activists of their 1939 strike against GM, while another explored the subculture of ham radio operators, who defied the centralizing tendencies of network radio. Even an activity as simple and ubiquitous as kids playing a game of marbles was not beyond *Friday*'s seemingly boundless interest in the participatory dimensions of popular culture.[71]

While these entertainment features accounted for roughly half of the content in the average issue of *Friday*, the other half consisted of articles that squarely addressed the labor movement, domestic politics, and the troubled international scene in the early stages of the Second World War. When possible, writers for the magazine attempted to sensationalize their coverage of these topics, often applying the tone and plotting of the *noir* thriller to appeal to readers habituated by the conventions of crime and detective fiction. An early exposé by Boyer on the unsolved murder of CIO organizer Laura Law, for instance, read like it could have been a treatment for a Hollywood mystery. Numerous articles on industrialist Henry Ford, his firm's notorious hostility to unionism, his support for violent right-wing vigilante groups like the Black Legion, and his anti-Semitic proclivities took a similar tack. "Out of the mouths of its own hired thugs," declared one story on the brutal tactics that Ford's euphemistically named "Service Department" utilized to keep the UAW at bay, it stood "accused of maintaining an industrial dictatorship based on violence, espionage, and homicide." A subsequent article described the company's "vast totalitarian automobile plant at River Rouge" on the outskirts of Detroit as "the center of the amazing empire of King Henry Ford." Another asserted that "Harry Bennett, Personnel Director of the Ford Motor Company, was Ford's Himmler," while "the secret army Bennett controls was but Ford's Gestapo." Extensive use of photographs, which graphically depicted the victims as well as the perpetrators of antiunion assaults, added a gritty realism to the coverage. When the tide finally turned in favor of the UAW, culminating in a hard-fought union victory in the spring of 1941, *Friday* championed it as a triumph for American democracy.[72]

Although the epic nature of the struggle between Ford and the UAW lent itself to dramatization, there was far more to the coverage of labor and politics in *Friday*. The magazine frequently profiled prominent union locals such as New York City's Transport Workers Union Local 100 and Wholesale and Warehouse Local 65. It also surveyed occupations with particularly hazardous conditions, like coal mining, in which the perils of catastrophic accidents and chronic ailments like black lung were well known, and hat making, in which mercury poisoning remained a common malady. The magazine also exposed the foundations of the quasi-feudal order that prevailed throughout most of the South. Articles on the poll tax and the crop-lien system of debt peonage demonstrated how these institutional arrangements not only oppressed the majority of Southerners but also undergirded much of the political power that business and conservatives used to thwart the CIO and its legislative agenda.[73] Furthermore, *Friday* appealed to the labor-oriented wing of the consumer movement, occasionally running material repurposed from LWS and CU, as well as a series of ads by CU soliciting new members. Like CU, *Friday* lent its support to cooperative initiatives for augmenting economic security and welfare, such as the Los Angeles–based Ross-Loos Clinic's experiment in group practice medicine. In the magazine's reporting on the 1940 elections, Gillmor, Boyer, and the other writers often articulated an uneasy progressive agnosticism that likely resonated with many in *Friday*'s core readership. They were critical of Roosevelt's foreign policy and his acquiescence to conservatives on domestic matters in the wake of the 1938 midterm elections. They were much harsher in their attacks on his Republican opponent Wendell Willkie, however, whom they roundly excoriated as a tool of Wall Street. Only the candidates of the Communist and Socialist Parties received favorable, although limited, coverage in the magazine.[74]

FIGURE 3.1 January 1941 cover of *Friday* targeting automobile magnate Henry Ford. This feature was part of a series of articles in the magazine supporting the United Auto Workers' dramatic campaign to organize his firm, which was the industry's last major holdout against the union.

The unfolding global catastrophe of the Second World War also received extensive attention in *Friday*, perhaps more than Gillmor and his associates might have liked. From the outset, the magazine espoused uncompromising neutrality, which was succinctly captured in a small cartoon of a man wearing a sandwich-board sign that read "Let God Save the King" that appeared in the corner of the cover of the first issue. Gillmor and Boyer condemned early efforts at American defense mobilization, which they cast as measures that would lead inevitably to intervention on behalf of the Allies and an eventual declaration of war by the United States. In this respect, Gillmor's editorial position was the opposite of Ingersoll's for *PM*, although Gillmor was also very careful to distinguish his brand of noninterventionism from that espoused by conservative isolationists like Charles Lindbergh. Only as the military situation for the Allies grew increasingly dire did Gillmor grudgingly come around to backing Lend-Lease by early 1941, but he still objected to the commitment of American troops. Meanwhile, *Friday's* loathing for Nazism and its resolute support for antifascist solidarity were roughly congruent with *PM's* editorial stance, as the magazine routinely reported on the suffering experienced by the masses living under fascist tyranny.[75]

Despite the enthusiasm and creativity of its staff, *Friday* struggled to establish itself in the media marketplace. Gillmor and his associates attempted not only to emulate the appearance and format of slick general-interest picture magazines, but also to follow crucial elements of what they assumed to be their business model. *Friday* launched with a newsstand price of ten cents, the same as *Life*. Gillmor and Gleason also assiduously solicited advertising from the national advertisers of branded goods that purchased space in general-interest magazines. The most immediately obvious discrepancy was that *Friday*, without the backing of an existing publishing venture on the order of Time Inc., had to begin modestly and then increase the scale of operations over time as revenue permitted. *Friday* offered space to advertisers at reasonable rates: $250 for a full black and white page in the first issue with a minimum circulation guarantee of just 40,000, which reflected the magazine's limited initial newsstand distribution to only the territory stretching from Maine to Ohio. Although *Friday* improved its distribution, it failed to attract the caliber of national advertisers that would make it a profitable media venture. Actual weekly circulation for *Friday* grew by the beginning of 1941 to about 180,000 copies—roughly 10 percent of the weekly sales of *Life* at that time—but any additional increase in readership, in the absence of substantial advertising revenue, would have likely just added to its losses. Advertising did not just make mass-circulation magazines lucrative; it was essential to keeping issue prices affordable for the mass market.[76]

As the magazine's losses mounted, Gillmor explored the possibility of labor patronage for *Friday*. In October 1940, he wrote to CIO president John L. Lewis with an unconventional proposal for securing the sponsorship of the industrial union center. Gillmor informed Lewis that he was in the process of creating a new magazine, called *Unbelievable*, that was "printed by rotogravure process and which will look very much like the ordinary detective magazines which you now see on the market." The demo issue consisted of rewritten and repurposed content that had already appeared in *Friday*, including extensive coverage of Ford's antiunion practices, as well as a new section, "The Album of Hate," with "pictures of the well-known anti-Semites, anti-union employers, and pro-Nazis in America." Gillmor wanted the CIO to purchase bulk orders of *Unbelievable* at cost in lots of 10,000 or more copies for use in the ongoing UAW organizing at Ford and other campaigns. Moving forward, *Friday* and the UAW would engage in "coordinated publicity in connection with the Ford Drive," in order "to make the material appearing in *Friday* as effective as possible from the standpoint of the UAW and as newsworthy as possible from the standpoint of *Friday*." Gillmor also hoped that the collaboration would furnish a means of circumventing the main commercial distributor in the Detroit metropolitan area, which had refused to make *Friday* available to newsstand vendors. Although he contended that all of the elements of his proposal were "mutually advantageous" for "the CIO and *Friday*," the CIO declined his offer.[77]

Gillmor continued his efforts to boost *Friday*'s sales, but he faced mounting obstacles. In January 1941, he purchased airtime on New York radio station WHN for a series of fifteen-minute news commentaries that aired on Mondays, Wednesdays, and Fridays at 7:45 p.m., as well as spot advertisements on stations in more than forty cities to plug the magazine. In an editorial in *Friday* that same month, he reiterated his willingness to make advertising space available to any entities willing to pay the magazine's going rate, as long as the advertiser did not contain fraudulent claims or expect to influence the magazine's content. By way of example, he pointed to a full-page ad by the Ford Motor Company that ran in the same issue as the first of a new series of articles assailing Ford. While *Friday* did carry more advertising lineage in its 1941 issues than it had in 1940, the ads still tended to be quarter-page or smaller and most were for pulp fiction, encyclopedias, correspondence courses, discount book clubs, budget vacation destinations, and novelty manufacturers who distributed heavily through direct response rather than through retail outlets; they were not the ads for the major branded goods that sustained the leading commercial publications. The intensified redbaiting of the magazine in the conservative press, including a high-profile attack by anticommunist journalist Benjamin Stolberg in the *Saturday Evening Post*, thwarted Gillmor and Gleason's efforts at attracting either the readers or the advertisers needed to stem the flow of red ink. Adding to their woes, in March 1941, William Randolph Hearst filed a libel suit seeking $500,000 in damages over allegations made in *Unbelievable* about his pro-fascist tendencies. Furthermore, as Depression conditions gave way to an inflationary economic boom fueled by the defense mobilization program, the magazine's production costs soared, putting even more pressure on the struggling enterprise.[78]

In an attempt to contain costs, *Friday* switched to a biweekly publication schedule and instituted various production changes, including a slightly smaller page size but more pages per issue. As the financial situation grew more desperate, the magazine also began to lay off employees; from a staff of forty-four in March 1941, *Friday* was down to just a skeleton crew of about fifteen by the end of August. Gillmor cut its frequency back to monthly, substituted low-grade pulp printing stock for the high-quality paper he had used previously, and in October rebranded it as *Scoop*, with a cover story by George Seldes on the underground resistance to Nazi rule within Germany. With his inheritance exhausted and circulation falling, Gillmor discontinued the venture the following month. As the United States entered the war, Gillmor briefly joined the staff of the federal government's Office of the Coordinator of Information, an intelligence and propaganda agency, but he was pushed out of his position in April 1942 in response to complaints over his procommunist associations.[79]

Leverett Gleason used the former offices of *Friday* for his own publishing enterprises, which prospered during the war from the sale of comic books, including the *Daredevil* and *Silver Streak* series as well as the more lurid *Crime Does Not Pay!* In 1944, Gleason launched a new publication on current affairs intended to attract supporters of the wartime Popular Front. Called *Reader's Scope*, it was an obvious knockoff of DeWitt Wallace's *Reader's Digest*, but with the original's pervasive conservative ideology supplanted entirely with progressive values. *Reader's Scope* was a monthly compendium of approximately two dozen brief articles, many of them abridged, in a compact format with no photographs. It offered subscribers a sampling of opinion from a diverse range of liberals and leftists; the August 1944 issue, for example, included selections such as "Post-War Jobs for All" by Senator Harvey Kilgore, "The Dead Will not Sleep" by Popular Front literary figure Howard Fast,

"The Goldwyn Saga" by Random House publisher Bennett Cerf, and "This Year Labor Means Business" by Julius Emspak of the CIO-affiliated United Electrical, Radio, and Machine Workers (UE). While some of *Reader's Scope's* content was written specifically for it by journalists formerly associated with *Friday*, it also excerpted material from *New Republic*, *New Yorker*, *PM*, *Colliers*, and *Saturday Review of Literature*, among other periodicals. *Reader's Scope* clearly lacked the imagination and creative verve of *Friday*, but its drastically lower production costs increased the odds of it subsisting on subscription revenue as *In Fact* did. Despite its no-frills approach, postwar inflation and renewed redbaiting eventually doomed the Popular Front digest. By May 1948, Gleason claimed that it had cumulative losses of $500,000, and that its current production costs were twice its monthly revenue. Unable to rectify the situation, Gleason suspended publication of *Reader's Scope* that October.[80]

Friday magazine's inability to sustain itself as a commercial enterprise in the American media marketplace of the early 1940s stemmed in large part from miscalculations by Gillmor and his associates regarding the economics of magazine publishing, although the timing of its launch also turned out to be somewhat inopportune. As with *PM*, the conception and planning of *Friday* reflected the growing confidence of progressives within the creative class in producing alternative media. It also reflected the increasing influence of organized labor and other movements for social justice, which the publishers, editors, writers, photographers, and art directors for *Friday* and *PM* hoped to represent as their principal subjects. Although the new periodicals sought to attract the partisans of the CIO and allied social movements as readers, who would support these media endeavors as consumers and feel empowered by their increased cultural visibility, *Friday* and *PM* appeared at an historical juncture in which progressives found themselves in disarray. Dissention over the advent of the Second World War and the apparent stalemate in domestic politics made it difficult for either publication to adopt a coherent editorial position capable of appealing to a community of like-minded readers that was as broad as that of the mid-1930s heyday of the initial Popular Front. Ingersoll and Gillmor each committed their respective publications to definite editorial stances, with *PM* backing intervention on behalf of Britain and the Allies as well as an unprecedented third term for Roosevelt, while *Friday* resisted the interventionist trend and expressed fatigue with FDR as the progressives' political standard bearer; in doing so, each alienated in its critical early months some of the potential readers necessary for commercial success.

Nevertheless, the commercial failure of *Friday*, regardless of its considerable journalistic achievements, demonstrated two major structural impediments that confronted all progressives interested in alternative modes of cultural production in the United States during the middle decades of the twentieth century. First, the magazine's difficulty in soliciting advertising for major branded goods illustrated the antipathy of the leading advertising agencies and their clients to any alternative media endeavor that consistently challenged the culture of consumer capitalism. Moreover, the mass-circulation periodicals that were the main beneficiaries of the advertisers' largess needed no enticement to impugn the motives of critical media projects like *Consumers Union Reports*, *PM*, *In Fact*, and *Friday* and accuse them of subversion. Yet *Friday*'s demise also revealed a second and more fundamental obstacle for the proponents of a social-democratic culture. If working-class Americans were supposed to be a core part of *Friday*'s ideal readership, how were they supposed to afford the price of the magazine, let alone to consume substantial quantities of the branded products, particularly durable goods, promoted through advertising? Like Rorty's hitchhiking magazine peddler, *Friday*'s travails called into question the commercial desirability of the Popular Front as a market segment, at least under Depression conditions.

4

Designing Radicalism

THE POPULAR FRONT, MODERNIST AESTHETICS,
AND THE PROBLEM OF PATRONAGE

THE MUSEUM OF Modern Art's retrospective exhibition on the Bauhaus that opened in December 1938 drew more visitors than any prior show in its brief history. Crowds thronged the museum's temporary galleries in Rockefeller Center to see sculptures, furniture, housewares, posters, and architectural models and drawings from the legendary German design school. Herbert Bayer, who had been one of the "master" instructors at the Bauhaus before the Nazis shuttered it in 1933, served as a guest curator for the exhibition, which highlighted the work of fellow masters Walter Gropius, Ludwig Mies van der Rohe, and Marcel Breuer. His collaborator, the museum's curator of architecture and industrial art, John McAndrew, marveled in the MoMA *Bulletin* that so few of the items on display "seem dated after a dozen years." Reflecting the supposedly timeless principles of modern design pioneered at the Bauhaus, "they were never meant to be 'in style' or 'the last word of 1926' but were honest and often distinguished."[1]

McAndrew intended for the exhibition to contribute to the definition of a modernist design canon, and he devoted much of his commentary to disassociating the functionalist modernism that it celebrated from the streamlined material and visual culture of Depression-era America. Although the prolific output of industrial design entrepreneurs like Norman Bel Geddes, Raymond Loewy and Henry Dreyfuss pervaded the imagery of modernity and progress in the United States during the 1930s, McAndrew maintained that their expressive commercial aesthetic was not truly "modern." Instead, they had imitated "superficially the forms of modern art, reducing them to decorative mannerisms." These industrial designers, engaged in "'restyling' almost everything, so that what we owned might look old fashioned as soon as possible," had seized upon streamlined forms "and misapplied them to a fantastic variety of objects." The designs in the MoMA exhibition, by contrast, "whether for chairs, lighting fixtures or ash trays, are free of both modernistic and streamlined aberrations; sound Bauhaus training would not permit them." By drawing sharp distinctions between the streamlined goods of American mass consumerism and the refined rationality on display in the retrospective, McAndrew articulated a new hierarchy of taste in which the austere functionalism of the emerging International Style became the cultural elite's preferred strategy for representing modernity in architecture, design, and the graphic arts.[2]

MoMA was by no means the only cultural institution in the United States attempting to promote modernist aesthetics or to define their possible connotations. Tucked away in a corner of the exhibition hall was a small display of work by students at the Laboratory School of Industrial Design in New York City. The curators included only a small sample of abstract experimental sculptures, rather than actual product prototypes, as a means of illustrating the far-reaching influence of Bauhaus pedagogical techniques. But the Design Laboratory was far more than a mere footnote in the narrative of modernism's genesis in America. When the school opened in 1935, it was the first educational institution in the country with open enrollment to offer comprehensive training in modern design. Throughout its existence, the school furnished a vibrant site of contact between multiple social and cultural currents, including the business culture of America's industrial design entrepreneurs, the experimental modernism of the Depression-era avant-garde, the unprecedented public arts bureaucracy of the New Deal, the militant industrial unionism of the CIO, and the progressive cultural politics of the Popular Front. Although its most immediate impact came through its pedagogical and curricular innovations, which were eventually adopted widely throughout American art and design education, the Design Laboratory's greater significance was as a key element of the efforts of progressives and radicals within the creative class to develop a modernist aesthetic strategy. The school's faculty and students aspired to establish a visual idiom that would signify both their desire for enhanced creative autonomy in the production of culture and their commitment to social consumerism. They shared this impulse with their like-minded counterparts in the white-collar unions' other educational and cultural programs, organizations like Consumers Union, and various endeavors to provide goods and services on a nonprofit basis under public, labor, or cooperative auspices. Through their

advocacy for a range of modernist design aesthetics—primarily a functionalist modernism, but also constructivism, surrealism, and hyperrealism—
they naturally adopted a highly critical stance toward the streamlined look
of American consumer capitalism that they shared uneasily with more elitist
proponents of modernism.

Exploring the Design Laboratory and the other modernist initiatives of
the Popular Front also elucidates the problem of patronage that confronted
those progressives and radicals who sought to establish alternative institutions
for the creation and dissemination of culture in mid-century America. Their
efforts to harness the symbolic and representational power of modernist
art and design in order to advance social-democratic objectives depended
upon garnering adequate financial support within a cultural environment
dominated by consumer capitalism. For the Design Laboratory, funding
through the Federal Art Project provided a steady, if meager, paycheck for a
dedicated faculty but also subjected them, and their students, to the organizational discipline of the project's administrators. After disagreements with
FAP officials and curtailments in appropriations by Congress combined to
eliminate public support for the school in 1937, the Laboratory's faculty and
students enjoyed greater autonomy during its period of union sponsorship as
well as in its final phase as an independent cooperative. Autonomy came with
a price as the school was forced to charge tuition, effectively commodifying
an educational experience intended to transcend existing capitalist relations
of cultural production. Beyond the immediate problem of securing adequate patronage for the Laboratory was the exponentially greater challenge
of getting its visions of a social-democratic modernism off the drawing board
and into production as actual buildings, furniture, appliances, housewares,
and graphics. The potential cost involved in large-scale construction, or the
mass production of durable goods, made the sums poured into media projects
like *PM* or *Friday* pale in comparison. For the most part, only the New Deal
state had the capacity to produce directly, or to procure from private firms to
its specifications, a built environment and material culture that manifested
the modernist design ethic espoused at the Laboratory, although ambitious
enthusiasts in the labor and consumer cooperative movements also aspired to
develop their own means of production.

By late 1938, with the school struggling to remain viable as an independent cooperative, the Laboratory's presence in the Bauhaus retrospective
increased the possibility that it might access the elite patronage networks that
enabled MoMA to fund the construction of its permanent home on Fifty-
Third Street. Although some leftist proponents of modernism fretted that

collaboration with elites compromised efforts to create social-democratic alternatives to the culture of consumer capitalism, the institutional instability of the Popular Front made such alliances attractive. Yet MoMA benefitted from the relationship as well. After all, some figures associated with the museum or with galleries that catered to wealthy art and design patrons were genuinely sympathetic to the goals of the Popular Front. Cultivating links with the Laboratory, and with the related modernist initiatives of the white-collar unions, enabled MoMA to enhance its own legitimacy. It also opened access to potential streams of public, labor, or cooperative patronage that might yet become reliable means of support in the years ahead.

From this perspective, MoMA's Bauhaus exhibition appears not as a teleological step toward the instantiation of a high modernist canon of art and design, but instead as a moment of flux in which artists, designers, curators, critics, and administrators both cooperated as well as competed to influence the development of modernist aesthetics in the United States. Explicating the role of the FAP, the white-collar unions in the culture industries, and progressive organizations like Consumers Union that contributed to discourses about design demonstrates the myriad ways that progressives and radicals in the creative class influenced American modernism over the course of the 1930s and 1940s. It also reveals the magnitude of the obstacles that the partisans of social-democratic modernism confronted, especially as war mobilization narrowed prospects for the direct public employment of culture workers. Even with the setbacks they encountered, they nonetheless continued to shape the built environment, material culture, and visual culture of the United States into the postwar years.

The Federal Art Project and Cultural Democracy

The four principal cultural projects that were funded in the initial appropriations for the Works Progress Administration in 1935—the Federal Art Project, the Federal Theater Project, the Federal Music Project (FMP), and the Federal Writers Project (FWP)—were unprecedented in the American experience for prioritizing the production of culture as a public good. Radicalized artists, designers, writers, editors, actors, musicians, and other performers and creative talent not only demanded better conditions in the existing jobs available in the culture industries, but also lobbied for the extension of public works relief to alleviate unemployment within the creative class. Throughout 1933 and 1934, organizations of unemployed creative, professional, and technical workers joined with militant white-collar unions, the John Reed Clubs, and other radical collectives of artists, writers, and performers to push for a massive expansion of government cultural patronage. "The purpose of this organization," New York's Artists' Union declared in its constitution, "is to unite all artists engaged in the practice of graphic and plastic art in their struggle for economic security and to encourage a wider distribution and understanding of art." Since "private patronage cannot provide the means to satisfy these needs in this period of grave economic crisis," the union demanded "that the Government fulfill its responsibilities toward unemployed artists" as part of its "responsibility toward providing for all unemployed workers." In doing so, it would "fulfill its responsibility toward the maintenance and furtherance of the cultural standards of this country by the proper use of artists' talents," establishing "the machinery necessary for the widest possible distribution of art to the general public."[3] In 1935, procommunist activists contributed to the formation of the League of American Writers, the American Artists Congress, and the Conference of Professional, Cultural, and White-Collar Workers, all of which reiterated the call for expanded public patronage for the production of culture. Although it may be tempting to see the WPA cultural projects as part of the inexorable expansion of state capacity during the Roosevelt administration, pressure from leftist activists was critical in overcoming the skepticism that many New Dealers harbored regarding relief employment for culture workers.[4]

Not only were the WPA cultural projects unlike anything that had come before, no major public program implemented since has followed their example. For the first and only time in the United States, tens of thousands of men and women were put directly on the government payroll to produce a wide array of culture for domestic consumption.[5] At their peak levels of employment in late 1936 and early 1937, the four WPA cultural projects together provided jobs to approximately 45,000 culture workers.[6] Despite the projects' modest size, their proponents within the ranks of the creative class saw them as a model upon which they hoped to build.

To supervise the new cultural projects, Secretary of the Interior Harold Ickes and WPA chief Harry Hopkins selected individuals who combined practical administrative experience, a commitment to cultural democracy, and enthusiasm for an eclectic range of genres and styles. Holger Cahill, their choice for the position of national director of the FAP, exemplified this approach. Born Sveinn Kristjan Bjarnason, he emigrated as a boy from Iceland to the Great Plains with his homesteading family, and as a young man he made his way to New York City in the 1910s, changed his name, and proceeded to reinvent himself as a journalist, art critic, and curator. From 1922 to 1931,

Cahill assisted John Cotton Dana at the Newark Museum, and from 1932 until he joined the FAP in 1935 he served as the director of exhibitions for MoMA. Cahill espoused an expansive conception of modernism, which led him to champion the surrealist and abstract painting produced by artists in New York's radical avant-garde as well as the vernacular aesthetics of folk art. As head of the FAP, he tirelessly strove to provide "art for the millions" by dramatically increasing accessibility to art through programs like the FAP Community Art Centers that operated in regions of the country isolated from the circuits of private patronage as well as by promoting more egalitarian attitudes about the social uses of art.[7]

Cahill invariably found himself contrasting the efforts of the FAP with prevailing modes of artistic patronage and appreciation prior to the Depression. Speaking in 1939 at a celebration of the eightieth birthday of renowned philosopher John Dewey, Cahill lamented that "from the middle of nineteenth century up to very recent times art has tended to become an activity sharply segregated from the everyday vocations of society." While "the art object has become more and more a minor luxury product," American art patrons frequently looked to Europe, sustaining "a tremendous traffic in aesthetic fragments torn from their social background, trailing clouds of vanished aristocratic glories." With the coming of the New Deal, "the groups working for an art program which would release the creative forces of our country and make art participation possible for the whole people have found a powerful ally in the United States Government as art patron." Cahill contended that the FAP succeeded in stimulating the "creative drive" among both the artists it employed and the new publics for art by holding "to the idea of the unity of art with the common experience," encouraging the "closest possible collaboration between the artist and the public for which he works," and hewing to "the idea of the greatest degree of freedom for the artist."[8]

Although the FAP and the other WPA cultural projects provided employees with considerable creative autonomy, the projects' offices, studios, classrooms, and other workplaces nonetheless quickly became contested sites of production. Artists, writers, teachers, performers, and other white-collar employees on the WPA cultural projects often found themselves in an adversarial relationship with supervisors and administrators. They were frequently humiliated by the requirement that they demonstrate their destitution in order to be eligible for relief employment. They also resisted efforts to impose the discipline and regimentation they associated with commercial work; in the Fine Art Section of the New York FAP, for instance, painters continually squabbled with the timekeepers who were charged with making sure that they spent the required number of hours in front of their easels. Several of the white-collar unions that had pushed for the creation of the cultural projects subsequently found them fertile grounds for organizing. The Artists' Union, which represented individuals who had previously been engaged primarily as independent agents creating artworks that usually lacked a predetermined price, benefited in particular from the stability inherent in a large common employer willing to pay a uniform scale. Journalists, writers, and editors working on the publications and programs of the FWP joined the Newspaper Guild or other unions, stage performers in the FTP signed up with Actors' Equity, and the well-organized American Federation of Musicians asserted its jurisdiction over the employees of the FMP. Although none of these unions engaged in formalized collective bargaining with the WPA cultural projects, they effectively mobilized members to resist arbitrary discipline by project supervisors and to press for an expansion of employment on the projects. The unions also pushed for increases in the miserly pay earned by the vast majority of project workers, who held relief positions, but had little success given the uncertainty of appropriation levels.[9]

The instability that plagued the WPA cultural projects proved to be the most contentious issue, as employees resorted to work stoppages and sit-in occupations to protest threatened lay-offs and program curtailments. The first significant strike took place in St. Louis, in November 1936, where novelist Jack Conroy led his coworkers with the FWP on a two-week walkout.[10] With its concentration of project workers, New York City soon emerged as the center of the most sustained demonstrations to defend the public production of culture. On December 1, hundreds of FAP employees occupied the main WPA office in midtown Manhattan to fight proposed cuts. Police responded by storming the office and savagely beating the protestors before hauling 219 of them away to jail. While this demonstration and others staved off the curtailment of activities for a few months, a much larger wave of protests and strikes by workers on the WPA cultural projects in New York City the following spring ultimately failed to prevent deep cuts to federal expenditures in 1937. The thousands of culture workers who lost their WPA positions found themselves with few options, as the economic recession that was precipitated by the reduction in public spending limited their prospects for commercial employment. After the heady first two years of the cultural projects, employment levels drifted downward; in New York City the number of artists employed by the FAP, for example, declined from 2,200 in early 1937 to just 1,000 by July 1940.[11]

The projects' employees, their unions, and their Popular Front allies in organizations like the American Artists Congress and the League of American Writers lobbied hard for the establishment of permanent cultural projects in which public patronage would not be justified in terms of the expediencies of relief. They argued that the need for public patronage was not a temporary emergency, since even in conditions of prosperity the profit-driven culture industries and private patrons were incapable of supporting an adequate quantity and range of cultural activity.[12] Yet the political obstacles to the establishment of permanent cultural projects were immense. Advocates confronted not only the mood of fiscal restraint that characterized much of Roosevelt's second term, but also the mounting hostility to the WPA from congressional conservatives like Martin Dies and J. Parnell Thomas. Proposed legislation to establish permanent cultural projects was resoundingly defeated during the late 1930s. Even Cahill, despite his rhapsodizing about the marvelous accomplishments of the FAP, remained noncommittal when pressed for an endorsement of the bill, in part to avoid the kind of acrimonious relationship that FTP director Hallie Flanagan and FWP director Henry Alsberg had with congressional critics.[13] Although progressives in the creative class were frustrated in this campaign, the example of public patronage represented by the WPA cultural projects continued to inspire them for years to come.

The Federal Art Project in Practice: The Design Laboratory

The Design Laboratory was one of the boldest undertakings of the FAP, and its development demonstrated the challenges facing the cultural projects' proponents. By providing systematic training in art and design that emphasized "coordination in the study of esthetics, industrial products, machine fabrication and merchandising," according to its first brochure, the school was to "train designers, not specialized craftsmen, by correlating thorough instruction in the general principles of design and fine arts with shop practice." When the Laboratory opened on December 2, 1935, its classrooms and studios in a cramped loft in midtown Manhattan were swamped with 300 pupils enrolled and another 350 on a waiting list. Aspiring designers flocked to the school. Don Wallance, who recalled finding the industrial design course he had taken at Pratt Institute "mainly superficial and anecdotal," quickly enrolled at the Laboratory to partake in its "comprehensive industrially oriented curriculum based on the Bauhaus experience."[14]

Frances Pollak, whom Cahill had hired to coordinate all educational programs in New York City, assumed the responsibility of recruiting the Laboratory's advisory board. To secure the imprimatur of the commercial design entrepreneurs, she solicited Raymond Loewy, Walter Dorwin Teague, Donald Deskey, George Sakier, and Russel Wright to serve on the board, although only Sakier and Wright had even a passing involvement in the school's everyday operations. Richard F. Bach of the Metropolitan Museum of Art enlisted as an advisor, as did progressive architects William Lescaze, Percival Goodman, Harvey Wiley Corbett, and Ely Jacques Kahn. Pollak rounded out the advisory board with several figures from trade publishing, notably Alfred Auerbach, editor of the magazine *Retailing*, and Earl Lougee, editor of *Modern Plastics*. For the position of director, she hired furniture designer Gilbert Rohde, whose agency created numerous models for the Kroehler and Herman Miller companies.[15]

As part of the early planning for the Laboratory in November 1935, Pollak submitted to Cahill a prospectus for the school. The included bibliography featured major texts by American social theorists like John Dewey, Charles Beard, and Lewis Mumford, along with writings by important modernist architects and designers such as Frank Lloyd Wright, László Moholy-Nagy, and Le Corbusier. Yet in Pollak's estimation, one work on the list, Thorstein Veblen's *Theory of the Leisure Class* (1899), stood out above the rest.[16] Veblen's critique of what he held to be the anachronistic and ostentatious "conspicuous consumption" of Gilded Age elites pointed toward a functionalist theory of culture that undergirded progressives' hopes for promoting social change through aesthetics and design. The persistence of outmoded signifiers of status from the preindustrial past, he contended, threatened to "lower the industrial efficiency of the community and retard the adaptation of human nature to the exigencies of modern industrial life." In a subsequent article, Veblen disparaged the "sophisticated archaism" of the Arts and Crafts movement as running counter to "the requirements of modern business enterprise as well as of modern, that is to say democratic, culture." Any effort "for the reform of industrial art or for the inculcation of aesthetic ideals," he concluded, "must fall in line with the technological exigencies of the machine process" if it were to have a chance of "checking the current ugliness."[17]

Mumford was nearly as important of an influence on the school as Veblen, and Design Laboratory instructors regularly assigned his texts to their pupils. The progressive sensibility, Mumford wrote in his magisterial survey *Technics and Civilization* (1934), had revealed the potential to liberate "forces which were suppressed or perverted by the earlier development of the machine," bringing "a new synthesis in thought and a fresh synergy in action." While advances in technology and culture hinted at the promise of a modernist future, Mumford, like Veblen before him, bemoaned that as yet it existed "only in fragments." Evidence of the Gilded Age penchant for misapplying obsolete decoration to the products of industrial technology still abounded, while the "frantic attempts that have been made in America by advertising agencies and 'designers' to stylicize machine-made objects" were nonetheless "for the most part attempts to pervert the machine process in the interests of caste and pecuniary distinction." Functionalist modernism, rather than the expressive modern ornamentation of streamlining, evoked an emerging ethos of "conspicuous economy" that Mumford believed was appropriate for a mature society characterized by "dynamic equilibrium" rather than unregulated growth and cycles of industrial boom and bust. With its eloquent elucidation of the evolution of modernist aesthetics and bold call for cultural regeneration, *Technics and Civilization* captivated the Laboratory's progressives, even though Mumford evaded the thorny question of what system of political economy could realize the ideals he set forth.[18]

Despite the stringent restrictions imposed on all of the WPA cultural projects that mandated relief salaries of approximately $30 per week for the majority of instructional employees, Pollak succeeded in attracting a diverse core of talented young designers and artists to teach at the Laboratory. A few, like interior designers Hilde Reiss and William Priestly, and graphic designer Lila Ulrich, had actually studied at the Bauhaus. Others, like product design instructor Jacques Levy, held degrees from elite universities like Columbia and Yale. But the majority of the instructors, including product designers William Friedman and Joseph J. Roberto, painters Irene Rice Pereira and Jack Kufeld, and sculptor Chaim Gross, had patched together their training from a combination of coursework at local institutions like City College, NYU, Cooper Union, Pratt Institute, and the Art Students' League. For all but the three who had been at the Bauhaus, the pedagogy that they developed grew principally out of their workplace experiences and independent exposure to modernist styles, not from their formal education. With a few exceptions like the teaching of various types of modernist painting in the cooperative school run by the Art Students' League, as late as the mid-1930s most formal education in art and architecture in America reflected Beaux Arts traditionalism. For the instructors nearly as much as the students, the daily activities at the Laboratory were a pragmatist exercise in "learning by doing."[19]

The faculty began by taking a holistic approach to design education that stressed creativity and proficiency in a wide range of media and techniques and encouraged students to transcend staid boundaries between disciplines. In place of "the existing artificial distinction between interior decoration and designing of mechanical objects," according to the initial bulletin, classes at the Laboratory were "grouped according to present day trends in fabrication and design. In this manner, wood, metal and plastics are treated as a unit." Although the emphasis on improvisation and experimentation drew positive attention to the school and its progressive pedagogy, it also reflected the problem of developing a structured curriculum, with a logical sequence of assignments over multiple semesters, given the uncertain future of the FAP. Nonetheless, in August 1936 the Laboratory introduced a provisional three-year design curriculum. "It has been plain that an educational organization," the New York FAP office proclaimed in a press release, "founded to provide instruction in the best modern design, could not operate on a purely temporary basis." In the new Laboratory course of study, however, students would really be able to "learn by designing a clock, a chair, a table, an inkwell, an ashtray, a radio cabinet, an interior of a house; by drafting blue prints, and then by actually carrying out the design, either life-size or to scale in model." Such an approach was "no new principle in progressive education," but it nonetheless remained a novelty "when applied to industrial design." While the school remained the only one in the United States "to present in a coordinated fashion the standards of taste and style evolved elsewhere in the world in the so-called 'International Style,'" the intention was not "to hand down dogmas." Just because "Le Corbusier has made extremely handsome chairs of chromium-plated tubing on which bands of textiles hang in the perfect suspension," modern designers "need not reject wood as a basic material for a chair."[20]

Despite the Laboratory's tremendous promise, serious disagreements over the purpose of the school slowly eroded official support for the institution within the FAP hierarchy. Faced with the daunting task of staffing local programs in remote parts of the country, Cahill hoped that the school could furnish a reliable source of competent personnel. In one November 1935 memorandum, he explained that the Laboratory's purpose was not just to meet "the increasing demand of industry for designers," but also "to train teachers working on our projects" as well as to provide for the "rehabilitation and retraining of artists, teachers and craftsmen who have been displaced through the development of modern technology." Several months later, while assisting with the preparation of a report on the early accomplishments of the FAP for Hopkins and First Lady Eleanor Roosevelt, Cahill further emphasized personnel training, describing the Laboratory as a "master teaching project"

FIGURE 4.1 Design Laboratory faculty and students at work in the school's shop in 1936. From the Federal Art Project, Photographic Division Collection, Archives of American Art, Smithsonian Institution.

to supply instructors who would then reach "hundreds of adult and youth groups under the Federal Art Project and the Recreation Division."[21]

Throughout the first half of 1936, FAP administrators discussed a variety of schemes to employ both pupils and faculty of the Laboratory in far-flung extension projects. After learning of a vocational school workshop in Massachusetts that was idle in summer months, Cahill proposed using it as a base for a small detachment that "would inaugurate a program for retraining New England craftsmen." Acclaimed textiles designer Ruth Reeves, who was traveling the country as a consultant for the FAP, suggested linking the Laboratory with the regional efforts of the WPA Recreation Division, the National Youth Administration, and the Civilian Conservation Corps. Although she had drawn upon Guatemalan motifs in her own designs, she seemed less enamored with some of the folk art she saw closer to home. Appalled "at the lack of taste and general gimcrackeryness" of the crafts programs she surveyed on a field visit to South Carolina, Reeves suggested that the Laboratory could furnish personnel with a "socially creative point of view" to establish progressive craft activities in rural areas. Such a move would alleviate what she characterized as the "congestion" affecting the FAP programs in New York City. Using the Laboratory in cooperation with other federal agencies as part of a comprehensive system of newly available public goods and services, she hoped, would legitimate the FAP "in a popular way at least as it has never been justified before." None of these proposals, however, were implemented, and by the fall discussion of Laboratory extension projects largely ceased.[22]

These schemes reflected not just the logistical challenges confronting Cahill and his top associates, but also their own aesthetic and political sensibilities. This was perhaps most evident in the early relationship between the Design Laboratory and the Index of American Design, which eventually became the best-known FAP initiative in the field of material culture and accounted for the largest share of total project employment. Spearheaded by Pollak, Reeves, painter Romana Javitz, and cultural historian Constance Rourke, the Index hired hundreds of artists to produce renderings of a wide array of decorative and applied arts from the late seventeenth through early nineteenth centuries, ranging from implements like weather vanes, to household goods like toys and quilts, to furniture. Cahill and the administrators of the Index envisioned the artifacts documented by the project as the legitimate precursors of a distinctly American modernism, rather than as objects of antiquarian or antimodernist interest. In early 1936, Cahill extolled the potential for the Laboratory as a center for design innovation while also portraying its mission as fundamentally linked to the efforts of the Index to document and make available for new generations of Americans the vernacular design traditions of the nation's past. In a letter to *New York Times* art critic Henry Brock in January, Cahill portrayed the Index as "a continuation of the work of the Design Laboratory." Elaborating on this theme several weeks later in a publicity release on the early progress of the FAP, Cahill described the Index as "allied" to the Laboratory and claimed that the documentary initiative was "a project of incalculable importance to American manufacturers, scholars, and creative artists in the field of design." By placing "at the disposal for everyone interested in the field of American decorative and applied art, for the first time, a graphic record of the development of American design," the Index would provide grounding for the Laboratory's modernist experimentation.[23]

As it became evident to Cahill and other FAP administrators that the Laboratory was not going to become a significant source of staffing, nor fit into their plans for promoting an approach to representing modernity that was rooted in American vernacular design and folk-art traditions, their early enthusiasm for the school began to wane. For their part, the Laboratory's faculty and students had little apparent interest in being deployed elsewhere and instead looked to pursue opportunities in New York City. Student publications endorsed the Artists' Union, demanded the creation of a permanent public art project, and called for "professionals" and "workers" alike to join together in a "United Front against War and Fascism." Faculty and students both took part in numerous demonstrations and strikes over issues such as the continuation of funding for the school, instructors' salaries, and reductions in the cultural projects' quota of "nonrelief" personnel. FAP administrators and consultants who reviewed the Laboratory in the fall of 1936 were unsympathetic to the hardships that resulted from this austerity, and instead blamed Pollak and Josiah Marvel, an assistant director who had been hired to run the school on a day-to-day basis, for mismanagement. In addition, although it offered a unique curriculum and pedagogy, complaints from private art schools about the competition from a tuition-free public venture also undermined support for the Laboratory.[24] These tensions came to a head during the disruptive protests of December 1936, when the FAP suspended Marvel for writing directly to Hopkins and Secretary of Treasury Henry Morgenthau to demand greater funding for the WPA cultural projects. By early 1937, the national FAP office was even declining to furnish inquiring journalists with already existing publicity materials on the Laboratory. The steep reduction in WPA appropriations announced that spring sealed the school's fate, and in May the Laboratory was designated as one of the many programs to be discontinued.[25]

While supporters of the school joined in the largest wave of strikes and demonstrations yet to hit the WPA in New York City, instructor William Friedman scrambled behind the scenes to keep the school open after the June 30 termination date set by the FAP. Working with the Communist caucus among the students and faculty, Friedman's ad-hoc coordinating committee arranged for sponsorship by the Federation of Architects, Engineers, Chemists, and Technicians (FAECT). The union had launched its own Federation Technical School the year before, primarily to provide review courses for state certification exams in architecture, engineering, and various other technical fields, so affiliation provided the Laboratory with an easy way for it to continue its operations. After a hiatus of several weeks, on July 12 the faculty and students began summer classes at a new loft space off of Union Square.[26]

Modernist Organizing: The White-Collar Unions' Educational Programs

With its reorganization, the Design Laboratory became one of the brightest stars in a constellation of schools, public forums, and other extension programs sponsored by New York's white-collar unions as part of their organizing activities. Like the Laboratory, the classes and presentations on the applied graphic arts put on by the Book and Magazine Guild (UOPWA Local 18), the American Advertising Guild (UOPWA Local 20), United American Artists (UOPWA Local 60), and the UOPWA New York Joint Council provided training in cutting-edge modernist techniques in layout, illustration, and typography largely unavailable through conventional educational institutions. They also tended to emphasize functionalist, constructivist, and surrealist variants of modernism at odds with the streamlined style frequently used to represent modernity in America's culture of consumer capitalism during the 1930s and 1940s. These educational endeavors, especially those that featured leading creative figures, were crucial to the unions' efforts to enhance their reputations and to integrate themselves into the institutional and professional cultures of the advertising, publishing, and design fields. Along with the unions' prolific use of functionalist, cubist, and surrealist graphic elements in flyers, pamphlets, and periodicals, the educational programs helped to strengthen the association between modernist aesthetics and the radical white-collar unions. With hundreds of workers enrolling in classes every year in the late 1930s and early 1940s, and hundreds more attending forums, these activities enabled the unions to reach workers who might not otherwise come into contact with organizers.

Despite the numerous uncertainties that accompanied the Design Laboratory's transition to labor patronage, most of the students and faculty stuck with the school. Friedman, who became Chairman of the Faculty, later recalled that "practically everyone who was on the original staff continued" because they believed in the Laboratory "over and beyond its connection with WPA. It became a very important school educationally and there was a feeling of tremendous involvement on the part of both students and staff." Administration of the school was entrusted to a committee comprised of representatives from the union, the faculty, and the student body. Freedom from relief regulations opened new possibilities while posing new challenges. The school could admit any interested students regardless of their economic means, but it also became dependent on a meager stream of tuition—initially set at $40 per semester—to cover most expenses. Instructors earned less teaching for a labor school than they had on WPA payroll, but they could now pursue freelance opportunities to supplement their incomes. While the Laboratory could now conduct its affairs on an ostensibly permanent basis, instead of relying on the federal government's relief program, it now only had the backing of a scrappy white-collar union that was barely four years old.[27]

With the school's reorganization the faculty also revamped the curriculum. They instituted a compulsory Materials Laboratory course for all incoming students regardless of their major program or prior training. Influenced by the Foundations course developed at the Bauhaus during the 1920s, the new course provided a more effective introduction to the school's interdisciplinary methods by forcing aspiring designers to experiment with a wide range of materials and shop techniques. The committee also instituted a two-semester Design Synthesis course intended to familiarize new students with the panoply of modernist styles and techniques as a way of teaching fresh approaches to the conceptualization of design tasks. In the fall of 1937, the school committee announced that it was extending the existing three-year program of study into a four-year design program comparable to the 120 credit-hour Bachelor of Arts degree programs at standard colleges and universities. As part of the four-year curriculum, the committee mandated new requirements in social studies, including courses in American labor history, economic history, and the cultural ramifications of industrial modernity. With enrollment rising to 400 pupils, the school's boosters were not unrealistic in their hopes that the Laboratory might serve as the cornerstone for a "labor university."[28]

The Design Laboratory's success depended in large part on the maintenance of a community of dedicated faculty and students. The school hosted a regular series of lively rent parties, which served to instill a degree of radical élan while helping the Laboratory survive financially. Students and faculty participated actively in the larger Popular Front movement culture that flourished in New York City during the late 1930s. To supplement its own offerings, the school encouraged students to take classes at reduced fees at the cooperative school sponsored by the American Artists Congress.[29] The school newspaper featured reviews of local art exhibitions and articles on shop methods alongside calls for aid to the embattled Spanish Republic and notices of boycotts against firms that resisted CIO organizing drives. One group of students and faculty met regularly during the fall of 1937 and the winter of 1938 to assist with various organizing campaigns being conducted by the FAECT and other CIO unions of culture workers in New York City. Sustaining this level of commitment, however, proved an arduous task. "We hear much about the progressive character of the Design Laboratory," a student

FIGURE 4.2 Collage of work by Design Laboratory students from its 1938 catalogue demonstrating the ways in which they applied the school's functionalist pedagogy in practice. From the Donald Wallance Archive, Gift of David and Gregory Wallance, Cooper Hewitt, Smithsonian Design Museum.

wrote in a January 1938 editorial. "Such terms as 'student-faculty relations,' 'cooperation,' etc. have been heard so often that they are taken for granted by everyone." Yet there remained a "definite lack of understanding among students as to their role" in the school. "We must feel that we are not just isolated individuals attending classes and receiving instruction from teachers who have little in common with us, but that all of us are part of this cooperative scheme, with every phase of school activity of concern to each of us." Product design instructor Jacques Levy concurred in an open letter, in which he combined a call for greater discipline with an appeal to the Laboratory's ideals. "Let us remember this: the school is no more important nor valuable to society than the students and teachers make it," he admonished. "Great things must be in store for a school with such principles as ours has. We're in at the beginning, a responsibility is ours—let's not muff it."[30]

Although many Laboratory faculty and students saw the FAECT as a more suitable patron than the FAP in political as well as aesthetic terms, after just one year the union and the design school parted ways. The FAECT had expanded as part of the first major wave of CIO growth, but like many unions it struggled as the Roosevelt Recession deepened. At the same time that its private-sector organizing stalled, WPA cutbacks resulted in the layoffs of members of the union's public-sector locals, exacerbating its financial woes. As the FAECT became less able to assist the school materially, some with the Laboratory began to wonder if sponsorship by the leftist union might jeopardize the school's quest for state accreditation as a degree-conferring institution. Conservative legislators and officials in New York were already fulminating about the presence of Communists in education, and within the next several years the state's Rapp-Coudert investigative committee mandated the purge of leftist professors and teachers from the public education system.[31] After the school was independent from the union and had changed its name to the Laboratory School of Industrial Design, it obtained a charter from the New York State Board of Regents that enabled it to award official Bachelor of Arts degrees to students who completed 120 credit-hours of study. This second reorganization was far less disruptive than the first one, as the school remained in its loft space next door to the FAECT office.[32]

While the Laboratory's particular requirements of equipment, materials, and dedicated shop and studio space had imposed a significant financial burden on the FAECT during its year of sponsoring the school, other white-collar unions needed fewer resources for their educational undertakings. The Book and Magazine Guild started its series of classes in 1935, although for the first two years it held them in members' apartments or in cafeterias. When it affiliated with the UOPWA in 1937, it moved its classes into the parent union's meeting space. As part of its expanded schedule that fall, the BMG added to its mundane offerings on proofreading and editing a course on typography with noted book designer and union president Robert Josephy, a course on literary criticism taught by *Fortune* editor Louis Kronenberger, and a course on magazine layout and design taught by *Harper's Bazaar* art director Alexey Brodovitch. BMG class offerings for 1939 and 1940 also included *New Republic* editor George Soule's course on the role of progressive media in mass society and a revamped course on magazine layout and design taught by Irving Simon, a production manager for pulp powerhouse Macfadden Publications.[33]

Beginning in the fall of 1938, educational initiatives sponsored by the Ad Guild and United American Artists supplemented the BMG's program. As part of a series of standing-room-only forums for commercial artists held at the UAA meeting hall in early 1939, Morris Rosenblum, art director for Bamberger's department store in Newark, presented a short movie, "A Day in the Life of an Ad," that documented the entire process involved in the production of a single print advertisement and highlighted the use of new styles and techniques. In the fall of 1939 and winter of 1940, the local again drew packed audiences to a series of forums on the comparative evolution of contemporary aesthetics and the fine arts chaired by Design Laboratory instructor Elizabeth McCausland, and featuring artists such as Stuart Davis, Philip Evergood, Irene Rice Pereira, and Joseph Solman.[34] Following the transfer of the Commercial Artists Section from the UAA to the Ad Guild in the fall of 1939, that union assumed the lead in sponsoring labor-based programs on the applied graphic arts. The Ad Guild's courses on copywriting, graphics, illustration, advertisement layout, production, and sales attracted a growing following, with enrollment surpassing 200 students by November 1940. Significantly, 30 percent of the students in its courses were not union members, although for many who did join the classes had been their first serious introduction into unionism. As Esther Handler of the UOPWA Joint Council's education department pointed out, the classes brought into the union fold "many unorganized advertising workers who had to admit that here was an opportunity for expert professional training offered nowhere else at this price." The Ad Guild's most expensive course, taught by renowned art director and former Laboratory instructor Paul Rand in the fall of 1941, charged tuition of $15 for members and $25 for nonmembers.[35]

Perhaps even more prestigious for the Ad Guild than Rand's course was its long-running educational collaboration with émigré graphic designer Herbert Bayer. Shortly after curating the MoMA retrospective exhibition on the Bauhaus, Bayer joined with Lila Ulrich, who had studied with him at the Bauhaus and subsequently taught at the Design Laboratory, to cochair a wildly successful forum on modernist design jointly sponsored by the Ad Guild and the UAA. Building on the positive response, Bayer and Ulrich agreed to team-teach a regular series of workshop classes for the Ad Guild that continued from the middle of 1939 through end of 1941 that stressed the practical application of constructivist, functionalist, and surrealist approaches to graphic design. These proved extremely popular, with sections continually oversubscribed by commercial artists in the advertising industry. In the spring of 1941, the New York Art Directors' Club recognized the contribution made by the Ad Guild courses by hosting an exhibition of student work at its gallery and reproducing a sample from the show in its journal.[36] Although it never had the structured curriculum of the Design Laboratory, the educational programs of the Ad Guild, like those of the other unions, made an important but generally overlooked contribution to the development of American modernism.

FIGURE 4.3 This emblem (most likely by Ad Reinhardt) that was utilized by the UOPWA Greater New York Joint Council in 1938 to promote its pioneering healthcare program for its members exemplified the embrace of modernist aesthetics by New York's white-collar unions. Represented here (clockwise from top) are UOPWA Local 18 (Book and Magazine Guild), Local 30 (insurance workers), Local 16 (general clerical), Local 60 (United American Artists), Local 19 (Social Services Employees Guild), Local 20 (American Advertising Guild), and the UOPWA Financial Employees Organizing Committee.

Use, Value, and Aesthetics: Consumers Union's Critique of Consumer Capitalist Design

In addition to the Design Laboratory and the other educational programs sponsored by white-collar unions in the culture industries, Consumers Union also contributed in important ways to Popular Front discourses on modernist material and visual culture. As part of its campaign against advertising practices that misinformed consumers by conveying false impressions of value or utility, CU was unsparing in its criticism of the design and aesthetics of American products during the 1930s and 1940s. The attention to the experiences of everyday use that pervaded its reviews countered the glamorized images of goods offered by manufacturers and retailers. The writers and technicians at CU objected to what they judged as the excessive ornamentation and decoration inherent in streamlined styling, much as the Design Laboratory's faculty and students did, and instead favored an organic functionalism. In doing so, they hoped to define the aesthetic as a signifier of social consumerism.

The emphasis on everyday use was quite apparent in the case of domestic appliances, which CU portrayed not as symbols of middle-class status, but simply as the implements of housework. Early appliance reviews in *Consumers Union Reports* often opened with scathing indictments of marketing hype. "Conservador—Shelvador—Eject-O-Cube—Adjusto-Shelf—Foodex—Handi-bins—Touch-A-Bar ... With these magic words, mechanical refrigerator makers persuade the American public to buy their product," a July 1936 review began. "Yet these words have absolutely nothing to do with the essential qualities of a refrigerator." Deflating the pretensions of some of the leading industrial designers, it noted that "streamlining, the art department's contribution to most makes of refrigerators, has no functional value unless, as someone has suggested, one contemplates throwing the box out of the window." Although General Electric had hired designer Henry Dreyfuss with much fanfare in 1934 to supplant its distinctive "monitor-top" refrigerator with a new "cleanlined" model that relocated the condenser beneath a starkly rectilinear cabinet, CU preferred the GE monitor-top, as its visible roof-mounted condenser was "more apt to be kept clean and thereby maintain its radiating effectiveness." Harsher judgment was rendered on the streamlined Coldspot refrigerator designed for Sears-Roebuck by Raymond Loewy's agency. *Business Week* heralded Loewy's redesign as one of the great success stories of the young industrial design profession, crediting his development of a streamlined low-priced model for Sears with a dramatic improvement in sales. Loewy himself touted the Coldspot design—with its successive annual model changes to encourage premature style obsolescence—as a major accomplishment throughout his career. Nonetheless, CU found the Coldspot 3324 to be one of the worst refrigerators on the market, with a shoddily assembled and inadequately insulated cabinet as well as high operating expenses that offset the model's low $99 list price.[37]

This reassessment of the relationship between use, value, and aesthetics was also readily apparent in the institute's approach to automobiles. Surveying the evolution of auto design in the mid-1930s, CU observed that mechanical components "have been improved from year to year, but far slower than would be the case if a large part of the car's cost were not diverted into features which make it easier to sell, but which do not add to the durability of the vehicle as such." For the 1938 models, it found that "the usual meaningless changes have been made in front-end sheet metal and instrument design." Status and style were dismissed as irrelevant. "To some buyers the prestige that a particular automobile has in the marketplace may be a major item," a subsequent review admonished, but, "with this, or with esthetic preferences, CU cannot deal. Regarding the latter, it should be borne in mind that all the 1939 cars, like their predecessors will be made to look obsolete before they wear out unless factory stylists fall down on their job." Essential values for CU were "comfort, not luxury; economy, not high top speed; durability, not flashy performance; safety, not streamlining and deluxe fittings; mechanical improvements, not gadgets." For the 1940 model year, it likewise found that the new cars still fulfilled "the industry's unspoken program" of " 'more for the money but never less money.' This means chiefly more size, weight, chromium strips and pseudo-streamlining, plus considerable additions to comfort, easy riding and handling, plus what additions to durability and economy the engineers have been able to 'sell' to managements hell-bent—at least at the motor shows—on merchandising a 30,000-part transportation machine as though it were face cream."[38]

New automobiles and major home appliances were beyond the economic means of many of the working-class consumers that CU aspired to reach, but the institute applied the same standards in its evaluation of lesser appliances and minor durable goods. While it found that the Hoover 150 vacuum cleaner designed by Dreyfuss's agency performed acceptably, for example, it recommended several other brands offering superior suction for a third of the price for "those who want ruggedness and long life in an efficient cleaner, and are not concerned about streamlining and gadgets." CU faulted electric irons with heel rests that "in order to increase the 'streamlining' effect of the design," had been made "so long and so low that they may interfere with the ironing." The relative mechanical simplicity of many small appliances, moreover, facilitated their maintenance and upkeep by informed owners. Whereas manufacturers encouraged artificial or premature obsolescence, CU taught owners ways to maximize efficiency and longevity. Readers who already owned vacuum cleaners, for instance, were advised to make "minor repairs and replacements on your present machine" before buying a new model. "Do not rely on a salesman to give you impartial advice on this. He makes his living selling new machines, not fixing up old ones." The easier accessibility of parts on older models that predated streamlining often made them preferable. "On the more old-fashioned cleaners, which have not received beauty treatment by eminent modern designers," the contact brushes on the motor "are usually on the outside of the case which encloses the motor, and brush replacement is a simple task." Other issues of the *Reports* included tips on the easy replacement of nickel-chromium heating elements for electric heaters, the safe mending of electrical appliance cords, and the testing and replacement of radio tubes.[39]

Whenever practical, CU encouraged consumers themselves to become competent in the evaluation of the functional utility of goods. The institute recommended in-home trials of appliances like vacuum cleaners. For furniture selection, CU consultant Roy Perry explicated the development of mass-production techniques in the industry and enumerated the signs of "borax" furniture that was "cheaply constructed, poorly finished, or produced in indiscriminate quantities for the sucker trade." Perry reiterated the importance of attempting to simulate the sensory experiences of everyday use. "If you are buying a dresser, make sure the drawer handles are large enough to grasp comfortably and aren't so delicate that a heavy tug on a well-filled drawer will cause them to snap off." Of particular help for its lower-income readers, the *Reports* also furnished advice for used car buyers. Given that "over half of the motorists in the United States have never owned a new car," it was essential to enable prospective buyers to assess aging vehicles with tens of thousands of miles already on them. Because "good used car values are very difficult to recognize," CU explained the tricks by which dealers temporarily concealed the evidence of serious mechanical problems. To illustrate these techniques of deception as just another part of the exploitation of poor Americans, the *Reports* accompanied one of its used car reviews with an excerpt from John Steinbeck's *The Grapes of Wrath* that portrayed the fleecing of naive Okies by unscrupulous dealers.[40]

In their quest for durable consumer goods that were free of streamlining and other unnecessary decorative elements, the writers and technicians of CU could point to the existing functionalist modernism of the appliances manufactured to government specifications for various New Deal programs. In early 1934, the Electric Home and Farm Authority (EHFA), initially a subsidiary of the Tennessee Valley Authority (TVA), began promoting the manufacture and distribution of no-frills models of refrigerators, stoves, and other appliances to consumers within its economically underdeveloped service area in southern Appalachia. Sales of major appliances had plummeted during the early 1930s, and while most firms turned toward the increased use of styling as a differentiation strategy to gain market share and increase profit per unit, some manufacturers were still willing to produce models that adhered to the austere specifications set by the EHFA if the government assisted with marketing. The advertising industry got a taste of the action as well, as the TVA hired the Young and Rubicam agency to develop publicity materials for the campaign. Wholesalers and retailers, however, balked. Even after their pressure scuttled an early EHFA plan to market its appliances directly at cost through its own outlets, merchants objected to the negligible profit margins included in the pricing structure for the special economy models—which sold for 15 percent to 25 percent below manufacturers' conventional offerings—and eventually prevailed upon the EHFA to offer discounted financing for all appliances. In 1935, the federal government reorganized the EHFA as a separate administrative entity to facilitate its work nationally with the Rural Electrification Administration, thereby making the economy models available on a wider basis. Additionally, units of new public housing constructed through the Public Works Administration, the Resettlement Administration (later the Farm Security Administration), and eventually the United States Housing Authority were typically outfitted with refrigerators, stoves, and heaters produced to economy specifications similar to those first laid out by the EHFA.[41]

For CU, appliances like these that were built to functional specifications at minimum cost represented a social-consumerist ideal. In an August 1937 review of refrigerators, the institute explicated the process by which the federal government selected a manufacturer to produce 16,600 economy units for installation in public housing. In addition to limiting accessories and proscribing ornamentation, the government made energy efficiency the overriding criteria in awarding the contract. Westinghouse beat bids by seven competing firms with a small model that cost the government $67.63 per unit—in contrast to the $137.50 list price the company charged regular consumers for a model with the same storage capacity—and that was projected to use only 1.32 kilowatt-hours of electricity per day. As CU pointed out, consumers who purchased refrigerators or other durable goods had to assess the value of their purchase on the basis of branding, advertising, styling, list price, and the salesman's persuasion, not objective performance standards as the government had.[42]

As war mobilization began, CU looked to the government's increasing regulation and management of the economy as an opportunity to promote functionalist design while also undermining the product differentiation strategies that were integral to the marketing of durable consumer goods. The institute expressed grave concern that the combination of increased demand and insufficient supply would lead to price inflation and declining quality for consumers, and it campaigned vigorously for an effective regime for controlling prices, rationing scarce commodities, and maintaining product standards. When restrictions on the use of certain materials with key military applications went into effect during 1941, CU writers hoped for an impending reduction in superfluous ornamentation. Already by June of that year, for instance, refrigerator manufacturers began replacing aluminum and stainless-steel parts, moldings, and trim with plastics or porcelain enameled steel. CU still noted the prevalence of conspicuous waste, since "the annual restyling of cabinets, which seems required to expedite obsolescence," was still "evident in most brands." In autos, however, substitutes were utilized "chiefly in details appealing to the eye, in gadgets, and in small miscellaneous parts," making new models "less gaudy than usual, for nickel and zinc are on strict priority lists." Following the attack on Pearl Harbor, as the War Production Board (WPB) directed that most factories manufacturing durable consumer goods be converted to military production for the duration of the conflict, CU advocated setting aside a small portion of the nation's total plant capacity for special "Victory" models of refrigerators, stoves, washing machines, and possibly even cars. Under the proposals, limited quantities of these unbranded models, designed to minimize use of restricted materials and free of decoration, would be manufactured. They would be subject to stringent price controls, and allocated to consumers according to rationing schemes similar to those used for food and nondurables. Most of the schemes for "Victory" models of major durable goods, with the exception of stoves, were not implemented; not only did the WPB object, but most manufacturing firms were unwilling to forgo highly profitable war contracts or encourage consumer acceptance of generic products. Even though most of the proposals that CU put forth in 1942 and 1943 went unrealized, the institute continued to link functionalist modernism with social consumerism.[43]

Contesting the Meanings of Modernism

As the designers, artists, educators, and activists involved with the Design Laboratory, the white-collar unions, and CU advocated for their preferred variants of modernist aesthetics, they competed against other individuals and institutions that had their own interests in shaping discourses regarding the representation of modernity. On the one hand, Popular Front modernists confronted the commercial proponents of streamlining, many of whom embraced the style explicitly as a technique for reinvigorating consumer capitalism in the midst of the Depression. Progressives generally saw the expressive modernism of streamlining not only as visual evidence of the deceptive and wasteful aspects of consumer capitalism, but also as indicative of the stifling or exploitative labor relations prevalent in industrial design offices, advertising agencies, and media firms. On the other hand, they encountered figures associated with elite cultural institutions like the Museum of Modern Art who shared their aesthetic affinities but who were ambivalent about the political and social meanings of modernism. Some within this second group perceived high-modernist art and design as signifying privileged status and refined taste rather than the ideals of social consumerism; over time, particularly as the Second World War gave way to the early years of the Cold War, others of them came to see high modernism as the embodiment of supposedly transcendent notions of freedom in need of defense from totalitarianism. Through the 1930s and 1940s, commercial designers for the mass market, cultural elites, and partisans of the Popular Front all contested the meanings of modernism.

The tensions that had existed between the Design Laboratory and FAP administrators during the school's initial period of public sponsorship in part reflected their diverging aesthetic politics. By the time the school reorganized under the auspices of the FAECT in 1937, its experimental pragmatist pedagogy had generated a more systematic and polemical analysis of modern design among its faculty, students, and supporters. In particular, Laboratory partisans turned away from their original aesthetic eclecticism and more explicitly articulated their commitment to functionalist modernism as an aesthetic strategy for representing the labor involved in the design, manufacturing, distribution, and use of goods. They also became more pointed in their criticisms of the streamlined style of modernity popularized by the industrial design entrepreneurs. In the declaration of principles that opened the first new catalog following the reorganization, the school's committee asserted that "mass production, being dependent on mass consumption, necessitates designs to meet the social needs of the consumer." To avoid "waste," conscientious designers were to place "as little emphasis as possible on ornament," and in particular to avoid "arbitrary" decorative elements that "have no genetic connection to the functional and mechanical properties of an object whose surfaces they adorn superficially." Rather, the school declared, "fabrication for function produces forms which have an inherent quality revealing both material and purpose." Within the Laboratory community, these principles were not just understood dogmatically, but were also a subject for occasional levity, as evident in a cartoon in the school newspaper that depicted a student being roasted on a spit after he was "caught streamlining a coffee pot."[44]

Streamlining was an easy target for the Laboratory's supporters. It was more difficult, however, for them to distinguish between their radical modernist initiatives and the formalist approach to modernist design espoused by many enthusiasts of the International Style. A few weeks after classes at the Laboratory resumed under union sponsorship, the American Contemporary Artists gallery hosted an exhibition of new student work. The gallery, run by leftist art dealer Herman Baron and BMG organizer Clara Grossman, was an important Popular Front venue, and the show exemplified both the school's increasing emphasis on functionalist modernism and its closer alignment with the ongoing white-collar insurgency in New York's culture industries.[45] In her review of the show, art educator and critic Elizabeth McCausland contended that "the original Bauhaus, germinal as it was, suffered somewhat from the romantically individualistic self-expression of the men of genius who founded and conducted it," as their formalistic preoccupation with "style" had overshadowed the proper social objectives of modern design. The Laboratory, by contrast, belonged to "a later generation than the Bauhaus," which "understands that the most beautiful architecture, design, and art is not built by the individual, but by the coordination of talents and technics of individuals within the containing envelope of social relations." While fawning acolytes of Gropius or Breuer might appropriate "the outward form of the Bauhaus" and recapitulate the "intellectual errors" of its masters, McCausland argued that the exhibition demonstrated that Laboratory designers grasped that the question of whether "the men who man the machines are dissatisfied by reason of too long hours and too low wages," was as important of a functional consideration for the aspiring modern designer as the selection of materials and fabrication methods.[46]

Laboratory instructor William Friedman more bluntly asserted both the school's functionalist modernism and the obstacles to achieving autonomy under prevailing systems of design and mass production in a penetrating review of the high modernist Nikolaus Pevsner's influential *Enquiry into Industrial Art in England*. "The products of present-day technological enterprises," Friedman noted, "are not designed by a handful of individuals," as both the streamlining industrial design entrepreneurs and the admirers of the International Style masters typically claimed. Instead, the material culture of consumer capitalism was churned out by "thousands of unknown draftsmen" and "tool and die designers and makers" in factories who found "no romance in the process of designing, because designing is a hard-boiled proposition in which the designer is told what to design by the salesmen and the buyers." Aside from a few carefully culled examples, Friedman complained, "one looks in vain for further substantiation of Pevsner's thesis" that "good design pays" for the manufacturer. Improving the quality of material and visual culture required not the formalistic imitation of functionalist modernism advocated by Pevsner, Friedman insisted, but instead a multifaceted approach directed at the roots of contemporary social and economic problems. "For the public, the question of design taste will have to be treated along with the three Rs, as part of the basic training of every citizen" rather than as "an esoteric item completely separated from the common experience of living." For designers themselves, the remedy was "a more realistic concept of the practice of design." Thus, the Laboratory impressed upon aspiring designers that their creative mental labor was "just one part of the manufacturing process" and that they were "in no more exalted a position than the tool and die maker in the factory."[47]

With these analyses, McCausland and Friedman aimed to affirm the superiority of the Laboratory's activities over the efforts of elite curators and critics. MoMA had emerged as one of the most important promoters of modern art and design in the United States almost immediately upon its founding in 1929, and despite the drastic curtailment of private art patronage during the Depression, it had the backing of enough philanthropists to maintain an expanding level of exhibitions and programming throughout the 1930s. In some fields, most obviously painting, MoMA demonstrated a willingness to exhibit work in nearly every modernist and proto-modernist style; its first efforts at collecting films indicated a similarly inclusive eclecticism. Additionally, some of its early curators and administrators, including Cahill, had unswervingly democratic sensibilities. Yet like most museums, MoMA was also established as an arbiter of taste, and consequently the aesthetic judgments rendered by its experts were utilized to construct and police cultural hierarchies. Although the museum embraced the potential for provoking social and cultural transformation, its curators and administrators were often deliberately vague about the specific changes to be achieved and the means for bringing them about. This mix of institutional imperatives was manifested in a tendency toward formalist understandings of modernist design, an early instance of which can be seen in the museum's highly influential 1932 exhibition, *The International Style: Architecture Since 1922*. Curated by Philip Johnson, founder of the museum's Department of Architecture and Design, and architectural historian Henry-Russell Hitchcock Jr., the show had a tremendous impact on the development of a high-modernist design canon that focused on the work of leading European figures such as Le Corbusier, Mies van der Rohe, and Gropius. The formalistic trend was even more pronounced in a follow-up exhibition in 1934, *Machine Art*, in which the museum displayed pieces of machinery and industrial equipment that were selected on the basis of their appearance of functionality in the eyes of the curators, which primarily meant simple lines and an absence of ornament, rather than their actual purpose.[48]

Even as most of the museum's experts drifted toward a formalist conception of modern art and design that primarily signified refinement and distinction for elite consumers capable of purchasing expensive craft-made goods, they could not completely ignore the actual social transformations taking place within American life. Shortly after the *Machine Art* show, for instance, MoMA hosted an exhibition on the desperate need for public housing in the United States. Guest curated by Carol Aronovici, with considerable input from social housing activist Catherine Bauer, the provocatively titled *America Can't Have Housing* show included a mock-up of a deplorably substandard tenement apartment juxtaposed with a model apartment interior. On larger-scale matters of building construction and siting for new housing, the exhibit pushed high-modernist *Zeilenbau* structures as an ideal solution regardless of the spatial context, funding constraints, or wishes of potential residents.[49] In October 1938, MoMA attempted to appropriate the notions of utility and value that were central to Consumers Union's design critique with *Useful Objects under Five Dollars*, an exhibit of ordinary accessories, housewares, implements, and other items available from conventional retailers. Whereas CU emphasized the everyday experience of using goods, the museum's curatorial technique idealized the selected items as art and distanced them from the ordinary realm of work and use. Goods were deliberately exhibited in ways that differed from common representations in advertisements or retail displays, but the stripping away of these overtly commercial contexts in turn enabled the conversion of the formal appearance of utility into a new basis of commodity value. A touring version of the show was sponsored, as curator Elodie Courter boasted, by "an art association, three colleges, two large department stores and a small specialty store." Recognizing the marketing benefits of prestige, she continued, "many manufacturers, whose merchandise had not been included in the exhibition, wrote the Museum asking that their products be considered another year." In December 1939, MoMA obliged with *Useful Objects under Ten Dollars*. Curator John McAndrew, commenting on the objects selected, offered a perfunctory declaration that "form must follow function," but once again the emphasis was on appearances.[50]

The museum's handful of direct collaborations with the Popular Front modernists also fit into this pattern. The inclusion of the sample of student sculptures from the Design Laboratory in the MoMA retrospective on the Bauhaus, for example, not only furnished the curators with evidence of the German academy's impact on American modernism, but it also provided them with a means of recognizing the Popular Front's cultural aspirations. A year later, in December 1939, the UAA and the other artists' locals and divisions within the UOPWA held a national conference on the political and economic situation of artists in the United States at the museum. Thus MoMA, which sustained itself through philanthropic donations, came to host a meeting for the purpose of examining, according to one union representative, how the "curtailment of government assistance and continued narrowing of private art markets have raised, more sharply than at any time since the low ebb of the Depression," the problem of how artists could "secure a decent livelihood through the expression of their art."[51] Even as the Laboratory and the UAA engaged in these joint activities with MoMA, advocates for social-democratic modernism continued to fault the museum for its formalist tendencies. In a caustic review of the Bauhaus retrospective in *Architectural Record*, Laboratory instructor Jacques Levy charged that Bayer's installation did nothing to transcend the "discrepancy between theory and practice" that separated "Bauhaus ideas and principles" from "the work of the Bauhaus itself." Levy chided the Bauhaus masters for their failure to appreciate that "the change from handicraft production to automatic and semi-automatic mass production" entailed "much more than the mere use of simplified forms and novel materials" for goods that were not actually suited for mass production and could only be marketed to affluent consumers able to afford craft-made wares.[52] Nonetheless, the Laboratory's willing participation in the exhibition, as it attempted to trade on the museum's prestige to bolster its own search for private patronage, blurred the tidy aesthetic and political judgments that Levy, Friedman, and McCausland sought to make. As long as shared aesthetic affinities and the need to secure adequate support drove elite institutions like MoMA and Popular Front institutions like the Laboratory into joint activities, the meanings of modernism were bound to remain highly contested.

The fluidity of modernism's meanings in the United States during the 1930s and 1940s is illustrated by Herbert Bayer's career in the years immediately following his flight from Europe. He was simultaneously an authentic Bauhaus émigré, a commercial designer with a record of success that stretched from his visually innovative advertising for department stores in Weimar Germany to his work for the Container Corporation of America, a tastemaker for the cultural elites associated with MoMA, and an ally of progressive white-collar unionism. Numerous other modernist advocates shared potentially competing allegiances to the various commercial, elite, public, labor, and cooperative patrons that supported their creative activities. Consequently, the efforts of white-collar progressives to define particular modernist styles as signifiers of their twin ideals of creative autonomy for culture workers and the social-democratic provisioning of goods and services had to contend with the claims made by corporate ideologues, commercial art entrepreneurs, museum curators, enlightened philanthropists, and public art administrators.

Furthermore, contests over the meanings and purposes of refined modernist design were always mediated by the inescapable presence of the more crass representations of modernity produced by the culture industries. Despite their shared disdain for streamlining, Popular Front and elite proponents of modernism periodically looked for opportunities to engage directly with the material and visual culture of American consumer capitalism. The 1939 New York World's Fair proved to be an irresistible lure. The fair was a massive advertisement for a not-too-distant future in which the austerity and strife of the Depression would give way to abundance, convenience, and technological mastery made possible by corporate enterprise. Prominent industrial design agencies rendered this vision into a fantastical environment dominated by the expressive styling that characterized the firms' regular commissions for packaging, durable goods, and retail spaces. Henry Dreyfuss's agency designed the official Theme Center for the fair, which included the iconic "Trylon" and "Perisphere" structures and the elaborate "Democracity" exhibit. The most popular attraction during the first season was the "Futurama" pavilion and exhibit designed by Norman Bel Geddes's agency, in which visitors were transported on a tramway above a massive diorama of an imagined American landscape of 1960 before, in a theatrical sleight-of-hand, being deposited into a life-size replica of one of the street intersections they had just swept over.[53]

The Design Laboratory and the New York Art Directors' Club collaborated to offer a critical view of the exposition with *A Design Students' Guide to the New York World's Fair*. The *Guide* was spearheaded by design prodigy Paul Rand, already established as an influential practitioner of modernist graphic arts. Deliberately ignoring the main attractions, Rand and his team of student assistants scoured the fair for the relatively few examples of functionalist architecture and design. McAndrew, who had recently joined the Laboratory's advisory board, contributed an introduction to the *Guide* that recapitulated his earlier litany against streamlining in the MoMA *Bulletin*. Praising the students for finding instances of "good modern design among the pseudo-modern fantasies," he admonished visitors to be wary of the "soft corners and fungoid bulges on the buildings by some of our most celebrated industrial designers" as they gleaned the saving remnants of "honest" modernism "shaped by the exigencies of function and materials" and "free of mannerisms." Yet there was little in the *Guide* that moved beyond subjective complaints over the tastelessness of America's culture of consumer capitalism to articulate a critique of either its political economy or the conditions under which it was produced.[54]

For Consumers Union, involvement with the fair risked a more fundamental compromising of principles. CU was unrivaled in its relentless criticism of consumer capitalism, but it nonetheless saw the New York World's Fair as an opportunity to circumvent the blacklisting of its solicitations by most mass-circulation periodicals and reach potential members. Since the fair's management had announced its own plans for an Advisory Committee on Consumers Interests, in an obvious attempt at coopting the consumer movement, progressives with CU and other groups felt compelled to make their voices heard by signing on. As opening day drew near, they became increasingly frustrated that the fair "was using them neatly for a front," in the words of *Consumers Union Reports*, and twenty-one members of the committee, including Donald Montgomery, Rose Schneiderman, and Colston Warne, resigned in protest in March 1939. Nonetheless, on the same page that CU informed its members of this action it still asked them to look out for its own exhibit at the fair, which the institute billed as the "only non-commercial consumer exhibit on the grounds." Once the fair opened, CU was cutting in its aesthetic judgment. "The architecture puts one in mind more of frozen cash than of frozen music," it jibed in a humorous play on Goethe's famous quote. "But that's as it should be, because the Fair is serving commerce and it knows no other master. The 'World of Tomorrow' that the Fair proposes to give a glimpse of is going to open to the strains of 'What's Good for Business is Good for You,' just as the National Ass'n of Manufacturers has been saying all along." Although the institute later claimed that it signed up 7,000 new members through its exhibit during the fair's first season, CU acquiesced to stringent conditions in order to take part. It was prohibited from endorsing or disapproving of any specific brands, thus turning the exhibit into an elaborate dramatization of scientific testing in the abstract in which the lab staff carefully removed the labeling from the products analyzed. In its attempt to raise its public profile, the institute's own political, social, and aesthetic vision was all but subsumed in the hegemony of American consumer capitalism.[55]

The Problem of Patronage from the First Popular Front to the People's War

Progressives' efforts at coherently articulating and advancing a social-democratic modernism gradually became more difficult as a consequence of developments in the late 1930s and early 1940s that disrupted the institutional and organizational arrangements upon which the realization of their aesthetic politics depended. Procommunists' acquiescence to the Nazi–Soviet pact created problems for initiatives in art and design that relied for support on a unified community of progressives, much as it did for print media endeavors like *Friday* magazine. Many noncommunist artists, designers, educators, commentators, and patrons withdrew, either temporarily or permanently, from the original Popular Front of the 1930s, sapping the strength of the networks required for endeavors like the Design Laboratory to survive. This political rift in the Popular Front coincided with escalating attacks on the FAP and the other WPA cultural projects by conservatives, which only accelerated the process of defunding activities that many progressives had hoped would grow into a permanent program for production of culture by the public sector. The cuts crippled the artists' locals within the UOPWA, since FAP employees accounted for the majority of their members. Although the federal government soon requisitioned wartime culture intended to boost morale, inform the American public about the Allies' democratic objectives, and compel compliance with home front mobilization programs, this failed to induce a revival of public patronage. The government opted to contract the bulk of this work to existing advertising agencies and media enterprises, in the process thwarting the UOPWA Ad Guild's program for using the wartime mobilization as a new basis for joint public-labor support for cultural production. Even as progressives continued to refine their ideas about how a modernist material and visual culture could be deployed as an alternative to the aesthetics of consumer capitalism, their inability to secure adequate patronage precluded the implementation of their proposals.

Operating independently after the Spring 1938 term made the Design Laboratory's continued existence increasingly precarious, but from an educational standpoint it was the school's most successful phase. The core faculty—Friedman, Reiss, Levy, Irene Rice Pereira, and William Priestly—made further enhancements to the curriculum while also recruiting a number of very talented artists and designers to carry out the Laboratory's mission. Some of the new faculty members brought fresh experience with artistic method and theory, like sculptor and designer Theodore Roszak, Hungarian émigré painter László Matulay, and muralist Burgoyne Diller, who had helped run the FAP Mural Division. Other new instructors brought experience from advertising and design agencies and the media. Industrial designer Peter Schladermundt had worked for Dreyfuss and Bel Geddes, while Danish architect and furniture designer Torben Muller had spent several years in Loewy's office. Harrison Murphy, a former art director at the *Chicago Tribune*, brought expertise integrating sales and marketing issues and the mechanics of print technology into the graphic design process, and research chemist John Heasty drew upon his ongoing work as a product-testing technician at CU for his courses on materials science.[56] Perhaps the two most important additions were Paul Rand and Elizabeth McCausland. At twenty-four, Rand had already worked as an art director for *Esquire* magazine and won acclaim for his covers for the leftist cultural review *Direction*, while McCausland replaced the earlier required courses on history and social science with a materialist survey of the cultural and social history of industrial development since the late seventeenth century.[57]

While the 1938–1939 catalog boasted that all instructors worked as designers in industry or supported themselves as freelance artists, giving them practical knowledge to pass on to their students, in reality the Laboratory's shaky finances made this a necessity. Jacques Levy, for example, freelanced for General Electric's home appliance styling division, wrote interior design guidelines for the New York City Housing Authority, and even worked for Norman Bel Geddes's agency on the elaborate dioramas for the Futurama exhibit at the 1939 New York World's Fair.[58] In the hopes of putting the Laboratory on sound financial footing, in August 1939 the school's governing committee of faculty and students announced an ambitious new fundraising drive. They set out to solicit from $25,000 to $40,000 in contributions with which they hoped to pay the school's new director, industrial designer George Sakier, improve salaries for the expanded faculty and staff, purchase new shop equipment, and relocate to larger quarters. To kick off the new campaign, the school opened a major exhibition of student work on October 12, the same day Sakier assumed his position. Prospective donors were invited to a special opening reception. Yet the event failed to generate sufficient funds even for continuation of the school on existing terms, and on November 14 the governing committee had no choice but to suspend formal operations. "You may be sure," wrote the committee, "that among teachers and students there is a group that will not permit the Laboratory School to go out of existence entirely even if the money we need is not received."[59] Many students and faculty continued to hold classes on an informal basis until the school could resume normal operations, but the sale of most of the Laboratory's shop equipment at a foreclosure auction in December made this increasingly unlikely. A dedicated nucleus of about fifty students and faculty convened into 1940 as they tried to organize another fundraising exhibition, but by May even this group saw the situation as futile. In a final letter to the student body, the school's committee announced the Laboratory's demise but noted proudly that "many of the basic ideas developed by the school during its four years of existence have already been incorporated in the teaching methods of other institutions and have certainly influenced the thinking of many individuals now working in the design field." Although conceding that the Design Laboratory was "technically dead," the committee claimed that much "that was most important of the school stays alive."[60]

To some extent, the school faltered in its turn toward more conventional channels of private art patronage because of its success in promoting its curricular and pedagogical innovations, which were gradually adopted—often piecemeal and usually without the Laboratory's political emphasis—by more traditional academic institutions. Although Walter Gropius's appointment as the dean of the revamped School of Architecture at Harvard in 1936 garnered considerable attention, modernism made little headway in other elite academic institutions until after the Second World War. Commercial and applied art programs at Pratt Institute and Carnegie Tech launched their first courses in "industrial design" in 1934 and 1935, but they only began substantively to incorporate modernist techniques between 1938 and 1941.[61] Among more vocationally oriented schools, Pratt and Carnegie were in the modernist vanguard; Cooper Union, an institution frequently identified with progressive education, remained in the thrall of Beaux-Arts traditionalism until the 1940s. László Moholy-Nagy, who supervised the Bauhaus Foundations course in the 1920s, established the Institute of Design in Chicago in the fall of 1937, although his "New Bauhaus" soon suspended operations due to lack of funds. It reopened in 1940 after a reorganization and was ultimately absorbed by the Illinois Institute of Technology (IIT) in 1949.[62] At many schools, former Laboratory faculty made important contributions to the development of modernist curricula. Abstract artist Irene Rice Pereira, for instance, brought her Design Synthesis course to Pratt during the 1940s, Friedman taught at the University of Iowa and the University of Minnesota prior to joining the Walker Art Center, and Priestly reunited with his mentor Mies van der Rohe at IIT in 1949. By the 1950s, Rand had become one of the nation's most renowned professors of modern graphic design at Yale.[63] As they scattered throughout America's systems of higher education, the Laboratory's faculty and students spread the strain of modernism that they had cultivated at the Laboratory.

Even as the Design Laboratory's demise demonstrated the continuing inadequacy of private art patronage in the late 1930s and early 1940s, the deep curtailment in federal appropriations gutted employment levels on the FAP, which in turn precipitated a crisis for the UAA. In February 1939, UAA Local 60 in New York had 1,428 members, of whom 1,142 were in the local's fine arts section, 256 were in the commercial section, and 30 were cartoonists. Nearly all of the members in the fine arts section were employed by FAP, so after the transfer of the commercial artists to the Ad Guild in September, the cuts in the public sector threatened the artists' union with terminal decline. By February 1940, more than half of the remaining 1,125 members in Local 60 claimed to be unemployed, while by May the shrinking pool of artists who remained on the project only earned an average weekly salary of $21.90. Activists in the artists' locals tried to conceive of new organizing strategies, possibly based on galleries as a point of sale for fine art created by freelance artists on a speculative basis, on the development of artists' cooperatives that were sponsored by the broader labor movement, or an artist placement service analogous to the preferential hiring arrangements used by numerous other unions.[64] None of these proposals, however, was able to furnish a viable alternative for organizing freelance artists comparable to the structure and stability of a regular employment relationship. The logic of industrial unionism offered another option, and by late 1940 and early 1941, Local 60 commenced organizing drives among commercial textile designers, museum and gallery employees, and workers at art supply stores. These drives did bring some new members into the fold, but not enough to offset the losses stemming from the gradual elimination of public patronage for the arts. By August 1941, the local's financial situation deteriorated to the point that the UOPWA suspended it for failing to pay its per capita dues assessments.[65]

Local 60 was briefly reinstated in October, but the continued existence of the seven artists' locals seemed increasingly tenuous. In a report to UOPWA president Lewis Merrill, international representative Richard Lewis described the UAA locals as a "drain" on the overextended white-collar union. "If we want to continue the art locals in affiliation," Lewis opined, "their program must be based on a campaign for converting WPA into a defense art medium for poster and camouflage work," since whatever possibilities "for preserving the Project as a cultural unit have all been frittered away." Regarding the ranks of unemployed artists, he continued, "the only practical solution I can see at this point is a vast retraining program which will convert them into draftsmen, camouflage workers, poster artists, etc., so that they can undertake the only kind of art that the government is ready to support during the present war," although he conceded that "this kind of program will represent a serious set-back to the people's cultural movement in which the Artists Union played a prominent part in the past." After reviewing the report, Merrill informed the fading art locals that they should either commit to the rapid implementation of the program outlined by Lewis or disband as trade unions. In response, Local 60's president, illustrator Rockwell Kent, conceded that the art locals had been a "failure," but still argued that "it would be a mistake to abandon the movement" of artists even though "the Projects have been slashed so that they are all but non-existent," and "their complete abandonment is being prepared."[66]

Other artists on the executive board of Local 60 interpreted Merrill's directive as a vote of no confidence. In March 1942, a majority of them voted to disaffiliate from the UOPWA and to merge the remnants of the local with the American Artists' Congress to form the Artists' League of America (ALA). The ALA sought to establish itself as a new organization for progressive artists to "make the most effective contribution possible to the war, through the exercise of our professional abilities and the mobilization of our talents, utilizing old forms of visual and plastic expression and creating new ones." Only by "making the artist a vital part of the social organism in flux," it maintained, "can art keep pace with the changing social structure and become an integral part of the world of the future." By the end of June, the ALA sponsored its first major exhibition, *Artists in the War*, at the American Contemporary Artists gallery, featuring work by a diverse range of artists, including Berenice Abbott, Philip Evergood, William Gropper, Chaim Gross, Rockwell Kent, Zero Mostel, Anton Refregier, Ad Reinhardt, John Sloan, Irene Rice Pereira, and Paul Strand. In early 1943, ALA planned another exhibition, *This Is Our War*, which Kent described as "aimed at keeping alive the artists' interest in picture painting during this war period, as distinct from poster making, it being our belief that, despite the desire of most of the artists to be of service in propaganda, they must, for their own sakes and in the public interest, not neglect their more enduring work." [67]

Although Merrill had initially suggested liquidation as an option, he was nonetheless miffed about the way in which Local 60 disaffiliated from the international union. Kent attempted to placate Merrill, emphasizing that progressive artists still hoped for "the political and cultural growth of the labor movement, the preservation and extension of democratic rights, the encouragement of art to be increasingly of service to labor and, in fact, a part of it, and the closest possible co-operation with labor for national unity in the prosecution of the war." But with Local 60 reduced by early 1942 to "a little, stubborn, die-hard remainder of that relatively small group of artists in New York who had the social vision to identify themselves as artists with labor and the very great courage to openly organize and fight for artists and for labor's rights," disaffiliation was the only practical move. Within months the ALA established a "fraternal" affiliation with the Greater New York Industrial Union Council. As an epitaph for the artists' unions, as well as evidence of the dispersal of the communities of radicalized artists that had sustained them, Local 60 vice president Norman Barr informed Kent in May that he had "just gotten a job as a draftsman in a concern doing defense work." Despite "the fact that I won't have any time to paint for a while, as I work on Saturdays and study Sundays," Barr added, "I'm very happy about it."[68]

While the UAA proved unable to adjust effectively to the demise of the FAP, activists in the Ad Guild devised a compelling program for joint labor-public patronage of cultural production with the Advertising Mobilization Committee (AMC). The initiative proposed to harness the talents of commercial artists, graphic designers, and copywriters who were employed in advertising and ancillary fields to produce informational materials and propaganda for mobilizing the home front, including pamphlets, posters, advertisements, publicity copy, scripts for radio programs or short films, and even entire periodicals. Through the AMC, the Ad Guild hoped to expand its organizing appeal, renew the government's commitment to sponsoring the white-collar radicals' cultural endeavors, and promote the social consumerism of the revitalized wartime Popular Front. Even though the activities of the AMC were subordinated to the war effort, they provided an opportunity for the Ad Guild to build upon its earlier educational programs and continue its efforts, however muted, to promote the ideal of autonomous creative work.

The AMC also furnished the wider Popular Front movement with one of its best opportunities to counter the ideological offensive being waged by business executives through their own embrace of patriotism. Many Americans old enough to remember the First World War still disapproved of the excesses of the government's Committee on Public Information, and their apprehensions had undercut attempts to modify WPA cultural projects to serve as a public program for wartime propaganda. Although the federal government did set up an Office of Facts and Figures (OFF) in 1941, which was reorganized the following year as the Office of War Information (OWI), these agencies outsourced much of the production of wartime information and propaganda. Media empires like Time Inc. supplied the

OWI with a considerable amount of the editorial content for magazines, newspapers, and newsreels, while radio networks NBC and CBS produced programming sponsored by the agency's Domestic Radio Bureau. The most conspicuous contribution to the wartime propaganda effort came from the Advertising Council, founded by the Association of National Advertisers and the American Association of Advertising Agencies. Because of the lavish tax deductions that the federal government bestowed upon corporations during the war for their advertising expenditures, American manufacturers and advertising agencies that had limited goods to sell to consumers were more than happy to channel their resources into a pro-business campaign that promoted support for the war while also rehabilitating the Depression-tarnished reputation of capitalism.[69]

By early 1942, Ad Council representatives had met with War Production Board chief Donald Nelson and OFF head Archibald MacLeish to offer their services and solicit specific assignments from the government. In its first major campaigns on the salvaging of scrap metal and the saving of household fats and greases to support the war, the Council established patterns of managerial direction and control modeled on routine agency practices. For the scrap metal campaign, the American Iron and Steel Institute contributed over $1.5 million to run a series of ads produced by prominent Council member Leo Burnett's agency, while McCann-Erickson served as the sole agent responsible for purchasing space for the ads in newspapers and magazines. Quickly, the Ad Council had cornered the market on propaganda projects assigned to nongovernmental entities through the OWI Bureau of Campaigns.[70]

Largely shut out from the OWI by the Ad Council, the AMC instead cultivated connections with the Office of Price Administration (OPA) and the Civilian Defense Volunteer Organization (CDVO) to produce materials encouraging compliance with price control, rent control, rationing, and other elements of wartime social consumerism. Unlike the Council, which farmed out projects to agencies, the AMC recruited individual illustrators, graphic designers, copywriters and publicists regardless of employer and pooled their talents to complete assignments, which also made it a vehicle for the Ad Guild to recruit potential members outside of the agencies' offices. At the Advertising for Victory Conference held by the Guild in June 1942, AMC chairman Howard Byrne emphasized that the Committee was "designed to mobilize advertising people, not only members of the Guild itself, for an aggressive campaign to win the war." Ad Guild President Howard Willard exhorted members to take an active role in the AMC as their way of joining "the whole democratic world" as it was "girding for a crushing blow against the fascist barbarians. Whether you use a gun or a brush or a type-writer," he insisted, "you have a place in the people's struggle." By July, hundreds of the AMC volunteers were hard at work on a series of posters, leaflets, pamphlets, and advertisements for sympathetic agencies within the wartime bureaucracy.[71]

The advertising trade press rendered a relatively favorable judgment on the AMC. *Advertising and Selling* lauded it for giving individual employees—who "quite naturally were not consulted" in whatever arrangements their bosses had made with the Ad Council—a chance to contribute directly. "It is reasonable to suppose that in mobilizing the little people of advertising for war jobs which they want, the Guild may have at last struck a responsive chord which will give it the boost it has so long desired." Unionization, the magazine continued, "may be a haunting idea to a few agency owners, but to most legitimate and fair-minded managements it promises little dislocation and may be an eventuality to be expected in the wake of the 'people's war.'" Noting that the wartime mobilization of advertising workers in Britain had led to widespread unionization there, it concluded that "if the Mobilization Committee does in the end succeed, and culminates in a functioning Advertising Guild with bargaining contracts throughout the industry," it would only illustrate "again to management that the modern union is not organized alone for financial-gain objectives," but is also "a club of like-minded people who want something business doesn't give them." *Tide* was more restrained in its assessment, yet it still promoted the AMC and approved the inclusion of token representation by liberal executives and entrepreneurs, such as Lord and Thomas agency vice president Walter Weir and prominent independent publicist Tom Fizdale, as explicitly "nonunion" members of the Committee's advisory committee.[72]

By early August, the Committee's volunteers had completed their first projects. One subcommittee, led by Ad Guild activist Harriet Gould, produced a series of five pamphlets touting price control, rent control, and other OPA policies, while another subcommittee headed by Guild activist Charlotte Willard turned out a booklet outlining family wartime budgets in the New York metropolitan area for the regional CDVO office. *PM* consumer editor Sidney Margolius assisted with another AMC pamphlet on clothing conservation. The UOPWA paid for the initial printing and distribution of the materials to members of CIO unions in New York City, but progressive administrators in the wartime mobilization agencies were sufficiently impressed with them to provide for wider distribution. In September the OPA agreed to print and circulate nationwide five million copies of each of the Committee's basic pamphlets on price control, rent control, and clothing conservation. AMC volunteers continued to take on localized projects through CDVO, such as the creation of an exhibit on the war that was installed on the boardwalk at Coney Island, a series of posters on fingerprinting, and posters calling for a second front in Western Europe that were displayed in New York department store windows. In addition, the Committee translated some OPA booklets into other languages and began work on a script for an OPA movie about the perils of inflation and ways to combat it through the community enforcement of price controls.[73]

During the fall of 1942, a delegation from the AMC met with representatives of the Ad Council to discuss the possibility of coordination, but the divergent objectives of the two groups prevented any collaboration. AMC activists wanted to tap into the deep pockets of the Council's corporate sponsors to pay for the widespread distribution of its materials throughout the mass media, while the Council hoped to absorb the Committee's volunteers and put them to work on its campaigns. For most of the second half of 1942, the rival initiatives of the Popular Front and corporate advertisers developed parallel channels of public patronage and influence, as the AMC benefited from the support of sympathetic officials like OPA Director of Information Robert Horton, OPA Deputy Price Administrator John Kenneth Galbraith, Department of Agriculture Consumer Counsel Donald Montgomery, and CDVO Consumer Division Director Persia Campbell. Nonetheless, the AMC faced clear material disadvantages. The agencies and corporations that underwrote the activities of the Ad Council spent millions of dollars promoting corporate stewardship of the war effort in the media, whereas the Committee's ability to reach the public with its rationale for home-front mobilization was limited to the distribution of its materials by the government or unions.[74]

Unfortunately for the AMC, Republican gains in the 1942 midterm elections compromised its tenuous links to the government's war mobilization bureaucracy. Even before the new Congress convened, the Roosevelt administration acquiesced to pressure to make its home front campaigns even more amenable to business interests. Leon Henderson's departure from the top post at the OPA in December 1942 and his replacement with advertising executive Prentiss Brown opened the way for the purging of progressive administrators who had facilitated the government's appropriation of AMC materials. Horton's replacement in early 1943 as OPA Director of Information by another ad exec, Lou Maxon, deprived the AMC of its most important outlet, while Galbraith and Montgomery were also pushed out of their positions.

Not content to let business dominate the government's apparatus for war-time propaganda, conservatives in Congress slashed the appropriations of both the OWI and the OPA in the summer of 1943. The cuts obliterated the OWI's in-house editorial and publishing programs, leaving little more than the Bureau of Campaigns to act as a clearinghouse for materials produced by the Ad Council or commercial media enterprises and indirectly subsidized through tax deductions. Given the recent experience with the WPA, the ease with which the logic of "free enterprise" prevailed to thwart public-supported production of culture and information in wartime America deeply dismayed liberals and leftists alike.[75]

For executives in the advertising-supported media and for conservative defenders of private patronage for the arts, there was seemingly no more appropriate epitaph for the government's experiments with cultural pro-duction than the discovery in early 1944 that several hundred paintings produced by the FAP Easel Division in New York City had been simply discarded when the project was liquidated. After being sold to a scrap dealer for four cents a pound, some of the paintings—including ones by renowned artists such as Refregier and Alice Neel—ended up for sale in a decrepit secondhand shop on Canal Street for as little as three dollars each. *Life* magazine, which generally provided positive coverage of the American art scene, insinuated that the unseemly fate of these works—which evi-dently had little or no commodity value in the existing private art market—demonstrated that the FAP had been a waste of taxpayers' money. Within days, Holger Cahill dashed off a lengthy rebuttal to *Life*'s editors that cast the legacy of the FAP in a far more favorable light, positing a different rela-tionship between public art, private patronage, and the commercial media than the one that was implicit in the article. Noting that eight artists then employed by the magazine had once painted for the FAP, as had another artist who was killed in action while covering the war for *Life*, he asked, "would it not be reasonable to assume that they, and their fellow artists, gave the American public good value for their government jobs?" Given that the FAP was first and foremost a "work relief program," he declared that "the remarkable thing is that so much of the project's work was found acceptable by institutions of the highest standing," and that only "a fraction of one percent of the work remained unallocated." In Cahill's estimation, "the value of the works of art" produced by FAP artists was "much greater than the sums paid for it by the government." The editors printed a heavily condensed version of Cahill's retort in the magazine, blunting his argument in the process.[76]

While Cahill offered a spirited defense of the FAP, progressive activists still wondered what the possibilities might be for funding their social-democratic initiatives in art and design in the future. McCausland, who had recently received a Guggenheim Fellowship to support her research on the social history of artistic patronage in the United States, wrote Cahill a letter of encouragement to express her faith that "good publicity will help cancel out the damage of articles which totally misrepresent the function and value of the government arts projects." Through the ALA as well as broader groups, like the Independent Citizens' Committee of the Arts, Sciences, and Professions (ICCASP), progressives continued to agitate for a permanent federal arts project, but the dismal results of even a modest wartime initiative like the AMC showed how difficult it would be to obtain adequate public or labor support. Surveying the prospects in a July 1945 article in *New Masses*, McCausland insisted that even under conditions of economic prosperity, conventional modes of private patronage would never be sufficient to enable the bulk of American artists to earn a decent living through their creative labor, or to furnish the American people with the quantity and quality of artwork they needed. She contended that the continuing orientation of the private art establishment toward speculation and elite status distinction rendered it incapable of adequate material support for artists. Museums, through their operation as "'grading' or 'labeling' agencies" served to channel most private art dollars into the pursuit of a select canon of valorized artists and styles, guaranteeing a dearth of funding for the majority of artists and resulting in "only negligible support for contemporary art." Given the slim chances of enacting a new public arts program, McCausland hoped that "the support of the arts by organized labor" would be "the next step in the democratization of American culture," although she conceded that "so far, the unions which have sought to incorporate art programs in their overall educational work are young and have been preoccupied with the struggle to survive." Eventually, she envisioned, "we may expect that organized labor will use its greater security and economic margin to broaden its support of cultural functions."[77]

As long as the terms of the postwar settlement between labor, capital, and the state remained uncertain, the aspirations of Popular Front activists could not be realized. Initiatives like the Design Laboratory had provided instructive models for the autonomous creative practices and modernist aesthetics that progressives sought to establish as widespread alternatives to the culture of consumer capitalism. Although the CIO had achieved impressive growth during a tumultuous decade of depression and war, it was still unclear whether the new industrial unions—particularly those like the UOPWA and Newspaper Guild that organized within the culture industries—could provide a sufficiently robust source of patronage, one that could sustain the production of social-democratic art and design and also provide remunerative employment.

5

New York's White-Collar Unions during Wartime and Reconversion

ON APRIL 2, 1947, *PM* readers encountered the latest installment in the tabloid's ongoing series on "the best dressed women on New York Avenues" that spotlighted the fashion sense of smartly dressed "workingwomen" on a budget. In keeping with the series' format, the paper ran an annotated photograph of Faith Illiva, identifying the stores at which she had purchased the items in her ensemble along with the prices she had paid, accompanied by her description of her personal style. Unlike the other women featured, Illiva was a striker on a picket line, pictured hoisting a sign that condemned the "un-American" pay at magazine publisher Parents Institute, where she worked as an editorial assistant in the art department. "I bought most of my present wardrobe with my mustering-out pay from the WACS [Women's Army Corps] last year," Illiva explained. "With prices so high now, I'd rather go without additions than wear something cheap."[1] Along with two hundred other members of the UOPWA Book and Magazine Guild, she had walked off the job nine days earlier to gain union recognition. The strike against the publisher of titles aimed at parents, educators, and teenagers capped off years of organizing against substandard pay and autocratic workplace discipline. Parents Institute executives had waged a fierce campaign against the union in the weeks leading up to a certification election in which the union had been narrowly defeated. The election and strike had divided not only the workforce but also management, as eight editors with executive responsibilities refused to cross the union's picket line. Just the day before Illiva was featured in *PM*, the NLRB had voided the results of the election on account of the institute's unfair labor practices, providing a partial vindication for the strikers.[2]

FIGURE 5.1 *Parents* striker Faith Illiva's April 1947 fashion profile in *PM*, which succinctly linked white-collar labor activism, social consumerism, and women's empowerment.

For *PM* readers, Illiva's fashion profile was yet another reminder of working women's central role in the social transformations of the 1940s. With the dramatic expansion of defense employment and the enlistment of millions of men into the armed forces, the number of women in the paid labor force surged from 11.9 million in April 1940 to 19.6 million by July 1945.[3] In New York City's culture industries, which already employed many women, the war opened new possibilities for career advancement. Like Illiva, many white-collar women embraced unionism as a way of realizing their aspirations, and their activism drove the new surge of union organizing among culture workers between 1941 and 1947. As they confronted systemic gender discrimination, they saw collective action as the best way to secure dignity and respect on the job, improve access to promotions, and win the increases in pay necessary for maintaining an independent lifestyle. Illiva's own union local became a bastion of labor feminism, with a woman president as well as a female majority on its executive board. In many unionized workplaces, such as Time Inc., women forced issues of gender inequality onto the bargaining agenda to a greater extent than ever before.

The profile also offered commentary on the relationship between incomes, prices, and commodities that was familiar to the tabloid's readers and to white-collar unionists. Inflation eroded all Americans' living standards during the 1940s, but white-collar workers often felt this squeeze most acutely. With few exceptions, they lacked the opportunities that many workers in manufacturing enjoyed during the war to augment their earnings through overtime. Furthermore, while unions of blue-collar workers could petition for limited increases in pay rates under the system of wartime wage and salary controls administered by the National War Labor Board (NWLB), levels of unionization in most white-collar occupations remained low by comparison. Proponents of white-collar unionism contended that this economic squeeze only made organization and collective bargaining all the more vital, even as they also advocated for a relaxation of wage constraints and tightening of price controls. Once the war ended, white-collar unionists secured long-sought increases in pay and made significant gains in membership through the middle of 1947, but they failed in their campaign to get Congress to maintain the regulatory powers of the wartime Office of Price Administration. In this context, Illiva represented simultaneously an affirmative example of women's increased workforce participation, an endorsement of white-collar unionism, and proof of the benefits of price control.

Of course, plenty of white-collar workers would have disapproved of *PM*'s affirmation of labor feminism and social consumerism. Many opposed the assertiveness of women in their own offices, their challenges to longstanding patterns of gender inequality, and their demands for access to jobs above the clerical or paraprofessional level. Furthermore, many unorganized white-collar workers did not see unionization and price control as solutions to the skyrocketing cost of living; rather, they perceived the wage gains of unionized workers in wartime industry as coming directly at their expense. They resented the decline in their own purchasing power due to inflation and the relative increase in the purchasing power of blue-collar workers, which undermined their sense of their own middle-class status. These white-collar workers opposed the postwar labor insurgency as well as efforts to preserve the OPA, and they proved receptive to business ideologues' advocacy of "free enterprise." In November 1946, they responded affirmatively to the Republicans' midterm campaign slogan—"Had Enough?"—and helped to give the GOP control of Congress for the first time since before the New Deal. With a militant upsurge in white-collar unionism coinciding with an increasingly robust white-collar conservatism, the social strata of clerical, sales, technical, professional, and creative workers became increasingly polarized. As Illiva and her fellow strikers and supporters battled with Parents Institute through the spring of 1947, it remained to be seen whether their militancy represented the cresting of a wave of white-collar labor activism that had been rising since 1941 or just another milestone on unionism's onward march through New York's culture industries.

The Organizing Resurgence in New York's Culture Industries

By the early months of 1941, the accelerating defense mobilization program had finally accomplished what the New Deal, for all of its achievements, had been unable to do: it had ended the Great Depression. After enduring eleven years of brutally high unemployment, American workers finally saw jobs become more and more plentiful with each passing month. In offices as well as in factories, supporters of unionization took advantage of workers' newfound leverage to redouble their organizing efforts. Yet the return of prosperity brought new challenges as well. For the first time in two decades, Americans faced the onset of a period of sustained price inflation. This introduced new uncertainty into organizing and collective bargaining, as executives estimated the impact of price hikes for raw materials and intermediate goods, and unionists recalibrated their wage demands to account for the impact of inflation on workers' purchasing power. At the same time, the surge in military enlistments and quickening pace of employee turnover deprived the unions of some of their most dedicated activists, and resulted in an influx of workers who were new to the labor movement.

The renewal of organizational vigor was especially evident in the Newspaper Guild of New York. After a period of torpor during which the membership in "good standing" had fallen to just 2,411 in April 1940, commitment to the union picked up again, with membership in good standing increasing to 4,122 twelve months later.[4] In August 1941, the Guild won an NLRB certification election at the *New York Times* for 587 employees in the paper's editorial departments, garnering 295 votes against 202 votes for an AFL affiliate and just 38 for no union. Combined with its victory the previous August in balloting by employees in the commercial departments, the *Times* editorial election effectively completed the local's organization of its core jurisdiction of daily newspapers, with the fading *Sun*, which had fewer than 200 white-collar employees, remaining the city's only major paper without a Guild contract.[5] The win also finally eliminated the possibility that the AFL might establish itself as a viable rival among white-collar workers in the city's print media. Furthermore, the Guild effectively leveraged its increasingly solid membership to compel employers to accede to its demand for a union shop. In 1935, J. David Stern, then publisher of the *New York Post*, had been the first newspaper owner in New York to agree to a union shop, but by 1941 even conservative tabloids like the *Daily News* and *Daily Mirror* accepted comparable union security clauses in their new contracts with the Guild. Increasingly, it seemed, the union shop was becoming the standard within the city's organized print media.[6]

During this period, the Newspaper Guild encountered some of the most determined management resistance from Time Inc. Unionists at the media conglomerate had settled for meager improvements when they negotiated their second contract in 1939, and they approached their third round of negotiations determined to obtain significant salary increases and some form of union security, given management's continuing harassment of Guild supporters. In February 1941, the Guild's negotiating committee proposed a boost in the minimum salary schedule, a 10 percent general increase for all employees, and the implementation of a union shop.[7] Despite Time's highest-ever net profits of nearly $3.5 million in 1940, executives rejected the Guild's demands. In an illegal attempt to short-circuit the collective bargaining process, Time president Roy Larsen presented management's counteroffer directly to the staff prior to notifying the union's negotiating committee. Fearful that the filing of unfair labor practice charges with the NLRB would only delay a contract settlement, Time unionists continued to press ahead.[8] Under the guidance of lead negotiator Alexander Crosby, who had worked for several years at Consumers Union before rejoining the staff of the Newspaper Guild, they surveyed prices at their neighborhood markets. While executives pointed to the apparently modest increase of 1.4 percent in the cost-of-living index calculated by the federal government's Bureau of Labor Statistics (BLS) during the first quarter of 1941, Guild members found much larger hikes in the cost of staple foods, with sugar up 15 percent, eggs up 13 percent, and butter up 10 percent over just the first three months of the year. Still, management refused to budge on the matter of a general salary increase, offering instead a paltry increase in the minimum salary schedule, even though only 25 percent of the staff in the editorial departments—mostly recent hires—earned the contract minimums for their job classifications in the spring of 1941.[9]

As inflation intensified during the summer, the Guild modified its position, calling for a progressively graduated scheme for salary increases, proposing a flat $5 weekly raise for all employees earning less than $40 per week, a 12 percent raise for those earning between $40 and $60, a 10 percent raise for those earning between $60 and $100, and 5 percent for creative talent earning over $100.[10] As negotiations stretched into the fall, longtime Guild activist Anna Goldsborough circulated a petition, signed by 216 editorial employees, demanding that the company agree to the Guild's proposals on salaries and union security or else face economic sanctions, either in the form of a strike or a union-organized boycott of Time Inc. publications. Tensions came to a head on November 27, when top executives summarily fired Goldsborough. Her dismissal over legally protected organizing activities outraged Guild proponents, who interpreted it as a challenge to the union's right to exist. On December 4, members of the Time unit voted to authorize a strike, but three days later the Japanese attacked Pearl Harbor, and the Guild immediately endorsed the decision by both CIO and AFL leaders to renounce the strike weapon for the duration of the war. Time unionists had little choice but to file unfair labor practice charges with the NLRB over Goldsborough's firing. Although the Time unionists' frustrating predicament stood out during a period in which the Guild solidified its organizational position, it underscored the continued efficacy of determined managerial intransigence.[11]

Equally as impressive as the Newspaper Guild's expansion during the early 1940s was the rapid growth of white-collar unionism in the New York offices of the major motion picture firms. In addition to several thousand clerical workers, the companies employed hundreds in advertising and marketing activities, and hundreds of technicians and clerks to manufacture and distribute prints to exhibitors throughout the eastern United States. In the late 1930s, publicity and advertising staff formed a Screen Publicists Guild (SPG), which in July 1940 joined forces with a similar group based in the studios' West Coast operations. By early 1941, the SPG felt confident petitioning the NLRB for representation at the New York offices of Columbia, Loew's, RKO, Paramount, Twentieth Century-Fox, United Artists, Universal, and Warner Brothers. In June, the Board finally authorized elections at all eight firms for full-time creative personnel employed in the advertising and publicity departments. The union failed in its first attempt at Warner and United Artists, but majorities voted in favor of the SPG at the other six firms. After protracted negotiations, the union and the companies finally agreed in May 1942 on a contract that granted substantial salary increases to the 169 employees covered, including an average of $200 in retroactive pay.[12]

Much larger groups of clerical workers in the studios' New York offices began to form independent union nuclei in an effort to raise salaries that still started as low as $18 per week in 1941. In October 1941, the 280 members of the Columbia Film Office Workers Guild voted unanimously to join the UOPWA, becoming the parent union's new Screen Office and Professional Employees Guild (SOPEG) Local 109. Within weeks, SOPEG petitioned the NLRB for elections at Columbia, Loew's-MGM, and Twentieth Century-Fox. Attempts to incorporate the SPG into SOPEG were rejected by the publicists, revealing ongoing divisions between the proponents of professional distinction and those who favored an inclusive industrial unionism. Only when the members of the New York SPG were guaranteed their own charter as a separate local of the UOPWA did they come into the CIO fold, severing their formal ties to the West Coast screen publicists in the process and becoming UOPWA Local 114 in June 1942.[13]

Although they were organized as separate UOPWA locals, the SPG and SOPEG frequently collaborated as they expanded throughout the entertainment industry in wartime New York. Within months of affiliating with the UOPWA, SPG won recognition at Warner Brothers and RKO. SOPEG also scored a series of decisive victories in representation elections at the New York offices of numerous motion picture companies, including Loew's, RKO, and Columbia. Film processing technicians at firms like DeLuxe also joined the union, eschewing the corrupt business unionism of the IATSE. By 1943, SOPEG had organized more than 3,000 of the industry's approximately 5,500 white-collar employees in the city.[14] Seeking to capitalize on the momentum of SOPEG and the SPG, in the summer of 1942 the UOPWA expanded both locals' jurisdictions to include any interested and eligible white-collar workers in New York's broadcasting, theater, and music industries. In some cases, integrated ownership facilitated the spread of unionization. While SOPEG was in the midst of negotiations for its first contract with Loew's, covering roughly 700 employees in its motion picture operations, the union was able to rapidly organize an additional 60 employees of the company's radio station WHN. Similarly, the unionization of white-collar workers in Paramount's core business sparked a successful organizing drive in the offices of its music-publishing subsidiary.[15]

The Radio Writers Guild, which had made little headway in its first few years, also gained traction during the early 1940s even though its members' varied working conditions posed unique organizing challenges. While some radio writers worked on a permanent salaried basis, including news and continuity writers employed directly by the networks, the majority were freelancers who were paid by the script. The more successful freelance writers had season-long commitments from producers to purchase a certain number of scripts, but in general they had a somewhat casual market relationship with the purchasers of their creative talents. To improve terms and conditions, the RWG developed a "minimum basic agreement" (MBA) which attempted, among its provisions, to establish ownership and residual rights for radio writers, to set minimum fees that they would receive from producers for each performance, to provide compensation for scripts written on a speculative basis, to stipulate circumstances under which producers would be obligated to purchase complete seasonal runs of scripts, and to guarantee on-air credit.[16] By persuading producers to adopt this model contract, RWG members hoped to both boost their incomes and secure their intellectual property rights.

The push to get producers to adopt the MBA coincided with an evolution in the RWG that paralleled earlier developments in the Newspaper Guild, as radio writers increasingly came to believe that their organization needed to function as a trade union rather than just as a professional advocacy association. Among the leaders of the new cadre of RWG activists was Peter Lyon, who established his professional reputation writing scripts for the *March of Time* radio series and for the historical docudrama series *Cavalcade of America*, which was sponsored by DuPont and produced by BBDO. Lyon had been active in the Newspaper Guild's initial organizing drive at Time Inc., and he drew upon that experience as he joined with other like-minded writers to reorient the RWG. In 1943, Lyon and his allies, including prominent dramatic writers Norman Corwin and Erik Barnouw and news commentators William Shirer and John Vandercook won control of the RWG Eastern Division based in New York, and the following year Lyon was elected national president of the RWG. The more assertive approach to organizing and collective bargaining resulted in the union's first contracts with the networks, as CBS, NBC, and the Blue Network all signed agreements covering staff writers for network-produced entertainment, news, and network continuity by 1944. To finance this organizing push, the RWG adopted a new increased dues schedule in which members paid 0.6 percent of their income to the union instead of an annual flat fee of $10, and it secured a $15,000 loan from the Guild's parent body, the Authors' League of America, to hire full-time staff and pay the legal and research expenses entailed in the expansion plans. As Lyon's cohort gained influence within the RWG, they also aligned the union with the wartime Popular Front; Lyon, for example, wrote many of the scripts utilized for the CIO-sponsored episodes in the *Labor for Victory* weekly radio series that aired nationwide in 1943 and 1944. This new orientation alienated a conservative minority of writers in the Guild, who perceived the emphasis on collective bargaining as an undignified loss of social status and disapproved of the leadership's public support for progressive causes.[17]

Even as RWG activists succeeded in negotiating contracts for network staff, they struggled to get producers to adopt the MBA for the freelance writers who comprised two-thirds of the membership. The advertising agencies that produced many of the most popular programs were particularly intransigent in their opposition to a collective bargaining agreement for scriptwriters, and RWG members found the agencies' prevailing terms and conditions to be especially pernicious. Advertising agencies often required writers to sign draconian release forms in which they relinquished virtually all of their rights. Not only did they refuse to grant on-air credit to radio writers, but they went to considerable lengths to conceal writers' identities, which hindered the Guild's organizing. Furthermore, many of the agencies had not substantially adjusted their pay rates since the end of the Depression, so many writers experienced significant declines in their real incomes due to wartime inflation. As one commentator noted in December 1943, "the freelance writer today has to sell two scripts to net what he did on one script last year." BBDO, for instance, still paid freelancers writing for *Cavalcade of America* anywhere from $100 per script to a maximum of $500, while Young and Rubicam paid only $100 to $200 per script for the *Kate Smith Hour* variety program. RWG activists received the run-around, however, when they attempted to get agencies to adopt the MBA: agency executives referred the union to the American Association of Advertising Agencies as the body entrusted to establish uniform practices throughout the industry, while the

4As maintained that as a trade group it had no legal standing to engage in collective bargaining on behalf of its member agencies.[18]

Although the advertising executives' categorical hostility to unionism impeded the efforts of the radio writers, the UOPWA Ad Guild found its drive to organize the bulk of agency employees completely squashed. The UOPWA estimated that New York's advertising industry employed roughly 20,000 men and women who were eligible for union membership in the early 1940s, between those who were on the agencies' payrolls as well as those working for ancillary firms that furnished various creative, technical, or administrative services. For the small core of Ad Guild activists, the prospect of building a significant following in this large jurisdiction was daunting in the absence of any commitment by the UOPWA to finance a sustained membership drive. Still, they hoped that as wartime inflation eroded the purchasing power of employees' meager salaries, especially at smaller agencies, support for unionism would grow. At Weiss and Geller, for example, harsh managerial discipline and a refusal to pay overtime spurred a group of women employed by the agency to begin meeting clandestinely after work in a nearby cafeteria before reaching out to the Ad Guild.[19]

Within the ambit of the agencies, a combination of ideological hegemony, managerial discipline, and structural factors prevented the proponents of white-collar unionism from achieving the organizational advances that they attained in other segments of New York's culture industries. The top advertising agencies, along with traditional lobbying groups like the National Association of Manufacturers, were the vanguard of business efforts to challenge an expanding regulatory state and an emboldened labor movement. The staunch faith in capitalists' benevolent stewardship of the economy and the voluntarist conception of market relations that pervaded wartime institutional advertising suffused the workplace ethos inside the agencies to a far greater extent than was the case in the offices of newspapers, magazines, motion-picture studios, or radio broadcasters. Many of the Ad Guild's supporters reflected the industry's infectious boosterism in their own calls to organize; to a greater extent than most other white-collar unionists in the city's culture industries, they still tended to represent the Guild primarily as an association dedicated to elevating professional standards. Organizers focused on seemingly nonadversarial initiatives like the union's educational programs and the Advertising Mobilization Committee, but they could not turn enthusiasm for professional development and progressive politics into membership gains or union contracts. Although the Ad Guild succeeded in organizing several smaller agencies, it could never muster the energy for a single coordinated drive in one of the city's medium-sized agencies, let alone firms like J. Walter Thompson or BBDO that had hundreds of employees. Of the 600 previously unorganized advertising employees who had participated in the AMC by November 1942, only 100 ultimately joined the union. Following the evaporation of public patronage for the AMC, in April 1943 the UOPWA merged the Ad Guild, which then had fewer than 200 members in good standing, into its much larger and more stable Book and Magazine Union. For all practical purposes, the effort to organize advertising workers had been put on an indefinite hiatus.[20]

The Ad Guild's failure stood in conspicuous contrast to the relative success of so many other white-collar unions in New York's culture industries during the war years. The copywriters, commercial artists, and public relations professionals who joined the Screen Publicists' Guild performed creative tasks similar to their far more numerous counterparts in the advertising agencies, while many Newspaper Guild units in the city included commercial artists as well as advertising sales agents. Legions of secretaries, stenographers, bookkeepers, and other clerical staff in the agencies had jobs that were virtually identical to those held by several thousand union members at daily newspapers, magazines, motion picture companies, and radio broadcasters. Many agency employees had worked previously for media enterprises, just as many employed in the media had some experience on the agency side of the production and distribution of America's culture of consumer capitalism. Despite the similarities in workers' jobs and the considerable overlap in personnel, advertising executives accomplished what their peers in other segments of the culture industries could not by completely routing the proponents of white-collar unionism. The unionists' inability to establish a viable presence within the advertising agencies had lasting consequences for the entire movement to organize the creative class, as the agencies not only remained citadels of antiunion ideology, but also retained their power to threaten union gains throughout the media.

Guns and Butter Too: The Culture Industry Unions and the Wartime Popular Front

As the white-collar unions in New York's culture industries expanded, they took a leading role in the social unionism of the wartime CIO. Progressives lacked the deep pockets and domination of the media that their business adversaries enjoyed, but they had a potential advantage in their ability to mobilize the swelling ranks of union members and supporters. Building upon the legacy of grassroots organizing established during the 1930s by labor, tenant, and consumer activists, the Greater New York Industrial Union Council organized workers at the neighborhood level in support of effective price control and rationing as a means of combatting wartime inflation. White-collar unionists were well represented in CIO Community Councils, which aspired to unite workers as a class regardless of employer or occupation. Creative workers associated with the CIO in New York were uniquely qualified to use their talents to advance the progressive agenda. Although the copywriters and graphic artists who participated in the AMC failed to secure lasting public sponsorship, the expansion of the labor movement during the war held out the possibility that the unions might yet become dependable patrons of culture. In particular, radio broadcasting became a more promising mode of cultural production during the war years. Progressives in the Newspaper Guild of New York succeeded in obtaining commercial radio time in 1943 and 1944 to launch their own weekly program, and they joined with activists from the Radio Writers Guild, the UOPWA, other CIO unions, and other Popular Front organizations to try to establish their own station on the newly opened Frequency Modulation (FM) broadcast spectrum.

The Greater New York Industrial Union Council coordinated the efforts of the city's CIO affiliates to promote social consumerism through community organizing. In the months following Pearl Harbor, the New York Council, like the national CIO and other state and municipal Industrial Union Councils, called for an economic stabilization program from the federal government that included robust measures to contain price inflation without any compulsory limits on wages and salaries. Progressive unionists were disappointed by both the shortcomings of the OPA, which significantly restrained inflation but ultimately failed to achieve its stated goal of stabilizing prices at the May 1942 level, and the decision of the NWLB to impose stringent wage controls. At first, they pressed their demands through conventional lobbying, with the New York Council imploring union members to barrage their congressmen with letters and telegrams. These efforts resulted in some changes, such as the rescheduling of local rationing board meetings from the daytime to evenings in order to facilitate greater involvement by working people. By the end of 1942, however, the New York CIO increasingly encouraged workers to engage in participatory grassroots actions to make the most out of the existing scheme. The Council furnished workers with special booklets for collecting data on local retailers' compliance with OPA regulations, and it began to organize pickets and boycotts against merchants found to be in violation by the working-class consumers who served as volunteer "price wardens."[21]

To more effectively mobilize workers, the New York CIO called for unionists to join the block committees sponsored by the Civilian Defense Volunteer Organization as well as the neighborhood branches of the leftist New York City Consumers Council. In the spring of 1943, the Greater New York Industrial Union Council supplemented these institutional structures by establishing its own network of CIO Community Councils, which were inaugurated with a series of neighborhood rallies throughout the five boroughs. As the UOPWA newspaper explained, involvement in the Community Councils was imperative, since they organized "every CIO member where he lives rather than where he works" and furnished "an instrument for the effective organization of workers as consumers." UOPWA and Newspaper Guild stalwarts participated heavily in the Community Councils, as did white-collar activists from the CIO-affiliated unions of department store workers and public-school teachers. Writer Ann Petry, for instance, a Newspaper Guild member employed by the *People's Voice*, an African American newspaper edited by Adam Clayton Powell Jr., served as the secretary of the Harlem and Riverside CIO Community Council, while John McManus, *PM* media critic and newly elected president of the Newspaper Guild of New York, chaired the Downtown CIO Community Council. Through these councils, workers demonstrated against recalcitrant merchants, supported new union organizing campaigns, and agitated for expanded public services, including free child-care centers for working mothers.[22]

UOPWA and Newspaper Guild activists also took a leading role in promoting social consumerism within the CIO more broadly. In the fall of 1942, a group of CU employees revamped the UOPWA New York Joint Council's course on consumer issues into a "lab" class designed to prepare unionists to serve on community price-control enforcement panels. Within a few months, the approach had been adopted for training programs run by the New York City Consumers Council as well as the nascent CIO Community Councils. CU promoted this model of grassroots consumer education on a wider basis through *Home Front: A Victory Program for Trade Union Consumers*, a booklet that it distributed to labor activists nationally. *Home Front* called on all union bodies to develop consumer cooperatives and to encourage members to take an active role in OPA enforcement. "Since labor has voluntarily suspended use of the strike as a means of protecting the living standards of its members," it asserted, "it has become all the more necessary for unions to organize their members as consumers to promote and support price control, democratic rationing, quality standards and other measures to protect the families of workers."[23]

The Newspaper Guild of New York advocated for the wartime Popular Front's social and political agenda with its weekly radio program, *The News and What to Do about It*. Broadcast locally on Friday evenings beginning in May 1943, the program gave CIO progressives a prime opportunity to reach New Yorkers outside of the unions' regular channels of communication. An early episode that July, for example, focused on how listeners could "take direct action to stop inflation" and safeguard their earnings "against the profiteers, the black markets, and the price chiselers" by participating in their local CIO Community Councils. Representatives of the New York CIO, who were featured guests that week, used a conversational format to explain common violations of OPA regulations and how to work through the Councils to submit formal complaints against noncompliant merchants. Other episodes consisted entirely of sketches that dramatized the activities of the CIO Community Councils. In one, a member of UAW Local 365 phones his neighborhood CIO Council in the Rockaways to arrange for an emergency delivery of coal to restock his home furnace, while in another a woman recounts her involvement in the Brownsville CIO Council's campaign of protests and boycotts against grocers who violated OPA price ceilings that forced them to lower the prices of staple food items like potatoes.[24]

The Newspaper Guild cadre who produced *The News and What to Do about It* grounded their advocacy within a broader progressive analysis of America's wartime political economy. A July 1943 episode, for instance, condemned Congress for slashing $10 million from the budget for OPA enforcement, among other transgressions, and explained the formation of the CIO Political Action Committee (CIO-PAC) as a necessary response. During the fall, the program assailed fiscally regressive wartime tax policies and demanded revisions to NWLB wage controls, contending that additional increases in workers' purchasing power would not be inflationary if OPA price ceilings were stringently enforced. An episode in February 1944 followed up on Senator Claude Pepper's investigative hearings on lagging white-collar incomes by examining the efforts of the CIO-affiliated United Federal Workers to win desperately needed raises for its members. Over that summer, episodes hosted by Irving Gilman, a journalist and former department head at the *New York Times* who had become a vice president of the New York Guild, extolled the Wagner-Murray-Dingell Bill, which would have expanded Social Security to include health care coverage, as well as the Murray-Truman-Kilgore Bill, which would have established economic planning mechanisms

FIGURE 5.2 New York's Popular Front unions utilized posters like this one during the Second World War to promote their vision of social consumerism.

for the reconversion period following the war and provided supplemental unemployment benefits to war-industry workers.[25]

In addition to advocating a permanent shift toward a greater regulation of businesses and markets, an expanded role for labor unions, increased provisioning of public goods and services, and fiscal policies intended to facilitate a more egalitarian distribution of income and wealth, the Newspaper Guild of New York also used its radio program to address the ways in which the structure of the culture industries made it difficult for organized labor to promote its political and social agenda. In September 1943, local president McManus hosted an episode of that focused on network executives and station managers' frequent invocation of the National Association of Broadcasters' code of standards and practices to prevent the airing of pro-labor programming. Nine major stations, including the Blue Network's flagship station WJZ in New York, had just refused to sell airtime to the UAW for a series of brief messages calling for more vigorous enforcement of price control. In each case, station management cited the NAB proscriptions against "controversial" programming that had been used routinely since the 1930s to deny labor access to the nation's supposedly public airwaves. After he explained the situation to the audience, McManus and several other Guild members read the scripts of a few UAW spots, each of which concluded with instructions for listeners to write to their congressman to demand that prices be rolled back to May 1942 levels. "Were they so controversial? Not to us, they weren't," McManus continued, "or to you out there—to you whose pay checks have been slashed by the mounting cost of living. They are controversial only to those who don't want a control over prices—who want only to make all the profit they can out of this war."[26]

As president of the Newspaper Guild of New York, McManus guaranteed that his own militant antiracism and his belief in the media's responsibility to combat discrimination and prejudice influenced the local's broadcasting endeavors. One of the first episodes, for instance, highlighted efforts by the National Committee to Abolish the Poll Tax to end voter disfranchisement in the South. Closer to home, on August 20, 1943, McManus and several Guild activists on the staff of the *People's Voice* hosted an episode that examined the civil disturbances that had recently rocked Harlem. Marvel Cooke, a feature reporter with the paper, asserted that the upheaval was a sad replay of what had occurred in the community in 1935, reflecting the reality that almost nothing had been done to ameliorate conditions in the overcrowded and impoverished African American neighborhood. The unrest was "the violent and terrible expression of the community against unjustified discrimination in housing, education and employment," and "against the unjustified discrimination in the armed forces at a time when unity is vitally necessary for America's win-the-war program." *People's Voice* theater reporter Fredi Washington characterized the disturbances as "the kind of drama that never reaches the stage—the drama of a people resenting their second-class citizenship."[27]

Although the broadcast aired several weeks after the disturbances, Washington, Cooke, and McManus hoped to shape the ongoing public debate about their meaning. Cooke contextualized the upheaval in terms of prevalent Popular Front discourses of antiracism and social consumerism. "These weren't hoodlums that I saw roaming the streets, looting the stores," she claimed. "Many of them were solid citizens—women, housewives who did not know how to spend their ration points to get the most for the coupons and their money. They were the victims of small incomes made smaller by the soaring cost of living. Food was the biggest item on that night." McManus emphasized the differences between the Harlem disturbances and the racial violence in Detroit earlier in the summer, when white mobs had wantonly attacked African Americans, resulting in thirty-four confirmed deaths and hundreds of serious injuries. "This was *not* a race riot," he insisted. "This was not a planned riot, as Detroit's riot was planned by the fifth columnists. Detroit is the arsenal of democracy, and the Negro is doing a fine job in the war plants there. Disturbing even for one minute the flow of essential war material from Detroit's factories gave Hitler that much more time to fight against us."[28] As their efforts to influence perceptions of the Harlem unrest—and to manage its ramifications for race relations in wartime New York—indicate, progressives in the city's unions of culture workers espoused a capacious vision of social solidarity that united factory and office workers and aspired to racial equality as well.

Activists in the Newspaper Guild, the RWG, and the UOPWA also backed a far more ambitious project for establishing a Popular Front radio station in New York City. Proposals by the FCC to allocate portions of the broadcast spectrum for transmissions using FM technology offered the hope of redressing progressives' marginalization and exclusion from the airwaves. In anticipation, the People's Radio Foundation (PRF) was established in late 1944 to secure one of the new licenses authorized for the New York metropolitan area. Its initial board of directors included McManus, former United American Artists president Rockwell Kent, Congressman Powell, International Labor Defense attorney Joseph Brodsky, actor Charlie Chaplin, poet Langston Hughes, Wholesale and Warehouse Local 65 president Arthur Osman, and *Reader's Scope* publisher Leverett Gleason. According to its prospectus, the PRF sought to establish a "powerful, progressive FM radio station" by selling up to $100,000 worth of stock to pay for the construction of suitable studio and transmission facilities. Eventual operating expenses for the nonprofit venture were to be financed from selling a limited portion of the station's available airtime to politically acceptable enterprises and organizations, and the station would prohibit the advertising of any products rated "not acceptable" by CU.[29] Left-led CIO unions acquired a substantial portion of the shares, with the United Electrical, Radio, and Machine Workers of America (UE) investing the largest sum in the PRF. The International Workers Order, a Popular Front insurance association that had nearly 200,000 members, and its affiliated ethnically based mutual-aid societies also made significant stock subscriptions, with the remaining PRF shares purchased by individuals like Gleason. As it raised funds, the PRF enlisted an advisory committee that featured RWG activists Norman Corwin, Peter Lyon, and Millard Lampell to develop program content, with an emphasis on dramatizations of current social and political issues clearly inspired by the Federal Theater Project's Living Newspaper productions. As they prepared to file their license application with the FCC in 1946, PRF backers were confident that they had adequate financing to compete against existing corporate heavyweights like the *Daily News* and the Hearst Corporation that were also seeking FM licenses in New York City.[30]

The PRF was far from the only progressive group with high hopes for the new FM broadcast spectrum. Its promotional materials highlighted the efforts nationally by community-based coalitions, and by larger CIO affiliates like the UAW and UE, to establish similar stations throughout the country in order to indicate to potential backers that the Foundation was part of a broad movement for media democracy. Indeed, the advent of FM seemed latent with utopian possibilities for countering the structural disadvantages that proponents of unionism, social consumerism, antiracism, and international antifascist and anti-imperialist solidarity had long faced as they attempted to disseminate their views. "We are convinced," the sponsors of the PRF declared, that the station would "meet the long-felt needs of the radio audiences and artists" in the New York metropolitan area by "providing a democratic voice to express the community life; to present honest news and responsible comment; to give labor a place in the broadcast world; to offer artists of the radio and theater an opportunity to create cultural and educational programs of the highest standards; and to experiment in the new FM medium for techniques which will improve the radio art." Through such forays into FM broadcasting, progressives aspired to build upon their wartime efforts to mobilize community-based support for the Popular Front agenda.[31]

New York's Culture Industry Unions and the National War Labor Board

White-collar unionists in New York's culture industries increasingly emphasized the importance of social consumerism and the organization of workers for political action away from the job partly in response to the impositions of the wartime labor regime. Like the rest of organized labor, they were constrained by the NWLB in their efforts to improve salaries and working conditions. The widespread suspension of sanctioned strike activity by American unions only marked the beginning of far-ranging deviations from the patterns of industrial relations instituted under the New Deal. In January 1942, as part of its efforts to promote economic stabilization, the federal government established the NWLB with new powers to intervene in collective bargaining between unions and employers. Unlike the existing NLRB, the NWLB had a tripartite composition, consisting of four representatives of organized labor, four representatives of business, and four "public" representatives including the chairman. While the NLRB had been charged with guaranteeing unions' rights to organize and to collective bargaining upon certification, the NWLB had the power to dictate the specific terms of labor contracts in the interest of maximizing production and fighting inflation.[32]

In July 1942, the NWLB gave the wartime labor regime a definite shape with its precedent-setting ruling in the "Little Steel" cases involving the CIO steelworkers' union and several key steelmaking firms. Despite the union's contention that actual increases in consumer prices had significantly surpassed the 15 percent rise in the Bureau of Labor Statistics' cost-of-living index between January 1941 and the supposed stabilization of prices by the OPA in May 1942, all of the management and public representatives on the NWLB accepted the validity of the official inflation figures. On this basis, they declared that the sum total of increases in the base rate of pay for any job from January 1941 until the end of hostilities could not exceed 15 percent. Exceptions could still be authorized if unions could demonstrate that workers needed to be reclassified to reflect accurately the work that they were actually doing, or if unions could prove that workers with comparable experience were receiving different rates for the same job. Fearful that these wage controls and other sacrifices by organized labor might sap workers' morale and foment unrest on the factory floor, the union representatives on the NWLB persuaded the public representatives to side with them on the issue of union security. The NWLB ordered that the steelworkers' contracts include clauses that required workers to maintain their union membership as a condition of continued employment, and that permitted voluntary payroll deductions for union dues, known as the "check-off."[33] The provisions of the ruling set forth the framework under which all of organized labor—including the UOPWA, the Newspaper Guild, and even the Radio Writers Guild— would be compelled to conduct collective bargaining until August 1945.

The NWLB policy was controversial from the outset, as many within the labor movement believed that maintenance of membership and dues check-off inadequately compensated unions for surrendering the strike weapon and accepting the Board's stingy wage controls. Even as the NWLB concessions guaranteed unions a more stable membership base and a more predict-able stream of income, some rank-and-file activists faulted these measures for expanding the power of unions to discipline workers. Contemporary commentators like Daniel Bell contended that submission to the wartime labor regime was a recipe for the bureaucratic sclerosis of the nation's unions, as organizations intended for workers' self-empowerment became subordi-nated to the imperatives of a militarized state.[34] Although activists in the UOPWA, Newspaper Guild, and the RWG criticized the NWLB wage constraints, they still hoped that the scheme could be manipulated to serve their members' interests.

With its vast, and largely unorganized, jurisdiction stretching into fields like insurance, banking, social services, direct mail, and general clerical work, the UOPWA stood to gain or lose the most from the Board's stance toward white-collar workers. As an agency established primarily to guarantee har-monious relations within the arsenal of democracy, it initially appeared that the NWLB might ignore white-collar unionists entirely. Once the Board clarified in September 1942 that it would in fact process white-collar workers' requests for salary adjustments, UOPWA leaders quickly developed a new organizing strategy that stressed the potential for securing salary increases from the NWLB. In marked contrast to the anti-inflation propaganda from the Ad Council and the NAM, UOPWA organizing materials assured office workers that it was still "patriotic to ask for a raise."[35]

After the NWLB created a series of regional War Labor Boards to cope with the deluge of applications for wage and salary adjustments, UOPWA leaders Peter Hawley and Aaron Schneider secured appointments as labor representatives to the New York WLB, which gave them a unique opportu-nity to advocate for white-collar workers. Hawley also advised his comrades on the Greater New York Industrial Union Council of the importance of solid research and analysis for winning cases. He stressed the ways that unionists could attain pay increases in excess of the Little Steel formula through job reclassifications, demonstrations of inequitable variations in rates within a workplace or an industry, and, more controversially, through incentive pay schemes linked to labor productivity. Some workers backed incentive proposals as a way to put more money in their weekly pay envelopes, but many saw little difference between these schemes and the various forms of piecework exploitation that the unions had fought hard for years to eliminate. Even as the UOPWA utilized all available means to secure the largest salary hikes permissible, by September 1943 national president Lewis Merrill was calling for a revision of NWLB wage controls to allow increases in pay rates of up to 35 percent for white-collar workers.[36]

The Newspaper Guild of New York also pushed for NWLB approval for salary hikes, but in addition it took advantage of the Board to enhance the union security provisions of its contracts. Irving Gilman's research was critical to the union's fight for wage increases. His analysis revealed that the average pay at most of the city's publishers had stagnated since 1941 on account of labor turnover. Guild contracts, like those of other white-collar unions, set minimum salaries for each job classification with step increases for the first two to four years of experience. When long-term employees earning salaries above the contract minimums left for military service or for other employment opportunities, their replacements often started at or near the bottom salaries. This tendency, Gilman found, was accentuated at firms that increased total employment, so that average salaries slightly declined. At Time Inc., for instance, where the number of workers in the editorial departments had swelled from around 350 in January 1941 to nearly 550 by December 1944, average weekly salaries slipped from $45.35 to $44.87 over the period, despite general increases of roughly 10 percent that management had grudgingly conceded. By comparison, at the *New York Times*, where the number of workers covered by the Guild contract remained relatively steady at around 1,400, average weekly salaries crept upward from $44.92 in January 1941 to $47.44 in May 1944.[37] Although the NWLB and its Newspaper Commission moved slowly on the Guild's applications for salary adjustments, Gilman's research eventually bore fruit. In May 1944, the NWLB authorized a modest combination of general increases and boosts in minimum salaries for the 840 Guild members at the *Daily News*. While the first raises in more than two years at the tabloid increased the publisher's expenditure for Guild labor by an average of 7.5 percent, the biggest increases went to workers in the lowest-paid classifications. In the case of the *New York Post*, Gilman used the concessions that the union had made in 1941 and 1942 in consideration of the paper's shaky financial condition under new owner Dorothy Schiff to convince the NWLB of the existence of pay inequities. Subsequently, in March 1945 the Board approved a contract between the Guild and the *Post* with one of the city's highest minimum salary schedules, making the agreement the new standard as the union began to formulate its postwar bargaining demands.[38]

In exchange for these modest improvements in salaries, the Newspaper Guild expected enhanced union security. It already had obtained some form of a union shop provision in two-thirds of its contracts by the middle of 1943, but it looked to convince the NWLB to order the inclusion of maintenance of membership in its contracts with two highly visible holdouts: the *New York Times* and Time Inc. When Time Inc. president Roy Larsen testified before the NWLB in August 1943, he declared "that no form of union shop or modification of it, such as maintenance of membership, has or can ever have any proper place in the editorial department of any news organization dedicated to the task of forthrightly reporting the news events of the world for the information of the American public." Any rulings that might establish such a precedent for the media would "inevitably lead to an impairment of the complete freedom with which news reports should be prepared and circulated." Here, he continued, "a fundamental right is at stake which far outweighs any possible benefit to the cause of unionism," since the "infinitely more basic interest of the public and labor in the maintenance of an uncontrolled press must take precedence in this case over the interest of protecting and promoting unionism in the field of journalism."[39]

Larsen proceeded in his testimony to recount the history of collective bargaining at Time, observing that the "Guild has demanded for the past six years that the Company agree to some form of compulsory union membership" but to no avail. It was taking advantage of wartime exigencies in an attempt "to obtain from the National War Labor Board what it could not otherwise secure." Completely glossing over management's record of hostility to the union, he claimed that because "the relations between the Company and the Guild have been amicable and generally harmonious, the Guild needs no protection against the Company." Instead, the integrity of management's editorial prerogatives needed to be defended. "If reporters and editorial writers should be required to remain members of the Guild in order to hold their jobs, conflict between duty to the publication and subservience to the Guild is bound to arise because of differences in the political and economic and social views and policies of the two." Larsen contended that it was "self-evident that the Guild does not intend to confine itself to matters of collective bargaining," but that "it intends to take an active stand in politics and to take very definite stands with regard to an infinite variety of matters of broad public interest, all of which constitute day to day subject-matter of news of vital interest to the public." The "freedom of the press" guaranteed by the First Amendment would be compromised "if any outside organization were to have a say as to who is to work or not to work" for a publisher, since "that organization and its aims and policies would have the inevitable tendency to influence, directly or indirectly, and on the part of the employee perhaps unconsciously, the content of the copy that is produced and printed and the editing of it." To demonstrate that this was not an abstract concern for management, Larsen recounted the actions of local president John McManus during the recent disturbances in Harlem. Even as city officials, police, and community leaders were working to restore order in the neighborhood, McManus had dispatched a telegram to the city editors of all of New York's major daily newspapers seeking to shape the coverage of the events. Using language that he would reiterate in his subsequent radio broadcast, McManus recommended that editors frame the unrest in Harlem as an understandable, if misguided, protest against racial discrimination in housing, employment, consumption, and matters of law enforcement, and that they refrain from describing it as a "race riot."[40]

Despite Larsen's pleading, the regional War Labor Board in New York began to process the Newspaper Guild's request for maintenance of membership at Time Inc. in anticipation that the NWLB would soon set a national precedent in the print media. Aaron Schneider of the UOPWA, the labor representative on the regional arbitration panel, persuaded the public representative to concur in a preliminary finding in favor of the Guild. They affirmed the Guild's claim that "all democratic and responsible unions which have subscribed and loyally adhered to the no-strike agreement, the rules and procedures of the War Labor Board, and the wage stabilization program" were "entitled in fairness to maintenance of membership as partial compensation for the handicaps they have voluntarily assumed at the Government's request." As for the constitutional issues raised by Larsen, Schneider and his colleague concluded that they were "unable to find any realistic relation between the relatively narrow issue" of union security and "the preservation of the freedom of the press." Management's appeals delayed but did not reverse the arbitration finding, which was finalized on March 14, 1944. Within fifteen days of the ruling, all employees of the firm's editorial departments who did not explicitly opt out of union membership were automatically enrolled in the Guild for the duration of its current contract, as were all new employees hired before the next contract period.[41] Larsen and other Time Inc. executives circulated memoranda to the staff in which they lamented the decision, but they also began to lay the ideological groundwork to renew the fight in the not-too-distant future. Several weeks after the NWLB ruling, Luce cast himself as a leading defender of the First Amendment by committing tens of thousands of dollars to an academic inquiry into the free press headed by University of Chicago president Robert M. Hutchins. In announcing his decision to charter the commission, Luce asserted that because "we have more government today than the theorists of the eighteenth century considered necessary or even anticipated, when freedom of the press was first established," it was imperative "to inquire into the whole question once again, to reaffirm first principles, and possibly to arrive at new definitions and a new set of codes and practices." Luce and his team of executives hoped that when they resumed their struggle with the Guild over union security after the war, the public reputation that they cultivated as guardians of liberty would work to their advantage.[42]

The implementation of solid union security measures in nearly all of the Newspaper Guild of New York's contracts greatly augmented the local's organizational strength, and the widespread adoption of dues check-off finally put the local on a solid financial footing.[43] Yet even as the Guild tried to make the most of the problematic wartime labor regime, its efforts served as grist for the political tensions that existed between the local and the anticommunist leadership of its parent union. Within months of McManus' election as president of the New York Guild, officers of the American Newspaper Guild began to attack the local over its collective bargaining record. Despite the New York Guild's use of sophisticated statistical analysis to wring every drop of additional pay permissible under the strictures of the NWLB, members of the ANG executive board accused the local's leadership of selling out the membership through sweetheart deals with the publishers. Seeking to exploit frustration over the measly salary increases authorized by the NWLB, in 1943 some ANG officers advocated repudiation of the union's no-strike pledge. Although they were overruled by the majority of delegates at the ANG annual convention, squabbling between the New York Guild and the national union regarding the proper stance toward the NWLB continued for the remainder of the war. In March 1945, anticommunists in the ANG again condemned the leadership of the New York local for extending its contracts with the Hearst-owned *Daily Mirror* and *Journal-American* through the end of the year, alleging that the move undermined the national union's wage program. McManus and other New York officials countered that the extension gave white-collar workers at the two papers a modest pay increase approved by the NWLB, and strategically aligned the contracts' expiration dates with other major agreements in order to augment the local's leverage in future collective bargaining.[44]

For the Radio Writers Guild, which obtained its first contracts with the broadcast networks during the war, the NWLB proved instrumental in establishing a coherent pay scale for its members. Salaries for radio writers and news commentators varied widely, reflecting actual differences in talent as well as managerial caprice. The general bargaining strategy of the RWG, which focused on eventually getting all producers and broadcasters of scripted content to recognize the union and adhere to its Minimum Basic Agreement, sought to reduce the pay disparities among radio writers. The implementation of the Little Steel formula limited pay hikes for those writers who were top earners, but the wide variations in writers' salaries made it easy for the RWG to persuade the NWLB that pervasive inequalities required remediation in the form of upward salary adjustments for many of its members. In an exceptional move, the NWLB in 1944 approved hefty pay boosts for many RWG members employed by the networks; staff writers in the NBC Shortwave division, for example, were granted raises in their annual salaries ranging from $700 to a top increase of $2,400, which was roughly equivalent to the median annual income in the United States at the time. Once these gains had been secured, the RWG continued to promote salary equalization. In the renegotiation of its contract for NBC newswriters, for instance, the union proposed that the network pool the revenues from all of its sponsored news programs in order to narrow the remaining salary disparities within the department. At the same time, the generous directives from the NWLB made the potential benefits of collective bargaining more attractive to freelancers, thus fueling their demands that the ad agencies and independent package producers adopt the MBA.[45]

While activists in all three unions—the UOPWA, the Newspaper Guild, and the RWG—engaged with the NWLB under differing circumstances, they all tended to view their dealings with the wartime labor regime as a complementary strategy to their robust social unionism and community organizing, not as a substitute for it. They were constantly frustrated by the glacial pace at which the NWLB and its subsidiary panels worked and, except for the radio writers, they grew increasingly impatient with the miserly wage adjustments permitted under the Little Steel formula. Yet the tripartite administrative bodies of the NWLB, with direct participation by labor representatives, still appeared to these unionists—along with the regulated consumerism of the OPA—to be latent with potential as the basic public planning mechanisms necessary for developing a social-democratic mixed economy in the United States. Negotiating the wartime labor regime did not automatically constitute an endorsement of industrial pluralism, with its emphasis on social harmony; from the perspective of most white-collar union activists, it represented the opening of another venue for struggle between labor and management. Moreover, engagement with the NWLB, and the enhanced union security that resulted, abetted social unionism in practical ways. Union cadre could devote the time and energy previously expended collecting dues from existing members to organizing new members or building the CIO Community Councils. Growing streams of dues income could support hiring additional organizers, offering more vibrant educational programs, sponsoring new cooperatives, and increasing labor patronage for cultural endeavors. At the same time, the new administrative apparatuses of the NWLB and the OPA, and the overt politicization of virtually all economic activity that they represented, made the continued strengthening of the Popular Front social movement absolutely critical. Only a broad coalition of blue-collar and white-collar workers could sustain the ongoing combination of grassroots mobilization, direct action, and political pressure needed to prevent labor's enemies from either dismantling those elements of the wartime regime that progressives hoped to employ to their advantage or, more ominously, using the augmented power of the state as a weapon in a business-led counteroffensive.

The Great Compression: White-Collar Incomes and Perceptions of Class and Status

Proponents of the revived Popular Front of the 1940s struggled to forge an alliance of blue-collar and white-collar workers under economic conditions very different from those they had faced in the 1930s. During the Great Depression, unionists had organized in an environment of extremely high unemployment and reduced earnings. American entry into the Second World War brought the tightest labor market of the twentieth century, but it also generated sudden and dramatic alterations in the distribution of income. The wartime years constituted the most intense phase of the "great compression," an extended period from the 1930s through the 1970s during which the proportion of national income earned by very affluent Americans declined, and the general distribution of income became, in relative terms, more egalitarian than it was in the decades before or since. The share of national income earned by the top decile shrank from 41 percent in 1941 to less than 32 percent by 1944, a figure that remained fairly stable for the next thirty-five years.[46]

This shift punctuated a broader trend in the functional allocation of national income, as wage and salary earnings accounted for 66.5 percent of all national income in 1944, an increase from labor's 58.1 percent share in 1929.[47]

This modest compression of the overall distribution of income in the United States coincided with a second type of income compression within the middle and lower strata that had important social and political consequences. The differential between the earnings of clerical, sales, technical, and professional workers, on the one hand, and the earnings of manufacturing workers, on the other, had narrowed gradually during the 1910s and 1920s. This gradual trend of income convergence continued intermittently through the Depression years but then sharply accelerated during the war. In 1936, after several years of anemic economic recovery and on the cusp of the first major industrial union breakthroughs, average annual earnings per full-time employee (or equivalent) in American manufacturing stood at $1,287, while the average annual earnings of full-time employees in the nation's finance, insurance, and real estate (FIRE) sectors, with their overwhelmingly white-collar workforce, was $1,747. Intense labor demand in war-related manufacturing swelled the ranks of blue-collar workers and dramatically pushed up their incomes, so that workers in manufacturing earned on average $2,517 per year in 1943, compared to $2,203 for employees in the FIRE sectors. Public school teachers, whose average annual incomes were still slightly greater than those of manufacturing workers as recently as 1940, earned less than two-thirds of manufacturing workers' yearly wages by 1943.[48] Workers in New York's culture industries also experienced this compression between blue-collar and white-collar earnings. Newspaper Guild members employed by the city's major publications earned on average between $44 and $48 per week in 1944, while professional staff employed by the broadcast networks averaged approximately $50. By contrast, average weekly earnings for production workers in durable-goods manufacturing—even with the constraints imposed by the Little Steel formula—had jumped from $30.48 in January 1941 to $51.52 by March 1944.[49]

Price inflation compounded the effects of this compression, especially for low-paid white-collar workers like retail clerks, whose average weekly earnings were still only $26.34 in March 1944.[50] Although OPA spokespersons never tired of reminding the American public that the rate of inflation was less than half of what it had been during the First World War, this was cold comfort to consumers who felt the constant erosion of their living standards. Price control regulations together with grassroots activism had restrained inflation, but had not prevented a jarring increase in the cost of living. From January 1941 to

October 1943, the BLS cost-of-living index jumped 23.4 percent, well beyond the 15 percent margin allowed for increases in pay rates under the Little Steel formula. Philip Murray and other CIO leaders charged that wartime inflation was in fact far worse than the official statistics indicated, and that by the end of 1943 its members had faced an increase of 45 percent in their cost of living over the previous three years. Rising prices diminished the impressive gains scored by workers employed in wartime manufacturing, but for many white-collar workers they led to a painful reduction in real purchasing power.[51] These shifts in the relative earnings of various occupations, and the resulting status anxiety among many Americans, were manifested vividly within the culture of wartime consumerism. In magazine publishing, the media sector in which the process of market segmentation was most advanced by the 1940s, titles with circulations that skewed toward blue-collar households were quick to tout their readers' increased purchasing power. To convince media buyers of the value of space in *True Story* magazine, for example, Macfadden Publications ran a series of advertisements in trade publications that juxtaposed the rising living standards of manufacturing workers with the concomitant austerity endured by white-collar consumers. The advertisements, along with numerous similar depictions of wartime disruptions to conventional hierarchies of status, refuted a core premise of the Popular Front. Rather than blue-collar and white-collar workers mutually benefiting from their organization into a social-democratic alliance, gains by factory workers were portrayed as coming at the expense of office workers in a zero-sum competition over consumer goods and social status.[52]

White-collar resentment over the rising living standards of workers in wartime industry was exacerbated by the demographic recomposition of the manufacturing workforce. At first, the expansion of military production in 1940–1941 primarily absorbed white male workers from lower-paying occupations or the ranks of the unemployed. After Pearl Harbor, however, as military enlistments increased and unemployment for white men practically vanished, the war industries increasingly turned to women and African Americans, many of whom had previously been outside of the labor force or on its margins, to satisfy their demand for workers. As late as April 1942, the 577,000 women employed in durable-goods manufacturing accounted for just 8.9 percent of the total workforce in that sector; by June 1943, this figure had more than tripled to more than 1.8 million, or 22 percent of the total. In the critical airframe and aircraft parts industries—the domain of "Rosie the Riveter"—the proportion of women in the workforce leapt from 6 percent to 39 percent during the same period. Gender discrimination remained

FIGURE 5.3 This trade advertisement for *True Story* magazine emphasized the increased purchasing power of its blue-collar readership and relative decline in the attractiveness of white-collar readers to advertisers as a result of wartime wage compression.

systemic throughout all of America's workplaces during the 1940s, but there was often less pay inequity in war work than in other occupational settings; average straight-time hourly wage rates for female riveters and assemblers in the metal-airframe industry in the eastern and central regions of the country, for example, were about 90 percent of the rates for men.[53] African Americans also achieved significant employment gains, with the number of Blacks employed as either craftsmen or operatives doubling from 500,000 in April 1940 to 1 million by April 1944. Despite the mixed record of the industrial unions and of agencies like the Fair Employment Practice Committee (FEPC) as advocates for racial justice in the workplace, in those factories in which the FEPC or NWLB intervened, Black workers saw their earnings increase during the war at twice the rate of white workers.[54] From the vantage point of many employed in clerical, sales, technical, and professional occupations, the relative decline in their standard of living meant not only a loss of social status to blue-collar workers in general, but often to women and minorities in particular.

Conservatives and anti-labor activists campaigned to harness white-collar resentment over wartime economic conditions. They frequently invoked the public good and castigated unionized blue-collar workers as selfish and unpatriotic, even though they had no more claim on civic virtue than those they criticized.[55] A November 1943 classified advertisement in the *New York Times* was typical, with its solicitation of "successful and altruistic business and professional men" to "create a national organization of the millions of unorganized, inarticulate and struggling office workers and professional men, etc., known as the 'White Collar Class.'" As the ad explicitly stated, "the plan is not for a labor union but for a non-sectarian, non-political, non-profit organization, ideally patriotic, which will make itself an unselfish public service factor in the life of the nation—seeking the welfare of *all* people, not alone small organized groups." In some cases, these efforts were supported more directly by business interests, such as the NAM-backed White Collar League investigated by Betty Goldstein (later Betty Friedan) in the spring of 1944 while she was a reporter for the leftist Federated Press. As American industry began the process of reconversion to civilian production and organized manufacturing workers fought to defend their living standards in the face of layoffs and reduced hours, conservatives continued these attacks unabated. In 1945 and 1946, a new group initially called White-Collar Majority (later National Majority) formed in the Westchester County suburbs of New York City as an "organization directly representing through its members the 'middle class group' of America." Directly contesting the labor movement's claims to speak for the American people, the group declared in the midst of the postwar strike wave that its members "deeply resent being included in the statements by Philip Murray of the CIO that he and his unions represent the public."[56]

The proponents of white-collar unionism, especially in the UOPWA, clearly saw the deteriorating living standards of clerical, sales, technical, and professional workers and the resulting tide of status anxiety as political dynamite that could destroy any chance of realizing the aims of the Popular Front. The UOPWA Book and Magazine Union condemned a series of articles in the *New York Times* in November 1943 that highlighted the plight of millions of supposedly "forgotten" white-collar workers as an appeal to "reactionaries and appeasers" who sought "to drive a wedge between white collar workers and the labor movement." To show office workers that "the only way to push salaries up is by working with the organized labor movement, not against it," the local union touted how it had already obtained $385,000 in wage and salary increases for its members in its first eleven months of access to the NWLB.[57] Similarly, when UOPWA president Lewis Merrill testified in January 1944 before Senator Pepper's subcommittee, he noted that recently there had been "a tremendous amount of discussion about the white-collar workers" stemming from the widespread "recognition that they are caught in the vice of fixed incomes and rising prices," but that given the "failure of the economic stabilization program" it was "little wonder" that "defeatist forces, open and concealed, have seized upon the recent discussion to further inflame the situation and to create hostility against the Government." Although Merrill represented the UOPWA as an advocate for all of the nation's white-collar workers, he nonetheless stressed "that our country and the salaried employees themselves will be stronger if they use on a wider scale the democratic collective bargaining process, take up membership in a union and through their union bring to their cause the support of the great and vital forces of labor."[58]

In actuality, Merrill's union faced serious limitations on its ability to bring disaffected office workers into its ranks. The CIO under Murray proved no more willing or able than it had under John L. Lewis to provide financial assistance and other tangible support for white-collar organizing. Forced to rely on the dues and assessments levied on a membership that only numbered in the tens of thousands, the UOPWA simply lacked the resources to assist all of the clerical, technical, and professional workers who were receptive to unionization. Sizeable groups of office workers in the burgeoning war industries presented ripe targets, but the UOPWA respected the jurisdictional claims of CIO manufacturing affiliates like the autoworkers and steelworkers, even when those unions were not viable means for white-collar organization. The largest organizing breakthrough by the UOPWA in wartime industry, at the Curtiss-Wright aircraft plant in Buffalo, New York, indicates both the possibilities and constraints that the union faced. After the UAW lost a hotly contested certification election among the blue-collar production workers at the complex to the rival International Association of Machinists in early 1943, a nucleus of clerical and technical workers at the plant reached out to the CIO to inquire if they could still organize with the industrial union center. The involvement of the UOPWA led to a series of certification elections through which the union came to represent approximately 4,000 of Curtiss-Wright's white-collar employees, a major addition at a time when the entire national membership had only recently topped 50,000.[59] Scattered UOPWA victories like this one revealed that even away from the fervid political environment of New York City, some groups of office workers were willing to view unionism as the solution rather than the cause of their economic problems.

Although the threat of a mounting conservative backlash against the wartime Popular Front lent an air of urgency to UOPWA organizing rhetoric during the mid-1940s, the union's resources were spread too thinly to have a dramatic impact. On the whole, the labor movement failed to take advantage of the opportunities during these years to expand the social frontiers of unionism deep into the white-collar occupational strata. Merrill's lobbying for a liberalization of NWLB procedures was driven in part by recognition that the overwhelming majority of the nation's clerical, sales, technical, and professional workers remained unorganized, which made it very difficult for them to petition for upward salary adjustments. Following the investigation by Senator Pepper's subcommittee, the NWLB did revise its procedures, so that white-collar workers who were not in a union could form "single-purpose" salary committees to seek approval for wage increases, and in some offices these committees did lead to subsequent unionization drives. The UOPWA nearly doubled its national membership during the war, but this represented just a fraction of the growth that might have been possible with a more substantial commitment of organizing resources to match the union's calls for "raises instead of reaction."[60]

Outside of the unions, progressive efforts to build support for the Popular Front agenda among clerical, sales, technical, and professional workers also focused on the realm of electoral politics. Republican gains in Congress during the 1942 midterm elections—when voter turnout declined by more than 40 percent from 1940 levels—had further diminished the influence of progressives on domestic policies, resulting in the final termination of the last vestiges of the WPA cultural projects, the purging of sympathetic administrators from the top ranks of the OPA, a tightening of wage controls, and the introduction of threatening new anti-labor legislation. If the expanded state apparatus of the war years was to serve the ends desired by white-collar progressives, then clearly it was essential to reverse the conservative electoral tide. To bolster white-collar support at the ballot box, in 1944 the CIO established a National Citizens Political Action Committee (NCPAC) as an auxiliary to the CIO-PAC that served as the principal electoral vehicle for its affiliated unions. As an early NCPAC advertisement asserted, the organization offered "farmers, workers, business and professional men and women" an opportunity to join with the CIO in a broad coalition to elect "Roosevelt and a progressive Congress" and ensure "total victory, a just and durable peace, and full employment."[61] In a complementary move, a group of cultural and academic figures with ties to earlier Popular Front organizations launched the Independent Voters Committee of the Arts and Sciences for Roosevelt, with sculptor Jo Davidson as its chair and Hollywood actor Frederic March as treasurer.[62] Like the Popular Front organizations of the mid-1930s, both NCPAC and the Independent Voters Committee drew their support dispro-portionately from the ranks of the culture industries, suggesting that the cre-ative class remained a portion of the white-collar occupational strata that was particularly receptive to progressive politics. Numerous artists, writers, and other creative professionals directly contributed their talents to the electoral effort, with perhaps the most notable examples being painter Ben Shahn's re-markable series of posters for CIO-PAC and Norman Corwin's direction of a nationwide election-eve radio broadcast over all four networks in which public figures ranging from the philosopher John Dewey to entertainers like Lucile Ball made personal appeals for a fourth term for FDR.[63]

As with the activities of CIO-PAC, the efforts at mobilizing the white-collar electorate through NCPAC and the Independent Voters Committee brought mixed results. From the outset, the disconnect between the hopes of the Popular Front and the actual compromises and contradictions of the Democratic Party was demonstrated by the inability of the CIO and its allies to prevent Vice President Henry Wallace from being unceremoniously dumped off the ticket in favor of Senator Harry Truman.[64] Redbaiting of the progressives' electoral front, led by lame-duck Representative Martin Dies and professional anticommunist J. B. Matthews, also took a toll, as some liberal candidates for the House and Senate who were endorsed by NCPAC opted to distance themselves from the organization.[65] Ultimately, the progressives' commitment of unprecedented organizational and financial resources during the 1944 election cycle did little more than maintain the political status quo while highlighting the deepening political polarization in the country.[66]

NCPAC and the Independent Voters Committee—which continued after the election as the Independent Citizens Committee of the Arts, Sciences, and Professions—served as vital organizational hubs for white-collar supporters of the Popular Front during the middle years of the decade.[67] Through their efforts, the two groups provided Americans who considered themselves middle class with a compelling alternative to the ominous mix of wartime economic constraints, simmering status anxiety, grassroots conser-vative activism, and "free enterprise" rhetoric espoused by business lobbies like the NAM. Like the wartime organizing breakthroughs by the UOPWA, the new political groups demonstrated that progressive ideals of industrial democracy, economic security, and social consumerism still resonated with many in the white-collar occupational strata. The ongoing support for white-collar unions and Popular Front political organizing, and the heavy fire their endeavors incited, challenge assumptions of a middle class that was solidly set against progressive policies and programs. At the same time, however, neither the white-collar unions nor NCPAC and the ICCASP could catalyze the fundamental political realignment that their proponents sought. Whether the setting was a single office or the expansive realms of American politics, society, and culture, the divisions between white-collar progressives and their anti-union, status-conscious adversaries remained as pronounced as ever.

"The Case of Mary X": Opportunities and Obstacles for White-Collar Women during the 1940s

Progressives' hopes for the Popular Front during the 1940s hinged not only on issues of class and status, but also of gender, as the large increase in the number of women in the labor force touched every aspect of American life. Much of the contemporary interest in female workers focused on the unprecedented influx of women into heavy manufacturing jobs, but the women employed in white-collar occupations during the war and reconversion periods arguably had a greater long-term impact on the gendering of work. In November 1943, when employment in wartime industry was near its peak, nearly 2.2 million women labored in production jobs in durable-goods manufacturing, but by April 1947, following the reconversion to civilian production and discriminatory layoffs of women to make way for returning veterans, only 824,000 women did. In non–durable manufacturing, such as textiles and food processing, in which wages had always been lower and the employment of women had always been more prevalent, the number of women workers remained fairly steady, declining only slightly from a wartime peak of over 2.6 million in October 1943 to just under 2.4 million in April 1947. With the rolling back during the reconversion period of many of the advances in earnings and status that women had made in wartime durable goods manufacturing, prior patterns of gender discrimination in blue-collar work largely reemerged.[68]

In white-collar occupations, existing patterns of gender discrimination were also reinforced by the war and subsequent reconversion, but the consequences were magnified over the coming decades as these occupations comprised a rapidly growing proportion of total employment. Women's clerical employment nearly doubled from 2.5 million in April 1940 to 4.9 million in April 1945, followed by only a modest decline to just over 4.1 million by April 1947. A similar pattern prevailed in sales employment over the same period, as the number of women workers grew from 830,000 in 1940 to 1.45 million in 1945, before dipping slightly to 1.3 million two years later.[69] These wartime shifts cemented long-term trends toward the feminization of clerical and retail work that had long been underway. Clerical and retail occupations in which women already predominated, such as file clerk and cashier, became even more overwhelmingly female, and earnings in these occupations lagged further behind median wages and salaries as the 1940s progressed. In those occupations that still employed significant numbers of both men and women, gender-based pay inequities were particularly evident. Among bank tellers in 1943, for example, average hourly earnings for female tellers were only two-thirds of the average hourly earnings for males; for general clerks in department stores, the pay gap was slightly wider, with women making only 60 percent of the hourly figure for men.[70] At the same time that women filled clerical and retail positions in growing numbers, women's upward career mobility into more remunerative and more fulfilling professional employment was thwarted. In 1940, 1.57 million women worked in professional and semiprofessional occupations, with the bulk still employed as either teachers or nurses. This number remained virtually unchanged through the war years, when women's overall employment surged, indicating the lack of improvement in women's woefully circumscribed opportunities for professional advancement. In fact, the percentage of women in the labor force who held employment in professional and paraprofessional occupations was actually lower in 1947 than before the war. For the growing numbers of women who would enter the labor force in subsequent decades, the range of employment options available to them was profoundly shaped by the outcome of the struggles over women's white-collar work during the 1940s.[71]

Women in New York's white-collar unions did not passively accept employers' efforts to reinscribe longstanding patterns of sex-based discrimination. They took advantage of the disruptions of the war and reconversion years to fight against pay inequity and to clear a path for their career advancement. As had been the case during the initial wave of white-collar organizing during the 1930s, female union activists saw issues of class and gender as inextricably intertwined. They continued to challenge the sexist norms that personnel managers used as the basis for women's lower salaries, a fight that became all the more pressing as skyrocketing prices compromised their already tenuous ability to maintain an autonomous lifestyle with their own earnings. In the New York locals of the UOPWA in particular, the proportion of women serving as paid full-time organizers, executive board members, and local officers increased significantly over the course of the 1940s.

One can get a sense of the consciousness that these activists sought to cultivate from "The Case of Mary X," a UOPWA organizing pamphlet that represented young white-collar women as avatars of urban modernity. The protagonist, "Mary X," was "the symbol of the Big City, the independent white-collar girl—the breadwinner" struggling to get by on her meager wages. "During the war Mary's boss told her the War Labor Board would not let him give her more than a 15 percent cost-of-living increase, and she didn't have the union's advice on how to get increases based on reclassification, merit increases, inequities, etc." At first, she "considered herself lucky at that, for many people she knew didn't get any increases." Eventually, however, she confronted her boss, telling him that "her salary of $28.75 today bought less than the $25 she began on five years ago" even though "her five years' experience made her worth a lot more to the firm." The boss retorted that the firm was unable to give any raises because the OPA refused to let it boost prices, and that "with all this government interference in business" he was struggling too. " 'You see,' " he claimed, " 'we're both in the same boat.' " Mary wondered about that, given that she had "ordered theatre tickets and made dinner reservations for him, while she'd been bringing her lunch to the office in order to pay her dentist bill." Unconvinced by his attempt to elide the class divisions between them, the everywoman heroine of this organizing tale turned to the UOPWA, like "lots of Mary Xs and John Qs all over the country" who "realized that the practice of individual bargaining was as outdated as a Model-T flivver." In addition to the salary demands in the union's collective bargaining program, the pamphlet stressed the goals of "classification scales to assure a salary commensurate with ability" as well as "equal pay for men and women for equal work."[72]

The systematic reclassification of office jobs—sometimes described by white-collar unionists as "job slotting"—was particularly important to women. The advent of the NWLB and its procedures for administering salary adjustments, while cumbersome, nonetheless provided an important impetus, since reclassification permitted white-collar workers to obtain raises beyond the constraints of the Little Steel formula. As UOPWA and Newspaper Guild analysts demonstrated in the evaluations of firms' salary structures that they submitted to the NWLB, the perverse intersection of ongoing sex-based discrimination and war-induced labor turnover contributed to the stagnation of women's earnings. When male employees left office jobs during the war, managers frequently shifted their responsibilities onto women who had initially been hired into lower-rank and lower-salary positions. In many cases, women who acquired additional skills or took on additional tasks received no commensurate enhancement in their title or pay. The salary figures for the fictional Mary X during the mid-1940s were all too real. In April 1943, the median weekly salary for file clerks in major American cities was just $22, for example, with three-quarters earning $25 or less; stenographers' salaries fit into a similarly narrow band, with $30 for the median weekly salary, and three-quarters earning $33 or less. Women's low salaries also contributed directly to high turnover, as some women forsook white-collar employment altogether between 1941 and 1945 for higher-pay jobs in wartime manufacturing. The constant churning among the ranks of white-collar women only served to further depress wages.[73]

Following the termination of the NWLB at the war's end, women activists in New York's culture industry unions demanded the incorporation of reclassification schemes into the collective bargaining agenda during the reconversion period. At the network headquarters of CBS, the "single-purpose" salary committee that workers had formed late in the war to petition the NWLB evolved into a full-fledged organizing drive under UOPWA auspices. When the union won certification in 1946, Myra Jordan and the other women who led the campaign insisted on the completion of the reclassification project they had instigated during the war. Under the terms of the union's first contract with the broadcaster, reclassification ultimately led to promotions for one out of every three covered employees, with women receiving the bulk of the upgrades.[74] In the home offices of the motion-picture firms, the UOPWA also utilized NWLB procedures to begin a reclassification program in 1942 that finally bore fruit in 1945 and 1946, with women being the prime beneficiaries of the resulting promotions.[75] Similarly, at Time Inc., women on the Newspaper Guild's negotiating committee utilized an analysis of the firm's salary structure carried out for the NWLB as the basis for successfully negotiating the establishment in 1946 of new job classifications for library clerks, copyreaders, production assistants, and other specialized support staff that significantly elevated their salaries.[76] The specialized expertise required for reclassification remained the domain of a handful of paid union staff and the most intensely active members, but the information generated by these analyses empowered a much wider circle of unionists who deployed this knowledge in everyday organizing and bargaining to improve their working conditions. On the whole, the trend toward greater gender equity under the

NWLB revealed the potential for harnessing the administrative apparatus of labor relations to serve the interests of workers.[77]

Reclassification, of course, had its limits as a tool for combatting gender discrimination. Although it could ensure that women in clerical and para-professional roles received compensation in line with the actual administrative and support tasks performed, it could not open opportunities for advancement into professional and supervisory positions. At Time Inc., women activists also demanded new contract language guaranteeing women equal opportunity for promotion. College-educated women employed as researchers for the firm's magazines led the charge. As a November 1945 management memorandum regarding procedures for *Fortune* asserted, "except for literary quality, all the writer's responsibilities are shared by the researcher on a senior-junior partnership basis." It was the researcher's duty to ensure the "thoroughness and quality of the research and reporting," management continued, that made the "writer-researcher team" so "unique" and gave "*Fortune* its authority." Yet this collaboration at the core of Time Inc.'s vaunted "group journalism" was explicitly a gendered division of creative labor.[78] As *Life* researcher and Newspaper Guild negotiator Gertrude Epstein contended during a January 1946 bargaining session, "it is our feeling that the presumption on which a woman gets a job and is promoted is a different one than in the case of many men who come to work in the editorial department." While there was "a systematic policy of giving the male researchers a break and letting them try their hand at writing early in the game, say after three months," she continued, no woman could become a writer on *Life* "unless she proves herself over a period of many years," so the handful of women writers—just over 10 percent of the writing staff on Time Inc. publications—were "extreme exceptions." Consequently, the union sought a formal process to guarantee that people were "given the opportunity for a promotion on the basis of qualification and not on the basis of sex, which is the way it often is now."[79]

From the other side of the bargaining table, Time's labor relations chief Louis Gratz responded with precisely the kind of flagrant sexism that Epstein and her fellow unionists were fighting against. He bluntly asserted that there were far fewer women than men who were qualified to write for the firm's magazines, and that the firm had had "poor experience" with the "women who have had an opportunity to write." For every "woman that makes the grade" as a writer, Gratz continued, "there are two hundred that don't." To the extent that they encountered prejudice, "the people who have created the prejudice are the girls themselves." The appalled Guild negotiators offered multiple refutations of Gratz's ludicrous claims. "We are not saying you have to wind up with a statistical proportion," Epstein explained. "All we want to do is create an atmosphere in which the women who are qualified will have as much opportunity to advance as the men who are qualified." As she pointed out, "the prestige of writing is so much greater than that of researching, whereas actually in the final production of the story, the researchers may have done much more of the creative work than the writer whose only relation to it may be of counseling on her work," but "she gets no recognition at all for the process of creating the story."[80] Unfortunately, Epstein and the other women at Time Inc. failed to obtain through collective bargaining the equal opportunity clause that they sought from management. A quarter of a century would pass before a new generation of women at the media giant would press the demand for equal opportunity with as much vigor. Nonetheless, the resolve that Epstein and her colleagues demonstrated in their attempt to break through the barriers of overt discrimination suggested that white-collar women in New York's culture industries had reached a heightened level of feminist consciousness by the 1940s.

This new assertiveness by white-collar women sustained one of the longest and most arduous unionization drives in the city's culture industries, as employees of Parents Institute struggled for eight years to organize with the UOPWA Book and Magazine Guild. While these women labored to produce highly influential representations and discourses of femininity in the American mass media, they also fought tenaciously for the economic means necessary to sustain their personal autonomy and fulfillment. Founded in 1926 as a research and publishing consortium sponsored by Columbia University Teachers College, Yale University, the University of Minnesota, and the University of Iowa, Parents Institute furnished authoritative expertise on family and educational matters. Under the management of publisher George Hecht, it became a thriving commercial enterprise, with its flagship *Parents Magazine*, educational trade periodicals, and a growing roster of magazines targeted at children and adolescents. Through its various publications, Parents Institute marketed a carefully tempered version of liberal pedagogy and domestic ideology designed to attract both a mass following of middle-class readers and corporate advertisers, eventually earning it the enmity of Consumers Union and other Popular Front consumer groups. During the Second World War, Parents embarked upon an ambitious expansion that included the launching in 1941 of a new magazine, *Calling All Girls*, which pioneered the teenage female magazine genre. Within two years it attained a monthly circulation of more than 400,000 issues, and by the end of 1946 its circulation neared the 1 million mark. Its success inspired competitors, most notably *Seventeen*, which first appeared in 1944. Although tame enough to offend neither parents nor advertisers, *Calling All Girls* still included progressive fare such as a series on fashion by feminist designer and union organizer Elizabeth Hawes in 1943 alongside features on bobbysoxer heartthrobs like Frank Sinatra.[81]

Parents Institute had provided greater opportunities than most publishers for women to advance into editorial and supervisory positions. Clara Savage Littledale, who in 1913 had become the very first woman reporter for the *New York Post*, had served as the editor-in-chief of *Parents Magazine* since its founding and was a vice president of the institute by the 1940s, while Frances Ullman DeArmand became the first editor-in-chief of *Calling All Girls* and was largely responsible for its rapid success. For most of the women employed in support and clerical roles, however, working conditions at Parents Institute remained poor, even as circulation and revenues grew. The Book and Magazine Guild recruited its first members at Parents in 1939 and 1940 during the union's campaign for a five-day workweek for all publishing workers. During the wartime expansion, as real salaries declined due to price inflation, the pace of organizing gradually gained momentum. By February 1944, a slender majority of workers had signed authorization cards, prompting the union to petition the NLRB for a certification election. Supporters hoped that a victory at Parents could be the kind of dramatic breakthrough at a large firm that would pave the way for organizing other mass-market magazine publishers like Macfadden and give new impetus to the union's organizing toeholds inside of huge book publishers like Doubleday and Macmillan.[82]

Hecht responded with a series of anti-union measures, including mandatory meetings where he and other top managers lectured workers on the evils of unionization and threatened to fire union activists. He cynically applied for a salary increase with the NWLB after the union had filed for an election and then blamed the union for preventing the raises from being implemented, even though it was federal labor law that prevented such moves during the run-up to an election in order to ensure a fair vote free of managerial attempts to manipulate the outcome. Hecht also hired notorious anti-labor attorney Walter Gordon Merritt, who ingeniously subverted the NLRB process and delayed the election. When an election finally occurred on June 1, after months of stalling, the union was defeated by a crushing 169–42 margin. The union subsequently filed charges of widespread unfair labor practices with the NLRB and requested that the vote be set aside, but Board examiner Charles T. Douds petulantly replied that "the charges are piecemeal and would compel exhaustive investigation." In October, the UOPWA yielded to pressure and withdrew its charges.[83]

Over the next several years, a core of pro-union women at Parents kept the organizing impulse alive. Although the publisher doubled its workforce between 1944 and 1947, salaries remained inadequate and pay inequities abounded in the absence of a union contract. A new UOPWA organizing committee, headed by Annette Turngren, an assistant editor for *Calling All Girls*, signed up a narrow majority of the staff, leading the union to petition for a second certification election. Borrowing a tactic used by women in other offices, union supporters staged repeated mass water cooler breaks at work in order to disrupt production and challenge managerial authority. Hecht's reaction to the new union push was even nastier than in 1944. In another round of captive meetings in early 1947—including one convened just an hour before the start of balloting on March 6—he attacked the union as a Communist front, slandered the 42 Parents employees on the organizing committee as "paid outside agitators," and threatened them with termination. As before, the intimidation precipitated another defeat in the March election, albeit by a much closer margin of 256–213. The union immediately filed unfair labor practice charges with the NLRB, and activists began a daring strike for recognition on March 24.[84]

Not surprisingly, the largest strike to date by the staff of a magazine publisher proved to be a highly contentious affair. Littledale, DeArmand, and six other editors who sympathized with the union refused to cross the picket line outside the institute's offices or to perform their managerial duties, crippling the production of magazine content even though roughly half of the staff remained on the job. Hecht was livid, accusing the eight of disloyalty and violating the principle of management unity. His attempts at replacing them during the strike were confounded as potential new hires backed out when they learned about the dispute. As Littledale recounted, "it was heartening, the way a man who had been managing editor of the *Elks Magazine*, for instance, called, explained he had been ill, had a wife and two children and needed work desperately," but declared, " 'I need a job, but I don't need a job so much that I'm willing to be a strikebreaker.'"[85] Numerous contributors to the institute's magazines, including Frederic March, who had just won an Academy Award for *The Best Years of Our Lives*, withdrew articles slated for publication to show solidarity. When the NLRB voided the election results on account of Hecht's conduct, Turngren hailed the ruling as proof that the union's "strike to end threats and intimidation was justified," while Hecht denounced it as an "astonishing" violation of "freedom of speech for employers."[86] Finally, on May 2, the New York State Mediation Board brokered a truce between the strikers and Hecht in which all employees who had been away from their jobs—the striking union members along with the eight supportive editors—were to return "without prejudice," salaries were to be increased by 10 to 20 percent, but union recognition was deferred pending the possible scheduling of yet another certification election.[87]

Hecht immediately violated the terms of the arrangement by firing DeArmand and several of the other editors who had refused to cross the picket line, as well as some of the most outspoken unionists. Additional firings of union supporters occurred in the coming weeks. Yet there was scant possibility that the strikers could have achieved a better outcome given the paucity of resources at their disposal. Despite the progressive rhetoric of the UOPWA and the genuine opportunities for women activists within the union, it still followed a double standard on gender when it came to allocating its limited funds. Major strikes and organizing initiatives involving groups of predominately male workers tended to receive greater financial backing from the national union than ones involving mostly female workers; in the case of the Parents strike, the national UOPWA furnished only a pitiful $7.30 from its Organizing and Defense Fund to support the struggle. Although organizers from the national union staff were quite active in the strike, the financial burden rested entirely on the local, which lacked the resources to provide even minimal strike benefits. The willingness of the strikers to stay out for six weeks under such difficult circumstances demonstrated their determination and resolve.[88]

Not only did the disappointing conclusion of the Parents strike frustrate their efforts to support an autonomous lifestyle, but it also diminished the influence that progressive women on the institute's editorial staff could exert over the discourses of femininity and domesticity that were propagated in its magazines. Even before the strike, *Parents Magazine* had increasingly committed to an ideological valorization of traditional gender roles that both reflected and reinforced the trends evident in postwar American society and culture. Echoing the blatantly antifeminist sentiments expressed by Ferdinand Lundberg and Marynia Farnham in their bestselling *Modern Woman: The Lost Sex* (1947), Vassar College anthropologist Dorothy Lee asserted in a typical article from the January 1947 issue of *Parents* that women needed to unlearn their previous work experiences outside of the home in order to properly appreciate their innate calling as mothers and homemakers. "In the classroom, in the office, in the factory," Lee claimed, "we all learned standards of efficiency." Yet many women felt "dissatisfaction with homemaking" as a result of applying "to the home these standards of the business world." She contended that no job could provide women with genuine satisfaction, even though promoting domesticity on such terms implicitly devalued the work of the women who produced the magazine. In Lee's vision, the vocation of motherhood required women to be actively cultivating democracy through their participation in community groups to combat social ills such as "slums, poor sanitation, unemployment, race discrimination, [and] bad public schooling," but democracy apparently did not require women to have the same access as men to opportunities to earn a decent living or obtain professional fulfillment.[89] The "Mary Xs" active in the white-collar unions in the culture industries—women like Gertrude Epstein and Faith Illiva—seldom appeared in the representations of femininity and domesticity that became increasingly hegemonic in the postwar media.[90]

During the reconversion period, women interested in promoting a labor-feminist alternative to the resurgence of traditionalism came together to establish the Congress of American Women, which drew heavily from the ranks of the white-collar unions and the Popular Front. Participants in the founding of the new organization in the spring of 1946 selected anthropologist Gene Weltfish, who had coauthored the multiculturalist wartime pamphlet *Races of Mankind*, to serve as president, and Josephine Timms, the secretary-treasurer of the CIO-affiliated American Communications Association, as executive secretary. The CAW board of vice presidents included longtime radical activist Elizabeth Gurley Flynn, a member of the Communist Party's national committee, and Ruth Young, the executive secretary of UE District 4 and the first woman to sit on that union's international executive board. The UOPWA represented the small CAW office staff, and within its first months of existence the CAW helped to mobilize public support for several strikes by white-collar women. In addition, Eleanor Flexner, who had previously held educational and organizing positions within the UOPWA, became heavily involved in the development of CAW programming and organizing materials.[91]

Within the CAW, the Commission on the Status of Women, chaired by Susan B. Anthony II, held primary responsibility for formulating a coherent public policy agenda to advance the interests of working women. From the outset, it distinguished its program from the elitist feminism of the National Woman's Party and the National Association of Business and Professional Women by condemning their proposed Equal Rights Amendment (ERA) to the Constitution. CAW activists claimed that the ERA offered women an abstract equality that would be of little use to most of them in their actual material circumstances while disallowing protective legislation, often passed at the state or local level, that addressed the consequences of endemic sexism by providing working women with practical benefits. Instead, the CAW advocated a "Woman's Status Amendment," endorsed by Representative Helen Gahagan Douglas, which stated that "there shall be no economic, legal, political, or social discrimination because of sex or marital status in the United States of America or territories subject to its jurisdiction," while also stipulating that "nothing in this article shall be so construed as to invalidate or prevent the enactment of legislation benefiting women in their work or family status." The Commission's legislative program also included support for the Pepper-Norton Bill for family welfare, which would have provided a permanent program of public child-care for working mothers; endorsement of the Wagner-Murray-Dingell proposal for national health care; a demand that proposals to reestablish a federal-level FEPC also include prohibitions against employment discrimination on the basis of sex as well as race; and backing for plans to extend Social Security coverage to agricultural, domestic, and other occupations with substantial proportions of women workers who were still excluded. In addition, CAW activists assisted women who had lost their jobs as part of the postwar wave of discriminatory layoffs, and deplored the discrimination that blocked career-minded women from admission to many graduate and professional schools.[92]

Besides pushing for a comprehensive program to promote the material conditions conducive to women's social equality and equal employment opportunity, the CAW Commission on the Status of Women assailed the derogatory representations of women that were commonplace within the mainstream culture of consumer capitalism. "A checkup of radio programs, magazine articles, [and] motion pictures," it reported, revealed many "offensive" portrayals. The typical woman was cast as either "an absolute moron, a silly feminist, an illiterate, or a clinging vine totally dependent upon a man," or a housewife capable only of thinking "in terms of her washing, ironing, cooking and sewing." By mobilizing progressive women to apply pressure on the purveyors of popular culture, CAW activists hoped that they could compel the media to begin to represent women like themselves.[93] In their analysis of both the material basis of women's oppression and its cultural manifestations, and their advocacy of a comprehensive program to provide the means for women's autonomy, they anticipated by a generation the movement of the late 1960s and 1970s.

Winning the Peace: The White-Collar Progressives' Postwar Ambitions

"We've Won the War, Let's Win the Peace," exclaimed the banner head-line across the front-page of the "Special V-J Issue" of the UOPWA *Office and Professional News* in August 1945. "The war for freedom and democracy has brought to the world the opportunity to make the peace lasting," the accompanying editorial implored, "but there can be no lasting peace unless the economic causes of war are brought under control. That means that there can be no lasting peace if our country, the most powerful in the world, becomes a land of poverty and hunger and mass unemployment." It was essential that "the program of labor and other forces of the people must be directed in every way to maintaining and expanding the purchasing power" of every segment of the public, particularly "the white-collar and professional workers." Without continued union growth, along with policies for full employment and economic stabilization during the reconversion period, "the future for white-collar workers is a grim one indeed."[94]

The tone of the editorial captured both the bold social-democratic ambitions of the white-collar Popular Front, including the activists in New York's culture-industry unions, and their grave sense of the momentous economic and political stakes in the tumultuous aftermath of the war. White-collar unionists achieved robust gains during the roughly two-year period from V-J Day through the summer of 1947, with total UOPWA membership increasing by more than 50 percent despite layoffs in war industries that eliminated thousands of organized office workers.[95] In New York City, the UOPWA scored important breakthroughs in radio broadcasting and in the engineering and design field, while its existing locals in publishing and in motion pictures consolidated their positions. The Newspaper Guild and the Radio Writers Guild likewise made considerable progress, although the continued recalcitrance of some employers frustrated activists in both of these unions. Within the city's culture industries, only the advertising agencies remained largely union-free.

Although the economic circumstances of most white-collar workers differed in key respects from those of blue-collar workers during the reconversion period, the CIO manufacturing affiliates' high-profile struggles significantly influenced the environment in which the UOPWA and the Newspaper Guild organized. To preserve members' purchasing power, the major CIO affiliates—now freed from the stringent wage controls imposed during the war by the NWLB—proposed a 30 percent increase in basic wage rates to establish a new postwar industrial wage pattern.[96] In doing so, they attempted to lock in the relationship between blue-collar and white-collar earnings that had been established during the peak of wartime demand for manufacturing labor. In March 1944, for instance, workers employed in durable-goods manufacturing earned on average 13.3 percent more per week than workers in the insurance industry; by November 1945, in the midst of reconversion layoffs and on the cusp of the massive postwar strike wave, insurance workers on average made 6.8 percent more per week than workers in durable-goods manufacturing.[97] Consequently, many unorganized white-collar workers did not see themselves as disinterested spectators as the strike wave of 1945–1946 unfolded. From their perspective, the conflict between the industrial unions and corporate giants like GM, GE, and US Steel represented a continuation of their own wartime competition with organized labor over consumption and status.

While this dynamic contributed to the antipathy that many unorganized clerical, sales, technical, and professional workers felt toward the more than five million Americans who walked off the job during the first year of peace, it also affected the white-collar unionists' prospects for improving conditions for their existing members, organizing new members, and taking progressive political action. Most white-collar workers did not experience any significant change in their working hours with the end of the war, nor, with the exception of clerical and technical workers in the offices of wartime manufacturing plants, did they experience a significant wave of reconversion layoffs. Unlike blue-collar workers, who fought to preserve their wartime levels of weekly earnings, white-collar workers sought gains to make up for their comparatively stagnant earnings since 1941. In late 1945 and early 1946, most of the white-collar CIO unions in New York opened the first postwar round of collective bargaining by demanding a 20 percent general pay increase. "The difference in the 20 percent that we ask and the 30 percent that basic industry is asking," the Newspaper Guild's Irving Gilman explained to Time Inc. management in January 1946, "rises out of the same motivation, to maintain a parity of the dollar value with what it was prior to the war and also to recapture as nearly as possible the take-home pay of the people in that industry." White-collar workers, Gilman continued, "have not basically suffered a cut in take-home pay because of the fact that we didn't work excessive amounts of overtime and didn't have unusual premium pay for work performed."[98]

Despite notable exceptions like the bitter walkout by telegram clerks and operators at Western Union in early 1946, most of the white-collar CIO unions in New York reached contract settlements with major employers in the first postwar round of collective bargaining without resorting to strike action. While the unions in many cases accepted more modest pay hikes than they had demanded, in percentage terms they tended to be roughly equivalent to the eighteen-and-a-half cents per hour increase that emerged as the first-round bargaining pattern for the CIO manufacturing affiliates. Among the most important of these settlements was the deal reached in February 1946 between the Newspaper Guild of New York and the *New York Times*, *Daily News*, *World-Telegram*, *Journal-American*, and *Daily Mirror* that covered more than 4,500 clerical, sales, and creative workers. The agreement, which fulfilled the local's longstanding objective of setting a citywide pattern, provided a 22 percent average increase in the minimum pay schedule as well as a general increase of 13 percent. As part of the pattern settlement, the *Times*, which remained the largest employer in the Guild's jurisdiction, acceded to the continuation of maintenance of membership despite its fierce opposition when it was first mandated by the NWLB.[99]

For some existing UOPWA locals in New York's culture industries, the commitment of limited resources to new organizing initiatives weakened their position at the bargaining table. In October 1946, after lengthy negotiations the UOPWA Screen Office and Professional Employees Guild reached a two-year master agreement that covered close to 4,000 employees in the New York offices of Columbia Pictures, Loew's-MGM, Movietone News, National Screen Service, Paramount, Republic Pictures, RKO, Twentieth Century-Fox, and United Artists. Only a few firms with which the local had already negotiated contracts, such as William Morris Agency, Warner Brothers, and Universal, remained outside the new pattern. The master agreement, which included a continuation of the reclassification program and the maintenance of membership provision, awarded workers an average general pay increase of 15 percent. Starting minimum salaries for the lowest clerical classifications still ranged from $25 to $32 per week, while minimums for the middle clerical grades ran from $33 to $43. Although the terms were comparable to the citywide pattern negotiated by the Newspaper Guild earlier in the year, the inflationary spurt during the summer had eroded much of these raises' value by the fall. Despite the dissatisfaction of many rank-and-file members within SOPEG, the determination of the UOPWA to concentrate on organizing new members in the promising economic climate of reconversion led the national union to squelch a strike mobilization for higher pay by one of its larger established locals.[100]

Among the major firms in New York's culture industries that had already been organized, Time Inc. was one of the most obstinate during the first postwar round of collective bargaining. As discussions of a new contract be-tween the Newspaper Guild and the company began in November 1945, the union looked to leverage its strengthened wartime position to win substantial enhancements in salaries and conditions. Guild activists hoped that an im-pressive contract could lift the bar in the union's negotiations with *Newsweek*, *Look*, and the other magazines already within its jurisdiction, as well as at-tract employees of the city's many unorganized magazines. Moreover, Time Inc. was in no position to argue that it was too poor to afford the terms that the Guild was seeking. The company's flagship publication, *Life*, had reached a weekly circulation of nearly 4 million by 1945, nearly overtaking rival *Saturday Evening Post*, the nation's top general interest weekly. Despite wartime restrictions on paper utilization, the annual net pages of advertising in *Life* nearly doubled between 1939 and 1945, while the quantity of adver-tising in *Time* leapt by almost 50 percent over the same period. Net profits for Time Inc. did actually slip slightly from $3.75 million in 1941 to just over $3 million in 1945, but the return to peacetime conditions pointed to rapid growth in profits in the coming years. The Guild's opening proposal to the company contained the same 20 percent general salary increase and union security provisions as its proposals to the daily newspapers, along with spe-cific provisions to promote equal opportunity and codify employees' rights to engage in outside activities. In addition, the Guild requested an expansion of the bargaining unit, which at the time contained roughly 600 employees in the editorial departments, to include nearly 1,000 employees in the New York commercial departments.[101]

Time management flatly rejected the Guild's initial proposal, and in doing so set forth a vision of creative labor within the company that was fundamen-tally at odds with that of the unionists. "The reputation that Time, Inc. has built," Gratz insisted, "attracts ambitious, energetic, intelligent persons," who "know that they have the best opportunity to achieve advancement and to be well paid in their chosen field," as well as to "develop ideas, their energies, and their minds to further their careers." As he depicted it, employment at Time was, for members of its creative elite, an endeavor that transcended the realm of necessity. The fact that "last year we interviewed approximately nine thou-sand people for jobs" simply affirmed his assessment, and in no way reflected the vicissitudes and structural inequalities inherent in the markets for var-ious occupational skills. Only flexibility, and not the new constraints that the union was attempting to impose, Gratz contended, could ensure that freedom for both management and employees would continue.[102] Time management also advanced counterproposals designed to reclaim certain prerogatives and roll back the union's influence in several crucial areas. To diminish the Guild's appeal to the better-paid writers, photographers, editors, and other creative professionals within the bargaining unit, the company refused to extend any general increases to employees already earning over $100 per week. The "cut-off" would make them entirely dependent on merit raises awarded by management on an individual basis. Also, management requested the exclusion from the existing bargaining unit of nearly forty non–executive editors, bureau heads, and department heads, including many longtime Guild stalwarts, even though these positions had previously been deemed eligible for union membership.[103]

No issue, however, divided the Guild and Time management more deeply than union security. Management rejected the Guild's proposal for a union shop, as it had in every round of collective bargaining since the 1930s, but also insisted on the elimination of maintenance of membership as mandated in 1944 by the NWLB. Even as publisher Henry Luce lent his name and support to the National Committee to Aid the Families of General Motors Strikers, his executives endeavored to strip his organized employees of the same union security measures that the UAW was fighting to preserve. Although 340 editorial employees signed a public petition demanding the continuation of maintenance of membership, management refused to budge.[104] By the end of March 1946, negotiations had completely deadlocked over union security. The Guild responded by staging a series of highly visible rallies outside the corporate headquarters, running advertisements in several newspapers, and sponsoring several five-minute broadcasts on local radio condemning the company's intransigence. In an attempt to undermine the unionists' resolve, Time president Roy Larsen announced that employees in the unorganized commercial departments would immediately be receiving general salary increases in accordance with management's most recent proposal, insinuating that the Guild was preventing editorial employees from sharing in the raises. As in 1941 following Anna Goldsborough's firing, Guild activists responded to the provocations by mobilizing for a strike. "I do know we're in a fight and that we have to close ranks and hold firm," wrote Time journalist Theodore White to Guild unit chair Gertrude Epstein, but if the union surrendered, "it is being weakened and forced backwards." Although he hoped "with all my heart that we won't have to strike," he recognized, like hundreds of his colleagues, that "it's the only tool we have left."[105]

At the end of a three-hour membership meeting on May 2, an overwhelming majority of 248 to 40 voted in favor of a resolution that authorized a strike as well as the use of state and federal mediation in the hopes of compelling Time management to sign a contract that included some form of union security. "The issue is simple," declared *Time* journalist and strike supporter Penn Kimball at the meeting; "we vote for our self-respect." Their strong desire for union security was rooted in their everyday experiences of supervisory discipline, and the intimidation and harassment that some members still experienced on account of their union support, particularly in the commercial departments. Guild leaders worried that if the union accepted a contract without at least maintenance of membership it would jeopardize the emerging bargaining pattern, as other organized publishers would undoubtedly seek similar terms moving forward, and unorganized publishers might stiffen their resistance to new unionization efforts. At the same time, activists at Time and local leaders alike had doubts about whether a protracted strike could force the deep-pocketed company to relent, or whether adequate financial support could be arranged from the national union. On May 13, mediators persuaded Guild negotiators to accept an arrangement that swapped maintenance of membership for a voluntary dues check-off provision and arbitration regarding resignations from the Guild. Other important issues of contention, such as the equal opportunity clause sought by women on the staff, the upper boundary of the bargaining unit, and the granting of general pay increases to employees in the upper salary ranges above the cut-off were left unaddressed when the full agreement was finalized over the summer.[106]

While the outcome of the first postwar bargaining round at Time Inc. demonstrated that resolute corporate power could stymie even an experienced and established cadre of white-collar unionists, new organizing breakthroughs were still possible at some of the larger corporate employers in New York's culture industries. The success of the UOPWA in introducing its brand of unionism into the New York headquarters of the radio networks was particularly promising for white-collar progressives, given the networks' economic clout and enormous cultural influence. By the 1940s, the networks were the most potent oligopoly in the culture industries; only four firms— NBC, CBS, ABC, and Mutual—offered programming over a nationwide network of stations. Between 1935 and 1945, radio doubled its share of all advertising expenditures from 17 percent to 34 percent, with the networks accounting for roughly half of that figure, or about $190 million annually from the sale of airtime.[107] Within the corporate entities that dominated network radio, legions of white-collar creative, professional, technical, and clerical workers labored to turn out a constant stream of content. The spread of talent guilds like the RWG and the American Federation of Radio Artists (AFRA), and the organization of technicians involved in the transmission of broadcast signals into craft unions like the International Brotherhood of Electrical Workers (IBEW), had resulted in piecemeal organization of the workforce, with the majority of network employees excluded from the benefits of collective bargaining. As the networks' unorganized employees saw the gains made by the writers, performers, and broadcast engineers and technicians, they formed salary committees late in the war to petition the NWLB. These committees constituted the nucleus of support for the UOPWA, and in September 1945 the union's members publicly announced the creation of the UOPWA Radio Guild to organize all workers at the four networks who did not already belong to the technical craft unions or talent guilds.[108]

As the UOPWA drive progressed, it benefitted from the support of other organized creative personnel, both inside and outside the networks. Members of the UOPWA Screen Publicists Guild held a series of social mixers with their counterparts in the networks' promotional and public relations departments. Writers and directors also proved to be valuable allies, particularly at CBS. Myra Jordan's role as head of the CBS organizing committee was made easier by the support she enjoyed from her immediate supervisor, highly rated news commentator and RWG activist William Shirer. Another RWG activist with CBS, respected writer and director Norman Corwin, as well as Leo Hurwitz, a director in the network's embryonic television studio, also encouraged unorganized white-collar employees to join the UOPWA. The union applied for certification at CBS at the end of 1945, but managerial resistance, along with the intervention of several AFL affiliates, led to NLRB hearings that delayed an election. In May 1946, the Board finally approved the bargaining unit requested by the UOPWA and directed an election for more than 700 creative, professional, technical, and clerical workers. Scores of members from other UOPWA locals in New York pitched in with the election organizing by visiting CBS employees at home in the evenings to share their positive experiences with unionization. When the vote was held in June, the UOPWA defeated its rivals and established itself as a force to be reckoned with in the New York hub of the broadcasting industry.[109]

As the prospect of an organizing sweep throughout New York broadcasting appeared increasingly likely, the networks stiffened their resolve. Encouraged by executives at the other networks, CBS management stalled contract negotiations in the hopes of breaking the spirit of union supporters without reaching a first contract settlement. More ominously, NBC intensified its antiunion campaign by firing at least a dozen UOPWA supporters over the summer. The union initially responded by filing unfair labor practice charges, but its inability to get the NLRB to order the workers' immediate reinstatement had a chilling effect on the pace of organizing at NBC as well as at ABC and Mutual. Even after the UOPWA Radio Guild finalized contract terms with several independent stations in New York, CBS still dragged its feet, only agreeing to terms in late November. The final deal with CBS included a 25 percent general increase as well as additional pay boosts through reclassifications and other adjustments, plus union security and individual job security provisions. Although the contract set a model for other broadcasters to follow, it remained unclear whether unionists at NBC, ABC, and Mutual would be able to regain their organizing momentum in the face of dogged management opposition.[110]

Not as glamorous perhaps as the breakthrough in radio was the beachhead the UOPWA attained in large-scale engineering and design with the organization of the professional and technical staff of Ebasco Services. A large design operation with several hundred employees, Ebasco Services was a subsidiary of Electric Bond and Share, the world's largest utilities conglomerate. The design subsidiary performed not only in-house work for the parent company's far-flung utility and infrastructure projects but also produced designs and plans for domestic projects by major corporate clients such as retailer R. H. Macy & Co. A group of Ebasco employees began organizing with the FAECT in late 1945, and in March 1946 the union surprised its AFL rival, Architectural Guild Local 66, and the Ebasco management by petitioning the NLRB for a certification election. In the balloting in April, shortly after the FAECT merged with the UOPWA, it handily defeated both the AFL and the opponents of unionism.[111]

Despite the election victory, Ebasco management resisted granting recognition to the union, now part of the UOPWA as Local 231. Only after unfair labor practice rulings from the NLRB, a strike authorization vote by the membership, and solidarity actions by unionized workers at several of Electric Bond and Share's Latin American subsidiaries did management agree to a one-year contract in September 1946. The first contract included raises of 15 percent retroactive to June, with salary arbitration provisions that awarded additional gains to many Ebasco employees in January 1947. Activists in the local hoped that their success would provide the catalyst for a new wave of organizing in New York's expanding architectural, design and engineering firms. In a number of small- and medium-sized firms headed by progressive architects who acceded to their employees' wishes for union recognition, Local 231 was able to establish collective bargaining relations in 1946 and early 1947. Executives with the other large-scale design firms in the city, however, reacted to the union victory at Ebasco by intensifying their resistance to unionism.[112]

Although workers in radio, design, newspapers, magazines, and motion pictures continued to demonstrate their receptiveness to unionism, the advertising agencies remained the one critical segment of the culture industries seemingly impervious to organization. In the summer of 1946, the UOPWA reconstituted Advertising Guild Local 20 to commence a new drive among commercial artists and designers, copywriters, publicists, and clerical staff employed by the agencies. Following the other white-collar unions in New York's culture industries, the Ad Guild's program called for extended vacations, a thirty-five-hour workweek, automatic yearly raises, the implementation of classification, merit, and seniority systems, and the elimination of sexual and racial discrimination. As one pamphlet exhorted, agency employees needed to band together, "just as movie actors and bookkeepers, press agents and filing clerks, scientists and stenographers!" Like the radio workers who had "taken their first steps to security and freedom through the Radio Guild at Columbia Broadcasting System," and the members of the Newspaper Guild who "took these steps in their stride long ago," ad workers needed to "get in step" with a union "organized by and for all advertising workers—creative, clerical, and production."[113] Despite its compelling pitch, the postwar Ad Guild was only able to win recognition at several smaller agencies during the reconversion period. The union apparently signed up about seventy-five employees at a medium-sized agency in early 1947, but the employers' use of surveillance and infiltration by antiunion operatives from American Business Consultants helped to defeat the organizing effort.[114]

On the whole the white-collar unionists in New York's culture industries enjoyed a moderate degree of organizing success during the reconversion period, but their hopes for advancing progressive politics at the national level were dashed.[115] The relationship between earnings and prices—a source of political polarization during the war—only became more divisive in the run-up to the 1946 midterm elections. Most of the settlements reached by major CIO and AFL unions during the first half of 1946 were predicated on price increases, which put increasing strain on the system of controls administered by the OPA. Manufacturers joined with farmers and food processors to lobby Congress for the relaxation of price controls. Although the white-collar unions and progressive groups like the NCPAC, ICCASP, and CAW joined with the rest of the labor movement and consumers' organizations in an all-out crusade to maintain effective controls, Congress ultimately voted to gut the OPA.[116] The relaxation of controls at the end of June sparked an immediate spike in inflation. The BLS consumer price index, which had only risen 3.1 percent between V-J Day and June 1946, shot up 15 percent in the second half of the year.[117] Not only did the inflationary surge cancel out most of the gains unionists attained in the first round of postwar collective bargaining, it also dealt a serious blow to the possibility that wartime social consumerism would be permanently embedded in the peacetime polity. Never again would progressives have access to a regulatory tool with such potential for fundamentally reshaping America's culture of consumer capitalism.

The chaotic lifting of price controls and the ensuing inflationary spiral added to the already sour mood of the electorate. The NAM, the Chamber of Commerce, the Ad Council, and other business groups mounted a massive publicity drive that shrewdly conflated the democratic rights and liberties for which Americans had fought and sacrificed during the war with conservative ideological tenets, including opposition to government regulation of markets, public programs for economic security, and, of course, trade unionism.[118] This message found a receptive audience among millions of Americans who aspired to middle-class status and who bristled at the postwar strike wave, the fitful process of domestic reconversion, and the modestly elevated social standing of women and African Americans during the war. While conservative voters grew increasingly energized in the run-up to the 1946 midterm elections, pro-labor and progressive constituencies were in disarray. Despite the efforts of the ICCASP, NCPAC, and unions like the UOPWA to convince white-collar voters to back progressive candidates, this segment of the electorate increasingly lined up behind the Republicans. Meanwhile, among blue-collar voters, frustration with the Truman administration, including its coolness toward the labor movement, made many indifferent to the electioneering of the CIO-PAC. Although six million more Americans voted in November 1946 than in the previous midterm elections, when the ballots were tallied the Republicans had gained control over both houses of Congress. In New York, despite the success of the CIO and its Popular Front allies in mobilizing urban voters, a deluge of Republican votes from rural and suburban areas assured Governor Thomas Dewey's reelection. By any measure, the midterms were a disaster for progressives.[119]

The backlash against the progressives' political agenda was fueled primarily by the economic pressures and social tumult of the war and reconversion period, but it was also driven by the renewed virulence of anticommunist sentiments. Although the wartime alliance with the Soviets had temporarily dampened public antagonism toward avowed Communists and the redbaiting of progressive organizations and causes, anticommunism was resurgent by late

1946. The fate of the People's Radio Foundation—one of the most important cultural initiatives of New York's Popular Front during the 1940s—furnished one indication of the rapid intensification of anticommunism in the months surrounding the midterm elections. After eighteen months of organizing and fundraising, the PRF had a well-developed plan for station operations and programming by the time that FCC hearings for the first FM broadcasting licenses commenced in July 1946. The PRF would, according to a solicitation from the ICCASP, "not only champion all democratic rights, but would serve as a channel for those liberal groups heretofore prevented from obtaining 'freedom of the air.'" It represented "many trade unions, fraternal organizations, and minority groups who have been unable to find their needed place in the radio world," and who finally had a shot at winning "one of the five available channels, thus defeating such applicants as the *Daily News*, the Hearst press, etc. . . . if they can rally popular support."[120]

Backers of the PRF also hoped to capitalize on the wave of public interest in radio reform. As part of their efforts to obtain airtime and fight against the National Association of Broadcasters' restrictive code of conduct, labor and progressive groups had started contesting the license renewals for existing AM stations that had consistently denied them access. Other reform-minded listeners challenged license renewals for stations that aired excessive quantities of advertising. In response to public pressure, in March 1946 the FCC issued a report, formally titled *Public Service Responsibility of Broadcast Licensees* but known colloquially as the "Blue Book," which strongly criticized existing industry practices. It affirmed the desirability of diversity in station ownership, the value of live programming originating within local communities, and the importance of maintaining a wide range of programs, including ones that might not attract commercial sponsorship.[121] Evaluated in terms of the criteria established in the Blue Book, the PRF could claim to be a strong applicant on account of its varied and innovative programming and its diverse array of owners. After the hearings concluded, the PRF moved forward to develop programming as it awaited the decision of the FCC. On several occasions in late 1946 and early 1947, the PRF staged public performances, complete with remote broadcasting equipment, of its socially conscious dramas on topics such as lynching and atomic warfare in order to continue to build support and facilitate fundraising.[122]

Meanwhile, the NAB, along with many station owners and advertisers, vehemently denounced the Blue Book's recommendations and attacked both the FCC and the progressive advocates of broadcasting reform as subversive threats to free enterprise. For the PRF, the intensified scrutiny proved to be particularly damaging. While the *Daily News*, the Scripps-Howard owned *World-Telegram*, and the Hearst-owned *Journal-American* had publicized the procommunist associations of some of the Foundation's key figures since its inception, these attacks escalated as the FCC hearings drew near. The PRF fought back, most notably by using the hearings to argue that the racist and anti-Semitic reportage common in the *Daily News* should disqualify the paper from receiving an FM license, but the FCC commissioners found themselves compelled to examine the Foundation's procommunist links. Investigators from the House Committee on Un-American Activities furnished the FCC with their files on many of the individuals and organizations involved with the PRF. The probing by the FCC provided the embattled agency with a convenient opportunity to deflect the media campaign to portray it as subversive, although it also set a dangerous precedent for making an applicant's political beliefs a legitimate criterion for approval or denial. In April 1947, when the FCC announced its first round of allocations of FM broadcast licenses, the application from PRF was one of the dozen that it rejected.[123]

The PRF still hoped to receive a license in a second round of allocations by the FCC, but it quickly became clear to the Foundation's supporters that no group with its political complexion could attain permission to broadcast over the public airwaves at the dawning of the Cold War. In October, its directors voted to dissolve the PRF, ending the possibility that the Popular Front social movement might establish a radio analogue to *Friday* magazine that could propagate progressive political and cultural content while providing an alternative site of cultural production and creative employment outside of the circuits of consumer capitalism.[124] More ominously, it showed just how quickly during 1946 and 1947 the procommunist affinities of certain elements of the Popular Front went from being mere liabilities to insurmountable obstacles to organizational growth. By the early 1950s, the ferocity of the anticommunist attacks would make the bold ambitions of progressives in the culture industries during the reconversion period seem a distant memory.

6

The Cold War in New York's Culture Industries

ON APRIL 8, 1952, Everett Rosenthal, the executive producer of the NBC primetime television series *Treasury Men in Action*, summoned writer Abram Ginnes into his office. "It has hit you, Abe," Rosenthal informed him. "The usual. Like Arnold." With that, Ginnes suddenly found himself out of a job. The quality of his scripts had not been the issue, as Rosenthal's firm, Prockter Productions, had recently given Ginnes additional assignments for the series. Instead, like his former colleague Arnold Perl, he was fired on account of his progressive politics. Rosenthal admitted to Ginnes that he had been pressured by the Borden Company, which sponsored *Treasury Men in Action*, and its advertising agency, Young and Rubicam. Although Rosenthal claimed that he deplored the circumstances, he insisted that he had no choice. In addition to Perl and Ginnes, during 1951 and 1952 the company dismissed writers Allan Sloane, Jack Bentkover, Ernest Kinoy, and Sheldon Stark, as well as directors David Pressman and Daphne Elliot, along with dozens of actors, due to allegations of subversion leveled by anticommunist activists.[1]

Such efforts to police the political activities of the creative class were common throughout the culture industries from the late 1940s through the end of the 1950s. Within the broadcast media, hundreds of actors, performers, writers, and directors, along with other craft, technical, and professional personnel involved in the production and distribution of radio and television programming, lost their jobs or were denied employment—blacklisted—on account of their links to the Popular Front. Hundreds more in the Hollywood motion picture industry found their careers ruined completely or put on hiatus for as long as ten or fifteen years. Numerous progressives who worked in the print media, the art and design fields, or in education likewise found their employment prospects adversely affected by their political activism. Even clerical workers in the culture industries were not immune, as CBS proved in January 1951 when it fired a secretary who refused to sign the loyalty oath that the network introduced as part of its new "security" program.[2] Some of these men and women were blacklisted after the FBI or witnesses testifying before Congress had identified them as having belonged to the Communist Party, or after they had refused to answer questions during their own appearances before congressional investigators. The majority, however, had never belonged to the CP, but had supported organizations such as the League of American Writers, the Joint Anti-Fascist Refugee Committee, the Artist's League of America, the People's Radio Foundation, the Civil Rights Congress, or the Congress of American Women. Quite a few had supported Henry Wallace's 1948 presidential campaign as the candidate of the Progressive Party. Many were also blacklisted on account of their militant unionism, including their vocal opposition to the practice of blacklisting.

This political inquisition within the culture industries became one of the defining features of the early years of the domestic Cold War. Actors, directors, writers, artists, journalists, and other creative professionals who were targeted by the anticommunist crusade often emphasized the inviolability of their civil liberties.[3] Sympathetic chroniclers of their ordeals have generally recapitulated their focus on individuals' prerogatives to harbor their own personal political beliefs.[4] Less charitable commentators have impugned the motives and integrity of those whom they held insufficiently strident in their condemnations of Stalinist totalitarianism.[5] Partisans in these continuing public debates over anticommunism have tended to frame the era in moralistic terms, with "the judges and judged" fighting to defend their competing conceptions of freedom.

Frequently obscured in these portrayals is the extent to which blacklisting was part of a larger struggle for control over the means of cultural production. The firing of Ginnes and his colleagues constituted just one of many examples of the assertive tactics used by employers in a series of ongoing contests over labor relations, political economy, and creative autonomy during the period. After a decade and a half in which progressives had instantiated themselves within the culture industries, through expanding white-collar unions, alternative media projects that criticized consumer capitalism, experiments with noncommercial forms of cultural patronage, and sporadic interventions by sympathetic federal officials, the surging tide of domestic anticommunism shifted the balance of power decisively in favor of management. In the environment of the early Cold War, executives of consumer goods manufacturers, advertising agencies, broadcasters, and mass-circulation print media were able to cripple the progressive movements within the creative class. The UOPWA, which remained under procommunist leadership, was annihilated, while unions like the Newspaper Guild were quarantined within their existing jurisdictions. Business interests used their dominance over the media to discredit proposals for expanding government programs, thereby dashing any hopes for the resumption of publicly supported cultural production. Within the ranks of progressives themselves, divisions between those who wished to continue Popular Front alliances and those who insisted on anticommunism as a test of political orthodoxy ruptured the personal and institutional linkages that had sustained their political and cultural initiatives prior to the late 1940s.

Prockter Productions' blacklisting typified the corporate counteroffensive in the culture industries. All six writers dismissed for their progressive politics had been active members of the Radio Writers Guild, which in 1948 had persuaded Prockter to sign a letter of adherence to the union's minimum basic agreement. In addition to committing the firm to matching the minimum salary schedule for comparable writers employed directly by the networks, the letter of adherence provided job security for regular writers, a joint arbitration board for grievances, and guarantees of writers' subsidiary and residual rights for their scripts. While Prockter took advantage of the rapid expansion of television, the firm's success depended on a core of highly talented writers and directors. Perl, Prockter's most prominent writer prior to blacklisting, had helped make the television version of *The Big Story*, a series which dramatized the efforts of newspaper journalists on the crime beat to advance the cause of justice, often through investigative reporting that exonerated those wrongfully accused, into one of the top-rated programs on NBC in 1949. He also contributed to the development of *Treasury Men in Action* and *Police Story*, which also became lucrative properties for Prockter. Pressman, a solidly progressive member of the Radio and Television Directors Guild (RTDG), devised innovative techniques in his work on *Treasury Men in Action* that combined scenes performed live in the studio with filmed sequences into a seamless program.[6]

Despite these writers and directors' high salaries and creative autonomy, they were not insulated from management's campaign to reassert control. Perl, for example, earned between $750 and $1,000 for each hour-long episode of *The Big Story*; after he was dismissed, Prockter Productions replaced him with writers who received $500 or less per script. By the spring of 1952, as the firm was under pressure from sponsors to jettison Ginnes, Pressman, and others, it began to rely more heavily on writers who were classified as independent contractors. These writers submitted scripts on a "single-shot" basis, without the job security, grievance procedure, or salary scales included in the RWG minimum basic agreement. While Prockter executives insisted on flexibility to react to sponsor complaints about controversial talent, Ginnes, Kinoy, Bentkover, and Stark argued that their blacklisting constituted an attack on union standards that adversely affected all writers, not only those who were denied employment.[7] Ultimately, the ramifications of the turmoil at Prockter, and of similar disturbances throughout the broadcasting, publishing, design, and advertising industries, stretched far beyond the creative class, as these conflicts defined the parameters of America's postwar culture of consumer capitalism.

The Ascent of Anticommunism in the Postwar United States

The potency of the campaign against progressives in the culture industries during the early years of the Cold War derived in large part from the dramatic intensification of anticommunist sentiments in American political life. Fear of Soviet belligerence and principled outrage over Stalinism furnished justifications for anticommunism, but domestic concerns drove its use by business interests and their conservative allies as an exceptionally effective political weapon. Invocations of the Communist menace provided a means for the multifaceted deployment of state power to dismantle the Popular Front. Moreover, the efforts of politicians and government agencies validated a network of professional anticommunists and conservative grassroots organizations, whose activism amplified the official crusade against subversion. Even as the anticommunist wave of the late 1940s put supporters of the Popular Front on the defensive, progressive political activism hardly ceased. The political situation still remained highly volatile, and the 1948 elections demonstrated that the social-democratic agenda of the CIO could still garner widespread public approval. Yet even as the Popular Front continued to mobilize its remaining adherents, by the end of the decade it was badly overmatched, fending off attacks from conservatives as well as anticommunist liberals.

Business interests eager to check the power of organized labor and roll back the New Deal harnessed the political power of anticommunism as part of their successful push in 1947 for new labor legislation from the Republican-led Congress. The NAM had long advocated revisions to the

National Labor Relations Act that would curtail the rights and protections that it provided for unions and pro-union workers, and Republicans incorporated many of the business lobby's proposals into the bill sponsored by Senator Robert Taft of Ohio and Representative Fred Hartley of New Jersey. Passed over President Truman's veto in June, the new law fundamentally altered the legal environment in which labor unions operated.[8] It redefined unfair labor practices, which had previously referred only to prohibited conduct by employers, such as the intimidation or firing of pro-union workers, or refusal to bargain with a certified union. Employers could now bring charges against unions for a range of activities, including participation in secondary strikes and boycotts, which essentially criminalized forms of working-class militancy and solidarity that had been crucial for the growth of organized labor.[9] The Taft-Hartley Act explicitly banned the unionization of supervisory employees, and while it stipulated that professional and technical employees retained the right to pursue collective bargaining, its ambiguities created further impediments for white-collar organizing.[10] The new law also required an additional consent election apart from certification in order to institute a union shop agreement. In addition, Section 14(b) permitted individual states to ban the union shop entirely. Southern states in particular took advantage of this provision to pass misleadingly named "right-to-work" measures in order to lure manufacturing firms away from the well-organized Northeast and Midwest.[11]

The provision of the Taft-Hartley Act that had the most immediate impact was Section 9(h), which required unions to submit affidavits affirming that their top officers were not members of the Communist Party as a condition for accessing the services of the National Labor Relations Board. Initially a wide array of noncommunist unions refused to comply as a protest against the use of state power to police the labor movement, although they opted to sign the affidavits once the reconstituted NLRB signaled that it would interpret the new law in ways that abetted the decertification of noncompliant unions. The unions that continued to hold out were those with procommunist leaders who could not file without risking indictment for perjury. Section 9(h) noncompliance devastated the UOPWA, including its units in New York-based broadcasting, design, publishing, and motion picture distribution and marketing. While the effects of Section 9(h) were not as dire for the Newspaper Guild of New York and the RWG, the provision nonetheless had significant consequences for these two unions, as it contributed to the purging of leaders who were politically aligned with the Popular Front and complicated the unions' organizing and bargaining efforts.[12]

Anticommunism also furnished a highly convenient rationale for opponents of the Popular Front presence in the culture industries to harness the government's investigative and law enforcement powers. Although Martin Dies had been temporarily chased from office, the anti-subversive committee he had chaired was granted permanent standing as the House Committee on Un-American Activities (HUAC). During 1945 and 1946, the committee requested the scripts of many of the liberal news commentators on network radio in a transparent attempt to stifle the broadcasting of political views that conservatives found disagreeable, and it held damaging hearings on several of the most conspicuously procommunist organizations in the Popular Front orbit.[13] Following the GOP takeover of the House, the new HUAC chair, Representative J. Parnell Thomas of New Jersey, and a pack of hungry young Republicans, including freshman legislator Richard Nixon, dramatically escalated their attacks. While the committee devoted considerable attention to exposing Communist infiltration within the government, much of its energies went into investigations of radicalism in the labor movement and in the media and entertainment fields.[14] Often the two overlapped, as with the HUAC hearings in September 1947 concerning alleged leftist subversion in the motion picture industry. HUAC subpoenaed anticommunist "friendly" witnesses including Screen Actors Guild (SAG) president Ronald Reagan as well as procommunist "unfriendly" witnesses, mostly activists in the Screen Writers Guild (SWG) or Screen Directors Guild, who invoked their First Amendment rights and refused to cooperate with their interrogation. Congress cited the "Hollywood Ten" for contempt. Federal courts upheld the charges and sentenced them to prison.[15] The career boost that many HUAC members received from their anticommunist crusading only guaranteed that other legislators would emulate this path to political celebrity. In 1950, new legislation established the Senate Internal Security Subcommittee of the Judiciary Committee (SISS) as an analog of HUAC for the senior chamber, while Republican Senator Joseph McCarthy eventually commandeered the Senate Government Operations Committee's Permanent Subcommittee on Investigations to engage in some of the most notorious anticommunist inquisitions of the Cold War.

The political points scored by the Republicans prompted the Truman administration to embark upon its own anticommunist initiatives in an attempt to neutralize the issue. In March 1947, President Truman established a Federal Employee Loyalty Program to screen several million government workers, with FBI interrogations and firings for those deemed security risks. Various media enterprises, including CBS, subsequently appropriated elements of this review process to develop their own security programs based on the federal model. The administration also created a revised and expanded List of Subversive Organizations promulgated by the attorney general in March 1948, which encouraged the tendency to construe participation in Popular Front activism as prima facie evidence of subversive intent.[16] Just a few months later the Department of Justice obtained its first indictments against top leaders of the Communist Party under the 1940 Alien Registration Act, indicating the government's position that procommunist affinities were tantamount to participation in a criminal conspiracy, and not a form of political expression protected by the First Amendment.[17]

Even as anticommunist pressure intensified during the late 1940s, proponents of the Popular Front continued to mobilize. Following the 1946 midterm elections, the National Citizens Political Action Committee formally severed its link with the CIO-PAC and merged with the Independent Citizens Committee of the Arts, Sciences, and Professions to form the Progressive Citizens of America (PCA) to provide a unified political vehicle for the late Popular Front.[18] In early 1947, the PCA responded to the cancellation of many liberal radio commentators, most conspicuously RWG activist William Shirer, by organizing a series of conferences and public forums to address the "crisis in radio" that included numerous figures from New York's culture industry unions.[19] PCA also launched the Voice of Freedom Committee (VOF), chaired by writer Dorothy Parker, to fight for the restoration of progressive perspectives to the airwaves and to condemn those radio personalities who were especially venomous in their anti-labor and anticommunist fusillades. The VOF set up a network of volunteer "monitors" who tended to see their activities as a continuation of the Popular Front's efforts to politicize the culture of consumer capitalism. "I do not think liberals are very intelligent," wrote one monitor in a letter that was reprinted in the December 1947 issue of the VOF newsletter, "if they continue to buy the products being sold by their fascist-minded enemies." The newsletter's editor was even more blunt. "Our news sources in radio are strictly commercial ventures. It is what they sell—not what they tell—that counts."[20] As the year drew to a close, activists in the PCA and its various initiatives, as well as in organizations like the CAW and left-led unions like the UOPWA, began preparing for the Popular Front's most audacious political endeavor, the independent presidential campaign of former Vice President Henry Wallace.[21]

The embattled Popular Front's continuing organizing efforts only incited anticommunists to escalate their campaign. The network of professional anticommunists that had crystalized in the late 1930s in opposition to the rise of the CIO and progressive consumer organizations revived and expanded in the late 1940s and early 1950s. In early 1947, three former FBI agents founded American Business Consultants, whose weekly newsletter, *Counterattack*, was intended to provide, as it proclaimed on its masthead, "facts to combat Communism." Their firm obtained its "facts" in large part by combing through Communist publications like the *Daily Worker*, sifting through the ephemera of Popular Front organizations, poring over hearings transcripts from HUAC and other governmental investigative bodies, and engaging in direct surveillance of alleged procommunists. American Business Consultants initially concentrated on leftist influence in the labor movement, producing a special report on the UOPWA, but gradually focused more squarely on Popular Fronters in the media and entertainment fields. Its best-known publication was *Red Channels*, released in June 1950, which it billed as "the report of Communist influence in radio and television." The volume detailed the Popular Front affiliations of 151 actors, performers, composers, writers, directors, and journalists, listing the petitions they had signed for various causes, organizations to which they had belonged, and rallies at which they had appeared. Despite the firm's insinuations, the report did not furnish any conclusive proof that any of the people included in the volume definitely belonged to the Communist Party, but it greatly facilitated the practice of blacklisting in the broadcast media.[22]

In addition, an array of political committees, civic groups, and grassroots organizations propagated and reinforced the efforts of government figures and professional anticommunists. Some of the influential anticommunist organizations of the early Cold War, like Americans for Democratic Action (ADA) and the Association of Catholic Trade Unionists (ACTU), grounded their attacks in liberal conceptions of social justice.[23] Many others, however, like the American Legion, reflected deeply conservative impulses in the American polity.[24] By the beginning of the 1950s, new groups joined the Legion's fight, such as the Veterans Action Committee of Syracuse Super Markets backed by upstate New York grocer Laurence Johnson. These associations all encouraged protests to sponsors, advertising agencies, and broadcasters against the employment of alleged subversives on radio and television. Like their progressive opponents in the VOF, conservatives saw their activities as a politicization of the culture of consumer capitalism. In a letter to the president of the Block Drug Company disapproving of the continued employment of progressives on a program that it sponsored, for example, Johnson suggested placing a customer questionnaire alongside the firm's products on store shelves that asked, "Do you want any part of your purchase price to be used to hire Communist fronters?"[25] Even though professional anticommunists often orchestrated the harassing letters, phone calls, and picketing by conservative activists, these efforts fulfilled a crucial role in the campaign against the Popular Front by enabling media and advertising executives to point to them as evidence of public support for blacklisting and union-busting within the culture industries.

Nonetheless, while anticommunism rapidly became Cold War orthodoxy in the United States, its ascendancy hardly assured that conservatives would be able to exploit fears of subversion to achieve a fundamental political realignment against the New Deal order. Truman's increasingly muscular foreign policy, along with his domestic security initiatives, dampened conservative accusations that he was "soft" on Communism, while his Taft-Hartley veto shored up his support with the mainstream of organized labor heading into the 1948 campaign. Yet he faced a significant challenge on his left flank from Wallace's campaign. In addition to calling for an easing of tensions with the Soviets and a concomitant reduction in defense expenditures, Wallace and the Progressive Party proposed the nationalization of railroads and utilities, a major expansion of Social Security to include national healthcare and childcare, the establishment of new regional development agencies modeled on the Tennessee Valley Authority, large-scale construction of public and cooperative housing, and a new program for permanent federal patronage of arts and culture. The Progressive Party also promised bold action on African American civil rights, and Wallace personally subjected himself to physical abuse and intimidation from racist hoodlums in the South as he stumped before integrated audiences.[26] To blunt Wallace's appeal, the Democrats embraced several key recommendations of the President's Committee on Civil Rights, including the desegregation of the armed forces, and emulated the Progressive Party's positions on national healthcare and public housing.

Despite defections on both the right and the left from the electoral coalition that had backed FDR, Truman confounded most prognosticators by scoring an upset victory.[27] Not only did the Democrats keep the White House, but they also picked up nine seats in the Senate and 75 in the House, canceling out the GOP gains during the previous midterm election. CIO-PAC, which had underperformed in 1946, contributed to the Democrats' successes. Wallace had dreamed of receiving 5 million votes in the presidential tally, and while the half-million votes that he received in the state of New York were enough to shift its 47 electoral college votes from Truman's column into Dewey's, the conspicuous influence of Communists in Wallace's campaign repelled many voters, so that nationwide the former vice president only won 1.15 million ballots.[28]

The Democrats' victory in November 1948, running on the party's most liberal platform yet, reflected the fluidity of American politics at this historical moment, but the latent possibilities of Truman's "Fair Deal" evaporated in the year ahead. Republicans continued their obstructionist coalition with Dixiecrats in Congress, killing any chance for Taft-Hartley repeal or the enactment of national healthcare. The main legislative achievement was the passage of the deeply compromised 1949 Housing Act, which provided ample new financing for suburban growth and subsidies for private interests to pursue urban renewal, but only funded an austere public housing program to serve solely those residents too poor to obtain shelter in the private rental market.[29] Conservatives escalated their anticommunist attacks and directed their fire at a wider range of targets, with McCarthy's ascent epitomizing the tendency toward indiscriminate and sensationalist demagoguery. With the outbreak of armed conflict in Korea in June 1950 and the deployment of American combat forces to the peninsula, the public mood turned alarmist, as virtually all progressive causes and movements came to be tainted by possible Communist association. For liberals and leftists alike, a darkness descended that would not lift until the end of the decade. Anticommunist conservatives failed in their ultimate goal of rallying broad public support to roll back the New Deal. They did, however, establish a climate that doomed not only any new proposals for progressive social or cultural programs, but also the careers of those members of the creative class who had most staunchly advocated for these types of initiatives in the past.

Defiance and Defeat: The Destruction of the United Office and Professional Workers of America

The intensifying anticommunism of the late 1940s and early 1950s pummeled all labor unions that retained leftist leadership, but it proved particularly devastating for the UOPWA. Even as many workers in the white-collar occupational strata leaned rightward in their political orientation, many others still favored unionism, and the UOPWA had grown at a robust pace during 1946 and the first half of 1947 despite its limited resources. At its peak, which roughly coincided with passage of the Taft-Hartley Act, it had approximately 80,000 members. Although other unions in the culture industries, such as the Newspaper Guild and the talent guilds in broadcasting and motion pictures, contained nuclei of procommunists as well as wider circles of members who were still receptive to the Popular Front, only in the UOPWA were procommunists able to outmaneuver their opponents and maintain control over the national organization. For fifteen months after the deadline for compliance with Section 9(h) of the Taft-Hartley Act, the union's officers refused to submit the required anticommunist affidavits, depriving its locals—including those in publishing, architecture and design, motion pictures, and broadcasting—of NLRB access. Yet the UOWPA was ill prepared to cope with the consequences of noncompliance. Many employers used noncompliance as grounds to withdraw recognition and terminate bargaining, secure in the knowledge that the union could not file unfair labor practice charges. By 1948, some frustrated members plotted secession from the crumbling union, while others collaborated with compliant unions looking to raid UOPWA shops. Even after the UOPWA finally submitted Section 9(h) affidavits in November 1948, employers and competing unions still challenged its legal status. In early 1950, the CIO expelled the UOPWA as part of its comprehensive purge of the left wing of the labor movement. Within another eighteen months, little remained of the union's presence in New York City's culture industries.

Following the 1946 midterms, UOPWA national president Lewis Merrill, who had been one of the staunchest procommunists in the American labor movement, became convinced that the union's political orientation was rapidly becoming untenable. He resigned his positions on the advisory boards of the procommunist magazine *New Masses* and the Jefferson School of Social Science, which was the Communist Party's primary educational endeavor in New York. He also publicly affirmed the importance of the union maintaining an autonomous political course driven by the interests of the membership. Through early 1947, rumors circulated of dissention within the UOPWA international executive board, as the procommunist majority stymied Merrill's attempt at political realignment.[30] In June he announced his resignation due to an undisclosed medical condition and abruptly withdrew from union affairs. The executive board selected James Durkin, a procommunist stalwart from the insurance division to complete the remainder of Merrill's term as president.[31]

As the August 22, 1947, deadline for Taft-Hartley compliance drew near, the UOPWA proceeded to renew as many of the union's contracts as possible before the hated "slave labor law" took effect. Holdout employers, like Ebasco Services, immediately demonstrated the cost of noncompliance. Days before Ebasco's first contract with UOPWA Local 231 expired, its management informed the union that it would not continue collective bargaining. Unable to file unfair labor practice charges with the NLRB, the pro-union draftsmen, designers, and engineers voted to strike for continued union recognition beginning September 5.[32] Ebasco responded to the walkout by the majority of its 375 design employees with an aggressive strategy for maintaining production. Within weeks, it began outsourcing design work to several subcontractors it had established. In response, the union relied upon longstanding tactics and strategies of mass mobilization. The strikers, with their ranks swelled by sympathetic members of AFL engineering and design unions as well as numerous supporters from the Greater New York Industrial Union Council, expanded their picketing to include the subcontractors' shops as well as the annual shareholders' meeting of Ebasco's corporate parent, Electric Bond and Share. UOPWA Local 231 also began to organize the miserably underpaid replacement workers in Ebasco's subcontracting shops to join the strike.[33] By late November, Ebasco management conceded that more than half of the employees of one of its subcontractors were respecting the picket and staying away from work. To break the strike, Ebasco became one of the first employers to avail itself of its enhanced legal standing under Taft-Hartley. It charged Local 231 with unfair labor practices, claiming that the picketing of the allegedly independent subcontractors constituted a secondary action prohibited by the new law. On December 2, the NLRB directed the United States District Court to issue an injunction against the union that drastically restricted its activities.[34]

Although an appeal by the union lifted the injunction a few weeks later, the strikers' resolve gradually collapsed. On February 2, 1948, they finally voted to end the strike after five months. Many of the striking draftsmen, designers, and engineers lost not just their union, but their jobs as well. Several months later, the Local 231 newsletter included a cautionary tale from an Ebasco striker who wrote under the pseudonym "Pushing Forty." He had been recently hired in one of the "job shops" that only existed "for the contract of the moment," and offered hourly design work at low rates with no vacation or sick days. He started alongside another new hire, "well past sixty," who "hadn't been in a strike," but "had been in something far worse." A lifetime of toil had left him with unsteady hands, and Pushing Forty was sure that he had hidden them during his interviews. While the "green velvet was faded to white" on the lining of his drafting case, decades of economic insecurity forced him to compete against men half his age. In a place where "get-the-job out is the motto; get it out, get it done, sweat first and quality afterwards is the rule," the older man did not stand a chance. At the end of a harried first day during which he had been repeatedly admonished for making errors, he was asked by the boss to stay until after the other draftsmen had left. When the writer said "goodnight" to him, the older man quietly replied "goodbye." The defeat of the Ebasco strike crippled Local 231, marking its demise as an organizational base for architectural, design, and engineering workers.[35]

Other New York employers that had contracts with the UOPWA noted Ebasco's multifaceted use of the Taft-Hartley Act to beat a well-organized and determined group of white-collar unionists. The looming expiration of major contracts in 1948 only raised the stakes. At its biennial convention in March, the union's procommunist cadre outflanked the fragmented anticommunist opposition. Over the objections of many delegates, the leadership recommitted the union to noncompliance with Section 9(h).[36] By midyear, the union began to crack up under the strain. In the insurance field, which accounted for 30 percent of the union's total membership, disaffected agents revolted and solicited the backing of CIO President Murray for their secession scheme. The UOPWA leadership responded by conducting a membership referendum on Taft-Hartley compliance in July 1948. Although they implored the members of locals suspended for secessionist activities to arrange for reinstatement so that they could participate in the poll, the union nonetheless reported that a majority of participants favored continued noncompliance.[37]

The referendum allowed the union's leaders to pretend that their continued defiance had the backing of a resolute membership, but such posturing did little for workers facing the loss of collective bargaining. The UOPWA Screen Office and Professional Employees Guild and Screen Publicists Guild had master contracts covering more than 4,000 workers in New York City that expired in September, but found that employers refused to open negotiations. Paramount Pictures president Barry Balaban's position was typical. In a letter to the SOPEG president, Balaban asserted that all the studio executives, "as those who share the responsibility for the welfare of our industry," were adamantly "opposed to Communist infiltration into our ranks." Although the union might exercise its right not to comply with the Taft-Hartley Act, he noted that "under the same law, we are relieved of any obligation to deal with you if you fail to file the affidavits." Balaban rejected the union's claim that the motion picture companies were attempting to dictate its political orientation, but he nonetheless insisted that it was a time "to stand up and be counted." "Why," he asked, "should any American hesitate to stand up and state, 'I am not a member of the Communist Party and I'm glad to swear to it!' What opprobrium is there involved in the act of signing an affidavit that one is not the agent of a foreign government?" In addition, Balaban and other industry executives colluded with American Business Consultants and the corrupt but staunchly anticommunist IATSE to undermine the SOPEG. Under these circumstances, there was little that the beleaguered local, which had succeeded a few years earlier in organizing the New York offices of nearly all of the major studios, could do to shield its members from the economic impact of the restructuring of the motion picture industry that came with the government-decreed separation of motion picture production and exhibition.[38]

The continued procommunist political orientation of the UOPWA also increased friction with the CIO. Many in the CIO felt the Truman administration had provided inadequate support for the labor movement and its legislative agenda, but determined that despite their reservations, the prudent course was to stick with Truman and the Democrats.[39] The left-led affiliates, including the UOPWA, instead backed Wallace and opposed Marshall Plan assistance for Europe. The Greater New York Industrial Union Council posed a particular problem for Murray and the national CIO, given the strength of Wallace support in the city and the critical importance of New York in the presidential campaign. Since the fall of 1946, many CIO affiliates, including locals of the Amalgamated Clothing Workers, the UAW, and the National Maritime Union, had withdrawn from the city's IUC to protest the dominance exerted by procommunists. By January 1948, its remaining affiliated locals were concentrated in the UOPWA, the UE, the United Public Workers (which represented public schoolteachers as well as city workers in welfare, sanitation, and other departments), the Transport Workers, and the distributive trades. Within the city, the IUC furnished the backbone for Wallace's presidential campaign, countering the official CIO-PAC effort for Truman.[40]

Moreover, these disputes over political strategy intersected with deepening disagreements with the CIO over organizational tactics. Since the end of the war, the Greater New York IUC had continued to mobilize workers by promoting a class-conscious social agenda that sought to transcend the narrow boundaries of employment inscribed by American labor law. By 1948, leftist networks of tenant and consumer activists, many of whom had participated in wartime CIO Community Councils, not only furnished a vital part of the Progressive Party campaign apparatus, but also an important source of neighborhood support for the UOPWA and other noncompliant unions in their battles to maintain collective bargaining. The *New York Tenant News*, for instance, publicized the plight of members of SOPEG and SPG who faced the termination of collective bargaining, imploring readers to boycott the motion picture companies that refused to negotiate with the left-led locals, and write to the companies in protest of their labor policies. Advertisements from SOPEG and SPG reinforced editorial support, with one spot in the *Tenant News* informing consumers that their "movie dollar" was being used to "deprive white-collar workers of job security; to keep salaries down while prices, including box-office profits, zoom; and to destroy collective bargaining."[41]

As part of its advocacy of a broad working-class interest, the IUC endorsed the continuation of the city's five-cent subway fare, even though the left-led Transport Workers Union contended that the hike was necessary to pay for a raise for its members. The conflict helped push Michael Quill, the longtime procommunist head of the union, to break with his former allies and quit the Council in March 1948.[42] Over the next few months, the rump IUC led by Durkin assisted the efforts of eight left-led CIO department store, retail, and distributive locals in New York as they fought to continue collective bargaining with major employers, including Macy's, Gimbel's, and Bloomingdale's, despite the unions' noncompliance with Section 9(h) and investigative attacks from House committees. When the anticommunist leadership of the parent union condemned the leftists' mass picketing and boycotts, and subsequently attempted to put the locals into receivership, the IUC backed the insurgents' secession from their international union.[43] In response, the CIO revoked the Greater New York Industrial Union Council's charter. In its report recommending the dissolution of the Council, the CIO trial board concluded that "as presently constituted," it functioned "not as an agency of the CIO," but rather "for all intents and purposes as an instrumentality through which the Communist Party is interfering in the affairs of the CIO and its unions in New York City."[44]

The success that anticommunists in the labor movement had in isolating the pro-Wallace minority precluded any possibility of the Progressive Party establishing itself as a viable force in American politics. Within days of the disappointing election results, the UOPWA executive board reversed its earlier position and prepared to submit Section 9(h) affidavits to the NLRB. Yet compliance brought little succor to the embattled white-collar union. Submission of the affidavits finally reopened access to the NLRB in early 1949 and allowed the UOPWA to appear on the ballot in a slew of upcoming certification elections. Raiding continued unabated, however, as the AFL-affiliated Office Employees International Union (OEIU) picked off numerous groups of clerical workers that the UOPWA had organized in the New York metropolitan area. Other AFL unions targeted groups of UOPWA members in insurance and motion pictures.[45] Even as the UOPWA sought to remain the collective bargaining representative for tens of thousands of white-collar workers, it devoted a growing share of its dwindling resources to fighting to remain within the CIO. When it convened a national organizing strategy conference in January 1949, it barred the press and representatives from the CIO, including UOPWA members employed in the CIO national office.[46]

In addition, Catholic social unionists in the CIO increasingly called for expulsion of the left-led affiliates. Father Charles Owen Rice of the ACTU circulated an open letter to UOPWA members in December 1948 in which he pleaded with them to repudiate Durkin and the other leaders. Rice maintained that submission of the Section 9(h) affidavits was merely a cynical ploy to take advantage "of the period of preparation before the CIO reveals its specific plans to organize all white-collar workers" through a new organizing committee. In correspondence to Durkin, Rice accused the UOPWA leadership of being "in the back pocket of the Communist Party." When Durkin demanded that Rice accept the consequences of his attacks on the union, the Catholic labor activist replied that his followers would build a "real organization" that would be "ten times as strong as under your selfish, short sighted and defeatish leadership." Employers would "no longer deal with a Red-tainted, bragging, but weak, outfit," he contended, but rather have to "deal with the full might of the CIO."[47]

By the fall of 1949, Murray and the rest of the CIO leadership finally determined to purge all of the unions that remained under leftist control. For each of the unions facing expulsion, the CIO executive board conducted formal proceedings that eerily paralleled HUAC investigative hearings. In the proceedings for the UOPWA, the CIO examiners demonstrated the union's adherence to the Communist line by showing how the editorial positions of its newspapers and its officials' public statements had shifted abruptly in response to changes in the Party's policies. Far more damning in retrospect were the letters by individual members protesting their union's opposition to CIO policy. At a meeting of the CIO Executive Board in February 1950, the final move was taken to expel the UOPWA.[48]

The barrage of attacks on the UOPWA from employers and from other unionists impeded the ability of even its well-organized units to advance members' living standards and assure a modicum of workplace autonomy. At CBS, where the initial two-year contract that the UOPWA Radio Guild signed in 1946 and the subsequent arbitration of a wage-reopening clause had resulted in many white-collar employees receiving salary increases of 40 percent or more by 1948, the union found that it could accomplish far less in the face of intensifying Cold War animosity. The last-minute submission of Section 9(h) affidavits with the NLRB ensured a settlement at the end of 1948 for a new one-year deal, albeit one substantially weaker than the original agreement. Network executives' hostility toward the union, increasingly evident in their harassment of activists on the staff, eventually led them to challenge the legal standing of the UOPWA in October 1949 by demanding a new certification election prior to any further negotiations. In January 1950, amidst management intimidation and the union's impending expulsion from the CIO, a majority of the CBS office and nontalent professional staff still voted to recertify the UOPWA. Following the lead of so many other employers, however, CBS refused to recognize the election, claiming that the union's political orientation constituted Taft-Hartley noncompliance. Union members at CBS organized mass picketing outside the network's offices and studios with supporters from other UOPWA locals, but they were unable to compel continued recognition from the network.[49]

Following its expulsion from the CIO, the UOPWA continued to disintegrate. The supplemental assessments the union levied as it struggled to survive made membership an increasingly costly proposition. Organizers' confidential assessments of a series of home-visits that they made in July to members in one formerly militant unit, for instance, revealed considerable anticommunist sentiment and a widespread desire to belong to a union still inside the CIO. In fact, the organizers conceded, the major force keeping this unit in the UOPWA was management's reluctance to permit the workers to switch to a new union that would likely be in a stronger position to improve salaries and benefits. With its resources dwindling, the UOPWA sought a merger with other left-led unions now outside the CIO. In October 1950, the remnants of the UOPWA combined with the renegade retail and distributive locals in New York and the remnants of the Food, Tobacco, Agricultural and Allied Workers (FTA) to form a new international union, the Distributive, Processing, and Office Workers of America (DPOWA). Reflecting the relative strength of the distributive division, Arthur Osman, who had helped build Wholesale and Warehouse Local 65, presided over the national union, while David Livingston, another Local 65 leader, headed an expanded District 65 that incorporated most of the new organization's New York membership, including all UOPWA units in the metropolitan area. A membership audit conducted shortly after the merger revealed the disarray of the white-collar union during its last few months of independent existence. While 88 percent of the members formerly in Local 65 and 85 percent of the department store members were current in their dues payments, only 43 percent of the members in the ex-UOPWA units were. The situation in the motion picture offices organized by SOPEG was typical: out of 2,900 workers under contract at the time of the merger, only 1,300 paid membership dues on a regular basis.[50]

Numerous employers contended that the merger simply proved the continuation of procommunist influence and balked at dealing with District 65, including many firms in the culture industries that faced increased scrutiny as part of the domestic Cold War. Some firms, including filmmaker Twentieth-Century Fox and book publisher Knopf, simply maintained that the UOPWA was defunct and that they had no obligation to bargain with District 65 until it had been certified in an election. Others claimed that the new organization was not in compliance with Section 9(h). Random House publisher Bennett Cerf, who had once supported the Popular Front and had recognized the UOPWA Book and Magazine Guild until its expulsion from the CIO, subjected his editorial and clerical staff to mandatory meetings in late 1950 in which he denounced District 65 as "the most thoroughly Communist-dominated union in the entire country." Cerf suggested the press would be ruined by recognizing such a union, and insinuated that workers who remained members of District 65 risked imprisonment under the Internal Security Act for knowingly supporting a subversive organization. Although a majority of the employees at Random House, as well as at Knopf and Viking, had still belonged to the union at the time of the merger, a torrent of resignations occurred in the following months. As the last president of the BMG, Estelle Levine, bitterly noted in April 1951, unless organizers recognized "that we do not have these shops now, we will continue to kid ourselves and continue to hang on to contracts but no workers."[51]

In a new round of certification elections, District 65 squared off against AFL and CIO affiliates that desired to scavenge the remains of the UOPWA. One of the most significant contests took place at CBS, where the Newspaper Guild, OEIU Local 153, and an independent organization all challenged District 65's right to represent the former UOPWA bargaining unit of roughly 700 employees. Although a majority of the employees opted for some form of union representation in the first phase of balloting on March 7, 1951, they split their support among the various contenders. There were 169 employees who voted for the Newspaper Guild, while 117 chose Local 153. District 65 received a paltry 54 votes. Ominously, however, 286 selected the option of no union, forcing a run-off election. CBS management, meanwhile, revealed how easily its objections to the procommunist affinities of the UOPWA could be redeployed more generally against any white-collar union. In the second poll, the Newspaper Guild narrowly lost by a margin of 308–290, putting an end to the drive for industrial unionism in the broadcast media that Myra Jordan and her colleagues had launched with so much promise.[52] Elsewhere, the Newspaper Guild's supporters were more fortunate, as the union beat

District 65 in representation elections for employees of Consumers Union and the *Saturday Review of Literature*.[53]

As the DPOWA confronted the loss of most of its former UOPWA members, as well as organizing difficulties even in its core processing, distributive, and retail divisions, it embarked upon a program of retrenchment. During the summer of 1951, it halved its paid staff. Former UOPWA organizers who had spent years fighting to build militant white-collar unions found themselves unemployed and largely unemployable on account of their radical pasts. In October, the DPOWA executive board voted to replace former UOPWA leaders James Durkin, Norma Aronson, Aaron Schneider, and Victoria Garvin with new board members from previously underrepresented segments of the union.[54] Beyond the impact of anticommunism on workers' opinions of the DPOWA, the union faced intensifying official pressure. By early 1952, both SISS and the House Education and Labor Committee were investigating the DPOWA and District 65. Livingston and other top union officers were also charged with contempt and obstruction of justice for refusing to testify before a federal grand jury regarding contributions of union funds to the Civil Rights Congress and other groups on the attorney general's list of subversive organizations. Later that year, the grand jury recommended that the NLRB strip the DPOWA and District 65 of certification.[55]

The multipronged campaign by the state to compel anticommunist political orthodoxy within the American labor movement overcame the union's resistance. In May 1952, Osman and Livingston publicly disavowed Communism at a District 65 convention at which it was decided to expel those members who were employed either by the handful of other leftist unions that still refused to capitulate to the federal government, or by organizations with clear links to the CP. This conspicuous, if perfunctory, repudiation of Communism satisfied the CIO enough to open discussions with the DPOWA and District 65 regarding possible readmission. While the DPOWA at first sought affiliation as a fully autonomous international union, its weakness enabled the CIO to dictate terms. Although a temporary charter in 1953 permitted CIO affiliates in New York City to furnish official assistance in strike situations, the permanent arrangement the following year forced the DPOWA to subsume itself within the CIO-affiliated Retail, Wholesale, and Department Store Union that Local 65 had bolted from six years earlier. Osman became a vice president of the international union, while Livingston remained head of District 65, which enjoyed partial autonomy.[56]

The return to the CIO fold came far too late for unionists in most of the cultural fields in which the UOPWA had organized during the 1930s and 1940s, but one of the notable exceptions was in the field of motion picture promotion and marketing, in which activists rebuilt the Screen Publicists Guild under the auspices of District 65. Prior to August 1947, the SPG had won contracts covering artists, copywriters, publicists, and other promotional and marketing employees in the New York offices of nine major motion picture studios and several independent publicity agencies. Between 1948 and 1951, however, most of these employers withdrew recognition from the SPG due to the union's actual or alleged noncompliance with Section 9(h) of the Taft-Hartley Act. Although AFL Sign Painters Local 230 and the IATSE succeeded in raiding some of the shops, in others a core of SPG activists remained committed. Organizing as a division of District 65, they regained NLRB certification and negotiated new contracts with Columbia, United Artists, Twentieth-Century Fox, Universal, and Warner Brothers between October 1951 and April 1954.[57] As District 65 rejoined the CIO, United Artists publicist and SPG executive council member George Nelson tried to recapture the movement culture that had animated the militant white-collar unionism in the city's culture industries during the heyday of the Popular Front. Nelson implored his colleagues not only to "take an active part in the 65, CIO, and CIO-PAC legislative and electoral campaigns to strengthen our ties with the rest of labor," but also to use the rapprochement to "undertake an organizing campaign within the film industry and in allied fields where advertising and publicity people are employed—in agencies and similar places." Nonetheless, his enthusiasm could not compensate for the disintegration of the dense network of unions and organizations necessary for these mobilizations. The SPG remained a vibrant division within District 65 into the 1970s, but as a group of just a few hundred members of the creative class holding their own within a declining jurisdiction—as motion picture firms outsourced promotional and marketing activities or relocated them to Southern California—it was a smoldering ember of the Popular Front in New York's culture industries rather than a spark for new organizing.[58]

Ultimately, the destruction of the UOPWA had ramifications that stretched far beyond its impact on New York's culture workers, as it adversely affected the much broader prospects for organizing in the rapidly expanding clerical, technical, and professional occupational sectors in the postwar United States. While its leaders' procommunist affinities had impeded its growth and eventually proved fatal, the union's demise nonetheless left a huge void. The CIO promised that it would charter a major new white-collar organizing committee with the jurisdiction formerly assigned to the UOPWA but failed to follow through. The AFL-affiliated rival of the UOPWA, the OEIU grew slowly during the late 1940s and early 1950s, partly through the raiding of UOPWA shops and partly through the transfer of groups of white-collar workers that other AFL internationals had organized outside of their craft jurisdictions, as was the case with CBS office personnel in Los Angeles. The merger of the AFL and CIO in December 1955 did little to stimulate the OEIU; by 1962, it still had only 66,000 members nationwide, fewer than the UOPWA had in 1947.[59]

The AFL-CIO Industrial Union Department, headed by UAW president Walter Reuther, encouraged the organization of office staff employed by manufacturing companies whose blue-collar workers were already unionized. At its conference on white-collar organizing held in December 1956, Reuther declared that this approach could lead to a subsequent wave of new organizing among "the tremendous mass of unorganized white-collar workers who make up the personnel of commercial offices, insurance offices, the retail industry, and the other service industries."[60] Even though the industrial unions made modest gains, the second phase of white-collar organizing that he hoped would enable the labor movement to push its social frontiers beyond its traditional domain and into the dynamic new sectors of the economy failed to materialize. During the late 1950s and early 1960s, white-collar union density in the private sector fluctuated at between one-half and one-third of the union density of blue-collar workers in manufacturing, but outside of retail the bulk of unionized white-collar workers remained concentrated in sectors facing limited growth potential or outright decline. The response from the labor movement as a whole was anemic; in no single year between 1957 and 1962 did American unions successfully organize more than 6,000 new office workers, and the disbanding of several small independent unions suggested that the idea of organization was actually losing ground among many groups of white-collar workers.[61] Viewed in this context, the end of the UOPWA was a key development within the larger political and social processes through which class consciousness was quarantined during the early Cold War. It squelched any near-term possibilities for organizing in fields such as broadcasting, advertising, design, and book and magazine publishing. But it also helped to diminish any sense of solidarity or collective action within the clerical, sales, technical, and professional occupations that made up the postwar middle class that was represented as the idealized subject of the culture of consumer capitalism.

Fit to Print: The Newspaper Guild in Cold-War New York

Unlike the UOPWA, which was obliterated by the rising tide of anticommunism, the Newspaper Guild of New York had by 1949 adjusted to the political imperatives of Cold War liberalism. Although it had long been an integral component of the city's Popular Front, the union's highly democratic structure gave anticommunist dissidents ample opportunity to challenge local president John McManus and his supporters. An anticommunist coalition won a slim majority in the December 1947 local elections, and within less than a year Popular Fronters had relinquished all positions of power within the New York Guild. The reorientation had far-reaching consequences, reinforcing a tendency toward bureaucratic sclerosis evident in many CIO unions by the 1950s. The local's new leadership regime, anchored by Thomas J. Murphy, a former bookkeeper with the *New York Times* who held the office of executive vice president in the local from 1948 until 1971, concentrated its energies on maintaining its primary jurisdiction in daily newspaper publishing. In doing so, however, the Guild neglected to solidify and expand its uncertain position in magazine publishing or to establish a major presence in broadcast media. Furthermore, the Newspaper Guild of New York found that conformity to Cold War anticommunist orthodoxy not only conflicted with contractual grievance and job security provisions, but also fundamental notions of journalistic autonomy, rooted in the First Amendment, that had been central to the Guild's mission from its birth.

During 1947 the long-simmering tensions between the ANG and the New York local that had existed since anticommunists had gained control of the national union in 1941 finally reached a boil. In March, ANG head Milton Murray appeared before the House Education and Labor Committee to blast the Popular Front leadership of the union's largest locals in New York and Los Angeles, and to insist that journalists with procommunist political inclinations were incapable of objective reporting. The furor in the months following Murray's testimony ultimately led him to withdraw his nomination for another term as ANG president, and when the Taft-Hartley Act took effect, the national union joined with much of the labor movement in refusing initially to submit the controversial Section 9(h) affidavits. Yet despite the stance taken by the national leadership in an attempt to defuse factional conflict, the issue of Taft-Hartley compliance presented an irresistible opportunity to anticommunists in New York. In September, the anticommunist slate of candidates in the local's upcoming elections declared that regardless of the

ANG position on Taft-Hartley, they would file affidavits with the NLRB if they won. Their move forced the hand of the national executive board, which "reluctantly" voted in early November to comply with Section 9(h).[62]

In making the elections a referendum on the politics of the local leadership, the anticommunists in the New York Guild linked the local's political orientation directly to matters of organizing and collective bargaining. These concerns tipped the balance in favor of the anticommunists, who won the December balloting, although the results revealed a deeply divided membership. John McManus, who had led the New York local for five years and had been one of the most prolific advocates of the city's Popular Front, lost the presidency to George Holmes, a picture caption editor who chaired the *Daily News* unit, by 3,041 votes to 2,748. McManus's running mates, including incumbent executive vice president John Ryan, lost by slightly larger margins. Popular Fronters still carried many units within the local, as McManus beat Holmes by tallies of 516–256 at the *New York Times*, 193–171 at Time Inc., and 139–22 in his home unit at *PM*. Holmes easily carried his home unit at the *Daily News* with 491 votes to just 170 for McManus, and routed the incumbent by margins of 394–70 at the *Journal-American* and 296–78 at the *Herald Tribune*.[63]

Supporters of the Popular Front immediately struck back. In January 1948, the local's Representative Assembly rejected the recommendations of the newly elected officers and instead appointed an executive board that included both McManus and Ryan. The delegates' rebuke to the anticommunists paralyzed the local for the next seven months. Finally, the suppression of the leftists' organizational base in the Greater New York Industrial Union Council forced a resolution to the standoff. Responding to pressure from the ANG as well as the national CIO, Murphy declared in July that the New York Guild was withdrawing from the Council despite union bylaws that clearly empowered the local executive board to set policy regarding such affiliations. Convinced that their position was no longer tenable, McManus and the other leftists on the executive board resigned. Within the next year, Murphy and the new executive board purged the local staff of all unionists with Popular Front loyalties.[64]

Compliance with the Taft-Hartley Act guaranteed a continuity of collective bargaining, and the Guild made strides toward its long-run goal of instituting a uniform bargaining pattern in daily newspaper publishing, even as employers sporadically attempted to take advantage of its internal disarray.[65] The logic of pattern bargaining sought to eliminate competition between firms on the basis of labor costs, assuming that other aspects of their operations were roughly the same. In actuality, some of New York City's newspapers earned handsome profits while others were slowly sinking in a sea of red ink. The possibility that a firm's failure might result in unemployment for Guild members became a reality with the end of *PM*. After earning a small profit in 1945, the progressive tabloid's losses resumed as prices for newsprint and ink skyrocketed while circulation remained flat. In November 1946, publisher Marshall Field III determined that *PM* would begin to accept advertising like all other newspapers, conceding its inability to subsist solely on circulation revenues. Although he hoped the move would put *PM* on a solid footing, the paper's politics still made it an unattractive medium for many retailers, while the addition of advertising alienated many longtime subscribers. By 1948, Field was unwilling to continue subsidizing the paper's operating deficit of roughly $15,000 per week. In March, he announced that he was selling *PM* to California-based publisher Clinton McKinnon, who planned on ceasing publication unless the Guild accepted drastic concessions, including cuts in pay and the abrogation of contract provisions on staffing, seniority, job security, and severance.[66]

Aware of McKinnon's poor reputation and fearful that accepting concessions would invite similar demands from other publishers, the New York Guild scuttled the deal, gambling with the livelihoods of its 162 members at *PM*. The union instead persuaded Field to continue the tabloid for an additional few weeks until another buyer could be found. At the end of April, Field sold controlling interest in the paper to Bartley Crum, who renamed it the *New York Star*. While the union greatly preferred Crum to McKinnon, the transition still resulted in the elimination of one quarter of the Guild positions at the *Star* even as the basic framework of the contract was preserved.[67] Crum and his staff were unable to boost the circulation, and in 1949 Field withdrew his remaining financial support. Ted Thackeray, recently divorced from *New York Post* owner Dorothy Schiff, interceded with new investors to purchase the *Star*, which he relaunched as the *Daily Compass*. Run with a skeletal staff of leftist journalists that included *PM* stalwarts such as I. F. Stone and former Guild activists like Irving Gilman, the *Compass* struggled to keep the presses rolling as a voice for the imploding Popular Front.[68]

Although *PM* had only employed a tiny fraction of the local's nearly 8,000 members, its passing reverberated throughout New York's newspaper industry. Even in the most fraught years of the early Cold War, economic restructuring, not political infighting, represented the most serious threat. The *Herald Tribune*, which increasingly trailed the *Times* in their competition for upscale, educated readers in the morning news market, tested the union in the aftermath of *PM*'s demise by laying off more than eighty Guild members between November 1948 and September 1949. Only a robust strike mobilization by the membership halted the stream of dismissals.[69] A more serious challenge came in 1950 following the demise of the *New York Sun*—the city's sole daily that had never recognized the Guild—and its acquisition by the Scripps-Howard chain's *World-Telegram*. Executives of the amalgamated *World-Telegram and Sun* announced their plans to combine the workforces of the two papers, provoking a showdown with the unions. After the Guild failed to get management to provide enhanced severance pay, guarantees against economy layoffs, and stronger union security, its 500 members at the paper struck on June 13. The AFL-affiliated mechanical unions, including the printers and pressmen, directed their 1,000 members employed by the *World-Telegram* to honor the Guild picket line, forcing the paper, with the third-largest circulation of any afternoon daily in the United States, to suspend publication until it came to terms on August 23. The two-year agreement met nearly all of the Guild's demands, including a freeze on layoffs in the first year of the contract and arbitration of any layoffs in the second year, pay increases, a thirty-five-hour workweek, and maintenance of membership. The Guild's unity with the mechanical unions helped to secure its bargaining pattern in the city and nationwide. By 1953, it had negotiated a top minimum salary of $130 per week for reporters and photographers with seven years of experience at all of the major daily newspapers in Manhattan. The higher rates won by the New York Guild set the bar for locals elsewhere, propping up a structure of metropolitan salary scales that ranged from the $125 weekly top minimum for reporters and photographers with the *Philadelphia Inquirer* and the *St. Louis Post-Dispatch* to $100 at the *Indianapolis Star* and the *Memphis Commercial Appeal*.[70]

Nonetheless, the alliance that enabled the Newspaper Guild to maintain its bargaining pattern ultimately pointed toward an increasingly defensive posture, rather than the realization of the Popular Front ideal of unity between manual and mental labor. The Murphy regime's focus on daily newspaper publishing, and its dependence on solidarity with the mechanical unions, precipitated a collective bargaining cold war with the publishers. In an attempt to counter the united front on labor's side of the bargaining table, all seven Manhattan-based papers pledged to suspend publication and lockout their unionized employees if any one of them were struck in the future. Most publishers also began to purchase strike insurance to prepare for a potential showdown. Maintaining the pattern, moreover, still cost jobs. Although the New York Guild had by 1953 secured roughly equivalent contract terms on salaries and benefits from the seven major dailies, the faltering *Brooklyn Eagle* remained below the city pattern. In January 1955, the *Eagle*'s 315 Guild members struck in an attempt to win the same contract terms enjoyed by the union's members at other papers. After several weeks, ownership announced that it was calling it quits instead of meeting the Guild's demands.[71] While the former employees of the *Eagle* searched for other jobs and pursued litigation against the defunct paper to obtain full severance pay, the Guild approached its next round of contract negotiations in 1956 assured that none of the city's major papers could point to the substandard terms at the *Eagle*.

As Murphy and his followers committed most of the Guild's finite resources to fortifying its position in daily newspaper publishing, they compromised the union's capacity for growth in more dynamic sectors of the media. While surging expenditures by national advertisers led to significant increases in the number of editorial, artistic, and clerical staff employed by magazines in New York during the late 1940s and 1950s, the union encountered serious difficulties organizing new groups of magazine employees or even sustaining its existing units. The continuing hostility of executives at Time Inc. proved to be the most serious impediment. Although Guild activists had attempted to represent the 1946 contract settlement as a draw between the union and management, over the next several years the magnitude of the union's defeat became clear. The weakened union security provisions allowed the company to use a variety of tactics to erode support for the Guild. As part of the comprehensive strategy that Time executives developed to contain the union, the company utilized the Taft-Hartley Act's more rigid definition of supervisory personnel to further its drive to remove department heads and upper-level editors from the bargaining unit. To drive a wedge between the highest-paid segment of creative personnel and the bulk of the unit's membership, Time management continued to insist that all employees earning more than $120 per week be exempted from any general salary increases, even as the union negotiated the elimination of similar cut-off points at the *Herald Tribune* and the *Times*. More ominously, Time Inc. management responded to the Guild's efforts to expand the bargaining unit to encompass the commercial departments by firing some of the more strident union supporters in these areas.[72]

Despite management's tough stance, Guild activists at Time Inc. kept pushing to improve working conditions and recover maintenance of membership. Postwar inflation undercut the company's strategy for diluting union support among the better-paid creative personnel. *Time* writer Gilbert Cant, who served as the unit chairman during the late 1940s, used his own situation as an example in arguing for the elimination of the salary cut-off for general increases. He noted that while the BLS consumer price index had jumped 25 percent in the three years since the magazine hired him in June 1944, his two merit raises during that period only totaled 19 percent. *Fortune* writer Dero Saunders, another employee earning over $120 per week, was more blunt. "It isn't worth this management's time," he pleaded in one bargaining session, to expend so much energy "on wage negotiations about such an infinitesimal sector of its total cost," since "we are less than ink, less than the black marks on the piece of paper of the magazine you put out." Nonetheless, management refused to accede to the Guild's salary demands.[73]

Even without the benefits of a general increase, writers for its magazines received over $180 per week on average in 1948, with the highest paid among them pulling down more than $300 weekly, making them among the top earners in New York's culture industries. For many of the company's affluent writers, editors, photographers, art directors, and other creative professionals, issues of personal autonomy furnished a more compelling rationale to back the Newspaper Guild. Since its earliest days at Time, the Guild had repeatedly sparred with management over the company's desire to regulate its employees' "outside activities," including public speaking—live or via radio broadcast— as well as freelance writing and artistic projects for other media enterprises. In May 1947, Luce and Larsen announced that all outside activities by employees required prior vetting by upper management, and they explicitly prohibited Time employees from selling any work to competing publications.[74] In part, management was responding to several recent cases in which prominent journalists closely associated with the company's media brands had not only profited from their connection to Time Inc. but also contributed to its rivals. Writer John Hersey, for example, had used material from his assignments as a wartime correspondent for *Time* and *Life* as the basis for his Pulitzer Prize-winning novel *A Bell for Adano* (1944) and had subsequently peeved Luce by reporting on the nuclear attack on Hiroshima and its survivors for *The New Yorker* in 1946, all while remaining a conspicuous Guild supporter.[75] If rigorously enforced, the policy would also ban projects with artistic merit if not profit potential, such as James Agee and Walker Evans's *Let Us Now Praise Famous Men* (1941), which was based upon material from an unsuccessful *Fortune* assignment to report on the rural South.[76] The new policy also sought to muzzle the company's remaining Popular Fronters. "Time, Inc.'s editorial policies are laid down after thoughtful deliberation," Larsen informed employees regarding the new policy, and if a journalist, "after equally thoughtful deliberation, finds that he fundamentally disagrees with those policies, then it seems an inevitable conclusion that he should not be writing for publication in Time Inc. magazines material with which he disagrees." In an increasingly polarized political environment, management was becoming less tolerant of intellectual or artistic independence within the interstices of the media empire.[77]

In their critique of the new policy, Guild activists at Time Inc. posited an alternative conception of writers and artists' roles that emphasized creative autonomy rather than managerial control. Acknowledging the company's right "to determine the framework of editorial policy which governs and shapes all writing done for Time publications," they nonetheless contended that "by the same token, any self-respecting individual in a society of free men must reserve the right to his own opinions and the expression of them." In contrast with Luce and Larsen's invocations of the First Amendment to justify their opposition to union security, they asserted, "as a citizen in a democracy," the journalist "has not only a right but a responsibility to voice and act upon his views whenever he believes that such expression and action may benefit society." Because "few writers can make a living by writing books alone, or find employment with publications that exactly coincide with their points of view," they continued, the overwhelming majority had no option other than "accepting employment within the structure of large-scale press, radio, and cinema organizations." In short, it was "unrealistic to suggest that a writer should not work for any publication in which he does not see eye to eye with the publisher." Furthermore, Guild activists maintained that diversity of opinion was in Time Inc.'s financial interest. "In a sense," they concluded, the company's "chief stock in trade, as its promotional activities recognize, is its readers' belief that Time writers are not slaves in mental bondage."[78]

Few moves by management could have generated more opposition from the company's creative staff. Two-thirds of the company's writers and photographers signed the Guild's petition condemning the new policy. Some objected primarily to the restrictions on the use of notes, interviews, or photographs that they produced while on assignment but that were not used directly by the company in its media content. They wondered if they would be prevented from leveraging their labors, as Hersey had, into substantial additional income as well as a degree of individual recognition that transcended Luce's vision of group journalism. Furthermore, these tensions over creative autonomy within Time Inc. occurred against the backdrop of Popular Fronters' concerns about the marginalization of progressive perspectives within the media. Signers of the union's petition were undoubtedly aware of the controversies surrounding the cancelation of prominent progressive radio commentators like William Shirer, and Guild activists were important early supporters of the Voice of Freedom committee. While still under McManus's leadership, the Newspaper Guild of New York joined with the UOPWA locals in the culture industries to hold a conference on the mounting threats to the "freedom of the press." Larsen responded to the criticism elicited by the company's more restrictive policy on outside activities by appearing to soften his stance, claiming that all cases would be reviewed on an individual basis, which, of course, still entailed largely unfettered managerial discretion. Top executives at Time remained sensitive to negative publicity; in September 1947, when journalist Don Hollenbeck planned to devote an episode of his weekly radio program *CBS Views the News* to examining the policy and its critics, Time executives contacted CBS chairman William Paley and president Frank Stanton to try to kill the show before it was scheduled to air. When Guild activists parodied *Time* magazine's "man of the year" with a mock cover featuring labor-relations executive Louis Gratz, management threatened the union with legal action for copyright infringement.[79]

Even as Guild members at Time continued to resist management's efforts to undermine the union and reassert control over the creative process, the changes in the local's leadership impeded their efforts. The purge of all local staff with Popular Front affinities eliminated those like Irving Gilman and Margaret March who appreciated the differences between newspaper and magazine publishing. Murphy took over as lead negotiator in the Guild's bargaining with Time, but his lack of expertise only made management's intransigence more effective. Following the end of the previous contract on October 1, 1948, negotiations on a new agreement dragged on for another full year as the company refused to compromise.[80] Murphy questioned magazine workers' dedication to the union, deriding the Time unit, for example, as a "minority" unit, even though Guild activists at Time insisted that they had 70 percent of the unit signed up. In the summer of 1949, Guild members began to publicize their bargaining deadlock and organize for a possible strike, as they had three years earlier. Despite their more careful preparations, there remained members who wavered on striking, while Murphy, who failed to grasp the Time unit's importance to the Guild's overall organizing prospects, declined to commit the necessary resources. Time management made a few late concessions on minimum salaries and job reclassifications, and Murphy pushed the unit to accept the settlement. In October, Guild members at Time Inc. ratified the new contract.[81]

Guild enthusiasts tried to put a positive spin on the agreement, but the dismal terms of the 1949 settlement set the course for subsequent decline. Better-paid employees increasingly saw the financial obligations of solidarity with other workers in the city's print media as being unwarranted by their limited personal gains from unionism. The local's imposition of a hefty 5 percent assessment in June 1950 to finance the strike against the *World-Telegram and Sun* sparked a wave of resignations by *Life* writers who earned well above the salary cut-off and had not benefitted from any negotiated general increase since the war.[82] Although its alliance with the printing and press unions had given the Guild leverage against the vertically integrated newspapers, there was no comparable means of exerting pressure on Time, which outsourced the printing of its magazines, primarily to virulently antiunion R. R. Donnelly and Sons. In subsequent contract negotiations through the 1950s, Time Inc. management kept its uncompromising stance on union security and individual job security. While the company did agree to raise the salary cut-off for general increases to $175 per week in 1951, it still exempted more than 20 percent of the employees in the editorial departments, including the majority of the writers, editors, photographers, artists, and other creative professionals whose labor was most essential. Unlike some of the struggling newspapers, Time maintained its opposition to the union's demands at a time when it enjoyed record profits and significantly expanded its editorial staff with new initiatives like *Sports Illustrated* magazine and Time-Life Books. By the end of the decade, as the number of employees in the bargaining unit increased to more than 1,200, fewer than half were Guild members in good standing.[83]

Time's relentless campaign to undermine the Newspaper Guild, and the union's apparent inability to overcome it, furnished a primer for other magazine publishers. *Newsweek* and *Look*, which had initially accepted the Guild's demands on union security in 1946, reversed course once the union accepted the end of maintenance of membership at Time Inc. without a strike. Although *Newsweek* consistently agreed to a slightly more generous minimum salary schedule than Time, in other regards it closely followed its rival in collective bargaining.[84] Other magazine publishers saw Time management's approach as way to prevent unionism from taking root in the first place, even as lagging salaries led many white-collar workers to favor organization. In the fall of 1950, employees of Macfadden Publications approached the Guild to initiate a membership drive at the down-market publisher. The union won a certification election there by a margin of 61–41 the following May, but for the first time in its history it failed to negotiate a first contract for a sizeable group of workers who had chosen the Guild as their bargaining representative. Macfadden executives stalled on negotiations while retaliating against Guild activists, daring the union to commit the resources necessary to either win a recognition strike or get the NLRB to take the publisher to court. With no contract after more than a year, the momentum for unionization fizzled. The Guild also conducted a much larger organizing drive at Fairchild Publications, which produced trade periodicals like *Women's Wear Daily*, *Retailing Daily*, and *Supermarket News*. Although some Fairchild employees had first expressed interest in joining the Guild back in the mid-1940s, the union only commenced a serious drive in early 1952. The Guild signed up a majority of the firm's roughly 650 employees at its New York headquarters, but the company succeeded in convincing the NLRB to include in the bargaining unit another 150 employees scattered in bureaus around the country, who had no contact with the organizing efforts. While hearings at the Board delayed balloting, Fairchild management intensified its antiunion activities. When the election was held that June, the Guild was defeated by a margin of 427 votes to 283, which ended for the remainder of the decade the union's attempts to organize new shops in the magazine field.[85]

The Newspaper Guild's compliance with the Taft-Hartley Act protected the union as an institution and the livelihoods of most of its members from the adverse effects of domestic anticommunism, but individual journalists with procommunist pasts found themselves under greater scrutiny. Since its birth in the 1930s, Guild proponents had argued that organization enhanced press freedom by securing journalists' autonomy, even as publishers insisted that unions of editorial employees contravened the First Amendment. As the pressures of the Cold War mounted, the Guild sometimes equivocated on its commitment to the right of journalists and other media workers to hold controversial political beliefs. Its official stance echoed the liberal anticommunism of groups such as Americans for Democratic Action, which condemned the excesses of demagogues like Senator McCarthy. Liberal anticommunist journalists and editors sometimes found themselves subjected to the very pressure tactics they deplored. In the early 1950s, for instance, McCarthy and his associates lashed out repeatedly at James Wechsler, the fiercely anticommunist editor of the *New York Post*, over his membership in the Young Communist League during the late 1930s as a way of retaliating for the paper's denunciations of the Senator. As part of his efforts to defend his reputation, Wechsler ultimately sued *Daily Mirror* columnist Walter Winchell for libel for insinuating that Wechsler had secretly remained a Communist despite his long public record as an opponent of Stalinism.[86]

Liberal anticommunists assailed McCarthy and his acolytes for their use of innuendo and hearsay evidence as well as their lack of concern for due process as they attacked their targets. Yet by casting Communists as not just political adversaries but as pariahs, these liberals contributed to the repressive climate that they found so disturbing. At its 1954 annual convention, the ANG executive board declared that the union must "resist by every means possible any discharge or discipline of Guild members on grounds that they refuse to sign a loyalty oath or that they exercise their rights of freedom of expression, or that they invoked the protection of the Bill of Rights." Simultaneously, however, it insisted, "the Guild recognizes that membership in the Communist Party represents more than a political conviction and is in fact participation in a criminal conspiracy to destroy the freedoms we uphold." Following the board's recommendation, delegates to the next year's convention ratified an amendment to the ANG constitution that absolved the union from responsibility for protecting the job security of members discharged on account of proven Communist activity within the previous six months. The issue of what constituted proof became a crucial matter as writers, reporters, and editors subpoenaed to testify before Congressional investigators invoked their Fifth Amendment protections against self-incrimination.[87]

For a number of journalists who had been active in New York's Popular Front, the inquisitorial powers of the Cold War state were brought to bear in 1955 and 1956, when the Senate Internal Security Subcommittee opened a new series of hearings following allegations of Communist infiltration leveled by CBS news correspondent Winston Burdett. Burdett had first admitted his past involvement with the Communist Party to CBS management in 1951 as a result of the network's security program. At the request of his superiors, he then met with the FBI to discuss his past radical activities. The matter seemed closed until Burdett, fearful of additional scrutiny, opted in 1955 to reach out to SISS and its chairman, the reactionary segregationist James Eastland of Mississippi. Burdett informed SISS that he had not been entirely forthcoming in his earlier disclosures to the FBI or CBS management and wanted to testify regarding the complete extent of his Communist associations. He claimed that he had joined the CP in the late 1930s while working for the *Brooklyn Eagle* and had been recruited for Soviet espionage through the Communist caucus within the Newspaper Guild of New York. Using his journalist credentials as cover, between 1940 and 1943 Burdett had traveled throughout Europe and the Middle East as an agent for Soviet intelligence before breaking with the Communists. Conforming to established practice by the mid-1950s, in his SISS testimony he named twenty-three journalists who he claimed had belonged to the CP. Nearly all of those Burdett identified were among the thirty-seven New York-based reporters and editors who received subpoenas from the committee. A few of those summoned to appear before SISS had remained active in the collapsing procommunist left, such as McManus, who had been the American Labor Party's candidate for governor of New York in 1950 and 1954 as well as coeditor of the *National Guardian*, but most had long ago distanced themselves from the CP.[88]

The hearings precipitated a crisis for the Newspaper Guild of New York, as publishers instantly fired journalists who invoked their Fifth Amendment privileges when questioned about their past Communist activities. For many, taking the Fifth was not only a way to protect themselves, but also a way to avoid informing on others. After *New York Times* copyeditor Melvin Barnet, one of the first witnesses called before SISS in July 1955, followed this reasoning in exercising his Fifth Amendment rights, publisher Arthur Hays Sulzberger notified him that "the course of conduct which you have followed since your name was first mentioned" had "caused *The Times* to lose confidence in you as a member of its news staff." Guild leaders and activists, like the publishers, were wary of appearing sympathetic to communism, but they also saw the firings as threatening the job security and grievance provisions in the union's major contracts. Between the first and second sessions of the SISS hearings, the New York Guild held a membership referendum regarding the local's obligation to journalists who took the Fifth. A majority of 3,185 voted that the local should consider each situation individually, while 2,064 favored automatic enforcement of the contract to defend the employment rights of all who were discharged.[89] When the hearings reconvened in January 1956, some additional witnesses invoked the Fifth Amendment, while four of them justified their refusal to answer the committee's questions by claiming their First Amendment liberties, earning them contempt citations and possible prison sentences. Three of the four—Robert Shelton, Alden Whitman, and Seymour Peck—worked for the *Times*, but unlike Barnet they retained their jobs while they awaited trial; the fourth, *Daily News* reporter William Price, was discharged, further complicating the New York Guild's quandary over contract enforcement.[90]

The local opted to pursue arbitration in an attempt to obtain reinstatement for some of its members who had been fired on account of their SISS testimony, but in the first cases adjudicated the arbitrators rejected the union's defense of its members and upheld the publishers' right to terminate employees who invoked the Fifth Amendment when questioned about Communist ties. In the case of Dan Mahoney, whom the *Daily Mirror* had fired from his position on its night rewrite desk, the arbitrator asserted that "a rewrite man can select the facts he considers important as relayed to him by the reporter in the field," and even though his work was subject to editorial supervision, he was nonetheless "in a position where he has the opportunity and capacity to do great harm." Although none of the articles that Mahoney had worked on in his twenty-two years with the paper were suspect, the arbitrator still concluded that Mahoney's SISS testimony had "raised a grave and gnawing doubt in the mind of his employer as to his association and connection with the Communist conspiracy," thereby providing *Mirror* management with "good and sufficient cause" for dismissal within the terms of the contract. In refusing to reinstate Mahoney, the arbitrator implicitly recapitulated the logic that publishers had unsuccessfully deployed earlier to obtain a press exemption from union security measures: that journalists' external political allegiances compromised their effectiveness. Although Burdett, who had actually been a Soviet agent, kept his job at CBS and was lauded by Senator Eastland for his patriotism, Barnet, Mahoney, and other witnesses who had only been named as former members of the CP had their careers ruined.[91]

The four journalists who had invoked the First Amendment in their SISS appearances all faced trial for contempt in 1957. Although they turned to the Guild for support, their union backed away from the strong commitment to journalistic autonomy and a positive conception of the First Amendment that had long motivated many Guild activists. Once the journalists' fight became a matter of civil liberties rather than contract enforcement, the Guild lost interest. All four were convicted and sentenced to prison terms of a few months, but their sentences were suspended as they appealed their cases in the more favorable legal climate of the late 1950s. Eventually all of them were able to win their appeals without serving any jail time, and their arduous legal victories furnished one indication of the thawing of the domestic Cold War.[92] Yet the Newspaper Guild of New York's feeble response to their plight, and to the more general allegations of subversion of which it was a part, illustrated poignantly the changes that the union's accommodation to the virulent anticommunism of the late 1940s and early 1950s had wrought. The journalists summoned before SISS had joined the CP largely out of their dedication to the Popular Front. For most of them, joining had seemed at the time a logical extension of the Guild's social unionism. By the second half of the 1950s, the Popular Front vision that had animated the Newspaper Guild and the other white-collar unions in New York's culture industries had atrophied to the point where the union was unwilling to defend members who had been among the most fervent proponents of social unionism in its heyday. Confined increasingly to its core jurisdiction of daily newspaper publishing, the Guild had largely eschewed any broader social vision in favor of a safe but stagnant contractualism.

Black Channels: Anticommunism, the Broadcasting Talent Guilds, and the Transition from Radio to Television

In broadcasting, several significant developments coincided to make the Cold War crusade against progressives during the late 1940s and early 1950s not only more conspicuous than in the print media, but also more effective. The surging tide of domestic anticommunism occurred at a time of substantial increases in advertising expenditures on the broadcast media. Unlike in the print media, in which it was always possible for a new publisher to enter the field and offer space to potential advertisers, the oligopolistic structure of American broadcasting placed finite limits on the inventory of airtime that could be sold. With the torrent of advertising dollars that poured into broadcasting during and after the Second World War, the costs of airtime spiraled upward. All of the enterprises involved in making radio and television content—commercial sponsors, advertising agencies, independent "package" producers, the major networks, and affiliated local stations—became increasingly averse to any form of negative publicity as they tried to orient programming toward acceptance by the largest audiences. Since multiple firms affected decisions about the employment of actors, directors, writers, and other talent, a veto from any of these entities could easily result in either the firing or the refusal to hire anyone who had drawn the attention of anticommunist activists.

The onset of the Cold War also overlapped with the rapid transition from radio to television as the primary broadcast medium for advertising-supported programming. Broadcasters' total gross revenue from the sale of airtime jumped from $433 million in 1946 to $913 million in 1953, but they funneled much of their increased earnings into their initial capital investments in television production, networking, and transmission facilities.[93] Consequently, broadcasters tended to be quite cost-conscious during the late 1940s, as the networks and the owners of major AM stations who had secured television licenses from the FCC looked to their radio operations to finance their shift into television for as long as possible. As television spread, advertisers soon decided that it was a more effective medium for selling than radio. In the New York market, the cost-per-thousand impressions (CPM) rates for evening prime-time television by 1950 already doubled those for the top radio programs. With the completion of the nationwide network infrastructure and the speedy proliferation of television receivers, the swing in the relative importance of the two media to the networks' fortunes was dramatic. In 1950, NBC still earned 75 percent of its gross revenues from radio, while rivals CBS and ABC earned 85 percent from radio; by 1954 CBS, the top-grossing network that year, earned more than 70 percent of its revenues from television, and many industry insiders began predicting the demise of network radio programming.[94] Even as broadcasting boomed, the fast pace of change in the industry led to instability both for firms involved in the production of broadcasting content and for the creative and technical professionals they employed.

Unionists in the broadcasting industry redoubled their organizing efforts during the late 1940s and early 1950s, and their struggles to gain greater control over the terms and conditions of their work shaped nearly every aspect of the anticommunist campaign in radio and television. Although managerial resistance had blunted the UOPWA Radio Guild's organizing push during the reconversion period, the talent guilds, whose members had more leverage than the range of white-collar workers organized by the UOPWA, proved to be more successful in strengthening their position in the industry. The Radio Writers Guild, which had only secured its first contracts for network staff writers in 1944, negotiated a minimum basic agreement that covered freelancers writing network-produced content in 1947. The following year, it compelled independent producers and the advertising agencies—which still directly produced many top shows—to begin signing memoranda of adherence to the terms of the network freelance MBA. Significantly, many RWG activists also supported progressive groups like the VOF as well as those within the FCC, like commissioner Clifford Durr, who wished to reform broadcasting practices. Anticommunism provided employers with a powerful weapon to use against unions like the RWG, but much of the redbaiting resulted from divisions within the creative ranks. By the late 1940s, jurisdictional conflicts over the representation of television talent led the Hollywood-based Screen Writers Guild to attack the RWG as "Communist," while Reagan's Screen Actors Guild made similar accusations against its rival, the American Federation of Radio Artists. Within the RWG itself, some of the more conservative writers, who had never been entirely comfortable with the organization's evolution into a labor union, leveled allegations of subversion against those activists who were the most forceful advocates of collective action.

As the RWG began its postwar growth, its supporters confronted a wide disparity in writers' working conditions. Writers for the most popular shows frequently earned handsome salaries of $10,000 to $15,000 per year, but the majority earned far less. According to the FCC, in 1946 staff writers employed by clear-channel 50 kilowatt stations earned $63.83 per week on average, compared with $88.75 for announcers, $224.76 for salesmen, and $299.00 for executives. For writers employed by small local stations, the situation was much worse, with weekly salaries averaging just $34.19 a week, barely above the pay for clerical staff.[95] Logistical issues and limited resources, however, led the RWG to focus its organizing efforts on the broadcasting centers of New York, Los Angeles, and to a lesser extent Chicago, where the largest concentrations of radio writers worked and the most valuable programming was produced. The RWG opened discussions with the advertising agencies at the war's end to try to obtain a satisfactory MBA for the freelancers who wrote scripts for agency-produced shows, but they found that the agency executives refused to accede to the writers' key demands, particularly with respect to employment stability, residual income, and intellectual property rights. After more than a year of fruitless talks, the RWG temporarily set aside its quest for a freelance MBA with the advertising agencies in late 1946 to concentrate instead on the freelancers who wrote network-produced entertainment programming. Since the networks' salaried staff writers had already established collective bargaining during the war without too much resistance, RWG leaders contended that adoption of a network MBA was a logical next step. Network executives initially balked for several reasons. While the law clearly defined their salaried staff as employees with the right to unionize, the position of freelancers, who could be construed as independent contractors, was far more ambiguous. Also, executives knew firsthand how their organized staff writers had been able to pressure them into raising salaries, at first with the help of the NWLB, and they feared that the payment scale proposed by the RWG would put them at a competitive disadvantage relative to the advertising agencies and independent producers. In addition, they were reluctant to agree to the intellectual property rights that the writers sought in the MBA.[96]

Having taken a low-key approach with the agencies as a way of preempting criticisms from the conservative minority of RWG members, the leadership vigorously pressed the fight for a network MBA for freelance writers. The RWG mounted a publicity campaign that included full-page ads in *Variety* and the *Hollywood Reporter* that listed all of the writers on leading programs who belonged to the Guild and backed its demands. In addition, for the first time ever, RWG members voted to authorize a strike against the networks.[97] Facing the loss of scripts for most of the entertainment programming that they produced directly, the networks in October 1947 finally accepted a free-lance MBA that included much of what the writers wanted. The agreement raised minimum fees to $500 per script for an hour-long sponsored program and $325 for an hour-long sustaining program, and it restructured the script procurement process to increase the share of writing done by freelancers on season-long contracts. The agreement also provided union security, as it required 90 percent of the freelancers hired to write for network-produced programs to be RWG members. Additionally, it guaranteed on-air credit for writers and enabled them to retain significant literary rights to their scripts. Buoyed by this achievement, by year's end RWG membership climbed to more than 1,600 writers.[98]

With contracts in place for one group of freelance writers, RWG activists turned their attention back to the advertising agencies only to find that they were as obstinate as ever. The agencies dismissed the initial RWG requests for negotiations with pro forma statements that they would only follow the lead of their trade association, the American Association of Advertising Agencies, in matters of labor relations, while the 4As in turn maintained that it had no standing to engage in collective bargaining since it was not an employer. Moreover, with the passage of the Taft-Hartley Act, some agencies began to use the Guild's lack of NLRB certification as yet another reason to refuse an agreement. The RWG countered that the agencies could legally recognize it without certification, and in May 1948 they solicited the services of the Federal Mediation and Conciliation Service to help break the deadlock.[99] As with the networks, it was ultimately the writers' own determination that produced a compromise settlement. A strike authorization in October convinced many of the agencies and independent producers to agree to a compromise in which the producers did not directly enter into collective bargaining with the RWG but instead signed memoranda of adherence in which they consented to abide by the terms of the network MBA. Several major agencies and sponsor-producers, including BBDO and Proctor and Gamble, still refused to sign, leading the writers for their shows to mount the first strike in the history of the RWG. After a few weeks of picketing and withheld scripts, the holdouts capitulated by the end of the year.[100] Although touted as another win for the writers, the lack of a legally binding contract between the RWG and these producers made it difficult to adjudicate formal grievances over rights and residuals, or to enforce job security provisions, which would eventually limit the union's ability to protect its members from blacklisting.

As the RWG came into its own as a representative of writers' economic and legal interests, it also became a more conspicuous participant in discourse about the proper role of the broadcast media in a democratic society. Many RWG activists believed that the fulfillment of progressive public service goals by the networks and station owners was inherently desirable for political reasons, but they also contended that a system of broadcasting that was more aligned toward public needs would be one in which writers and other culture workers would enjoy improved working conditions and expanded creative opportunities. When RWG members criticized the cancelation of progressive news commentators John Vandercook on NBC and William Shirer on CBS, they were not just protesting the loss of employment by two of their organization's leading activists, but also signaling their conviction that their own autonomy as writers was enhanced in a media environment in which voices like Shirer's could remain on the nation's airwaves. After RWG president Erik Barnouw testified before the FCC in March 1948 in favor of maintaining the Mayflower Doctrine, which was intended to prevent station owners from propagandizing solely their own political beliefs, he wrote to the other national officers to share his "own impression" of the hearings since "the papers (and radio) gave an inadequate and misleading account." Barnouw reported that the "FCC meets a long procession of lawyers and licensees" but "almost never anyone from the program side of radio." Once he had finished reading his prepared statement, the commissioners peppered him with questions about "the status of the radio writer, how much chance he has to express himself, to what extent he influences program content, how radio writers work, whether commercials are written by our members," and "whether I thought there was a growing trend for institutional commercials to express political philosophy."[101] Progressive activists interested in broadcasting reform also continued to look to the RWG as a natural ally. Stella Holt of the VOF, for instance, wrote to the union in July 1949 to offer support against blacklisting, and again in March 1950 in an attempt to enlist RWG backing for the VOF campaign to get the first African American news commentator onto network radio.[102]

Just as the RWG appeared on the verge of consolidating its position, it slid into a legal and jurisdictional morass that sapped its momentum. In January 1949, a federal district court ruled that a boycott by the Dramatists Guild, which like the RWG and SWG was part of the Authors' League of America, against a theatrical producer who violated its minimum basic agreement for playwrights constituted an unlawful restraint of trade since it had not been certified by the NLRB. Because the RWG had similarly sought voluntary recognition without certification, it found that most of its agreements with producers could not be enforced in their current form.[103] Moreover, the problem of NLRB certification was complicated by the matter of Taft-Hartley Section 9(h), as several members of the RWG national council, notably procommunists Peter Lyon, the union's most effective contract negotiator, and Sam Moore, could not sign the required affidavits and soon resigned in favor of writers who could comply. NLRB General Counsel Robert Denham exacerbated the situation by holding that not only the officers and national council members of the RWG had to file, but also the officers and council members of the Authors' League as its parent organization. Some of these individuals objected to filing on civil libertarian grounds, while others objected that the League was in fact not a labor union. Eventually the RWG attained compliance and certification, but in the interim the advertising agencies, independent producers, and networks all took advantage of the union's uncertain legal status.[104]

The union's difficulties with the NLRB also coincided with serious disputes between the RWG, the SWG, and the Authors' League over the organization of the swelling ranks of television writers. In December 1948, the League proposed chartering a new Television Writers Guild (TWG) to join its existing divisions, and it directed both the RWG and the SWG to refrain from any further organizing of writers who worked entirely in the new television medium. Neither group found the League's decision acceptable. The RWG argued that since it already covered network staff writers as well as freelancers writing for most of the firms currently producing television programming, it was only logical that it should have primary jurisdiction over television. Conversely, the SWG maintained that television writing was analogous to writing for motion pictures, and that filmed television content would become more prevalent in the future. In addition, many writers disliked the prospect of paying dues to multiple guilds. The rapid ascendancy of the new medium represented both the potential for increased membership and economic prominence as well as the risk of marginalization for these existing guilds. While the League tried to prop up its TWG with few members and no contracts, both the SWG and the RWG competed for the loyalty of newcomers to television writing.[105] As the League's clumsy meddling stymied the RWG's efforts to expand and to continue improving conditions, many members began to contemplate the possibility of becoming an independent union or affiliating with either the AFL or CIO.

As RWG activists tussled with employers, the NLRB, and rival groups of writers, the intensification of the anticommunist crusade created additional difficulties. Many key figures in the RWG had long identified with the Popular Front. While their progressive political orientation had not impeded the union's organizational growth in 1947 and 1948, their associations increasingly provided ammunition for their right-wing adversaries. During the late 1940s, the escalating anticommunist attacks on Popular Fronters in the entertainment fields that appeared in the pages of *Counterattack* or the Hearst press only sporadically resulted in their discharge or denial of employment. Early cases, such as the July 1949 firing of William Sweets, director of the radio crime thriller *Gangbusters*, garnered attention because they were so rare. Sweets had been president of the Radio and Television Directors Guild, but he had resigned his union post in late 1948 because he could not comply with Section 9(h). Eventually, negative publicity about his political associations led the production company that employed Sweets and the sponsors of the shows he directed, General Foods and Pepsi-Cola, to cut him loose. The VOF made him the public face of its protests against the onset of blacklisting, and some of the most outspoken figures in the broadcasting industry, like procommunist radio writer Millard Lampell, called for consumers to boycott the sponsors that had let Sweets go.[106]

As instances of blacklisting proliferated, the RWG, AFRA, and RTDG all formed "fact-finding" committees in the first months of 1950 to examine the problem, but employers began a systematic purge of the broadcast industry during the second half of the year. The publication of *Red Channels* in June stunned many of those who worked in radio and television; one RWG leader recounted that when an advance copy was passed around a membership meeting, "you couldn't hear anyone talk over the loud gasps."[107] North Korea's surprise invasion of the South within days of *Red Channels'* release only made the publication's insinuations of Communist subversion all the more alarming. At a July meeting of the RWG Eastern Region Council, anticommunist writer Welbourne Kelley introduced a resolution pledging the union's support of the United Nations' efforts at repelling the Communist assault in Korea. When a majority on the council tabled the resolution on procedural grounds, Kelley and other anticommunists both inside and outside the RWG howled that the incident proved the extent of Communist infiltration in the broadcasting unions. The accusations opened deep fissures within the union's leadership, as some figures who had previously aligned with the progressives tried to distance themselves. Noting in October that "during recent months there have been rumors to the effect that a small communist minority is trying to dominate the guild," Barnouw asserted that "many of our members are asking for reassurance on the matter" and that "they, as well as the public, are entitled to it." Conversely, RWG stalwart Hector Chevigny contended that "what is agitating the Guild today is a recrudescence of the old struggle between opposing viewpoints as to the Guild's objectives and destiny," and that most of those who "have charged the present Eastern Council with being Communist-dominated" had long resisted the movement toward militant tactics, including strikes, that had been "forced upon the Guild by the needs and demands of the members." Although the slate of candidates opposed by the anticommunists handily won the RWG national elections that fall, the redbaiters in the union—organized into a caucus known as "We The Undersigned"—publicly denounced many of the Guild's current and former leaders before HUAC and SISS over the next several years.[108]

In the first phase of systematic blacklisting after *Red Channels*, pressure from anticommunist activists on sponsors, advertising agencies, packagers, and networks about the continued employment of listed talent furnished the pretext for a wave of dismissals. The highly publicized firing of actress Jean Muir in August 1950 illustrated the new trend. Muir, who had nine citations in *Red Channels*, including her support for the Spanish Refugee Relief Campaign and her message of congratulations to the Moscow Arts Theater on its fiftieth anniversary, had been cast in *The Aldrich Family*, a television situation comedy produced by Young and Rubicam for General Foods and aired nationally by NBC. Just before the fall season of the series was to begin, anticommunist protests led to her last-minute replacement with another actress. Muir accepted a settlement in which she received her full salary of over $10,000 for the eighteen-episode season, but her career was effectively finished.[109] For Muir and similarly persecuted actors, performers, writers, and directors, acceptance of a financial settlement, when available, reflected a realistic assessment of the weakened grievance procedures in their union contracts and the anticommunist prejudices of likely arbitrators in the early 1950s. Philip Loeb, another prominent target of the blacklisters, had been a militant unionist in Actors Equity since the 1930s. Anticommunists' complaints regarding his citations in *Red Channels* led to his replacement on *The Goldbergs* in late 1951. Although the producer agreed to a settlement in which Loeb received nearly $40,000 over the next several years, his inability to work helped drive him to suicide in 1955.[110] Arnold Perl, the first writer fired from Prockter Productions for political reasons, had also been listed in *Red Channels*. When he was discharged in May 1951, Perl agreed to a settlement worth up to $20,000 over three years, reflecting both his writing for current shows as well as the potential value of several programs in development, although Prockter subsequently reneged on part of the deal.[111]

In all of these cases, the dismissal of well-known talent already under contract resulted in considerable expense for producers and sponsors in addition to adverse publicity. By the time Prockter Productions fired Abram Ginnes a year after Perl, blacklisting in radio and television was already moving into a second phase in which those who might be considered controversial were screened from hiring. Executive producers and others responsible for talent were required to check all prospects with the "security" offices of the networks and top advertising agencies, or to consult their own internal lists of acceptable personnel. Security staff euphemistically described blacklisted actors, writers, and directors as "not available," even when they were desperately seeking work. As blacklisting became an institutionalized practice, it affected a pool of people well beyond those listed in *Red Channels*. The ongoing investigations of broadcasting by HUAC and SISS generated a steady stream of suspects, while professional blacklisters scrutinized additional figures in the entertainment industry. When Prockter, for example, compiled its internal security list in June 1952 with guidance from the anticommunist AWARE Inc., it barred 138 out of the roughly 600 persons who had performed in the production company's programs since its inception. Until the end of the decade, this system of screening operated smoothly and discreetly, if not always consistently. Many individuals discovered that they could work on one network but not another, or that they could work on programs with some sponsors but not others—sometimes referred to as "graylisting"—although this only demonstrated further the system's capriciousness.[112]

The institutionalization of blacklisting only deepened the political schisms within the broadcasting unions. In both the RWG and the American Federation of Television and Radio Artists (AFTRA, as AFRA rebranded itself in 1952) a minority of vehement anticommunists abetted the process of blacklisting through their participation in AWARE, which counted professional blacklisters Vincent Hartnett and Laurence Johnson as members of its executive board. AWARE contended that any efforts to resist blacklisting were tantamount to assisting the Communist conspiracy and that actors, writers, or directors who had supported Popular Front causes and who refused to renounce their past commitments and embrace a muscular anticommunism deserved to be denied employment. The RWG's "We The Undersigned" caucus joined forces with AWARE in its ongoing efforts to unseat those officers it judged insufficiently anticommunist. After losing elections in 1950 and 1951, "We The Undersigned" escalated its attacks by publicizing an August 1952 report by SISS that slammed the RWG as "Communist-dominated." In response, the membership handed "We The Undersigned" its biggest defeat yet that November, as the overwhelming majority saw the caucus' tactics as weakening the union.[113]

In AFTRA, vocal anticommunists, including several associated with AWARE, gained a majority on the union's national executive board that they held from 1951 through 1955. AFTRA president George Heller maintained a publicly neutral stance that managed to prevent the union from splintering along its ideological fault lines, but his strained impartiality ultimately worked to the advantage of the anticommunist faction and badly undermined the union's resistance to blacklisting. Actors who were outspoken critics of blacklisting often found that their views were used to justify their loss or denial of employment. As AWARE became more active in encouraging blacklisted actors to "clear" themselves, AFTRA membership meetings by 1953 and 1954 frequently featured speeches in which actors seeking rehabilitation conspicuously affirmed their anticommunism. In June 1955, however, when the beleaguered opponents of blacklisting within the New York local of AFTRA finally succeeded in holding a secret-ballot referendum on a resolution condemning AWARE for its "smear methods," members voted in favor by a 982 to 514 vote margin, marking the beginning of the end of the union's complicity with blacklisting.[114]

While AFTRA made a weaker stand in protecting the employment rights of its members than the RWG did, it was more effective than the unions for radio and television writers in advancing its other collective bargaining objectives. Heller's ability to maintain a façade of unity paved the way between 1952 and 1954 for the negotiation of a comprehensive Pension and Welfare Plan for AFTRA members, tailored to their itinerant working patterns. Under the arrangement, producers paid a contribution equal to 5 percent of the "gross compensation" for actors and other on-air talent into a fund that furnished union members, who typically worked for many different firms and also experienced periodic gaps in employment, with access to healthcare, retirement income, and other benefits.[115] For the RWG, ideological turmoil and its interminable jurisdictional squabbles with the other divisions of the Authors' League made it difficult to build upon the gains it had won for writers in the late 1940s. In July 1952, the RWG struck the networks for the first time, as news, dramatic, and continuity staff writers fought to win improved compensation and rights, particularly for writers of sponsored news programs. Unfortunately, the worsening dysfunction hobbled the union's efforts to advance the interests of freelance television writers at a crucial juncture in the development of the new medium. When the SWG called a jurisdictional strike against West Coast producers of filmed television programming in August, most RWG writers employed by the targeted firms refused to participate on the grounds that the SWG was trying to impose an agreement that was inferior to the RWG standard. After the strike failed, largely because RWG members with no allegiance to the SWG continued working, recriminations within the League reached a fever pitch.[116]

On the West Coast, the ongoing jurisdictional feud in the midst of a boom in filmed television production forced many union-conscious writers to conclude that their interests could only be served by founding a new organization, the Television Writers of America (TWA). RWG members formed the initial nucleus of TWA, and they hoped to arrange for the RWG to secede from the League and join their new union. By spring 1953, the TWA had gained enough momentum to petition the NLRB for a certification election to represent freelance writers on network-produced programs. The Board's decision in favor of a single national bargaining unit for each of the networks only provided additional impetus for the new union's spread among New York-based writers. Even though two-thirds of the 425 writers eligible to vote in the election were working primarily in the East, a whirlwind organizing blitz headed by TWA president Dick Powell and TWA executive secretary Joan LaCour enabled the insurgents to win an upset victory in the balloting and wrest from the Authors' League and its constituent guilds the heart of the television writing jurisdiction. After the balloting had concluded, the TWA quickly assembled an Eastern Council that united the factions within the RWG, with Irve Tunick, a resolute anticommunist nearing the peak of his prominence as a writer for prestigious live dramatic programs, and Ernest Kinoy, one of the most militant unionists among the New York-based writers, publicly serving as cochairs.[117]

This fleeting harmony among television writers was shattered late in 1953 when a HUAC informer named LaCour as a former member of the Communist Party. She admitted to the TWA cadre that she had briefly belonged to the CP while she was working with the ICCASP and PCA in 1946 and 1947 but when she appeared before HUAC she invoked the Fifth Amendment in order to avoid naming others. When the TWA Western Region announced it would keep LaCour as its executive secretary despite her refusal to cooperate with HUAC, Tunick and other members of the executive council resigned. More ominously, the new union's negotiations for a new MBA for network freelancers ground to a halt. TWA supporters sought a substantial increase in minimum fees to over $700 per script for a sponsored half-hour program along with enhanced rights and a union shop, but after the latest schism the companies determined that they could break the union.[118] Even as several groups of network staff writers defected from the RWG and voted to certify TWA as their bargaining representative in early 1954, the new union could not compel the networks to agree to a new freelance contract. Fear of the Communist taint eroded freelancers' commitment to the TWA, as the network negotiators had calculated, so that when the new union was forced to call a strike in July in a last-ditch attempt to win a settlement, it soon collapsed.[119]

With both the TWA and the RWG in ruins, the Authors' League moved forward with a reorganization plan put forth by the SWG to establish a new guild that unified all writers for motion pictures, television, and radio. The Writers Guild of America (WGA) came into existence in September 1954, and by 1956 it had secured a substantial increase in pay for network freelancers, with the minimum fee for a half-hour sponsored television script raised to $1,100. While it was a huge boost over the terms of the last MBA negotiated by the RWG, it was still a relatively modest improvement given the vast sums of advertising money flooding into television by the mid-1950s. The new WGA effectively advanced the economic interests of the most successful film and television writers, but it did less for the larger number of staff writers and marginal freelancers. Until the end of the decade, WGA leaders generally avoided thorny political issues, particularly the ongoing blacklisting within the broadcasting industry.[120]

With the broadcasting unions ultimately unable to protect members who were denied employment on account of their progressive political orientation, the blacklisted responded in a variety of ways. Several of the most dedicated procommunists initially stepped up their political activism after they lost their jobs. After Prockter Productions fired Perl, for example, he put his skills to work on behalf of the left-led UE by writing and directing television programs that the union aired in the manufacturing centers of Schenectady and Erie prior to certification elections. Perl subsequently led the Progressive Party's radio and television activities for its 1952 campaign, including its efforts to obtain equal time free of charge from the networks for its candidates. Millard Lampell, another blacklisted writer, focused his energies on trying to unite all culture workers who were adversely affected by anticommunist repression, as he emceed rallies to "Crack the Back of *Counterattack*" that highlighted not only cases in motion pictures, radio, and television, but also the plight of creative professionals with leftist backgrounds in book and magazine publishing, the graphic arts, design, music, education, and other fields.[121]

As the practice of blacklisting became more entrenched, some of those who were denied employment found ways to work either under assumed names or behind "fronts" who represented their work. After her blacklisting, Joan LaCour wrote scripts for the family adventure series *Lassie* during the second half of the 1950s under the thinly veiled pseudonym Joanne Court. David Pressman, whose blacklisting followed a string of leftist associations stretching back to his professional debut directing *Thursdays Till Nine*, a 1947 theatrical review staged by the left-led CIO department store unions that eventually formed District 65, was a rare instance of someone who managed to help direct behind a front. Unable to work in his own right in television after Prockter fired him, Pressman consulted under the table, showing up at the set for *Philip Morris Playhouse* in New York during rehearsal and instructing the official "director" about staging the upcoming show and then leaving well before the actual televised performance.[122] Some of those who were targeted by anticommunists found positions within the apparatus of network broadcasting where their livelihood no longer depended directly upon advertisers. Ernest Kinoy, who was unable to obtain freelance work on sponsored shows for several years on account of his union activism, earned a more modest income as a network continuity writer with NBC until the political climate thawed. Others found that their only option was to turn toward less lucrative fields of cultural production. Peter Lyon, who became completely unemployable in the broadcasting industry after he invoked the Fifth Amendment before SISS, had earned roughly $20,000 in his last full year of writing for radio and television, but earned less than $3,000 annually from freelance magazine writing after being blacklisted. Pressman taught acting and directing at Boston University from 1954 until the end of the decade. Some who had been blacklisted fought for financial damages from producers for breach of contract, as Abram Ginnes did, but they were usually disappointed with the outcome. In May 1956, the New York State Supreme Court ruled that Prockter Productions did not have to submit to arbitration in its dispute with Ginnes and the WGA.[123]

For many who were blacklisted, the loss of creative opportunities in their chosen media, the loss of status, and the loss of income was too much to bear. Instead, they capitulated to the security officers in the networks and the agencies, the redbaiting journalists, and the professional anticommunist activists. Given the diffuse and furtive means by which they were labeled controversial or subversive, blacklisted individuals sometimes had difficulty determining precisely what allegations were preventing them from working or who needed to be placated. Was it someone like Laurence Johnson, the

Syracuse grocer turned anticommunist zealot? Was it a newspaper columnist like Victor Riesel of the *Daily Mirror* or Jack O'Brien of the *Journal-American*? Or was it a security officer at an advertising agency, like Jack Wren at BBDO, or at a network, like Dan O'Shea at CBS? Often, those who sought "clearance" to work openly in the industry again were required to become informers for the FBI or to testify before HUAC or SISS. They had to publicly renounce the progressive political stances they had espoused in the past and distance themselves from the movements and causes they had once supported. In doing so, they sundered whatever bonds of solidarity had united them with other members of the creative class who had shared their political and social values.[124]

Whether progressive writers, directors, actors, and other creative professionals in broadcasting attempted to defy the blacklist, cooperated in ways that abetted its operation, or sought to keep their reservations private and go about their work, most of them pursued their chosen course as individuals. In this sense, all three paths represented a victory for the forces that wished to eliminate the Popular Front presence in the culture industries. Like the members of the Newspaper Guild, creative talent in radio and television preserved unionism throughout the most intense years of the anticommunist onslaught, but the ambition and scope of their organizing narrowed considerably. Within the bounds of the contract, wage and salary demands tended to become more moderate, while provisions for greater equity among culture workers were compromised or disappeared entirely from the collective bargaining agenda. The most highly paid creatives in the print and broadcast media saw their earnings increase relative to other professionals in the culture industries, let alone the larger numbers of technical, paraprofessional, and clerical workers. Efforts to expand opportunities for employment and career advancement for women and minorities, pursued by the Popular Front in a piecemeal fashion during the 1930s and more consistently during the 1940s, diminished in the 1950s. In terms of the bottom line, anticommunism paid off for management: the owners of broadcast networks and affiliated stations, mass-circulation magazines and newspapers, design firms, and advertising agencies were able to keep more of manufacturers and merchants' largess for themselves.

Yet the Popular Front's demise had ramifications that reached beyond the capacity of culture workers' unions to boost salaries and promote equity. It weakened the unions' power to respond to structural changes and dislocations in New York's culture industries that not only jeopardized employment on any terms for thousands of their workers, but that also undermined a range of particular creative practices that were embedded in the city and its workplaces. Furthermore, it influenced the development during the postwar period of ideas about the nature of creativity itself, including considerations of the forms of mental labor that were defined as genuinely creative, the ideal relationship between autonomy and creativity for culture workers, and the fundamental role of creativity within American consumer capitalism.

7

Creativity and Consumer Capitalism in the Affluent Society

"LAST SATURDAY NIGHT I dislodged my sons from the family TV," wrote Design Laboratory alumnus Don Wallance in a February 1961 letter to John Kenneth Galbraith, in order to hear his debate with the Museum of Modern Art's Russel Lynes on the merits of public art patronage. "I was quite intrigued by the idea of an economist, and particularly the author of *The Affluent Society*, engaging in a public discussion of the arts." Although Wallance "felt that logic and right were on your side," he was not convinced that "you were sufficiently well informed to make the most of your case." Wallance concurred with Galbraith's assessment of the "mediocre level of American product design," but not with his reasoning or "the implication that government support would change this." Instead, Wallance contended, "your statement that the scientist and engineer have been made an integral part of American industry while the artist has been shut out does not really accord with the facts." Perhaps no other country, he informed Galbraith, made greater use of the "industrially oriented artist" than the United States. "The problem," Wallance noted, "is not so much one of the status and recognition of the artist in industry, as it is that of a society organized as a giant sales room." As intrinsically desirable as public patronage for the arts might be, it would not on its own enhance the aesthetic or functional characteristics of the material culture of postwar consumer capitalism. "I believe that if the economic and social proposals you made in *The Affluent Society* were realized," Wallance concluded, "this would do more to raise the level of design in America than merely increasing the number or status of artists in industry."[1]

At the heart of the analysis that Galbraith put forth in his 1958 bestseller was his claim that postwar abundance had resulted in the emergence of a new economic consciousness predicated on what he described as a "diminishing urgency of consumption."[2] As growing numbers of Americans passed through institutions of higher education, entered into professional careers, and earned enough discretionary income to put them beyond the bounds of necessity, he posited, their marginal utility from consuming ever-larger quantities of private goods declined. Members of this "New Class" transcended the economic rationality of utility maximization under conditions of scarcity, instead preferring quality—whether construed as aesthetic refinement and sophistication, superior performance, or ecological sustainability—to sheer quantity. They were also inclined to favor the increased availability of public goods, rather than just greater amounts of private goods, to restore what Galbraith termed the "social balance" of production. Yet this new economic consciousness shaped not only their attitudes as consumers, he argued, but their perception of their own labor as well. For them, "work, as it continues to be called" was assumed to be "enjoyable," as they were people who expected "to contribute their best regardless of compensation." Their status conferred numerous advantages, including "exemption from manual toil; escape from boredom and confining and severe routine; the chance to spend one's life in clean and physically comfortable surroundings; and some opportunity for applying one's thoughts to the day's work." Furthermore, Galbraith contended, "demand for individuals in the occupations generally identified with the New Class increases much more proportionately with increased income and well-being." If the growth of the New Class became "a deliberate objective of society," the "emphasis on education and its ultimate effect on intellectual, literary, cultural, and artistic demands, would greatly broaden the opportunities for membership." Meanwhile, the concomitant reduction in the number of people "who engage in work *qua* work" was a development "to be regarded not alone with equanimity but with positive approval."[3] Abundance thus entailed not simply a material surfeit of goods, but also a seemingly boundless expansion in the potential for people to lead lives of autonomy and creativity.

The Affluent Society exemplified what historian Howard Brick has described as the "postcapitalist vision" that animated much of liberal social thought in the United States from the onset of the Cold War through the economic shocks of the 1970s.[4] Expectations of abundance and its blessings informed the political agendas of Kennedy's New Frontier and Johnson's Great Society, justifying an expansion of the production of public goods along with bold antipoverty initiatives. The postcapitalist sensibility also inflected the emerging forms of grassroots liberalism in upscale suburbs, such as the communities along Route 128 ringing Boston, where the New Class predominated. Espousing a meritocratic worldview coupled with support for education, civil rights, environmentalism, and peace, many of these liberal professionals backed the "New Politics" of Eugene McCarthy and George McGovern during the late 1960s and early 1970s.[5] In addition, postcapitalist assumptions thoroughly suffused liberal understandings of creativity. The ideal of creative expression unfettered by the constraints of necessity furnished powerful ammunition in the cultural Cold War, demonstrating the superiority of the "free world" over the oppressive Soviet system. The autonomy often associated with artistic creativity, moreover, epitomized the conditions of fulfilling and remunerative mental labor that purportedly defined membership in the New Class.

Within America's culture industries, the influence of this postcapitalist vision on ways of thinking about creativity was most readily apparent in the fields of advertising and design. Although the purpose of advertisements, along with the bulk of product, packaging, and retail design, was to stimulate demand for branded goods, the lure of transcendence proved to be a powerful means for realizing this objective. Manufacturers and merchants' efforts to reinforce conventional market logic often sought to evoke sensations of comfort and convenience in which the hard realities of prices and finite incomes and resources melted away. Many of the artists and writers whose mental labor produced these inducements to buy also found elements of the New Class ideal and the larger postcapitalist vision personally appealing as well. For some veterans of the Popular Front, like Wallance and his cohort of progressive modernist designers, a postcapitalist sensibility helped to fill the void left by the demise of their social democratic hopes, and to reconcile their criticisms of postwar America's culture of consumer capitalism with their successful careers focused primarily on elevating consumer tastes. For some younger artists and copywriters, such as the proponents of advertising's "creative revolution" of the 1960s, New Class expectations of autonomy melded with their rejection of the rigidly conformist practices of most established agencies during the 1950s and their desire to assimilate countercultural styles and signifiers. Even blue-chip agencies eventually asserted their commitment to the new spirit of artistic innovation. As a 1966 promotional profile of the J. Walter Thompson Company declared, the "creation of advertising—at least outstanding advertising—depends on creative people, who almost instinctively rebel against the formal, structured organization, covet individuality, and thrive best in an atmosphere of freedom."[6] Celebrations of creativity in postwar advertising and design as an activity that was liberated from the realm of necessity thus tended to combine equal measures of self-affirmation and wish-fulfillment.

Despite the lofty rhetoric, the freedom inherent in the postcapitalist vision was constrained in numerous ways. Most glaringly, entrance into the professional occupations that conferred both autonomy and salaries high enough to slake the thirst for ever greater levels of private consumption depended in large part upon gender and racial privilege rather than merit. New York City's culture industries were hardly immune from the general patterns of white-collar employment discrimination in the postwar United States. By 1970, women made up fully 40 percent of the metropolitan area's advertising workforce, for example, but still held barely 20 percent of professional or managerial positions. Furthermore, the median salary for female professionals in advertising was only 63 percent of that of their male counterparts.[7] African Americans and other racial minorities were even more thoroughly excluded from access to the New Class ideal. A 1968 investigation by the New York City Commission on Human Rights revealed that while African Americans and Puerto Ricans together accounted for 28 percent of the area's population, they only accounted for a paltry 3.5 percent of its advertising workforce.[8] While the New Class ideal gestured toward forms of creative fulfillment that moved beyond prevailing notions of work, the ongoing segmentation of the occupational structure along lines of gender and race, and the resulting patterns of social and economic inequality, provided damning evidence of the persistence of capitalist labor relations.

Even those people—overwhelmingly white, disproportionately male— who were fortunate enough to gain employment as creative professionals in America's postwar culture industries usually discovered that in practice, the promise of autonomy simply evaded rather than transcended the constraints of capitalist production and exchange. In advertising and design, both fields in which white-collar unionism failed to establish a durable presence and disaffected individuals with talent could sometimes become entrepreneurs, or at least successful freelancers, obfuscations of "work *qua* work" were particularly evident. Only a small minority of creative professionals in these fields became their own boss, but even those who achieved this form of independence were not spared the frustrations of placating clients, passing projects through review committees, and accepting the disappointing compromises that often resulted. While compensation in advertising and design tended to be generous by postwar standards, high earnings often entailed periodic stretches of long hours and high stress. These and other dissatisfactions rooted in everyday experiences of alienated labor contradicted the postcapitalist conception of creativity in which the imagination and effort that went into producing culture were cast as activities beyond necessity. This irreconcilable tension profoundly shaped the evolution of advertising and design, and the culture industries more generally, during the postwar era. For many creative professionals, their desire for an imminent transition to a postcapitalist social order compromised their ability to improve either the conditions of their labor under still-existing capitalism, or the quality of the culture that they made.

Containment

The ascendance of postcapitalist notions of creativity and consumerism during the 1950s and 1960s stemmed in large part from the eclipse of the Popular Front. The intense domestic anticommunism of the early Cold War that crushed the UOPWA and enervated the Newspaper Guild and the broadcasting talent guilds had lasting cultural and intellectual ramifications. Attacks on these unions not only undermined their practical efficacy as a collective means for improving working conditions, but drastically curtailed their promotion of class-conscious understandings of modern mental labor and their advocacy of social consumerism. Other organizations and media ventures committed to propagating the Popular Front's social and political vision also faced tremendous pressure. Writers, artists, and other creative professionals who publicly displayed a continued affinity for the Popular Front risked ostracism or outright blacklisting. The withering anticommunist assault of the late 1940s and early 1950s not only discredited class-conscious and redistributive ideas about work, consumption, and political economy, but disrupted the networks through which leftist ideological currents could circulate. To be sure, numerous cultural and intellectual figures independently came to believe in the intrinsic superiority of the analysis of social and economic relations that Galbraith offered in *The Affluent Society*, especially given the nation's unprecedented postwar prosperity. The containment of class, however, provided them with multifaceted inducements to adopt a postcapitalist paradigm for framing their interpretations and criticisms of contemporary America.

The postwar trajectory of Consumers Union illustrates vividly the ways in which domestic containment impacted leftist cultural and intellectual endeavors. Surging consumer expenditures, especially for newly available big-ticket durable goods like autos and major household appliances, stimulated demand for the institute's objective testing and ratings of products. As buyers

turned to CU for expert guidance, circulation of its flagship monthly magazine, which simplified its title in 1942 to *Consumer Reports*, rose from 300,000
copies per issue in 1946 to 900,000 a decade later. This growth finally put CU
on solid financial footing, with an annual budget that exceeded $4 million by
1960.[9] Yet the expansion also coincided with intensifying attacks on CU from
anticommunist activists, pushing management eventually to distance the institute from its Popular Front roots. This ideological reorientation had far
reaching consequences, both for the institute's internal operations as well as
its critique of consumer capitalism.

At its founding, CU had been as much a collective experiment in white-
collar workers' empowerment as it was a challenge to consumer capitalism's
cultural hegemony. The UOPWA Book and Magazine Guild had represented
the CU workforce nearly since its inception, and the institute's bylaws
stipulated that the board of directors must include a representative from the
union's shop committee. Management and the union enjoyed cordial relations
during the early years, as ideologically committed staff members tolerated
meager salaries while helping to build the institute and the broader movement for social consumerism. By the end of the Second World War, however,
relations between staff and management became increasingly adversarial. "It
seems hardly necessary," the shop committee admonished in December 1945,
"to have to point out to the Board of Directors of Consumers Union that
high living costs, continued heavy tax burdens and the substandard quality of
consumer goods have lowered the 'real wages,' far outweighing any nominal
increase the workers have received." Management, which looked to expand its
budget for acquiring newly available consumer durables for laboratory testing,
grudgingly acceded to modest salary increases, but pay issues only grew more
acrimonious. In 1947, CU technical director Arthur Kallet convened an expanded executive committee in lieu of the board in order to exclude the staff
representative from having any involvement in decision-making.[10]

While labor relations at CU deteriorated, the institute also initiated a
gradual reorientation of its content to reflect changing postwar consumption patterns. Following the evisceration of wartime price control, CU discontinued its weekly *Bread and Butter* newsletter, which had focused on
economic data and policy developments of immediate interest to left-leaning
consumer activists, in April 1947. The institute introduced a "Bread and
Butter" section into *Consumer Reports* several months later, but buried it in
the back pages along with the shrinking section on labor conditions. In 1948
the magazine included a variety of feature articles that advocated for progressive measures, such as more stringent enforcement of broadcasters' public

service obligations and group medical practice. The following year, however, after several items slamming the American Medical Association for its fierce opposition to the Truman administration's proposal for national healthcare, the general trend away from social consumerism accelerated, and reportage of labor conditions vanished altogether.[11] In the absence of this political and social context, the expanding coverage of product reviews and ratings tended to provide consumers with information for maximizing their individual utility, not for aligning their purchase and use of goods with the values of the Popular Front.

As part of its editorial revamping, in June 1947 *Consumer Reports* inaugurated a new regular feature by designer Eliot Noyes titled "The Shape of Things." Noyes had studied with Walter Gropius and Marcel Breuer in the late 1930s, and in 1940 he joined the Museum of Modern Art as a curator of industrial design. When the series launched, he was working on his first major design commission for IBM, consummating a long-term relationship that deeply shaped the development of postwar corporate high-modernism. Noyes's series represented an attempt by CU to link functionalist aesthetics to its critiques of consumer capitalism, but it also reflected the ambiguities of both the cultural meanings of modernism and the institute's evolving approach to reforming consumer practices.[12] In his first column, Noyes set the tone by condemning most manufacturers of living-room radio sets for failing to make "any effort to find an appropriate form for a complex electronic instrument" and instead presenting the radio as "an eighteenth-century piece of furniture." A column in September on furniture touted the modernist designs of George Nelson, Charles Eames, and Alvar Aalto, insisting that it was "more practical and more rewarding" for savvy consumers "to search for the best that today offers than to revert to period reproduction." Noyes contended that these aesthetic judgments were not "just a form of snobbery" since historically styled pieces "almost always sacrifice important elements of usefulness, efficiency, or comfort in the effort to recapture old shapes and details." When he assessed the state of American automotive design in May 1948, however, he was unable to refrain from drawing invidious distinctions of taste. Automakers offered a "marvelous mass-produced transportation mechanism surrounded with inappropriate and costly sheet-metal shapes which are ineptly and trashify decorated and which often make the machine less efficient."[13] In some cases, even products that had the formal appearance of functionality, with simple lines and little in the way of applied ornamentation, in fact had limited utility: most of the portable radios that Noyes lauded in one early column, for instance, were rated "Not Acceptable" on the basis of testing. Overall, Noyes's series, which continued through the June 1950 issue, made little effort to define functionalist modernism as a clear signifier of social consumerism, and provided another indication of the ideological shift underway at CU.[14]

Despite the moderation evident in the pages of *Consumer Reports*, the institute's lingering procommunist associations gave its opponents ammunition that only increased in potency as the Cold War intensified. While the UOPWA disintegrated, the union's shop committee at CU remained militant, thwarting management's efforts at demoting or firing employees whose political affinities were a mounting liability for the institute. By 1950, however, the inability of the UOPWA to attain significant raises for CU staff spurred a group of employees to reach out to the Newspaper Guild of New York for assistance. Led by African American writer and labor activist Marian Minus, they objected to the UOPWA merger into District 65 and hoped instead to return to the CIO fold. The CU board of directors issued a formal pledge of neutrality in the contest between District 65 and the Guild, but organizers for District 65 alleged that supervisors were warning employees that a vote for that union in the upcoming certification election would lead to a precipitous decline in *Consumers Reports* circulation and layoffs. The Guild prevailed in the hard-fought election in early 1951 by a 66–57 margin, but unfair labor practice charges by District 65 delayed the negotiation of a new contract for several months. Once the deal was complete, the Guild collaborated with CU management to fire the remaining Communist Party members and District 65 stalwarts on the staff.[15]

The purge of the institute's remaining procommunists failed to restore comity to labor relations, as Kallet and his new personnel manager, Sidney Cahn, attempted to keep salaries at a minimum. In July 1952, an impasse in contract negotiations resulted in a five-week work stoppage that Kallet and Cahn claimed was a strike and that the Newspaper Guild described as a lockout. Given the institute's origins in the 1935 strike against Consumers' Research, the dispute was a major public embarrassment for CU management, and a source of *schadenfreude* for old nemeses like F. J. Schlink and J. B. Matthews. Kallet capitulated, firing Cahn and acceding to the Guild's demands.[16] Having been defeated by the Guild's show of solidarity, which encompassed laboratory staff and writers as well as clerical and distribution workers, Kallet and his managers tried to exclude engineers and technicians from the bargaining unit. Explicitly disavowing the class-conscious conception of modern mental labor that had been central to the Popular Front, they encouraged these highly skilled white-collar workers to see themselves as individuals whose autonomy and prospects for career advancement were reduced rather than enhanced by unionism, generating ongoing tension within the Guild unit.[17]

As part of Kallet's rightward drift, CU strove to appease its detractors by publicly affirming an explicitly anticommunist identity for the first time. An October 1951 editorial in *Consumers Reports* denied that the institute had "any truck with communism" and declared that "the organization is not and has not been fronting for anybody—communists, New Dealers, or conservatives." A more forceful attempt by CU to recant its past attacks on consumer capitalism and halt the relentless redbaiting came in April 1953, when the board of directors issued a statement refuting accusations that the institute was "sowing distrust of American business" or denigrating the "free enterprise system." They denounced "communism, and all other forms of totalitarianism" along with any "authoritarian guidance of production and consumption," while asserting that the "success of our efforts depends fundamentally upon high-level national income, upon the existence of a broad variety of widely distributed brands, and upon the maintenance of a competitive marketplace in which the consumer can exercise complete freedom of choice."[18] It was no coincidence that the board's statement read like the declarations offered by blacklisted actors and writers seeking "clearance," as Kallet and some of the other directors were working behind the scenes with HUAC. After several CU officers testified and submitted evidence to the committee in executive session, in early 1954 HUAC gave CU its seal of approval and formally rescinded the citations for subversive activity that the institute had received in 1939 and 1944.[19]

Eventually, many of Kallet's fellow directors grew dissatisfied with his acrimonious approach to labor relations and his abandonment of social consumerism. In June 1957 the CU board narrowly voted to oust Kallet as the institute's technical director, a position he had held since its founding. The following year, the board promoted Minus to become the institute's new personnel director, which deprived the Newspaper Guild of a key activist but resulted in more harmonious relations between the union and CU management.[20] Over the long term the new leadership brought a gradual return to consumer activism, but of a type more attuned to the postcapitalist liberalism of the New Class than the class-conscious consumerism of the Popular Front. By the early 1960s, CU was busy highlighting an array of threats to the public, including contamination of the food supply by radioactive fallout, the ecological impact of toxic pesticides, the health risks of cigarette smoking, the shocking inadequacy of auto safety, and merchants' exploitative marketing and credit practices. CU offered copies of Rachel Carson's *Silent Spring* (1962) as a bonus for new subscribers, and it provided financial support for the research behind David Caplovitz's *The Poor Pay More* (1963). Ralph Nader utilized the institute's automotive test results to dramatic effect in his *Unsafe at Any Speed* (1965).[21] While these new crusades led to the enactment of important environmental and safety regulations, as well as prohibitions of some deceptive and discriminatory marketing practices, they lacked the breadth of the institute's early ambitions to challenge America's culture of consumer capitalism and empower white-collar labor.

CU survived the harsh political climate of the early Cold War years as a result of its capitulation, accommodating itself to the narrowing of ideologically acceptable discourse and adjusting its consumer guidance accordingly. Resistance often proved to be untenable. George Seldes's *In Fact*, for example, remained indefatigable in its commitment to the ideals of the Popular Front and its critique of capitalist power, but it succumbed to the fragmentation of the progressive readership upon which it depended. Although the news bulletin's weekly circulation peaked in mid-1947 at 176,000 copies—more than double the combined circulation of *New Republic* and *The Nation*—it declined rapidly over the following three years in the face of anticommunist attacks. By January 1950, circulation for *In Fact* had plummeted to just 73,000, and additional cancelations from subscribers forced Seldes finally to suspend publication in October.[22] Seldes's style of radical journalism persisted, but only in a marginalized and vestigial form. I. F. Stone, who found himself unemployed (and likely unemployable) once New York's left-leaning *Daily Compass* newspaper shuttered in 1952, began his eponymous weekly news bulletin as an attempt to continue where Seldes left off, but it only reached a few thousand readers per issue in its first years of publication and still had a circulation that barely topped 20,000 in 1963.[23] Former Newspaper Guild of New York president John McManus teamed up with fellow leftist journalists James Aronson and Cedric Belfrage to launch the *National Guardian* in October 1948, but they fared little better. Combining critical news coverage with a spirited advocacy of the Progressive Party and American Labor Party, including McManus's campaigns for New York governor in 1950 and 1954, the weekly newspaper's circulation peaked at 75,000 copies in early 1950. By 1956, as the procommunist left commenced its final collapse, its circulation had fallen to under 35,000.[24] *I. F. Stone's Weekly* and the *National Guardian* preserved a Popular Front mode of radical commentary, and constituted an important bridge between the Old Left and the New Left, but they had little immediate influence beyond a residual and increasingly sectarian base of readers. Furthermore, neither of these publications had the aspirations that *PM*, *Friday*, or the stillborn People's Radio Foundation once had to provide a wide range of content that could challenge the capitalist media and effectively appeal to the expansive, diverse, progressive public of the Popular Front cultural imagination.

Progressives' hopes that organized labor would finally emerge as a more important sponsor for cultural production were also dashed. Although many unions attained a degree of institutional stability that they had never enjoyed before, their interest in undertaking new cultural initiatives seemingly declined in inverse relation to their expanded financial resources. Those unions that bucked the trend were often disappointed with their efforts. With more than a million members, the formidable UAW established its own FM radio stations in Detroit and Cleveland in 1949, but pulled the plug on their operation after only three years. While the UAW under Walter Reuther's leadership had a bolder social-democratic vision than perhaps any anticommunist union during this period, it still could not justify the continuing expenditure of dues revenue to keep the stations broadcasting.[25] The left-led UE and District 65 made some innovative and effective use of television on an occasional basis during the early 1950s, but the rapidly increasing cost of television airtime soon precluded these embattled unions' use of the new medium. During the late 1950s the recently merged AFL-CIO made its most substantial foray into television with *Americans at Work*, a syndicated public service documentary program that the federation hoped would counter the influence of the widely carried NAM series *Industry on Parade*. Despite the title, the AFL-CIO eschewed class-conscious representations of workers' experiences on the job or their political and social roles outside of the workplace; rather, it portrayed organized labor as a respectable partner that shared employers' commitment to free enterprise. Besides echoing key parts of *Industry on Parade*'s message *Americans at Work* also mirrored its staid format and visual conventions; the AFL-CIO program lacked the narrative and aesthetic creativity, let alone the provocative political content, which was apparent in so many Popular Front cultural endeavors.[26]

Even members of the Newspaper Guild shied away from the prospect of becoming media patrons. Since the 1930s, Guild activists had proposed that the union operate its own daily newspaper to counter the generally conservative and anti-labor bias of much of the commercial media. Facing a new wave of consolidation in the daily newspaper industry, in 1950 the ANG convention and executive board approved "Project X," a program to investigate the possibility of launching a nationally oriented newspaper backed by the

Guild and other unions. When members were given an opportunity to vote on the appropriation of up to $50,000 from the ANG defense fund for the project's initial development, however, a majority rejected the outlay. Within the New York Guild, the referendum was defeated by an overwhelming 2,726 to 335 margin. Although the lack of support for Project X in New York reflected the likelihood that any new paper established by the national union would be located outside the city, it also revealed deep skepticism about the venture in general.[27] As most members came to see the Guild's purpose as simply to obtain the best possible pay and benefits for employees of existing commercial media enterprises, there seemed little point in supporting an alternative media project either to provide a new model of creative labor or to produce content critical of consumer capitalism.

With the marginalization of class-conscious discourses about labor, consumerism, and political economy, American cultural and intellectual life came to be dominated in the 1950s by the triumphant reassertion of capitalist cultural hegemony. After two decades of grappling with the challenges posed by the insurgent social movements of the Popular Front and the liberal regulatory impulses of the New Deal, business found its legitimacy largely uncontested. Especially in the early years of the decade, when anticommunism was peaking, assertions that Americans should find freedom and fulfillment through capitalist markets, as sellers of labor to private firms and as the consumers of the goods they produced, were met with little rebuttal in the public sphere. Over time, discontent with the exuberant materialism of the decade's culture of consumer capitalism and with many employers' instrumentalist approaches to white-collar personnel management gradually resurfaced. Both creative professionals in the culture industries and intellectuals engaged in social and cultural analysis, however, increasingly framed their critiques and proposed remedies in new terms, emphasizing the potential for the transcendence rather than the socialization of existing relations of production and exchange.

In many cases, writers, artists, designers, and other creative professionals who embraced aspects of the postcapitalist vision were also rejecting the prevailing mid-century consensus regarding the nature of cultural dissemination and reception. Despite the intense ideological rancor of the early Cold War years, numerous commentators from across the ideological spectrum shared a highly mechanistic view of modern culture that stressed its power to manipulate popular consciousness. As the procommunist Left adopted a siege mentality during the late 1940s and early 1950s, for example, many of its more doctrinaire cultural activists began to insist ever more strongly on rigid adherence to the radical dictum of "art as a weapon." This renewed push for aesthetic and literary orthodoxy was most clearly demonstrated in the public reprimand of screenwriter Albert Maltz in 1946 for his contribution to a forum titled "What Shall We Ask of Writers?" in *New Masses* magazine. Opening with the disclaimer that he offered "the comments of a working writer, not the presentation of a formal esthetician," Maltz questioned the instrumental use of art to advance class struggle. This formula, he contended, had led to a "vulgarization of the theory of art" in which "the *nature* of art—*how* art may best be a weapon, and how it may *not* be" was too often disregarded, so that "creative works are judged *primarily* by their formal ideology." Within the procommunists' already contracting cultural domain, Maltz was pilloried for his affirmation of artists' autonomy and subsequently recanted.[28] These attempts at maintaining ideological discipline repelled many writers, artists, and intellectuals who were sympathetic to the Popular Front's domestic political and social agenda. But progressives who turned away from the Old Left not only recoiled from its increasing sectarianism and disregard for creative autonomy. They also objected to its general cultural sclerosis, including its tendency to valorize didactic works lacking in ambiguity or complexity, its diminishing acceptance of modernist currents in art and literature, and, most fundamentally, its dogma that following the right formula could produce cultural content capable of automatic indoctrination.

The mechanistic understanding of culture that prevailed in much of the Old Left during its waning years was closely mirrored in the activism of its anticommunist nemeses. Since the 1930s, opponents of the Popular Front had accused its various organizations of being nothing more than "transmission belts" that manipulated unwitting "dupes" through their cultural content and messaging. With the onset of the Cold War, anticommunists only amplified their fearful diatribes about Stalinist thought control through the mass media. "In an emergency," *Counterattack* warned its readers in 1950, "it would require only three persons (subversives)—one engineer in master control at a radio network, one director in a radio studio, one voice before a microphone—to reach 90 million American people with a message!" The "success the CP has had in penetrating the most powerful propaganda media in the U.S.," the newsletter's editors continued, posed a "great danger," which had to be exposed and combatted "if the American airwaves were to be kept free."[29] Thus the logic of blacklisting was predicated not only on hostility to the political positions and conduct of writers, artists, performers, and other creative professionals in the culture industries who had links to the Popular Front; it also rested on the theory that the products of mass culture—cinema, television, radio, newspapers, magazines, posters, and commercial design—had the power to overwhelm ordinary people's rational capacity to process and critically evaluate them. Ostensibly acting in defense of freedom, anticommunists instrumentalized the imagination and the labor of both the producers and consumers of culture.

The advertising agencies that channeled the patronage of manufacturers and merchants throughout the culture industries had clear pecuniary incentives to promote this consensus. Many agencies had embraced behaviorist psychology in the 1910s and 1920s in order to legitimate the advertising profession and demonstrate its practitioners' efficacy in molding public opinion. As advertising rehabilitated its reputation from the crisis of the Great Depression and attacks by the Popular Front, the industry not only redoubled its embrace of behaviorism's instrumentalist rhetoric, but also began to implement its precepts with more sophisticated methods. New varieties of motivational research and message testing guided copywriters as they devised what advertising executive Rosser Reeves of Ted Bates Incorporated termed a "unique selling proposition" for each branded product. These were formulaic statements designed not just to differentiate products from their competitors, but to manipulate consumers' purchasing habits in a direct and mechanistic fashion, often through heavy repetition.[30] Echoing the phrasing that anticommunists had utilized to describe the Popular Front's cultural endeavors, Reeves claimed that a successful agency was "nothing but a transmission belt designed to produce a piece of copy."[31]

Even the fiercest intellectual critics of postwar American culture tended to agree with ad men like Reeves about its instrumental efficacy. "Mass Culture," Dwight Macdonald wrote in 1953, was "solely and directly an article for mass consumption, like chewing gum" that was "imposed from above," and "fabricated by technicians hired by businessmen" for "passive consumers." The "whole field" of mass culture "could be approached from the standpoint of the division of labor." Since the areas that were "more advanced technologically" had the most extensive division of labor, "art workers" in television, for instance, were "as alienated from their brainwork as the industrial worker is from his handiwork." Yet despite his own personal experience working for Time Inc., Macdonald did not see this as meriting a detailed explication of the relations of production then prevalent in the culture industries. Instead, what mattered was the ways in which the "scientific and artistic technicians of Mass Culture" both "degraded the public by treating it as an object, to be handled with the lack of ceremony and the objectivity of medical students dissecting a corpse," and pandered "to its level of taste and ideas by taking these as the criterion of reality (in the case of questionnaire-sociologists and other 'social scientists') or of art (in the case of the Lords of *kitsch*)."[32] Frankfurt School émigré Theodor Adorno largely shared Macdonald's pessimistic judgment of mass culture as a corrupting force that contaminated traditional high culture, authentic popular culture, and the modernist avant-garde in addition to promoting latent totalitarian tendencies. In his essay "Television and the Patterns of Mass Culture," Adorno looked to expose "the social-psychological implications and mechanisms" of the medium, "which often operate under the guise of fake realism" so that "not only may the shows be improved, but, more important possibly, the public at large may be sensitized to the nefarious effect of some of these mechanisms." Although he acknowledged the actual conditions of television production only in passing, he asserted that the medium's adherence to formula justified a critical theory that focused on the ways in which programming manipulated viewers. "To study television shows in terms of the psychology of the authors," he quipped, "would almost be tantamount to studying Ford cars in terms of the psychoanalysis of the late Mr. Ford."[33]

Creative professionals in the culture industries who were amenable to aspects of the postcapitalist vision, however illusory it may have been ultimately, not only sought to overcome the constraints imposed by the logic of the market, but also to push beyond the mechanistic cultural discourses that accompanied the demise of the Popular Front and its aftermath. By regarding themselves as being at the leading edge of a transition to a new social order defined by abundance, they hoped to reassert their own autonomy as the agents, and not merely the instruments, of cultural production. They also looked to rehabilitate the agency of the millions of people who consumed the culture industries' enormous volume of output, and to affirm the conscious effort that went into reading newspapers and magazines, listening to the radio, watching television, using goods, or experiencing the built environment. At their most innovative and promising, the cultural initiatives of the Popular Front had likewise reflected their creators' desire to stimulate the imaginative power of ordinary people as they interpreted and constructed the meanings of the cultural products that they encountered, and to harness it to challenge the pervasive influence of consumer capitalism. Starting from different premises, those creative professionals after the Popular Front who pursued comparable attempts to liberate themselves and their audiences found that in most instances, the ideal of transcending rather than confronting capitalism merely imposed new limitations.[34]

Advertising Abundance: Hegemony and Creativity in Postwar America's Culture of Consumer Capitalism

The gradual emergence of postcapitalist sensibilities in the advertising industry not only ran counter to its primary function of stimulating demand even as consumers enjoyed greater and greater quantities of goods, but also to its crucial role as the vanguard of the campaign to restore the unopposed hegemony of American capitalism after the Second World War. The crusade sought to eliminate, or at least suppress, whatever doubts may have existed among the general public concerning the legitimacy of free enterprise, and it disciplined white-collar workers throughout all of the culture industries that depended on advertisers' patronage. Whether conducted under the auspices of the Advertising Council, or through the copious institutional advertising sponsored by the National Association of Manufacturers, the US Chamber of Commerce, or individual corporations, these propaganda initiatives had a profound impact.[35] Efforts to discredit the public provisioning of goods and services, for instance, extinguished any possibility of renewed government or nonprofit patronage for cultural production that might have furnished members of the creative class with alternative sources of employment. Advertising agencies, moreover, played a leading role in blacklisting progressives in radio and television, which seriously weakened the broadcasting talent guilds. Yet despite the agencies' forceful advocacy for capitalist cultural hegemony, tensions within their creative workforces persisted. "Nothing in their daily experience so disgusts the business executives of advertising," observed journalist Martin Mayer in 1958, "as the realization that some of the most valued members of their creative staff are out of sympathy with the purposes of the business, and regard the ad itself as more important than the success of the advertised product." Simultaneously, "the writers and artists struggle against their distaste for the businessmen who can measure the values of art only in terms of dollars paid and dollars received."[36]

The surge in advertising expenditures during the postwar boom also exercised a soft control over creative expression throughout the culture industries. Total annual advertising expenditures in the United States jumped from $4.2 billion in 1947 to $10.3 billion by 1957, and to $17.4 billion by 1967.[37] The vast sums that flowed from manufacturers and merchants through the advertising agencies and into the commercial media greatly magnified the opportunity costs of any mass-circulation periodicals or broadcast programs that were not oriented toward the largest potential audience. Nothing illustrated this tendency more clearly than the shifting patterns of television program sponsorship and procurement. In the first half of the 1950s, most primetime programs were still produced directly by the top advertising agencies on behalf of clients with deep pockets, or by independent package producers with heavy agency and sponsor involvement. By 1960, networks procured 80 percent of programs straight from production companies, eliminating most of the direct input by sponsors and agencies into the minutiae of scripting, casting, directing, and filming of television series.[38] Nonetheless, the astronomical value of prime commercial airtime virtually precluded any deviation from the narrow formulas of situation comedies and action-adventure series. The more varied and experimental range of programming, including serious dramas and other formats with more latitude for creative independence, that had flourished even in the midst of blacklisting was not financially justifiable to the networks by the late 1950s and early 1960s, when potential audiences numbered well into the tens of millions and a minute of primetime network advertising could cost $50,000. Thus, the most successful creative professionals encountered a paradoxical embarrassment of riches: while they earned more than ever before, their autonomy diminished.

J. Walter Thompson, consistently the nation's leading advertising agency in terms of billings, exemplified many of the industry's major trends during the 1950s and early 1960s.[39] Its New York offices served as headquarters for a multinational advertising empire that included 14 satellite offices around the United States as well as 22 foreign offices. Employment in the New York office swelled from 456 staff members in 1940 to 1,541 in 1959, while the company's total domestic workforce increased from 678 to 2,455. Overseas employment for JWT expanded even more, from 668 total staff outside the country in 1939 to 3,359 two decades later. While Western Europe accounted for much of the international growth, considerable hiring also took place in major markets in the developing world, such as Brazil, where JWT had 288 employees by 1959, and India, with 431 employees.[40]

With its extensive resources, JWT offered clients a range of services that few other agencies could match, such as its New York-based Television Workshop that the agency initiated in 1955. This facility consisted of a fully equipped studio capable of transmitting live takes of commercials via closed circuit to standard television sets located in a "Receiving Room" in which copywriters, art directors, producers, account executives, and clients could view the results under conditions that simulated the experience of viewers at home. The Television Workshop enabled a more effective evaluation of performing talent, set design, lighting, and staging prior to the final filming of a commercial. It also abetted experimentation with visual effects, ranging from the assorted studio tricks used to make food and beverages look appetizing on early black-and-white television screens, to animation and superimposition, to the electronic manipulation of images. As videotape recording came to be used for a small but growing proportion of commercials by the end of the 1950s, the facility added an Ampex video unit. By 1961, JWT was screen-testing hundreds of actors and performers annually, with the results being added to a film library that was available to all accounts. Most major JWT clients, including Ford Motors, Pan American Airlines, Lever Brothers, Liggett and Myers Tobacco, Standard Brands, Schlitz Beer, Eastman Kodak, and Blue Cross/Blue Shield utilized the Television Workshop's services.[41]

Like most other large agencies in these years, JWT had a highly structured organizational culture, with rigid guidelines circumscribing staff roles. In order to control contact between the agency and its clients, account executives were required to follow a detailed protocol when negotiating commissions and fees or presenting advertising. Creative professionals were clearly in a subordinate position. Account executives were generally barred from bringing creative staff, other than a group head, to meetings with clients, and copywriters and art directors were specifically prohibited from collaborating in the development of advertising content.[42] In addition, the creative angle was frequently subsumed in the agency's overriding emphasis on research. JWT utilized a variety of experimental techniques for testing copy, with the most elaborate involving measurements of consumers' coupon redemptions or other forms of direct response to particular sales propositions. It applied quasi-scientific methods to attempt to quantify the efficacy of pitches and to enhance, as it claimed, its capacity to "predict mass behavior." The agency sold clients the results of copy research as well as the appearance of rational control.[43] With the production process driven by account executives who pandered to clients, creative work under this type of bureaucratic regime, while lucrative, provided limited opportunities for autonomy.

JWT management adhered to a gendered division of labor that was commonplace in advertising at this time. Fully 60 percent of the personnel in the New York office were clerical workers, with women filling nearly all positions as clerks, typists, and secretaries. While many of them may have harbored aspirations to move into creative or managerial positions, rampant sex discrimination often blocked the path to career advancement. Although JWT did hire some women as copywriters, they were assigned almost exclusively to accounts for processed foods, kitchen gadgets, household cleaning products, cosmetics, and toiletries. In 1963, every single one of the forty-four copywriters assigned to these types of accounts at JWT was a woman. Some women at the agency during this period also worked as media buyers, but few women held professional positions in the television department, and professional jobs in the art department and accounts department were effectively off limits. Only a tiny fraction of the agency's female employees attained executive standing; out of 114 JWT vice presidents in 1957, just seven were women, and in 1963 Nancy Stephenson became the first woman since the wife of the late chairman Stanley Resor to sit on the board of directors.[44]

Even as total agency employment grew in line with advertisers' rising expenditures and salaries steadily increased, professionals in the industry faced considerable job insecurity. Account executives fawned so obsequiously over clients precisely because advertisers could and did take their business elsewhere with some regularity. Agencies went on hiring sprees when they signed new accounts, and the loss of major accounts nearly always resulted in layoffs. This instability resulted in a comparatively high level of employee turnover during the postwar era; in 1960, for instance, full-time salaried professional and technical employees in advertising were 35 percent more likely than their counterparts in publishing or broadcasting to have experienced unemployment during the previous twelve months.[45] Meanwhile, earnings for top professional talent were among the highest in New York's culture industries, with one leading placement service reporting in 1962 that among roughly forty agencies with annual billings greater than $25 million, salaries could range from $35,000 a year to as high as $60,000 for recently hired creative directors, from $12,000 up to $20,000 for experienced art directors in nonsupervisory roles, and from $8,000 to $18,000 for experienced copywriters. These impressive salaries masked the periodic stretches of unemployment—often six months or longer—that even talented professionals in the industry endured. Furthermore, many of these top earners still managed to live beyond their means, partly to project an image of liberation from the constraints of material necessity. While most Americans in the early 1960s would have been unlikely to sympathize with an account executive who complained, in an article in the trade magazine *Madison Avenue*, about "going broke on $25,000 a year," his circumstances were not uncommon within the industry's upper tiers.[46] As copywriter Jerry Della Femina recalled, the fear and anxiety bred by the uncertainty was part of the routine, especially in the larger agencies, which often employed "killers" whose job was to fire other employees.[47]

The incessant churn in employment, and the agencies' constant search for new blood, was largely driven by the very nature of the advertising business as a stimulant of new consumer desires and new product preferences. "The job mortality rate among creative people due to the ceaseless demands for fresh creative thinking," a personnel adviser averred, "is nothing short of fierce. When an old copy or art man loses his job he may have no place to go." Of "all of the young people who pour in one end of the advertising business and trickle out the other end at a relatively early age," most, he surmised, experienced a significant decline in income. The older adman who "suddenly finds himself on the beach must face up to the fact that he is a second-class citizen in an industry that makes a fetish of youth. He must be prepared to take a second-class job in a second-class company at a second-class salary. He just cannot expect to compete for top-drawer jobs and salaries with men ten and 15 years his junior." Many, he continued, were forced to take up new lines of work, "such as teaching, real estate, corporate sales, or consulting."[48] Whereas people employed in most professional occupations could reasonably expect that their incomes would continue to rise through their forties and fifties, advertising professionals confronted the probability of a substantial fall-off in their earning power as they advanced into middle age.

Discontented advertising professionals had few avenues for addressing their frustrations during the late 1950s and early 1960s, but they occasionally still imagined the possibility of collective remedies. In October 1960, the Newspaper Guild of New York received an anonymous letter from a disgruntled copywriter encouraging the union to organize the "advertising, promotion, and publicity writers," starting with his employer, the midsized Ellington and Company. The agency's president, the letter asserted, was "the perfect picture of the boss who originally made organization for protection necessary." He "threatens, bullies, salary-cuts, and fires according to whim," and after giving employees the pink slip, he took "sadistic glee in trying to keep anyone he fired from ever getting another job." Although the author of the letter surmised that "the only answer to such a menace is recruitment and organization of both the writers and the white collar people," he demurred from committing himself to assisting with any unionization effort. Instead, he recommended that the Newspaper Guild track down a copywriter named Julian Koenig, who had been fired from Ellington in 1958, for the information and contacts necessary to begin an organizing drive. "It's time," he concluded, that "the huckster racket stopped."[49]

There is no evidence that the Guild ever reached out to Koenig, whose career trajectory exemplified the trends that gave rise to advertising's "creative revolution" during the 1960s, in which copywriters and art directors founded countless new agencies that rejected both the style of conventional advertising as well as the restrictive policies and practices of established firms. After losing his job at Ellington, Koenig landed a job as a copy supervisor with the upstart

Doyle Dane Bernbach agency (DDB).[50] To a considerable extent, DDB had pioneered many of the practices associated with the creative revolution in the midst of the conservative 1950s. The agency had earned its reputation by producing offbeat advertising for clients like Levy's Rye Bread, Polaroid, and Volkswagen and by eschewing the deference that typified its rivals' approach to accounts management. DDB cofounder William Bernbach frankly stated in 1957 that "I feel that if the agency makes an ad and the client doesn't like it, the client ought to run it anyway." Agency policy stipulated that factual error and the inadvertent violation of a client's longstanding corporate standards were the only acceptable reasons for revisions. Whereas agencies like JWT strictly delineated and rationalized creative tasks, DDB encouraged its copywriters and art directors to collaborate freely in the development of advertising for its clients. As Bob Gage, who headed the art department at DDB during the late 1950s, explained, "A copywriter might have a good line, and I think how I can visualize it. I do a visual, and he looks at it, and that might give him still another idea for a line."[51] DDB and the agencies that it helped to inspire provided writers and artists with far greater freedom to determine their own work processes, and, more fundamentally, allowed them to valorize both their creative labor and the artistic qualities of the advertising they produced beyond just the quantifiable impact on sales.

After less than two years with DDB, Koenig departed to start his own agency with former DDB art director George Lois and copywriter Fred Papert as his partners. Their firm, Papert Koenig Lois (PKL), grew quickly, attaining more than $16 million in annual billings by early 1962 with a client roster that included the *New York Herald Tribune*, Peugeot automobiles, Xerox photocopiers, and Seagram's Wolfschmidt vodka. The three partners then took a step that was virtually unheard of at the time in the advertising business: raising outside capital through an initial public offering (IPO) of stock. In May of that year, PKL became the first publicly traded advertising agency since the 1920s when its shares became listed on the American Stock Exchange.[52] As PKL continued to expand, the rebellious and irreverent conduct of its creative leaders became legendary throughout the industry. During one presentation, for instance, a client repeatedly pestered Koenig about how a full-page advertisement might look in a half-page format; exasperated, he finally declared, "here's how it would look," as he ripped the ad in half. When copywriter Carl Ally grew irritated with Lois and Koenig's questioning during a job interview and blurted out, "fuck you, I don't need this horseshit," they decided that he was PKL material and hired him on the spot. The agency also demonstrated a more serious side of its creative ken with its political advertising, including television commercials for Jacob Javits's 1962 campaign for US Senate in New York and Robert Kennedy's Senate race two years later. By 1967, PKL had 200 employees and $41 million in annual billings.[53]

The postcapitalist impulses inherent in the efforts of figures like Koenig and Lois to transcend the logic of the market by emphasizing the importance of creativity beyond its mere monetary value eventually came into conflict, however, with their capitalistic means of realizing autonomy through entrepreneurship. In 1967 Lois, who had grown weary of his increasing management responsibilities as PKL expanded, decided to leave the firm. In September of that year, he and two of his former colleagues from PKL opened a new agency, Lois Holland Callaway (LHC), in which he insisted that his role would be primarily creative. "The only way I can do the work I like is to do it myself," Lois said when the new agency was announced. "I'd much rather do ads than be the boss." By the time he left PKL, he complained, the only time he was doing any creative work was "between seven and nine each evening at home," since "the rest of the time, at the office, I was supervising the other creative people." At LHC, "the three of us—Ron, Jim and me—we're going to do all the marketing and advertising. All the work, all the thinking is going to be done by us." Besides assuring prospective clients that they would be receiving the partners' full creative attention, the new arrangement promised to give Lois the autonomy he craved. "We intend to keep control of the product, the work," he insisted. Within a little more than a year, LHC had signed up major clients like the Edwards and Hanly investment brokerage and Braniff Airlines, and posted $22 million in gross billings for 1968.[54]

In addition to opening up new opportunities for autonomy for artists and writers, the creative revolution's proponents often subverted the rhetorical and representational conventions that had characterized most previous advertising content. In doing so, they called into question the mechanistic understandings of communication that were prevalent during the early years of the Cold War. Advertising produced by the creative revolution's most strident partisans frequently turned the axiom of Reeves's unique selling proposition on its head. At first the pitch was often minimalist, as with the "Think Small" tagline that Koenig coined for Volkswagen before leaving DDB.[55] By the mid-1960s, advertising copy and imagery from the upstart agencies frequently anticipated consumers' skepticism about hackneyed and fraudulent sales claims and incorporated the types of criticisms made by CU about the shoddiness and wastefulness of postwar consumer goods. In one of the most notable instances, Volvo, which was looking to follow in Volkswagen's footsteps and appeal to New Class consumers, turned in 1967 to Scali,

McCabe, Sloves to produce a campaign that skewered Detroit's excesses, including a parody ad that ran in *Life* featuring a "paper car" billed as the "logical next step in a continuing program of planned obsolescence."[56] Other ad campaigns from the creative agencies took a playful or whimsical approach, with some even humorously depicting imagined disadvantages of using a client's product. In all of these instances, the advertisements depended on prospective consumers' agency, as they interpreted their imagery and language and constructed their meanings, in order to be effective.

Some of the creative revolution's enthusiasts also hoped to harness the style and spirit of the increasingly rebellious 1960s to advocate for progressive social change. Carl Ally, who had launched his own agency after several years at PKL, produced advertising for Eugene McCarthy's 1968 insurgent campaign for the Democratic presidential nomination, which tapped into growing opposition to the Vietnam War, as well as promotional materials for the Poor People's Campaign that Martin Luther King Jr. had initiated prior to his assassination. Fred Papert led a pioneering advertising effort to build support for gun-control legislation. He and Jerry Della Femina, among others, contributed to a workshop course on "protest advertising" offered by the School of Visual Arts under the auspices of graphic designer Milton Glaser.[57] Perhaps most noteworthy was a campaign developed on behalf of the New York Urban Coalition by a team of young creative talent recently hired by Young and Rubicam. Featuring "Give a Damn" as its central slogan, it consisted of hard-hitting television commercials on various aspects of the city's deepening urban crisis that combined the gritty visual techniques of direct cinema with wry sarcasm. In one spot, a slumlord extols the supposed attributes of a horribly dilapidated apartment to a prospective Black tenant; in another, an announcer describes the wholesome recreational opportunities available at a summer vacation camp while viewers see minority children playing in squalid inner-city streets and trash-strewn vacant lots. The commercials won a slew of prestigious advertising awards and convinced struggling New York City Mayor John Lindsay to hire their creators to produce the television ads for his 1969 reelection campaign.[58]

Significantly, for all of its spontaneous, nonconformist, and countercultural tendencies, the creative revolution led by figures like Koenig, Lois, Ally, and Della Femina was not a movement in which talented women gained comparable access to opportunities for autonomy through career advancement or entrepreneurship. Mary Wells's meteoric rise in the industry was truly the exception that proved the rule. Wells first found employment in New York as a copywriter in the mid-1950s, and by 1958 she had been hired by DDB as copy group head for the agency's Max Factor cosmetics account. In 1964, Wells joined Jack Tinker and Partners, a special projects agency within the expanding Interpublic advertising and marketing conglomerate, as a partner responsible for its high-profile Alka-Seltzer and Braniff accounts. Two years later she founded her own agency, Wells Rich Greene (WRG), with two of her colleagues from Tinker, and several major clients, including Braniff, followed her. Wells married Braniff president Harrison Lawrence, but soon resigned her husband's account in order to pick up Trans World Airlines' more lucrative advertising business. By 1968, WRG had added accounts from American Motors, Philip Morris, Smith-Kline, and Proctor and Gamble; at year's end it had nearly $60 million in annual billings and 260 employees. When she committed the following year to serve as the agency's president for the next decade, her annual salary of $225,000 made her the country's highest paid female executive.[59] Yet Mary Wells Lawrence's stunning success did remarkably little, at least in the near term, to pave the way for other women to follow in her footsteps. Eventually, some feminists came to fault her for what they saw as her unwillingness to prioritize the promotion of women's career advancement, or to leverage her prestige to fight against the pervasiveness of sexist images and messaging in advertising.

While the new creative agencies of the 1960s succeeded in altering the style of American advertising, they did not dislodge the established agencies from their positions of dominance in the industry. By the end of the decade, the agencies with the highest annual gross billings—J. Walter Thompson, Young and Rubicam, McCann-Erickson, Ted Bates, BBDO—were mostly the same ones that had led the rankings ten years earlier.[60] Blue-chip agencies certainly felt the sting when important clients decamped for their parvenu competitors, but they nonetheless enjoyed considerable growth for three primary reasons. First, the established agencies responded to the creative challenge in part by expanding their array of client services to add new planning, marketing, media, design, and research activities. Account executives at the largest firms were quick to point out to clients that the burgeoning creative shops—which they typically dismissed as "boutiques"—lacked the resources to furnish such comprehensive support. Interpublic, for example, by 1967 included under its corporate umbrella the Market Planning Corporation (Marplan), Corporate Expansion Services, Infoplan (specializing in public relations), New Dimensions Design (specializing in product development), along with multiple advertising agencies. Although a cash crunch in late 1967 and early 1968 forced the conglomerate to jettison several of these ventures, Interpublic was soon growing again with new acquisitions such as Dataplan.[61]

Many of the larger advertising agencies, like BBDO, that had a heavy volume of accounts for nondurable consumer goods, like prepackaged foods, over-the-counter medicines, toiletries, and household cleaning products, developed their own design departments in order to offer a comprehensive range of services.[62] Not only did new subsidiaries and services meet the complex needs of major clients, they also generated lucrative additional sources of revenue beyond the standard 15 percent agency commission on gross billings.

A second key development was the technological transformation in advertising that resulted from the introduction of computerized data processing applications. Data processing made its first impact in the media departments of larger agencies, where the introduction of linear programming methods enabled a far more analytically robust and precise measurement of the relative efficiency of numerous time and space options than the crude formula-buying based on CPM that had been common practice during the 1950s. Computing was also used increasingly to generate sophisticated analyses of demographic and market survey data, which advertisers could deploy to mold consumers' preferences more effectively. The costs of mainframe computing hardware along with the specialized coding required for the industry's data processing applications, however, put the new technology beyond the reach of smaller agencies. Even as the creative revolution's partisans emphasized intuition, spontaneity, individuality, nonconformity, and skepticism, their efforts competed against computing's tendency to intensify the quantification and rationalization of advertising's primal capacity to stoke consumer demand and increase the marginal urgency of goods.[63]

The third major factor contributing to the continued dominance of the establishment agencies was the ease with which they could emulate the style of the creative revolution. Some of the large firms accomplished this by forming their own internal subsidiaries or divisions, such as Interpublic's Jack Tinker and Partners and J. Walter Thompson's Group 7, that were conspicuously emancipated from regimented workplace routines. More frequently, old-line agencies simply poached copywriters and art directors with creative reputations away from the new shops by offering hefty raises that the upstarts could not match. By 1966, it was not uncommon for account executives with the blue-chip agencies to take client representatives on office tours in order to show off their hip young creative talent.[64] Furthermore, while the proponents of the creative revolution assailed the establishment's lack of authenticity, most clients and consumers found the large agencies' appropriations of countercultural signifiers of youthful rebellion—psychedelic graphics, rock music, long hair, and flamboyant clothing—to be adequately compelling. For all of their professed commitment to breaking from the industry's conventional practices, the creative partisans did not fundamentally transform the experience of mental labor for most people employed in advertising, nor did they offer a coherent alternative to consumer capitalism. Displays of nonconformity, performances of authenticity, and even symbolic rejections of the logic of the market all still served one goal: to sell goods and services.

The surprisingly rapid decline of PKL furnished a coda for the creative revolution. After Lois's departure the agency began to lose major clients, including Xerox, Proctor and Gamble, and National Airlines, while the corporate board, lured by the conglomerate mania of the late 1960s, attempted to diversify into electronics and services. By the end of 1969, its annual billings had tumbled more than 80 percent in the previous two-and-a-half years, and the agency's workforce had been slashed from 185 employees in early 1968 to a skeleton crew of 35. Koenig severed his ties to PKL in 1970 and began a period of semiretirement, financed from his profits off of the company's stock during its boom years.[65] In the long run, the spread of public stock offerings within the advertising industry proved to be a more lasting legacy for PKL than its prodigious creative output. Although advertising executive Fairfax Cone criticized PKL in 1962 for its groundbreaking IPO, declaring that "an agency should be operated for the benefit of the officers and employees who devote their lives to it" and that he "wouldn't want to be a part of an agency that owed its primary obligation to outside stockholders," he nonetheless took his own agency (Foote, Cone, and Belding) public the next year.[66] DDB followed suit with its own IPO in 1964. Grey Advertising joined the trend in 1965, along with Ogilvy and Mather in 1967, WRG in 1968, JWT in 1969, Interpublic in 1971, and BBDO in 1973.[67] The need to maintain stock prices quickly became another force disciplining the industry's workers. Mary Wells Lawrence may have embraced "love power" as a slogan for her new agency in 1967, but by 1970 she extolled "the dynamism of public ownership of agencies." Her fiduciary responsibility to her shareholders necessitated an exacting system of cost-accounting that gave WRG "the stimulus it takes to fire people the agency cannot afford," since "fat is an agency's greatest threat," breeding "hierarchy, bureaucracy, and mediocrity." The copywriters and art directors at WRG, she continued, were "as interested in the American Stock Exchange as they are in the Clio Awards Dinner."[68]

The mild recession of 1970, which foreshadowed the economic woes to come in the middle of the decade, also helped to bring the creative revolution to a close. The rate of growth in agencies' billings slowed, so that by 1973 total advertising expenditures as a percentage of gross national product slipped to the lowest level since 1950.[69] Quite a few clients turned away from the visually and rhetorically innovative advertising of the 1960s in favor of the older types of formulaic product differentiation, with the more desperate manufacturers and retailers reverting to outright price competition in response to inflationary conditions. Advertisements in the 1970s became less likely to draw attention to their own stylistic innovation, or to represent consumers as rebels and nonconformists, and more likely to emphasize traditional conceptions of utility maximization. Already waxing elegiac in September 1971, advertising executive Marvin Sloves, one of the creative revolution's survivors, reminisced that "it was a time of great opportunity. There was a whole generation in their early thirties who were really ready at that moment." But, he added, "it's the last time it's going to happen—too many pressures now. Business is tough, the national expansion has slowed. New product introduction is down."[70] Furthermore, the trend toward public shareholding had other unintended consequences. Initial public offerings raised working capital while simultaneously enabling existing partners in advertising agencies to monetize their ownership shares. Over time, public shareholding facilitated acquisition by conglomerates, which were often attracted by the agencies' comparatively large revenue streams relative to their limited capital requirements. As the 1970s progressed, New York increasingly became a center for the direction of diversified and far-flung advertising and marketing activities, with the result that the city's advertising workforce became more heavily weighted toward managerial personnel and the proportion of creative staff plateaued. After many decades in which the metropolitan area had accounted for nearly one-third of all white-collar employment in the American advertising industry, New York's share declined to just a quarter of the national total by 1980.[71] Although median salaries in advertising remained higher than in most other predominately white-collar sectors of the metropolitan economy, the restructurings of the 1970s still limited the horizons of most of the industry's employees. The visions of workplace autonomy and freedom from the constraints of the market that had motivated the creative revolution proved more elusive than ever.

"The Man in the Middle": Design, Autonomy, and Aesthetics in an Age of Abundance

The people who designed the multitude of products that advertisements were intended to sell, along with their packaging and the retail environments in which buyers made their purchases, encountered many of the same frustrations and pressures as their counterparts on Madison Avenue. Postwar industrial design in the United States advanced far beyond its early years during the Great Depression, becoming a routine component of all phases of manufacturing, marketing, and distribution. As the field evolved between the late 1940s and the early 1970s, the range of design practices and workplace settings became increasingly varied. Designers worked for substantial consulting firms that emulated aspects of the larger advertising agencies, within advertising or marketing conglomerates, for the in-house design departments incorporated into most mass-production manufacturing operations, for specialized manufacturers engaged in serial production utilizing craft methods, or in some cases as freelancers whose creative talents enabled them to enjoy a modicum of independence within the interstices of the dynamically expanding economy. While career opportunities abounded, many designers nonetheless yearned for greater creative autonomy, including greater control over the aesthetic and material qualities of the goods they helped to develop as well as the prospect of design for social needs, or at least design unconstrained by sales imperatives.

The experiences of designers who had been involved with the Design Laboratory, the FAECT, or other Popular Front initiatives as they adapted to postwar conditions of abundance illustrated many of the larger trends in the design field with particular clarity. While the prospects for progressive social transformation collapsed with the onset of the domestic Cold War, these designers retained a critical perspective on mental labor and its role within complex systems of cultural production. Yet their earlier faith in workers' collective empowerment and the socialization of production gave way to a new vision—both more expansive and more limiting—in which fortunate individuals could attain autonomy by transcending relations of production and exchange. Moreover, this shift in these designers' understanding of creativity influenced their aesthetic sensibilities as well. They remained proponents of a functionalist modernism relatively free of expressive ornamentation, but they no longer strove to establish this aesthetic as a signifier of incipient social democracy. Instead, they found themselves as the embodiments of a New Class creative ethos, designing upmarket goods in a refined modernist style intended to appeal to affluent consumers.

In the late 1940s, progressive designers, art educators, curators, and critics often promoted their preferred variants of modernist aesthetics in an ideologically ambiguous manner that reflected both their lingering hopes for a renewal of public, labor, or cooperative sponsorship and their vexing struggles to secure such patronage in the past. Former Design Laboratory faculty William Friedman and Hilde Reiss exemplified this trend with their efforts to boost modern design while on the staff of the Walker Art Center in Minneapolis. The institution had emerged as one of the nation's leading supporters of modernism in the visual arts under the direction of architect Daniel Defenbacher. As an FAP administrator, he had made it into one of the project's largest and most successful Community Art Centers, appropriating WPA funds to enhance its facilities and collections. When control over the Walker Art Center reverted to private trustees after the WPA was terminated, they retained Defenbacher and authorized him to hire Friedman as assistant director in 1944 and Reiss as a curator the following year.[72] Arriving at the institution on the cusp of manufacturers' reconversion for postwar civilian production and the massive consumer binge that followed, Reiss quickly set about establishing a program to channel the pent-up demand toward the purchase of furnishings, housewares, appliances, and other items that reflected a refined modernist aesthetic. In January 1946, she opened her first exhibition in the Walker's new Everyday Art Gallery, and later that year she founded an eponymous quarterly journal to advocate for modern design on a wider basis. The debut issue described the Everyday Art Gallery as a "permanent addition to the Center" that was "devoted to selecting and displaying the best ideas concerning the home and the many articles that go into it," with exhibitions intended to "give practical information about design, materials, costs, and sources of supply."[73] In addition, Reiss hired former Design Laboratory colleague Elizabeth McCausland, who was still based in New York, to take care of national publicity for the initiative.[74]

From the outset, Reiss sought out commercial collaborators for her cultural mission. The Everyday Art Gallery partnered with local retailers as well as with furniture manufacturers Herman Miller, Knoll, and Artek-Pascoe to obtain sample items for exhibition. These firms, along with appliance manufacturers, regional utilities, and even a local Chrysler dealer whose product offerings undoubtedly violated the *Quarterly*'s aesthetic principles, also helped to sustain her publication with their advertising. While most manufacturers and merchants saw postwar housing as simply a lever for consumer demand, Reiss and her colleagues contended that the home must also be a site of creative engagement and enrichment. To demonstrate their concepts for modern living more clearly, in 1947 she and Friedman designed and constructed Idea House II on the Walker Art Center's grounds. They presented it not as a prototype for direct emulation or as a formalist art object in its own right, but rather in the spirit of a laboratory experiment for testing their hypotheses about possible combinations of modernist architectural elements and furnishings. Several families as well as a pair of young women lived in Idea House II in consecutive stints following its initial public exhibition as a means for assessing the suitability of its innovative features. Habitation also assured continuing publicity, as did manufacturers' interest in having their products photographed within the experimental dwelling. For the next twenty years, Idea House II periodically provided housing for guest lecturers, curatorial staff, and visiting artists.[75]

Although Reiss, Friedman, and McCausland still continued their Popular Front activism into the early postwar years, including their advocacy for public arts sponsorship and other public goods and services, their progressive politics found less and less direct connection to their affinity for modernism.[76] The tension that had existed during the 1930s and early 1940s between those who labored to establish functionalist modernism as a signifier of social democracy and those who embraced it primarily as a marker of cultural sophistication largely dissipated. Reiss and her associates envisioned an aesthetic capable of signifying the autonomy and creative engagement sought by both designers and discerning consumers; nonetheless, like Noyes in his columns for *Consumer Reports*, they increasingly avoided explicitly linking modernism to social democracy's prospects. Moving away from the austerity that had characterized much of the Design Laboratory's output of renderings and models as well as its critiques of material culture, the Everyday Art Gallery instead aimed to put some fun into function. Ceramicist Eva Zeisel articulated the new mood in an article she contributed to the second issue of *Everyday Art Quarterly*. "Regardless of function, color and lines evoke associations in us," she contended. "We respond to them emotionally." Until recently, "for functionalists, this expressiveness" was not considered a legitimate part of the "avowed purpose" of objects, as users "were expected to appreciate form from the aspect of function," not become absorbed "in contemplation of the form."[77] While emphasizing the playful and improvisational dimensions of modernism, the *Quarterly* still carefully distinguished the designs that it promoted from the crass exuberance of much of postwar mass consumerism. In an article on plastics, Friedman and Reiss's former student Don Wallance, who was gradually establishing his own reputation as a creator of furniture and housewares, reminded readers that "good design does not necessarily follow from sleek surfaces, transparent materials, strident color, heavy ornament, or bulbous forms." These decorative tactics "may endow an object with temporary 'shelf appeal,'" but ultimately products "which retain their freshness with familiarity and use depend on more intrinsic qualities of design." Recapitulating the modernist catechism of functionality for a growing market of affluent and educated consumers, Wallance asserted that the "form of a well-designed object is expressive of its purpose, material, and structure. Its shape and outline are agreeable to eye and hand. In a well-designed object, texture, ornament, and color are integrated with and subordinated to form." Wallance's views, aligned with Reiss's editorial position, offered a critique of consumer capitalism's impact on mass taste, but not of its political economy.[78]

The ideological compromises necessitated by the eclipse of Popular Front hopes for public, labor, or cooperative patronage were even more pronounced for progressives' actual design practice, as was evident in the development of George Nelson's firm during the postwar years. Although he received a traditional training in architecture at Yale in the late 1920s, Nelson became an early and influential convert to modernist principles.[79] He was also an enthusiastic supporter of the FAECT, penning an essay for the union's magazine on the proletarianization of architects and designers and the importance of organization as a response.[80] More substantive union involvement came through his active membership in the Newspaper Guild during a stint at Time Inc., where Nelson was an editor of *Architectural Forum* and a periodic contributor to *Fortune*. In early 1945, an article on wall storage concepts that he coauthored with fellow editor Henry Wright got the attention of Herman Miller furniture company president D. J. De Pree.[81] The company had been one of the few American furniture manufacturers to embrace modern design during the 1930s, which executives had hoped would enable the firm to stand out within an increasingly competitive industry. As Herman Miller began planning its initial postwar product line, De Pree offered Nelson the position of design director for the company.

While Nelson and De Pree shared aesthetic tastes, their politics could not have diverged more sharply. Like many heads of medium-sized Midwestern manufacturing firms, De Pree was a staunch conservative who was deeply hostile to the progressive agenda. Nonetheless, Nelson accepted the offer. With a major client in hand, he proceeded to assemble an agency, which he eventually incorporated as George Nelson Associates. Neither he nor the other progressive designers he hired objected too strenuously to their client's ardent conservatism, while De Pree did not seem too troubled by the leftist pasts of designers like Irving Harper, who like Nelson had been a supporter of the FAECT, or Design Laboratory alumna Suzanne Sekey. Nelson's relationship with Herman Miller lasted into the 1970s, and the work that his agency performed for the furniture maker, or that he contracted out to other leading designers—most notably Charles and Ray Eames—on a freelance basis, came to define the aesthetic of refined modernism in postwar America.[82] Although

Nelson's agency adopted the aesthetic affinities and the autonomous creative practices advanced by the Design Laboratory, its approach became divorced from earlier progressive aspirations to harness the visual power of modernism to represent social democracy. Instead, the refined modernism of the furnishings, interiors, graphics and other design work produced by the agency became indicators of New Class affluence and status.

Industrial design for the postwar mass market, as exemplified by Raymond Loewy Associates, contrasted dramatically with both the aesthetic standards and workplace practices associated with Nelson's agency. Loewy adroitly used the celebrity aura he had first cultivated before the war to personify his agency's brand, which through its prolific commissions shaped the products, packaging, and retail spaces targeted at millions of American consumers who would have scoffed at Galbraith's belief in the diminishing marginal urgency of goods and who still believed that more, not less, was more.[83] Loewy's appearance on the cover of *Time* in 1949 indicated his iconic cultural status, while the accompanying profile touted his agency's pervasive impact on the material culture of everyday life. Nearly 150 designers, architects, and draftsmen worked full-time for Loewy, with numerous supplemental design staff contracted for various projects on a temporary or freelance basis. Scores more worked for the agency in clerical, sales, and other support roles. In addition to the main New York office, Loewy maintained branch offices in Chicago and Los Angeles, along with a special office at the Studebaker auto factory in South Bend, Indiana, where the agency was an on-site design contractor. Foreign offices in London and São Paulo provided entry into international markets. With its substantial scale of operations, Loewy offered clients a wider range of services than other design agencies. Its bread-and-butter remained the periodic updating and restyling of products, packaging, and graphic design for an array of firms. The agency enjoyed lucrative long-term relationships with major home appliance manufacturers—first Sears and then Frigidaire—for which it created numerous models over successive years. It also earned a reputation as a designer of retail spaces. Following its well-received design of Lord and Taylor's first suburban branch store on Long Island, department store design became another one of the agency's staples.[84] Eventually, by the late 1950s and 1960s, Loewy began offering clients sophisticated marketing analyses and motivational research comparable to that available from large advertising agencies. In several instances, major trade associations turned to the agency to map the socioeconomic contours of major market segments, and to prescribe appropriate design and marketing solutions targeted toward particular groups of consumers.[85]

Designer Irving Harper's early career path highlighted the stark differences between working conditions at Raymond Loewy Associates and the conditions in agencies like Nelson's. Harper had started his career with Gilbert Rohde's small agency in the late 1930s, contributing to the development of some of Herman Miller's first modern furniture as well as several exhibits for the 1939 New York World's Fair. Following the war, the first job available to him was with Loewy's burgeoning department store division. As the agency expanded to take advantage of the postwar consumer boom, it increased its output of completed design commissions not just by adding personnel, but also by implementing a highly rationalized division of labor. When Harper joined the agency, department store projects were partitioned between a planning unit, an estimate unit, a design unit, and a detailing unit. In detailing, where he worked, managers parceled out discrete elements of a general interior plan produced by the estimate and design units for completion, so that some staff worked only on cabinets and fixtures along the bases of walls, others on lighting fixtures, others on trim, and still others on stand-alone floor displays. In effect, Harper and his coworkers contributed their mental labor without necessarily having any conception of the entire project.

FIGURE 7.1 Creative labor in one of the drawing rooms at Raymond Loewy Associates' main offices in New York during the 1950s. From the Raymond Loewy Archive, Gift of Betty Reese, Cooper Hewitt, Smithsonian Design Museum.

Harper recalled it as "a conveyor-belt operation." Loewy's business partner William Snaith, who headed the department store division, augmented the rationalization with old-fashioned sweating of labor, as he and his managers paced the large drawing room, constantly haranguing Harper and the other designers to complete their assigned tasks more quickly. The job's only redeeming aspect, according to Harper, was the pay.[86]

Although the FAECT briefly seemed to be gaining momentum in the war's immediate aftermath, as it organized Ebasco along with a handful of smaller architectural firms in New York, Harper did not see much potential for a successful unionization effort to improve working conditions at Loewy's agency. His deliverance from the alienation of Loewy's regimented drawing room instead stemmed from his winning a competition sponsored by Bloomingdale's department store to design a model suburban home. The prize of $5,000 surpassed his annual salary, but financial constraints still loomed. One of the judges, architect Edward Durell Stone, was so impressed that he offered to hire him, but Harper declined because the move would have entailed a cut in pay. Fortunately, in 1947, Nelson made him a more generous offer which allowed him to leave Loewy's design factory.[87]

George Nelson Associates provided Harper and the other designers there the substantive creative autonomy that was conspicuously lacking at workplaces like Loewy's. Although the tempo could become hectic with long hours when projects were due for delivery, to a considerable degree the designers were free to tackle assignments as they saw fit. Members of the staff often collaborated, but in most cases a designer on a project was involved with all steps of its development and completion. Responding in 1949 to a research query from Don Wallance, Nelson explicated the design philosophy that emerged from his early years running his own agency. "I have tried to run the thing at the highest possible level, as far as integrity is concerned," he remarked, "but I am coming to the conclusion that we may never reach solutions that are more than superficial unless designing and making are merged into a single process. How to do this is another matter." Nelson dismissed the popular image of the industrial designer as "a character who can turn from locomotives to toothbrushes with equal competence and ease," which in his mind represented "the antithesis of the craftsman's approach." There was no substitute for specific craft knowledge and artistic experimentation. Yet the purpose of integrating intellectual and manual tasks was to elevate the designer's creativity. Ideally, Nelson maintained, "the designer has to be a craftsman to develop his capacities as a designer, not because he has to make the prototype." In trying to adhere to this principle in his own agency, he acknowledged the pervasive "social disease" of alienation in postwar America; "it isn't only the craftsman," he reminded Wallance, "who has been divorced from meaningful work (in a social sense) but practically everyone."[88] Nelson's enlightened approach in some regards foreshadowed the thinking behind many of the "creative" advertising agencies of the 1960s, although even the relative autonomy afforded to the designers he employed had its boundaries. For publicity and marketing purposes, Nelson took credit for the work of his designers, much as advertising agencies took credit for the work of their graphic artists and copywriters. Only trade insiders might know, for instance, that Harper had in fact created Herman Miller's iconic logo or some of the company's most distinctive furniture designs.[89] While Harper's job with Nelson made him one of the few designers privileged to develop his own work practices free from the division of labor that was prevalent elsewhere, his creativity, like that of most others in his profession, did not garner widespread public recognition.

The creative anonymity of postwar American design was experienced most acutely by designers employed directly by major manufacturers, most of which by mid-century had integrated activities related to product appearance and styling directly into the firm. These designers easily outnumbered those working in consulting design agencies, whether those like Raymond Loewy Associates that molded mass tastes or those like George Nelson Associates that offered a more refined vision of modernity. By far the largest of the in-house design units were those maintained by the Big Three automakers in Detroit, each of which employed hundreds of stylists, design engineers, and draftsmen. Although many of the industry's designers had embraced unionism during the 1930s and early 1940s by joining the Society of Designing Engineers, factional disputes had weakened the organization and enabled management to reassert control over the studios and drawing rooms. By the 1950s, when General Motors relocated the bulk of its several hundred auto stylists to its new Technical Center, a modernist suburban office campus, the foothold that the SDE once had inside the company had been eliminated.[90] As product differentiation became increasingly important in the postwar market, the automakers expanded their design staffs accordingly. GM, which had employed just 90 designers in 1934, had a design staff of 1,400 by 1965, whose responsibilities included not just its multiple automotive makes and models, but also home appliances for its Frigidaire division (where in-house personnel took over from Loewy in 1953), its overall corporate identity, and special exhibits such as the GM pavilion at the 1964–1965 New York World's Fair.[91] The auto designs created by these workers, including the flamboyant tailfins that they popularized in the late 1950s, were among the most potent symbols of the visual culture of postwar American consumerism, and heavily influenced the vernacular architecture of suburban spaces defined by automobility.

Somewhat more typical than the automakers' large but insular design departments were the design units of home appliance manufacturers like General Electric. By the late 1940s, GE employed a permanent staff of 50 designers and 17 skilled model makers in a centralized "Appearance Design" department at its massive appliance factory in Bridgeport, Connecticut. As part of its strategy of dispersing manufacturing capacity away from established centers of labor militancy, during the early 1950s GE divided the Bridgeport group into multiple design and styling units attached to each of its consumer appliance and electronics divisions. Project managers at the division level coordinated the work of each design unit with the divisional engineering and sales personnel involved with particular product lines, such as refrigerators, television sets, and washing machines.[92] As the firm's head design supervisor, Arthur BecVar, explained in 1953, this ongoing association gave what he termed the "corporation designer" the "opportunity to recognize design problems that the engineer or manufacturing man or the business executive might miss." Furthermore, "the constant association of the corporation designer with executives of the company, the ease with which they can consult him, the lack of consideration regarding fees to be paid, and most of all, their acceptance of him as a full-time member of the company," was mutually beneficial. The inclusion of designers within the firm's social circles and their insulation from immediate market calculations regarding the cost of their mental labor thus assured GE a steady flow of suitable designs for its products. Although BecVar believed that consultant designers could still make valuable contributions to firms with their own design staffs, he felt it was imperative that they should only be brought in on the recommendation of the head of the design department and that they coordinate all of their work directly with him.[93] Even under these conditions, the results could be disappointing, as GE discovered several years later when BecVar retained George Nelson Associates for the company's effort to develop cabinet-hung horizontal refrigerators that could be installed inside kitchen walls or partitions.[94] As GE continued its decentralization program, the total number of designers within the company increased even as they became more geographically dispersed. The Major Appliance unit in Louisville employed 45 designers and model-makers in 1965, while a design staff of 24 focused on smaller appliances like vacuum cleaners and toasters in the Bridgeport Housewares Division, and a third group of 21 designers worked in a Consumer Electronics Unit.[95]

Wallance hoped to explicate this increasing diversity of designers' work practices and to analyze the ways in which these practices affected the aesthetic and functional qualities of goods with his book *Shaping America's Products*, which he published in 1956. He had initiated his research in the late 1940s as part of a comprehensive project to examine "design and craftsmanship in today's products" that he and his mentors Friedman and Reiss had conceived under the auspices of the Walker Art Center. Their ambitious plans to produce several research volumes involving input from social scientists, along with public exhibitions and an educational motion picture, were drastically curtailed after Friedman and Reiss's departure from the Center cost the endeavor much of its financing. Nonetheless, Wallance pushed forward to produce a study based on the research, balancing his writing with his ongoing work as a freelance designer.[96] *Shaping America's Products* bore the indelible mark of the Design Laboratory's commitment to functionalist aesthetics along with its materialist methodology and its curiosity about the condition of creative labor that typified Popular Front cultural analyses more generally. Yet Wallance's survey conspicuously avoided the Popular Front's encouragement of cultural workers' collective empowerment, as well as its critiques of cultural patronage and the broader political economy of mass consumerism. Instead, anticipating Galbraith, Wallance claimed that "the most significant contribution to the growth of democracy made by 20th century America has been not in politics or government, but in the widespread distribution of material goods." With rising affluence, the "preoccupation with sheer quantity of production and distribution has been tempered by a growing interest in the design and quality of ordinary objects." Moreover, he continued, "rising standards of taste and increasing selectivity on the part of the general public are making product design and quality not only a matter of cultural interest, but also a matter of increasing concern to business managements—a decisive factor in the competition for markets."[97]

Shaping America's Products provided a kaleidoscopic view of nearly every venue in which designers worked, with a series of detailed case studies in which Wallance effectively utilized his trove of research to illuminate the varieties of contemporary design practice. "Insofar as product creation is inevitably bound up with technical skills and with the human 'instinct of workmanship,'" he asserted, his study was inherently also "an inquiry into the nature of craftsmanship and how it finds its expression in some areas of our industrial society." Following Friedman and Nelson's lead, Wallance identified the separation of "design" (which he defined as "essentially abstract procedures—analysis, synthesis, planning, invention") and "craftsmanship" (the realm of "concrete execution—delineation, model fabrication, tool and die making and actual production") in modern industry as the book's central organizing principle.[98] Quality products, he contended, resulted from concerted efforts to bridge this gap, even in large-scale industrial settings in which design and craftsmanship were fragmented into an array of discrete tasks and "the individual is subordinated to the group." Despite "the current practice of featuring designers' names," which "can be attributed in part to the undoubted sales promotional value of associating an otherwise anonymous and impersonal product with a colorful personality," most goods were created by numerous skilled workers, each of whom "must subordinate his own personality to the exigencies of a complex industrial process and his personal taste to the requirements of a mass market." Yet these same market forces also led to the "distractions of superficial outer styling" that undermined attempts at maintaining design integrity. "The onus for this state of affairs," Wallance maintained, "has at various times been placed on the manufacturer, the designer, the advertising profession, the retailer, or the consumer," even though "each is caught in a complex of pressures and inertia which cannot be readily modified from any one quarter." Ultimately, he concluded, these tensions would likely be resolved "only when the designer, producer, and consumer achieve a common outlook and response to visual form."[99]

Wallance thus offered a paradoxical assessment of design work in postwar America. His case studies convincingly demonstrated the agency that designers still exercised, even within complex systems of production. The workplace practices of designers at General Electric or Raymond Loewy Associates could be plausibly situated along a spectrum of creative autonomy that also included designers in experimental studios like the Eameses', freelance designers like himself, and independent designer-artisans. Simultaneously, however, he represented the conditions in which most designers worked as the inexorable result of deterministic technological or sociological processes, such as industrialization or the impact of affluence on consumer taste. Nowhere in the text does Wallance suggest that designers' agency might extend to union organizing as a means of improving their work practices, or to participating in broader social movements to promote alternatives to consumer capitalism. While this implicit legitimation of the status quo reflected a realistic assessment of the political landscape following the Popular Front's demise, it also indicated his expectations that ongoing technological and sociological processes would inexorably enable the transcendence of the economic relations that thwarted quality design. Hence the importance of Wallance's educational mission: as affluent consumers increasingly came to appreciate products with design integrity that embodied quality rather than quantity, manufacturers would be compelled to respond by providing more well-designed goods, which would in turn generate more opportunities for designers to work under conditions conducive to creative autonomy and design integrity.

Two years later, sociologist C. Wright Mills offered a more pointed critique of the state of the design profession in an address to the annual meeting of the International Design Conference in Aspen. The conference had first been launched largely through the sponsorship of Container Corporation of America's president Walter Paepcke as a means of promoting refined modernist design along with liberal cultural commentary to an elite audience.[100] In his remarks, which he revised for publication in *Industrial Design* magazine as an article titled, "The Man in the Middle," Mills observed that designers stood at the intersection of "two great developments of twentieth-century America": first, the "shift in economic emphasis from production to distribution, and along with it, the joining of the struggle for existence with the panic for status"; and second, "the bringing of art, science, and learning into subordinate relation with the dominant institutions of the capitalist economy and the nationalist state." Designers were thus integrated into the modern "cultural apparatus," which he defined as "all those organizations and milieux in which artistic, intellectual, and scientific work goes on" along with "all the means by which such work is made available to small circles, wider publics, and the great masses." Within this system for the creation and propagation of culture, Mills contended, the majority of designers had opted to turn the "arts and crafts and skills of the cultural apparatus" from "adjuncts of advertising" into "advertisements" themselves. "By brand and trademark, by slogan and package, by color and form," they gave "the commodity a fictitious individuality," so that, ultimately, "the silly needs of salesmanship are thus met by the silly designing and redesigning of things." Echoing Veblen, Mills identified industrial design as symptomatic of the "waste of human labor and material" that had become "irrationally central to the performance of the capitalist mechanism." American society had been transformed into "a great sales room, a network of public rackets, and a continuous fashion show" in which "the image of beauty itself" was "identified with the designer's speed-up and debasement of imagination, taste, and sensibility."[101]

Mills's caustic assessment of postwar design practice might have surprised the cultural elites assembled in Aspen, who were likely expecting the approbation typical of professional conferences, but he held out the possibility of redemption through a renewed commitment to the ideal of craftsmanship.

"The cultural workman," he opined, "in particular the designer, tends to become part of the means of distribution, over which he tends to lose control." Moreover, "in this situation of increasing bureaucratization" combined with "the continual need for innovation," the "cultural workman tends to become either a commercial hack or a commercial star." The star found himself fortunate that his "productions are so much in demand" that he was able "to some extent at least, to make distributors serve as *his* adjuncts." The majority of designers, however, were "hacks" relegated to anonymity and a modest salary. While Mills conceded that he was "describing the role of the designer at what I hope will be its worst," he acknowledged that the "autonomy of all types of cultural workmen has in our time been declining." Craftsmanship "as an ideal and a practice" could provide a basis for "all the designer ought to represent as an individual and all that he ought to stand for socially and politically and economically." It stood for "the creative nature of work, and for the central place of such work in human development as a whole," as well as the elimination of the invidious divisions "of work and play" and "of work and culture."[102] Although Mills was more explicit than Wallance in finding fault with consumer capitalism, both identified alienation as the fundamental source of the many shortcomings they found in American material culture. Yet neither Wallance nor Mills presented a specific program for combating the conditions that generated alienation, instead offering affirmation to those enlightened enough to appreciate their critiques.

These critical discourses on the relationship between creative autonomy, design integrity, and consumerism gained influence in the coming years. Sophisticated modern design, influenced by functionalist principles and largely free of applied ornamentation, more than ever served to aestheticize the New Class ideal. A 1966 profile in *Industrial Design* of Eliot Noyes and Associates, then at the apex of its professional prestige with major long-term consulting relationships with IBM and Westinghouse, noted the "relaxed, deceptively casual air" of the firm's offices in New Canaan, Connecticut, free from New York's "hard-edge of hustle." The offices were "light and comfortably furnished," suggesting "a sensitivity to men who can and must want to work there" while also providing "room to think beyond engineering considerations, color chips, and production requirements." As Noyes's senior associate explained, they believed that "the concept of design as a means of expression holds equally true for the designer as for his client," a principle that he conflated with their adherence to "the notion of the industrial designer as a professional, working to professional standards and not just creating a service organization for industry." To drive home the message, Noyes denigrated the "ID profession" as "not very professional," given the predominance of designers whose work was, in his estimation, not "based on any philosophical attitudes or social values." In his view, his agency's consulting role was to be "the conscience in design for the client," relating its activities to a "philosophy of design worked out to reflect the client" and how it wanted "to be seen and known in society."[103]

With just a dozen industrial designers on staff, Noyes's agency realized an ideal of creative autonomy that the majority of designers, let alone the broader occupational strata of professionals and technicians, were unlikely to attain in their own jobs. Nonetheless, consulting agencies like Eliot Noyes and Associates and George Nelson Associates had a massive impact on the consciousness of white-collar workers in postwar America through their innovative and far-reaching contributions to the postwar office. The most significant new development was the widespread introduction of computerized data processing, which was already transforming an enormous range of clerical, sales, professional, and technical occupations. No mainframe computers of the era were more successful from either a design or a sales standpoint than the IBM System/360, which made its debut in 1964. Noyes and his staff, in collaboration with the corporation's own engineers and designers, created the consistent form and appearance of all of the components, including operator consoles, processing units, drum memory units, tape drives, card readers, and display terminals. Modular design enabled customers to configure System/360 to meet a wide range of specific needs.[104] The equipment's sleek, unadorned look epitomized what Noyes described as the client's "corporate character"; as he explained, "it's easy to say that IBM is simply a maker of business machines. But if you get to the very heart of the matter, what IBM really does is to help man extend his control over his environment."[105] The modular design of computer hardware also influenced the physical configuration of office space, as the 1960s saw the proliferation of movable partitions and cubicles, including flexible office storage and partitioning systems created by Nelson's agency.[106] In addition, architectural firms creating modernist skyscrapers to serve as corporate headquarters often found existing stock furniture options to be disappointing, leading them to design their own functionalist desks, cabinets, and other pieces. A line of office furniture created by Skidmore, Owings, and Merrill (SOM) as part of a 1959 commission for a Manhattan tower, for instance, was widely copied by numerous steel fabricators, making its austere, angular forms an ordinary aspect of white-collar workplaces across the country during the 1960s and 1970s.[107]

Gradually, the critiques put forth by the idealistic proponents of modernist design integrity began to have some effect on the aesthetics of mass-market consumerism. When the federal government looked to present the bounty of American capitalism abroad, it turned to agencies like George Nelson Associates to create tasteful pavilions and exhibits for international fairs, including the model home that served as the backdrop for the 1959 "kitchen debate" in Moscow between Vice President Richard Nixon and Soviet Premier Nikita Khrushchev.[108] American automakers, responding both to mounting criticisms of their garish designs and consumers' fickle craving for novelty, eliminated tailfins at the start of the 1960s along with much of the chrome and applied ornament that had signified mass prosperity in the prior decade. Many major home appliances, including refrigerators, stoves, and washing machines, likewise lost most of the chrome and rounded corners that were a legacy of streamlining in exchange for a cleaner, sleeker appearance. Efforts to promote a refined modernism were also apparent in the landscape and built environment of suburban consumerism, as evident in the look of the large, planned shopping malls designed by Victor Gruen Associates and in exurban "new towns."[109] High modernism also entered the visual culture of everyday life through the proliferation of new corporate logos, such as those that former Design Laboratory instructor Paul Rand designed for IBM, Westinghouse, and ABC among many other clients. Unlike earlier corporate iconography, which had often been rendered in an expressive style and included some visual referent to the firm's products, the new wave of logos tended toward abstract symbols or abbreviations, providing corporations with a basis for a meta-identity that was distanced from actual production or other aspects of their activities as a capitalist enterprise. These logos graced corporate lobbies and letterheads, but they also were printed on countless boxes and cans, flashed across television screens in millions of homes, and mounted on thousands of roadside signs across the landscape.[110]

Despite these trends, however, those who advocated for improvements in both the quality of mass-market design and the tastes of average consumers still found much to disparage in what critic Peter Blake labeled "God's own junkyard."[111] As one commentator in *Industrial Design* noted, "designers and architects attending professional design conferences," had "the curious habit" of "condemning the ugliness of a dehumanized, brutalized, profit-dominated, man-deteriorated environment which they are in part responsible for" while implying "that *other* designers, architects and money-grabbing speculators are *really* responsible." Noyes put it more bluntly in his remarks as the 1964 chairman of the International Design Conference in Aspen: "This conference," he declared, "is based on one simple premise. The general state of design in this country and perhaps in the world is a mess."[112] Proponents of refined modernism continued to be disappointed by the persistence of low design standards for many products. A 1965 survey of "design lag" in television manufacturing in *Industrial Design*, for example, lamented that showrooms were still brimming with models in period-style cabinets "that disguise, in every possible way, the precise mechanisms that they house." Although the reviewer found that some of the portable sets revealed "a closer application of the concept of functional design," on the whole she observed that "any awareness of what the well-heeled consumer is buying in furniture and housewares" would indicate "that the consumer is far more knowing and sophisticated" than the manufacturers' corporate design staffs believed.[113]

The 1964–1965 New York World's Fair revealed with particular clarity this conflict between the impulse to engage with the mass market as a means of elevating design standards and educating consumers and the countervailing impulse to seek critical distance. Staged to mark the quarter-century anniversary of the previous fair, the 1960s reprise was intended both to highlight how much of the Depression-era "world of tomorrow" had already been realized by postwar consumer capitalism and to tantalize visitors with coming advancements that were just beyond the horizon. Major corporate and government participants contracted with leading consultant designers to give their exhibits a future-oriented look that was distinctive and dignified. In keeping with its overall corporate image program, IBM turned to Noyes's agency to design its exhibit, which featured a large spheroid auditorium that housed a dazzling multimedia spectacle produced by Charles Eames. George Nelson Associates created an especially elaborate exhibit for Chrysler, which architecture critic Vincent Scully lauded in *Life* magazine as "pop art at its best," presenting "Detroit with welcome wit and irony."[114] Yet whatever uplifting effects came from the contributions of designers like Noyes and Nelson were seemingly countered by the fair operators' determination to exploit every commercial opportunity, so that high-concept modernist structures and spaces were juxtaposed with a carnival midway. Overall, Scully decried the fair for recapitulating "exactly the kind of world we are building all over the U.S. right now," one "created by and for the automobile in which everything permanent and solid melts away in favor of fugitive constructions bedizened with flapping pennants, neon signs, and screaming colors." A postmortem in *Industrial Design* amplified his assessment. "In its closing days, the Fair, which had never been a knock-out, was in a run-down, honky-tonk state," wrote Judith Miller. More fundamentally, she continued, its troubled two seasons called into question whether "fairs of this kind and size serve a purpose any longer." While international expositions once "confirmed and promoted" the "optimistic view that technological progress would solve the problems of the world," she asserted, "that view is less than tenable today. Technology, we have learned, creates as many problems as it solves."[115]

The fair's poor reception foreshadowed a creeping skepticism toward modernist projects of improvement and uplift in general. One dimension of this trend was the emergence of a new critical discourse within design circles that tended to validate vernacular styles and popular tastes. Modernism's progressive partisans had long believed in the power of design to provoke a constructive engagement with material culture and the built environment. This faith in the capacity of ordinary citizens and consumers to interact with modernist design, rooted in pragmatist pedagogy, stood in contrast to the widespread acceptance of mechanistic conceptions of cultural manipulation and control during the mid-century totalitarian moment. But progressive modernists' democratic convictions rested upon their assumption that an educated public would choose "good design" over premodern styles or the tawdry offerings of the mass market. While this belief aligned well with their expectations regarding the ascendancy of the New Class, it also furnished a basis for design critiques that reinforced status distinctions in postwar society. Instead, proponents of the new sensibility were inclined to agree with architects Robert Venturi and Denise Scott Brown in *Learning from Las Vegas* (1972) that the commercial vernacular of the roadside strip was "almost all right." Venturi and Scott Brown argued that despite modernism's pretenses of functionalist design integrity, it actually operated as just another system of visual symbols, with no intrinsic superiority to the symbols prevalent in vernacular landscapes, interiors, and objects. "In dismissing Levittown," they declared, "Modern architects, who have characteristically promoted the role of the social sciences in architecture, reject whole sets of dominant social patterns because they do not like the architectural consequences of those patterns." As "Experts with Ideals," modernists designed "to suit their own particular upper-middle class values, which they assign to everyone." Yet it was not necessary "to agree with hard-hat politics to support the rights of the middle-middle class to their own architectural aesthetics." Those who wished as Venturi and Scott Brown did "for a reallocation of national resources toward social purposes," they concluded, "must take care to lay emphasis on the purposes and their promotion rather than on the architecture that shelters them."[116]

In addition to this incipient postmodernist cultural critique of American design practice, growing concerns about the ecological impact of consumer capitalism furnished another potent basis for censure. Social critic Vance Packard pointed in this direction with *The Waste Makers* (1960) which drew upon information furnished by CU to make a scathing indictment of postwar industrial design. While much of Packard's polemic focused on the ways in which designers abetted the planned obsolescence of products, effectively swindling consumers, he also bucked one of the key tenets of abundance by acknowledging the existence of limits. He warned of the "dangerous decline in the United States of its supply of essential resources" and the importance of "all enduring societies" maintaining "a tolerable balance between their population and their supporting environment."[117] By the late 1960s and early 1970s, the design profession, which still subsisted in large part through the marketing of product differentiation and novelty, responded to the rise of the modern environmental movement in conflicted and contradictory ways. Within the pages of *Industrial Design*, periodic articles addressing pollution, sustainability, and ecological degradation were surrounded by trade advertising for packaging, materials, and processes that exacerbated all of these problems. An article from the April 1970 issue, for instance, suggested that "a glance at a few of the types of solutions to pollution problems—systems for recycling sewage and garbage, advanced agricultural practices, equipment for filtering industrial wastes, research into pesticide development, installation of automatic garbage collection systems—indicates that increased production and technological development are necessary to bring about these types of solutions." In an implicit swipe at more radical environmentalists, it also asserted that "if pollution control means more decreases in the standard of living, then many people will oppose" it. Ultimately, "the environmental crisis which everyone is talking and writing about exists approximately to the same extent that there is a general crisis in the type of research, development, and production that improves the quality of life."[118] In this and similar analyses, the recognition of ecological constraints spurred a new cycle of techno-utopianism, rather than a reassessment of the commitment to economic expansion and increasing production that undergirded commercial design practice in the postwar era.[119]

In addition, as in the advertising industry, impulses in the design field that emphasized autonomy, intuition, authenticity, or ecological harmony were undercut by countervailing technological and structural forces. One early proponent of computerization, for example, wrote in *Industrial Design* that while current practitioners tended to be "reasonably adept at solving object problems," as was evident in the "overabundance of reasonably functional and attractive chairs, automobiles, packages, [and] appliances," in too many cases, "there is failure at the systems level where design must be considered as an integral function within the marketing/merchandising/management system." Data processing made it possible to draw "in depth on mathematics, the social sciences and operations research" to enable the designer to "create a scientific base for the design/marketing process that parallels established procedures in natural sciences and military and space programs." In response to those who saw computerization as "a threat to the creative designer," the author maintained that computing "should be viewed as a tool that becomes powerful in the hands of the designer." Nonetheless, the move toward systems and operational analysis only accentuated the ongoing trend toward the designer's labor becoming hidden within the cultural apparatus.[120] Furthermore, some types of industrial design jobs actually were vanishing by the 1970s. As manufacturers began to move production out of the country and imports of many goods—particularly consumer electronics but also some larger durables like automobiles—surged, design-related employment grew in Japan and other countries at the expense of jobs in the United States.[121]

As the age of abundance reached its end, Don Wallance reflected on his long career to offer a succinct assessment of design work within consumer capitalism that captured its fundamental dilemmas and constraints. Responding to a questionnaire from the Industrial Design Society of America in the late 1970s, Wallance remarked that "where large investments, the jobs of thousands and the figure on the bottom line are all at stake, sales considerations necessarily take precedence over all others, and are often in conflict with the designer's inner convictions and esthetic standards." He had been an exception, he pointed out, as one of "a few designers" who had "attempted to resolve this problem for themselves by limiting their work to those few areas (and clients) where quality work to reasonably high esthetic standards is accepted." He was fortunate to have made for himself "a way of life and work which enables me, on a modest scale, to do work I enjoy doing, that I am not ashamed of, and which contributes to the quality of life and the pleasure of others."[122] The ideal of creative autonomy endured for the minority of designers like Wallance who could subsist as selective freelancers, or establish an agency dedicated to modernist integrity as Nelson did, or find remunerative and fulfilling employment in such an agency. Yet the ideal remained out of reach for most designers, as it did for most of their counterparts employed throughout the culture industries.

8

The Cultural Deindustrialization
of New York

IN 1960, *LIFE* magazine ostentatiously dedicated itself to the rediscovery of "our national purpose" with a series of essays by major American political, intellectual, and cultural figures, including two-time Democratic presidential candidate Adlai Stevenson; columnist Walter Lippmann; poet, playwright, and former Time Inc. editor Archibald MacLeish; evangelist Billy Graham; and historian Clinton Rossiter. In his introduction to the forum, *Life's* chief editorial writer John Jessup asserted that while "the U.S. has hitherto been a country associated with great purpose," many worried that the nation had strayed from the mission of spreading liberty and democracy that publisher Henry Luce had set forth in 1941 in his *Life* editorial on "The American Century." "Is there not a connection," Jessup warned, "between the rise of nations and great purposes," or "between the loss of purpose and their decline?"[1] Upon completing his editorial on the need for a vigorous public debate regarding the country's values and objectives, readers would have scanned the last photo in the essay, a shot of the United Nations headquarters in New York gleaming at twilight, along with an accompanying caption touting Franklin Delano Roosevelt's role in the creation of the UN, before turning the page to see a full-page, four-color advertisement for Frigidaire air conditioners.[2] Such were the circumstances under which millions of *Life* readers contemplated Americans' national purpose.

During the coming decade, the social fabric of the United States was rent by conflicts that made Jessup's handwringing seem overwrought and insignificant. As any kind of consensus that Americans might have had regarding their national purpose fractured, the prospects for any periodical with such a unifying preoccupation became increasingly tenuous. After Luce's death in

1967, Time Inc. executives and their managing editors at *Life* tried to steer a middle course for the magazine. Editorials endorsed Richard Nixon for the presidency in 1968 over his rivals Hubert Humphrey and George Wallace, and again in 1972 over George McGovern. Yet in 1969 *Life* acknowledged mounting public discontent with the war in Southeast Asia when it ran horrifying photographs documenting the massacre of Vietnamese civilians by American soldiers the previous year at My Lai. In its attempts at representing and somehow reconciling Americans' disparate views of the world, *Life* sought not only to remain faithful to Luce's political legacy by promoting an amalgam of Eisenhower's Modern Republicanism and Kennedy's New Frontier, but also to hold together a cohesive mass readership for the benefit of the advertisers who provided most of the magazine's revenues.[3]

Since its earliest years, *Life* had been one of the nation's most lucrative media ventures. During the late 1940s, it generated more gross advertising revenue than any single commercial media outlet. By 1954 the television network operations of CBS and NBC had greater annual gross advertising revenues than *Life*, but it still far surpassed any other periodical. Although its share of total magazine advertising had declined, *Life* still earned more from advertising than any other magazine, with its gross advertising revenue peaking at $170 million in 1966.[4] Over the course of the 1960s, it triumphed in its long circulation war against its principal rivals for the middle-income, general-interest readership, Curtis Publishing's venerable *Saturday Evening Post* and Cowles Communications' *Look*. When the *Post* trimmed its circulation in 1968 as part of a series of retrenchments that failed to stave off the magazine's demise in February 1969, *Life* purchased a portion of its subscriber list to attain its maximum guaranteed weekly circulation of 8.5 million copies. The only national periodicals with higher circulation during the late 1960s were the down-market *Readers' Digest* and *TV Guide*, neither of which could offer a readership as affluent as *Life*, or the page formats that leading advertisers sought.[5]

Even as its circulation reached new heights, *Life* confronted economic pressures that threatened its viability. A substantial portion of the circulation of *Life*, *Look*, and the *Saturday Evening Post* had been accumulated through years of deep promotional discounts to subscribers. As circulation furnished a diminishing share of total earnings, all three titles became ever more dependent on advertising to sustain revenues and profits. After *Life* hit its maximum circulation in 1968, it raised its price for a full-page, four-color advertisement to $64,000, more than it cost to buy a full-minute commercial on primetime network television. Many advertisers balked, leading to a 13 percent decline in the total number of advertising pages carried in *Life* during 1969 and the magazine's first operating deficit since the late 1930s. Time Inc. management also faced escalating costs, coming not just from salaries and benefits, but also from soaring outlays for paper, inks, printing, and postage. In an attempt to restore profitability, it cut *Life*'s circulation guarantee to 7 million copies in October 1970, and again to 5.5 million in November 1971 as it shed marginal subscribers. While this brought significant reductions in advertising rates, first to $54,000 for a full-page, four-color advertisement in late 1970 and then to $43,000 a year later, advertisers remained dissatisfied since these prices masked actual increases in the cost-per-thousand impressions (CPM).[6]

For the editors, writers, photographers, artists, researchers, and other creative professionals at Time Inc., as well as the sizeable support staff, the first signs of the media giant's belt-tightening were not necessarily alarming. Once lavish expense accounts gradually became less generous. Editors and correspondents for *Fortune*, who had long been accustomed to flying first class, found themselves booked in coach. Sumptuous buffets laid out to sustain staffers on the late nights that they frenetically worked to close the week's issues and transmit them to the printers gradually became more meager until vanishing in the early 1970s. Eventually, more troubling signs became evident. Top creative talent who had long enjoyed salaries and merit raises well above the minimum salary schedule stipulated in the publisher's contract with the Newspaper Guild suddenly found raises harder to get. Rival *Look*, which had also instituted a series of circulation curtailments in an attempt to regain its profitability, folded in October 1971. Most ominously, in the fall of 1970, Time Inc. management initiated the first of several rounds of layoffs and transfers, including one that eliminated roughly 20 percent of all *Life* employees in December 1971. To everyone in the company, and in the media and advertising industries generally, it was increasingly evident that the iconic record of Luce's American Century was dangling by a thread.[7]

Nonetheless, the December 8, 1972 announcement that the company would cease publication of *Life* at the end of the year still stunned employees and industry observers. Within hours of the public announcement, the magazine's offices on the twenty-ninth floor of the Time-Life Building were inundated by reporters from television stations, newspapers, and other magazines looking for a personal angle to the story. The atmosphere was akin to that of a wake, with quite a few of the dismissed employees sharing midday cocktails as they contemplated the magazine's demise. Some reminisced about their lengthy careers with *Life*. Others retreated behind closed doors, with one staff member nearly getting into a fistfight with an overly intrusive television cameraman. *Life* itself contained no notice of the end until the final issue, which opened with editor-in-chief Hedley Donovan lamenting the four straight years of losses that had doomed the magazine while also commemorating its achievements. In its thirty-six years *Life* had, as Donovan claimed, been the "creator of so much of the visual vitality that is all around us." It was more or less accurate that "magazines all over the world are different because of *Life*," as was "the pictorial makeup of the newspapers, the look of advertising," and "even some of the technique of TV."[8]

The elimination of the remaining 325 positions at *Life* contradicted many of the assumptions about postwar American abundance that the magazine had been devoted to propagating. To be sure, even in their unemployment the former staffers experienced nothing remotely like the deprivation endured by millions of impoverished Americans unable to partake in the consumer bonanza that had been depicted in *Life's* pages, or the austerity already being inflicted upon blue-collar workers in declining manufacturing sectors by the early 1970s. Thanks to thirty-five years of collective bargaining between the Newspaper Guild and Time Inc., they had generous severance packages. A *Life* veteran with twenty years of service, for example, received a total of seventy-six weeks of regular pay and qualified immediately for a company pension. Yet even the magazine's highly paid creative professionals still suffered significant economic losses. For middle-aged staff in their prime earning years, new jobs were available, but often at much lower salaries. On the day that *Life's* closure was announced, one long-time photographer for the magazine remarked that "a wire-service guy" he knew had told him "to come around and he'd try to fix me up with a job. I thanked him for the thought, but I'm on $40,000 a year. Where," he wondered, "can I get that money again?"[9]

Although he was among the most affluent employees at the apex of New York's culture industries, this photographer's predicament demonstrated that the creative class had not in fact been able to transcend economic necessity. Despite the assertions by Time Inc. alumni John Kenneth Galbraith and Daniel Bell that the well-paid creators of knowledge and culture were at the forefront of a massive shift in societal norms beyond the narrow modes of economic rationality that had characterized the industrial epoch, these workers still experienced insecurity. The ordinary vicissitudes of market competition, together with long-term structural transformations in the mass media and in the American economy more generally, resulted in numerous dislocations throughout the age of abundance that affected white-collar workers of all occupational and income levels. The containment of white-collar progressives during the early Cold War limited the extent to which New York's creative class could influence the course of change within the culture industries. In television, the various talent guilds and technicians' unions survived the blacklisting era, unlike the UOPWA Radio Guild, but a legacy of fragmentation and acquiescence prevented an effective response to the westward relocation of production or to programming trends that constrained creative autonomy. In the city's print media, the Newspaper Guild was unable to cope with the magnitude of the structural crisis confronting many of the city's newspapers and magazines during the 1960s and 1970s.

White-collar workers employed in New York's broadcasting and publishing industries, or those who hoped to find work in these sectors, encountered prospects that were more constrained than those facing their counterparts in advertising and design. While employment in the latter two fields became more geographically dispersed over the postwar period, the metropolitan area continued to be a vital hub of production. Madison Avenue remained the focal point of the American advertising industry. Although it accounted for a gradually declining proportion of the nation's total advertising workforce, net white-collar advertising employment in the New York metropolitan area swelled to more than 37,000 by 1970, even as the pace of job growth slowed considerably in the next decade.[10] The much smaller field of industrial design, which only employed 10,000 designers nationally in 1970 in addition to thousands more in administrative, sales, and other supporting roles, became even more deconcentrated, especially with the significant expansion of manufacturers' in-house design staffs during the 1950s and 1960s.[11] The New York metropolitan area was still home to many consulting design agencies, and it retained its prominence in the subfields of packaging, graphics, and corporate image, with Chicago as its only legitimate rival as a locus of creative activity. In addition, as the manufacturing of consumer durables in the United States declined in the 1970s and 1980s, design jobs in New York were frequently more secure than those scattered around the country. By contrast, in television and the print media, developments in technology, logistics, consumer preferences, and labor relations induced major firms to either shift the production of cultural content away from New York or to terminate operations. The relocation of primetime television production away from the city took thousands of jobs with it, and greatly reduced television employment opportunities in New York for decades to come. Printing and publishing still accounted for 105,000 white-collar positions in the metropolitan area in 1970, but the closing of numerous newspapers and magazines eliminated thousands of jobs.[12] Lean times at many other publishers further curtailed employment opportunities in the largest of the city's culture industries, resulting in anemic salary growth and heightened insecurity for most of its workforce, even as total employment increased at a slower rate than previously. In a larger sense, the deindustrialization of New York broadcasting and publishing pointed to the city's fading hegemony over America's culture of consumer capitalism.

Furthermore, the advent of cultural deindustrialization in New York's publishing and broadcasting sectors coincided with the resurgence of activism by women and minorities to fight against employment discrimination. Women comprised a majority of the white-collar workers employed in printing and publishing in the metropolitan area in 1970, but more than two-thirds of them were relegated to clerical positions. Within publishing's clerical ranks, the median salary for women was 71 percent of that for men. For those women who managed to overcome the tremendous obstacles to their career advancement and enter professional roles in publishing, the median salary was only 61 percent of that of their male colleagues. In broadcasting the situation was comparable, as the median salary for female professionals in that sector was just 65 percent of that of men.[13] While white women in New York's culture industries during the postwar era endured gross pay inequities and other forms of sex-based discrimination and harassment, minorities—both women and men—found themselves largely excluded from the creative class except for the circumscribed sphere of minority-owned and—oriented media. Much as the advertising and media portrayal of women in domestic or otherwise submissive roles mirrored the marginalization of women employed in cultural production, the near absence of nonwhite faces paralleled the very low rates of minority employment in advertising, publishing, and broadcasting. A 1968 survey of 388 newspapers, magazines, and radio and television stations throughout the United States found that African Americans accounted for 4.2 percent of all employees in the editorial and commercial departments. New York publications that responded to the questionnaire largely conformed to the national pattern; Cowles Communications, which included *Look*, reported 18 African Americans out of 352 white-collar employees, for example, while McGraw-Hill's *Business Week* reported only four out of 200.[14] Just as women and minorities finally began to make progress toward equal employment opportunities in the media, however, overall job prospects deteriorated markedly. Ultimately, they found themselves both empowered and constrained by the intersectionality of gender, race, and class as they struggled to combat discrimination in media workplaces and to reform representations of women and minorities within America's culture of consumer capitalism.

Television's Geographical Division of Labor

A confluence of factors drove television production away from New York during the 1950s and 1960s, but perhaps the most critical of these was the networks' growing power over the procurement and scheduling of programming. To a greater extent than any of the other culture industries, postwar television was an oligopoly. Following the demise of the DuMont network in 1955, three nationwide networks—NBC, CBS, and ABC—dominated and structured American broadcasting.[15] The extremely high initial costs of starting a new network from scratch and the federal government's regulatory framework established barriers to entry that were practically insurmountable. Even though a substantial portion of television programming was produced by independent entities, the networks' program procurement decisions effectively determined their activities.[16] Opportunities to produce original programming for syndicated distribution to unaffiliated local stations declined by the late 1950s as station owners came to prefer the lower-cost options of old Hollywood films or reruns of former network shows. As a result, creative professionals in television faced unique restrictions on their autonomy. In advertising, design, and publishing, gifted and fortunate professionals could sometimes establish or find employment at small- and medium-scale enterprises that privileged certain creative practices or served specific market segments. Programming for network television, however, had to be oriented toward a massive general audience. Noncommercial alternatives remained largely limited to programming produced by local educational broadcasters, or the various initiatives backed by the Ford Foundation and its subsidiaries, including the network program *Omnibus*, which aired during the 1950s, and the more substantial efforts of National Educational Television, which furnished the kernel for the Public Broadcasting Service that commenced operations in 1969.[17]

As television entered into a period of rapid expansion during the 1950s, network executives gradually came to prefer filmed programming over the live performance of primetime broadcast content. The limitations of early cameras and transmission equipment, the slow spread of the coaxial cable that physically connected the stations into a network, and proximity to the advertising agencies that produced or owned many programs all guaranteed New York's primacy in live programming origination during television's first years. Within a few years, technological advances made the use of filmed programming more appealing. Film, of course, could be edited, allowing not only multiple takes and the elimination of mishaps, but also the use of more and larger sets and the option of shooting on location. Filmed programming also had the advantage of being repeatable without an actual encore performance.

To exploit the full potential of "telefilms" required more expansive studio space than was readily available for producers in New York, which led the industry to adopt a geographical division of labor that had a tremendous impact on the employment prospects of not just writers, directors, actors, and other performers in the city, but also a wide array of technical, administrative, and support personnel. In a shift that mirrored the migration of early motion-picture production to Hollywood, the leading networks began to construct large new studio facilities in southern California. CBS broke ground on its Television City production complex in Los Angeles in 1950, while NBC followed suit shortly thereafter in nearby Burbank.[18] When the initial phase of Television City became operational in 1952, CBS explained to industry observers that while "miracles" had occurred in the improvisational first years of live television originating from New York, it was now necessary for programs to "come off more easily, speedily, economically, so we built a factory for them to happen in," where "program product could flow on an assembly line, from idea to show-time."[19] Existing Hollywood studios also quickly emerged as important sources of filmed content for television. As box-office receipts plunged, the studios responded by producing fewer feature-length films for theatrical release, which in turn left them with underutilized sound stages and back lots, and threatened much of the filmmaking work-force with underemployment or outright unemployment. Entering into the production of filmed television programming, either by leasing facilities to independent producers or by launching their own television subsidiaries, as Columbia did with its highly successful Screen Gems division, offered a path to continued viability. In some cases, television production companies simply acquired faltering Hollywood studios lock, stock, and barrel, as Desilu did when it bought RKO. As early as 1954, West Coast producers churned out roughly 900 hours of telefilm. Moreover, Class A members of the Screen Actors Guild earning less than $7,500 a year were paid nearly as much that year from their television work as from movies for theatrical release.[20]

As West Coast television production began its boom, the functional inadequacy of New York facilities was brought into starker relief. From the inception of network operations, live performances were frequently staged under makeshift conditions, with vacant Broadway theaters pressed into service for many television shows.[21] In its quest for space, NBC acquired and redeveloped a portion of the disused Vitagraph movie studio in the Midwood section of Brooklyn to produce a range of programming, including many of the elaborate color "spectaculars" that president Sylvester "Pat" Weaver hoped would enable the network to best CBS and sell new color sets manufactured by its corporate parent RCA. Despite its remoteness from network headquarters in midtown Manhattan, the lack of adequate parking, and other limitations, NBC spent several million dollars upgrading the facility and constructing a second color studio at the site in 1956, which remained the network's largest for many years. The westward drift of television production left the Brooklyn facility underutilized, and by the 1959–1960 season, NBC used it mainly for the production of daytime soap operas and the occasional primetime special.[22] Independent producers of filmed content in New York faced similar impediments. Filmways, for example, opened a modest studio on West 54th Street in Manhattan in early 1954 in the hopes of utilizing it to produce primetime programming, but found that it was instead booked primarily by advertising agencies to shoot filmed commercials. By 1959, Filmways converted a former garage in East Harlem into a pair of sound stages, but the facility's shortcomings dampened its appeal for producers of either filmed television programming or feature-length films for theatrical release.[23]

As early as 1952, various firms within New York's television industry began calling for municipal government to take a more active role in promoting production by providing space for the construction of state-of-the-art studio facilities. The Film Producers' Association of New York wanted the city to utilize its powers of eminent domain to assemble a site for a major complex on the West Side of midtown Manhattan. Key officials, including Robert Moses, who served as the local administrator for the federal Title I urban renewal program as well as chairman of the city's Slum Clearance Committee, instead proposed the former grounds of the 1939 World's Fair in Flushing, Queens and similar vacant or underutilized sites in outlying areas. After several years of impasse and inaction, in 1956 City Council president Abe Stark advocated for a revised proposal for a twenty-two acre "Television City" on the West Side to be constructed through Title I. "The same unsolved dilemmas," he declared, "which caused the motion picture industry to be lost to our city thirty years ago now threaten New York's leadership as the television capital of the world. The broadcasting industry, which spends $300,000,000 a year in the City of New York and provides employment opportunities for tens of thousands of people" deserved assistance "through the cooperative efforts of government and private enterprise." Moses, however, prioritized the use of Title I funds for the Lincoln Center performing arts and educational complex, effectively tabling Stark's plan.[24]

The massive commercial success of network television, and the torrents of advertising dollars flowing into the industry, only exacerbated the crisis of New York-based production during the second half of the 1950s. By 1958, television accounted for 37 percent of all expenditures by advertisers of nationally available branded goods, with primetime network programming absorbing the bulk of sponsors' dollars. The massive audiences that the three networks could deliver were simply irresistible. Fully 86 percent of American homes had at least one television set by 1959, and average daily viewing time within these homes exceeded five hours.[25] The steep increases in the value of primetime by the second half of the 1950s gave the networks enormous leverage that they had previously lacked when dealing with sponsors and advertising agencies. For the first time the networks asserted full control over the procurement and scheduling of programming for nationwide broadcast, dispossessing their remaining time-franchised legacy sponsors. Furthermore, they increased the price of airtime to levels that induced most advertisers to opt for short, usually sixty-second, commercial spots instead of ongoing sponsorship during the late 1950s and early 1960s.

The new patterns of sponsorship and program procurement proved especially disadvantageous for the mix of programs that originated from New York.[26] The city was closely associated with the live performance of original dramatic teleplays as part of prestigious anthologies, along with live comedy and variety programs like *Texaco Star Theater*, hosted by Milton Berle, and *Your Show of Shows*, hosted by Sid Caesar and Imogene Coca. Sponsorship of live anthology drama had functioned essentially as a form of institutional advertising for major corporations, such as the *United States Steel Hour*, *Celanese Theater*, *Armstrong Circle Theater*, *Westinghouse Studio One*, and *General Electric Theater*. By 1957, the networks were replacing many of these anthologies in their primetime schedules with filmed adventure-action or situation comedy series produced on the West Coast. Even some of the live dramatic anthologies that remained on the air, like *Playhouse 90*, originated from the West Coast to take advantage of the networks' continuing studio investments there. Early live comedy and variety programs that were rooted in urban experiences and ethnic traditions had made their debut when the network was limited to the major cities on the East Coast and had a diminishing appeal as the networks came to encompass a national viewership. Even quiz shows, the one New York-produced genre that did become more prevalent in network schedules during the mid-1950s, rapidly declined in popularity following the scandals that embroiled *Twenty-One* and several other programs. By the fall of 1957, more than 70 percent of the programming in the networks' primetime schedules originated on the West Coast.[27]

In 1958, leading creative talent still based in New York attempted to reverse the trend by organizing the Television Action Committee (TAC), which included among its more prominent backers producers David Susskind and Herbert Brodkin; writers Paddy Chayefsky and Reginald Rose; directors Sidney Lumet and Elia Kazan; and newsman Fred Friendly. Susskind emerged as the group's most prominent spokesman. In a letter to Chayefsky that June, in which he attempted to enlist him to write a script for the New York-based *Du Pont Show of the Month*, Susskind asserted that he was "deeply concerned about the miserable state of television today." It represented the "absolute nadir of creativity, imagination, challenge and responsibility to an important entertainment medium."[28] Shortly after his letter to Chayefsky, the TAC issued its manifesto, which Susskind largely shaped. "The continuing loss to tv of quality programs, traditionally presented from New York, constitutes a serious threat to the efficacy and prestige of the country's most important medium of communication and entertainment." The westward migration, the TAC continued, had resulted in "a breach of responsibility on the part of the tv industry and its leaders to the millions in the viewing audience who are hungry for quality," as well as the "millions more whose appetite for this kind of program might be whetted." The broadcasters instead provided "small, trite entertainments," which the committee attributed to the industry's affliction by "mass productionitis" and the "western flu." By explicitly linking issues of genre, form, subject matter, aesthetics, and poetics with the political economy of television and its material conditions of production, the committee furnished the potential basis for a critical theory of cultural deindustrialization. To remediate the cultural shortcomings of late-1950s television, they advocated a material solution: calling upon New York's incumbent governor, Averell Harriman, a Democrat seeking reelection, to circumvent Robert Moses and provide direct state subsidies for the construction of a television production complex on Manhattan's West Side.[29]

The TAC activists' lamentations about television's emphasis on "quizzes, lackluster films, Westerns and giveaways" only bore a superficial resemblance to the condemnations of mass culture by Theodor Adorno, Dwight Macdonald, and other like-minded critics. Unlike these intellectuals, the members of the TAC believed in the practical possibilities for improving programming within a commercial framework. They contended that a more sophisticated mix of original and repertory drama, performing arts, edgy sketch and stand-up comedy, straight news, panel discussions, and documentaries could find a profitable viewership within America's culture of consumer capitalism. Furthermore, they would have taken exception to Macdonald's snide assertions that "there is nothing more vulgar than sophisticated kitsch," and that efforts at improving mass culture only rendered a "tepid, flaccid Middlebrow Culture that threatens to engulf everything in its spreading ooze," which denigrated the cultural aspirations of the performers, writers, directors, and producers who formed the TAC, as well as the millions of Americans who had been enthusiastic viewers of their work.[30] For the committee's backers, the westward migration of production was not just an economic crisis for those who counted on New York-based television for their livelihoods, but also a crisis for an artistic movement that had flourished with early television's experimentation. Yet while the TAC served to formulate and amplify a particular critique of the television industry that would be influential in the years to come, it did little in the short term to arrest the decline of production within the city. Susskind and other key figures in the group had hoped to make cultural deindustrialization into a significant issue in the gubernatorial contest, but Nelson Rockefeller's victory, combined with growing concerns over the coercion and corruption inherent in the implementation of the Title I program in New York, doomed any proposal for using public resources to build a major new television complex in Manhattan. By 1960, the dearth of work in the city, except for the thriving business in commercials, had grown so dire that both AFTRA and IATSE were offering substantial wage and salary concessions to any employer willing to film a television series in New York.[31]

Despite its mandate to oversee the broadcast industry and ensure that licensees served the public interest, the FCC had a fairly muted response to the changes in television programming during the second half of the 1950s. With the Democrats' return to the White House, the agency adopted a more activist regulatory posture that drew significantly upon the analysis advanced by the TAC. President Kennedy's new FCC chairman, Newton Minow, shocked industry observers in May 1961 with his scathing address to the National Association of Broadcasters, in which he declared that the programming then available on television constituted "a vast wasteland." Although he maintained that "when television is good, nothing—not the theatre, not the magazines or newspapers" could surpass it, "when television is bad, nothing is worse." Broadcasters, Minow continued, furnished a scheduled tedium in which the viewer would "see a procession of game shows, violence, audience participation shows, formula comedies about totally unbelievable families, blood and thunder, mayhem" along with "Western badmen,

Western goodmen, private eyes, gangsters, more violence, and cartoons. And, endlessly, commercials—many screaming, cajoling, and offending." Minow recognized that while he could utilize his position as chairman of the FCC as a bully pulpit to encourage the networks to elevate the quality of the programming, his real leverage was in the licensing of broadcast stations. "The people own the air. They own it as much in prime evening time as they do 6 o'clock Sunday morning. For every hour that the people give you—you owe them something." While he acknowledged that "in the past licenses were often renewed pro forma," Minow warned that there was "nothing permanent or sacred about a broadcast license."[32]

Minow initiated investigative hearings conducted by the FCC Office of Network Study that were designed to focus critical attention on the broadcasting industry. During the summer of 1961, members of the Office of Network Study convened in New York City, taking testimony from many of the prominent figures involved with the TAC, including Susskind, Brodkin, Chayefsky, and Friendly, along with other luminaries of television's "golden age," such as leading anthology drama producers Fred Coe and Worthington Miner, and *Omnibus* producer Robert Saudek. The hearings also featured several writers who were at the forefront of broadcasting unionism, notably Erik Barnouw, a member of Writers Guild of America (WGA) East's executive board and former RWG president; Ernest Kinoy, who had led the RWG fight against blacklisting; and WGA national chairman David Davidson.[33] For the pro-union writers, it was their first substantive opportunity to contribute meaningfully to the formulation of FCC policy since the late 1940s, and a refreshing chance to be cooperative witnesses at public hearings on media and entertainment.

Most of the writers, directors, and producers who shared their views on the state of television focused on their loss of creative autonomy, which they identified as a primary cause of the dismal quality of television and the lack of program variety. Susskind testified, with more than a touch of nostalgia, that in the early 1950s the new medium had been "a wonderful artistic matter. It was daring, it was exciting, it was innovating, it was experimental, and you had license, you had freedom to function and do your best thinking and do your best work." By the second half of the decade, as "costs became astronomical," the "whole structure of television and the temper of television underwent a complete metamorphosis." He quipped that "if it weren't for the fact that I have seen next year's schedule, I would say that this year marked the nadir of television in terms of balance and diversification." With the exception of "some quite wonderful public affairs programs" which constituted, "at most,

10 percent of the total programming," television was "a travesty." A "large minority" of viewers, Coe contended, was not getting its "fair shake on television today," since nearly all entertainment was oriented toward "a fantastically
large majority" to the exclusion of other market segments. Brodkin echoed
Coe and Susskind's complaints about the loss of creative autonomy and their
dismay at the disappearance of serious drama from television, but was more
hopeful about the near-term prospects for getting more quality programming
on television. The "many small men in television who are afraid" to air "hard-
hitting" or "downbeat" drama were having their inhibitions eroded by the
acclaim earned by some of the public affairs programming from the networks'
news and documentary divisions as well as their new wariness of the FCC.[34]

The writers who testified before the Office of Network Study furnished, if
anything, an even bleaker portrayal of the creative environment within television than the producers and directors had. Many of them had been among the
most renowned writers for the premier live drama anthologies of the 1950s.
The cancelation of these programs by the networks had diminished their
professional status and drastically reduced their artistic freedom. Instead of
developing unique characters and plots, and addressing subject matter that
they found suitably intriguing, most of their employment opportunities involved writing for filmed action-adventure series with continuing characters,
formulaic plots, and vapid subject matter. "Nobody is asking that quality
drama be forced on people who don't want it," Davidson contended, "only
that some proportion of airtime be turned back to that great quality audience
of 20 millions who are also owners of the air waves whose use is given free to
the broadcasting industry." Kinoy detailed how writing for action-adventure
series during the early 1960s entailed submitting to a "handcuffs formula."
Producers of series that network executives had deemed likely to attract the
largest possible audience sent established writers a précis that described the
overall theme, the main characters, and key details about the setting. In many
cases, producers invited prospective writers to a screening of the pilot episode.
For writers in these circumstances, there was "no point in bringing an original
idea" to the producers "which does not meet their type-pattern because they
have no need for it." Kinoy readily conceded that he was fortunate to have
already established his reputation, so he could turn down work that he found
unacceptable. Writers entering the field, however, had limited options to earn
a living in television; they had to be "journeymen and workmen" who had
"to do the job for this employer they work for" since they had "no alternative." He concluded that there was "virtually no opportunity for writers in the
television medium who have not already attained some reputation to attain

it," since "you cannot build a reputation either in the trade or in the public eye as a writer of episodes of a crime show or a western when your product is indistinguishable from the week before and the week after."[35] Significantly, the producers, directors, and writers who tended to idealize early television overlooked the rampant blacklisting within the industry and its far-reaching ramifications. Their rhetorical strategy to pressure the networks to reform their programming practices suppressed the history of how the crusade against domestic subversion had badly weakened the unions in the industry, and compromised their ability to exert a more constructive influence on the production process.

In addition to shining a spotlight on the networks, Minow intervened in the sale of a station in the New York metropolitan area to demonstrate to owners that his comments to the NAB regarding license renewals and transfers were not an idle threat. Channel 13 was licensed to National Telefilm Associates (NTA), which had planned to use it as the hub for a pseudo-network of stations that would broadcast a slate of syndicated original filmed programs, but a lack of investor interest stymied the scheme. Although it featured *The Play of the Week*, which was produced by Susskind's company, Talent Associates, and was one of the only dramatic anthologies still originating from New York, most of Channel 13's schedule consisted of old Hollywood movies and syndicated reruns of former network shows. In early 1961, NTA put the struggling station up for sale. Several prospective buyers made offers in the $6 to $7 million range, including a group headed by Susskind that wanted to use the station as a platform for filmed programs produced in New York, while a noncommercial consortium, Educational Television for the Metropolitan Area, Inc. made a much lower bid of $4.2 million.[36] New York still had no broadcast outlet for National Educational Television, hobbling the organization's ability to establish itself as a viable purveyor of noncommercial programming.

Minow made it publicly known that any commercial buyers would face lengthy hearings on the license transfer, thereby applying unprecedented pressure on NTA to sell to the educational group. To compensate NTA and to buy goodwill from the FCC, all of the other television broadcasters in the New York market chipped in to cover the difference between the educators' offer and the commercial ones, with most stations in the region contributing $250,000 to the purchase. When completed, the deal represented one of the few instances in which the FCC used its authority to arrange for the transfer of a lucrative commercial portion of the broadcast spectrum to a noncommercial entity; given New York's importance, few actions by the federal government in the postwar period provided as much tangible public support for noncommercial television production. Friction with AFTRA over contract terms delayed the station's opening by several months in 1962, but in the long run the acquisition of Channel 13 by the educational group opened up additional television employment in the city, both for above-the-line performers, writers, directors, and other creative personnel, and for below-the-line technicians and craft workers.[37]

Minow's actions also encouraged the networks to consider New York-based options for dramatic series when procuring programs for their primetime schedules. CBS had responded to some of Minow's initial criticisms by purchasing a twenty-six-episode season of *The Defenders*, a show developed by several figures from the TAC. Created by Reginald Rose, the hour-long legal drama about a father-son team of criminal defense attorneys was produced by Herbert Brodkin's company, Plautus Productions, and shot at the Filmways studio in East Harlem. The following season, CBS added a second New York-produced filmed dramatic series from Plautus, *The Nurses*, one of the few primetime network programs in the postwar era based around women's workplace experiences.[38] Both of these series introduced an element of New Frontier liberalism into the CBS schedule, as episodes confronted a range of social issues including racial discrimination, religious prejudice, civil liberties, mental illness, domestic violence, drug and alcohol abuse, and urban street crime. Writers who had backed the TAC or testified before the FCC proved essential to realizing this vision for a new kind of socially conscious television drama. Kinoy, for instance, wrote numerous episodes for *The Defenders*, including "The Man with the Concrete Thumb," which pilloried an imperious urban renewal czar obviously modeled on Robert Moses, and "Blacklist," the first television program to dramatize the practice, which earned Kinoy his first Emmy award.[39]

Perhaps no series more boldly expressed the aspirations of the TAC than *East Side/West Side*, which CBS purchased from Susskind's Talent Associates for its 1963–1964 primetime schedule. Susskind and his creative collaborators began developing the idea of a dramatic series with a social worker protagonist in 1962. In an early character sketch, writer Robert Alan Aurthur described him as a figure with a heroic capacity to cure social ills, not just those caused by "poverty," but those stemming from "society as a totally encompassing giant machine, a 'system' which seems to be so big that an ordinary human being is powerless." The social worker was "dedicated to helping, dedicated to the idea that there *is* change, there *is* promise, there *is* hope," and responsible, moreover, for proving that hope was "valid and feasible." Susskind, in his pitch to CBS executives, portrayed the "young, well educated, sensitive, and dynamic" lead as working in a field that "has changed from one in which it was just giving relief and assistance to the poor and needy to one in which qualified, trained and educated professionals help *everyone* in every economic class with the problems that are foisted upon them by this society of ours." He assured them that "the social service worker in New York City can go anywhere, do anything and administer to every imaginable human problem. I think we have one helluva show in the making!"[40] Network executives were intrigued enough to approve the expenditure of $175,000 on a pilot episode, filmed in New York in January 1963 with George C. Scott cast as social worker Neil Brock, and eventually to commit to twenty-six hour-long episodes, with an option for six more to extend the first season if CBS wished to renew the series.[41]

East Side/West Side echoed many of the themes and concerns evident in the Popular Front culture of the 1930s and 1940s. In promoting the show to potential writers, Talent Associates' production supervisors presented a clear directive: "Very simply, we want social problems. And because we intend to stress *themes* before *plots*, we insist that the social problem be made explicit and urgent." The social issues were to furnish "the superstructure upon which a moving drama can be evolved. The problems of life in the 1960s are very real; we want the writer to make them *live*, to provide that shock of recognition that that will make them compelling" without "either preaching or slopping around in creeping maudlinism." They did not expect that "the social problem of our time will be solved on each week's program. Because of that, this will not be a 'happy-ending' series."[42] Beyond its commitment to the idea of drama as a catalyst for progressive social change, *East Side/West Side* also had direct personal links to the Popular Front presence in broadcasting, with two previously blacklisted writers, Arnold Perl and Millard Lampell, contributing to the series. Perl first joined *East Side/West Side* as a script editor, but he was soon elevated to interim executive producer in August 1963 as the staff struggled to prepare scripts for filming. His episode "Who Do You Kill?" offered a searing examination of racial discrimination in employment and slum housing conditions, winning him an award from the WGA. Lampell wrote perhaps the second-most acclaimed episode, "No Hiding Place," which exposed the hypocrisy of northern, middle-class whites when confronted with the racial integration of their neighborhood and the possibility of blockbusting by unscrupulous realtors. Additionally, both Perl and Lampell rewrote or revised numerous other scripts used for the program, sometimes without credit, so their overall influence on the series was pervasive.[43]

If *East Side/West Side* showed the promise of New York-based "quality" dramatic series on commercial television, it also demonstrated the continuing impediments to television production in the city. While working on location in East Harlem for the pilot episode, the crew antagonized several community groups that objected to having their neighborhood used as a backdrop for fictional reproductions of urban crime and disorder. The president of the East Harlem Merchants Association complained directly to Susskind about the filming of scenes involving "a window being broken, a man stabbed and apparently killed and a young man being apprehended and being taken into custody by the police." This disruption, he continued, had "created much apprehension and resentment in a community which is so sensitive to bad publicity by the press and TV networks."[44] The regular production of the series only brought additional logistical and financial difficulties. Since Filmways and the few other studios were already booked, interior filming for *East Side/West Side* took place at another remnant of the city's silent movie past, the old Biograph studio near Crotona Park in the Bronx. Biograph's dilapidated condition and its location far from midtown in a rapidly deteriorating neighborhood were a constant source of irritation for Susskind and his production staff.[45]

Ultimately, the fate of *East Side/West Side* was determined not by these production hassles, but by the responses of advertisers and viewers. The advertising sales department at CBS succeeded in signing up Philip Morris and American Home Products as major sponsors by May 1963, but it could not secure additional long-term commitments prior to the series' debut in September. During the first few episodes a substantial portion of the available commercial airtime, cumulatively worth hundreds of thousands of dollars, went unsold. Making matters worse, *East Side/West Side* struggled in its crucial first weeks against lackluster competition on NBC and ABC in its Monday 10:00 p.m. time slot, failing to draw consistently the minimum Nielsen share of 30 sought by network executives. Susskind used his influence to help boost the show, arranging an advance screening of Perl's "Who Do You Kill?" episode for Senator Jacob Javits and then prodding him to plug the broadcast from the floor of the chamber.[46] Such efforts increased ratings overall, but they only added to the series' difficulties in obtaining clearance from CBS affiliates in the South. Some southern stations refused to air a program that featured an African American woman, Cicely Tyson, as a principal character in a racially integrated, professional workplace environment, and that repeatedly condemned racial discrimination throughout society. American Home Products dropped its sponsorship after 13 weeks, but numerous other advertisers stepped in to make smaller ad buys, enabling the show to be 90 percent sold by January 1964. Nonetheless, CBS announced it would not renew *East Side/West Side* for a second season. The final episode, "Here Today," which depicted a campaign to keep a liberal newspaper from being put out of business, furnished an obvious allegory for the series' demise.[47]

The cancellation of *East Side/West Side* marked the beginning of the end of the brief revival in New York television production spurred by the TAC and the FCC. In March, a dispute between Brodkin's Plautus Productions and United Scenic Artists led the company to temporarily relocate the filming of *The Defenders* and *The Doctors and the Nurses* to the West Coast. Brodkin had been a vocal backer of the TAC, but by the mid-1960s even he had become frustrated with the drawbacks of television production in New York, and his maneuver was clearly intended as a threat to all of the various craft and technical unions. Plautus resumed regular production of both series in New York, but a year later CBS dropped them from its primetime schedule. By September 1965, out of the 96 entertainment programs that comprised the three networks' primetime schedules, only ten originated in New York, most of them music, variety, or game shows.[48] This decline in production had a substantial economic impact. Each regular episode of *East Side/West Side*, for example, had a budget of approximately $135,000, with roughly $55,000 going toward above-the-line costs for the production supervisors, writers, directors, actors, and final production tasks, and the remaining $80,000 or so for below-the-line items including studio rental, equipment, materials, and the technicians and craft workers involved in staging, filming, and film processing. While a generous slice of the above-the-line costs went to the star, with Scott receiving $10,000 per episode, most of it went to a wider circle of creative talent in New York. The sum total for all other actors was roughly equal to Scott's take. The original script writers, nearly all based in the New York region, usually received around $4,000 per episode, while somewhat more money was allotted to those involved in reviewing, editing, and rewriting scripts. Independent television producers in New York tried to hold the line on below-the-line costs, which tended to be higher than on the West Coast. Despite the willingness of some unions to accommodate television producers, many of the unions representing craft and technical workers, including cameramen, scenarists, and electricians, took a hard line in collective bargaining, due to the high cost of living and members' alternative employment opportunities on television commercials or Broadway theater. On the whole, the region lost $3 to $4 million for every season of an hour-long filmed primetime series produced on the West Coast rather than in New York during the 1960s.[49]

Although New York Mayor John Lindsay devoted considerable resources during his two terms to enticing producers of motion pictures for theatrical release to use the city for exterior location shooting, his administration did little to follow through on his campaign pledge to improve the situation for television production. During the late 1960s, only Susskind's Talent Associates was able to develop a filmed dramatic series made in New York and successfully sell it to one of the networks for primetime scheduling. Susskind and Talent Associates' Dan Melnick again collaborated with Perl to develop a new series, *N.Y.P.D.*, that they pitched to ABC as an updated action-drama derived from the police department's files. Although Talent Associates produced a one-hour pilot for the network, ABC executives only committed to a half-hour series in the 1967–1968 schedule, and a minimum order of seventeen episodes. Partly the change reflected executives' concerns about New York production costs, but it also reflected their determination not to repeat the experience of *East Side/West Side*. "While a number of stories will deal with 'adult' themes," the ABC executive vice president for network programming assured the Foote, Cone, and Belding advertising agency in May 1967, "the intent of the series is not to preach or deal in social commentary; rather, the intent is to attract and entertain the viewing audience by offering them exciting police-detective stories."[50] Melnick looked to dispel any preconceptions that *N.Y.P.D.* would be another round of agitprop, instead portraying it as a bit of art-house cinema in primetime television. "Audiences are more sophisticated than given credit in terms of what kind of story will interest them and in terms of film technique," he maintained. "They've all seen Antonioni and Fellini and Resnais." Unlike other programs, *N.Y.P.D.* was filmed on 16mm color stock, which permitted the crew to utilize hand-held cameras for the first time in location shooting around the city, giving it some of the visual immediacy of direct cinema. Despite its innovative techniques and Melnick's faith in viewers' tastes, *N.Y.P.D.* struggled to attract a full complement of sponsors or to reach the 30 Nielsen share threshold. Although it was given a reprieve for a second season, ABC dropped the series in March 1969.[51]

The industry's geographic division of labor became even more pronounced during the early 1970s. The need for proximity to the top advertising agencies as well as to providers of specialized financial and administrative services kept the networks' corporate headquarters on the East Coast, which guaranteed that thousands of related professional, technical, sales, and clerical positions remained in the city. The network news divisions also remained anchored in New York, providing roughly 1,500 additional jobs. The production of filmed or videotaped commercial spots for television continued to flourish, furnishing yet another important source of employment. Beyond that, the situation was bleak. Even some of the remaining talk, variety, and game shows either moved to the West Coast, as *The Tonight Show* did, or were canceled. The production of daytime soap operas with their simple sets and modest budgets, which had remained concentrated in New York, also began to drift away, with several prominent daytime series—including *General Hospital, Days of Our Lives*, and *The Young and the Restless*—originating from Los Angeles where costs were lower. By 1972, the leadership of the 7,500-member New York local of AFTRA indicated its resignation concerning the deindustrialization of the city's television sector and the apparent permanence of job loss by launching a Supplemental Training and Employment Program designed to furnish unemployed actors with new skills that might lead to them finding work outside of the performing arts.[52] While television still furnished a solid livelihood for many within the city's creative class, the industry had lost thousands of jobs as New York's share of total production plummeted.

The Structural Crisis of New York's Print Media

Most New Yorkers outside the television industry were unaware of the economic consequences of the draining away of production. Viewers encountered a seemingly constant stream of programming on their sets, even if less and less of it originated inside the city. Much of the economic impact, moreover, registered in jobs that were not created, or in sales of ancillary services by local firms that were not made, rather than in conspicuous mass layoffs or business failures. It was impossible for ordinary residents to ignore the structural crisis of New York's print media during the 1960s and 1970s. Strikes and lockouts hobbled the city's newspaper industry and subjected readers to periodic blackouts of daily print journalism. Between 1963 and 1967, four newspapers—the *Daily Mirror, Herald Tribune, Journal-American*, and *World-Telegram and Sun*—ceased publication, depriving thousands of New Yorkers of their livelihoods. Stagnant advertising revenue, declining circulation, rising costs, and technological changes damaged the newspaper industry, although some of these problems also afflicted the national news and general-interest magazines headquartered in the city. The retrenchment within the print media exposed the limitations of the Newspaper Guild of New York's collective bargaining strategy, which was predicated on the conditions of industrial unionism in a stable or expanding market. Furthermore, the continued direction of the local by a cadre of leaders who had come to power in the late 1940s resulted in a widening generation gap within the union. Not only did some younger members disagree with the leadership's firm insistence on seniority in layoffs and its resistance to automation, but the union establishment's Cold War liberalism also clashed with many younger members' opposition to the Vietnam War and their support for the struggles of women and minorities for equality and empowerment.

During the postwar years, print media nationally grappled with the effects of competition from television, regional population shifts, and suburbanization on circulation and revenue. Between 1947 and 1958, American newspapers' share of national advertising expenditures declined only slightly from 28 percent to 26 percent, whereas magazines' proportion plummeted from 41 percent to 27 percent. Television posed the greatest threat to the general-interest magazines, since they justified themselves to national advertisers as offering a comparable mass audience, with publications like the *Saturday Evening Post*—in which short fiction comprised a significant portion of the editorial content—feeling the competition most acutely. The growing number of special-interest magazines that could deliver niche markets of consumers selectively to advertisers had less to fear from the new broadcast medium. Among metropolitan daily newspapers, those published in the afternoon tended to be more vulnerable to competition from television than those published in the morning. The migration of millions of Americans to the Sunbelt allowed newspapers in the fastest-growing parts of the South, Southwest, and West Coast to buck national trends and increase circulation, while only adding to the market pressures facing papers in the urban Northeast and Midwest. On the fringes of major cities like New York, Chicago, and Philadelphia, new or expanded suburban newspapers also experienced lucrative growth, typically at the expense of the established metropolitan papers.[53]

Even within specific metropolitan markets, not all publishers of daily newspapers felt the pinch to the same extent. In New York, the *Times* gained circulation during the postwar years and expanded its editorial and commercial departments accordingly, so that the paper's white-collar workforce grew by about 60 percent between the Second World War and the mid-1960s. Others newspapers experienced a troubling decline in their health. The *Herald Tribune* had long been considered the *Times'* principal rival for morning readers interested in serious journalism, but poor management and deteriorating quality hurt the paper's circulation and advertising revenues. When John Whitney acquired control of the *Herald Tribune* in 1958 and began an attempt at revitalizing it through an infusion of younger writers and editors, it was barely treading water. The two Hearst papers in the city, the morning tabloid *Daily Mirror* and the afternoon *Journal-American*, each lost about 15 percent of their readership during the 1950s, leading many observers to wonder how committed the media conglomerate was to remaining in the market.[54]

The squeeze made labor relations in New York's daily newspaper industry increasingly acrimonious by the late 1950s and early 1960s. The alliance between the Newspaper Guild and the eleven unions that represented workers involved in printing and distribution had imposed a consistent collective bargaining pattern in the city, but the publishers' mounting financial woes as well as divisions among the various groups of workers caused it to unravel. Within the biennial routine of negotiations, the Guild contracts came up for renewal first, with the union's agreements with all seven of the major dailies expiring on November 1 of even-numbered years. Strategically the Guild might have preferred to strike one or more of the publishers selectively in order to obtain a more favorable settlement as the basis for the new pattern, but employer unity precluded that course. In every round of bargaining, disagreements over pay, health insurance, and other benefits led Guild members to authorize strike action. Organizers rented storefronts near each of the papers to serve as strike headquarters, designated picket captains, and on several occasions made plans for the publication of the Guild's own newspaper to guarantee that the public still had access to news and information in the event of a city-wide lockout. Nonetheless, until 1962 the Guild always reached a last-minute deal.[55] The other unions, whose contracts with the publishers expired on December 8, found it difficult to obtain more for their members than what the white-collar workers had settled for a few weeks earlier, so the Guild's contract effectively set the terms for all of the industry's unionized employees.

Many newspaper workers grew dissatisfied with the Guild leadership's willingness to accept modest improvements in pay and benefits. Some of the craft workers whose skills were critical to the printing process, such as typographers and photoengravers, became convinced that they could win a better deal for themselves through their own strike action. By the early 1960s, these militants were pressing their leaders to hold out for more than the Guild settlement. Discontent existed within the Guild's ranks as well. While the 1958 contract with the *Times*, for instance, included the addition of a Major Medical plan to augment the existing Blue Cross/Blue Shield coverage as well as an average weekly raise of $7.00 over two years, more than 125 Guild members at the paper signed a petition denouncing the settlement as inadequate.[56] Writers, editors, photographers, illustrators, and other creative professionals with the city's newspapers envied the higher salaries earned by their counterparts at the leading national magazines, the television networks, and the advertising agencies for seemingly comparable work. Clerical employees, who comprised two-thirds of the Guild membership at the major papers, generally earned more than comparable office workers in New York, so they tended to be more supportive of steady incremental gains.

As the publishers attempted to hold the line in the fall of 1962, the Newspaper Guild acted on its biennial strike threats, hitting the profitable *Daily News*. When *News* management arranged to print a highly abbreviated edition of the paper, comprised mostly of wire reports and a few articles written by managing editors, on the presses of the *Journal-American* on November 2, the Guild inveighed upon the manufacturing unions to violate normal protocol and handle the struck copy in order to preclude a lockout elsewhere. With so little content at its disposal, *News* management suspended publication for the duration of the strike. A few days later, a settlement was reached that provided the 1,200 Guild members at the paper with an average raise of $4.25 a week in the first year of the contract and an additional $3.75 a week in the second year. It was quickly matched by other papers in town, and most in the industry assumed that the Guild settlement would again serve as the basis for terms with the other unions when their contracts with the Publishers' Association expired on December 8.[57]

Instead, the Big Six local of the International Typographical Union (ITU) initiated the most disruptive work stoppage in the history of the New York press. Its members were highly skilled linotype operators who had long been able to leverage their essential role in production into some of the best pay and conditions of any of the city's craft workers, but by the early 1960s, technological changes threatened their livelihoods. Newspaper publishers were increasingly eager to take advantage of "teletypesetting," in which punched tape fed instructions into automatic linotype machines that could set hot metal type four times as quickly as a human operator. More ominously, publishers also wanted to introduce new photo-offset printing methods that eliminated hot type completely. Together, the two developments rendered the linotype operators' prized skills obsolete. In response, they mobilized to delay implementation of the new technologies while extracting as much as possible from the publishers in the interim. From December 1960 through September 1961, the local had worked without a contract, only to have the union accept a settlement that many found unacceptable. A majority of the union's members at all seven of New York's dailies rejected the master agreement, which was only ratified due to the strong support from members employed by book printers and job shops. The local's new president, Bertram Powers, promised that in 1962 he would insist upon a pay hike greater than whatever the Newspaper Guild obtained. When Powers's bargaining team failed to reach a new agreement with the Publishers' Association by the contract expiration date, the Big Six struck *Daily News*, the *Times*, the *Journal-American*, and the *World-Telegram and Sun*, leading to an immediate lockout at the *Daily Mirror*, the *Herald Tribune*, and the *Post*.[58]

The protracted strike and lockout left millions of newspaper readers deprived of their regular sources of news and information, while the city's merchants lost their principal means of reaching customers. Department store sales in most of the Northeast showed modest year-over-year gains of roughly 5 percent during both the holiday rush and the slack winter months that followed, but sales in New York City were off by an average of 7 percent during the labor dispute. Other kinds of economic activity suffered even more serious losses due to the interruption in the regular flow of information. Apartment brokers in the city, for example, reported that rental activity was off anywhere from 25 percent to 75 percent. The strike also hurt attendance at Broadway theaters, concerts, and other types of entertainment. Competing media tried to fill the vacuum. Local television stations expanded their news coverage from 30 percent to 70 percent, as dozens of otherwise idled reporters and columnists for the papers took their journalistic talents to the airwaves. Time Inc. began to print a weekly news digest filled solely with news items of local interest that it sold at the city's newsstands and major transit hubs. Several entrepreneurs published rudimentary "strike papers" in an abbreviated sixteen-page tabloid format, often printed on the presses of struggling local papers in New Jersey. They aspired to provide daily reporting, often by moonlighting Guild members, for the news-deprived metropolis, and also to earn windfall revenues from local advertisers. While these publications existed temporarily, other cultural adaptations to the strike were not as fleeting; the absence of the Book Review section of the Sunday *Times* inspired a group of intellectuals led by Robert Silvers, Barbara Epstein, and Elizabeth Hardwick to launch the *New York Review of Books* in February 1963.[59]

As the strike and lockout dragged on with no end in sight, both the unions and the newspaper owners began to crack under the strain. The first major break came on management's side, when the *New York Post*'s Dorothy Schiff announced on February 28 that she was withdrawing from the Publishers' Association and ending the paper's lockout of the ITU, with the union's members promised whatever terms were eventually agreed to by the other owners. Schiff resented the sexism of the other management representatives on the negotiating committee, and the *Post*'s precarious financial position convinced her that the paper could not survive if it did not resume publication. For the remaining thirteen years that she owned the paper, the *Post* pursued an independent course in labor relations.[60] The bonds of labor solidarity frayed as the strike entered its third month, as the other unions began to question why they were sacrificing so the typographers could get a premium contract. The Newspaper Guild of New York, with 6,000 members out of work, bore the largest financial burden. By the middle of February, the Guild had already paid out $1.7 million in lockout benefits, but even with the parent union picking up 70 percent of the tab, the drain on the local was unsustainable. Even the ITU, which had one of the labor movement's most ample strike funds, began to press Powers and the New York local to reach a settlement. In late March the typographers ratified a deal that raised their wages by an average of $12.63 a week, and the presses began rolling again at all six suspended papers on April 1.[61]

The millions of dollars in losses that the publishers sustained, even with the payouts from their strike and lockout insurance, and the prospect of spiraling labor costs in the years to come triggered a series of closings and consolidations in New York's newspaper industry. First came the surprise announcement on October 15, 1963 that the *Daily Mirror* was immediately terminating operations. Even though the *Mirror* still had the second highest daily circulation in the market, it had lost a greater percentage of its readership over the previous decade than any of its competitors. Additionally, multiple circulation surveys during the late 1950s and early 1960s indicated that a substantial share of *Mirror* readers bought it in addition to another morning paper, which diminished its value in the eyes of advertisers and compelled the publisher to offer discounted rates in order to compensate. Hearst Corporation executive Richard Berlin contended that the *Mirror* would have been profitable if it could have increased its newsstand price from five to seven cents, but such a price hike was out of the question as long as the *News* continued to sell for five cents, leaving the company with no choice but to kill the paper. Hearst management provided no advance warning; instead, it intended for the *Mirror*'s 1,500 employees to learn of the shutdown only when the final issue came off the presses, although word leaked out from the composing room once the closing notice arrived to be set into type. Even gossip columnist Walter Winchell had no idea his employer was about to fold.[62] Although Winchell and a handful of other high-profile writers received transfers to the *Journal-American*, most of the 496 Newspaper Guild members at the *Mirror* were out of work. The severance provisions in the Guild contract provided roughly $2.3 million in termination payments, which helped to ease the transition as the union tried to find new positions for former *Mirror* employees. By January 1964, slightly more than 200 of them had found new jobs, while another 100 or so, typically older employees with more than twenty-five years of service at the *Mirror* and limited prospects, opted for early retirement. The remaining 175 were still seeking gainful employment.[63]

The Guild's leadership had difficulty formulating a coherent response to the structural crisis facing New York's daily newspapers, in part because of the increasingly divergent interests of the various segments of the newspaper workforce. Newspaper Guild of New York executive vice president Thomas Murphy called on Congress to investigate whether the *Daily News* had violated antitrust law by selling below cost in order to drive the *Mirror* from the field. In turn, more than 170 members at the *News* signed a petition protesting that it was not their employer's responsibility to keep its competitors afloat and that it was the price-fixing advocated by Murphy that actually violated antitrust statutes.[64] In addition to the rift between employees of the profitable *News* and *Times* and employees of the struggling *Herald Tribune, Post, World-Telegram and Sun*, and *Journal-American*, issues of automation and job security divided workers as well. The most obvious cleavage existed between the typographers, who were clearly willing to jeopardize the financial viability of the weaker publishers in order to forestall technological change, and the white-collar employees, but the specter of automation haunted many in the Guild's jurisdiction. By the mid-1960s the introduction of computerized data processing threatened to eliminate many clerical positions. Reporters, writers, editors, photographers, illustrators, and others who created content had little to fear from automation, and instead tended to see the possible merger or closing of newspapers as the primary threat to their livelihoods.

The fragmentation of the industry's collective bargaining pattern with the 1962–1963 strike made labor relations even more chaotic, as leaders of the various union locals, often responding to restiveness within the rank-and-file, vied with each other to win the largest pay increases for their respective members. As they approached negotiations in 1965, Murphy and the other leaders of the New York Guild proposed an average weekly salary boost of $12 over two years, along with tough new contract language to enhance union security, protect members from layoffs due to automation, guarantee transfers and retraining for those displaced by new equipment, and establish Guild jurisdiction over any new technological processes that might be introduced into the editorial or commercial departments. The publishers offered little resistance to the Guild's salary demands, but they dug in on the other issues. Management at the *Herald Tribune*—which lost $2.5 million in 1964—fought especially hard against the Guild's proposals on automation and job losses, while the *Times* rejected the union's proposal to include the top echelon of editorial employees within a modified union shop.[65] As reports surfaced that the *Herald Tribune*, the *Journal-American*, and the *World-Telegram and Sun* had held preliminary merger discussions, the Guild requested additional contract language protecting members from layoffs due to the combination of newspaper staffs. When the Guild finally struck the *Times* in September 1965, the *Herald Tribune* opted to continue publication along with the *Post*, while the *Daily News*, *Journal-American*, and *World-Telegram* locked out their employees and suspended publication, even though they had long ago acceded to the union security provisions that *Times* management was fighting. After twenty-five days, the Guild and the *Times* reached a settlement that resolved little and only magnified the uncertainties facing the industry and its workers.[66]

In February 1966 the owners of the *Herald Tribune*, *Journal-American*, and *World-Telegram and Sun* finally unveiled their unification scheme. Initially the new company planned on publishing the *Herald Tribune* on weekday and Saturday mornings, an amalgamated *World-Journal* on weekday afternoons, and a single paper, the *World-Journal-Tribune*, on Sundays. The unions balked at publishers' proposals for combining the staffs of the three papers and insisted on strict adherence to seniority. Murphy and other Guild leaders rejected the pleas from *Herald Tribune* publisher John Whitney, who had made his paper and its *New York* Sunday magazine supplement into an incubator of the New Journalism, to allow the joint-operating enterprise to keep talented young writers like Tom Wolfe and Jimmy Breslin who would be crucial to its survival.[67] The issue sharply divided the Guild units at the merging newspapers, with clerical workers providing the decisive margin in favor of striking when the arrangement took effect on April 25. Dissent in the ranks surfaced immediately. On the first day of the walkout, a group of reporters and writers staged a brief sit-in protest, with Breslin, along with his *Herald Tribune* colleagues Dick Schaap, Walt Kelly, and Peter Axthelm, publicly proposing the creation of a new journalists' union to supplant the Guild. "Editorial people want to work on newspapers," their statement declared, "not have them shut down while the guild negotiates ways for its phone clerks to leave the business." Even after 300 Guild members at the struck papers offered to quit or take early retirement in order to expedite a settlement, several of the manufacturing and distribution unions still held out for more.

When talks with the pressmen, the last of the unions involved, broke down in early August, management terminated the *Herald Tribune*, whose daily circulation had barely topped 300,000 copies during its last few months. After the presses finally began rolling again on September 4, the company published just a single paper, the *World-Journal-Tribune*, on weekday afternoons and Sundays.[68]

In a eulogy for the *Herald Tribune* that Breslin penned for *Life* magazine, he blamed the unions for the death of the paper, singling out Murphy for special condemnation. Noting that the Guild was "comprised 70 percent of business department workers," Breslin charged that Murphy, "a former bookkeeper for the *Times*," had only "hearsay" knowledge of "the product of a newspaper—the thinking and writing." In its talks for a contract covering the white-collar staff of the merged papers, the Guild was represented by a team of five negotiators, none of whom, Breslin claimed, "had ever worked in a city room." Adherence to strict seniority, as the Guild insisted, would have "wrecked" the *Herald Tribune*'s "only asset, its young staff." He found Murphy's alleged assertion, during negotiations with the paper's management, that " 'we're all the same in our union . . . we're all just composing room helpers' " to be an absurd denial of the centrality of creative talent to the success of any media enterprise. By contrast, Breslin portrayed his relations with the publisher with more than a touch of sentimentality. "Jock Whitney is the only millionaire I ever rooted for," he wrote. "The guy hired me while I was drunk at a bar."[69]

Journalistic complaints about the Newspaper Guild's industrial unionism were hardly new; Breslin's critique, however, was articulated not by a conservative in the Westbrook Pegler mold, but by a liberal journalist. As his article suggested, the diverging interests of professional and clerical employees in the print media required a rethinking of the Guild's approaches to organizing and collective bargaining. Still, Murphy and most other local leaders had difficulty grasping the shortcomings of a strategy that may have preserved standards at the profitable *Times* and *News* but that accelerated the contraction of the city's newspaper industry. In addition to the 450 Guild positions that the joint-operating enterprise had initially wanted to eliminate, the strike resulted in the loss of another 400 Guild positions with the decision to terminate the *Herald Tribune*, and finally the jobs of 750 more members when the feeble *World-Journal-Tribune* expired on May 5, 1967.[70]

Belatedly the Newspaper Guild of New York responded to these membership losses in its primary jurisdiction—and the concomitant disappearance of over $100,000 annually in routine dues and assessments—by considering ways it could revitalize its organizing efforts. To many members of the local executive board, the obvious opportunities for growth were the suburban newspapers, particularly *Newsday*, then the largest nonunion daily paper in the metropolitan area, as well as a chain of weekly and semiweekly papers in Westchester County owned by Gannett Publications. While the Westchester papers had many employees who had once been with publications in the city and were consequently veterans of the Guild, they also had a large pool of low-wage, part-time workers who, some unionists suspected, might be difficult to organize. Others on the board wanted to focus the Guild's resources in Manhattan on magazines and, if possible, on book publishers as well. The proponents of this course were mostly activists within the Guild's existing magazine units, many of which were effectively open shops, who argued that the easiest path for quick growth was to sign up new members at those publishers like Time Inc. where it already pursued collective bargaining. More than 1,300 clerical and professional employees in the editorial departments— ranging from secretaries and file clerks to top writers and photographers for *Time*, *Life*, *Fortune*, and *Sports Illustrated*—fell within the Guild's jurisdiction at the media giant, but only 450 belonged to the union as it struggled to negotiate a new contract in early 1967. Besides the immediate boost to membership and dues revenue, building membership in these shops, proponents contended, would spark new organizing at other magazines and in the offices of major book publishers like Macmillan, where low salaries exerted a downward pull on standards in magazine publishing. Skeptics on the board, however, saw the anemic membership figures at Time Inc., *Newsweek*, and *Look* as evidence of a lack of enthusiasm for unionism.[71]

These disagreements within the Guild over organizing strategy reflected deeper generational, political, and social fault lines within the white-collar union. In their focus on the local's core jurisdiction, Murphy and his allies on the executive board often failed to appreciate just how much of the Guild's leverage in its dealings with the daily newspapers stemmed from these employers' vertical integration of production, and how expansion into less integrated sectors of the print media required different organizing approaches. They were also unmoved when representatives from the magazine units pointed out how the additional dues and assessments levied to finance the Guild's war of attrition with the newspaper publishers discouraged membership in units that lacked union security provisions. In effect, the local leadership privileged older workers' immediate interest in job security over a younger and more diverse group of workers' career aspirations and future employment opportunities.[72] The generation gap within the Newspaper Guild also manifested itself in disagreements over the era's major political and social issues. Murphy and his supporters on the local's executive board had largely eschewed the robust social unionism that characterized the Guild during its early years; when several hundred members of the New York Guild traveled to Washington, DC, in August 1963 for the March for Jobs and Freedom, their participation was only facilitated by the efforts of the UAW and District 65 to mobilize unionists from the city. Younger Guild activists, many of whom identified with the new progressive movements and countercultural currents, believed that engaging with a broader range of issues and struggles beyond the collective bargaining relationship would attract potential members and practically facilitate organization and growth.[73]

The Guild leadership's tepid racial liberalism came under increasing strain as the civil-rights campaigns of the 1950s and early 1960s gave way to empowerment struggles. When the United Federation of Teachers (UFT) struck in September 1967 to protest a series of personnel actions by an experimental community school board in the largely African American neighborhoods of Ocean Hill and Brownsville in Brooklyn, the Guild's executive board backed the union. After the *New York Post* sent several reporters into the community-controlled schools as replacement teachers in order to cover the dispute from the inside, top Guild officials prevailed upon the paper's management to withdraw them on the grounds that their contract prohibited them from doing struck work.[74] As the conflict dragged on, paralyzing public education throughout the city, many Guild members began to express their support for the community school board and to see the UFT as an obstacle to racial justice. In September 1968, when the executive board of the New York Guild endorsed the renewal of strike action by the UFT, the Time Inc. unit council condemned the strike and called for a membership referendum on the Guild's position. Although the referendum was moot when it was held in early 1969, nearly half of the Guild members who took part voted to repudiate their leadership.[75] In some cases, the emergence of a militant racial consciousness complicated the Guild's own organizing efforts. In 1970, as part of its tentative forays into book publishing, Guild organizers at Harcourt and Brace encountered a group of Black employees in the firm's Department of Urban Education who initially wanted to form their own separate unit, and who were skeptical of the union's commitment to racial empowerment.[76]

In addition, a growing number of Guild members came to oppose their leadership's continued backing of Cold War foreign policies, particularly the war in Vietnam. In February 1967, it was revealed that training courses conducted by the American Newspaper Guild's International Affairs

Program in collaboration with the South Vietnamese Union of Journalists and with various press unions throughout Latin America had been indirectly financed by the Central Intelligence Agency. Some members took this opportunity to criticize the union's position on the conflict in Southeast Asia, while others were more concerned about how the arrangement had subverted the Guild's claims to promote journalistic integrity.[77] The war again roiled the local in the spring of 1970 with the American invasion of Cambodia and the protests that followed, including the killing of four students by National Guardsmen at Kent State in Ohio on May 4, and the infamous assault on antiwar demonstrators by construction workers in lower Manhattan on May 8. Guild activists at Time Inc. and at the *New York Times* blasted the local executive board for its generic statement lamenting the "violence at home" and calling for "a just peace" in Southeast Asia. They implored it instead to disavow the pro-war stance of the AFL-CIO and endorse a joint labor-student antiwar rally on May 21 sponsored by District 65, Drug and Hospital Union Local 1199, District 37 of the American Federation of State, County, and Municipal Employees, and District 3 of the International Union of Electrical Workers. The local leadership refused to yield to the activists' demands, although subsequent debates over the appropriate policy for the New York Guild highlighted the divisions within its membership. Older local officers and executive board members from the daily newspaper units reaffirmed their support for the AFL-CIO line on foreign affairs and backed the peaceful pro-war rally held by the construction unions not long after the "hard-hat riot." Younger activists and activists from the struggling magazine units pushed for the local to embrace the politics of the antiwar movement. As Wilton Woods, the unit chair for Time Inc. pointed out, "lacking a union shop, new members had to be recruited through issues, and the issues necessarily had to be close to the people." The "signing up of new members and the payment of dues by them," he continued, "signified an endorsement of policy."[78]

Although the war in Southeast Asia gradually receded in importance in the internal politics of the New York Guild, the divisions over the issue in many ways epitomized the general discord within the union in the early 1970s. Economic uncertainty led to renewed interest in the union in various unorganized corners of the media, but the local's entrenched leadership seemed determined to squander the opportunity. Murphy finally retired at the end of 1970, but his followers continued his policies. The local leadership continued to build the defense fund in preparation for a cataclysmic showdown with the *Times* or the *Daily News*, but frowned on the expenditure of funds to hire additional organizers for the magazine or book publishing sectors. The local's few organizing positions, moreover, were treated by the officers as sinecures for their loyalists, so they were mostly held by older white men who had difficulty relating to workers in their twenties and thirties, often women or minorities, whom the union was trying to enlist. Even the organizing pamphlets that the union made available were woefully out-of-date. Jean Davidson, the only woman among the local's full-time staff organizers in 1971, and the only organizer familiar with the problems facing the magazine units, contended that the union was failing to take account not just of "the importance of keeping up with the changes in contracts," but of the "change in the social climate, and the change in the kind of membership now in the Guild."[79]

The New Radicalism: The Resurgence of Feminism in New York's Culture Industries

Of all of the social transformations of the 1960s and 1970s, none had a greater impact on the Newspaper Guild of New York or on the city's culture industries in general than the revitalization of the movement for women's equality and empowerment. Like the women who were active in the Popular Front, feminists of the 1960s and 1970s believed that the improvement of working conditions in the culture industries would result in the creation of cultural content that was more socially and politically progressive. Actions like the occupation of the *Ladies Home Journal*'s editorial offices on March 18, 1970, were intended to drive home the connection: media workplaces rife with sexism produced sexist representations of women. Yet in other crucial respects second-wave feminists differed from the labor feminists of the 1930s and 1940s. Most importantly, while most Popular Front women tended to view and interpret sex discrimination and inequality through the lens of class, activist women of the 1960s and 1970s frequently prioritized aspects of their gender identity over their class identity in their thinking and practice. This fundamental shift in the consciousness of women in the culture industries was congruent with legal developments, as the passage of the 1964 Civil Rights Act, with its Title VII prohibitions on sex-based employment discrimination, conferred upon working women certain rights and potential claims for redistributive justice that surpassed those available under the National Labor Relations Act, let alone what many women believed they could realize through the labor movement. Women in publishing and broadcasting often initiated their campaigns for pay equity, fair opportunities for career advancement, and an end to rampant sexual harassment in the workplace by organizing outside of union channels. Over time the two modes of collective action overlapped and intersected, so that the spread of feminist consciousness and activism stimulated renewed interest in white-collar labor organizing in New York during the 1970s. Women's influence within these unions increased, most remarkably with Betsy Wade's election as the first woman president of the Newspaper Guild of New York in 1978. Nonetheless, many women, especially educated professionals, remained skeptical of class-based solidarity, instead embracing the meritocratic ethos of New Class liberalism as more aligned with their own personal career and lifestyle aspirations. To a certain extent, these differences among women in New York's culture industries during the 1970s simply recapitulated the ambivalence over unionization that had run through the creative class since its emergence.

The rapid growth and radicalization of the resurgent feminist movement during the late 1960s involved many women employed in the city's media. New York feminists established one of the first local chapters of the National Organization for Women (NOW) in 1966, and within several years the chapter's Image Committee and its Employment Committee, which focused much of its attention on the discrimination experienced by women in publishing, broadcasting, and advertising, were among its most active endeavors. By the end of the 1960s, more militant groups like New York Radical Feminists (NYRF) and Redstockings attracted many of the younger, well-educated women in the culture industries who were growing increasingly outraged by the pervasive discrimination they encountered.[80] Participation in these groups formed a basis for consciousness-raising, networking, and coordination outside of the white-collar unions. For many of the women, previous involvement with New Left groups like Students for a Democratic Society contributed to their skepticism, if not outright disdain, for organized labor, which some of them saw as a reactionary force in American life. Moreover, their personal experiences with sexist behavior by men with whom they had worked in the civil rights and antiwar movements also motivated them to pursue an independent path. Media Women, for example, came into existence in the second half of 1969 as a feminist secession from the New York Media Project, which had been formed to develop antiwar cultural content and to promote criticism of mainstream press coverage of contemporary events. In its initial phase, the group tried to enlist women working in the city's culture industries to support a broad range of feminist and radical activism, even as it focused on issues related to America's sexist media. Media Women encouraged participatory forms of resistance, such as distributing stickers reading "This Ad Insults Women" which feminists could affix to offensive advertisements in public places. It was also an early proponent of the American Civil Liberties Union's Women's Rights Project, headed by attorney Eleanor Holmes Norton, which sought to encourage and coordinate the filing of sex discrimination complaints with the Equal Employment Opportunities Commission (EEOC).[81]

It did not take long for women in the New York media to seek out Norton's guidance. The first legal challenge to discriminatory practices in pay, hiring, and promotions came at *Newsweek*, where a group of women began organizing in late 1969. Most of the women involved were researchers, who resented being stuck in a sex-segregated occupational ghetto with few chances to move up into more prestigious, higher paying, and more creative roles as reporters, writers, or editors. Some members of the group were involved with Media Women or the New York City chapter of NOW and, through these contacts, learned of the ACLU initiative. Meanwhile, the upsurge in feminist workplace activism within the culture industries coincided with a conspicuous increase in media coverage of women's liberation, and in many instances the activism and the coverage intersected in significant ways. At *Newsweek*, women organized as the magazine's male editors developed a cover story on the new wave of feminist activism without soliciting their input. Simultaneously undercutting their employer's editorial content and capitalizing on it, they timed the announcement of their complaint for the same day that the "Women in Revolt" issue hit the newsstands. On March 16, 1970, the forty-six women who filed the complaint declared that they had been "systematically discriminated against in both hiring and promotion" and "forced to assume a subsidiary role" on account of their sex. They also petitioned Katherine Graham, president of the Washington Post Company, which owned *Newsweek*, for a voluntary program for integrating men into the research department and substantially increasing the number of women in reporting, writing, and editing positions.[82] Their complaint, one of the first lodged with the EEOC over sex discrimination, inspired subsequent charges by women in New York's culture industries, including one that 140 women at Time Inc. filed with the city's Human Rights Commission, which Norton was appointed to chair in May.[83] As the charges of sex discrimination against publishers and broadcasters multiplied, media enterprises frequently became the news.

The dynamic relationship between feminist activism and its representation within sexist media itself became a subject of radical critique within the movement. Coverage in the mainstream media, although frequently biased against feminists, nonetheless spread public awareness of their challenges to

FIGURE 8.1 Women employees of *Newsweek* and attorney Eleanor Holmes Norton (center) announcing their groundbreaking sex discrimination complaint in March 1970 on the same day that the magazine's "Women in Revolt" special issue (foreground) hit the newsstands. From the Bettmann Archive/Getty Images.

patriarchy and entrenched sexism throughout American society and culture. Many feminist activists adopted the practice of only granting interviews to women journalists, in the hopes that this would result in coverage that was more favorable while also encouraging media enterprises to alter their sexist employment practices. Yet some radical feminists maintained that much of this coverage in fact narrowly served the interests of a handful of relatively privileged women whose reportage advanced their own careers more than it promoted a militant conception of women's solidarity. Susan Brownmiller, a mainstream journalist and a member of both NYRF and Media Women, found herself at the center of the debate. Brownmiller had struggled to build her media career, which included a stint as a *Newsweek* researcher, and by the beginning of 1970 she had achieved enough renown as a freelance writer to be selected by the *New York Times* to write a feature article surveying the women's liberation movement for its Sunday magazine. At the same time, she was also playing a key role in planning the *Ladies Home Journal* protest and occupation by activists from a coalition of groups that included Media Women, NYRF, Redstockings, NOW, and the Gay Liberation Front. Brownmiller's article, entitled "Sisterhood Is Powerful," appeared on March 15, the day before the *Newsweek* women announced their EEOC complaint, and three days before the *Journal* action. The group of women who invaded the *Journal*'s offices issued a wide range of demands designed to benefit women employees as well as to reorient its content along feminist lines. They called for the immediate replacement of editor-in-chief John Mack Carter with a woman, the hiring of an exclusively female editorial and advertising staff, the elimination of all pay inequities, and the installation of a child-care center on the premises. They also called for management to grant them complete control over a special "Liberated" issue of the *Journal*, as well as the elimination of regular features like "Can This Marriage Be Saved?" that they deemed offensive, along with all advertising that demeaned women.[84]

After eleven hours of negotiations, including a pivotal moment when feminist theorist Shulamith Firestone lunged at Carter, the sit-in came to an end, with the occupiers accepting a limited settlement in which they received complete editorial control over an eight-page section in the August 1970 issue. Management failed to accede to any of the demands related to working conditions, which fed rumors within the movement that organizers such as Brownmiller had sacrificed the interests of women employed in clerical and support roles to promote themselves as writers. Before long, some radical feminists began to attack the right of prominent feminist journalists to speak on behalf of the movement. When the Second Congress to Unite Women convened in May in New York City, members of the Class Workshop, who proclaimed themselves in opposition to all forms of occupational, income, or property privilege, denounced Brownmiller specifically and castigated all women who set themselves above the mass of oppressed women through their reporting on the movement. During the Congress' plenum, Rita Mae Brown, who had recently broken with the New York City chapter of NOW over what she saw as its classism and homophobia, affirmed the Class Workshop's resolution in pointed language. "We don't need spokespeople and we don't need leaders," Brown declared. "All women can speak, and all women can write."[85]

While the rancor at this intense moment of movement building was especially acute, a basic tension between individual achievement and collective empowerment ran through the resurgence of feminist activism in New York's culture industries. Nothing illustrated these strains more clearly than the feminists' engagement with the existing white-collar unions. In principle the unions functioned as the institutional embodiment of workplace solidarity, but many women in the print media were wary of enlisting the Newspaper Guild in their fight. At *Newsweek*, where the Guild had an open-shop contract and only a small fraction of the covered employees were members in good standing, the unit was dominated by men in the production departments during the late 1960s. Few of the *Newsweek* women who filed the discrimination complaint had previously belonged to the Guild, and they did not initially see it as a means for attaining workplace equity. At Time Inc., where the Guild also had an open-shop contract, women who worked as researchers or in clerical and support positions comprised a larger proportion of the unit membership, but there too the women who enlisted the EEOC initially organized outside of the union. Women in other newspaper and magazine offices who organized against sex discrimination during 1970 and 1971 often followed this pattern, with aspiring writers or editors frequently viewing the Guild as irrelevant to their struggle, if not actually a part of the patriarchal structure that impeded their advancement.[86]

The men who led the Newspaper Guild were not wholly indifferent to women's renewed efforts for empowerment and equity, but their limited support frequently appeared perfunctory to feminists in the print media. After prodding by NOW and a shift by many other unions that had long supported sex-protective legislation, the New York Guild finally endorsed the proposed Equal Rights Amendment to the United States Constitution in early 1970. When the Newspaper Guild held its first national conference on sex discrimination and women's rights that fall, the New York local sent one of the most prominent delegations. Yet when some of these delegates subsequently proposed at the Guild's 1971 convention to establish a permanent paid position for a "women's rights coordinator" on the international union's executive board, the local leadership balked.[87] Even when women who were organizing against their employers' discriminatory practices worked closely with the Guild, the local leadership's response was lukewarm. In 1972, a women's caucus at the *New York Times*, headed by longtime Guild activist Betsy Wade, began meeting with management in an attempt to remediate the pervasive discrimination in hiring, pay, and promotions at the paper. Wade had been the first female copyeditor permanently assigned to the city desk at the *Times*, and had faced continual discrimination as she struggled to advance. Wade and the other caucus activists consulted with the union, with attorney Harriet Rabb of Columbia University Law School's Employment Rights Project, and with the New York City chapter of NOW. The payroll data obtained by Wade through her role as a union trustee for the *Times* pension plan revealed that women in professional positions typically earned at least $60 to $70 less per week than men performing comparable work, due primarily to the unequal awarding of merit pay. Yet the consensus on the local's executive board was that since every employee received at least the negotiated minimum for their job classification, the paper had not violated the equal pay provision of the contract. The board had a similar reaction to findings regarding women's difficulties in obtaining promotions. Even though women only accounted for 11 of 199 managerial employees at the paper, and 85 out of 789 nonsupervisory professional employees, members of the local board contended that the matter was not subject to arbitration under the Guild's contract with the *Times*. Although several members of the board recommended that the local contribute financially to Rabb's project and encourage women to avail themselves of the EEOC when collective bargaining proved inadequate, they generally failed to grasp the moral urgency of women's demands.[88]

Nevertheless, the difficulties involved in enforcing consent agreements reached as a result of complaints filed with the EEOC or comparable state and city agencies led some women in the print media to reassess their initial diffidence regarding unionism. At *Newsweek*, for instance, women activists reached an initial settlement with the publication in August 1970 in which management made only vague assurances that it would give women more opportunities for career advancement and address some of the more glaring salary inequities among the staff. Although the agreement established a committee of editors and women employees that met on a bimonthly basis to implement and monitor its provisions, women at the magazine soon grew frustrated with their inability to hold management accountable for the lack of progress. By the beginning of 1972, as they prepared for a second sex-discrimination complaint against *Newsweek*, most of them decided to join the Newspaper Guild in the hopes of strengthening their position. *Newsweek* Women's Committee organizer Nancy Stadtman, who had been promoted from researcher to a writing role on account of her activism, became chair of the magazine's Guild unit. By the time Rabb filed their new complaint in May, 44 of the 51 women who signed it were Guild members in good standing. Pointing to recent federal court decisions in Title VII cases that mandated robust affirmative action programs, Rabb and the women pressed for an agreement that included specific quotas and timelines. Facing the prospect of litigation and an unfavorable outcome, management capitulated. The memorandum of understanding reached in June 1973 stipulated that the percentage of men working as researchers be made approximately equal to the percentage of women working as writers, that women constitute one-third or more of all domestic reporters, that by December 1974 one-third of all writers were to be women, that two of the next domestic bureau chiefs would be women, and that by December 1975 at least one woman would be a senior editor. In addition, it set forth a comprehensive training program to ensure that female staffers would be in line for most of the new openings. Enforcement was provided by an arbitration provision designed to complement the existing arbitration language in the Guild contract.[89]

Women employed in television encountered similar patterns of discrimination, but several historical and institutional factors specific to the broadcast media led them to pursue different approaches in their fight for equity. First, the circumscribed and fragmented extent of unionization in broadcasting meant that for many women, seeking assistance from an existing labor organization was not a practical option. Since the destruction of the UOPWA Radio Guild, the talent guilds and the technicians' craft unions had been the only unions in New York broadcasting. Most women toiled in clerical, paraprofessional, and professional positions that were unorganized. Second, the regulatory apparatus of American broadcasting offered women another tool beyond either labor law or civil rights law for pressuring employers. The FCC's general definition of licensee's public service responsibilities virtually invited feminists to link their opposition to broadcasters' sexist employment practices with their condemnation of sexist programming. Much as progressives in the 1940s had appealed to the FCC to challenge the renewal or transfer of licenses held by broadcasters hostile to organized labor or the expansion of social democracy, women's groups within broadcasting joined forces with NOW in the early 1970s to pressure licensees. By the fall of 1970, several NOW chapters around the country began organizing members to serve as "monitors" to help compile program surveys and assessments for use as supporting evidence in FCC complaints and petitions. Furthermore, in 1971 the FCC required licensees to begin submitting data on their employment of women.[90]

In New York, feminists used this tactic against WABC-TV, the local owned and operated station and programming hub for the ABC network. In several regards, ABC had been a leader in offering opportunities to talented women and in its representations of women. ABC correspondent Marlene Sanders had been the first woman to anchor a network television news program, and she had given the burgeoning second-wave feminist movement some of its most thoughtful and favorable coverage, including a special documentary that she produced in May 1970.[91] Yet other aspects of the network's programming and employment practices revealed pervasive sexism, and monitors pegged WABC as marginally more offensive than the metropolitan area's other broadcasters. By the time the station's license came up for renewal in 1972, a caucus of female employees who had organized for workplace equity had joined with NOW to petition the FCC to deny its application for renewal. The FCC deferred action on the renewal application, which would normally have been automatic. Short of actual revocation, it was the strongest regulatory action the FCC could take to compel the licensee to respond to the criticisms. While the status of the renewal remained unresolved, the network found that it had to pursue discussions with NOW and the employee's caucus.[92]

After several months of meetings, in July 1972 the New York City chapter of NOW proposed a consent agreement with ABC that was remarkable for its analysis of the materialist basis for patriarchal cultural hegemony, and for its ambitious expectations of the capacity of public regulation of the airwaves to promote equal employment opportunity and reform broadcast content. The first half of the proposal addressed issues of employment opportunity and stipulated a specific set of goals and timelines for hiring and promoting women into executive, creative, professional, and sales positions at the network. Within eighteen months, at least one quarter of the employees in most categories were to be women, with fully half to be women within five years. The NOW proposal also confronted the near total exclusion of women from unionized craft and technical jobs, calling for the opening of positions as camera operators, film editors, sound technicians, electricians, and transmission engineers to women and the establishment of accelerated training and apprenticeship programs to prepare women to fulfill the staffing quotas. Additionally, it demanded a robust recruitment program to "encourage women to enter all phases of the broadcast industry" and provide "preferential treatment for hiring or promotion" in all occupational categories in which the goals had not yet been met. Outreach to potential applicants was to be carried out in part through NOW, Gloria Steinem's recently founded *Ms.* magazine, and other feminist organizations and publications. Finally, women employed in clerical and paraprofessional roles who did not benefit directly from this affirmative action program were to have their jobs subject to "reevaluation" in order to ensure that their titles and salaries actually reflected their actual job content and responsibilities.[93]

The second half of the proposal focused on television programming. While it echoed many of the demands that the *Ladies Home Journal* occupiers had made two years earlier, it insisted on an array of new initiatives in the areas of news, public affairs, and documentaries. WABC-TV was to include in its local evening newscasts at least two five-minute segments per week that were "devoted to news of the women's rights movement and/or investigative reports on the problems of women." ABC was also to commit to at least ten hours per year of primetime public affairs and documentary programs that would express feminist viewpoints in a "persuasive, hard-hitting, and polemical" manner. Topics were to be selected in consultation with a Women's Advisory Committee, and women were to be employed in all aspects of production. The network's obligation to ensure "that any particular viewpoint be 'balanced'" in accordance with the FCC Fairness Doctrine was to be met "through other programming vehicles." Rounding out its public affairs demands, New York NOW sought the creation of a daytime women's program, with a magazine format, that would counter the sexist content of most daytime programming directed toward homemakers.[94]

NOW made further demands pertaining to entertainment and advertising content that cut to the sexist core of America's culture of consumer capitalism. The organization called for ABC to develop new primetime series starring feminist protagonists, to introduce two female physicians to the daytime soap opera *General Hospital* "who participate fully in their professional capacities and do not merely assist the male surgeons," and to ensure that *The Rookies* include "frequent parts for policewomen in action." Also, the network was to guarantee that "the next host hired for a game show shall be a woman, and at least every other host hereafter hired shall be female," and that "children's programming shall have an equal balance of boys and girls, and adult male and female characters," which "shall not be sex stereotyped." Regardless of the impact on revenues, ABC was to "inform its advertisers of its commitment to eliminate all broadcast material which tends to denigrate women or depict women solely in the role of housewife/mother, sex object, or as servile or subservient to men," with several commercials, including National Airlines' notorious "Fly Me" spots and the "Olivetti Girl" ads for office equipment, to be specifically banned from the network. To advance these reforms, network executives responsible for improving the image of women were to "provide ongoing service and advice to advertisers and their agencies in developing campaigns and commercials consonant with sex-neutral guidelines." By accepting the proposed terms, ABC would be seizing "an opportunity to project a new image of women more in conformity with women's expanding roles in society."[95]

ABC management responded with a paltry assortment of concessions. The network announced that it was creating a position of Equal Employment Opportunity Director, and although it vaguely assented to an affirmative action program in which "WABC-TV will establish specific goals and timetables for the employment of women and minorities," the actual terms were left undefined. Management promised to encourage women to apply for technical and professional positions in which they were severely underrepresented, and it dropped from its employment application forms "questions relating to marital status, number of children, height, weight, and number of persons dependent upon the applicant." Additionally, the company declared it would "urge unions with which it has agreements to cooperate in the development of programs to assure qualified female persons equal opportunity in employment," while "new or renegotiated union contracts will include a provision designed to eliminate discrimination on the basis of sex." The network accepted almost none of the feminists' demands regarding program content. It committed only to four special primetime programs over a period of three years "which will focus on matters of special significance or primary interest to women," as well as the establishment of an "experimental" production unit to develop a regular public affairs program "designed to respond to the interests of women" with no guarantee that the results would be approved for airing. ABC ignored all of the specific NOW demands regarding entertainment and advertising, offering only the perfunctory assurance that the network's standards and practices department would "undertake, in its review of programming and commercials, to make suggestions and recommendations encouraging the affirmative portrayal of women and discouraging the unnecessary portrayal of women in sex-stereotyped roles or other portrayals which depict women as inferior or secondary to men."[96] As it became increasingly clear that the FCC would not revoke the station's license, the limited leverage that NOW had with ABC management evaporated; ultimately, the NOW petition languished in limbo until the FCC, responding to a court order, officially rejected it in March 1975.[97]

As radical hopes for rapid cultural change began to wane, some professional women refocused their energies on the more immediate goals of career advancement within media enterprises. This perspective received its most elaborate exposition in *Rooms with No View: A Woman's Guide to the Man's World of the Media* (1974), an anthology compiled by the Media Women's Association. "In light of the power of the media to affect women's views of themselves," the organization noted in the foreword, "it is particularly ironic that women have traditionally had so little power within the media." Although the members of Media Women "all were aware that every branch of the media discriminated against women," they determined that "since our own experiences varied and since cold statistics often do not reveal the essence of a situation," the best course was "to assemble and publish as many individual articles as we could about representative publishers and broadcasters."[98] A collection of mostly anonymous participant-observer studies of the different ways in which sexism pervaded New York's culture industries, the volume reflected the contributors' diverging approaches to the problem of discrimination. Multiple essays explicated aspects of the development and filing of EEOC complaints, with particular focus on *Newsweek*, as models for subsequent collective action. Several entries, most conspicuously the account of the three-week strike staged in June 1974 by an independent union of employees of book publisher Harper and Row that subsequently affiliated with District 65, extolled collective bargaining as a means of fighting for equity.[99] Yet some of the accounts betrayed a subtle shift from militant assertions of solidarity grounded in women's shared oppression toward individualized tactics for addressing the inequities and injustices rooted in systemic sexism, as authors suggested that upward occupational mobility was attainable for women of merit who made an extra effort at overcoming discrimination.

In December 1974, Media Women organized a conference to coincide with the publication of *Rooms with No View* and to draw attention to the issues it raised. In her keynote address, Marlene Sanders of ABC News asserted that the future of women in the culture industries was contingent on the outcome of a "two-front war" over "employment and image." Acknowledging the deep roots of sexism in the media, she observed that "the men we work for judge us by how they saw their mothers and by the kind of women their wives are. You can be sure that the women in their lives served them and took care of them." With respect to her own employer, she maintained that women at ABC "enjoy excellent relations with management, as a group," although she added, "we intend to keep the pressure on." As part of her case for expanded employment opportunities, she appealed both to management's self-interest and to notions of individual merit, contending "it costs the network nothing, really, to put a good woman in a good job which either a man or woman could fill." Changing television's representation of women, Sanders argued, would likely be more daunting than changing discriminatory employment patterns. "People—men and women, boys and girls—need to see our various possibilities in life," but instead "the image of women now on the screens of motion pictures and television sets is severely limited by the imaginations of men."[100]

Other participants, who saw a harder fight ahead for women who were not star talent like Sanders, used the conference to advocate for an updated labor feminism. Journalist Claudia Dreifus, representing Media Women's steering committee, excoriated Macmillan for laying off nearly two hundred employees as retaliation for "feminist and trade-union activities" and blaming the job cuts on the worsening economic recession. Although the publishing giant had recently selected *Rooms with No View* for distribution through its women's book club, Dreifus indicated that Macmillan's actions were "in direct contradiction to the spirit and intent of the book."[101] Kitty Krupat, an organizer for District 65, made a presentation on behalf of her union that explicitly positioned it as an agent of feminist empowerment. *New York Times* reporters Joan Cook and Grace Glueck, who, along with their colleague Betsy Wade, had just filed a sex-discrimination lawsuit against their employer, presented on their fight against the well-documented inequities in pay and promotions at the newspaper, but were interrupted by Yetta Riesel, the international human rights coordinator for the Guild. Contradicting Cook and Glueck, Riesel incorrectly maintained that existing language standard in Guild contracts (including at the *Times*) adequately addressed the issue. A few days after the conference, Wade admonished Riesel. "You set the whole process back about 20 years. Grace was appalled and Joan was speechless with rage to see their own union undercutting their presentation." In Wade's judgment, Riesel's comments showed her "ignorance of what affirmative action is all about." Instead, Wade continued, Riesel "could have talked about job security or maternity leave," which were "rallying cries" in a recession, or she "could have pointed out that the New York Guild is supporting the *Times* women's action, with money for the law group and with strong clerical support and loan of meeting rooms." Either would have been preferable to her blustering intervention, which only "made the Guild look like an organization of fools."[102]

Wade was especially sensitive to the way the union presented itself in forums like the Media Women conference precisely because of her simultaneous immersion in both labor activism and women's expanding professional networks. She had been one of the founders of the Coalition of Labor Union Women (CLUW) in 1974, and the following year she joined the Newspaper Guild's international executive board. Yet her role as the lead named defendant in the *New York Times* Women's Caucus lawsuit against the newspaper also made her an important personality within the circles of professional women in New York media. Despite the *Times'* liberal reputation, the paper's management took a hard line and resisted reaching a negotiated settlement with the plaintiffs.[103] As the litigation slowly moved through the initial discovery phase, to the federal court's certification of the suit as a class action on behalf of all female employees of the *Times*, and into the lengthy pretrial deposition of witnesses, Wade found herself sought out by professional women who admired her efforts to break through the glass ceiling but who had little awareness of—or necessarily any interest in—labor organizing. Although Wade belonged to the Women's Media Group, which had formed to provide networking and career support, in an August 1976 memo for her files she characterized the majority of its members as "elitist, status-conscious, union-hating, [and] anti-activist." Even the minority of the women in the group who were more attuned to the systemic aspects of sex-based pay inequities and the potential for unionization to bring about equal employment opportunities seemed, from Wade's perspective, shockingly unfamiliar with the practical aspects of organizing. In part, their lack of experience was a legacy of the social containment of unionization at the dawn of the Cold War; most had come of age in communities in which affluent white-collar professionals generally did not belong to unions, and they had made their careers in media workplaces in which there had been no apparent organizing efforts.[104]

The resolution of the sex-discrimination lawsuit against the *Times* was intertwined with Wade's ascent in the New York Guild. After years of intransigence, the company finally tendered a settlement offer to the Women's Caucus and attorney Harriet Rabb in the early fall of 1978, which the plaintiffs reluctantly accepted. In many respects, its terms encapsulated the larger struggle for women's equal employment opportunity during the decade: the women who initiated the suit gained very little, while most of the benefits accrued to younger, well-educated women who were just starting their careers or would do so in the future. The *Times* expended a paltry $350,000 in settlement costs, with two-thirds of the sum paid to the 550 women covered in the class action based on their tenure of employment. Women who had been with the newspaper twenty or more years received $1,000, while women with 15 to 20 years received $500, women with 10 to 15 years received $300, women with 5 to 10 years received $200, and women employed for less than five years received $100. The seven named plaintiffs and eight key witnesses were awarded an additional $1,000 each, and the company contributed $100,000 to Rabb's Employment Rights Project in lieu of attorney's fees. For all of the women, the payments were a pittance. Plaintiffs Wade, Cook, and Glueck received amounts that were just a fraction of the annual gap between their salaries and those of their male colleagues with comparable (or inferior) skills and experience. The majority, who held clerical and service positions at the paper, received payments that could not even begin to compensate for the wholesale devaluation of their labor as "women's work." Looking forward, the paper committed to a significant affirmative action program that guaranteed that by the end of 1982 women would hold one-eighth of all executive-level corporate positions and one-quarter of the top news and editorial positions, with increased proportions of women in all other professional classifications as well. Implementation of this section of the agreement opened doors for numerous younger women with talent and ambition, and facilitated the slow and halting process of breaking down the culture of workplace sexism not only at the *Times*, but throughout the print media.[105]

Most New Yorkers were unaware of the settlement, which occurred in the midst of another lengthy newspaper strike in the city that shut down the *Times* and the *Daily News* for 88 days. The publishers entered the 1978 round of collective bargaining demanding concessions from their unionized workers, with the pressmen's union and the Newspaper Guild emerging as the principal targets. The New York Guild's paid staff and elected leadership appeared unprepared to respond to the onslaught. A short strike by the Guild against the *Daily News* in June, while the pressmen and several of the other blue-collar unions continued negotiating, yielded a contract with poor terms for the union, including the removal of more than 100 positions from the bargaining unit, reductions in the paper's clerical staff, and the introduction of a two-tiered schedule of minimum salaries for new hires. These provisions hit the women and minorities within the Guild's jurisdiction the hardest. When the new owner of the *New York Post*, Australian-born media tycoon Rupert Murdoch, began firing Guild members during negotiations, the union proved unable to act decisively to protect its members before the pressmen struck, suspending operations at all three of the remaining major daily newspapers published in Manhattan.[106] Murdoch initially led the Publishers Association's united front against the unions, but withdrew once he suspected that the negotiators for the *News* and the *Times* might be cutting deals behind his back. His decision to settle separately with the pressmen and the Guild in October and resume publication only placed greater pressure on the *News* and *Times* strikers. When the pressmen suddenly settled in early November and the blue-collar unions indicated that they might not respect the Guild's picket lines at the *Times*, the white-collar local hastily accepted a substandard contract.[107]

Membership dissatisfaction with the contract settlements at the three daily newspapers in the New York Guild's jurisdiction combined with many younger unionists' enthusiasm for the empowerment of women and minorities to propel Wade and her allies to victory in the December 1978 local elections. As a respected editor, a long-time Guild activist, and an embodiment of the fight for workplace equity, she was a natural to head the Responsibility Slate that challenged the local's ossified leadership. Wade's slate campaigned on a promise to "give the Guild back to its members" and to curtail the power of the paid local staff who had mishandled the union's affairs and squandered opportunities for new organizing in the recessionary economic climate of the 1970s.[108] Her election as local president, coming on the heels of the landmark settlement with her employer, represented the cresting of a wave of progressive activism to make media workplaces more egalitarian and more attuned to the social mores of an increasingly diverse workforce, although Wade and her supporters would find that their adversaries—in the ranks of management and within their own union—remained tenacious.

Yet the advent of effective affirmative action programs, the gradual lessening of prejudice in personnel decisions, and other developments that gave women and minorities more equal access to employment in New York's culture industries occurred when the range of existing opportunities was far more limited than it had been at any time since the Great Depression. The seemingly boundless economic growth of the 1950s and 1960s was receding into memory by the late 1970s. Although postwar affluence failed to eliminate insecurity, even for educated professionals, and its fruits were unevenly distributed across the occupational spectrum, it nonetheless offered a generation of white men prospects for enhanced earnings, wealth, and socioeconomic status that would not be available to subsequent generations of women and minorities. Conditions in the city's culture industries were not as dire as in American manufacturing, but economic constraints nonetheless restricted the gains that women and minorities would be able to achieve. The print media's woes continued unabated, television production other than news programming and daytime serials remained at low ebb, and the increased prevalence of conglomerate ownership in advertising and in book publishing led to layoffs at many firms in these industries as well. While the movements to combat discrimination against women and minorities and to promote social and economic equality won numerous victories, they could not overcome the overall limits imposed by the course of capitalist development, even in those creative endeavors that were frequently imagined to be beyond the realm of necessity.[109]

Epilogue

NEW YORK'S CULTURE INDUSTRIES
IN THE TWILIGHT OF FORDISM

AMERICANS TRIED THEIR best to be enthusiastic about the nation's bicentennial, but many found little reason to celebrate. The United States was still suffering the effects of its most severe economic recession in nearly forty years, one that had been triggered in large part by the global oil shock of 1973–1974. The supply shortages and price spikes that followed the embargo imposed by the Organization of Petroleum Exporting Countries revealed the real constraints on postwar abundance, heralding the arrival of a new era of limits and the eclipse of the social vision promoted by thinkers like Galbraith and Bell. Americans who conflated automobility with personal liberty suddenly encountered epic lines at the gas pump.[1] President Nixon's resignation in August 1974, and the collapse of American-backed regimes in South Vietnam, Cambodia, and Laos the following spring only added to the impression among much of the public that the nation had slid into an epoch of decline. The affluent confidence that had inspired *Life* magazine's inquiry regarding America's purpose in 1960 was hard to find by 1976.

The unprecedented coincidence of unemployment and inflation focused the attention of most Americans on immediate material concerns that affected them personally, such as the staffing level at their workplace, the price of a pound of ground chuck at the grocery store, or their ability to make their monthly mortgage payment on time. In sum, these microeconomic pressures constituted a macroeconomic inflection point for the United States. The long, slow trend toward a more equal distribution of income and wealth sputtered to a halt during the middle of the 1970s. By the decade's end, the economy had started along a different trajectory characterized by increasing levels of inequality, as the share of national income accruing to the top 1 percent of earners surged from less than 10 percent in the mid-1970s to more than 20 percent four decades later.[2] In addition, the annual rate of growth in real gross domestic product per capita, which had averaged 2.4 percent between 1947 and 1973, declined significantly, only averaging a little more than 1.5 percent from 1979 through 2016.[3] The economic basis of the mass consuming public that America's culture industries had summoned into being through decades worth of advertisements, newspapers and magazines, product and packaging design, and radio and television programming gradually started to disintegrate. Even as myriad technological innovations, the deregulation of the telecommunication and mass media, and the diffusion of diverse lifestyles made it easier for advertisers and media enterprises to represent and target specialized market segments, the logic of the mass market became less compelling due to tectonic shifts in the composition of consumer demand.[4] The Fordist era, in which comparatively high wages enabled workers to purchase growing quantities of mass-produced, mass-marketed consumer goods, had drawn to a close.

For New York City, the economic restructuring was brutal. Although its industrial base had not been oriented toward the kinds of mass-production activities that typified Fordism, manufacturing, distribution, and transportation nonetheless accounted for a formidable share of the city's employment in the postwar years. Despite considerable wage restraint by many of the city's unions, the steady loss of employment in these sectors accelerated during the 1960s and 1970s. Between 1969 and 1976, fully 650,000 jobs vanished in the city, with half of the losses occurring in manufacturing.[5] Meanwhile, suburban development, subsidized by the federal government, lured white middle-class families and corporate headquarters out of New York City, weakening the municipal tax base. As it struggled to provide public services, particularly for a growing population of disadvantaged minorities who suffered discrimination in housing, education, and employment, the municipal government increasingly relied upon short-term debt. When major banks refused to continue underwriting the city's bonds in 1975, it precipitated a catastrophic fiscal crisis. Pleas for federal assistance were initially rebuffed, as the *Daily News* dramatically conveyed in its "Ford to City—Drop Dead" headline of October 30. With New York City teetering on the brink of bankruptcy, its creditors insisted on harsh austerity measures, forcing the city to slash its payroll and drastically curtail services.[6] The cuts only exacerbated the effects of the nationwide recession, pushing up unemployment in the city's poor and working-class neighborhoods to Depression-era levels. Factory lofts, warehouses, and docks stood empty, while 30,000 units of housing in the city were destroyed annually through arson and abandonment.[7]

Many viewed New York's decline as laden with symbolic meanings about the state of American politics and culture in the 1970s. For an emerging co-terie of neoconservative intellectuals, the city's woes furnished an object lesson on the profligate folly of Great Society liberalism, a view expressed with particular potency by the neoconservative intellectual Midge Decter in her essay on "Looting and Liberal Racism" following the July 1977 electrical blackout.[8] When President Jimmy Carter visited the rubble-strewn lots of the South Bronx several months later, he invoked his postapocalyptic backdrop not to tout a new round of federal aid to rebuild America's suffering cities, but largely to reiterate Decter's central point: the character deficiencies of inner-city residents, rather than structural economic and social forces, were the leading causes of urban decay.[9] Three years later, presidential candidate Ronald Reagan also visited the South Bronx, not only as a way of driving home his rival's inability to resolve the crisis of America's cities through mere moralizing, but also as a way of reinforcing the federal government's retreat from the cities. To Reagan, government intervention—in the form of social welfare programs, not the massive public subsidies and other inducements for suburbanization and white flight—had somehow produced the devasta-tion of the South Bronx and other ravaged inner-city areas. His election in 1980 only accelerated the withdrawal of federal support for the cities, and for disadvantaged Americans more generally. These moves, along with the Reagan administration's tax cuts for the wealthy and its punitive treatment of organized labor, propelled the nation on its course toward greater economic inequality.

The transition from Fordism to a post-Fordist political economy predicated upon an increasingly bifurcated distribution of income and wealth, which proved so wrenching for New York as a whole, also had a dis-ruptive impact on the city's culture industries and their workers. *The Saturday Evening Post*, *Look*, and *Life*—three magazines that had done so much to de-fine the American mass consumer market at mid-century—succumbed to the constantly increasing importance of television, the increased costs of printing and distribution, and the diminished desirability of a readership largely attracted by steep promotional discounts. The network television oligopoly of NBC, CBS, and ABC supplanted general-interest magazines as the essen-tial advertising medium that defined the mass market, but network executives continued to procure most of their primetime entertainment programming from producers based on the West Coast, limiting employment opportunities within New York. Overall employment levels remained stable in the city's advertising industry in the wake of the creative revolution of the 1960s, and while advertising remained a lucrative pursuit, it also continued to be a volatile business, with high rates of personnel turnover, attrition, and burnout. Contraction within the city's daily newspaper industry failed to resolve its long-term structural problems, jeopardizing the employment prospects of its remaining workforce.

During the 1970s and 1980s, however, additional new developments accentuated the precarity of labor in the city's culture industries. The most important of these changes stemmed from the "financialization" of global capitalism, which originated in the proliferation of conglomerate forms of corporate ownership, and subsequently accelerated in response to the inflation and instability of the 1970s.[10] Firms in the culture industries, such as advertising agencies and book publishers, became attractive targets for acquisition, while the shortening of investors' time horizons magnified the pressure on the executives of these cultural subsidiaries to increase profits. The restructuring of firms acquired by conglomerates often resulted in significant layoffs, particularly among clerical and support personnel, while executive ranks swelled with individuals who had financial and accounting expertise, or who had managed other corporate divisions, but who often lacked practical experience as creative talent engaged in the production of cultural content. When new owners and managers came from within an industry, the impact on workers tended to be the same, and even in firms that were not bought or sold, managers still had a heightened preoccupation with increasing productivity and cutting costs. Although the economic tumult within New York's culture industries sparked new organizing initiatives among their hard-pressed workers, a confluence of political and social factors in the 1970s and early 1980s precluded a repeat of the union advances of the 1930s and 1940s.[11]

And yet New York City still enjoyed unique forms of metropolitan privilege. Despite the loss of thousands of jobs in the television industry, the city remained the country's second most important site of production. Likewise, even with the contraction or outright failure of numerous newspapers and magazines, New York was still the nation's leading publishing center. Although numerous major corporate headquarters fled Manhattan during the period, some aspects of financialization generated new incentives to stay in the city. The increased dominance of finance devastated American manufacturing, and disrupted the culture industries that had developed in order to maintain consumer demand for manufactured goods, but New York's continued importance as a hub of global capitalism ensured that the city would be attractive for the types of firms and entrepreneurs engaged in producing cultural commodities for a new millennium.

Already by the late 1970s, when New York was still reeling from the most severe consequences of the fiscal crisis and deindustrialization, some commentators envisioned its resurgence. An article in the *New York Times Sunday Magazine* in January 1979, for example, proclaimed that the city was on the cusp of a momentous transformation into a magnet for affluent white-collar professionals who craved urban authenticity and excitement. "People often snicker when they first hear of it," it opined. "A renaissance in New York City? The rich moving in and the poor moving out? The mind boggles at the very notion." Nevertheless, the article insisted, "New York and other cities in the American Northeast are beginning to enjoy a revival as they undergo a gradual process known by the curious name of 'gentrification.'" With the fundamental shift in the metropolitan economy from "manufacturing goods to providing services and generating ideas," the "nature of the jobs the city has to offer are changing," and, consequently, "so is the population the city attracts." While it held out little promise for its displaced working class, and had diminishing appeal to the conventional middle class that had been fleeing to the suburbs, New York seemed "to be attracting a new professional upper class, an achievement-oriented gentry" that included "the best and the brightest" in fields such as law, international finance, advertising, communications, and publishing.[12]

From the vantage point of the early twenty-first century, the article might appear prophetic. Throughout the city, industrial and residential districts that experienced extensive disinvestment and abandonment during the 1970s have, decades later, been rejuvenated. Former manufacturing and warehouse lofts have been repurposed by new internet and digital media ventures that employ tens of thousands of persons engaged in creating the latest iterations of the culture of consumer capitalism. Discarded sites such as the Silvercup Bakery in Long Island City, or portions of the vast Brooklyn Navy Yard, have been converted into studios for film and television production. Throughout Brooklyn's brownstone belt, substantial three- and four-story townhouses that might have been purchased for less than $50,000 during the 1970s could sell in the 2010s for one hundred times their earlier market value. Led by the film and television industry and the emergent digital media, the New York metropolitan area could claim half of all job gains in the media sector in the entire United States between 2011 and 2014.[13] Although the renewed prosperity of the city's most intensively gentrified areas might seem to furnish prima facie evidence of the central role of affluent, educated urban professional and creative workers as catalysts of the city's transformation into a leading node of post-Fordist economic circulation and accumulation, it is imperative to resist the temptation of teleological interpretations and to focus instead on the pervasive uncertainty that affected New York's culture industries at this crucial moment in the twilight of Fordism.

While film and television production grew to provide over 100,000 annual full-time equivalent (FTE) positions in New York City by the mid-2010s, in the 1970s any predictions of a significant expansion in the city's television output would have seemed premature if not preposterous. The network news divisions, which essentially functioned as marketing loss leaders, remained firmly ensconced in New York. Yet even key variety and interview programs of the kind that had remained in the east, often airing during early fringe or late-night segments of network airtime, or as first-run syndicated programs, began to drift away by the 1970s. A similar decline was apparent in the production of daytime soaps, which had also remained a mainstay of New York television on account of the programs' compact space requirements, as well as their ability to utilize a pool of actors who also performed in Broadway theater or in the television commercials produced by the city's advertising agencies. Producer David Susskind, who throughout the postwar period had been one of the most dedicated boosters of East Coast television, remarked in 1977 that there was "an impetus, particularly at CBS, to do New York product—to get away from the uniformity, the plasticity, of California's shows. They all look alike. We've got eastern writers, and we're also finding West Coast writers and directors who want to come back to New York." But he also complained that the New York unions "involved in film are absolutely intransigent. They are implacable in work rules, in featherbedding. So for the same film pilot, it costs us, if you are very lucky and do good bargaining, 25 percent more at a *minimum* to shoot film in New York City." Another independent producer was blunt. "You know what a Teamster is? A Teamster is someone who knocks on your door at 2 a.m. and threatens you if you don't hire unnecessary people."[14]

Although the administration of Mayor Ed Koch began to take a more active role in attempting to lure television production back to New York, the paltry results of its initial efforts showed that the continued inadequacy of the city's limited studio facilities, rather than labor difficulties, was the major impediment. In 1981, the networks finally agreed to pick up two primetime situation comedies originating from New York, yet both were stymied from the outset. One of the series, carried by NBC, faced the prospect of sharing Studio 8H at Rockefeller Center with *Saturday Night Live*, one of the few network programs to commence production in the city during the previous decade. The new series' star, Tony Randall, observed that there was "a terrible shortage of space" in New York, unlike in the vast, integrated West Coast facilities in which "the crews, the commissaries, the print shop, the scenery docks, the prop shop are all in one place." An executive producer of the other new series, slated to air on CBS, readily conceded that "we're in a studio half the size we want and we're in it half the time we want." Looking forward, the Mayor's Office of Film, Theater, and Broadcasting and the unions hoped that several pending construction projects to build new studio space, along with the nascent demand for original programming by emerging cable broadcasters would provide a basis for future gains in production.[15]

Both of New York's 1981 sitcoms were cancelled after one season, but their brief presence, along with a flurry of made-for-television movies and miniseries, convinced public officials and property owners of the potential to expand production. In 1982, work began on two major projects in Queens: the reconstruction of Astoria Studios, another decrepit and underutilized remnant of the city's early twentieth century moviemaking past, and the conversion of the former Silvercup Bakery site. Sporadic use of the Astoria location during the late 1970s, despite its very dilapidated condition, made it the initial target for redevelopment. The financing arrangement for the first phase of reconstruction, which included two spacious sound stages and a support facility, encompassed $2 million in federal funding from an Urban Development Action Grant, another $2.5 million federal grant through the Economic Development Administration (EDA), a direct loan of $2,250,000 from the EDA, and $1,750,000 from the city's capital budget to enable acquisition of the site by its Public Development Corporation, which then leased it to its private operators. Real estate developer George Kaufman advanced the first private commitment of $2.5 million to the project, although once the initial financing was secure, additional investors, including director Sidney Lumet, writer Neil Simon, and television host Johnny Carson—whose own iconic late-night show had abandoned New York in 1972—contributed millions more to permit subsequent phases of expansion to proceed.[16] Silvercup's owners had purchased their three-block-long complex in 1980 with the intention of leasing its industrial loft spaces to manufacturing tenants, but after these plans fell through they discerned the possibility of repurposing the structure for film and television production. "Our decision to develop the building as a film and video center," one of the owners remarked, "is directly related to the momentum that has brought the production of film and television back to New York and the expansion of cable television." Here too, early financial support from the public sector was a catalyst for the first phase of the conversion project, which yielded ten new sound stages, as well as film and video editing and postproduction facilities.[17] Only in the mid-1980s, when New York-produced sitcoms like *Kate & Allie* and *The Cosby Show* became primetime network hits, did the city's television industry finally begin to turn a corner.

The tentative efforts to resuscitate New York television production furnished one measure of the uncertainty that characterized the city's culture industries in the twilight of Fordism; the effect that changes in ownership and managerial practices had on advertising and publishing provided another. While the market tumult of the 1970s and 1980s spurred a tremendous volume of mergers and acquisitions throughout the culture industries, as throughout the American economy generally, much of the commentary focused on the role of corporate conglomerates. Unlike the industrial corporations of the late nineteenth and early twentieth centuries that expanded by implementing strategies of horizontal or vertical integration, these conglomerates were diversified owners of disparate and functionally unrelated subsidiaries. These firms grew partly in response to the constraints that antitrust regulation imposed on traditional integrative strategies, partly as a way to counter the rise of industrial unionism, and partly as a way of spreading financial risk more generally, but they were defined primarily by their more intensive approach to capital accumulation. Conglomerate executives tended to administer their subsidiaries much as an individual investor might manage the securities in their portfolio to maximize returns. They looked to established operations that generated substantial revenues but had limited growth potential to serve as "cash cows" that could furnish capital for investment in emerging businesses with high potential for growth in revenues and profits. Although their methods primarily spurred disinvestment in old lines of manufacturing like steelmaking and meatpacking and redirected resources to defense, electronics, computing, and other advanced technology fields, these executives often saw firms in the culture industries as attractive acquisitions that had potential for increased revenue without long-term commitments to fixed capital investment in plant and equipment.

In few areas of cultural production was the entry of conglomerates more conspicuously disruptive than in book publishing. Except for a handful of large publishers like Doubleday and Macmillan, until the 1960s most houses were relatively small firms, often structured as proprietary partnerships, with fewer than 150 employees. Run by men who envisioned themselves as genteel stewards of American literary quality and taste, book publishers' staid business practices generated steady but modest profits. The first major conglomerate acquisition came in 1966, when RCA, the vertically integrated manufacturer of television sets and owner of NBC, purchased Random House and its various imprints. The pace of conglomerate-led restructuring in the industry quickened during the 1970s, transforming virtually every aspect of book publishing, even for firms that were not bought out. First and foremost, conglomerates inculcated a more abstract way of thinking about books that diminished the specificity of writing and the printed word and instead emphasized their circulation as cultural commodities. Richard Snyder, who became president of Simon and Schuster following its purchase by former auto parts maker Gulf and Western, which also owned Paramount Pictures, succinctly articulated the new mindset when he remarked in 1978 that books were just "the software of the television and movie media."[18] In practice, this meant that publishers internalized the logic of financialization, resulting in a dramatic surge in the advances offered to best-selling authors, as firms competed for the next blockbuster title, while the bulk of authors experienced advances that were cut or eliminated altogether, reduced promotional support, and curtailed distribution. The intensified focus on profitability also introduced a heightened degree of career insecurity into publishing. "Now you have a situation where you have valuable editors who are working in an atmosphere of fear and anxiety and who have been turned to marking up profitable production records instead of spending their time looking for literary excellence," noted one publishing insider. "When I started in publishing, during the sixties," she continued, "the advertising business had that reputation, but now the kind of anxiety we used to associate with advertising has permeated the publishing business itself."[19]

Resistance by authors actually helped to scuttle conglomerate acquisitions of publishers in several cases. In 1978, protests led by Archibald MacLeish, John Kenneth Galbraith, and other authors published by Boston-based Houghton Mifflin staved off its purchase by a railroad holding company, while the following year objections by the Authors Guild to the proposed acquisition of McGraw-Hill by American Express contributed to the cancelation of the financial services company's hostile takeover attempt.[20] Smoldering discontent over the declining terms and conditions for most authors in the conglomerate era led to a series of organizing conferences that culminated in the chartering in 1983 of the National Writers Union (NWU), which counted Galbraith, Norman Mailer, E. L. Doctorow, Susan Brownmiller, and Alice Walker among its early members and supporters. District 65 provided initial backing for the endeavor, which dovetailed with its organizing efforts among publishing employees, but ultimately the NWU proved unable to gain for book authors the bargaining clout that the Writers Guild of America secured for television writers.[21]

In the advertising industry, the rising tide of mergers and acquisitions added yet another source of volatility and workplace insecurity. The trend toward public stock offerings that commenced during the creative revolution forced agency executives to worry both about pleasing fickle clients and maintaining share price. When stock performance failed to meet expectations, these publicly traded firms became takeover targets, sometimes with deleterious consequences for agency operations. Between 1973 and 1978, more than 100 agency mergers occurred nationwide, as industry leaders bought smaller agencies, many of which had been regionally based firms outside of New York. To boost profits, executives attempted to cap salaries, so that payrolls, measured as a percentage of agencies' gross revenues, steadily declined over the course of the decade, even in years in which gross revenues and net profits grew handsomely; by 1979, the percentage had reached its lowest level since the late 1920s.[22] In the 1980s, a new wave of acquisitions by firms from outside the conventional domain of American advertising brought further tumult. In some instances, the new owners were media firms, as when Lorimar, a producer of television programming for networks and syndication, purchased the Kenyon and Eckhart agency in 1983.[23] Far more disruptive were the British firms that moved aggressively into the American market in the middle of the decade as the leveraged buyout frenzy reached its peak. The brash Saatchi and Saatchi agency, known for its campaign ads for Margaret Thatcher and her Conservative party in their victorious 1979 election campaign, acquired a slew of American firms, culminating in the purchase of Ted Bates Worldwide in 1986 in a deal worth more than $450 million.[24] Another group of British investors, led by Martin Sorrell, purchased the Wire and Plastic Products Company (WPP), a firm that had manufactured shopping baskets and grocery carts. They issued new securities to raise capital and transformed it into a communications conglomerate that in 1987 successfully executed a takeover of the venerable J. Walter Thompson Group.[25] The client conflicts that resulted from these consolidations, along with a sense that many of the acquired agencies were providing lackluster service, led to a wave of account terminations that triggered more than 4,000 layoffs in New York advertising during the second half of the decade. As executives obsessed over the financial machinations that undergirded the merger mania, commentators lamented that advertising had lapsed into a creative torpor not seen since the 1950s.[26]

In the newspaper and magazine publishing industries, which already faced long-term structural problems, ownership changes compounded the pressures workers faced. Rupert Murdoch's arrival into the New York media market was perhaps the most unsettling development. Murdoch first purchased *New York* magazine and the *Village Voice* alternative weekly, which spurred its staff to organize with District 65, but his major coup came late in 1976 when he bought the *New York Post* from Dorothy Schiff for $31 million. What had been a pillar of the city's postwar liberalism quickly became a vehicle for advancing a hard-nosed view of the urban crisis, providing important backing for Ed Koch's successful run for mayor. While Murdoch brought a conservative slant to the *Post*'s editorial page, he also introduced a harsher working climate to the newsroom.[27] In addition to his targeted firings of Newspaper Guild activists, he attempted to intimidate unionists during contract negotiations by showing that he could operate successfully without any of them. On a weekend in April 1978 when the paper's building would normally be dormant, Murdoch flew in a skeleton crew of journalists and editors from his nonunion media properties outside the city and had them produce the content for a dummy issue as armed guards prevented any regular employees from setting foot on the premises.[28] The exercise marked a sharp departure from four decades of labor relations in the city's newspaper industry. Although relations had grown increasingly contentious, no employer had yet threatened to eliminate an established union.

The meager results of a renewed wave of organizing by the Newspaper Guild at Time Inc. also illustrated the obstacles that unionists encountered in the tougher economic environment. Following the layoffs and reassignments that accompanied the termination of *Life*, activists found it much easier to recruit new members. Employees whose positions were secure nonetheless felt aggrieved by the company's increasingly stingy approach to salaries as it marshaled its resources for various initiatives, including the launch of *People* and *Money* magazines, the expansion of its fledgling cable television subsidiaries, and diversification into several real estate ventures. For the first time since the 1950s, a sizeable majority of the workforce belonged to the union; as the Guild approached contract negotiations in 1976, fully 63 percent of the roughly 1,000 employees remaining within the bargaining unit were dues-paying members in good standing. In addition to their standard request for an agency shop and a substantial increase in the cut-off, then $22,000 annually, above which employees were exempt from any general salary increases, the union negotiators also demanded a more robust equal opportunity program for women and minorities and a halt to the company's plan to relocate its Time-Life Books division to Alexandria, Virginia. Management's counterproposal included an actual reduction of the salary cut-off, an expansion of discretionary merit pay, and a paltry general increase that lagged behind the rampant pace of price inflation. When the company refused to budge, Guild supporters struck the publisher on June 2.[29] Whereas an earlier generation of activists had ultimately backed down in their crucial showdowns with Time management in the 1940s, these unionists pressed forward with the first work stoppage in the company's history.

Their defiance had little impact on management's stance. It soon became apparent that as many Guild members in the 1940s had feared, the strikers could not prevent the company from publishing. On June 4, management announced that *Time* magazine would make its first weekly closing, as managers and workers who stayed on the job toiled around the clock to prepare content for the printers. The magazine issues produced during the dispute were skimpy and rough-hewn, but they nonetheless still appeared on newsstands and in subscribers' mailboxes. Furthermore, as with many of the labor struggles of the 1970s, the clerks, secretaries, researchers, writers, photographers, illustrators, and editors who struck Time Inc. waged their battle largely in isolation. Unlike their earlier counterparts, they were not integrated into a broad social movement that could mobilize other workers in solidarity, or link their efforts to improve working conditions within the culture industries to efforts to reform the culture of consumer capitalism, or promote the public provisioning of goods and services. CLUW furnished valuable backing for the strike, but the leadership of the Newspaper Guild of New York did little to coordinate support from even its own members, while the rest of the city's labor movement was overwhelmed by the collapse of manufacturing employment and the assault on public-sector unionism that accompanied the fiscal crisis. On June 21, the strikers voted overwhelmingly to accept a contract settlement with Time Inc. that was only marginally better than the one they had previously rejected. The company pushed ahead with the relocation of Time-Life Books, which included many of the unit's most committed activists, and it expanded the use of merit pay based on capricious judgments by supervisors, which undermined some of the most basic forms of job and income security that the Guild had established at Time decades earlier.[30] For those who had walked off the job, and to workers throughout the city's culture industries who might have looked to them for inspiration, the outcome was demoralizing.

Even as the economic squeeze and the spirit of the new social movements continued to make many workers receptive to unionism, the Newspaper Guild often proved unable to convert that interest into successful organizing drives and membership growth. At the *New Yorker* magazine, for example, where a Guild drive in the 1940s had fizzled, management's austerity in the wake of slack revenues and rising production costs spurred a number of the editorial staff to form a new organizing committee in 1976. Although they contemplated reaching out to District 65, they turned to the Guild for guidance as the nucleus of union enthusiasts began to expand. By October a majority of the staff had signed union authorization cards and the Guild informed the magazine's management that it was seeking to represent its workers for purposes of collective bargaining. *New Yorker* editor William Shawn at first tried to moderate his opposition to unionization in his public statements; like countless other employers in the culture industries stretching back to the early twentieth century, he maintained that the interposition of an outside party to negotiate a binding contract would destroy the magazine's unique collegial environment and throttle creativity. Privately he subjected members of the organizing committee to intense pressure and, more ominously, hired the anti-union Proskauer Rose law firm. Once it became clear to the Guild's full-time paid organizers that the union would have to commit significant resources to help the magazine's employees overcome Shawn's resistance, the Guild backed away from the drive. Adrift, the organizing committee accepted an advisory role, but its members soon found that Shawn was unwilling to accede to their requests for improvements in pay and benefits, or to the introduction of a transparent process for promotions and other personnel actions. The opportunity to unionize the *New Yorker* melted away, as did numerous similar organizing possibilities involving employees of other media firms during the 1970s and early 1980s.[31]

Frustration with the Newspaper Guild of New York's failure to tap into the simmering workplace discontent throughout the city's culture industries contributed to the insurgent victory by Betsy Wade and her Responsibility Slate in the union's December 1978 elections. Although they grasped the union's urgent need to appeal to a younger and more diverse group of workers as well as to expand its membership within magazines, book publishers, and other media ventures, Wade and her supporters encountered numerous impediments. The recent strikes against the *New York Times*, the *Daily News*, and the *Post* drained more than $2 million from the international union's strike fund. Saddled with debt to the international, the New York local was forced to boost its already high dues and assessments without being able to deploy these funds to new organizing drives. In several instances, promising organizing opportunities faded when workers realized that Guild dues and assessments would account for almost 2.5 percent of their gross earnings if they joined. These costs also sparked resignations from existing units, a problem that became more serious in the wake of the Supreme Court's 1978 ruling in favor of conservative pundit William F. Buckley Jr., who had sued AFTRA to escape its union security provisions.[32] The obstinacy of the union's ensconced paid staff was perhaps a greater problem. Most were products of the old regime, and many of them did not share Wade's commitment to expanding beyond the embattled daily newspaper industry, protecting smaller units under attack, and using the union's resources to advance the cause of equal employment opportunity for women and minorities.[33] Some of the older white male members in the newspaper units resented Wade's staunch backing of class action litigation against their employers over race- and gender-based discrimination in hiring, pay, and promotions, particularly when they felt that the affirmative remedies ordered by the courts adversely affected their own employment prospects.[34] Finally, the continued financial woes of major employers within the Guild's jurisdiction undercut the progressive reformers. While the *Times'* long-term strategy of solidifying its role as the paper-of-record for a national readership had ensured its profitability for the time being, the head-to-head competition between the *News* and the *Post* resulted in heavy losses for their owners. In 1982, the Tribune Company announced that it might sell or close the *News* if it could not reduce the flow of red ink, precipitating buyouts for 160 Guild members at the paper to help stabilize the situation.[35]

At the same time that Wade and her allies were burdened by the past—the sclerosis of the Guild's previous regime, its inadequate approach to organizing, the overall weakening of the labor movement, and the print media's structural difficulties—they also faced new technological developments. The widespread introduction of video display terminals, for instance, as mainframe-based applications for word processing and other office tasks proliferated, raised occupational health concerns among many Guild members.[36] While improvements in screens, keyboards, and software have lessened the physical toll of utilizing new digital technologies to create cultural content, the union's engagement with these occupational health issues nonetheless foreshadowed a future in which desktop computers, laptops, smartphones, tablets, and other devices came to be completely incorporated into almost every material aspect of performing creative labor. During Wade's tenure, the Guild's members also had their initial encounter with the electronic distribution of their creativity, as they confronted an early partnership between the *New York Times* and CompuServe, a first-generation internet service provider utilizing dial-up modem connections over legacy telephone lines. As she described it in early 1981, the arrangement was "still in the R&D stage," with the *Times* and its collaborator "moving mostly material from news service and special features, a separate division that buys material from non–*Times* writers, freelancers, etc." The system "puts on 110–20 stories a time" which were "edited (by either regular desks and then news service editors) and then further cut for CompuServe." Not all types of content were disseminated equally: "all movie and theater reviews" were "used, uncut," and were " 'permanent' " to the database of articles, while other items were designated as " 'transient,' " although the eventual goal was to make the full text of the entire newspaper available. Subscribers paid $5 an hour after 6:00 p.m. for access to the day's updated set of articles, a steep price that undoubtedly limited the market for the service even within the still small pool of American households with personal computers and modems. To demonstrate the service, Wade arranged for a computer to be connected to the phone lines at the union's headquarters "so we can let it run for an hour or so and see what's moving on it" and also gauge the reactions of members "watching their electronic byproduct."[37] As rudimentary as this online news service was, it nonetheless represented the dawn of a digital future in which new systems for content distribution, new mechanisms for content aggregation, and even new forms of artificial intelligence have been utilized to devalue content and to make it increasingly difficult for journalists, as well as other culture workers, to be adequately remunerated for their creativity.

Wade's caucus within the New York Guild was ultimately foiled in its efforts to revitalize the union. Her opponents challenged her narrow reelection as local president in December 1980, filing complaints with the US Department of Labor. After a lengthy investigation of the balloting, in May 1982 the government ordered a rerun of the election. In the interim, the local was paralyzed as it had not been since the late 1940s, when Cold War liberals ousted Popular Front supporters from its leadership. As the internal strife thwarted its ability to respond to pressing issues, backing for Wade began to erode.[38] Recognizing that she had become a politically polarizing figure within the Guild, she declined to stand in a September 1982 special election for new union officers. Instead, her supporters, organized as the Membership Slate, nominated *Times* foreign desk copyeditor Don Bacheller as their candidate for local president, *Post* reporter and copyeditor Joy Cook for first vice president, *Amsterdam News* columnist and editorial cartoonist Mel Tapley for second vice president, and *People* computerized typesetter Key Martin for third vice president. Their campaign literature highlighted their involvement with civil rights, feminist, and peace movements, their engagement with the struggle for reform within the Guild, and their hopes for a progressive and expansive future for the union. Likening the old guard that had ruled until 1978 to "one-party states from Poland to Mississippi," they insisted that "affirmative action for women and minorities must be a priority, in our jobs, and in our union leadership" and emphasized the imperative to "organize the unorganized in our industry," starting "with our greatest untapped resource: our open shops." Additionally, they held that "workers must get their share of the dramatic improvements flowing from technological change" and pledged that as "technology blurs the distinctions" among occupations "we must renew the Guild's commitment to arrive at one industrial union for the entire newspaper, magazine, and electronic information industry."[39]

Despite the Membership Slate's efforts, they lost the special election by a slender margin, effectively ending any possibility in the near term that the New York Guild might reestablish itself as a force within the city's media capable of mobilizing large swaths of its creative class. In the years following their defeat, the local stagnated, failing not only to organize new groups of workers in the magazine, book publishing, or nascent digital media sectors, but even to defend its core jurisdiction in the daily newspaper industry. The Guild did persevere in a long and bitter strike against the *Daily News* in 1990–1991 as the Tribune Company divested itself of the money-losing tabloid, only to face ultimate defeat two years later when real-estate developer Mort Zuckerman acquired the bankrupt paper. Taking advantage of its lapsed contract with the Guild, Zuckerman fired more than 170 of the paper's 540 remaining Guild members and unilaterally terminated collective bargaining with its white-collar workforce.[40] Rupert Murdoch, who had sold the *New York Post* in the late 1980s to comply with FCC regulations against media concentration when he purchased New York Channel 5 for his planned Fox television network, acquired the bankrupt tabloid for a second time in 1993; following a poorly strategized strike by the Guild, Murdoch locked out the union, carrying through on the threat he had made fifteen years earlier and operating the paper with a newsroom full of permanent replacements.[41] By the turn of the new millennium, the Guild was a shell of what it once had been, with its future organizing revival of the 2010s and early 2020s still far over the horizon.[42]

Despite the waning fortunes of the Newspaper Guild of New York during the late twentieth century, the values and aspirations that have motivated its ardent supporters, as well as other pro-union culture workers, are as important as ever. While the Fordist political economy that drove the initial development of the American creative class has given way to more flexible relations of production and exchange, the need remains for collective solutions to improve the terms and conditions of labor in the culture industries, to maintain workplace autonomy, and to affirm diversity and equal opportunity. The economic contingency and precarity that increasingly characterize the making of our culture mirror the far more extensive, and more exploitative, forms of contingency and precarity prevalent for workers throughout our world in the early twenty-first century.[43] The political and social logic of the Popular Front of the mid-twentieth century—if not necessarily all of its specific tactics, institutional structures, or ideological precepts—may yet provide a guide for culture workers to become more effective allies with other workers throughout the economy. Contemporary concerns about the state of the media and popular culture likewise point to the continuing significance of the linkage between the labor relations of cultural production and the actual characteristics of cultural content, even when that content now includes podcasts, blog posts, emails, tweets, text messages, and video clips filmed by random participant-observers on their smartphones. People who believe that democratic control over the production and distribution of news and information is crucial for preserving genuine political democracy—let alone advancing a progressive agenda that includes a radical response to the climate emergency, universal healthcare, free public higher education, new public housing programs, and the public or nonprofit provisioning of other goods or services—can look to the alternative media and cultural endeavors of the Popular Front era for inspiration as well as cautionary lessons.

This book traces long-term developments in the political economy, cultural production, and labor relations of the twentieth-century United States, but beneath these abstractions it is fundamentally a collection of personal stories. Myra Jordan's leading role in organizing her coworkers at the New York headquarters of the CBS network during the 1940s is relevant not because her experience was unique, but because it was commonplace in the city's culture industries at the time. Figures as varied as Susan Jenkins, Heywood Broun, Morris Watson, Jane Benedict, James Rorty, Mildred Edie, George Seldes, William Friedman, Don Wallance, Elizabeth McCausland, Anna Goldsborough, John McManus, Norma Aronson, Faith Illiva, Peter Lyon, and Arnold Perl—just to name a few—used their creative and organizational talents to try to bring about fairer workplaces, a more democratic culture, and a more just society. Their actions and commitments serve as instructive examples for those today, in our era of inequality, who seek to restore democratic and egalitarian values.

Appendix

Table 1 Major Occupational Categories in the United States, 1880 and 1900[1]

| | Numbers of persons and percentages of the total paid labor force | | | |
| | 1880 | | 1900 | |
Occupational Category	N	%	N	%
Proprietors	553,492	3.4	1,039,661	3.8
Managers and Officials	269,291	1.6	591,941	2.1
Professionals	584,940	3.5	1,126,205	4.1
Clerical Workers	263,931	1.6	1,054,110	3.8
Sales Workers	436,293	2.6	1,000,987	3.6
Craft Workers	1,703,847	10.3	3,141,081	11.4
Semiskilled Operatives	2,273,682	13.8	3,824,089	13.9
Nonagricultural Laborers	1,980,787	12.0	3,503,834	12.7
Farmers	4,490,111	27.2	5,824,546	21.1
Agricultural Laborers	2,554,056	15.5	3,465,130	12.6
Domestic Workers	1,094,249	6.6	2,105,943	7.6
Service Workers	274,238	1.7	876,528	3.2
TOTAL	16,478,917		27,554,086	

[1]*Source*: Matthew Sobek, "New Statistics on the U.S. Labor Force, 1850–1990," *Historical Methods* 34, no. 2 (Spring 2001): 71–87; and Sobek, Table Ba1033-1046, in *Historical Statistics of the United States, Earliest Times to the Present, Millennial Edition: Volume Two, Part B: Work and Welfare*, ed. Susan B. Carter, Scott Sigmund Carter, Michael R. Haines, Alan L. Olmstead, Richard Sutch, and Gavin Wright (New York: Cambridge University Press, 2006), 2/133.

Table 2 Major Occupational Categories in the United States, 1920 and 1940[1]

| | Numbers of persons and percentages of the total paid labor force | | | |
| | 1920 | | 1940 | |
	N	%	N	%
Occupational Category				
Proprietors	1,586,186	3.4	2,029,575	4.3
Managers and Officials	1,121,201	2.8	1,784,823	3.7
Professionals	2,261,078	5.6	3,398,320	7.1
Clerical Workers	3,263,382	8.1	4,927,067	10.4
Sales Workers	2,001,550	5.0	2,968,019	6.2
Craft Workers	5,681,921	14.2	5,476,776	11.5
Semiskilled Operatives	6,352,824	15.8	8,586,887	18.0
Nonagricultural Laborers	4,607,487	11.5	4,373,802	9.2
Farmers	6,569,911	16.4	5,216,903	11.0
Agricultural Laborers	3,398,866	8.5	3,003,540	6.3
Domestic Workers	1,490,405	3.7	2,113,392	4.4
Service Workers	1,778,456	4.4	3,377,546	7.1
Unclassified	0		363,588	0.8
TOTAL	40,113,274		47,584,238	

[1]*Source*: Sobek, "New Statistics on the U.S. Labor Force, 1850–1990," 71–87; and Sobek, Table Ba1033-1046, in *Historical Statistics of the United States, Earliest Times to the Present, Millennial Edition*, ed. Carter et al., 2/133.

Table 3 Gender Distribution Within Selected Professional and Clerical Occupations, 1900[1]

	Numbers of persons and percentages of each occupation		
	N	% Male	% Female
Occupation			
Engineers (all types)	30,400	100.0	0.0
Physicians	131,300	97.7	2.3
Editors and Reporters	28,800	92.40	7.6
Photographers	25,800	91.1	8.9
Architects	6,100	100.0	0.0
Artists and Art Teachers	22,800	66.7	33.3
Teachers (except art and music)	409,000	24.7	75.3
Nurses (professional)	9,900	0.0	100.0
Shipping and Receiving Clerks	28,100	97.2	2.8
Bookkeepers	239,100	79.0	21.0
Office Machine Operators	800	n/a	n/a
Secretaries, Stenographers, and Typists	100,200	29.5	70.5
Telephone Operators	22,000	10.5	89.5

[1] *Source*: Sobek, Tables Ba1159-1395, Ba1440-1676, Ba1721-1957, in *Historical Statistics of the United States, Earliest Times to the Present, Millennial Edition*, ed. Carter et al., , 2/142–2/149, 2/152–2/159, 2/162–2/169.

Table 4 Gender Distribution Within Selected Professional and Clerical Occupations, 1920[1]

	Numbers of persons and percentages of each occupation		
	N	% Male	% Female
Occupation			
Engineers (all types)	146,400	n/a	n/a
Physicians	135,300	99.3	0.7
Editors and Reporters	34,200	86.5	13.5
Photographers	27,700	86.3	13.7
Architects	15,500	n/a	n/a
Artists and Art Teachers	33,800	61.2	38.8
Teachers (except art and music)	736,600	16.6	83.4
Social and Welfare Workers	12,600	27.0	73.0
Nurses (professional)	114,300	3.6	96.4
Shipping and Receiving Clerks	126,000	94.5	5.5
Bookkeepers	524,500	47.0	53.0
Office Machine Operators	15,400	10.4	89.6
Secretaries, Stenographers, and Typists	660,300	11.9	88.1
Telephone Operators	187,900	5.4	94.6

[1]*Source*: Sobek, Tables Ba1159-1395, Ba1440-1676, Ba1721-1957, in *Historical Statistics of the United States, Earliest Times to the Present, Millennial Edition*, ed. Carter et al., , 2/142–2/149, 2/152–2/159, 2/162–2/169.

Table 5 Gender Distribution Within Selected Professional and Clerical Occupations, 1940[1]

	Numbers of persons and percentages of each occupation		
	N	% Male	% Female
Occupation			
Engineers (all types)	252,700	98.7	1.3
Physicians	172,300	95.5	4.5
Editors and Reporters	59,200	76.4	23.6
Photographers	34,900	90.8	9.2
Architects	19,000	98.4	1.6
Artists and Art Teachers	55,800	69.0	31.0
Teachers (except art and music)	1,056,100	25.1	74.9
Social and Welfare Workers	73,900	38.6	61.4
Nurses (professional)	327,300	3.6	96.4
Shipping and Receiving Clerks	226,300	92.9	7.1
Bookkeepers	867,700	48.4	51.6
Office Machine Operators	73,200	22.1	77.9
Secretaries, Stenographers, and Typists	1,109,700	6.9	93.1
Telephone Operators	197,400	6.5	93.5

[1]*Source*: Sobek, Tables Ba1159-1395, Ba1440-1676, Ba1721-1957, in *Historical Statistics of the United States, Earliest Times to the Present, Millennial Edition*, ed. Carter et al., , 2/142–2/149, 2/152–2/159, 2/162–2/169.

Table 6 Distribution of Major White-Collar Occupational Categories By Industrial Sector, 1920

	Numbers of workers			
	Clerical	Sales	Professional[2]	Management[3]
Industrial Sector				
Agriculture, Forestry, and Fisheries	3,700	0	22,900	2,800
Mining and Fossil Fuel Extraction	21,500	0	8,400	15,400
Construction	26,100	300	26,000	31,300
Durable Goods Manufacturing	405,400	1,200	84,600	100,700
Nondurable Goods Manufacturing[4]	373,900	1,300	49,200	111,400
Transportation	445,300	500	34,600	195,000
Telecommunications and Utilities	300,300	2,200	16,700	26,000
Wholesale Trade	144,600	344,500	8,100	90,600
Retail Trade	257,000	1,342,800	85,700	220,600
Finance, Insurance, and Real Estate	327,100	265,200	18,800	119,000
Legal Services	37,300	0	106,600	100
Accounting and Auditing Services	57,800	0	25,200	100
Engineering Services	5,600	200	53,300	200
Healthcare	32,400	100	344,200	5,100
Education	20,600	1,200	866,800[5]	2,800
Social Welfare, Religious, and Nonprofit Services	19,200	200	178,200	12,400
Public Sector	319,700	900	50,500	108,600

(*continued*)

Table 6 Continued

	Numbers of workers			
	Clerical	Sales	Professional[2]	Management[3]
Culture Industries[6]	90,800	28,900	195,400[7]	38,200
Other Services and Unclassified	375,100	12,100	85,900	40,900
TOTAL	3,263,400	2,001,600	2,261,100	1,121,200

[1]Calculations made by the author using US Census data samples from Steven Ruggles, J. Trent Alexander, Katie Genadek, Matthew B. Schroeder, and Matthew Sobek, *Integrated Public Use Microdata Series: Version 5.0 Machine-Readable Database* (Minneapolis: University of Minnesota Press, 2010).

[2]Figures for professionals do not include architects, artists, authors, designers, editors, and reporters except for Education and the Culture Industries (see notes e and g).

[3]Salaried managers and officials only. Does not include individuals classified as proprietors.

[4]Figures for Nondurable Manufacturing exclude all white-collar workers employed in Printing, Publishing, and Allied Trades.

[5]Figure for professional employees in Education includes all architects, artists, authors, designers, editors, and reporters specifically classified by the US Census as employed in this industrial sector.

[6]Figures for the Culture Industries include all white-collar workers classified by the US Census as employed in Printing, Publishing, and Allied Industries; Advertising; Radio Broadcasting; Theaters and Motion Pictures; and Miscellaneous Entertainment and Recreation Services.

[7]Figures for professional workers in the Culture Industries also include all additional architects, artists, authors, designers, editors, and reporters in the US labor force except for those employed in the Education category.

Table 7 Distribution of Major White-Collar Occupational Categories By Industrial Sector, 1940[1]

	Numbers of workers			
	Clerical	Sales	Professional[2]	Management[3]
Industrial Sector				
Agriculture, Forestry, and Fisheries	19,800	5,300	21,800	7,900
Mining and Fossil Fuel Extraction	34,400	3,300	18,100	16,300
Construction	100,400	7,800	68,000	36,100
Durable Goods Manufacturing	518,800	117,600	161,100	134,100
Nondurable Goods Manufacturing[4]	481,400	184,500	90,100	141,800
Transportation	333,400	11,000	26,800	134,000
Telecommunications and Utilities	353,400	16,500	48,200	50,800
Wholesale Trade	251,100	266,400	9,800	124,000
Retail Trade	554,300	1,788,900	117,200	444,000
Finance, Insurance, and Real Estate	546,300	347,600	21,400	205,300
Legal Services	n/a	n/a	126,700	n/a
Accounting and Auditing Services	n/a	n/a	n/a	n/a
Engineering Services	n/a	n/a	27,200	n/a
Healthcare	116,300	2,200	590,000	10,400
Education	131,300	4,000	1,224,800[5]	11,200
Social Welfare, Religious, and Nonprofit Services	48,600	2,400	195,300	29,800
Public Sector	682,100	5,700	187,400	246,300

(*continued*)

Table 7 Continued

	Numbers of workers			
	Clerical	Sales	Professional[2]	Management[3]
Culture Industries[6]	199,700	118,400	326,700[7]	69,000
Other Services and Unclassified	555,800	86,400	137,700	87,800
TOTAL	4,927,100	2,968,000	3,398,300	1,748,800

[1]Calculations made by the author using US Census data samples from Ruggles et al., *Integrated Public Use Microdata Series.*

[2]Figures for professionals do not include architects, artists, authors, designers, editors, and reporters except for Education and the Culture Industries (see notes e and g).

[3]Salaried managers and officials only. Does not include individuals classified as proprietors.

[4]Figures for Nondurable Manufacturing exclude all white-collar workers employed in Printing, Publishing, and Allied Trades.

[5]Figure for professional employees in Education includes all architects, artists, authors, designers, editors, and reporters specifically classified by the US Census as employed in this industrial sector.

[6]Figures for the Culture Industries include all white-collar workers classified by the US Census as employed in Printing, Publishing, and Allied Industries; Advertising; Radio Broadcasting; Theaters and Motion Pictures; and Miscellaneous Entertainment and Recreation Services.

[7]Figures for professional workers in the Culture Industries also include all additional architects, artists, authors, designers, editors, and reporters in the US labor force except for those employed in the Education category.

Table 8 Major Occupational Categories in the United States, 1950 and 1970[1]

	Numbers of persons and percentages of the total paid labor force			
	1950		1970	
	N	%	N	%
Occupational Category				
Proprietors	2,544,012	4.5	1,511,976	2.0
Managers and Officials	2,557,926	4.5	4,500,219	5.9
Professionals and Technicians	5,047,198	8.9	11,859,938	15.5
Clerical Workers	7,139,285	12.5	13,290,216	17.9
Sales Workers	3,979,498	7.0	5,520,037	7.2
Craft Workers	7,954,410	14.0	10,351,231	13.6
Semiskilled Operatives	11,489,205	20.2	13,601,511	17.8
Nonagricultural Laborers	3,540,518	6.2	3,347,564	4.4
Farmers	4,350,507	7.6	1,402,232	1.8
Agricultural Laborers	2,298,610	4.0	947,136	1.2
Domestic Workers	1,400,662	2.5	1,159,022	1.5
Service Workers	4,446,612	7.8	8,379,443	11.0
Unclassified	225,306	0.4	0	
TOTAL	56,973,749		76,270,515	

[1]*Source*: Sobek, "New Statistics on the U.S. Labor Force, 1850–1990," 71–87; and Sobek, Table Ba1033-1046, in *Historical Statistics of the United States, Earliest Times to the Present, Millennial Edition*, ed. Carter et al., 2/133.

Table 9 Major Occupational Categories in the United States, 1990[1]

	Numbers of persons and percentages of the total paid labor force	
	1990	
	N	%
Occupational Sector		
Proprietors	2,128,820	1.8
Managers and Officials	12,536,174	10.9
Professionals and Technicians	23,561,866	20.5
Clerical Workers	21,560,507	18.7
Sales Workers	7,870,883	6.8
Craft Workers	12,062,085	10.5
Semiskilled Operatives	13,373,392	11.6
Nonagricultural Laborers	4,948,573	4.3
Farmers	1,040,236	0.9
Agricultural Laborers	771,036	0.7
Domestic Workers	521,839	0.5
Service Workers	14,724,463	12.8
TOTAL	115,083,094	

[1]*Source*: Sobek, "New Statistics on the U.S. Labor Force, 1850–1990," 71–87; and Sobek, Table Ba1033-1046, in *Historical Statistics of the United States, Earliest Times to the Present, Millennial Edition*, ed. Carter et al., 2/133.

Table 10 Gender Distribution Within Selected Professional and Clerical Occupations, 1950[1]

	Numbers of persons and percentages of each occupation		
	N	% Male	% Female
Occupation			
Engineers (all types)	550,600	98.1	1.9
Physicians	197,500	94.1	5.9
Editors and Reporters	88,800	72.2	27.8
Photographers	54,100	82.1	17.9
Architects	25,200	98.0	2.0
Artists and Art Teachers	78,800	63.3	36.7
Teachers (except art and music)	1,152,500	25.5	74.5
Social and Welfare Workers	84,700	31.2	68.8
Nurses (professional)	404,600	2.3	97.7
Shipping and Receiving Clerks	293,600	94.0	6.0
Bookkeepers	749,400	22.8	77.2
Office Machine Operators	151,600	16.8	83.2
Secretaries, Stenographers, and Typists	1,630,000	5.3	94.7
Telephone Operators	380,100	7.4	92.6

[1]*Source*: Sobek, Tables Ba1159-1395, Ba1440-1676, Ba1721-1957, in *Historical Statistics of the United States, Earliest Times to the Present, Millennial Edition*, ed. Carter et al., 2/142–2/149, 2/152–2/159, 2/162–2/169.

Table 11 Gender Distribution Within Selected Professional and Clerical Occupations, 1970[1]

Occupation	Numbers of persons and percentages of each occupation		
	N	% Male	% Female
Engineers (all types)	1,210,600	98.4	1.6
Physicians	278,400	90.7	9.3
Editors and Reporters	221,200	63.9	36.1
Photographers	64,400	86.3	13.7
Architects	56,100	96.3	3.7
Artists and Art Teachers	100,800	63.9	36.1
Teachers (except art and music)	2,764,800	32.3	67.7
Social and Welfare Workers	217,900	36.9	63.1
Nurses (professional)	917,900	7.5	92.5
Shipping and Receiving Clerks	408,900	85.7	14.3
Bookkeepers	1,534,600	17.9	82.1
Office Machine Operators	549,200	26.4	73.6
Secretaries, Stenographers, and Typists	3,806,000	3.3	96.7
Telephone Operators	410,600	5.5	94.5

[1]*Source*: Sobek, Tables Ba1159-1395, Ba1440-1676, Ba1721-1957, in *Historical Statistics of the United States, Earliest Times to the Present, Millennial Edition*, ed. Carter et al., 2/142–2/149, 2/152–2/159, 2/162–2/169.

Table 12 Gender Distribution Within Selected Professional and Clerical Occupations, 1990[1]

| Occupation | Numbers of persons and percentages of each occupation | | |
	N	% Male	% Female
Engineers (all types)	1,972,800	87.6	12.4
Physicians	573,100	79.3	20.7
Editors and Reporters	421,900	45.9	54.1
Photographers	135,900	69.8	30.2
Architects	152,500	84.9	15.1
Artists and Art Teachers	203,300	47.1	52.9
Teachers (except art and music)	4,465,700	26.7	73.3
Social and Welfare Workers	641,400	30.9	69.1
Nurses (professional)	2,114,500	9.0	91.0
Shipping and Receiving Clerks	793,900	70.3	29.7
Bookkeepers	1,846,400	10.3	89.7
Office Machine Operators	1,378,200	27.4	72.6
Secretaries, Stenographers, and Typists	4,594,500	2.0	98.0
Telephone Operators	224,900	13.3	86.7

[1]*Source*: Sobek, Tables Ba1159-1395, Ba1440-1676, Ba1721-1957, in *Historical Statistics of the United States, Earliest Times to the Present, Millennial Edition*, ed. Carter et al., 2/142–2/149, 2/152–2/159, 2/162–2/169.

Table 13 White-Collar Labor Force in New York's Culture Industries, 1950, 1970, and 1980[1]

	Numbers of Persons		
	1950	1970	1980
Advertising:			
Management and Ownership	7,555	7,428	11,819
Professional and Technical	6,922	12,408	12,625
Sales	4,743	5,809	7,106
Clerical	13,612	13,725	13,693
TOTAL	32,822	39,370	45,243
Printing and Publishing:			
Management and Ownership	12,813	14,690	22,214
Professional and Technical	16,445	28,985	40,714
Sales (Nonretail)	5,140	10,078	10,511
Clerical	38,111	51,253	50,047
TOTAL	72,509	105,006	123,486
Broadcasting:			
Management and Ownership	2,099	3,630	6,468
Professional and Technical	6,322	9,306	9,689
Sales	181	937	576
Clerical	2,594	5,375	5,689
TOTAL	11,196	19,248	22,422

[1]Calculations by the author using data from Ruggles et al., *Integrated Public Use Microdata Series*. New York Metropolitan Area defined as New York, Kings, Queens, Bronx, Richmond, Westchester, Nassau, Suffolk, and Rockland Counties in New York State; Hudson, Bergen, Essex, Passaic, Morris, Union, and Somerset Counties in New Jersey; and Fairfield County in Connecticut.

Table 14 Distribution of Men and Women in the White-Collar Labor Force in New York's Culture Industries, 1970[1]

	Numbers of Persons	
	Men	Women
Advertising:		
Management and Ownership	5,850	1,580
Professionals and Technicians	9,650	2,760
Sales	4,760	1,050
Clerical	2,710	11,010
TOTAL	22,970	16,400
Printing and Publishing:		
Management and Ownership	12,940	1,750
Professionals and Technicians	15,640	13,350
Sales (Nonretail)	8,840	1,240
Clerical	12,980	38,270
TOTAL	50,400	54,610
Broadcasting:		
Management and Ownership	2,930	700
Professionals and Technicians	7,570	1,740
Sales	840	100
Clerical	1,550	3,830
TOTAL	12,890	6,370

[1]Calculations by the author using data from Ruggles et al., *Integrated Public Use Microdata Series*. Data based on household survey, not establishment survey. New York Metropolitan Area defined as New York, Kings, Queens, Bronx, Richmond, Westchester, Nassau, Suffolk, and Rockland Counties in New York State; Hudson, Bergen, Essex, Passaic, Morris, Union, and Somerset Counties in New Jersey; and Fairfield County in Connecticut.

Table 15 Distribution of Annual Salaries for Male and Female Clerical and Professional Employees in New York's Culture Industries and Throughout the Metropolitan Economy, 1970[1]

	Figures in 1970 Dollars			
	Male Clerical	Female Clerical	Male Professional	Female Professional
Advertising:				
Lower Quartile	$5,750	$4,975	$10,050	$7,350
Median	$8,050	$6,000	$15,050	$9,550
Upper Quartile	$11,950	$7,125	$19,050	$17,800
Printing and Publishing:				
Lower Quartile	$4,550	$4,050	$9,050	$5,100
Median	$7,350	$5,250	$12,050	$7,350
Upper Quartile	$11,700	$6,650	$17,050	$9,825
Broadcasting:				
Lower Quartile	$4,300	$5,550	$10,425	$7,675
Median	$6,650	$6,350	$15,050	$9,100
Upper Quartile	$11,100	$7,250	$19,300	$13,050
Entire New York Metropolitan Economy:				
Lower Quartile	$5,750	$4,250	$8,350	$5,050
Median	$7,750	$5,550	$11,550	$7,550
Upper Quartile	$9,750	$7,050	$15,450	$9,950

[1]Calculations by the author using data from Ruggles et al., *Integrated Public Use Microdata Series*. Data based on household survey, not establishment survey. New York Metropolitan Area defined as New York, Kings, Queens, Bronx, Richmond, Westchester, Nassau, Suffolk, and Rockland Counties in New York State; Hudson, Bergen, Essex, Passaic, Morris, Union, and Somerset Counties in New Jersey; and Fairfield County in Connecticut. All figures based on the salaries of persons who were at least 21 years of age and who worked a minimum of 30 hours per week. Figures for male and female professionals based on positions classified as Professional and Technical in the 1970 US Census.

Notes

MANUSCRIPT AND ARCHIVAL COLLECTIONS

AFAE 66   American Federation of Architectural Engineers Local 66 Records, Wagner Collection 9, Tamiment Institute Library/Robert F. Wagner Labor Archives, New York University Libraries, New York.

BW-NG   Betsy Wade Files on the Newspaper Guild of New York, Wagner Collection 45, Tamiment Institute Library/Robert F. Wagner Labor Archives, New York University Libraries, New York.

CIO-C   Congress of Industrial Organizations Central Office Records, American Catholic History Research Center and University Archives, Mullen Library, Catholic University of America, Washington, DC.

CIO-JLL   Congress of Industrial Organizations Files of John L. Lewis. University Publications of America, Frederick, MD.

CIO-ST   Congress of Industrial Organizations, Office of the Secretary-Treasurer Records, Archives of Labor and Urban Affairs, Walter P. Reuther Library, Wayne State University, Detroit.

CLA-CRF   Church League of America Collection, Series I: American Business Consultants, Inc. *Counterattack* Research Files, Tamiment Collection 148, Tamiment Institute Library/Robert F. Wagner Labor Archives, New York University Libraries, New York.

CM   Clarina Michelson Papers, Tamiment Collection 240, Tamiment Institute Library/Robert F. Wagner Labor Archives, New York University Libraries, New York.

CR   Consumers' Research Records, University Archives and Special Collections, Alexander Library, Rutgers University, New Brunswick, NJ.

CSL   Clara Savage Littledale Papers, Schlesinger Manuscript Library, Radcliffe Institute, Harvard University, Cambridge, MA.

District 65   United Automobile, Aircraft, and Vehicle Workers of America, District 65 Records, Wagner Collection 6, Tamiment Institute Library/Robert F. Wagner Labor Archives, New York University Libraries, New York.

DM   Donald Montgomery Papers, Archives of Labor and Urban Affairs, Walter P. Reuther Library, Wayne State University, Detroit.

DS   David Susskind Papers. Wisconsin Center for Film and Theater Research, Wisconsin Historical Society, Madison.

DW   Donald Wallance Collection, Henry and Doris Dreyfuss Research Library, Cooper-Hewitt National Design Museum, Smithsonian Institution, New York.

EM   Elizabeth McCausland Papers, Archives of American Art, Smithsonian Institution, Washington, DC.

FAP   Federal Art Project Records, Archives of American Art, Smithsonian Institution. The contents of this collection are extracted from the Records of the Works Progress Administration, Records Group 69, National Archives and Records Administration, College Park, MD.

FUD   Frances Ullmann DeArmand Papers, Schlesinger Manuscript Library, Radcliffe Institute, Harvard University, Cambridge, MA.

GNYIUC   Greater New York Industrial Union Council Minutes, Tamiment Institute Library/Robert F. Wagner Labor Archives, New York University Libraries, New York.

HC   Holger Cahill Papers, Archives of American Art, Smithsonian Institution, Washington, DC.

IRP   Irene Rice Pereira Papers, Archives of American Art, Smithsonian Institution, Washington, DC.

JBM   J. B. Matthews Collection, David M. Rubenstein Rare Book and Manuscript Library, Duke University, Durham, NC.

JWT-IC   J. Walter Thompson Company, Information Center Records, David M. Rubenstein Rare Book and Manuscript Library, Duke University, Durham, NC.

JWT-JD   J. Walter Thompson Company, John Devine Collection, David M. Rubenstein Rare Book and Manuscript Library, Duke University, Durham, NC.

JWT-NL   J. Walter Thompson Company, News Letter Collection, David M. Rubenstein Rare Book and Manuscript Library, Duke University, Durham, NC.

JWT-SM   J. Walter Thompson Company, Staff Meeting Minutes, David M. Rubenstein Rare Book and Manuscript Library, Duke University, Durham, NC.

JWT-TO   J. Walter Thompson Company, Treasurers' Office Records, David M. Rubenstein Rare Book and Manuscript Library, Duke University, Durham, NC.

LC	Lewis Corey Papers, Rare Books and Manuscripts Division, Butler Library, Columbia University, New York.
NA	Norma Aronson Papers, Tamiment Collection 209, Tamiment Institute Library/Robert F. Wagner Labor Archives, New York University Libraries, New York.
NGNY	Newspaper Guild of New York (American Newspaper Guild Local 3) Records, Wagner Collection 125, Tamiment Institute Library/ Robert F. Wagner Labor Archives, New York University Libraries, New York.
NLRB	National Labor Relations Board Records, Records Group 25, National Archives and Records Administration, College Park, MD.
NOW-NYC	National Organization for Women, New York City Chapter Records, Tamiment Collection 106, Tamiment Institute Library/Robert F. Wagner Labor Archives, New York University Libraries, New York.
OEIU 153	Office Employees International Union Local 153 Minutes, Tamiment Institute Library/Robert F. Wagner Labor Archives, New York University Libraries, New York.
PHJB	Peter K. Hawley and Jane Benedict Papers, Tamiment Collection 338, Tamiment Institute Library/Robert F. Wagner Labor Archives, New York University Libraries, New York.
RBSKL	Rabinowitz, Boudin, Standard, Krinsky, and Lieberman Legal Files, Tamiment Collection 287, Tamiment Institute Library/Robert F. Wagner Labor Archives, New York University Libraries, New York.
RK	Rockwell Kent Papers, Archives of American Art, Smithsonian Institution.
RWG	Radio Writers' Guild Records, Special Collections and Archives, Library of Performing Arts, New York Public Library, New York.
USA-829	United Scenic Artists Records, Wagner Collection 65, Tamiment Institute Library/Robert F. Wagner Labor Archives, New York University Libraries, New York.

PERIODICAL TITLES

Periodicals Used as Primary Sources

AA	*Advertising Age*
AF	*Art Front* (Artists' Union organ)
AmFed	*American Federationist* (AFL organ)
ArchFor	*Architectural Forum*
ArchRec	*Architectural Record*
A&D	*Arts and Decoration*
A&S	*Advertising and Selling*

BCAW	*Bulletin of the Congress of American Women* (including *Womanpower*)
BMoMA	*Bulletin of the Museum of Modern Art*
BW	*Business Week*
B&B	*Bread and Butter*
CION	*CIO News*
CRB	*Consumers' Research Bulletin*
CUR	*Consumers Union Reports* (*Consumer Reports* after 1942)
DE	*Designing Engineer* (Society of Designing Engineers organ)
DNLRB	*Decisions of the National Labor Relations Board*
E&P	*Editor and Publisher*
EAQ	*Everyday Art Quarterly*
GN	*Guild News* (BMG organ)
GR	*Guild Reporter* (ANG organ)
ID	*Industrial Design*
IF	*In Fact*
MA	*Madison Avenue*
MLR	*Monthly Labor Review*
NG	*National Guardian*
NM	*New Masses*
NR	*New Republic*
NYDN	*New York Daily News*
NYGN	*New York Guild News* (NGNY organ prior to *Frontpage*)
NYHT	*New York Herald Tribune*
NYmag	*New York (Magazine)*
NYP	*New York Post*
NYT	*New York Times*
NYW-T	*New York World-Telegram*
NYer	*The New Yorker*
OPN	*Office and Professional News*
OW(BS&AU)	*Office Worker* (BS&AU Local 12646 organ)
OW(OWU)	*Office Worker* (OWU organ)
ProgArch	*Progressive Architecture*
PI	*Printer's Ink*
PP	*Pencil Points*
PW	*Publishers' Weekly*
RS	*Reader's Scope*
SEP	*Saturday Evening Post*
SM	*Sales Management*
TA	*Technical America* (FAECT organ)
TT	*Tech Talk* (FAECT organ)
TW	*The TV Writer*

| WW | *Working Woman* (CPUSA organ) |
| WSJ | *Wall Street Journal* |

Secondary Literature—Scholarly Journals

AAAJ	*Archives of American Art Journal*
ACH	*American Communist History*
AHR	*American Historical Review*
AQ	*American Quarterly*
BHR	*Business History Review*
DI	*Design Issues*
FS	*Feminist Studies*
G&S	*Gender and Society*
HM	*Historical Methods*
ILRR	*Industrial Relations Research Review*
ILWCH	*International Labor and Working-Class History*
JAH	*Journal of American History*
JAS	*Journal of American Studies*
JDH	*Journal of Design History*
JEH	*Journal of Economic History*
JEP	*Journal of Economic Perspectives*
JPE	*Journal of Political Economy*
JPH	*Journal of Policy History*
LH	*Labor History*
PSQ	*Political Science Quarterly*
QJE	*Quarterly Journal of Economics*
RAH	*Reviews in American History*
SSH	*Social Science History*

INTRODUCTION

1. "CBS Certification Spurs Radio Drive as NYC Organizing Barometer Rises," *OPN*, October 1946, 6; Radio Guild Press Release, October 31, 1946, Trade Union Vertical File, "UOPWA—Publishing, Artists, and Radio Guild," Tamiment Library/Wagner Labor Archives, New York University; Myra Jordan, "Cut Out Static," *OPN*, November 1946, 4.

2. "CIO Moves Toward Large-Scale Organization of Net Personnel," *Broadcasting*, May 28, 1945; "CIO and AFL in Competitive Race to Organize Network Office Workers," *Broadcasting*, June 4, 1945; "CBS Group Asks Salary Boosts," *Variety*, September 9, 1945; "CIO Unit Edges AFL Organizations in Pitch for Network Collarites," *Variety*, September 12, 1945.

3. "Union Grows in Radio Networks," *OPN*, October 1945, 3; "Local 16 Members Aid Radio Guild CBS Victory," *Memo*, July 1946, 1; "UOPWA Wins CBS Radio Poll," *OPN*, July 1946, 1.

4. "CBS Signs with CIO Unit: Wage Rise and Compromise on Union Status in 2-Year Pact," *NYT*, November 22, 1946, 5; "Radio Guild (CIO) Wins 2-Year Contract with CBS Covering White-Collar Group," *Broadcasting*, November 25, 1946, 101.

5. On the development of a new middle-class standard of consumption in the United States during the late nineteenth and early twentieth centuries, see Roland Marchand, *Advertising the American Dream: Making Way for Modernity, 1920–1940* (Berkeley: University of California Press, 1985), 1–87, 117–205; William Leach, *Land of Desire: Merchants, Power, and the Rise of a New American Culture* (New York: Vintage, 1993), 3–12, 35–190; Jackson Lears, *Fables of Abundance: A Cultural History of Advertising* (New York: Random House, 1994), 196–234; Marina Moskowitz, *Standard of Living: The Measure of the Middle Class in Modern America* (Baltimore: Johns Hopkins University Press, 2004); Walter Friedman, *Birth of a Salesman: The Transformation of Selling in America* (Cambridge, MA: Harvard University Press, 2004), 88–116, 151–71; Charles McGovern, *Sold American: Consumption and Citizenship, 1890–1945* (Chapel Hill: University of North Carolina Press, 2006), 1–131; and Julia Guarneri, *Newsprint Metropolis: City Papers and the Making of Modern Americans* (Chicago: University of Chicago Press, 2017), 54–101.

6. Claudia Goldin, "Egalitarianism and the Returns to Education during the Great Transformation of American Education," *JPE* 107 (December 1999): S65–S94. Also see Matthew Sobek, "Work, Status, and Income: Men in the American Occupational Structure since the Late Nineteenth Century," *SSH* 20, no. 2 (1996): 169–207.

7. For historical perspective on the social position of people in professional, technical, or artistic occupations, see Barbara and John Ehrenreich, "The Professional-Managerial Class." *Radical America* 11, no. 2 (March–April 1977): 7–31; Jean-Christophe Agnew, "A Touch of Class," *democracy* 3, no. 2 (1983): 59–72; Michael Denning, *The Cultural Front: The Laboring of American Culture in the Twentieth Century* (New York: Verso, 1996), 96–104, 110–14; Andrew Ross, "The Mental Labor Problem," *Social Text* 18 (Summer 2000): 1–31; and Robert D. Johnston, "Historians and the American Middle Class," in *The Middling Sorts: Explorations in the History of the American Middle Class*, ed. Burton J. Bledstein and Robert D. Johnston (New York: Routledge, 2001), 296–306.

8. On women's circumscribed opportunities in the media during the early twentieth century, see Julia Golia, "Courting Women, Courting Advertisers: The Woman's Page and the Transformation of the American Newspaper, 1895–1935," *JAH* 103 (2016): 606–28.

9. For a survey of the history of minority-owned news media in the United States, see Juan Gonzáles and Joseph Torres, *News for All the People: The Epic Story of Race and the American Media* (New York: Verso, 2011).

10. James Rorty, *Our Master's Voice: Advertising* (New York: John Day Co., 1934), 348–52; J. Walter Thompson Research Department, "J. Walter Thompson Company Personnel as of May 15, 1934," Box 11, JWT-IC; Marchand, *Advertising the American Dream*, 288.

11. See, for example, Catherine McNicol Stock, *Main Street in Crisis: The Great Depression and the Old Middle Class on the Northern Plains* (Chapel Hill: University of North Carolina Press, 1992); and Mary C. McComb, *The Great Depression and the Middle Class: Experts, Collegiate Youth, and Business Ideology, 1929–1941* (New York: Routledge, 2006).

12. For a theoretical assessment of Fordism as a mode of capitalism, see David Harvey, *The Condition of Postmodernity* (New York: Basil Blackwell, 1993), 125–40.

13. The scholarly literature on the history of white-collar unionism in the United States remains surprisingly thin, but see Everett M. Kassalow, "White-Collar Unionism in the United States," in *White-Collar Trade Unions: Contemporary Developments in Industrialized Societies*, ed. Adolf Sturmthal (Urbana: University of Illinois Press, 1967), 305–64; Daniel Leab, *A Union of Individuals: The Formation of the American Newspaper Guild, 1933–1936* (New York: Columbia University Press, 1970); Carl Snyder, *White-Collar Workers and the UAW* (Urbana: University of Illinois Press, 1973); Joseph E. Finley, *White-Collar Union: The Story of the OPEIU and Its People* (New York: Octagon Books, 1975); Jürgen Kocka, *White-Collar Workers in America, 1890–1940: A Social-Political History in International Perspective*, trans. Maura Kealey (Beverly Hills, CA: Sage Publications, 1980); Mark D. McColloch, *White-Collar Labor in Transition: The Boom Years, 1940–1970* (Westport, CT: Greenwood Press, 1983); Sharon Hartman Strom, "'We're No Kitty Foyles': Organizing Office Workers for the Congress of Industrial Organizations, 1937–1950," in *Women, Work and Protest: A Century of Women's Labor History*, ed. Ruth Milkman (Boston: Routledge, 1985), 211–26; Denning, *Cultural Front*, 49–50, 87–90; and Daniel Opler, *For All White-Collar Workers: The Possibilities of Radicalism in New York City's Department Store Unions, 1934–1953* (Columbus: Ohio State University Press, 2007).

14. For forceful explications of "missing wave" advocacy of Popular Front labor feminism from the period, see Elizabeth Hawes, *Why Women Cry? Or, Wenches with Wrenches* (New York: Reynal and Hitchcock, 1943); and Hawes, *Hurry Up Please, It's Time* (New York: Reynal and Hitchcock, 1946). For historical context and analysis, see Ellen DuBois, "Eleanor Flexner and the History of American Feminism," *G&S* 3, no. 1 (1991): 81–90; Denning, *Cultural Front*, 136–51; Kate Weigand, *Red Feminism: American Communism and the Making of Women's Liberation* (Baltimore: Johns Hopkins University Press, 2001); Dorothy Sue Cobble, *The Other Women's Movement: Workplace Justice and Social Rights in Modern America* (Princeton, NJ: Princeton University Press, 2004), 1–68; and Daniel Horowitz, "Feminism, Women's History, and American Social Thought at Midcentury," in *American Capitalism: Social Thought and Political Economy in the Twentieth Century*, ed. Nelson Lichtenstein (Philadelphia: University of Pennsylvania Press, 2004), 191–209.

15. See, for context, Denning, *Cultural Front*, 104–10; Ellen Schrecker, *Many Were the Crimes: McCarthyism in America* (Princeton, NJ: Princeton University Press, 1998), 3–41; and Landon Storrs, *The Second Red Scare and the Unmaking of the New Deal Left* (Princeton, NJ: Princeton University Press, 2013), 1–85.

16. See, for example, Lawrence Glickman, "The Strike in the Temple of Consumption: Consumer Activism and Twentieth-Century American Political Culture," *JAH* 88 (June 2001): 99–128; Lizabeth Cohen, *A Consumers' Republic: The Politics of Mass Consumption in Postwar America* (New York: Knopf, 2003), 20–53; Meg Jacobs, *Pocketbook Politics: Economic Citizenship in Twentieth-Century America* (Princeton, NJ: Princeton University Press, 2004), 122–35, 150–75; Kathy Newman, *Radio Active: Advertising and Consumer Activism, 1935–1947* (Berkeley: University of California Press, 2004); Inger Stole, *Advertising on Trial: Consumer Activism and Corporate Public Relations in the 1930s* (Urbana: University of Illinois Press, 2006); and McGovern, *Sold American*, 186–217, 241–53, 302–13.

17. On the WPA cultural projects, see Richard McKinzie, *The New Deal for Artists* (Princeton, NJ: Princeton University Press, 1973); Joanne Bentley, *Hallie Flanagan: A Life in the American Theater* (New York: Knopf, 1988), 183–348; Denning, *Cultural Front*, 44–45, 77–83; Susan Platt, *Art and Politics in the 1930s: Modernism, Marxism, Americanism* (New York: Midmarch Arts Press, 1999), 173–200; Andrew Hemingway, *Artists on the Left: American Artists and the Communist Movement, 1926–1956* (New Haven, CT: Yale University Press, 2002), 147–88; Jerrold Hirsch, *Portrait of America: A Cultural History of the Federal Writers' Project* (Chapel Hill: University of North Carolina Press, 2003); A. Joan Saab, *For the Millions: American Art and Culture Between the Wars* (Philadelphia: University of Pennsylvania Press, 2004), 15–83; and Sharon Musher, *Democratic Art: The New Deal's Influence on American Culture* (Chicago: University of Chicago Press, 2015), 100–71. On labor education in the first half of the twentieth century, see Richard Altenbaugh, *Education for Struggle: The American Labor Colleges of the 1920s and 1930s* (Philadelphia: Temple University Press, 1990).

18. On the development of modernist design aesthetics in the United States, see Jeffrey Meikle, *Twentieth-Century Limited: Industrial Design in America, 1925–1939* (Philadelphia: Temple University Press, 1979); Arthur J. Pulos, *American Design Ethic: A History of Industrial Design to 1940* (Cambridge, MA: MIT Press, 1983); Pulos, *American Design Adventure, 1940–1975* (Cambridge, MA: MIT Press, 1988); Terry Smith, *Making the Modern: Industry, Art, and Design in America* (Chicago: University of Chicago Press, 1993); David Gartman, *Auto Opium: A Social History of Automobile Design* (New York: Routledge, 1994); William B. Scott and Peter Rutkoff, *New York Modern: The Arts and the City* (Baltimore: Johns Hopkins University Press, 1999); Platt, *Art and Politics*, 201–57; Shelley Nickles, "'Preserving Women': Refrigerator Design as a Social Process in the 1930s," *Technology and Culture* 43, no. 4 (2002): 693–727.

19. For background on the early development of the RWG, see Catherine Fisk, *Writing for Hire: Unions, Hollywood, and Madison Avenue* (Cambridge, MA: Harvard University Press, 2016), 89–98.

20. Claudia Goldin and Robert Margo, "The Great Compression: The Wage Structure in the United States at Mid-Century," *QJE* 107 (February 1992): 1–34; and Thomas Piketty and Emanuel Saez, "Income Inequality in the United States, 1913–1998," *QJE* 118 (February 2003): 1–39. Between 1940 and 1947, the income share (excluding capital gains) going to the top 1 percent of earners in the US decreased from 15.73 percent to 10.95 percent, while the share received by the top decile declined from 44.43 percent to 33.02 percent.

21. For an intriguing macroeconomic survey of the compression within the heart of the American income distribution during the mid-twentieth century, see Wojciech Kopczuk, Emmanuel Saez, and Jae Song, "Earnings Inequality and Mobility in the United States: Evidence From Social Security Since 1937," *QJE* 125 (February 2010): 91–128.

22. On the OPA and progressives' social and economic proposals during the 1940s, see Alan Brinkley, *The End of Reform: New Deal Liberalism in Recession and War* (New York: Knopf, 1995), 227–64; Cohen, *Consumers Republic*, 63–109; Jennifer Klein, *For All These Rights: Business, Labor, and the Shaping of America's Public-Private Welfare State* (Princeton, NJ: Princeton University Press, 2003), 116–202; and Jacobs, *Pocketbook Politics*, 179–231.

23. For classic treatments of McCarthyism and its impact on the culture industries, see David Caute, *The Great Fear: The Anti-Communist Purge under Truman and Eisenhower* (New York: Simon and Schuster, 1978); and Victor Navasky, *Naming Names* (New York: Viking Press, 1980).

24. For prime examples of this analysis, see John Kenneth Galbraith, *The Affluent Society* (Boston: Houghton Mifflin, 1958); C. Wright Mills, "The New Left," (1960) in *Power, Politics, and People: The Collected Essays of C. Wright Mills*, ed. Irving Horowitz (New York: Oxford University Press, 1963), 247–59; and Daniel Bell, *The Coming of Post-Industrial Society: A Venture in Social Forcasting* (New York: Basic Books, 1973). On the history of twentieth-century intellectuals who posited a widespread transition beyond the realm of necessity to the realm of freedom without resorting to revolutionary socialist upheaval, please see Howard Brick, *Transcending Capitalism: Visions of a New Society in Modern American Thought* (Ithaca, NY: Cornell University Press, 2006).

25. For surveys of television production and distribution in the United States during the 1950s and 1960s, see Erik Barnouw, *The Image Empire: A History of Broadcasting in the United States, Volume III—from 1953* (New York: Oxford University Press, 1970); William Boddy, *Fifties Television: The Industry and Its Critics* (Urbana: University of Illinois Press, 1992); Lynn Spigel and Michael Curtin, eds., *The Revolution Wasn't Televised: Sixties Television and Social Conflict* (New York: Routledge, 1997); and

James Baughman, *Same Time, Same Station: Creating American Television, 1948–1961* (Baltimore: Johns Hopkins University Press, 2007).

26. On the advent of "second-wave" feminism and women's renewed struggles for equal employment opportunity in white-collar workplaces, see Alice Echols, *Daring to Be Bad: Radical Feminism in America, 1967–1975* (Minneapolis: University of Minnesota Press, 1989); Alice Kessler-Harris, *In Pursuit of Equity: Women, Men, and the Quest for Economic Citizenship in Twentieth-Century America* (New York: Oxford University Press, 2001), 239–96; Cobble, *Other Women's Movement*, 168–222; Nancy MacLean, *Freedom Is Not Enough: The Opening of the American Workplace* (Cambridge, MA: Harvard University Press/Russell Sage Foundation, 2006), 117–54; Bonnie Dow, *Watching Women's Liberation, 1970: Feminism's Pivotal Year on the Network News* (Urbana: University of Illinois Press, 2014); Nancy Woloch, *A Class by Herself: Protective Laws for Women Workers, 1890s–1990s* (New York: Oxford University Press, 2015), 191–234; and Katherine Turk, *Equality on Trial: Gender and Rights in the Modern American Workplace* (Philadelphia: University of Pennsylvania Press, 2016), 1–101.

27. Capitalist philanthropies such as the Rockefeller, Carnegie, and Ford Foundations also became increasingly important patrons of noncommerical cultural projects in the postwar era, but insisted that those they funded hewed to the philanthropies' ideological commitments and programmatic objectives. See, for example, Karen Ferguson, *Top Down: The Ford Foundation, Black Power, and the Reinvention of Racial Liberalism* (Philadelphia: University of Pennsylvania Press, 2013), 169–209.

28. On radical cultural initiatives from the mid-1960s through the early 1970s, see, for example, Dan Georgakas and Marvin Surkin, *Detroit: I Do Mind Dying: A Study in Urban Revolution* (1975), rev. 3rd ed. (Chicago: Haymarket Books, 2012), 13–22, 107–30; Echols, *Daring to Be Bad*, 103–202; Julia Bryan-Wilson, *Art Workers: Radical Practice in the Vietnam War Era* (Berkeley: University of California Press, 2009), 13–39; and John McMillan, *Smoking Typewriters: The Sixties Underground Press and the Rise of Alternative Media in America* (New York: Oxford University Press, 2011), 82–114. On advertisers' capacity for appropriating and co-opting the symbols of countercultural rebellion, see Thomas Frank. *The Conquest of Cool: Business Culture, Counterculture, and the Rise of Hip Consumerism* (Chicago: University of Chicago Press, 1997).

29. On the demise of Fordism and the emergence of a post-Fordist regime of political economy in the United States predicated upon flexible accumulation of capital and a bifucated distribution of consumer purchasing power, please see Mike Davis, *Prisoners of the American Dream: Politics and Economy in the History of the U.S. Working Class* (New York: Verso, 1987), 136–53, 181–230; Kim Moody, *An Injury to All: The Decline of American Unionism* (New York: Verso, 1988), 95–146; Harvey, *Condition of Postmodernity*, 141–97; David Harvey, *A Brief History of Neoliberalism* (New York: Oxford University Press, 2005), 5–63; and Judith Stein,

Pivotal Decade: How the United States Traded Factories for Finance in the 1970s (New Haven, CT: Yale University Press, 2010).

30. E. B. Weiss, "Individualized Society Turns to Narrowcast Marketing," *AA*, January 6, 1969, 46.

CHAPTER I

1. C. Wright Mills, *White Collar: The American Middle Classes* (New York: Oxford University Press, 1951), ix, xvi. Also see Irving Louis Horowitz, *C. Wright Mills: An American Utopian* (New York: Free Press, 1983), 69, 136–37, 226–55; Richard Pells, *The Liberal Mind in a Conservative Age: American Intellectuals in the 1940s and 1950s* (New York: Vintage, 1985), 249–61; Daniel Geary, *Radical Ambition: C. Wright Mills, the Left, and American Social Thought* (Berkeley: University of California Press, 2009), 106–42; and Robert Genter, *Late Modernism: Art, Culture, and Politics in Cold War America* (Philadelphia: University of Pennsylvania Press, 2010), 157–58.

2. David Riesman with Nathan Glazer and Reuel Denney, *The Lonely Crowd: The Changing American Social Character* (New Haven, CT: Yale University Press, 1950), 21. Also see Pells, *Liberal Mind in a Conservative Age,* 238–47; Wilfred McClay, *The Masterless: Self and Society in Modern America* (Chapel Hill: University of North Carolina Press, 1994), 236–57; Brick, *Transcending Capitalism,* 172–80; and Daniel Horowitz, *Consuming Pleasures: Intellectuals and Popular Culture in the Postwar World* (Philadelphia: University of Pennsylvania Press, 2012), 122–36.

3. William H. Whyte Jr., *The Organization Man* (New York: Simon and Schuster, 1956), 4, 7. Also see Pells, *Liberal Mind,* 232–38.

4. Daniel Bell, *Work and Its Discontents: The Cult of Efficiency in America* (Boston: Beacon Press, 1956), 50, 54. Also see Pells, *Liberal Mind,* 130–46; and Howard Brick, *Daniel Bell and the Decline of Intellectual Radicalism* (Madison: University of Wisconsin Press, 1986), 193–211.

5. Richard Hofstadter, *The Age of Reform: From Bryan to F.D.R.* (New York: Vintage, 1955), 3, 5, 135, 144, 217. Also see Alan Brinkley, "Richard Hofstadter's *The Age of Reform:* A Reconsideration," *RAH* 13, no. 3 (1985): 462–80; Pells, *Liberal Mind,* 150–55; and David Brown, *Richard Hofstadter: An Intellectual Biography* (Chicago: University of Chicago Press, 2006), 99–119.

6. Hofstadter, *Age of Reform,* 11, 218, 315, 325.

7. Riesman, *Lonely Crowd,* 287. Also see Genter, *Late Modernism,* 73–89.

8. Whyte, *Organization Man,* 12–13.

9. Galbraith, *Affluent Society,* 340, 344–45. Also see Pells, *Liberal Mind,* 162–74; Kevin Mattson, "John Kenneth Galbraith: Liberalism and the Politics of Cultural Critique," in *American Capitalism,* ed. Lichtenstein, 88–108; and Brick, *Transcending Capitalism,* 180–85.

10. Bell, *Work and Its Discontents,* 38–41.

11. Mills, "The New Left," 255–56. Also see Geary, *Radical Ambition,* 162–68, 179–89.

12. Bell, *Coming of Post-Industrial Society,* 14, 26–28, 75–76, 127, 374. Also see Howard Brick, *The Age of Contradiction: Amercian Thought and Culture during the Sixties* (Ithaca, NY: Cornell University Press, 2000), 1–13, 54–57; and Brick, *Transcending Capitalism,* 189–200, 212–18, 228–35.

13. Bell, *Coming of Post-Industrial Society,* 148–54, 164.

14. Mills, *White Collar,* 301–23; and Mills, "The Cultural Apparatus" (1959), in *Power, Politics, and People,* ed. Horowitz, 406. Also see Daniel Geary, "The 'Union of the Power and the Intellect': C. Wright Mills and the Labor Movement," *LH* 42, no. 4 (2001): 327–45; Geary, *Radical Ambition,* 189–97; and Genter, *Late Modernism,* 287–94.

15. "New Officers," *On Time* (Time Inc. unit shop paper), February 2, 1949, 1, Folder 38, Box 61, NGNY; Lolita Brown to New York Local of the Newspaper Guild, June 16, 1950, Folder 33, Box 58, NGNY; Newspaper Guild of New York, "Committee Assignments," 1953, Folder 5, Box 133, NGNY; William H. Whyte Jr., to New York Newspaper Guild, January 1950, Folder 33, Box 58, NGNY; Time, Inc. Guild Unit, "Petition to Time Inc. Management," October 31, 1947, Folder 14, Box 60, NGNY; "Members of the Unit Council," *Guild Shop News* (Time Inc. Unit), April 7, 1939, 2, Folder 32, Box 61, NGNY; Minutes, Time, Inc. Guild Unit, December 5, 1940, Folder 2, Box 58, NGNY; Judith Pequignot to Guild Members, May 22, 1941, Folder 13, Box 58, NGNY.

16. For perhaps the most significant example of the lasting influence of thinkers like Bell, Galbraith, Mills, and Riesman, on popular discourse in the early twenty-first century, see Richard Florida, *The Rise of the Creative Class* (New York: Basic Books, 2002).

17. Mills, *White Collar,* 63–65, 71–76.

18. Claudia Goldin, "America's Graduation from High School: The Evolution and Spread of Secondary Schooling in the Twentieth Century," *JEH* 58 (June 1998): 345–74.

19. See Ileen DeVault, *Sons and Daughters of Labor: Class and Clerical Work in Turn-of-the-Century Pittsburgh* (Ithaca, NY: Cornell University Press, 1990), 73–104, 172–77; and Sharon Hartman Strom, *Beyond the Typewriter: Gender, Class, and the Origins of Modern American Office Work, 1900–1930* (Urbana: University of Illinois Press, 1992), 273–313. For a different view of the "collar line," see Olivier Zunz, *Making America Corporate, 1870–1920* (Chicago: University of Chicago Press, 1990), 125–48.

20. Goldin, "Egalitarianism and the Returns to Education during the Great Transformation of American Education"; and Sobek, "Work, Status, and Income: Men in the American Occupational Structure since the Late Nineteenth Century."

21. Matthew Sobek, "New Statistics on the U.S. Labor Force, 1850–1990," *Historical Methods* 34, no. 2 (2001): 71–87; and Strom, *Beyond the Typewriter,* 331–42.

22. National Industrial Conference Board, *Clerical Salaries in the United States* (New York: National Industrial Conference Board, 1926), 11–21, 29; Goldin, "Egalitarianism and the Returns to Education."

23. Mills, *White Collar,* 195.

24. Strom, *Beyond the Typewriter,* 172–269.

25. See David F. Noble, *America by Design: Science, Technology, and the Rise of Corporate Capitalism* (New York: Knopf, 1977), 33–49; Burton Bledstein, *The Culture of Professionalism: The Middle Class and the Development of Higher Education in America* (New York: Norton, 1978); Clark Davis, *Company Men: White-Collar Life and Corporate Cultures in Los Angeles, 1892–1941* (Baltimore: Johns Hopkins University Press, 2001), 67–120; Friedman, *Birth of a Salesman,* 153–71; and Jeffrey Hornstein, *A Nation of Realtors: A Cultural History of the Twentieth-Century American Middle Class* (Durham, NC: Duke University Press, 2006) 1–117.

26. See Alfred D. Chandler Jr., *The Visible Hand: The Managerial Revolution in American Business* (Cambridge, MA: Belknap Press, 1977), 285–376; and Martin Sklar, *The Corporate Reconstruction of American Capitalism, 1890–1916: The Market, the Law, and Politics* (New York: Cambridge University Press, 1988), 86–332.

27. Calculations on employment levels made by the author using US Census data samples from Steven Ruggles, J. Trent Alexander, Katie Genadek, Matthew B. Schroeder, and Matthew Sobek, *Integrated Public Use Microdata Series: Version 5.0 Machine-Readable Database* (Minneapolis: University of Minnesota Press, 2010). See Tables A.6 and A.7 in the appendix.

28. Friedman, *Birth of a Salesman,* 88–105.

29. Daniel Pope, *The Making of Modern Advertising* (New York: Basic Books, 1983), 33–111; Marchand, *Advertising the American Dream,* 120–21; McGovern, *Sold American,* 25–48.

30. On the rise of mass-circulation newspapers, see Frank Luther Mott, *American Journalism: A History, 1690–1960* (New York: Macmillan, 1962), 411–612; Michael Schudson, *Discovering the News: A Social History of American Newspapers* (New York: Basic Books, 1978); Richard Kluger, *The Paper: The Life and Death of the* New York Herald Tribune (New York: Knopf, 1986), 145–52, 160–67, 181–86; Susan Tifft and Alex Jones, *The Trust: The Private and Powerful Family behind* The New York Times (New York: Back Bay/Hachette, 1999), 31–46, 52–58, 63–77; Gerald Baldasty, *E. W. Scripps and the Business of Newspapers* (Urbana: University of Illinois Press, 1999); David Nasaw, *The Chief: The Life of William Randolph Hearst* (New York: Mariner, 2001), 98–112; Guarneri, *Newsprint Metropolis,* 13–53; and Michael Stamm, *Dead Tree Media: Manufacturing the Newspaper in Twentieth-Century North America* (Baltimore: Johns Hopkins University Press, 2018), 31–53, 115–18.

31. Pope, *Making of Modern Advertising,* 30; and Charles Kinter, "The Changing Pattern of the Newspaper Publishing Industry," *American Journal of Economics and Sociology* 5, no. 1 (1945), 43–63.

32. Matthew Schneirov, *The Dream of a New Social Order: Popular Magazines in America, 1893–1914* (New York: Columbia University Press, 1994), 67–124; Michele Bogart, *Artists, Advertising, and the Borders of Art* (Chicago: University of Chicago Press, 1995), 20–26; Roland Marchand, *Creating the Corporate Soul: The Rise of Public Relations and Corporate Imagery in American Big Business* (Berkeley: University of California Press, 1998), 130–201; McGovern, *Sold American*, 88–94.

33. "Hard Boiled Year," *Tide*, July 1930, 5–6; Rorty, *Our Master's Voice*, 23–24.

34. Pope, *Making of Modern Advertising*, 112–83; Marchand, *Advertising the American Dream*, 25–32; and Fisk, *Writing for Hire*, 33–50.

35. Marchand, *Advertising*, 7–9; Lears, *Fables of Abundance*, 142–83, 196–234; McGovern, *Sold American*,

36. On music, see David Suisman, *Selling Sounds: The Commercial Revolution in American Music* (Cambridge, MA: Harvard University Press, 2009).

37. See Lary May, *Screening Out the Past: The Birth of Mass Culture and the Motion Picture Industry* (New York: Oxford University Press, 1980).

38. Michael Stamm, *Sound Business: Newspapers, Radio, and the Politics of New Media* (Philadelphia: University of Pennsylvania Press, 2011), 29–45.

39. Erik Barnouw, *A Tower in Babel: A History of American Broadcasting to 1933* (New York: Oxford University Press, 1966), 61–64, 91–160; Susan Douglas, *Inventing American Broadcasting, 1899–1922* (Baltimore: Johns Hopkins University Press, 1987), 240–322; Robert McChesney, *Telecommunications, Mass Media, and Democracy: The Battle for Control of U.S. Broadcasting, 1928–1935* (New York: Oxford University Press, 1993), 12–18, 38–47, 63–80; Nathan Godfried, *WCFL: Chicago's Voice of Labor, 1926–78* (Urbana: University of Illinois Press, 1997), 1–135; William Boddy, *New Media and Popular Imagination: Launching Radio, Television, and Digital Media in the United States* (New York: Oxford University Press, 2004), 7–43; Susan Douglas, *Listening In: Radio and the American Imagination* (Minneapolis: University of Minnesota Press, 2004), 55–82; and Elena Razlogova, *The Listener's Voice: Early Radio and the American Public* (Philadelphia: University of Pennsylvania Press, 2011), 33–97.

40. Marchand, *Advertising the American Dream*, 89–94; McGovern, *Sold American*, 48–50.

41. Barnouw, *Tower in Babel*, 125, 229.

42. "Radio: Air Chains," *Tide*, March 1929, 7–8; JWT Representatives Staff Meeting, January 13, 1931, Folder 3/3, Box 3, JWT-SM; Barnouw, *Tower*, 154–58, 190–91, 222; McChesney, *Telecommunications, Mass Media, and Democracy*, 29; Bruce Lenthall, *Radio's America: The Great Depression and the Rise of Modern Mass Culture* (Chicago: University of Chicago Press, 2007), 5–13.

43. McChesney, *Telecommunications*, 18–29, 196–239; Stamm, *Sound Business*, 45–58, 66–75, 85–92.

44. "Radio: Air Chains"; JWT Representatives Staff Meeting, August 11, 1931, Folder 4/3, Box 4, JWT-SM; JWT Representatives Staff Meeting, February 2, 1932, Folder 4/9, Box 4, JWT-SM; Rorty, *Our Master's Voice*, 349; Erik Barnouw, *The Golden Web: A History of Broadcasting in the United States, 1933–1953* (New York: Oxford University Press, 1968), 111; Marchand, *Advertising the American Dream*, 105–10; McGovern, *Sold American*, 50–59.

45. Barnouw, *Tower*, 239.

46. Martin Green, *New York, 1913: The Armory Show and the Paterson Strike Pageant* (New York: Scribner, 1988), 9–61, 74–86, 129–91; Leach, *Land of Desire*, 285–90; John Loughery, *John Sloan: Painter and Rebel* (New York: Henry Holt, 1995), 169–247.

47. A Commercial Art Manager, "Futuristic Monstrosities Are All the Rage," *PI*, November 12, 1925, 57–60; A Commercial Art Manager, "Futurism Breaks into Newspaper Advertising Art," *PI*, November 18, 1926, 145–50; "Advertising Art: No Isms, No Ists," *Tide*, December 1928, 1–2; "McMurtrie Tells How to Make a Modern Layout," *AA*, February 22, 1930, 6; Marchand, *Advertising the American Dream*, 140–48; Bogart, *Artists*, 137–43.

48. For examples of turn-of-the century mass-produced material culture, see *Sears Roebuck and Company Catalogue for Fall 1900*, rpt. ed. (Northfield: Digest Books, 1970), esp. 142–164, 824–847, and 1059–1095. Also see Gwendolyn Wright, *Moralism and the Model Home: Domestic Architecture and Cultural Conflict in Chicago, 1873–1913* (Chicago: University of Chicago Press, 1980), 79–114; Pulos, *American Design Ethic*, 142–181, 228–250; Eileen Boris, *Art and Labor: Ruskin, Morris, and the Craftsman Ideal in America* (Philadelphia: Temple University Press, 1986), 53–81; Adrian Forty, *Objects of Desire* (New York: Pantheon, 1986), 94–113; Witold Rybczynski, *Home: A Short History of an Idea* (New York: Penguin, 1987), 173–179; and Miles Orvell, *The Real Thing: Imitation and Authenticity in American Culture, 1880–1940* (Chapel Hill: University of North Carolina Press, 1989), 40–69.

49. David Nye, *Electrifying America: Social Meanings of a New Technology, 1890–1940* (Cambridge, MA: MIT Press, 1990), 238–86.

50. David Hounshell, *From the American System to Mass Production, 1800–1932* (Baltimore: Johns Hopkins University Press, 1984), 217–62; James Flink, *The Automobile Age* (Cambridge, MA: MIT Press, 1988), 40–59; Richard Tedlow, *New and Improved: The Story of Mass Marketing in America* (New York: Basic Books, 1990), 120–30; Gartman, *Auto Opium*, 23–49.

51. Stephen Bayley, *Harley Earl and the Dream Machine* (New York: Knopf, 1983), 27–45; Hounshell, *From the American System to Mass Production*, 263–302; Flink, *Automobile Age*, 229–44; Tedlow, *New and Improved*, 147–58, 176–75; Gartman, *Auto Opium*, 64–66, 73–77.

52. "Bel Geddes," *Fortune*, July 1930, 51–57; Fred Suhr, "A Check List for Selecting a Product Designer," *SM*, September 13, 1930, 386; "Advertising Men as Designers,"

AA, July 23, 1932, 4; Norman Bel Geddes, *Horizons* (Boston: Little and Brown, 1932), 3–5, 13–23, 44–46, 249–58; "Stoves Learn from Autos: New Models Rouse Apathetic Dealers," *SM,* January 15, 1933, 63; "Both Fish and Fowl," *Fortune,* February 1934, 40–43, 88, 90, 94, 97, 98; Mary Siff, "A Realist in Industrial Design," *A&D,* October 1934, 44–48; "Industrial Design Comes of Age (Part 1)," *BW,* May 23, 1936, 16–18; Meikle, *Twentieth Century Limited,* 19–67; Smith, *Making the Modern,* 353–84.

53. On the processes by which the culture of consumer capitalism can become "popular," see Lawrence Levine, "The Folklore of Industrial Society: Popular Culture and Its Audiences," *AHR* 97, no. 5 (1992): 1369–99; Robin Kelley, "Notes on Deconstructing 'The Folk,'" *AHR* 97, no. 5 (1992): 1400–108; Natalie Zemon Davis, "Toward Mixtures and Margins," *AHR* 97, no. 5 (1992): 1409–16; Jackson Lears, "Making Fun of Popular Culture," *AHR* 97, no. 5 (1992): 1417–26; Janice Radway, *Reading the Romance: Women, Patriarchy, and Popular Literature,* rev. ed. (Chapel Hill: University of North Carolina Press, 1991); and Raymond Williams, *Culture and Materialism: Selected Essays* (London: Verso, 1980).

54. Calculations on employment levels made by the author using US Census data samples from Steven Ruggles, J. Trent Alexander, Katie Genadek, Matthew B. Schroeder, and Matthew Sobek, *Integrated Public Use Microdata Series: Version 5.0 Machine-Readable Database* (Minneapolis: University of Minnesota Press, 2010).

55. On the early development of the *Daily News,* see Stamm, *Dead Tree Media,* 132–36.

56. "Hard Boiled Year"; "All at Once," *Tide,* July 1932, 12–13; Mott, *American Journalism,* 666–73; Marchand, *Advertising the American Dream,* 53–63; Kluger, *Paper,* 211.

57. "Briton Hadden," *Tide,* January 1931, 5–7; Alan Brinkley, *The Publisher: Henry Luce and His American Century* (New York: Knopf, 2010), 108–44; Robert Vanderlan, *Intellectuals Incorporated: Politics, Art, and Ideas inside Henry Luce's Media Empire* (Philadelphia: University of Pennsylvania Press, 2010), 61–80.

58. "Hard Boiled Year."

59. Marchand, *Advertising the American Dream,* 32–38; Lears, *Fables of Abundance,* 197.

60. American Woman's Association, *The Trained Woman and the Economic Crisis: Employment and Unemployment Among a Selected Group of Business and Professional Women in New York City* (New York: American Woman's Association, 1931), 16–21, 38–43.

61. "Who Shall Slow Down? A Few? Or All?" *BW,* October 19, 1929, 8–9; "Auto Industry Nervous, But Is Optimistic," *AA,* February 1, 1930, 1–2; Martha L. Olney, *Buy Now, Pay Later: Advertising, Credit, and Consumer Durables in the 1920s* (Chapel Hill: University of North Carolina Press, 1991), 135–89; Colin Gordon, *New Deals: Business, Labor, and Politics in America, 1920–1935* (New York: Cambridge University Press, 1994), 35–45.

62. "Hard Boiled Year."

63. Marchand, *Advertising the American Dream,* 288–312; Lears, *Fables of Abundance,* 238–40.

64. "All at Once"; "March Advertising Lineage in Magazines," *AA,* March 25, 1933, 14; Rorty, *Our Master's Voice,* 348; Kinter, "The Changing Pattern of the Newspaper Publishing Industry."

65. "Sale of Radio Time in 1932 Hits New High," *AA,* January 28, 1933, 9; "Scheme to Find Circulation of Radio Outlined," *AA,* February 25, 1933, 1, 8; "Radio Notes," *Flash* (JWT internal newsletter), June 25, 1937, Box DO8, JWT-NL; Barnouw, *Golden Web,* 16–17.

66. Barnouw, *Golden Web,* 69, 88; Lenthall, *Radio's America,* 1–3, 177–205.

67. "Mass Production and Advertising," *AA,* May 24, 1930, 4; L. R. Boulware, "How Price Competition Destroys a Specialty Market," *SM,* March 21, 1931, 494–95, 518–19; "Has Industry Gone Price Crazy?" *SM,* February 27, 1932, 290–92; J. J. Nance, "Frigidaire Backs Dealer Drive with National Advertising," *PI,* May 12, 1932, 103–104; Edmond S. LaRose, "How to Commit Suicide by Cutting Prices," *SM,* July 15, 1932, 55–57; H. W. Newell, "Frigidaire's $2,000,000 Campaign," *PI,* March 23, 1933, 56, 58.

68. Roy Dickinson, "Advertising and the New Economics," *PI,* July 1, 1933, 3–4, 6, 84, 86–87; "Price-Fixing," *BW,* August 19, 1933, 12–13; "Appliances," *BW,* September 2, 1933, 12–13; Saunders Norvell, "A Frank Talk to Salesmen about the NRA," *SM,* September 15, 1933, 250–51; Allen Rucker, "Pricing Goods to Protect Profit under NRA Codes," *SM,* October 20, 1933, 397–98; Edward A. Filene, "New Deal Makes Business Policy Fit Today's Conditions," *PI,* January 11, 1934, 78, 80, 82; Meikle, *Twentieth Century Limited,* 68–133. On the NRA, see Ellis Hawley, *The New Deal and the Problem of Monopoly: A Study in Economic Ambivalence* (Princeton, NJ: Princeton University Press, 1966), 19–146; and Gordon, *New Deals,* 166–203.

69. Kinter, "The Changing Pattern of the Newspaper Publishing Industry."

70. "End of the World," *Tide,* March 1931, 5–6; Mott, *American Journalism,* 674–77; Kluger, *The Paper,* 256–61, 269–71; Nasaw, *The Chief,* 426–33, 534–47.

71. "Will Advertising Come Back?" *AA,* May 21, 1932, 4; "Study Plans to Aid Unemployed in Advertising," *AA,* January 14, 1933, 13; Marchand, *Advertising the American Dream,* 285–88; Lears, *Fables of Abundance,* 236–38; McGovern, *Sold American,* 223–41.

72. "New Handicap Seen in Trend to Cheap Art," *AA,* June 27, 1931, 9; Rorty, *Our Master's Voice,* 352; "FAECT Four Years Old!" *TA,* September 1937, 10.

73. Robert Margo, "The Microeconomics of Depression Unemployment," *JEH* 51, no. 2 (1991): 333–41; Robert Margo, "Employment and Unemployment in the 1930s," *JEP* 7, no. 2 (1993): 41–59; Goldin, "Egalitarianism and the Returns to Education during the Great Transformation of American Education."

74. League of Professional Groups for Foster and Ford, *Culture and the Crisis: An Open Letter to the Writers, Artists, Teachers, Physicians, Engineers, Scientists, and other Professional Workers of America* (New York: n.p., 1932), 7, 18, 28–29. Also see

Richard Pells, *Radical Visions and American Dreams: Culture and Social Thought in the Depression Years* (New York: Harper and Row, 1973), 76–77; Paul Buhle, *A Dreamer's Paradise Lost: Louis C. Fraina/Lewis Corey (1892–1953) and the Decline of Radicalism in the United States* (Atlantic Highlands, NJ: Humanities Press, 1995), 133–34; and Denning, *Cultural Front,* 98–99.

75. See Platt, *Art and Politics,* 88, 90; Helen Langa, "Elizabeth Olds: Gender Difference and Indifference," *Woman's Art Journal* 22, no. 2 (Fall 2001/Winter 2002): 5–11; Hemingway, *Artists on the Left,* 137, 182–84.

CHAPTER 2

1. See *Historical Statistics of the United States, Earliest Times to the Present: Volume Two, Part B, Work and Welfare* (New York: Cambridge University Press, 2006), Table Ba4783-4791, 2–337.

2. A. M. Bayes and Arlo Wallace, "Application to the C.I.O. for a Local Union Charter," June 15, 1937, Folder 72, Box 58, CIO-C; M. E. Benderlari to Bayes, August 6, 1937, Folder 72, Box 58, CIO-C; J. R. Bell to Wallace, May 29, 1941, Folder 72, Box 58, CIO-C.

3. Harris Nelsen and Ray Veio, "Application to the C.I.O. for a Local Union Charter, May 8, 1937," Folder 26, Box 53, CIO-C; John Brophy to Nelsen, May 13, 1937, Folder 26, Box 53, CIO-C; Edward Washer to Brophy, September 3, 1938, Folder 18, Box 15, CIO-C.

4. "The Heart of Milwaukee," *WW,* February 1935, 3, 6–7.

5. For an overview of the history of this conception of craft in the United States during the Gilded Age and Progressive Era, see David Montgomery, *The Fall of the House of Labor: Workers, Employers, and the State, 1865–1925* (New York: Cambridge University Press, 1987).

6. See, for example, ITU, *A Study of the History of the International Typographical Union* (Colorado Springs: ITU Executive Council, 1964); George Seltzer, *Music Matters: The Performer and the American Federation of Musicians* (Metuchen, NJ: Scarecrow Press, 1989); IATSE, *One Hundred Years of Solidarity, 1893–1993* (n.p., 1993).

7. "Plea for Women's Unions," *NYT,* July 8, 1907, 7; "Women out Strong in Labor Parade," *NYT,* September 6, 1910, 9; Helen Marot, *American Labor Unions* (New York: Henry Holt, 1914), 65–77; Ann Hogan, "Delegate's Report of A.F. of L. Convention," *OW(BS&AU),* February 1918, 1; "Mass Meeting an Inspiration," *OW(BS&AU),* May 5, 1918, 1; "Hits Politicians," *OW(BS&AU),* June 1918, 2–3; "Motions in Aid of Socialists Are Denied; Submission of Evidence Begins Today," *NYT,* January 22, 1920, 1, 2.

8. "Gompers Outlaws a Union of Reds," *NYT,* July 11, 1922, 5; Henry Fruchter, "The Crisis," *OW(BS&AU),* July 1922, 2–3; Leonard Bright, "A Heart-to-Heart Talk," *OW(BS&AU),* September 1922, 1–4; Ernest Bohm, "The Bank Clerks," *OW(BS&AU),* January 1923, 1, 3; "Try Again to Form Bank Clerks' Union," *NYT,*

August 26, 1923, E13; "Bookkeepers' Union Ousts 23 Members," *NYT*, March 1, 1927, 28; "Union to Invade Insurance Field," *NYT*, October 17, 1927, 42; "Bookkeepers' Unions Expels 23 in Row," *NYT*, February 21, 1928, 22. For an sharp analysis of the conservative drift within the labor movement of the 1920s, albeit in a different local context, see Dana Frank, *Purchasing Power: Consumer Organizing, Gender, and the Seattle Labor Movement, 1919–1929* (New York: Cambridge University Press, 1994), 163–246.

9. On the TUUL, see Edward Johanningsmeier, "The Trade Union Unity League: American Communists and the Transition to Industrial Unionism, 1928–1934," *LH* 42 (May 2001): 159–77.

10. "Our First Issue," *OW(OWU)*, November 1928, 1; "The Objects of the Union," *OW(OWU)*, November 1928, 2.

11. H. Robin, "The O.W.U. Leads the Unemployed Office Workers," *OW(OWU)*, April 1930, 3; "Draft Resolution and Directives of the TUUL Board on the Role and Work of the Revolutionary Unions in the Movement and Struggle of the Unemployed," 1931, Folder 20, Box 3, CM; "Department Stores Cut Wages," *OW(OWU)*, July 1931, 1; "Department Store Workers Organize!" *OW(OWU)*, July 1931, 1–2; "Book Publishers Cut Wages," *OW(OWU)*, September 1931, 1; "Vast Decrease in Office Jobs," *OW(OWU)*, October 1931, 1; "Mobilize for the Hunger March," *OW(OWU)*, November 1931, 1, 4; "Union Organizes Publishing and Bookselling Section," *OW(OWU)*, January 1932, 2; "'Liberal' *World-Telegram* Shows the Way," *OW(OWU)*, April 1932, 1–2.

12. "Technicians Petition for Larger CWA Fund," *NYT*, February 5, 1934, 2; "Plan Neighborhood Clubs: White Collar and Professional Groups Discuss Forming Chain," *NYT*, July 21, 1934, 2; "For Jobs and Adequate Relief," *AF*, November 1934, 4–5; "FAECT Four Years Old!"

13. "Authors Arrested as Strike Pickets," *NYT*, June 7, 1934, 21; "Book Strike Settled by Job Agreement," *NYT*, June 9, 1934, 13; "Union Wins Macauley [sic] Strike," *OW(OWU)*, June-July 1934, 1, 3; "Macaulay Strike Solid in Sixth Week," *OW(OWU)*, November 1934, 1, 4; "The Macaulay Ruling," *NM*, March 12, 1935, 7.

14. "Klein Workers Win," *OW(OWU)*, November 1934, 1, 3; "29 Store Pickets Seized," *NYT*, December 18, 1934, 18; "Store Pickets Limited," *NYT*, December 20, 1934, 5; "Writers in Union Square," *NM*, February 5, 1935, 7; "Klein Strike Ends in Victory," *OW(OWU)*, February 1935, 1, 3. Also see Opler, *For All White-Collar Workers*, 22–41.

15. "The Mercury Staff Goes on a Strike," *NYT*, May 1, 1935, 23; "The Scab Mercury," *NM*, May 14, 1935, 4; "Other Office Strikes," *NM*, May 14, 1935, 4; "On the *Mercury* Picket Line," *NM*, July 2, 1935, 6; John Buchanan, "White Collars Organize," *NM*, April 7, 1936, 22–23. Russell T. Limbach, "Artists Union Convention," *NM*, May 19, 1936, 28;

16. Lewis Corey, *The Crisis of the Middle Class* (New York: Covici, Friede, 1935), 15, 23, 266, 272–73, 344; Corey, "The Minds of the Middle Class," *NM*, April 1936,

15–16; Corey, "Labor and the Middle Class," *Ledger,* June 1936, 11–13. Also see Pells, *Radical Visions,* 91–93; Buhle, *Dreamer's Paradise Lost,* 128–31; and Denning, *Cultural Front,* 99–104.

17. Gilbert Mines to Corey, January 10, 1935, Box 13, LC; William Chase to Corey, January 24, 1935, Box 13, LC; Chase to Corey, February 7, 1935, Box 13, LC; Chase to Corey, May 3, 1935, Box 13, LC.

18. "Trade Union Unity," *OW(OWU),* April 1935, 2–3; "Draft Program and Structure of the Joint Unity Committee of Independent Unions as Adopted at the Conference of Independent Trade Unions," May 10, 1935, Folder 20, Box 3, CM; Interview with Clarina Michelson by Debra Bernhardt, October 29, 1979, Folder 3, Box 3, CM; OWU, "For One Strong Union," 1935, Folder 7, Box 3, CM; Richard Lewis, "Office Workers Need Unity," *OW(OWU),* November 1935, 3; "For One Union of Office Workers," *Ledger,* January 1936, 8–9; "BS&AU elections," *Ledger,* October-November 1936, 7–8, 10; Lewis Merrill, "The Union Looks Forward," *Ledger,* October-November 1936, 7.

19. Heywood Broun, "It Seems to Me," *NYW-T,* August 7, 1933, 21; "Newspaper Guild Adopts Constitution," *NYT,* October 19, 1933, 10; "Newspaper Guild Begins to Function," *NYT,* November 16, 1933, 30; "Newspaper Guilds Unite Nationally," *NYT,* December 16, 1933, 15; "Guild Hears Union Debate," *NYT,* April 23, 1934, 3. Also see Leab, *Union of Individuals,* 33–133.

20. "Asks Writers to Unite," *NYT,* November 23, 1934, 17; Heywood Broun, "An Army with Banners," *OW(OWU),* April 1935, 12–13; "Newspaper Guild for Vertical Union," *NYT,* June 6, 1935, 19; "Guild Vote Indicates Defeat of A.F.L. Tie," October 16, 1935, 25; "Guild Votes 84 to 5 to Join A.F.L.," *NYT,* May 31, 1936, 25; "Green Gives Charter to Newspaper Guild," *NYT,* August 8, 1936, 2. Also see Leab, *Union of Individuals,* 134–283.

21. Alfred Bingham, *Insurgent America: The Revolt of the Middle Classes* (New York: Harper, 1935). Also see Pells, *Radical Visions,* 74–76, 94–95; and Robert McG. Thomas Jr., "Alfred Bingham, 93, Dies; Once-Radical Intellectual," *NYT,* November 5, 1998, D4.

22. "Book Notes," *NYT,* June 1, 1935, 13; "Consumer Group Formed," *NYT,* February 6, 1936, 9; "Book Notes," *NYT,* June 24, 1936, 21; Robert Josephy, "How to Start a Trade Union: Five Years of the Book and Magazine Guild," *GN,* May 1940, 14–15.

23. "News and Notes of the Advertising World," *NYT,* November 6, 1936, 47; "News and Notes of the Advertising World," *NYT,* November 16, 1936, 28; "Press Agents Convene," *NYT,* February 10, 1937, 18; "Advertising News and Notes," *NYT,* April 6, 1937, 42; "Randau Addresses Admen," *New York Guild News,* May 22, 1937, 3.

24. Luise Sillcox to multiple recipients, July 12, 1937, Folder 2, Box 1, RWG; Kenneth Webb, "Report of President," November 7, 1938, Folder 3A, Box 1, RWG; "Objectives of the Radio Writers' Guild," February 1939, Folder 4, Box 1, RWG; Webb to Peggy Scheuerman, November 11, 1940, Folder 5, Box 1, RWG.

25. See Montgomery, *Fall of the House of Labor,* 370–464.

26. See Davis, *Prisoners of the American Dream*, 55–65; Steven Fraser, *Labor Will Rule: Sidney Hillman and the Rise of American Labor* (New York: Free Press, 1991), 328–52; Robert Ziegler, *The CIO, 1935–1955* (Chapel Hill: University of North Carolina Press, 1995), 22–65.

27. L. P. Lindelof to Fred Marshall, April 19, 1937, Folder 16, Box 1, USA-829; Marshall to Edward Ackerley, April 20, 1937, Folder 16, Box 1, USA-829; Marshall to Lindelof, April 22, 1937, Folder 16, Box 1, USA-829; Lindelof to Frank Morrison, April 28, 1937, Folder 16, Box 1, USA-829; Morrison to William Collins, April 28, 1937, Folder 16, Box 1, USA-829.

28. Jules Korchien to George Holland, October 5, 1936, Folder 68, Box 9, AFAE 66; John Rannells to FAECT, October 9, 1936, Folder 68, Box 9, AFAE 66; Executive Council, International Federation of Technical, Engineering, Architectural, and Drafting Unions, "Report and Recommendations," December 14, 1936, Folder 12, Box 7, AFAE 66; C. L. Rosemund to All Local Unions, January 5, 1937, Folder 12, Box 7, AFAE 66; "Rosemund Bars Entry into AFL," *TA*, January 1937, 2–3.

29. Jules Korchien, "Apply for CIO Membership," *TA*, March 1937, 2; Marcel Scherer to John Brophy, April 16, 1937, Folder 20, Box 2, CIO-C; Guy K. Young, "Another Letter, From the Federation of A.E.C.&T.," *PP*, April-May 1937, 52 suppl.; "Technicians Join CIO," *NYT*, May 28, 1937, 10; Young, "CIO Leads the Technician," *TA*, June 1937, 4.

30. "Affiliation Facts," *DE*, September 1937, 4; Adolph Germer to Walter Smethhurst, September 21, 1937, Folder 15, Box 49, Part I, CIO-ST; "New Election Voted," *DE*, February 1938, 2; "SDE to Conduct another FAECT Referendum," *TA*, February 1938, 6; "Affiliation," *DE*, April 1938, 2; Walter Johnson, "SDE Affiliates," *TA*, April 1938, 5.

31. "Office Guild Jams Huge Astor Hall," *NYGN*, May 22, 1937, 1, 3; Louis Stark, "A.F. of L. Prepares to Declare a War to Finish on C.I.O.," *NYT*, May 24, 1937, 1, 13; "CIO Affiliation Approved: Industrial Unionism Resolution Adopted by Members, 304-46," *NYGN*, June 5, 1937, 1, 3; "Newspaper Guild Votes to Join C.I.O.," *NYT*, June 9, 1937, 5.

32. ANG, "19,000 Newspaper Men," 1940, Folder 34, Box 17, NGNY.

33. Lewis Merrill to John L. Lewis, July 31, 1936, Frame 873, Reel 8, Part I, CIO-JLL; Lewis to Merrill, August 5, 1936, Frame 872, Reel 8, Part I, CIO-JLL; "Tampa Delegates Plan National Union," *Ledger*, December 1936, 6; "Merrill Outlines Growth and Plans of National Office Committee," *Ledger*, March 1937, 6; Merrill to Brophy, May 13, 1937, Folder 12, Box 15, CIO-C; "Clerks Vote for C.I.O.," *NYT*, May 18, 1937, 6; Lewis to Merrill, June 1, 1937, Folder 12, Box 15, CIO-C; "C.I.O. Admits Office Workers," *NYT*, June 2, 1937, 8; "CIO Charters National Union of Office and Professional Workers," *Ledger*, June 1937, 1–2.

34. "Book Guild Joins CIO; Opens Drive," *Ledger*, July 1937, 8; "PM Shorts," *PM* (the publication of the New York Art Director's Club, not the tabloid examined that commenced publication in July 1940 and is examined in chapter 3), September

1937, 34; "Three Artists' Organizations to Form One Big Union and Affiliate to UOPWA, CIO," *Ledger*, January 1938, 3; "Artists Cheer Presentation of New UOPWA Charter," *Ledger*, February 1938, 5; "Ad Guild Spurs Membership with 'Pioneer Contest,'" *Ledger*, March 1938, 1–2; "PM Shorts," *PM*, April 1938, 16.

35. "Film Office Workers Seek Featured Roles in Unionization Drama," *Ledger*, August 1937, 2; "Joint White Collar Council Launched in Metropolis; Numbers 15,000 Members," *Ledger*, March 1938, 3; Eve Harrison, "Portrait of a Joint Council," *NM*, April 11, 1939, 14–15; "SPG Sees Victory as Hearings End," *SPG News*, March 1941, 1, 3, Folder 21, Box 24, NGNY; "Screen Publicists Will Have Election," *NYT*, June 19, 1941, 24; "Publicists Guild Wins," *NYT*, July 18, 1941, 36; "Movie Guilds Join UOPWA, Ask Columbia Office Poll," *OPN*, October 1941, 1–2; "Separate Screen Guilds United in the UOPWA," *OPN*, October 1941, 10; "Screen Publicists Get UOPWA Charter," *OPN*, July 1, 1942, 1; "UOPWA Wins CBS Radio Poll," *OPN*, July 1946, 1; "CBS Signs with CIO Unit," *NYT*, November 22, 1946, 5.

36. George Nelson, "Mechanizing the Architect," *TA*, April 1938, 3–4. Also see "White Collar Union Veterans," *NM*, October 26, 1937; and Meyer Schapiro, "Architecture and the Architect," *NM*, April 1936, 30–31.

37. George Seldes, *Lords of the Press* (New York: Julian Messner, 1938), 370–71, 374–75.

38. NLRB, Decision and Certification of Representatives, Case R-467, February 17, 1938, *DNLRB* 5 (1938): 362–71; NLRB, Decision and Certification of Representatives, Case R-809, July 5, 1938, *DNLRB* 8 (1938): 76–83; Application for Approval of a Wage or Salary Rate (NWLB Form 10), March 14, 1945, Folder 34, Box 17, NGNY; Dennis Flanagan to Robert Stern, February 25, 1947, Folder 28, Box 58, NGNY.

39. "Book and Mag Guild Members Win Raise in 'Modern Age,'" *Ledger*, January 1938, 3; "BMG Winning New Contract," *Ledger*, January 1938, 3; "Mag Guild Finds Union Key to Phi Beta Kappa," *Ledger*, April 1938, 8; "BMG Signs Up Viking," *Ledger*, June 1938, 2; "NLRB Certifies Guild at Knopf," *Ledger*, July 1938, 2; "Random House Signs Contract," *GN*, September 1938, 1; "Book Guild Renews All Contracts During Year," *UOPWA News*, December 1939, 2; "PM Shorts," *PM*, December 1939, 90; "Walden Signs With BMG; Picket Line Spurs Agreement, Pay Raises," *GN*, January 1940, 1,5; "Saturday Review Employees Ask BMG Contract," *GN*, February 1940, 1; "PM Shorts," *PM*, February 1940, 84; "Union Organizes Doubleday Stores," *Proof*, May 1942, 1.

40. "PM Shorts," *PM*, September 1937, 34; "Artists Cheer Presentation of New UOPWA Charter," *Ledger*, February 1938, 5; NLRB, Decision and Direction of Elections, Cases R-715 and R-866, December 5, 1938, *DNLRB* 10 (1938): 197–217; "Artists' Union Transferred," *NYT*, October 29, 1939, 3.

41. Leo Huberman, "CIO Unions Here to Form Council," *PM* (the tabloid newspaper), June 28, 1940, 15; Saul Mills to All Council Delegates and Union Secretaries, March 14, 1945, Folder 14, Box 9, NGNY; "Hillman Union Joins CIO Council Here," *NYT*, March 19, 1945, 20.

42. See Book and Magazine Guild, *Report of the Salary Survey of the Book Publishing Industry* (1940), Folder 3, Box 1, PHJB.

43. "News and Notes of the Advertising Field," *NYT*, October 17, 1940, 45; "At Benton and Bowles," *S&T*, October 21, 1940, 1, Folder 6, Box 504, JBM.

44. "Movie Studio Strike Voted by 100 Workers," *NYT*, May 7, 1937, 5; "Betty Boop and Popeye," *NM*, June 1, 1937, 19; "Three Artists' Organizations to Form One Big Union and Affiliate to UOPWA, CIO," *Ledger*, January 1938, 3; "UAA Reopen Negotiations at Fleischer," *Ledger*, July 1938, 2; UAA Executive Board Minutes, August 17, 1938, Frames 562–64, Reel 5242, RK; "Studio Negotiates with UAA— Popeye Goes South," *Ledger*, August 1938, 5.

45. Willard Smart to John Brophy, January 5, 1937, Folder 20, Box 2, CIO-C; FAECT, "Draft Report to Executive Meeting of C.I.O, April 12–13, 1938," Folder 22, Box 2, CIO-C; Marcel Scherer to Van Bittner, July 19, 1938, Frame 152, Reel 1, Part I, CIO-JLL; NLRB, Decision and Direction of Election, Case R-1407, July 31, 1939, *DNLRB* 13 (1939): 1326–35; Lewis Alan Berne to Allan S. Haywood, April 29, 1940, Folder 24, Box 2, CIO-C; Lewis Merrill to Haywood, November 11, 1943, Folder 2, Box 16, CIO-C.

46. Leo Bollens, *White-Collar or Noose? The Occupation of Millions* (New York: North River Press, 1947), 68–203.

47. CIO Executive Board, Schedule of Receipts and Disbursements, May 7, 1940, Frames 167–70, Reel 6, Part II, CIO-JLL; "Report of the United Office and Professional Workers of America, C.I.O. for the Period June 1, 1937 to September 30, 1937," Folder 15, Box 15, CIO-C; Lewis Merrill to John Brophy, February 11, 1938, Folder 17, Box 15, CIO-C; A. D. Lewis to John L. Lewis, April 10, 1939, Frame 10645, Reel 8, Part I, CIO-JLL; UOPWA, General Executive Board Minutes, October 18, 1940, Frames 704–10, Reel 5243, RK. Also see Zieger, *CIO*, 92–98.

48. "Advertising News and Notes," *NYT*, February 8, 1937, 24; advertisement for mAD Arts Ball, *NM*, April 5, 1938, 29; "Arts Ball Rolls Around as Sober Citizens Batten Down Their Hatches," *Ledger*, April 1938, 8; "PM Shorts," *PM*, February 1940, 87; "mAD Arts Ball Success," *OPN*, May 1940, 7; "mAD Arts Ball—Crazy," *OPN*, March 1941, 5.

49. "Low Cost Health Plan Begun by N.Y. Council," *UOPWA News*, February 1939, 5; "16,000 in Union Get Group Health Care," *NYT*, February 2, 1939, 17; Anne Berenholz, "A Health Plan for the UOPWA," *UOPWA News*, December 1939, 4; Klein, *For All These Rights*, 152.

50. "Summary of Senate's Sub-Committee Report on the Use of Espionage in Industry," *NYT*, December 22, 1937, 22–23; "Sen. LaFollette to Talk on Labor Spy at BMG Conference," *Ledger*, March 1938, 8.

51. Irving Harper, interview by author, March 16, 2004; "Ad Guild Spurs Membership Drive with 'Pioneer Contest,'" *Ledger*, March 1938, 1–2.

52. See Katherine Van Wezel Stone, "The Post-War Paradigm in American Labor Law," *Yale Law Journal* 90, no. 7 (1981): 1509–80; Christopher Tomlins, "The New

Deal, Collective Bargaining, and the Triumph of Industrial Pluralism," *ILRR* 39, no. 1 (1985): 19–34; Stone, "The Legacy of Industrial Pluralism: The Tension between Individual Employment Rights and the New Deal Collective Bargaining System," *University of Chicago Law Review* 59, no. 2 (1992): 575–644; Gordon, *New Deals,* 204–39; Jean-Christian Vinel, *The Employee: A Political History* (Philadelphia: University of Pennsylvania Press, 2013), 48–62, 71–85; Joseph McCartin, "'As Long as There Survives': Contemplating the Wagner Act After Eighty Years," *Labor* 14 (Summer 2017): 21–42; Dorothy Sue Cobble, "A Wagner Act for Today: Save the Preamble but Not the Rest?" *Labor* 14 (Summer 2017): 43–47; Craig Becker, "A Wide View of the Wagner Act at Eighty," *Labor* 14 (Summer 2017): 49–53; and Stone, "Imagining a New Labor Law for a New Era of Work," *Labor* (Summer 2017): 55–59.

53. "Associated Press Served in Guild Case," *NYT,* December 5, 1935, 23; "Labor Relations Act Challenged by A.P.," *NYT,* December 19, 1935, 2; "A.P. Asks Injunction in Guild Dispute," *NYT,* January 4, 1936, 13; Elmer Rice, "The Federal Theater Hereabouts," *NYT,* January 5, 1936, IX, 1; "WPA Drama," *NYT,* January 19, 1936, IX, 2; "A.P. Loses Ruling in Labor Dispute," *NYT,* April 25, 1936, 6; Decision and Direction of Election, Case R-26, May 6, 1936, *DNLRB* 1 (1936): 686–95.

54. "Court Hears Case of AP and Guild," *NYT,* January 18, 1936, 16; "News Guild Wins Point in Labor Suit," March 18, 1936, 18; "Decision Reserved in A.P.-Guild Case," *NYT,* April 9, 1936, 32; "A.P. Loses Ruling in Labor Dispute"; "A.P. Staff to Vote on the Guild Issue," *NYT,* May 8, 1936, 16; "A.P. Labor Dispute is Taken to Court," *NYT,* May 27, 1936, 21. Also see Vinel, *Employee,* 40–45.

55. "Associated Press Tests Labor Act," *NYT,* September 15, 1936, 13; "Government Seeks Wagner Act Ruling," *NYT,* September 30, 1936, 14; "Labor Issue Looms In Supreme Court," *NYT,* October 4, 1936, 45; "Freedom of Press at Stake, Says A.P.," *NYT,* January 23, 1937, 15; "Labor Act Scored Before High Court," *NYT,* February 10, 1937, 1, 12; *Associated Press v. National Labor Relations Board* 301 U.S. 103, 132–33 (1937); Arthur Krock, "Five Cases Decided," *NYT,* April 13, 1937, 1, 15.

56. "Watson Resumes Job in A.P. Office Here," *NYT,* April 14, 1937, 14; "Watson Quits A.P., Returns to Theater," *NYT,* May 18, 1937, 6; "Guild Asks A.P. Elections," *NYT,* September 25, 1937, 5; Certification of Representatives, Case R-536, March 16, 1938, *DNLRB* 6 (1938): 4–7.

57. "Advertising Men Begin Campaign of Picketing" *NYT,* March 18, 1939, 8; "No Strike Is Called, but Union Pickets," *NYT,* March 19, 1939, 19; "History in Advertising Row," *Commercial Artists Bulletin,* March 1939, Frame 703, Reel 5242, RK; "Labor Troubles," *Tide,* April 1, 1939, 42; "Ad Guild Says G-Kahn Kahn't," *UOPWA News,* April 1939, 1–2; "Gussow-Kahn Before NLRB," *UOPWA News,* May 1939, 2; "Gussow-Kahn Co. Firing Breaks Truce," *UOPWA News,* October 1939, 7.

58. Brinkley, *Publisher: Henry Luce and His American Century,* 181–89, 216–24; and Vanderlan, *Intellectuals Incorporated,* 61–90.

59. NGNY, "1937 Negotiations—Exhibit 4," Folder 35, Box 58, NGNY; NGNY, "1937 Negotiations—Exhibit 5," Folder 35, Box 58, NGNY; Time, Inc. Report to Stockholders, November 25, 1941, Folder 10, Box 58, NGNY; Minutes of 1937 Negotiations, Folder 35, Box 58, NGNY; Cameron Mackenzie to Milton Kaufman, June 22, 1937, Folder 37, Box 58, NGNY; Kaufman to Roy Larsen, Folder 37, Box 58, NGNY.

60. Ralph Ingersoll to All Employees, July 15, 1937, Folder 5, Box 58, NGNY; Minutes, Time Unit of the Newspaper Guild, August 5, 1937, Folder 1, Box 58, NGNY; Cameron Mackenzie to Milton Kaufman, September 7, 1937, Folder 37, Box 58, NGNY; Kaufman to Henry R. Luce, September 13, 1937, Folder 37, Box 58, NGNY; "Time Hears Parley Report," *NYGN*, October 20, 1937, 2; Luce to All Members of All Divisions of Time Inc., November 17, 1937, Folder 5, Box 58, NGNY; "Post Signs Guild Pact," *NYT*, July 27, 1935, 11.

61. Minutes, Time Unit of the Newspaper Guild, December 2, 1937, Folder 1, Box 58, NGNY; Ralph Ingersoll to Staff, December 23, 1937, Folder 5, Box 58, NGNY; "Time Unit in Deadlock: Management's Counter Proposal Rejected," *NYGN*, December 28, 1937, 1; Ingersoll to All Employees of Time Inc., April 6, 1938, NGNY, Box 58, Folder 7; *Guild Shop News* (Time Unit), April 12, 1938, NGNY, Box 61, Folder 32; "Tasks before the Guild," *Guild Shop News* (Time Unit), May 12, 1938, NGNY, Box 61, Folder 32; Contract between Time Inc. and the Newspaper Guild of New York, July 15, 1938, NGNY, Box 61, Folder 39; Ingersoll to Staff of Time Inc., July 25, 1938, NGNY, Box 58, Folder 5.

62. Dwight Macdonald, "Fortune Magazine," *Nation*, May 8, 1937, 529–30; "The Truth Is: The Publishers' Association Doesn't Like the Guild," *Guild Shop News* (Time Unit), July 28, 1937, Folder 32, Box 61, NGNY; "Time Hears Parley Report." Also see Michael Wreszin, *A Rebel in Defense of Tradition: The Life and* politics *of Dwight Macdonald* (New York: Basic Books, 1994), 47–53; and David Witwer, "Westbrook Pegler and the Anti-Union Movement," *JAH* 92, no. 2 (2005): 527–52.

63. "The Memo," *Guild Shop News* (Time Unit), February 24, 1939, Folder 32, Box 61, NGNY; Editorial, *E&P*, March 4, 1939, 22; "*Editor and Publisher* Likes It," *Guild Shop News* (Time Unit), March 10, 1939, Folder 32, Box 61, NGNY.

64. Henry Luce to Anna Goldsborough, September 25, 1939, Folder 8, Box 58, NGNY; Goldsborough to Luce, October 5, 1939, Folder 8, Box 58, NGNY; Luce to Goldsborough, October 12, 1939, Folder 10, Box 58, NGNY; Contract between Time Inc., and the Newspaper Guild of New York, December 12, 1939, Folder 39, Box 61, NGNY.

65. "Unit Officers Elected," *Guild Shop News* (Time Unit), December 21, 1939, Folder 32, Box 61, NGNY.

66. On "missing wave" labor feminism, see Ruth Milkman, *Gender at Work: The Dynamics of Job Segregation by Sex during World War II* (Urbana: University of Illinois Press, 1987), 1–26, 84–98, 128–52; Nancy Gabin, *Feminism in the Labor Movement: Women and the United Auto Workers, 1935–1975* (Ithaca, NY: Cornell

University Press, 1990), 1–142; Denning, *The Cultural Front*, 136–51; Daniel Horowitz, *Betty Friedan and the Making of* the Feminine Mystique: *The American Left, the Cold War, and Modern Feminism* (Amherst: University of Massachusetts Press, 1998), 102–52; and Cobble, *Other Women's Movement*, 1–68.

67. "New BMU Health Plan Saves $$," *Proof*, May 1943, 4; and "Knopf Contract is Trail Blazer," *Proof*, July 1943, 1, 3. Also see Weigand, *Red Feminism*, 1–17, 46–64, 110–11, 140–48.

68. "11 Book Strikers Enlist 11 Authors," *NYT*, June 6, 1934, 19; Arthur Kallet, "Consumers' Research on Strike," *NM*, September 17, 1935, 12–13; "Consumers Union," October 22, 1948, Folder 28, Box 6, CLA-CRF; "New York City Consumers' Council," 1948, Folder 3, Box 8, CLA-CRF; Interview with Clarina Michelson by Debra Bernhardt, October 29, 1979, Folder 3, Box 3, CM; Norma Aronson scrapbook, NA; "Re: UOPWA-CIO," November 14, 1946, Folder 10, Box 11, CLA-CRF; "Anne Berenholz," January 3, 1950, Folder 30, Box 18, CLA-CRF.

69. Rose Wortis, "Women, Protect the Union of Your Choice," *WW*, January 1934, 4; Wortis, "Miss Schneiderman of the NRA," *WW*, July 1934, 13.

70. See, for example, K., "Woman's Voice: Driving to Victory," *WW*, March 1933, 14; F. Reish, "Woman's Voice: We Win Lower Rent," *WW*, March 1933, 15; Clara Licht, "Councils Fight Against High Cost of Living," *WW*, October 1933, 10; A Detroit Woman Auto Worker, "N.R.A.—What It Means to Women," *WW*, April 1934, 13; "Toledo Strike Lessons," *WW*, September 1934, 9; One Who Knows, "A Salesgirl's Life," *WW*, November 1935, 3, 14; P. M., "The Detroit Meat Strike," *WW*, November 1935, 12.

71. "The Working Woman: Changes to a Magazine," *WW*, March 1933, 2; "Letters Received by the American Birth Control League," *WW*, April 1933, 13; "Can You Afford Another Baby?" *WW*, April 1933, 13; Sasha Small, "Life a la *Ladies Home Journal*," *WW*, July 1934, 10, 15; Small, "Love Leads the Way," *WW*, October 1934, 12, 15; "Birth Control Knowledge Needed," *WW*, November 1934, 4.

72. Rebecca Pitts, "Women and Communism," *NM*, February 19, 1935, 14–18.

73. Josephine Wertheim, "The League of Women Shoppers," *WW*, July 1935, 5.

74. "N.Y. Joint Council Launches Varied and Interesting Program," *Ledger*, September 1938, 5; "Forums, Classes, Arts and Sports, 1939–1940," Trade Union File—United Office and Professional Workers, Tamiment Institute, New York University; Ruth McKenney, "It Takes All Kinds of Anniversaries," *GN*, May 1940, 3; Shirley Jackson, "One of the Boys," *GN*, March 1941, 3, 10. Also see Bettina Birch, *Radical by Design: The Life and Style of Elizabeth Hawes* (New York: Dutton, 1988), 62–88.

75. "Jane Benedict Chosen by Membership as New Executive Secretary," *GN*, April 1941, 1; "Benedict Gets New GEB Post," *Proof*, October 1942, 1; and Jane Benedict Interview with Debra Bernhardt, New Yorkers at Work Oral History Collection, December 6, 1983, 7–9; "Portrait of a Shop Chairman," *GN*, August 1940, 3; "Irene: Key to Phi Beta Kappa," *GN*, Oct. 1940, 6, 7; "Report on the Treasurer

and the Figure She Cuts," *GN*, January 1941, 3; "That's Some Shop, Consumers' Union—35 Members Work, Get Results," *Proof*, July 1942, 3.

76. Benedict Interview, 10–11; "Guild Undertakes First Wage Census; Publishing Workers Get Questionnaire," *GN*, February 1940, 1, 5; "Low-Paid Workers Welcome Census," *GN*, March 1940, 1, 3; "Grand Finale for Survey," *GN*, May 1940, 3, 8; "Survey Findings Rouse Industry; Letters, Comments Spur Organization," *GN*, June 1940, 1.

77. See Harvey Klehr, *The Heyday of American Communism: The Depression Decade* (New York: Basic Books, 1984); and Schrecker, *Many Are the Crimes*, 3–41.

78. UOPWA Press Release, April 16, 1938, Frame 982, Reel 8, Part I, CIO-JLL; "Frey Story Answered by President Merrill," *Ledger*, September 1938, 1, 5.

79. Benjamin Stolberg, "Communist Wreckers in the Labor Movement," *SEP*, September 2, 1939, 5–6, 32, 34.

80. "Red Growth Swift, Matthews Asserts," *NYT*, August 23, 1938, 2; "Dies Investigator Says Reds Utilize Consumer Groups," *NYT*, December 11, 1939, 1.

81. UOPWA Press Release, January 26, 1938, Folder 17, Box 15, CIO-C; Richard Lewis to Wesley Stout, October 4, 1939, Frames 1024–27, Reel 8, Part I, CIO-JLL; Benjamin Stolberg to Lewis, October 12, 1939, Frames 1028–30, Reel 8, Part I, CIO-JLL; Lewis Merrill to Stout, December 11, 1939, Frames 1037–39, Reel 8, Part I, CIO-JLL; "Guild Uses Stolberg Charges to Restate Aims," *GN*, January 1940, 1, 2.

82. "500 in C.I.O. Union Bolt to the A.F.L.," *NYT*, March 21, 1939, 1, 18; "Split in Office Union Called Spite Action," *NYT*, March 23, 1939, 15; "Locals Deny AFL 'Raid' on UOPWA—N.Y. Clique out of Local 16," *UOPWA News*, April 1939, 2.

83. Milton Kaufman, Report of Executive Secretary to Enlarged Meeting of the Executive Committee together with Discussion on the Report, June 4, 1939, Folder 13, Box 17, NGNY.

84. Minutes, Time Unit of the Newspaper Guild, May 8, 1940, Folder 2, Box 58, NGNY; Minutes, Time Unit of the Newspaper Guild, June 13, 1940, Folder 2, Box 58, NGNY.

85. Whittaker Chambers, *Witness* (New York: Random House, 1952), 269, 475. On this point, please also see Denning, *Cultural Front*, 85, 105–106.

86. See Harvey Klehr, John Earl Haynes, and Kyrill Anderson, *The Soviet World of American Communism* (New Haven, CT: Yale University Press, 1998), 48–84; and Haynes and Klehr, *Venona: Decoding Soviet Espionage in America* (New Haven, CT: Yale University Press, 1999), 76–77, 223–24, 262, 326–27.

87. For a recent assessment of the difficulties that Roosevelt and other proponents for intervention on behalf of the Allies faced in 1939–1941 as they struggled to move public opinion, see Ira Katznelson, *Fear Itself: The New Deal and the Origins of Our Time* (New York: Norton, 2013), 276–316.

88. Peter Hawley to John L. Lewis, October 29, 1940, Frame 606, Reel 20, Part I, CIO-JLL; Norma Aronson to Lewis, November 5, 1940, Frame 607, Reel 20, Part I,

CIO-JLL; Norman Barr to Lewis, November 8, 1940, Frame 585, Reel 20, Part I, CIO-JLL; Jane Benedict to Lewis, November 11, 1940, Frame 587, Reel 20, Part I, CIO-JLL. Also see Zieger, *CIO,* 102–10.

89. Gladys Bentley to Unit Chairmen, Controllers, and Shop Paper Editors, August 8, 1940, Folder 11, Box 58, NGNY.

CHAPTER 3

1. Susan Jenkins to John L. Lewis, November 20, 1935, Frame 7, Reel 9, Part I, CIO-JLL; Jenkins to Lewis, October 21, 1935, Frame 19, Reel 9, Part I, CIO-JLL; and Jenkins to Executive Council of the American Federation of Labor, October 21, 1935, Frames 20–21, Reel 9, Part I, CIO-JLL.

2. "Consumers Union Reports," *CUR,* May 1936, 2, 24.

3. Barnouw, *Golden Web,* 22–36; Lizabeth Cohen, *Making a New Deal: Industrial Workers in Chicago, 1919–1939* (New York: Cambridge University Press, 1990), 136–42; McChesney, *Telecommunications, Mass Media, and Democracy,* 188–270; Godfried, *WCFL: Chicago's Voice of Labor,* 19–194; Godfried, "Struggling over Politics and Culture: Organized Labor and Radio Station WEVD during the 1930s," *LH* 42, no. 4 (2001): 347–69; Newman, *Radio Active,* 65–66.

4. Barnouw, *Golden Web,* 137–38; Newman, *Radio Active,* 105–106; Elizabeth Fones-Wolf, *Waves of Opposition: Labor and the Struggle for Democratic Radio* (Urbana: University of Illinois Press, 2006), 63–86.

5. Thorstein Veblen, *The Theory of Business Enterprise* (New York: Scribner and Sons, 1904), 36, 39, 54–55, 216. Also see Thorstein Veblen, *The Theory of the Leisure Class* (New York: Macmillan, 1899); Dorothy Ross, *The Origins of American Social Science* (New York: Cambridge University Press, 1991), 204, 216–17; Martha Banta, *Taylored Lives: Narrative Productions in the Age of Taylor, Veblen, and Ford* (Chicago: University of Chicago Press, 1993), 91–92; John Jordan, *Machine-Age Ideology: Social Engineering and American Liberalism, 1911–1939* (Chapel Hill: University of North Carolina Press, 1994), 13–19, 106–108; Gary Fine, "The Social Construction of Style: Thorstein Veblen's *The Theory of the Leisure Class* as Contested Text," *Sociological Quarterly* 35, no. 3 (1994): 457–72; and McGovern, *Sold American,* 138–49.

6. Thorstein Veblen, *Absentee Ownership and Business Enterprise in Recent Times* (New York: B. W. Hubesch, 1923), 300, 304, 306, 314–15.

7. Stuart Chase, *The Tragedy of Waste* (New York: Macmillan, 1925), 42. Also see Robert Westbrook, "Tribune of the Technostructure: The Popular Economics of Stuart Chase," *AQ* 32, no. 4 (1980): 387–408; and Daniel Horowitz, *The Morality of Spending: Attitudes Towards the Consumer Society in America* (Baltimore: Johns Hopkins University Press, 1985), 110–13, 152–53; McGovern, *Sold American,* 167–70.

8. Stuart Chase and F. J. Schlink, *Your Money's Worth: A Study in the Waste of the Consumer's Dollar* (New York: Macmillan, 1927), 245. Also see Glickman, " 'Strike

in the Temple of Consumption'"; McGovern, *Sold American*, 170–78; Jacobs, *Pocketbook Politics*, 89–90; Stole, *Advertising on Trial*, 23–26.

9. Robert and Helen Lynd, *Middletown: A Study in Modern American Culture* (New York: Harcourt and Brace, 1929), 7, 80–82, 499–500. Also see Robert Lynd with Alice Hanson, "The People as Consumers," in *Recent Social Trends in the United States*, ed. Wesley Mitchell (New York: McGraw-Hill, 1932), 857–911; Pells, *Radical Visions*, 24–27; Richard Fox, "Epitaph for *Middletown*: Robert S. Lynd and the Analysis of Consumer Culture," in *The Culture of Consumption: Critical Essays in American History, 1880–1980*, ed. Richard Fox and Jackson Lears (New York: Pantheon, 1983), 101–41; and Sarah Igo, *The Averaged American: Surveys, Citizens, and the Making of a Mass Public* (Cambridge, MA: Harvard University Press, 2007), 23–102.

10. "Cellophaned Editor," *Tide*, June 1931, 26–27; "Anthony against the Ads," *Tide*, July 1931, 22; "Ballyhoo," *Tide*, October 1931, 20; "Doings of *Ballyhoo*," *Tide*, February 1932, 19–20; Rorty, *Our Master's Voice*, 382–84. Also see Marchand, *Advertising the American Dream*, 312–14; McGovern, 242; Stole, *Advertising on Trial*, 29–30.

11. Masthead/Editorial Statement, *CRB*, September 1931, 1; addendum to E. B. White, "What Advertising Works at and How: The Urgency of an Agency," *CRB*, September 1931, 10–11. Also see Glickman, "'Strike in the Temple of Consumption'"; McGovern, *Sold American*, 186–217.

12. "The Buyer's Baedeker," *NR*, November 26, 1930, 32–33; Stuart Chase, "The Age of Distribution," *Nation*, July 25, 1934, 93–95; Matthew Josephson, "The Consumer Consumed," *NM*, March 12, 1935, 22–23.

13. F. J. Schlink and Arthur Kallet, *100,000,000 Guinea Pigs: Dangers in Everyday Food, Drugs and Cosmetics* (New York: Vanguard Press, 1932); M. C. Phillips, *Skin Deep: The Truth about Beauty Aids* (New York: Vanguard Press, 1934); J. B. Matthews and R. E. Shallcross, *Partners in Plunder: The Cost of Business Dictatorship* (New York: Covici, Friede, 1935); F. J. Schlink, *Eat, Drink, and Be Wary* (New York: Covici, Friede, 1935); and Arthur Kallet, *Counterfeit: Not Your Money but What It Buys* (New York: Vanguard Press, 1935). Also see McGovern, *Sold American*, 245–53.

14. "Durstine Challenges Consumers' Research at Washington Meet," *AA*, May 6, 1935, 1–2; "When They Ask about *Skin Deep*," *JWT News*, January 15, 1935, 9–10, Box DO8, JWT-NL; "Review of *Partners in Plunder*," JWT Junior News Letter, March 18, 1935, 11–12, Box DO8, JWT-NL. Also see "Advertising Ethics Non-Existent, Chase Tells N.U. Students," *AA*, April 19, 1930, 10; "'Guinea Pigs' Called Danger to Advertising," *AA*, March 11, 1933, 15; "Consumers Have Faith in Advertising," *AA*, January 20, 1934, 4; McGovern, *Sold American*, 253–60; Stole, *Advertising on Trial*, 32–36, 58–65.

15. "Advertising is Parasite, View of R. G. Tugwell," *AA*, June 10, 1933, 8; "Professor Tugwell on the Competitive System," *AA*, June 17, 1933, 4; "U.S. Officials Reassure Advertisers," *AA*, July 1, 1933, 1, 19; "Notes on NIRA—For Consumers," *CRB*,

October 1933, 1–5; "Quality Standards Requested for Codes," *NYT*, October 30, 1933, 2; "Needed: A Department of the Consumer," *CRB*, January 1934, 1–3; "200 Liberals Ask a Powerful NRA," *NYT*, May 24, 1934, 10; "Self-Regulation Endorsed by Advertising Federation," *AA*, June 23, 1934, 1, 34; "Economist Asks New U.S. Department to Represent Consumer," *AA*, June 30, 1934; Donald W. McDonnell, "Consumers and the Consumer Advisory Board," *CRB*, July 1934, 1–4; J. B. Matthews, "The Great NRA Illusion: The Consumers Advisory Board," *CRB*, October 1934, 5–7. Also see Cohen, *Consumers' Republic*, 19–20, 28–31; Jacobs, *Pocketbook Politics*, 104–35; and Stole, *Advertising on Trial*, 36–8, 65–79.

16. "Advertising is Parasite, View of R. G. Tugwell," *AA*, June 10, 1933, 5; "Prof. Tugwell on the Competitive System," *AA*, June 17, 1933, 4; Rexford Tugwell, "The Idea of the New Deal," *NYT*, July 16, 1933, VI, 1–2, 17; "Toward a Planned Society," *BW*, January 6, 1934, 5–6; "Government Grades Versus Advertised Brands," *AA*, February 3, 1934, 4; "TVA to Compete with Businesses in Many Fields," *AA*, February 3, 1934, 16; "Tugwell Sees End of Laissez-Faire," *NYT*, February 16, 1934, 15; "Kallet Flags Copeland Bill as Caricature," *AA*, March 3, 1934, 19; "Asks Grade Rules in All NRA Codes," *NYT*, March 25, 1934, N17; "Professor Tugwell's Address to Newspaper Editors at the Capital," *NYT*, April 22, 1934, 30; "Opposition to TVA Appliance Program Grows," *AA*, June 8, 1934, 1, 26; "Tugwell Dropped in AAA Councils," *NYT*, October 26, 1934, 17.

17. Daniel Pope, "His Master's Voice: James Rorty and the Critique of Advertising," *Maryland History* 19 (Spring/Summer 1988): 5–16; Newman, *Radio Active*, 58–63; and McGovern, *Sold American*, 243–44.

18. James Rorty to Lewis Corey, November 25, 1932, "Correspondence—1932" folder, Box 9, LC; League of Professional Groups, "Lecture Series: Culture and Capitalism," January 1933, "Correspondence—1933" folder, Box 9, LC; "Program of the League of Professional Groups (1933)," "Correspondence—1933" folder, Box 9, LC; James Rorty, "League of Professional Groups Reorganization Memo," June 16, 1933, "Correspondence—1933" folder, Box 9, LC.

19. Rorty, *Our Master's Voice*, v, ix, 14–18, 32. See also John Chamberlain, "Books of the Times," *NYT*, May 11, 1934, 19.

20. Rorty, *Our Master's Voice*, 133, 173.

21. "New School Offers 100 Adult Courses," *NYT*, September 15, 1935, 28; "Rorty Rips Up," *AA*, October 14, 1935, 6.

22. James Rorty, *Where Life Is Better: An Unsentimental American Journey* (New York: Reynal and Hitchcock, 1936), 92–97. "Sweeney" was in fact a stock character from *Daily News* trade advertising, but *True Story* made essentially the same claims about its readers' demographics and purchasing power as Rorty insinuates.

23. "New Organizations to Rate Labor Conditions," *CRB*, January 1933, 9. Also see "Producers Organize—Consumers Must," *CRB*, September 1932, 2; F. Reish, "Woman's Voice: We Win Lower Rent," *WW*, March 1933, 15; Clara Licht, "Councils Fight Against High Cost of Living," *WW*, October 1933, 10; Anna

Cohen, "We Stick Together and Win!" *WW*, January 1934; "How Consumers Can Organize for Their Own Protection," *CRB*, April 1934, 1–3; "Bread Strike," *WW*, September 1934, 9; Rose Nelson, "We Strike for Cheap Meat," *WW*, July 1935, 3; P. M., "The Detroit Meat Strike," *WW*, November 1935, 12. Also see Glickman, " 'The Strike in the Temple of Consumption' "; and McGovern, *Sold American*, 302–04.

24. "Kallet Flays Copeland Bill as Caricature"; Kallet, *Counterfeit*, 94–95; "Consumers' Union" (internal research memo), October 22, 1948, Folder 28, Box 6, CLA-CRF.

25. Mildred Edie to F. J. Schlink, August 31, 1935, Folder 5, Box 196, CR; "Strike at Consumers' Research," *Ledger*, September 15, 1935, 1–2; Arthur Kallet, "Consumers' Research on Strike" *NM*, September 17, 1935, 12–13; "Later Strike Developments at CR," *CRB*, October 1935, 18–24; J. B. Matthews, Deposition, October 10, 1935, "Brady, Mildred Edie, n.d." folder, Box 593, JBM; David Munro, "Consumers Right and Left," *S&T*, May 22, 1939, 1–3, Folder 5, Box 197, CR. Also see McGovern, *Sold American*, 304–309; and Stole, *Advertising on Trial*, 80–92.

26. "The Strike at Consumers' Research," *NR*, October 9, 1935, 230–31; "Fixing the Blame at CR," *NR*, November 13, 1935; "The C.R. Strike," *Nation*, December 4, 1935, 637; "Kallet vs. Schlink," *BW*, September 7, 1935, 8; "Thunder on the Left," *Tide*, September x, 1935, 22–23; "CR: Comedy Relief," *BW*, October 12, 1935, 30. Also see Glickman, " 'The Strike in the Temple of Consumption.' "

27. See "Waking Up!" *Ledger*, September 15, 1935, 5; Local 20055, "Strike Bulletin," October 17, 1935, Frames 11–13, Reel 9, Part I, CIO-JLL; "CR Strike News," *Ledger*, October 24, 1935, 12; Local 20055, "Strike Bulletin," October 25, 1935, Frame 14, Reel 9, Part I, CIO-JLL; "CR Theatre Party," *Ledger*, October 24, 1935, 12.

28. Masthead, *CUR*, May 1936, 2; "Consumers Union Reports," *CUR*, May 1936, 2, 24. Also see Stole, *Advertising on Trial*, 92–98.

29. "Consumers' Goods Makers Unfair to Labor," *CUR*, May 1936, 20–21; "Broad Campaign to Sell Public on Union Label," *AA*, August 18, 1934, 6. Also see Frank, *Purchasing Power*, 193–251; and Lawrence Glickman, *A Living Wage: American Workers and the Making of Consumer Society* (Ithaca, NY: Cornell University Press, 1997), 95–146.

30. "Low- and Medium-Priced Automobiles," *CUR*, June 1936, 3–11; "The Automobile Industry's Workers," *CUR*, June 1936, 11–12; "The Refrigerator Industry's Workers," *CUR*, July 1936, 9–10; "The 'Sitdown,'" *CUR*, March 1937, 27–28; "Workers in the Automobile Plants," *CUR*, March 1938, 30. Also see, "Labor in the Baking Plants," *CUR*, August 1936, 6; "In the Soap Factories," *CUR*, August 1936, 9; "Labor in the Washing Machine Factories," *CUR*, May 1937, 26; "Labor in the Typewriter Industry," *CUR*, November 1937, 12; "Labor in the Radio Industry: A Report on Wages and Unionization," *CUR*, December 1937, 32; "Workers in the Chain Stores," *CUR*, April 1938, 8–10; "Autos—the Companies and the Union," *CUR*, February 1939, 30–31; "Textiles—the 'Sick Giant,'" *CUR*, January 1939, 25–26.

31. "Consumers Union Reports," *CUR*, May 1936, 2, 24; "Strike Against Hearst," *CUR*, June 1936, 2.

32. "Good Housekeeping Institute," *CUR*, July 1936, 2, 24; CU advertisement, *NYT Magazine*, November 22, 1936, 28; CU advertisement, *NYT Magazine*, December 20, 1936, 20; "The Attacking Stage," *CUR*, December 1937, 2; George Seldes, "Do Advertisers Dominate the Press?" *CUR*, January 1939, 17.

33. "Nothing Wrong with Consumers Union Copy," *AA*, February 19, 1940, 30; CU advertisement, *NR*, December 21, 1938, 209; CU advertisement, *Nation*, October 2, 1937, 351; CU advertisement, *Daily Worker*, April 30, 1938, 5; CU advertisement, *Soviet Russia Today*, March 1937, inside back cover; Susan Jenkins to Wyndham Mortimer, May 15, 1937, Folder 14, Box 86, CIO-C; Arthur Kallet to John L. Lewis, November 3, 1938, Folder 15, Box 86, CIO-C.

34. Alexander Crosby to Len De Caux, December 31, 1937, Folder 15, Box 86, CIO-C; Lydia Altschuler to Kathryn Lewis, February 23, 1938, Frames 129–30, Reel 4, Part I, CIO-JLL; Kallet to Lewis, November 3, 1938; "CU's Members Report," *CUR*, October 1939, 8–9.

35. Ira Cottins, "CD," *CUR*, July 1936, 21–22; Henry Davis, "Building a Cooperative," *CUR*, September 1936, 22–23; "The 1938 Radio Sets," *CUR*, December 1937, 26–30; "The Cooperators Meet," *CUR*, November 1938, 9; "Electric Irons," *CUR*, May 1939, 15–16; "1939 Refrigerators Are Cheaper," *CUR*, July 1939, 3–6; "Vacuum Cleaners," *CUR*, October 1941, 257–61; Ella Roller, "Are Frozen Foods Good Buys?" *CUR*, August 1941, 219–20; Kingsley Roberts, "Group Health Associations," *CUR*, April 1940, 32–33; Roberts, "Group Health Plans," *CUR*, May 1940, 26–27; Joan David, "I Am a Member of Group Health," *CUR*, May 1941, 132–33. Also see Klein, *For All These Rights*, 149–61.

36. "That's How Prices Are Made," *CUR*, April 1939, 6–7; "Waste and Want—An Answer," *CUR*, June 1939, 30–31; "Surpluses and Need," *CUR*, November 1939, 15–16; "The A.M.A. Claims," *CUR*, June 1940, 25–26; "What Consumers Want," *CUR*, April 1941, 106–107. Also see Fraser, *Labor Will Rule*, 349–440; and Brinkley, *The End of Reform*, 65–85, 106–74.

37. "What Should a Label Say?" *CUR*, March 1938, 20–21; "Mr. Barton vs. the Truth," *CUR*, March 1940, 1, 4; "The Consumer Witness," *CUR*, February 1941, 52–53. Also see Stole, *Advertising on Trial*, 138–58.

38. David Munro, "Changing Guard," *S&T*, November 21, 1938, Folder 5, Box 196, CR; J. A. Malloy to L. M. Whiting, November 27, 1939, Folder 6, Box 504, JBM; Munro, "Masters at Meeting," *S&T*, May 13, 1940, Folder 6, Box 504, JBM; Munro, "Braucher, Edie, Etc.," *S&T*, November 18, 1940, Folder 6, Box 504, JBM; "Munro Suits," *Tide*, April 1, 1941, 28, 30; "Advertising Isn't 'Institutionally' Evil, It's Just Used Anti-Socially by Some Admen: Masters," *AA*, October 4, 1965, 104.

39. J. B. Matthews to George Sokolsky, February 24, 1938, Folder 2, Box 196, CR; "Hearst Writer Sees CR as a Public Menace," *CRB*, April 1934, 23; "Good House," *Tide*, September 1, 1939, 36, 38. Also see Murray Kempton, *Part of Our Time: Some Ruins and Monuments of the Thirties* (New York: Simon and Schuster, 1955), 151–79; and McGovern, *Sold American*, 316–22.

40. "Faith in Advertising," *CUR*, August 1939, 14–15; U.S. Federal Trade Commission, Docket No. 3872, In the Matter of Hearst Magazines, Inc., Complaint, August 17, 1939, Folder 5, Box 3, DM; "*Good House*," *Tide*, September 1, 1939, 36, 38; "*Good Housekeeping* Stands Indicted," *CUR*, September 1939, 3–5; "The Way It Looks to Us," *CUR*, November 1939, 32; Richard Berlin to Advertisers and Manufacturers, December 9, 1939, Folder 18, Box 2, DM; "*Good House* V," *Tide*, December 15, 1939, 14–15; David Munro, "The Dies Plot, Detail," *S&T*, December 18, 1939, Folder 15, Box 2, DM; "'Report' by Mr. Matthews," *CUR*, January 1940, 24–25; "The Case Against Good Housekeeping," *CUR*, January 1940, 26–27; Munro, "How it Happened," *S&T*, January 31, 1940, Folder 6, Box 504, JBM; Munro, "You Can Count on ANA," *S&T*, April 1, 1940, Folder 6, Box 504, JBM; "FTC Docket No. 3872," *CUR*, April 1941, 103–105.

41. "Report of the Director of Research, J. B. Matthews, to the Special Committee on Un-American Activities on Communist Work in Consumer Organizations, December 11, 1939, 1–3, 11, Folder 18, Box 2, DM. On the deployment of "free enterprise" in opposition to the New Deal and its supporters, see Lawrence Glickman, *Free Enterprise: An American History* (New Haven, CT: Yale University Press, 2019), 79–110.

42. "Sticks and Stones," *CUR*, October 1939, 32; "New Tack," *Tide*, November 15, 1939, 23–24; Susan Jenkins, Statement, December 11, 1939, Folder 15, Box 2, DM; Donald Montgomery, Statement, December 12, 1939, Folder 17, Box 2, DM; David Munro, "Dies and Consumers," *S&T*, January 10, 1940, Folder 6, Box 504, JBM; Munro, "Dies Okayed," *S&T*, January 24, 1940, Folder 6, Box 504, JBM; Dexter Masters to Montgomery, April 10, 1940, Folder 1, Box 3, DM; Montgomery to Masters, April 11, 1940, Folder 1, Box 3, DM; Montgomery to Martin Dies, April 22, 1940, Folder 18, Box 2, DM; Munro, "4-As Take Castor Oil," *S&T*, May 20, 1940, Folder 6, Box 504, JBM; Munro, "ANA (Hearst) vs. FTC," *S&T*, July 15, 1940, Folder 6, Box 504, JBM; Munro, "The 'Stop *Space & Time*' Suit," *S&T*, November 4, 1940, Folder 6, Box 504, JBM.

43. Ralph Ingersoll, *Point of Departure: An Adventure in Autobiography* (New York: Harcourt and Brace, 1961), 163–67, 185–204; Roy Hoopes, *Ralph Ingersoll: A Biography* (New York: Athaeneum, 1985), 62–186; Paul Milkman, *PM: A New Deal in Journalism* (New Brunswick: Rutgers University Press, 1997), 10–14; Brinkley, *Publisher*, 158–66, 195–201, 208–27; and Vanderlan, *Intellectuals Incorporated*, 96–120. For perspective on an early twentieth century experiment with advertising-free news, see Duane Stoltzfus, *Freedom from Advertising: E. W. Scripps's Chicago Experiment* (Urbana: University of Illinois Press, 2007).

44. "Manhattan Daily," *Tide*, December 15, 1939, 38, 40; Hoopes, *Ralph Ingersoll*, 157–59, 187–217; Milkman, PM, 22–43; and Marilyn Nissenson, *The Lady Upstairs: Dorothy Schiff and the New York Post* (New York: St. Martins, 2007), 51–53.

45. "*PM*," *Tide*, May 15, 1940, 9–10; "*PM* Signs with the Newspaper Guild," *PM*, October 9, 1940, 10; John P. Lewis to Ad Reinhardt, April 1, 1947, Folder 6,

Box 2, AR; Hoopes, *Ralph Ingersoll*, 217–20, 225–28; and Milkman, PM, 6–10, 14–21, 43–51.

46. News for Living Masthead, *PM*, June 18, 1940, 25; "Federal Trade Commission Renews Heating On Good Housekeeping Magazine," *PM*, June 18, 1940, 25; Elizabeth Hawes, "CU Reports Can Stretch Your Money—They Can Also Drive You Crazy," *PM*, June 24, 1940; "Grain of Salt," *CUR*, July 1940, 1; Roger Dakin, "Tenant Assns. Watch Court Fight Over Knickerbocker Village Leases," *PM*, July 11, 1940, 25; Amos Landman, "Civil War 'Slave Markets' Survive in the Bronx," *PM*, July 15, 1940, 14; Berch, *Radical by Design*, 88–97.

47. David Munro, "*PM*'s First," *S&T*, June 17, 1940, Folder 6, Box 504, JBM; "Birth of *PM*," *Tide*, July 1, 1940, 52, 54; "*PM*," August 15, 1940, 24; "*PM* to Field?" *Tide*, October 1, 1940, 76, Hoopes, *Ralph Ingersoll*, 225–31, 235–37; Milkman, PM, 51–57.

48. Ralph Ingersoll, Memorandum to All Writers and Editors, December 21, 1940, NGNY, Box 54, Folder 17; Hoopes, *Ralph Ingersoll*, 232–35, 241–44.

49. Field Publications, Comparison of Payrolls 1/17/41 and 9/15/44 by Classification (Company Exhibit No. 12), February 1, 1945, Folder 20, Box 54, NGNY; NGNY PM Unit, Report on PM Negotiations, April 23, 1941, Folder 32, Box 54, NGNY; NWLB Daily Newspaper Printing and Publishing Commission, Report and Rulings of the Commission, Case No. 111-12603-D, October 15, 1945, Folder 20, Box 54, NGNY; Field Publications, Guild Production Costs (Company Exhibit No. 20), February 1, 1945, Folder 20, Box 54, NGNY.

50. Henry Luce, "The American Century," *Life*, February 17, 1941, 61–65; Henry Wallace, "Common People March Toward Fuller Freedom, And Won't Be Stopped," *PM*, May 10, 1942, 12–13. Also see Graham White and John Maze, *Henry A. Wallace: His Search for a New World Order* (Chapel Hill: University of North Carolina Press, 1995), 162–64; Milkman, PM, 67–75, 165–76; and Brinkley, *Publisher*, 267–73.

51. Field Publications, Net Paid Circulation Comparison (Company Exhibit No. 5), February 1, 1945, Folder 20, Box 54, NGNY; Milkman, PM, 137.

52. David Munro, "Field to Chicago," *S&T*, September 22, 1941, 4, Folder 7, Box 504, JBM; "AM for Chicago," *Tide*, October 1, 1940, 32, 34; John P. Lewis and Lowell L. Leake to the Employees of *PM*, 1945, Folder 35, Box 54, NGNY; Hoopes, *Ralph Ingersoll*, 315–18; Milkman, PM, 145, 177–79.

53. George Seldes, *Tell the Truth and Run* (New York: Greenberg, 1953), vii–xxiv, 1–41, 128–66, 179–200, 209–23. Also see Gilbert Seldes, *The Seven Lively Arts* (New York: Harper, 1924); and Michael Kammen, *The Lively Arts: Gilbert Seldes and the Transformation of Cultural Criticism in the United States* (New York: Oxford University Press, 1996).

54. George Seldes, *You Can't Print That: The Truth behind the News* (Garden City: Garden City, 1927); Seldes, *Sawdust Caesar: The Untold History of Mussolini and Fascism* (New York: Harper, 1935); and Seldes, *Freedom of the Press* (New York: Harper, 1935).

55. Seldes, *Lords of the Press*, 6, 47, 370, 374, 382, 399–402.

56. "How Advertising Kills," *IF*, May 19, 1941, 1–2; Seldes, *Tell the Truth and Run*, 227–55; and George Seldes, *Never Tire of Protesting* (New York: Lyle Stuart, 1968), 14–20.

57. Eugene Lyons, "Red Mouthpiece: The Facts behind *In Fact*," *Plain Talk*, March 1947 (reprint), Folder 5, Box 264, JBM; Seldes, *Tell the Truth*, 261; Seldes, *Never Tire of Protesting*, 21–22, 50–54, 197–205.

58. See, for example, "Mr. Dies in Service to Big Business," *IF*, November 3, 1941, 1–2; "NAM Meets to Plot Against Welfare of People," *IF*, December 15, 1942, 2–3; "The Fascist Fringe," *IF*, July 10, 1944, 2–3; "Press Suppresses Congress Exposé of NAM Plot to Control U.S. Radio as It Controls Newspapers," *IF*, November 12, 1945, 1–3; "U.S. Big Business Boasts It Corrupts Public Opinion Through Press, Radio, School, Church," *IF*, November 19, 1945, 1–3; "Press Lord Runs Big Fascist Outfit," *IF*, August 6, 1945, 1; "FFE Smells of Texas Oil and Oranges," *IF*, August 6, 1945, 4; Shaemas O'Sheel, "The First American Legion—The Untold Story," *IF*, September 24, 1945, 3–4; and "Legion Fights Liberalism, Socialism, PAC, Trade Unionism in 'Isms' War; Omits Fascism," *IF*, December 30, 1946, 1–3. Also see Seldes, *Never Tire*, 36–41, 100–13.

59. See, for example, "Venal? Corrupt? Unfair?" *IF*, September 1, 1941, 1–3; "J.P. Morgan's Beauty Cream," *IF*, October 27, 1941, 1–2; "80 Years of *Chicago Tribune* Unbroken Record of Falsehood by this Outstanding Enemy of the People," *IF*, November 24, 1941, 1–4; "News is Suppressed 365 Days a Year," *IF*, October 8, 1945, 2–3; "Newspapers Suppress A&P Expose," *IF*, October 15, 1945, 3–4; "Collusion: *Detroit Free Press* and General Motors," *IF*, December 3, 1945, 3–4; and "'Stop Cancer' Drive Suppresses Scientific News Linking Disease to Well-Advertised Cigarettes," *IF*, July 28, 1947, 1–3. Also see Seldes, *Never Tire*, 29–35, 66–69, 83–92.

60. David Munro, "New Medium," *S&T*, January 6, 1941, Folder 7, Box 504, JBM, Box 504; Morris Watson and Frances Watson, "America First NYC in Coughlin's Control," *IF*, December 1, 1941, 3–4; Naomi Michelson to Tom Murphy, May 3, 1943, Folder 11, Box 40, NGNY; Urcel Daniels to Murphy, May 10, 1943, Folder 11, Box 40, NGNY; Daniels to Murphy, May 18, 1943, Folder 11, Box 40, NGNY.

61. "Price of *In Fact* Goes to $1 a Year Jan. 1," *IF*, December 15, 1941, 4; and Seldes, *Tell the Truth*, 269; Seldes, *Never Tire*, 26–27, 52.

62. "Dies Will Quit Seat in Congress," *NYT*, May 13, 1944, 1; "Dies the Center of Many Storms in Six-Year House Investigation," *NYT*, May 13, 1944, 10; Elizabeth Donahue, "Dies Retirement Spells Doom of Witch-Hunt Agency," *PM*, May 14, 1944, 5; "Ex-Judge Is Only Candidate for Dies' Seat," *PM*, May 14, 1944, 5; and "To *In Fact* Readers: Fourth Annual Report," *IF*, May 22, 1944, 1–3. Also see Seldes, *Never Tire*, 41–49.

63. "To *In Fact* Readers: Fourth Annual Report."

64. "New 10-Cent Weekly Due," *NYT*, February 14, 1940, 30; "*Friday*: A Report on a New Magazine," *Tide*, March 1, 1940, 21; Benjamin Stolberg, "Muddled Millions,"

SEP, February 15, 1941, 6–10; Seldes, *Never Tire*, 20; and Hoopes, *Ralph Ingersoll*, 220, 234.

65. Daniel Gillmor, "Dear Reader," *Friday*, March 15, 1940, 20. Also see Denning, *Cultural Front*, 156–59.

66. "Magazine to Make Bow," *NYT*, March 7, 1940, 21; *Friday* masthead, March 15, 1940; *Friday* masthead, June 14, 1940; *Friday* masthead, July 5, 1940; "Braucher, Edie, Etc," *S&T*, November 18, 1940, Folder 6, Box 504, JBM; *Friday* masthead, December 27, 1940; "Cameron MacKenzie" (internal research memo), October 19, 1948, Folder 23, Box 13, CLA-CRF; "Leverett S. Gleason" (internal research memo), December 19, 1950, Folder 3, Box 14, CLA-CRF; Bradford Wright, *Comic Book Nation: The Transformation of Youth Culture in America* (Baltimore: Johns Hopkins University Press, 2003), 41; John Ryan to D. S. Gillmor, March 15, 1941, Folder 47, Box 35, NGNY; Gillmor to Ryan, March 22, 1941, Folder 47, Box 35, NGNY; Charles Beard, "Time and Archibald MacLeish," *Friday*, September 27, 1940, 16; Franz Boas, "We Are Starving Democracy," *Friday*, September 20, 1940, 17–18; and Theodore Dreiser, "The Story of Harry Bridges," *Friday*, October 4, 1940, 1–7, 28.

67. "Hollywood Fights Back," *Friday*, March 15, 1940, 12–13.

68. Ella Winter, "Charlie Chaplin and 'The Dictator,'" *Friday*, August 30, 1940, 22–23; "*The Devil and Miss Jones*: Jean Arthur Joins the Union and Signs up the Devil," *Friday*, April 4, 1941, 24–25. Also see Michael Rogin, "How the Working Class Saved Capitalism: The New Labor History and *The Devil and Miss Jones*," *JAH* 89 (June 2002): 87–114.

69. "Wellesapoppin," *Friday*, September 13, 1940, 14; "Orson Delivers," *Friday*, January 17, 1941, 24–27; Orson Welles, "Orson Welles Tells His Side of *Citizen Kane* Controversy," *Friday*, February 14, 1941, 8–9.

70. "10,000 Girls and a Little Man," *Friday*, April 5, 1940, 2–4.

71. Jack Freel, "Baseball's Migratory Workers," *Friday*, March 22, 1940, 5; "Baseball Needs Them," *Friday*, April 12, 1940, 10–12; "$25,000,000 Nickel Business: The Pinball Craze is a Depression Baby Who Came to Stay," *Friday*, April 11, 1941, 24–25; "Who's Afraid of the Big Bad Walt?" *Friday*, July 25, 1941, 38–39; "A Union Makes a Movie," *Friday*, June 7, 1940, 14–17; "Calling All Hams," *Friday*, April 4, 1941, 26–27; and "Mibbs, Miggs, and Aggies," *Friday*, July 25, 1941, 32–35.

72. Richard Boyer, "Who Killed Laura Law?" *Friday*, March 22, 1940, 1–4; Boyer, "Who Killed Laura Law? (Part Two)," *Friday*, April 5, 1940, 19; "M-Day at Dearborn," *Friday*, April 12, 1940, 7–9; "M-Day at Dearborn (Part Two)," *Friday*, April 19, 1940, 12–13; "The Case Against Ford," *Friday*, May 3, 1940, 11–13; "King Ford's Empire," *Friday*, October 25, 1940, 11–13; Dan Gillmor, "Ford's Fascism: Proof," *Friday*, January 24, 1941, 3–9; Gillmor, "Ford's Fascism: Proof (Part Two)," *Friday*, January 31, 1941, 3–7; Gillmor, "Ford's Fascism: Proof (Part Three)," *Friday*, February 7, 1941, 15–20; Gillmor, "Ford's Fascism: Proof (Part Four)," *Friday*, February 14, 1941, 11–15; "Detroit Sees Change," *Friday*, February 28, 1941, 3–9; "News Pictures: Ford Strike," *Friday*, May 9, 1941, 4.

73. Ruth McKenney, "The Transport Workers," *Friday*, March 22, 1940, 9–11; "Union Now: American Style," *Friday*, September 20, 1940, 14–16; "Dirt and Death," *Friday*, April 4, 1941, 6–10; Charles Calkins, "Mercury Spells Death in Danbury," *Friday*, February 14, 1941, 21–23; "Peonage in Georgia," *Friday*, April 12, 1940, 22–23; "Ten Million Americans Can't Vote," *Friday*, April 19, 1940, 1–4, 25; "These Are Their Lives," *Friday*, March 29, 1940, 2–4. On the visual representation of labor more generally during the 1930s and 1940s, see Carol Quirke, *Eyes on Labor: News Photography and America's Working Class* (New York: Oxford University Press, 2012), 3–107.

74. Dexter Masters, "Light on Utility Bargains," *Friday*, May 3, 1940, 28; Consumers Union ad, *Friday*, April 4, 1941, 32; "Can You Afford to Pay Your Doctor's Bill?" *Friday*, October 11, 1940, 9–11; Dan Gillmor, "A Letter to You," *Friday*, June 14, 1940, 2; "Socialist Party," *Friday*, November 1, 1940, 9; "Communist Party," *Friday*, November 1, 1940, 13.

75. *Friday* cover, March 15, 1940; Richard Boyer, "Zero Hour for Uncle Sam," *Friday*, May 24, 1940, 1–7, 24; Gillmor, "This Man is Not for Peace," *Friday*, August 30, 1940, 2; Gerald Nye, "The Same Old Game," *Friday*, August 30, 1940, 3–4; and Winston Burdett, "Hitler Sells Out Mussolini," *Friday*, April 25, 1941, 3–7.

76. "*Friday*: A Report on a New Magazine," *Tide*, March 1, 1940, 21; and "*Friday*," *Tide*, January 15, 1941, 24–25.

77. D. S. Gillmor to John L. Lewis, October 21, 1940, Folder 18, Box 91, CIO-C; and Ralph Hetzel to Gillmor, October 31, 1940, Folder 18, Box 91, CIO-C.

78. "*Friday*," *Tide*, January 15, 1941, 24–25; Display ad, *NYT*, January 13, 1941, 30; Display ad, *Friday*, January 17, 1941, 27; Stolberg, "Muddled Millions," 6–10; Dan Gillmor, "Greetings from San Simeon," *Friday*, March 7, 1941, 2; Gillmor, "A Reply to a Letter," *Friday*, April 11, 1941, 2; "*Friday* answers Hearst," *IF*, April 21, 1941, 3–4.

79. Dan Gillmor, "Annual Report to Our Readers," *Friday*, March 14, 1941, 20; Nat Einhorn to Milton Kaufman, August 29, 1941, Folder 48, Box 35, NGNY; "New Name for *Friday*," *IF*, September 15, 1941, 3; "Gillmor out of OCI Post," *NYT*, April 10, 1942, 11.

80. *Reader's Scope* index August 1944; Harvey Killgore, "Post-War Jobs for All," *RS*, August 1944, 3–6; Howard Fast, "The Dead Will not Sleep," *RS*, August 1944, 58–59; Bennett Cerf, "The Goldwyn Saga," *RS*, August 1944, 70–73; Julius Emspak, "This Year Labor Means Business," *RS*, August 1944, 92–95; J. B. Matthews, Hearst Magazines Inc. memorandum, July 10, 1945, Folder 16, Box 475, JBM; Leverett Gleason, "Dear Subscriber" form letter, May 28, 1948, Folder 16, Box 475, JBM.

CHAPTER 4

1. John McAndrew, "'Modernistic' and 'Streamlined'," *BMoMA*, December 1938, 2. Also see Barbara Staniszewski, *The Power of Display: A History of Exhibition Installations at the Museum of Modern Art* (Cambridge, MA: MIT Press, 1998),

143–90; and Margaret Kentgens-Craig, *The Bauhaus and America: First Contacts, 1919–1936* (Cambridge, MA: MIT Press, 1999).

2. McAndrew, "'Modernistic' and 'Streamlined,'" 1–2. On the founding of MoMA and elite patronage for modernism, see Russell Lynes, *The Good Old Modern: An Intimate Portrait of the Museum of Modern Art* (New York: Athenaeum, 1973), 57–211; Scott and Rutkoff, *New York Modern*, 163–93; Platt, *Art and Politics in the 1930s*, 202–205; Sybil Gordon Kantor, *Alfred H. Barr and the Intellectual Origins of the Museum of Modern Art* (Cambridge, MA: MIT Press, 2002), 242–353; and Saab, *For the Millions*, 84–128.

3. Artists' Union Constitution, *AF*, November 1934, 8.

4. Charmion von Wiegand, "American Artists' Congress," *AF*, March 1936, 8; WPA, *Our Job with the WPA*, March 1936, Folder 60, Box 26, EM; Meyer Schapiro, "Public Use of Art," *AF*, November 1936, 4–6; Clarence Weinstock, "Public Art in Practice," *AF*, December 1936, 8–10. Also see Garnett McCoy, "The Rise and Fall of the American Artists' Congress," *Prospects* 13 (October 1988): 325–40; Patricia Hills, "1936: Meyer Schapiro, *Art Front*, and the Popular Front," *OAJ* 17, no. 1 (1994): 30–41; Denning, *Cultural Front*, 38–83; Platt, *Art and Politics in the 1930s*, 87–101, 147–65; and Hemingway, *Artists on the Left*, 20–24, 39–46, 85–88, 123–33.

5. By contrast, the National Endowment for the Arts (NEA), National Endowment for the Humanities (NEH), and Corporation for Public Broadcasting (CPB) that were established in the 1960s as part of the Great Society inject streams of public funding into networks and institutions that have been structured by conventional means of private cultural patronage. See M. David Ermann, "The Operative Goals of Corporate Philanthropy: Contributions to the Public Broadcasting Service, 1972–1976," *Social Problems* 25, no. 5 (1978): 504–14; James Ledbetter, *Made Possible By: The Death of Public Broadcasting in the United States* (New York: Verso, 1997); Michael Brenson, *Visionaries and Outcasts: The NEA, Congress, and the Place of the Visual Artist in America* (New York: New Press, 2001); and Donna Binkiewicz, *Federalizing the Muse: United States Art Policy and the National Endowment for the Arts, 1965–1980* (Chapel Hill: University of North Carolina Press, 2004).

6. WPA, "Employment on Federally Sponsored WPA Projects, By State," May 8, 1937, Frame 490, Reel 1107, HC, Reel 1107; and Elizabeth McCausland, "Save the Arts Projects," *Nation*, July 17, 1937, 67–69.

7. Interview with Holger Cahill by Joan Pringe, 1957, Frames 27–653, Reel 5285, HC. Also see Jane De Hart Mathews, "Arts and the People: The New Deal Quest for Cultural Democracy," *JAH* 62, no. 2 (1975): 316–39; Wendy Jeffers, "Holger Cahill and American Art," *AAAJ* 31, no. 4 (1991): 2–11; William Leuchtenberg, "Art in the Great Depression," in *A Modern Mosaic: Art and Modernism in the United States*, ed. Townsend Ludington (Chapel Hill: University of North Carolina Press, 1999), 227–55; Platt, *Art and Politics*, 177–80, 205–206; Hemingway, *Artists on the Left*, 79, 81, 84, 151–53; Saab, *Art for the Millions*, 20–23; and Andrew Hemingway,

"Cultural Democracy by Default: The Politics of the New Deal Art Programmes," *OAJ* 30, no. 2 (2007): 271–87.

8. The text of Cahill's remarks appears as the "Foreward" in *Art for the Millions*, ed. O'Connor, 33–44.

9. Holger Cahill to Rockwell Kent, May 22, 1936, Frame 846, Reel 5181, RK; "Full Report of the Eastern District Convention of the Artists' Unions," *AF*, June 1936, 5–7; C. A. Glassgold to Cahill, June 15, 1936, Frames 397–98, Reel NDA15, HC; Audrey McMahon to Cahill, October 14, 1936, Frames 1226–28, Reel 5285, HC; and Gerald Monroe, "Artists on the Barricades: The Militant Artists Union Treats with the New Deal," *AAAJ* 18, no. 3 (1978): 20–23.

10. St. Louis Writers' Union, Press Release, November 2, 1936, Frames 410–13, Reel 6, Part I, CIO-JLL; Milton Lomask to Katherine Lewis, November 12, 1936, Frame 406, Reel 6, Part I, CIO-JLL; Lomask to "Dear Friend," November 17, 1936, Frame 407, Reel 6, Part I, CIO-JLL; Jack Conroy, "Writers Disturbing the Peace," *WPA Writers Strike*, November 1936, Frames 398–99, Reel 6, Part I, CIO-JLL; and Lomask to Katherine Lewis, November 27, 1936, Frame 396, Reel 6, Part I, CIO-JLL.

11. "WPA Artists Fight Police; 219 Ejected, Many Clubbed," *NYT*, December 2, 1936, 1, 16; "Mayor Seeks to End Lay-Offs on WPA," *NYT*, December 3, 1936, 4; Morris Neuwirth, "219," *AF*, January 1937, 4–5; "Sit-In at Art Project," *NYT*, May 15, 1937, 8; "WPA Stoppage Due to Involve 20,000," *NYT*, May 27, 1937, 2; "10,000 Stop Work on WPA Projects," *NYT*, May 28, 1937, 1, 12; "WPA Here to Drop 12,000 Next Week," *NYT*, June 23, 1937, 1, 6; Financial Status of Federal Art Project, November 1, 1936, Frame 472, Reel 1107, HC; and Richard Lewis to the Executive Boards of All Art Locals, May 23, 1941, Frame 884, Reel 5243, RK.

12. "For a Permanent Art Project," *AF*, February 1936, 3; American Artists' Congress Executive Board, Policy Statement, February 1936, Frames 563–56, Reel 5154, RK; "Towards Permanent Projects," *AF*, May 1936, 5–6; Charmion von Wiegand to Rockwell Kent, June 21, 1936, Frame 849, Reel 5181, RK; Harry Gotlieb and Clarence Weinstock to the American People, May 24, 1937, Frames 1182–83, Reel 5158, RK; Marcia Coleman to Kent, February 18, 1938, Frame 479, Reel 5242, RK; and Kent to Franklin D. Roosevelt, May 13, 1939, Frames 549–51, Reel 5229, RK.

13. See Bentley, *Hallie Flanagan*, 304–48; and Hirsch, *Portrait of America*, 197–212.

14. FAP, "Design Laboratory," December 1935, Frames 563–65, Reel DC60, FAP; "WPA Establishes Free Art School," *NYT*, December 2, 1935, 19; and Don Wallance to Charles Hublitz, February 6, 1980, "Biographical Statements, Questionnaires, and Related Materials" folder, Box 1, DW.

15. Frances Pollak to Holger Cahill, October 22, 1935, Reel DC91, FAP; Cahill to Bruce McClure, November 2, 1935, Frame 377, Reel NDA15, HC; and Cahill to Pollak, November 18, 1935, Reel DC91, FAP. Also see Phyllis Ross, "Merchandising the Modern: Gilbert Rohde at Herman Miller," *JDH* 17, no. 4 (2004): 359–76.

16. Frances Pollak to Holger Cahill, "Design Laboratory Bibliography," December 5, 1935, Frames 181–83, Reel 1084, FO. Ralph Pearson, who supervised art programs at the New School for Social Research by the late 1930s, later claimed to Cahill that he had actually written the Laboratory prospectus; see Pearson to Cahill, January 6, 1938, Frame 193, Reel DC48, FAP.

17. Thorstein Veblen, *The Theory of the Leisure Class: An Economic Study of Institutions* (1899), rpt. ed. (New York: Random House, 1934), 157, 162, 244; and Veblen, "Arts and Crafts," *JPE* 11 (December 1902): 108–11.

18. Lewis Mumford, *Technics and Civilization* (New York: Harcourt, Brace and Co., 1934), 5–6, 345–55, 429. Also see Casey Blake, *Beloved Community: The Cultural Criticism of Randolph Bourne, Van Wyck Brooks, Waldo Frank, and Lewis Mumford* (Chapel Hill: University of North Carolina Press, 1990), 278–95; and Jordan, *Machine-Age Ideology*, 255–61.

19. Holger Cahill to Frances Pollak, September 18, 1935, Frame 46, Reel 1084, FO; "American Bauhaus," *ArchFor*, January 1936, 17, 34; Federal Project Number One, "Supervising Employees on Project Unit Payroll," August 1, 1936, Frames 715–16, Reel 1084, FO, Reel 1084; "Federation Technical School Design Laboratory, Catalog of Courses, 1937–1938," "Education—Design Laboratory, Circulars, 1936–1940" folder, Box 1, DW.

20. "Design Laboratory, New York" *American Magazine of Art*, February 1936, 117; "Classes at Capacity in WPA Art School," *NYT*, April 17, 1936, 5; WPA, "Design Laboratory," August 22, 1936, Folder 24, Box 26, EM; and Jacqueline A. Keyes, "WPA Educators Blazing Trail with School in Industry Design," *NYT*, October 25, 1936, II, 5.

21. Holger Cahill to Bruce McClure, November 2, 1935, Frame 377, Reel NDA15, HC; and Cahill to Jacob Baker, February 13, 1936, Frames 221–22, Reel DC54, FAP.

22. Jacob Baker to Harry Hopkins, February 14, 1936, Frame 953, Reel 5285, HC; Holger Cahill to Frances Pollak, February 13, 1936, Frame 201, Reel DC48, FAP; and Ruth Reeves to Cahill, June 1, 1936, Frames 552–54, Reel DC52.

23. Holger Cahill to Henry I. Brock, January 29, 1936, Frames 379–85, Reel NDA15, HC; "Holger Cahill Reports on Progress of Federal Art Program," February 16, 1936, Frames 31–32, Reel DC46, FAP; and "Holger Cahill Reports on Progress of Federal Art Project, 1937," Reel DC46, FAP. On the Index, see Virginia Tuttle Clayton, "Picturing a 'Usable Past,'" in *Drawing on America's Past: Folk Art, Modernism, and the Index of American Design*, ed. Virginia Tuttle Clayton, Elisabeth Stillinger, Erika Doss, and Deborah Chotner (Washington and Chapel Hill: National Gallery of Art/University of North Carolina Press, 2002), 1–43; and Doss, "American Folk Art's 'Distinctive Character': The Index of American Design and New Deal Notions of Cultural Nationalism," in *Drawing on America's Past*, 61–73. Also see Thomas Denenberg, *Wallace Nutting and the Invention of Old America* (New Haven, CT: Yale University Press, 2003), 1–21, 87–151, 185–93.

24. Lawrence Drake to Harry Hopkins, March 21, 1936, Frame 449, Reel 1086, FO, Reel 1086; *American Student Designer*, May 19, 1936, 1–3, "Education—Design Laboratory, Student Activities, 1936–1940" folder, Box 1, DW; Ruth Reeves to Holger Cahill, June 17, 1936, Frame 564, Reel DC52, FAP; Cahill to Audrey McMahon, July 7, 1936, Frame 839, Reel 1085, FO; McMahon to Cahill, July 15, 1936, Frame 838, Reel 1085, FO; Edith Halpert to Cahill and Thomas Parker, July 26, 1936, Frames 99–103, Reel DC52, FAP; Frances Pollak to McMahon, August 4, 1936, Frame 841, Reel 1085, FO; McMahon to Cahill, August 10, 1936, Frame 840, Reel 1085, FO; and E. M. Benson to Parker, November 4, 1936, Frame 284, Reel DC54, FAP.

25. Josiah Marvel to Harry Hopkins, December 4, 1936, Frame 73, Reel DC47, FAP; Marvel to Henry Morgenthau, December 4, 1936, Frame 845, Reel 1085, FO; Thomas Parker to Audrey McMahon, December 12, 1936, Frame 72, Reel DC47, FAP; McMahon to Parker, December 15, 1936, Frame 70, Reel DC47, FAP; Marvel to McMahon, December 16, 1936, Frame 71, Reel DC47, FAP; McMahon to Holger Cahill, December 18, 1936, Frame 854, Reel 1085, FO; McMahon to Cahill, December 21, 1936, Frame 84, Reel DC47, FAP; Parker to McMahon, December 23, 1936, Frame 69, Reel DC47, FAP; E. M. Benson to Parker, February 17, 1937, Frame 294, Reel DC54; and Cahill to Ralph Pearson, January 15, 1938, Frames 191–92, Reel DC48, FAP. Also see Karen A. Bearor, "The Design Laboratory: New Deal Experiment in Self-Conscious Vanguardism," *Southeastern College Art Conference Review* 13, no. 1 (1996): 14–31.

26. Milton Kalish to Suzanne Sekey, undated letter in Shannan Clark's possession (although clearly from May or June 1937); Milton Lowenthal to Dean Brimhall, June 21, 1937, Reel DC92, FAP; Audrey McMahon to Holger Cahill, June 25, 1937, Frame 164, Reel DC47, FAP; Lowenthal to McMahon, Reel DC92, FAP; "WPA Art School Goes On," *NYT*, July 4, 1937, 2; Cahill to Lowenthal, July 10, 1937, Reel DC92, FAP; Thomas Parker to McMahon, July 10, 1937, Frame 163, Reel DC47, FAP; and Parker to McMahon, July 27, 1937, Reel DC92, FAP.

27. Interview with William Friedman by Mary McChesney, June 16, 1965, A New Deal for Artists Interview Series, Archives of American Art, Smithsonian Institution, 6; Design Laboratory Brochure, Summer 1937, "Education—Design Laboratory, Circulars, 1936–1940" folder, Box 1, DW; "Design Laboratory Catalogue of Courses, 1937–1938," 14, "Education—Design Laboratory, Circulars, 1936–1940" folder, Box 1, DW; and Interview with Jack Kufeld by Avis Berman, October 5, 1981, Mark Rothko and His Times Oral History Project, Archives of American Art, Smithsonian Institution, 14.

28. Charmion von Wiegand, "The Fine Arts," *NM*, July 6, 1937, 30–31; Liame Dunne, "Learning Design and Production: The Methods Used in the Design Laboratory of the F.A.E.C.T. School," *PM* (the art directors' publication, not the newspaper), August 1937, 39–44; "Chapter School Grows in Influence," *TA*, September 1937, 10; Design Laboratory Catalogue of Courses, 1937–1938, 4–6; "Design Laboratory at

FAECT," *ArchRec*, October 1937, 41; and "Design Laboratory," *Design*, November 1937, VII.

29. See Virginia Marquardt, "The American Artists School: Radical Heritage and Social Content Art," *AAAJ* 26, no. 4 (1986): 17–23.

30. Ephemera, including invitations and flyers for various Design Laboratory events from 1937 through 1939 in "Education—Design Laboratory, Student Activities, 1936–1940" folder, Box 1, DW; "Student Responsibilities," *Design Laboratory Perspective*, January 1938, 1, "Education—Design Laboratory, Student Activities, 1936–1940" folder, Box 1, DW; Jacques F. Levy, "From a Faculty Member," *Perspective*, January 1938, 2; "Robot '38 Rocks 16th Street," *Perspective*, January 1938, 3; and "Council of Industrial Designers," *Perspective*, January 1938, 6.

31. See Stephen Leberstein, "Purging the Profs: The Rapp-Coudert Committee in New York, 1940–1942," in *New Studies in the Politics and Culture of U.S. Communism*, 91–122.

32. "Laboratory School of Industrial Design Provisional Charter," Folder 20, Box 27, EM.

33. "PM Shorts," *PM*, November 1937, 53; UOPWA Greater New York Joint Council, "Forums, Classes, Arts and Sports, 1939–1940," Trade Union File—United Office and Professional Workers, Tamiment Institute, New York University; "Class Enrollment High," *GN*, March 1940, 5; "The Guild School," *GN*, May 1940, 12; "BMG School Begins Fall Term," *OPN*, October 1940, 7; "Guild School Opens Second Term," *Proof*, March 1942, 3; "Publishing Courses Swell School List," *Proof*, November 1942, 4; "Ad-Mag-Pub School Opens Oct. 13," *Proof*, October 1943, 1, 4; "School Days Start at White Collar Center," *OPN*, October 1945, 10; and BMG, "Book and Magazine Guild School—Fall Term 1946," Folder 10, Box 11, CLA-CRF. In June 1940 when the progressive tabloid newspaper *PM* began publication in New York City, the Art Directors' Club changed the name of its cooperatively produced journal to *A-D* to avoid confusion.

34. "A Day in the Life of an Ad," *Commercial Artists Bulletin*, March 1939, Frame 702, Reel 5242, RK; "Three Locals Hold Forums," *UOPWA News*, April 1939, 5; UOPWA Greater New York Joint Council, "Forums, Classes, Arts and Sports, 1939–1940," Trade Union File—United Office and Professional Workers, Tamiment Institute, New York University; "Booklet Describes Cultural Program of New York Council," *UOPWA News*, October 1939, 7; UAA, 'United American Artists Lecture Series," 1939, Reel 2395, IRP, Reel; and "Artists Debate, But Surreally!" *OPN*, February 1940, 7.

35. Esther Handler, "This Is Our School," *OPN*, September 1940, 9; "A-D Shorts," *A-D*, Oct. 1940, 54; "Successful AAG Craft Classes Win Recruits," *OPN*, November 1940, 7; "Guild Begins New Ad Craft Classes," *OPN*, April 1941, 9; and "New York Dept. Set Up; Announces Fall Program," *OPN*, October 1941, 10.

36. UOPWA Greater New York Joint Council, "Special Series of Forums for those in the Art, Advertising, and Publishing Fields," Frame 717, Reel 5242, RK; "The

Bauhaus Revived," *Commercial Artists Bulletin*, March 1939; "Famous Ad Man Teaches Guild," *OPN*, March 1940, 5; "Luncheons Build Ad Union," *OPN*, January 1941, 3; "A-D Shorts," *A-D*, April 1941, 57; "Herbert Bayer's Design Class," *A-D*, June 1941, 18–30; and Percy Seitlin, "What Is Taught and Why," *A-D*, June 1941, 31–32.

37. "Mechanical Refrigerators," *CUR*, July 1936, 3–9; "Industrial Design Comes of Age," *BW*, May 23, 1936, 17–18. In 1937 and 1938 CU commented favorably on the improved design of midprice Coldspot models, in 1938 even ranking the Coldspot 3836 at $160 as a "Best Buy," but subsequent low-price models like the 3310 that were sales leaders were ranked "Not Acceptable." "Mechanical Refrigerators," *CUR*, July 1937, 15; "Mechanical Refrigerators," *CUR*, August 1937, 7–11; *CUR*, June 1938, 11–15. On Loewy's use of the Coldspot in his own self-promotion, see his widely read midcareer memoir, *Never Leave Well Enough Alone* (New York: Simon and Schuster, 1951); as well as his own later textbook, *Industrial Design* (Woodstock: Overlook Press, 1979). Also see Meikle, *Twentieth-Century Limited*, 104–106; Arthur J. Pulos, "Nothing Succeeds Like Success: Raymond Loewy: The Thirties and Forties," in *Raymond Loewy: Pioneer of American Industrial Design*, ed. Angela Schönberger (Munich: Prestel-Verlag, 1990), 75–86; Paul Jodard, *Raymond Loewy* (London: Trefoil, 1992); and Glenn Porter, *Raymond Loewy: Design for a Consumer Culture* (Wilmington: Hagley Museum and Library, 2002).

38. "Automobiles," *CUR*, March 1937, 16–27; "The 1938 Automobiles," *CUR*, December 1937, 8–13; "The New Cars Show More Improvements Than Usual," *CUR*, February 1939, 17–29.

39. "Vacuum Cleaners," *CUR*, December 1936, 5–9; "Electric Irons," *CUR*, December 1936, 9–11; "Electric Fans," *CUR*, July 1937, 3–6; "Your Electrical Appliances," *CUR*, January 1939, 33–35. Also see Glenna Mathews, *"Just a Housewife": The Rise and Fall of Domesticity in America* (New York: Oxford University Press, 1987), 157–71.

40. "Vacuum Cleaners," *CUR*, December 1936, 5–9; Roy Perry, "Wood Furniture: A Guide to Its Selection and Care," *CUR*, August 1940, 7–9; "The Great Used Car Market," *CUR*, June 1939, 23–27; and "The Radio Repairman," *CUR*, October 1941, 270–71.

41. "EHFA Incorporated; To Sell Appliances," *NYT*, January 21, 1934, 30; "Federal Agency Plans Campaign on Appliances," *AA*, April 28, 1934, 26; "EHFA Explains How Appliances Are to Be Sold," *AA*, June 2, 1934, 1, 28; "Opposition to TVA Appliance Program Grows," *AA*, June 9, 1934, 1, 26; "Financing of TVA Appliances is Criticized," *AA*, August 4, 1934, 16; "Utilities and Dealers Split over TVA Lines," *AA*, September 1, 1934, 12; "EHFA to Sell All Models of TVA Appliances," *AA*, September 8, 1934, 10; "Favors Extension of Electric Aids," *NYT*, December 27, 1934, 14; "EHFA to Seek Wider Markets for Appliances," *AA*, August 26, 1935, 8; Turner Catledge, "Vital Parts of New Deal to Get Second Term," *NYT*, January 24, 1937, IV, 3.

42. "Mechanical Refrigerators," *CUR* August/September 1937, 7–11. Also see Susie McKellar, "'The Beauty of Stark Utility': Rational Consumption in

America—*Consumer Reports*, 1936–1954," in *Utility Reassessed: The Role of Ethics in the Practice of Design*, ed. Judy Attfield (Manchester: Manchester University Press, 1999), 73–90.

43. "1941 Refrigerators," *CUR*, June 1941, 145–47; "Autos: Buy for the Long Pull," *CUR*, June 1941, 157–60; "Labor Asks One Refrigerator Line, Minus Brand Name," *AA*, February 9, 1942, 28; "These Additional Steps Must be Taken," *B&B*, May 1, 1942, 4; "'Concentration' Order Hits U.S. Stove Industry," *AA*, May 18, 1942, 6; and "Industries Will Decide Wartime Fate of Brands," *AA*, October 26, 1942, 1, 42.

44. "Design Laboratory Catalogue of Courses, 1937–1938," 4–6; and Cartoon, *Design Laboratory Perspective*, January 1938, 2.

45. On the ACA show see Exhibit List, Folder 34, Box 26, EM; "Laboratory Design Project Show at the A.C.A.," *NYT*, August 15, 1937, X, 7; and "Design Laboratory Exhibition, August 9th to 22nd, A.C.A. Gallery," Frames 334–38, Reel D375, EM. On Grossman, see "The Treasurer and the Figure She Cuts," *GN*, January 1941, 3. Also see Hemingway, *Artists on the Left*, 136–44.

46. Elizabeth McCausland, "An 'American Bauhaus': Design Laboratory on Permanent Basis," *Springfield Union and Republican*, August 22, 1937, 6E. Also see "Elizabeth McCausland, Critic and Idealist," *AAAJ* 6 (April 1966): 16–20; Platt, *Art and Politics in the 1930s*, 65–79.

47. William Friedman, "Book Review: *An Enquiry into Industrial Art in England*, by Nikolaus Pevsner," *PM*, December 1937, 59–60.

48. Henry-Russell Hitchcock Jr., and Philip Johnson, *The International Style: Architecture Since 1922* (New York: Norton, 1932); "Machine Art," *BMoMA*, November 1933, 1–2; Smith, *Making the Modern*, 385–404; Henry Matthews, "The Promotion of Modern Architecture by the Museum of Modern Art in the 1930s," *JDH* 7, no. 1 (1994): 43–59; and Jennifer Marshall, "In Form We Trust: Neoplatonism, the Gold Standard, and the *Machine Art* Show, 1934," *Art Bulletin* 90 (December 2008): 597–615.

49. Carol Aronovici, "Housing and Architecture," *BMoMA*, October 1934, 2–3; Carol Aronovici, ed., *America Can't Have Housing* (New York: Committee on the Housing Exhibition by the Museum of Modern Art, 1934). Also see Richard Pommer, "The Architecture of Urban Housing in the United States during the Early 1930s," *Journal of the Society of Architectural Historians* 37 (December 1978): 235–64; and Gail Radford, *Modern Housing in America, Policy Struggles in the New Deal Era* (Chicago: University of Chicago Press, 1996), 59–83.

50. Elodie Courter, "Notes on the Exhibition of Useful Objects," *BMoMA*, January 1940, 3–5; John McAndrew, "New Standards for Industrial Design," *BMoMA*, January 1940, 5–6. For a different interpretation, see Saab, *For the Millions*, 101, 105, 116–19.

51. "Artists to Hold Conference in N.Y.," *UOPWA News*, December 1939, 3; Richard Lewis to Officers and Members of All Art Local and Divisions, December 6, 1939, Frames 664–65, Reel 5243, RK.

52. Levy, "Bauhaus and Design, 1919–1939," *ArchRec*, January 1939, 71, 118. For more sympathetic reviews from the left, see "Bauhaus," *Direction*, December 1938, 23; and "Bauhaus Revived," *Commercial Artists Bulletin*, March 1939, 1.

53. On the central attractions of the 1939 World's Fair, see Meikle, *Twentieth Century Limited*, 188–210; Roland Marchand, "The Designers Go to the Fair II: Norman Bel Geddes, The General Motors' 'Futurama,' and the Visit to the Factory Transformed," *DI* 8 (Spring 1992): 23–40; David E. Nye, *American Technological Sublime* (Cambridge, MA: MIT Press, 1994), 199–224; Christina Cogdell, "The Futurama Recontextualized: Norman Bel Geddes' Eugenic 'World of Tomorrow,'" *AQ* 52 (June 2000): 193–245; and A. Joan Saab, "Historical Amnesia: New Urbanism and the City of Tomorrow," *Journal of Planning History* 6 (August 2007): 191–213.

54. *A Design Students' Guide to the New York World's Fair, compiled for P/M Magazine by the Laboratory School of Industrial Design* (New York: Laboratory School of Industrial Design, 1939), Box 1, DW.

55. "A Letter to Mr. Whalen," *CUR*, March 1939, 31; "Consumers Union at the World's Fair," *CUR*, March 1939, 31; "Consumers Union at the New York World's Fair," *CUR*, April 1939, 7; "CU at the World's Fair," *CUR*, June 1939, 5; "Last Night," *CUR*, November 1939, 7; Cohen, *Consumers' Republic*, 61; and Stole, *Advertising on Trial*, 96–97.

56. Laboratory School of Industrial Design (LSID), "New Appointments to the Faculty for Spring 1939," "Education—Design Laboratory, Correspondence, Announcements, Related Materials, 1934–1942" folder, Box 1, DW; LSID, "1939 Bulletin," "Education—Design Laboratory, Circulars, 1936–1940" folder, Box 1, DW; LSID, "Spring 1939 Course Listings," Frames 328–33, Reel D375, EM; LSID, "Exhibit by 9 Instructors Recently Appointed to the Faculty of their Professional Work in Industrial Design and Graphic Arts," Frames 317–38, Reel D375, EM; LSID, "Instructors for Basic Courses, Fall 1939–40," Folder 26, Box 27, EM; and McCausland, Lecture Notes, September 28, 1939, Laboratory School of Industrial Design, 1939," Folder 25, Box 27, EM.

57. "Paul Rand," *PM*, October 1938, 1–16; McCausland, "Cultural Morphology I—Syllabus," Reel D384G, EM; McCausland, Notes for course on 'Cultural Morphology,' Laboratory School of Industrial Design, 1939," Reel D384G, EM; and Interview with Suzanne Sekey by Shannan Clark, May 30, 2003.

58. Levy, Curriculum Vitae, February 1941, "Education—Design Laboratory, Correspondence, Announcements, Related Materials, 1934–1942" folder, Box 1, DW.

59. "LSID Report to the General Membership," August 22, 1939, "Education—Design Laboratory, Correspondence, Announcements, Related Materials, 1934–1942" folder, Box 1, DW; and Memorandum to All Students, LSID, November 14, 1939, "Education—Design Laboratory, Correspondence, Announcements, Related Materials, 1934–1942" folder, Box 1, DW.

60. Receipt of Foreclosure Sale, First District Court, Borough of Manhattan, December 8, 1939, "Education—Design Laboratory, Correspondence, Announcements, Related Materials, 1934–1942" folder, Box 1, DW; Minutes of Student Committee, LSID, December 27, 1939, "Education—Design Laboratory, Correspondence, Announcements, Related Materials, 1934–1942" folder, Box 1, DW; Anna Bogue, William C. Whitney Foundation, to Frances T. Schwab, May 24, 1940, "Education—Design Laboratory, Correspondence, Announcements, Related Materials, 1934–1942" folder, Box 1, DW; and Student Committee of Laboratory School of Industrial Design to students, June 6, 1940, "Education—Design Laboratory, Correspondence, Announcements, Related Materials, 1934–1942" folder, Box 1, DW.

61. On Carnegie and Pratt, see Peter Müller-Munk, "Industrial Design," *Design*, January 1939, 12–15; and Alexander J. Kostellow, "Design and Structure Program of the Pratt Institute Art School," *Design*, May 1940, 6–9, 24.

62. On Moholy-Nagy's Institute of Design in Chicago, see "Bauhaus Will Open In Chicago in Fall," *NYT*, August 22, 1937, II, 6; "Gropius Aide Here to Run Art School," *NYT*, September 2, 1937, 23; "Chicago's New Bauhaus," *NYT*, September 12, 1937, XI, 7; and "The New Bauhaus," *ArchFor*, October 1937, 22, 82. Also see James Sloan Allen, *The Romance of Commerce and Culture: Capitalism, Modernism, and the Chicago-Aspen Crusade for Cultural Reform* (Chicago: University of Chicago Press, 1983), 3–77; and Maggie Taft, "Better Than Before: László Moholy-Nagy and the New Bauhaus in Chicago," in *Chicago Makes Modern: How Creative Minds Changed Society*, ed. Mary Jane Jacobs and Jacquelynn Baas (Chicago: University of Chicago Press, 2012), 31–43.

63. On Pereira, see her undated c.v., "Personal Documents and Biographical Information," Reel 1296, IRP. On Rand's subsequent career, see Paul Rand, *From Lascaux to Brooklyn* (New Haven, CT: Yale University Press, 1996); Jessica Helfand, *Paul Rand: American Modernist* (New York: William Drenttel, 1998); and Steven Heller, *Paul Rand* (New York: Phaidon, 2000).

64. UAA Membership Analysis, February 1, 1939, Frame 591, Reel 5242, RK; UOPWA Joint Council Minutes, February 15, 1940, Frames 666–68, Reel 5243, RK; Rita Murphy to Rockwell Kent, May 23, 1940, Frame 799, Reel 5242, RK; Henry Biber to Dear Member, April 15, 1940, Frame 780, Reel 5242, RK; Richard Lewis to Members of National Advisory Committee on Art Locals, August 22, 1940, Frames 679–80, Reel 5243, RK; William Dove to Fellow Member, October 28, 1940, Frame 917, Reel 5242, RK; UAA Local 60, "Words and Pictures," December 1940, Frames 947–50, Reel 5242, RK; and Lynd Ward to Dear Member, February 7, 1941, Frame 1069, Reel 5242, RK.

65. Richard Lewis to Executive Boards of Art Locals, January 17, 1941, Frame 1048, Reel 5242, RK; "UAA Opens Drive in Art Supply Field," *OPN*, February 1941, 8; "Henschel Strike," *UAA Bulletin*, March 1941, Frames 1136–37, Reel 5242, RK; "Textile Designers Section," *UAA Bulletin*, March 1941, Frame 1137, Reel 5242,

RK; "UAA Strikes Henschel, Signs Other Art Firms," *OPN*, March 1941, 8; and "Henschel Contract Boosts Union in Art Supply Field," *OPN*, May 1941, 8.

66. Lewis Merrill to Presidents of All Locals with Artist Members, December 1, 1941, Frame 1443, Reel 5242, RK; Richard Lewis to Merrill, December 12, 1941, Frames 256–57, Reel 5243, RK; Rockwell Kent to Merrill, January 9, 1942, Frames 9–11, Reel 5243, RK; and Merrill to UOPWA Local 60 Executive Board, January 14, 1942, Frame 16–17, Reel 5243.

67. Norman Barr to Rockwell Kent, March 8, 1942, Frames 51–52, Reel 5243, RK; Barr to Kent, April 20, 1942, Frames 58–60, Reel 5243, RK; Kent to Barr, April 30, 1942, Frames 65–67, Reel 5243, RK; "A Call to Artists," *Joint Bulletin of the American Artists Congress and United American Artists*, May 1942, Frames 264–65, Reel D368, EM; "Artists Wanted," *Joint Bulletin*, May 1942; *Artists in the War: Catalog of Exhibition, June 14, 1942, A.C.A. Gallery*, Frames 128–33, Reel 5243, RK; and Kent to Victor D'Amico, December 11, 1942, Frame 253, Reel 5243, RK. Also see Hemingway, *Artists on the Left*, 191–95.

68. Lewis Merrill to Members of the Executive Board of Local 60, United American Artists, May 13, 1942, Frame 76, Reel 5243, RK; Merrill to All Members of Local 60, United American Artists, May 13, 1942, Frame 77, Reel 5243, RK; Norman Barr to Rockwell Kent, May 16, 1942, Frames 83–85, Reel 5243, RK; Kent to Merrill, May 23, 1942, Frames 93–95, Reel 5243, RK; Merrill to Kent, May 25, 1942, Frames 98–99, Reel 5243, RK; Kent to Merrill, May 28, 1942, Frames 106–107, Reel 5243, RK; Merrill to Kent, June 2, 1942, Frame 114, Reel 5243, RK; Daniel Koener to Kent, June 1, 1942, Frame 112, Reel 5243, RK; Kent to Koener, June 4, 1942, Frame 117, Reel 5243, RK; Barr to Kent, May 30, 1942, Frames 108–109, Reel 5243, RK; Kent to American Advertising Guild, May 20, 1942, Frame 400, Reel 5154, RK; and Betty Yohai to Kent, May 25, 1942, Frame 402, Reel 5154, RK.

69. See John Morton Blum, *V Was for Victory: Politics and American Culture During World War II* (New York: Harcourt Brace Jovanovich, 1976), 15–45; Robert Griffith, "The Selling of America: The Advertising Council and American Politics, 1942–1960," *BHR* 57, no. 3 (1983): 388–412; Marchand, *Creating the Corporate Soul*, 320–22, 328, 331, 359–60; and James Sparrow, *Warfare State: World War II Americans and the Age of Big Government* (New York: Oxford University Press, 2011), 74–77.

70. "Advertising Council," *Tide*, February 15, 1942, 13; "LaRoche Announces Makeup of New Ad Council," *AA*, February 16, 1942, 4; "Huge Salvage Campaign Begins to Take Shape," *AA*, May 4, 1942, 1, 35; "Salvage Drives," *Tide*, June 15, 1942, 28–29; "The Council Marches On," *A&S*, July 1942, 18–19; "Salvage Drive," *Tide*, July 15, 1942, 47; "Admen to Plan War Information Policy, Programs," *AA*, August 17, 1942, 19; "Bureau to Work With Council," *A&S*, September 1942, 19–20; "Six Months of the Advertising Council," *A&S*, November 1942, 26; and "Advertising Council Serves to Coordinate War Activities," *AA*, November 21, 1942, 24–28.

71. "Ad Guild Offers Skills to Build U.S. Morale," *OPN*, May 1, 1942, 2; "Advertising Volunteers Needed," *NYT*, May 6, 1942, 34; Howard Byrne to Rockwell Kent, May 20, 1942, Frame 401, Reel 5154, RK; "Ad Men Ask U.S.A. to Let Them Help," *PM*, June 5, 1942, 18; "Local 20 Gives Admen Chance to Help War," *OPN*, July 15, 1942, 3; and Howard Willard to Ad Guilders, July 27, 1942, Frame 407, Reel 5154, RK.

72. "The Advertising Guild on the March: A Stepchild of the CIO's UOPWA May Now Come into Its Own," *A&S*, July 1942, 19–20; and "Advertising Guild," *Tide*, August 1, 1942, 38, 40.

73. "AMC's Army of Admen Turns Out First War Jobs," *OPN*, August 1, 1942, 3; "14 War Jobs Done, AMC Starts on More," *OPN*, August 15, 1942, 2; "Advertising News and Notes," *NYT*, August 27, 1942, 31; "AMC Gets Inside Track as Ad Industry Welcomes War Projects," *OPN*, September 1, 1942, 4; "Advertising Workers Busy on Ideas That Will Help Sell and Win the War," *PM*, September 2, 1942, 4; "AMC Gets Big War Order," *OPN*, September 15, 1942, 2; "OPA Distributes 3 AMC Pamphlets," *War Copy* (Ad Guild publication), October 1942, 1, Frame 418, Reel 5154, RK; "Ad Mobilization Holds Open Check-Up Oct. 15," *OPN*, October 15, 1942, 6; and "Price Control Data Out," *NYT*, December 21, 1942, 16.

74. "OWI," *Tide*, September 15, 1942, 62; "Wire from Washington," *B&B*, September 18, 1942, 4; "Guild Activities," *Tide*, November 15, 1942, 14; and "Predicts More Grade Labeling, Victory Models," *AA*, November 23, 1942, 1, 47.

75. "Population Shifts Blamed for Gallup Error," *AA*, November 9, 1942, 36; "The Elections and the War," *B&B*, November 13, 1942, 2; "OPA," *Tide*, January 1, 1943, 58–59; "Advertising Tempest in the OWI," *Tide*, May 1, 1943, 15–16; "The OWI," *Tide*, July 15, 1943, 74.

76. "End of WPA Art," *Life*, April 17, 1944, 85–86; Holger Cahill to Editor of *Life*, April 20, 1944, Frames 665–68, Reel 5286, HC; Editors of *Life* to Cahill, May 1, 1944, Frame 679, Reel 5286, HC; and Cahill to Editors, *Life*, May 8, 1944, 4. Also see Peter Blume et al to the Editor, April 27, 1944, Frames 674–75, Reel 5286, HC; and Anton Refregier to Cahill, May 1, 1944, Frames 677–78, Reel 5286, HC.

77. Elizabeth McCausland to Holger Cahill, April 23, 1944, Folder 8, Box 3, EM; and McCausland, "Must Artists Starve?" *NM*, July 10, 1945, 8–10. Also see McCausland, "Why Can't America Afford Art?" *Magazine of Art*, January 1946.

CHAPTER 5

1. "*PM Picks the Best-Dressed Women on New York Avenues,*" *PM*, April 2, 1947, 15.

2. "Strike Slated Today at Parents' Magazine," *PM*, March 24, 1947, 10; "Magazine Guild Strikes," *NYT*, March 25, 1947, 22; "Magazine Strikers Ask Fair Pay—Fair Play," *OPN*, April 1947, 3; "NLRB Voids Magazine Vote," *PM*, April 1, 1947, 11; Frances Ullman DeArmand to Leonard Boudin, "History of Employment of Frances Ullman DeArmand at Parents Institute, Inc.," May 13, 1947, Folder 16, Box 2, FUD.

3. "Trend of Employment, Earnings, and Hours: Labor Force, August 1945," *MLR* 61 (September 1945): 829–30; and Harold Wool and Lester M. Pearlman, "Recent Occupational Trends: Wartime and Postwar Trends Compared: An Appraisal of the Permanence of Recent Movements," *MLR* 65 (August 1947): 139–47.

4. Gladys Bentley to All Unit Chairmen, Treasurers, Assistant Treasurers, and Shop Paper Editors, May 14, 1941, Folder 11, Box 58, NGNY.

5. Decision and Order, Case C-775, August 24, 1940, *DNLRB* 26 (1940): 1094–181; Decision, Order, and Direction of Election, Cases R-2278 and R-2279, June 20, 1941, *DNLRB* 32 (1941): 928–61; "News Guild Wins in *Times* Election," *NYT*, August 2, 1941, 13; Supplemental Decision and Certification of Representatives, Cases R-2278 and R-2279, August 27, 1941, *DNLRB* 35 (1941): 17–18.

6. "News Union Invokes 'Membership' Rule," *NYT*, July 6, 1941, 25; "43 on the *News* Face Ouster in Guild Move," *NYT*, August 9, 1941, 13; Barry Kritzberg, "An Unfinished Chapter in White-Collar Unionism: The Formative Years of the Chicago Newspaper Guild, Local 71, American Newspaper Guild, A.F.L.-C.I.O.," *LH* 14 (Summer 1973): 397–413.

7. Transcript of Time, Inc. Negotiations, January 31, 1941, 1–30, Folder 5, Box 59, NGNY Transcript of Time, Inc. Negotiations, February 4, 1941, 1–39, Folder 6, Box 59, NGNY; Minutes of Time Unit Meeting, February 13, 1941, Folder 3, Box 58, NGNY; Minutes of Time Unit Meeting, February 28, 1941, Folder 3, Box 58, NGNY.

8. Time, Inc. Report to Stockholders, November 25, 1941, Folder 10, Box 58, NGNY; Transcript of Time, Inc. Negotiations, March 27, 1941, 1–39, Folder 8, Box 59, NGNY; Roy E. Larsen to the Staff of Time, Inc., March 27, 1941, Folder 10, Box 58, NGNY; Time Unit Executive Committee to Time Inc. Employees, March 28, 1941, Folder 10, Box 58, NGNY; Abraham J. Isserman to Alexander Crosby, April 1, 1941, Folder 3, Box 59, NGNY; Transcript of Time, Inc. Negotiations, April 1, 1941, 1–35, Folder 9, Box 59, NGNY.

9. Minutes of Time Unit Meeting, April 10, 1941, Folder 3, Box 58, NGNY; Transcript of Time, Inc. Negotiations, April 15, 1941, 1–40, Folder 10, Box 59, NGNY; Transcript of Time, Inc. Negotiations, May 1, 1941, 1–70, Folder 11, Box 59, NGNY; "Cost of Living: Changes in Living Costs in Large Cities, December 15, 1941," *MLR* 54 (February 1942): 455–60.

10. Minutes of Time Unit Meeting, June 26, 1941, Folder 3, Box 58, NGNY; Minutes of Time Unit Meeting, September 11, 1941, Folder 3, Box 58, NGNY; Transcript of Time, Inc. Negotiations, September 12, 1941, 1–26, Folder 12, Box 59, NGNY; Transcript of Time, Inc. Negotiations, October 30, 1941, 1–17, Folder 13, Box 59, NGNY; Transcript of Time, Inc. Negotiations, November 18, 1941, 1–36, Folder 13, Box 59, NGNY.

11. Andrew Heiskell to Anna Goldsborough, November 27, 1941, Folder 14, Box 61, NGNY; Minutes of Time Unit Meeting, November 28, 1941, Folder 3, Box 58, NGNY; Minutes of Time Unit Meeting, December 4, 1941, Folder 3, Box 58,

NGNY; Roy E. Larsen to Nat Einhorn, December 12, 1941, Folder 3, Box 58, NGNY; Minutes of Time Unit Meeting, December 12, 1941, Folder 3, Box 58, NGNY.

12. "Screen News Here and in Hollywood," *NYT*, July 11, 1940, 23; Joseph Gould to Nat Einhorn, October 14, 1940, Folder 21, Box 24, NGNY; "SPG Sees Victory as Hearings End," *SPG News*, March 1941, Folder 21, Box 24, NGNY; "Screen Publicists Will Have Election," *NYT*, June 19, 1941, 24; "Screen Publicists Win Pay Increases," *NYT*, May 6, 1942, 22; Mort Frankel, "What's A Screen Publicist, Anyway?" *OPN*, August 1, 1942, 7.

13. "Movie Guilds Join UOPWA, Ask Columbia Office Poll," *OPN*, October 1941, 1–2; "Separate Screen Guilds United in the UOPWA," *OPN*, October 1941, 10; "Publicists Oppose C.I.O.," *NYT*, November 13, 1941, 25; "NLRB in Four-Star Ruling Orders Two Screen Polls," *OPN*, February 15, 1942, 8: "SOPEG Wins 3–1 at Loew's," *OPN*, March 15, 1942, 1; "SOPEG Scores Third Triumph in Fox Vote," *OPN*, April 1, 1942, 1; "Screen Publicists Get UOPWA Charter," *OPN*, July 1, 1942, 1.

14. "Publicists Sign With Warner Bros.," *OPN*, September 1, 1942, 3; "Screen Flacks Get Contract with RKO," *Billboard*, October 3, 1942, 5; Certification of Representatives, Case R-3628, June 10, 1942, *DNLRB* 42 (1942): 900–902; "Four Major Movie Firms Sign UOPWA Contracts," *OPN*, August 1, 1942, 1–2; "Paramount to Vote; SOPEG Signs Deluxe," *OPN*, November 1942, 1; "Republic Victory, United Artists and National Screen Pacts Bring Movie Organization to New High," *OPN*, January 1943, 2; Decision and Direction of Election, Cases R-4497, R-4498, and R-4499, January 8, 1943, *DNLRB* 46 (1943): 875–86; "SOPEG: Where? Why? When? How? Who? What?" pamphlet (1943), Folder 10; Box 11, CLA-CRF; UOPWA, *Report of the General Executive Board to the Fifth Constitutional Convention of the United Office and Professional Workers of America, CIO*, September 4, 1944, 28–29.

15. "CIO White-Collar Drive Threatens New York Stations," *Billboard*, August 1, 1942, 7; "White Collars Win Union Pact, N.Y. Drive Next," *Billboard*, August 8, 1942, 6; "2 Paramount Pubs Unionized from Clerks to Pluggers," *Billboard*, May 22, 1943, 21.

16. "Objectives of the Radio Writers' Guild," February 1939, Folder 4, Box 1, RWG; Katherine Seymour, "President's Report to the Membership," 1942, Folder 1, Box 4, RWG; "Bulletin from the Radio Writers' Guild," August 1944, Folder 9, Box 1, RWG.

17. Dorothy Bryant to Peter Lyon, December 27, 1943, Folder 8, Box 1, RWG; "Writers' Guild Plans Different Type of Operation," *Billboard*, March 18, 1944, 10; "Bulletin from the Radio Writers' Guild," August 1944; "Lyon Looks Set for RWG Prexy," *Billboard*, October 14, 1944, 7; "Peter Lyon," (unsigned and undated memo, probably from 1947 or 1948), "Lyon, Peter, 1939–947 and n.d." folder, Box 621, JBM. Also see Fones-Wolf, *Waves of Opposition*, 102–105.

18. Kenneth Webb to Peggy Scheuerman, November 11, 1940, Folder 5, Box 1, RWG; Katherine Seymour to Forrest Barnes, January 23, 1941, Folder 6, Box 1, RWG; Lou Frankel, "Midnight Lamps Writers' Cramps," *Billboard*, December 18, 1943, 6; Mabel Cobb, "We Cannot Find Your Script," *NYT*, April 9, 1944, X5; Peter Lyon, "President's Report to the Membership," 1944, Folder 1A, Box 4, RWG; "RWG New Contract Bid Plenty Stiff," *Billboard*, May 5, 1945, 9.

19. *Report of the General Executive Board to the Fifth Constitutional Convention of the United Office and Professional Workers of America, CIO*, September 4, 1944, 24–26; Decision and Direction of Election, Case R-3938, July 10, 1942, *DNLRB* 42 (1942): 281–84; Decision and Order, Case C-2607, May 7, 1943, *DNLRB* 51 (1943): 796–819.

20. "Ad Guild Office Tells Industry About Contract," *OPN*, July 1941, 2; "Ad Guild Scores Three Times," *OPN*, August 15, 1942, 1; "Ad Guild Talks for Five Fashion Studios," *OPN*, September 1, 1942, 4; "Guild Activities," *Tide*, November 15, 1942, 14; "Two Studios Sign Ad Guild Contracts," *OPN*, December 1942, 12; "Ad Guild, BMU Now One Union," *Proof*, April 1943, 1, 3; Rudy Bass to Ad Guild Members, September 30, 1943, Folder 10, Box 11, CLA-CRF.

21. GNYIUC Minutes, January 16, 1942; "Unions and Consumer Action," *B&B*, June 12, 1942, 3; "Help the War by Buying Wisely, OPA Urges Union Conference," *OPN*, July 1, 1942, 7; Gerald Blank, "Consumers and Unions Back Drive for Price Wardens," *PM*, July 2, 1942, 13; "CIO Council Asks OPA to Use Consumer Groups," *NYT*, July 6, 1942, 16; GNYIUC Minutes, August 6, 1942; GNYIUC Minutes, December 3, 1942; GNYIUC Minutes, December 17, 1942. Also see Jacobs, *Pocketbook Politics*, 180–209; and Cohen, *Consumers' Republic*, 63–83, for more about citizen participation in OPA policy formulation and enforcement.

22. GNYIUC Minutes, December 17, 1942; GNYIUC Minutes, January 21, 1943; GNYIUC Minutes, January 25, 1943; GNYIUC Minutes, February 4, 1943; Clifford McAvoy, "Become Price-Minded; Build Consumer Front," *OPN*, May 1943, 8; Ben Smith to Jack Ryan, April 28, 1943, Folder 8, Box 9, NGNY; "BMUers Busy in CIO Community Councils," *Proof*, May 1943, 4; GNYIUC Minutes, May 20, 1943; "CIO in Your Neighborhood," *Proof*, July 1943, 3. Also see Eimer, "The Challenge of Organizing the Organized: The CIO Greater New York Industrial Union Council and Working Class Formation," 106–23.

23. "UOPWA Consumers Set up 'Lab,'" *OPN*, November 1942, 6; "Union Trains Consumer Leaders," *OPN*, February 1943, 7; Milo Lathrop, *Home Front: A Victory Program for Trade Union Consumers* (New York: Consumers Union, 1942), 3; "AMC Gets Nod from Murray," *Proof*, May 1943, 1.

24. *The News and What to Do about It* (radio script), July 9, 1943, Folder 6, Box 22, NGNY; *The News . . .* (radio script), February 6, 1944, Folder 8, Box 22, NGNY.

25. *The News and What to Do about It* (radio script), July 23, 1943, Folder 6, Box 22, NGNY; *The News . . .* (radio script), October 15, 1943, Folder 7, Box 22; *The News . . .* (radio script), December 9, 1943, Folder 7, Box 22, NGNY; *The News . . .*

(radio script), February 13, 1944, Folder 8, Box 22, NGNY; *The News . . .* (radio script), July 16, 1944, Folder 9, Box 22, NGNY; *The News . . .* (radio script), August 13, 1944, Folder 9, Box 22, NGNY. On the Wagner-Murray-Dingell Bill, see Klein, *For All These Rights*, 175–77, 211.

26. *The News and What to Do about It* (radio script), September 24, 1943, Folder 6, Box 22, NGNY; "Radio Gag 'Rights' Put to Test," *PM*, July 6, 1944, 3; John Moutoux, "CIO Readies Fight on Radio Labor Gag," *PM*, August 10, 1944, 7; Moutoux, "UAW Fights for Right to Buy Time that NAM Gets for Free," *PM*, August 17, 1944, 13. Also see Fones-Wolf, *Waves of Opposition*, 100–101, 109–12, 119–24; and Victor Pickard, *America's Battle for Media Democracy: The Triumph of Corporate Libertarianism and the Future of Media Reform* (New York: Cambridge University Press, 2015), 33–35.

27. *The News and What to Do about It* (radio script), May 7, 1943, Folder 6, Box 22, NGNY; *The News . . .* (radio script), August 20, 1943, Folder 6, Box 22, NGNY. Also see Cheryl Greenberg, "The Politics of Disorder: Reexamining Harlem's Riots of 1935 and 1943," *Journal of Urban History* 18, no. 4 (1992): 395–441; Nat Brandt, *Harlem at War: The Black Experience in WWII* (Syracuse, NY: Syracuse University Press, 1996), 144–215; Cohen, *Consumers' Republic*, 83–100; and Cheryl Black, "'New Negro' Performance in Art and Life: Fredi Washington and the Theatrical Columns of the *People's Voice*, 1943–47," *Theater History Studies* 24 (June 2004): 57–72.

28. *The News and What to Do about It* (radio script), August 20, 1943, Folder 6, Box 22, NGNY.

29. Rockwell Kent to John McManus, October 20, 1944, Folder 18, Box 14, NGNY; Rockwell Kent to Dear Friend, November 2, 1944, Frame 491, Reel 5222, RK; Eugene Konecky, "Special Report on 'FM' Radio Developments," November 9, 1944, Frames 493–96, Reel 5222, RK; Joseph Brodsky to Dear Friend, December 8, 1944, Frame 498, Reel 5222, RK; People's Radio Foundation, "For a People's Radio Station in the Greater New York Area," 1945, Frames 592–96, Reel 5222, RK; Eugene Konecky, *The American Communications Conspiracy* (New York: People's Radio Foundation, 1948), 102–108.

30. Joseph Brodsky to Dear Stockholder, August 9, 1946, Frames 547–48, Reel 5222, RK; People's Radio Foundation, FCC Application, Answer to Question 8(n), Frames 555–57, Reel 5222, RK; J. Eliot Engelbourg, "People's Radio Foundation Inc., Statement of Assets, Liabilities and Capital at June 30, 1946," Frame 565, Reel 5222, RK.

31. Eugene Konecky, "Labor Must Avoid 'SNAFU' of FM Radio," 1945, Frames 508–509, Reel 5222, RK; Rockwell Kent and Muriel Draper to Dear Friend, October 1945, Frame 538, Reel 5222, RK; "Press Suppresses Congress Expose of NAM Plot to Control U.S. Radio as It Controls Newspapers," *IF*, November 12, 1945, 1–3. Also see Barnouw, *Golden Web*, 242; Douglas, *Listening In*, 261–62; Fones-Wolf, *Waves of Opposition*, 138–43; and Christopher H. Sterling and Michael C. Keith, *Sounds of*

Change: A History of FM Broadcasting (Chapel Hill: University of North Carolina Press, 2008), 37–66.

32. Department of Labor, *The Termination Report of the National War Labor Board: Industrial Disputes and Wage Stabilization in Wartime*, Vol. I (Washington, DC: G.P.O., 1947), 3–62. Also see Nelson Lichtenstein, *Labor's War at Home: The CIO in World War II* (New York: Cambridge University Press, 1982), 82–109; Howell John Harris, *The Right to Manage: Industrial Relations Policies of American Business in the 1940s* (Madison: University of Wisconsin Press, 1982), 47–58; Zieger, *CIO*, 146–47, 163–77; Brinkley, *End of Reform*, 209–17; Andrew Workman, "Creating the National War Labor Board: Franklin Roosevelt and the Politics of State Building in the Early 1940s," *JPH* 12, no. 2 (2000): 233–64; and Sparrow, *Warfare State*, 162–66.

33. *Directive Orders and Opinions of the National War Labor Board in the "Little Steel" Case* (Washington, DC: G.P.O., 1942); *Termination Report of the NWLB*, I, 80–104, 177–274.

34. Daniel Bell, "The Coming Tragedy of American Labor," *politics*, March 1944, 37–42. Also see Brick, *Daniel Bell*, 80–100; and Gregory Sumner, *Dwight Macdonald and the* politics *Circle: The Challenge of Cosmopolitan Democracy* (Ithaca, NY: Cornell University Press, 1996), 15–20. Many labor historians have largely recapitulated Bell's negative assessment of the NWLB. See Lichtenstein, *Labor's War at Home*, 67–81; Davis, *Prisoners of the American Dream*, 74–82; Moody, *An Injury to All*, 28–35; Fraser, *Labor Will Rule*, 496–503; and Lichtenstein's introduction to the new edition, *Labor's War at Home: The CIO in World War II*, rev. ed. (Philadelphia: Temple University Press, 2003), vii–xxviii.

35. Morris Yanoff, "Across the Desk," *Proof*, March 1942, 3; Aaron Schneider, "Wages Are Related to Production," *OPN*, January 1943, 2; "WLB Sets Precedent for All Non-War Workers in Donnelley Dispute," *Proof*, February 1943, 1, 3.

36. GNYIUC Minutes, February 18, 1943; Lewis Merrill, "In My Opinion," *OPN*, April 1943, 8; GNYIUC Minutes, April 15, 1943; Merrill, "Take Up the Wage Problems of the Unorganized—Now!" *OPN*, May 1943, 6–7; GNYIUC Minutes, May 20, 1943; Merrill, "Taking Stock," *OPN*, November 1943, 5–8; Testimony by Lewis Merrill, *Fixed Incomes in the War Economy: Hearings before the Subcommittee on Wartime Health and Education of the Committee on Education and Labor*, United States Senate, 78th Congress, 2nd Session, Part 3, Washington, DC, January 27, 1944 (Washington, DC: G.P.O., 1944), 1261–65.

37. Application for Approval of a Wage or Salary Rate Adjustment Schedule (NWLB Form 10) (Time Inc.), February 5, 1945, Folder 1, Box 60, NGNY; Application for Approval . . . (NWLB Form 10) (*New York Times*), March 14, 1945, Folder 34, Box 17, NGNY. Also see *Termination Report of the NWLB*, I, 1180–96, and III, 780–816.

38. Application for Approval of a Wage or Salary Rate Adjustment or Schedule (NWLB Form 10) (*Daily News*), March 15, 1945, Folder 34, Box 17, NGNY; Application for

Approval . . . (NWLB Form 10) (*New York Post*), April 24, 1944, Folder 34, Box 17, NGNY; Application for Approval . . . (NWLB Form 10) (*New York Post*), March 22, 1945, Folder 34, Box 17, NGNY.

39. "Case Against Guild Shop," *E&P*, January 16, 1943, 24; Minutes of Time, Inc. unit meeting, July 17, 1943, Folder 4, Box 58, NGNY; Morris Ernst, "ANG Statement on Maintenance of Membership and the Freedom of the Press," 1943, Folder 25A, Box 16, NGNY; "Statement Made by Roy E. Larsen on Behalf of Time Incorporated before a Panel of the National War Labor Board," August 1943, 4–5, Folder 12, Box 58, NGNY; Public Hearing before the National War Labor Board in the Case of the Newspaper Publishers and the American Newspaper Guild, CIO, Case Number 111-927-D, October 15, 1943, Folder 39, Box 17, NGNY; "WLB Hears 'Membership Maintenance' Debate," *E&P*, October 23, 1943, 14.

40. "Statement Made by Roy E. Larsen in Behalf of Time Incorporated before a Panel of the National War Labor Board," August 1943, 5, 8, 11.

41. Ralph T. Seward and Aaron D. Schneider, Preliminary Recital in the Matter of Time, Inc. and Newspaper Guild of New York, Case No. 2-D-440, NWLB 2nd Region, October 13, 1943, 9, 15–16, 27–28, Folder 21, Box 59, NGNY; Minutes of Time, Inc. unit meeting, October 21, 1943, Folder 4, Box 58, NGNY; "Member Maintenance Rule Won by Guild," *E&P*, March 11, 1944, 8; NWLB 2nd Region, Directive Order in the Matter of Time, Inc. and Newspaper Guild of New York, Case No. 111-2805-D, March 14, 1944, Folder 12, Box 58, NGNY; "Maintenance Rule Ordered for Time, Inc.," *E&P*, March 18, 1944, 11.

42. Louis P. Gratz to All Time Staff, March 6, 1944, Folder 12, Box 58, NGNY; Roy Larsen to All Staff, March 15, 1944, Folder 12, Box 58, NGNY; Philip Schuyler, "Government News Gag Press Freedom Problem," *E&P*, April 8, 1944, 7, 56. Also see Pickard, *America's Battle for Media Democracy*, 143–75.

43. Bentley to All Unit Chairmen, Treasurers, Assistant Treasurers, and Shop Paper Editors, April 9, 1941, Folder 11, Box 58, NGNY; Saul Mills, Certification of Voting Rights Based on Per Capita and Attendance, April 4, 1944, Folder 13, Box 9, NGNY; Mills, Certification of Voting Rights, July 1, 1946, Folder 15, Box 9, NGNY.

44. "Here Are Both Sides of Issue in Guild Probe of N.Y. Local," *PM*, November 18, 1943, 9; "Local Unit Assails National News Guild," *NYT*, November 20, 1943, 17; Sam Eubanks to Nat Einhorn, March 13, 1945, Folder 12, Box 4, NGNY; Eubanks to John McManus, March 20, 1945, Folder 12, Box 4, NGNY; McManus to Eubanks, April 4, 1945, Folder 12, Box 4, NGNY; and Einhorn to Margaret Wikle, April 27, 1945, Folder 12, Box 4, NGNY. On wartime strikes, the Smith-Connally Act, and national service proposals, see Lichtenstein, *Labor's War at Home*, 127–35, 157–71, 182–86; Sparrow, *Warfare State*, 184–200.

45. Lyon, "President's Report to Membership," 1944, Folder 1A, Box 4, RWG; "RWG Elects Lyon, 190 New Members in Eastern Division," *Billboard*, November 11, 1944, 8; "RWG Talking New Net Papers for Scribblers," *Billboard*, December 23, 1944, 22.

46. Goldin and Margo, "The Great Compression: The Wage Structure in the United States at Mid-Century"; Piketty and Saez, "Income Inequality in the United States, 1913–1998"; Piketty and Saez, "The Evolution of Top Incomes: A Historical and International Perspective," *American Economic Review* 96 (2006): 200–205; and Kopczuk, Saez, and Song, "Earnings Inequality and Mobility in the United States: Evidence from Social Security Data since 1937." For an historian's perspective, see Stein, *Pivotal Decade*, 1–22.

47. "Revised Estimates of National Income and Products," *MLR* 65 (September 1947): 325–28.

48. "Revised Estimates of National Income and Products"; Testimony by Donald DuShane, *Fixed Incomes in the War Economy*, 1186–90, 1205.

49. "Wage and Hour Statistics: Trend of Factory Earnings, 1939 to January 1944," *MLR* 58 (April 1944): 855–56; "Wage and Hour Statistics: Trend of Earnings among White-Collar Workers during the War," *MLR* 58 (May 1944): 1033–49; "Trend of Employment, Earnings, and Hours: Detailed Reports for Industrial and Business Employment, March 1944," *MLR* 58 (June 1944): 1320–34.

50. "Trend of Employment, Earnings, and Hours: Detailed Reports for Industrial and Business Employment, March 1944."

51. Testimony of Chester Bowles, *Fixed Incomes in the War Economy*, 1247–48; "Trend of Prices and Cost of Living in 1943," *MLR* 58 (February 1944): 244–68; Testimony of Philip Murray, *Fixed Incomes in the War Economy*, 1052–53; Frederick Barkley, "'White Collar' Pay Must Be Increased, Say Labor Leaders," *NYT*, January 26, 1944, 1, 38; Nathan Robertson, "Labor Says Living Cost Rise is Double U.S. Figures," *PM*, January 30, 1944, 4; John Crider, "Murray Denounces 'Hold-Line' Report," *NYT*, April 13, 1944, 36.

52. *True Story* trade ad in *Tide*, October 1, 1942, 6; also see similar *True Story* trade ad in *Tide*, October 15, 1942, 9.

53. "Women in Industry," *MLR* 57 (October 1943): 723–28; "Wage and Hour Statistics: Average Hourly Earnings in the Airframe Industry, 1943," *MLR* 58 (May 1944): 1050–68. Also see Milkman, *Gender at Work*, 49–98; Gabin, *Feminism in the Labor Movement*, 47–100; and Cobble, *Other Women's Movement*, 13–18.

54. "War and Post-War Trends in Employment of Negroes," *MLR* 60 (January 1945): 1–5; *Termination Report of the NWLB*, I, 150–55. Also see Robert Korstad and Nelson Lichtenstein, "Opportunities Found and Lost: Labor, Radicals, and the Early Civil Rights Movement," *JAH* 75, no. 3 (1988): 786–811; Thomas Sugrue, *Origins of the Urban Crisis: Race and Inequality in Postwar Detroit* (Princeton, NJ: Princeton University Press, 1996), 23–28; MacLean, *Freedom Is Not Enough*, 22–27; Clarence Lang, *Grassroots at the Gateway: Class Politics and Black Freedom Struggle in St. Louis, 1936–75* (Ann Arbor: University of Michigan Press, 2009), 43–63; Erik Gellman, *Death Blow to Jim Crow: The National Negro Congress and the Rise of Militant Civil Rights* (Chapel Hill: University of North Carolina Press,

2012), 165–211; and Lisa Phillips, *A Renegade Union: Interracial Organizing and Radical Unionism* (Urbana: University of Illinois Press, 2012), 66–90.

55. On popular understandings of wartime sacrifice and obligation during World War II, see Robert Westbrook, "'I Want a Girl, Just Like the Girl that Married Harry James': American Women and the Problem of Political Obligation in World War II," *AQ* 42, no. 4 (1990): 587–614; Mark Leff, "The Politics of Sacrifice on the American Home Front in World War II," *JAH* 77, no. 4 (1991): 1296–318; and Sparrow, *Warfare State*, 48–112, 166–84.

56. "Help Asked to Organize 'White Collar Class'" display ad, *NYT*, November 21, 1943, 12; "NAMzi White Collar League," *IF*, March 27, 1944, 4; Horowitz, *Betty Friedan*, 110–11; and contents of Folder 39, Box 19, CLA-CRF.

57. Louis Stark, "Lack Machinery to Raise 'White Collar' Pay," *NYT*, November 15, 1943, 1, 24; Arthur Krock, "Seeking a Way out for the Eighteen Million," *NYT*, November 16, 1943, 22; "BMU Salary Drive Answers Times Blast," *Proof*, December 1943, 1; "Action vs. Crocodile Tears," *Proof*, December 1943, 2; and Lewis Merrill, "Starch in the White Collar," *NM*, December 14, 1943, 20–22.

58. Testimony of Lewis Merrill, *Fixed Incomes in the War Economy*, 1255, 1263; and "Senate Hearings Turn Spotlight on White Collar Woes," *OPN*, January 1944, 1.

59. Lewis Merrill, "Taking Stock," *OPN*, November 1943, 5–8; "Curtiss Wright Goes UOPWA in Poll of 4,200 Workers," *OPN*, December 1943, 1, 3; "Curtiss Workers Get $30 Pay Floor in Contract for 4,500," *OPN*, March 1944, 3.

60. "Senate Body Says Lift Salary Freeze," *OPN*, May 1944, 1; "Ragged White Collars," *B&B*, May 13, 1944, 1.

61. Louis Stark, "New Political Unit Headed by Hillman," *NYT*, July 14, 1944, 8; John Moutoux, "Nationwide Liberal Committee to Help Re-Elect FDR," *PM*, July 14, 1944, 6; NCPAC advertisement, *NYT*, July 21, 1944, 8; "CIO Political Unit to Aid Campaign," *NYT*, July 23, 1944, 29. Also see Fraser, *Labor Will Rule*, 514–17.

62. "Jo Davidson Heads Unit for Roosevelt," *NYT*, August 24, 1944, 32; Tom O'Connor, "Stars to Join Wallace in Roosevelt Rally at Garden," *PM*, September 20, 1944, 17; "Artists, Writers Pledge Aid to Roosevelt in Visit to White House Led by Jo Davidson," *NYT*, October 6, 1944, 15.

63. On the contributions by Shahn, Corwin, and other artists, see Karl Pretshold, "PAC Out to Reach 'Grass Roots' U.S.A. on Vital Issues," *PM*, July 30, 1944, 7; John McManus, "Auto Workers' Film Roars Hell-Bent for FDR," *PM*, September 25, 1944, 15; "Corwin to Do Hour Show Election Eve with F.D.R. Pitch," *Billboard*, November 4, 1944, 5; Barnouw, *Golden Web*, 208–209; Zieger, *CIO*, 183–86; Denning, *Cultural Front*, 73, 418–19; and Hemingway, *Artists on the Left*, 194–97.

64. Nathan Robertson, "CIO Fights Appeasement of Democratic Reactionaries," *PM*, July 19, 1944, 4; James Reston, "Hillman Says CIO Will Back Truman," *NYT*, July 22, 1944, 10; James Wechsler, "Party Bosses' Fears Cost Wallace Nomination; Liberals Signal Full Support for Sen. Truman," *PM*, July 23, 1944, 11. Also see Fraser, *Labor Will Rule*, 530–34.

65. John Moutoux, "Hillman Talks Back, Pins Lie on PAC 'Slush Fund,'" *PM*, August 29, 1944, 14; "Biddle Gives NCPAC Clean Bill of Health," *PM*, September 26, 1944, 12; Louis Stark, "PAC Unit Is Called Communist Agency," *NYT*, October 4, 1944, 17; "Lists 119 of NCPAC with Communists," *NYT*, October 6, 1944, 13; Nathan Robertson, "Dies Refuses NCPAC A Fair Day in Court," *PM*, October 6, 1944, 13. Also see Fraser, *Labor Will Rule*, 523–30, 534–36.

66. C. P. Trussell, "Thirteen Million Elusive Voters," *NYT*, August 6, 1944, SM18–19; I. F. Stone, "Organized Labor Got out the Vote for Roosevelt," *PM*, November 8, 1944, 11. Also see Blum, *V Was for Victory*, 292–300; Fraser, *Labor Will Rule*, 536–38; Zieger, *CIO*, 187–88; and David Kennedy, *Freedom from Fear: The American People in Depression and War, 1929–1945* (New York: Oxford University Press, 1999), 782–93.

67. "Arts, Sciences Group Takes Political Role," *NYT*, December 20, 1944, 19; Jo Davison to Rockwell Kent, December 21, 1944, Frame 648, Reel 5192, RK; ICCASP introductory brochure, n.d., Frames 649–52, Reel 5192, RK; ICCASP, "January 1945—June 1946: The History of the First Eighteen Months of the Independent Citizens' Committee of the Arts, Sciences, and Professions," 1946, Folder 6, Box 5, CLA-CRF. Also see Fraser, *Labor Will Rule*, 557–60.

68. "Women in Industry: Changes in Women's Employment during the War," *MLR* 59 (November 1944): 1029–30; Harold Wool and Lester Pearlman, "Recent Occupational Trends: Wartime and Postwar Trends Compared," *MLR* 65 (August 1947): 139–47; Mary Elizabeth Pidgeon, "Women Workers and Recent Economic Change," *MLR* 65 (December 1947): 666–71. Also see Milkman, *Gender at Work*, 99–127; Gabin, *Feminism in the UAW*, 111–42; and Cobble, *Other Women's Movement*, 69–93.

69. "Women in Industry: Changes in Women's Employment during the War"; Wool and Pearlman, "Recent Occupational Trends: Wartime and Postwar Trends Compared"; Pidgeon, "Women Workers and Recent Economic Change."

70. "Wage and Hour Statistics: Earnings of Bank Employees, Spring and Summer of 1943," *MLR* 58 (April 1944): 816–21; Wage and Hour Statistics: Wages in Department and Clothing Stores in Large Cities, Spring and Summer of 1943," *MLR* 59 (November 1944): 1036–47.

71. "Women in Industry: Changes in Women's Employment during the War"; Wool and Pearlman, "Recent Occupational Trends: Wartime and Postwar Trends Compared"; Pidgeon, "Women Workers and Recent Economic Change."

72. UOPWA, "The Case of Mary X" (pamphlet), 1946, Folder 10, Box 11, CLA-CRF.

73. "Wage and Hour Statistics: Salaries of Clerical Workers in 20 Cities, April 1943," *MLR* 57 (August 1943): 348–49.

74. "'Blue' Collarites Follow CBS Lead Down Union Trail; NBC, MBS Next," *Variety*, June 6, 1945, 31, 36; "Classification of Jobs Weighed by CBS, CIO," *Billboard*, October 13, 1945, 5; "Union Grows in Radio Networks," *OPN*, October 1945, 3.

75. "Screen Case Settled; Still to Be Ratified," *OPN*, July 1945, 4; "Movie Workers Net Half Million in Job Plan," *OPN*, October 1945, 3.

76. Terry Lipani and Eleanor Smith to Gertrude Epstein, January 4, 1945, Folder 3, Box 60, NGNY; Helen Commander to Connie D'Amato, August 25, 1945, Folder 3, Box 60, NGNY; Transcript of Time, Inc. contract negotiations, January 4, 1946, 9–22, Folder 5, Box 60, NGNY; Transcript of Time, Inc. contract negotiations, March 1, 1946, 1–3, Folder 8, Box 60, NGNY; Transcript of Time, Inc. Negotiations, March 5, 1946, 21–29, 44–48, Folder 8, Box 60, NGNY; Transcript of Time, Inc. Negotiations, March 7, 1946, 1–10, Folder 8, Box 60, NGNY.

77. On the overall efficacy of the NWLB in diminishing gender discrimination in the workplace, see *Termination Report of the NWLB*, I, 290–98.

78. R. D. P. Jr. to *Fortune* Staff, November 7, 1945, 9–10, Folder 2, Box 60, NGNY; I. Benney to *Fortune* Researchers, January 28, 1946, Folder 2, Box 60, NGNY.

79. Transcript of Time, Inc. contract negotiations, January 31, 1946, 7, Folder 5, Box 60, NGNY.

80. Ibid., 9–20.

81. "The Postwar World," *Tide*, July 15, 1942, 31; "Calling All Girls," *Tide*, August 1, 1943, 38. On the teen female magazine genre, see Rachel Devlin, *Relative Intimacy: Fathers, Adolescent Daughters, and Postwar American Culture* (Chapel Hill: University of North Carolina, 2005), 88–102.

82. "Parents Workers Air Grievances," *Proof*, November 1943, 3; "Election at Parents!" *Proof*, February 1944, 1; Book and Magazine Union, Local 18, UOPWA-CIO, Petition for Investigation and Certification of Representatives, Case 2-R-4537, February 3, 1944, Formal and Informal Unfair Labor Practice and Representation Case Files, 1944, NLRB.

83. Clara Savage Littledale to MEG, February 18, 1944, Folder 65, Box 3, CSL; "Give-and-Take Meeting Spurs Parents Organizing," *Proof*, March 1944, 1; "Parents' Solid as Management Stalls Election," *Proof*, April 1944, 1, 3; NLRB Region 2, Tally of Ballots, Case 2-R-4537, June 1, 1944, Formal and Informal Unfair Labor Practice and Representation Case Files, 1944, NLRB; Samuel Sacher to NLRB Region 2, Case 2-R-4537, June 5, 1944, Formal and Informal Case Files, 1944, NLRB; Charles T. Douds to Oscar S. Smith, Case 2-R-4537, October 5, 1944, Formal and Informal Case Files, 1944, NLRB; Sacher to Douds, Case 2-R-4537, October 9, 1944, Formal and Informal Case Files, 1944, NLRB; Frances Ullman DeArmand to Leonard Boudin, "History of Employment of Frances Ullman DeArmand at Parents Institute, Inc.," May 13, 1947, Folder 16, Box 2, FUD.

84. "Magazine, Commercial, Film Workers Organize," *OPN*, February 1947, 10; "Parents Workers in Election March 6," *OPN*, March 1947, 3; "Strike Slated Today at Parents' Magazine," *PM*, March 24, 1947, 10; Clara Savage Littledale to Rosemary and Len Rieser, April 4, 1947, Folder 65, Box 3, CSL; Frances Ullman DeArmand to Leonard Boudin, "History of Employment of Frances Ullman DeArmand at Parents Institute, Inc."

85. "Employees Walk Out on 'Parents' Magazine'," *PM*, March 25, 1947, 11; "Magazine Strike Continues," *NYT*, March 26, 1947, 18; Clara Savage Littledale to Rosemary and Len Rieser, April 20, 1947, Folder 65, Box 3, CSL.

86. "NLRB Order Raises Free Speech Issue," *NYT*, April 1, 1947, 21; "Parents Institute Employees Strike for Guild Contract," *Publishers' Weekly*, April 12, 1947, 2024; Parents Strike Committee, "The Story of the *'Parents' Magazine'* Strike," April 1947, Frame 483, Reel 5243, RK; "Magazine Strike is Solid in Sixth Week," *OPN*, May 1947, 3.

87. Clara Savage Littledale to Rosemary and Len Rieser, April 28, 1947, Folder 65, Box 3, CSL; "Magazine Strike Ends," *NYT*, May 3, 1947, 8; Frances Ullman DeArmand to Leonard Boudin, "History of Employment of Frances Ullman DeArmand at Parents Institute, Inc."; "Parents Workers Settle Strike," *OPN*, June 1947, 5.

88. Frances Ullman DeArmand to Leonard Boudin, "History of Employment of Frances Ullman DeArmand at Parents Institute, Inc."; Clara Savage Littledale to Rosemary and Len Rieser, May 14, 1947, Folder 65, Box 3, CSL; Littledale to Riesers, June 7, 1947, Folder 65, Box 3, CSL; S. Jay Lassiter, CPA, Audit of UOPWA Organizing and Defense Fund Expenses, July 1, 1946 to June 30, 1947, February 14, 1948, Folder 15, Box 11, CLA-CRF.

89. Dorothy Lee, "What Does Homemaking Mean to You?" *Parents*, January 1947, 24, 88–89. Also see Ferdinand Lundberg and Marynia Farnham, *Modern Woman: The Lost Sex* (New York: Harper and Bros., 1947); Dorothy Parker, "A Book about 'Woman' Irks Miss Parker," *PM*, January 12, 1947, M13; and Eugene H. Kone, "Incubator of Democracy," *Parents*, January 1947, 26, 81–82. Also see Elaine Tyler May, *Homeward Bound: American Families in the Cold War Era* (New York: Basic Books, 1988), 16–36, 58–91; and Susan M. Hartman, "Women's Employment and the Domestic Ideal in the Early Cold War Years," in *Not June Cleaver: Women and Gender in Postwar America, 1945–1960*, ed. Joanne Meyerowitz (Philadelphia: Temple University Press, 1994), 84–100.

90. This assessment of the representation of women in postwar popular culture is central to Betty Friedan's argument in *The Feminine Mystique* (New York: Norton, 1963). For a differing perspective, see Joanne Meyerowitz, "Beyond the Feminine Mystique: A Reassessment of Postwar Mass Culture, 1946–1958," *JAH* 79, no. 4 (1993): 1455–82.

91. *BCAW*, June 24, 1946, 1–2; Estelle Reuter to Pauline Jones, July 17, 1946, Folder 15, Box 103, District 65; Jones to Reuter, July 30, 1946, Folder 15, Box 103, District 65; Amy Swerdlow, "The Congress of American Women: Left-Feminist Peace Politics in the Cold War," in *U.S. History as Women's History: New Feminist Essays*, ed. Linda Kerber, Alice Kessler-Harris, and Kathryn Kish Sklar (Chapel Hill: University of North Carolina Press, 1995), 296–312; Weigand, *Red Feminism*, 46–64; and Horowitz, *Betty Friedan*, 124–31.

92. "Woman's Rights Amendment," *BCAW*, June 24, 1946, 2; Anna Lee, "Now Is the Time for a Woman's Status Amendment," *BCAW*, July 28, 1946, 7; Eleanor

Vaughn, "C.A.W. Goes to Washington," *BCAW*, June 24, 1946, 3; Mary Murphy, "Commission Reports—Status of Women," *BCAW*, August-September 1946, 4; Mary Murphy, "Women and Unemployment—A Critical Problem," *BCAW*, June 24, 1946, 3. Also see Cobble, *Other Women's Movement*, 60–68.

93. Congress of American Women, "Program: The Commission on the Status of Women," 1947, Folder 30, Box 6, CLA-CRF.

94. "We've Won the War: Let's Win the Peace," *OPN*, August 15, 1945, 1.

95. *Officers' Report to the Seventh Constitutional Convention of the United Office and Professional Workers of America, CIO*, March 1948, 11.

96. On the CIO leadership's initial responses to the sudden resumption of conventional collective bargaining in the late summer and early fall of 1945, see Lichtenstein, *Labor's War at Home*, 216–21; Harris, *Right to Manage*, 111–18; Fraser, *Labor Will Rule*, 560–65; and Zieger, *CIO*, 214–19.

97. "Trend of Employment, Earnings, and Hours: Detailed Reports for Industrial and Business Employment, March 1944"; "Trend of Employment, Earnings, and Hours: Detailed Reports for Industrial and Business Employment, November 1945," *MLR* 62 (February 1946): 333–46.

98. Richard Lewis, "Battle of the Pay Envelope," *OPN*, July 1945, 7; "20 percent Pay Boost in Guild Demands," *E&P*, September 8, 1945, 50; Transcript of Time, Inc. Negotiations, January 4, 1946, 37, Folder 5, Box 60, NGNY. On the 1945–46 strikes in New York City, see Joshua Freeman, *Working-Class New York: Life and Labor since World War Two* (New York: New Press, 2001), 3–6.

99. GNYIUC Minutes, January 3, 1946, Folder 15, Box 9, NGNY; "Newspaper Guild Votes for 5 Pacts," *NYT*, February 5, 1946, 15; "Guild Contracts Negotiated for 5 N.Y. Dailies," *E&P*, February 16, 1946, 59; "*Times*, Guild Sign Pact," *NYT*, February 16, 1946, 11.

100. "Screen Guild Gets Ready for Industry-Wide Talks," *OPN*, April 1946, 8; "Emergency Conference Called on Film Talks," *OPN*, August 1946, 2; "Screen Talks Near Climax," *OPN*, September 1946, 8; *Agreement Made and Entered into between Motion Picture Industry in New York and Screen Office Professional Employees Guild, Local 109, U.O.P.W.A., CIO* (booklet), October 3, 1946, NA; "Victorious Screen Settlement Leads Month of NYC Bargaining Gains," *OPN*, October 1946, 7; Fred Hodgson, "To Members of the Paramount Unit" (open letter), October 14, 1946, Folder 11, Box 11, CLA-CRF.

101. Time Incorporated, *Annual Report to Stockholders for 1945*, 2–5, Folder 23, Box 59, NGNY; "Contract Negotiations Open on Friday, November 30," *On Time*, November 29, 1945, Folder 36, Box 61, NGNY; Transcript of Time, Inc. Negotiations, November 30, 1945, 5–10, Folder 23, Box 59, NGNY; Transcript of Time, Inc. Negotiations, December 7, 1945, 1–3, Folder 23, Box 59, NGNY; Transcript of Time, Inc. Negotiations, January 31, 1946, 7–28, Folder 5, Box 60, NGNY;

102. Transcript of Time, Inc. Negotiations, December 7, 1945, 3–6, 11–13.

103. Transcript of Time, Inc. Negotiations, March 1, 1946, 33–38, Folder 8, Box 60, NGNY; Transcript of Time, Inc. Negotiations, March 5, 1946, 1–21, Folder 8, Box 60, NGNY; Transcript of Time, Inc. Negotiations, March 7, 1946, 11–40, Folder 8, Box 60, NGNY; Transcript of Time, Inc. Negotiations, March 8, 1946, 22–29, Folder 9, Box 60, NGNY; Transcript of Time, Inc. Negotiations, March 26, 1946, 1–16, 28-Folder 9, Box 60. On the efforts of business to reassert its "right to manage" more generally after the war, see Harris, *Right to Manage*, 60–89, 95–104; and Sanford Jacoby, *Modern Manors: Welfare Capitalism since the New Deal* (Princeton, NJ: Princeton University Press, 1997), 228–35.

104. Transcript of Time, Inc. Negotiations, December 7, 1945, 4–5, 8–9, 13–16, 23–26; Transcript of Time, Inc. Negotiations, December 14, 1945, 4–22, Folder 23, Box 59, NGNY; Transcript of Time, Inc. Negotiations, January 4, 1946, 1–8; Transcript of Time, Inc. Negotiations, January 31, 1946, 38–39; Transcript of Time, Inc. Negotiations, February 21, 1946, 8–15, Folder 7, Box 60, NGNY; "Company Offers More Money, Insists on Open Shop," *On Time*, February 27, 1946, Folder 36, Box 61, NGNY; Transcript of Time, Inc. Negotiations, March 1, 1946, 6–22; Transcript of Time Inc. Negotiations, March 8, 1946, 31–42; "Guild Presses Case for Union Security," *On Time*, March 13, 1946, Folder 36, Box 61, NGNY; Nelson Lichtenstein, *Walter Reuther: The Most Dangerous Man in Detroit* (Urbana: University of Illinois Press, 1997), 237; "Petition on Behalf of Employees of Time, Inc.," n.d., Folder 4, Box 60, NGNY.

105. Transcript of Time, Inc. Negotiations, March 22, 1946, 1–23, Folder 9, Box 60, NGNY; Transcript of Time, Inc. Negotiations, April 4, 1946, 1–12, Folder 10, Box 60, NGNY; "Guild Takes Security Issue to Public," *On Time*, April 8, 1946, Folder 36, Box 61, NGNY; Newspaper Guild of New York to All City Editors, April 9, 1946, Folder 13, Box 60, NGNY; Newspaper Guild of New York press release, April 25, 1946, Folder 25, Box 58, NGNY; Roy Larsen to All Editorial Staff, April 26, 1946, Folder 4, Box 60, NGNY; Newspaper Guild of New York to NLRB Region 2, Unfair Labor Practice Charges, April 27, 1946, Folder 23, Box 58, NGNY; "Guild Weighs Luce Strike," *NYT*, April 28, 1946, 34; Gertrude Epstein to Dear Correspondent/Photographer, April 30, 1946, Folder 25, Box 58, NGNY; Theodore White to Gertrude Epstein, May 1, 1946, Folder 25, Box 58, NGNY.

106. "Resolution Adopted by Time, Inc. Unit," May 3, 1946, Folder 25, Box 58, NGNY; "Unit Votes Strike," *On Time*, May 3, 1946, Folder 36, Box 61, NGNY; "N.Y. Guild Votes Further Effort to Organize," *E&P*, May 4, 1946, 54; "That Great Big Wonderful Meeting," *On Time*, May 8, 1946, Folder 36, Box 61, NGNY; Gertrude Epstein to All Correspondents, May 10, 1946, Folder 25, Box 58, NGNY; "Security of the Guild," May 13, 1946, Folder 22, Box 58, NGNY; "Unit Rescinds Strike Vote," *On Time*, May 16, 1946, Folder 36, Box 61, NGNY; Transcript of Time, Inc. Negotiations, May 22, 1946, Folder 10, Box 60, NGNY; "Contract Still Unsettled," *On Time*, June 27, 1946, Folder 36, Box 61, NGNY.

107. "*The Billboard* Sizes up Media Battle for $," *Billboard*, January 26, 1946, 3, 8; "Webs' 1946 Take—193 Million," *Billboard*, December 28, 1946, 5; Barnouw, *Golden Web*, 168–81, 187–90, 227–36.

108. "CIO Moves Toward Large-Scale Organization of Net Personnel," *Broadcasting*, May 28, 1945; "'Blue' Collarites Follow CBS Lead Down Union Trail; NBC, MBS Next," *Variety*, June 6, 1945, 31, 36; "Union Grows in Radio Networks," *OPN*, October 1945, 3.

109. "Screen Publicity Guild Hosts Radio Flacks, Offers Help in Getting Salary Increases," *Billboard*, June 23, 1945, 4; "Hearings Start on Radio Poll," *OPN*, January 1946, 3; "CBS Campaigner Tells Why UOPWA Platform is Radio Office Choice," *OPN*, February 1946, 2; Decision and Direction of Election, Cases 2-R-5878 and 2-R-5884, May 24, 1946, *DNLRB* 68 (1946): 274–84; "UOPWA Polls Greatest Vote at CBS, but not Majority; Run-Off May Be Necessary," *Billboard*, June 22, 1946, 6, 51; "UOPWA Wins CBS Radio Poll," *OPN*, July 1946, 1; "Local 16 Members Aid Radio Guild CBS Victory," *Memo*, July 1946, 1, Folder 13, Box 103, District 65; Andrew Hertz, "I Went on a Home Visit for the Radio Guild," *Memo*, July 1946, 3; Second Supplemental Decision and Direction, Cases 2-R-5878 and 2-R-5884, September 20, 1946, *DNLRB* 70 (1946): 1368–75.

110. "UOPWA Charges NBC With Unfair Labor Practices," *Broadcasting*, June 23, 1946; "'Strategic' Retreat by CIO at NBC," *Billboard*, August 3, 1946, 5, 8; "Workers Fired, UOPWA Hits NBC with Boycott Threat; FCC & NLRB Seek an Out," *Billboard*, August 10, 1946, 6, 12; "NBC Fires Veteran as Radio Guild Grows," *OPN*, August 1946, 2; "CBS Hikes 900 Staffers' Wages; CIO Certification Pends; ABC Program Drawn," *Billboard*, September 7, 1946, 6; "3 More Nets Asked to Give Interim Hikes," *Billboard*, September 14, 1946, 5, 13; "WMCA-CIO Pact Ups 60 Employees' Pay," *Billboard*, September 21, 1946, 6; "CBS Certification Spurs Radio Drive as NYC Organizing Barometer Rises," *OPN*, October 1946, 6; "CBS White Collarites Ask 35 percent Pay Hike; Union Plans N.Y.C. Organization Drive," *Billboard*, October 26, 1946, 6, 18; "CIO White Collarites Plan Demonstration for NBC Aid," *Billboard*, November 2, 1946, 12; "CBS White Collars Picket NBC, MBS," *Billboard*, November 9, 1946, 15; Myra Jordan, "Cut Out Static," *OPN*, November 1946, 4; "Radio Guild (CIO) Wins 2-Year Contract With CBS Covering White-Collar Group," *Broadcasting*, November. 25, 1946, 101; "Radio Guild Wins 25 percent Increase at CBS," *OPN*, December 1946, 1.

111. "FAECT Votes on Merger with UOPWA," *OPN*, January 1946, 1; "Union Organizes at Ebasco," *Tech Talk*, March 1946, 2; J. Lawrence Raimist to NLRB Region 2, March 20, 1946, Folder 7, Box 13, AFAE 66; Howard F. LeBaron to Raimist, March 20, 1946, Folder 7, Box 13, AG 66; FAECT Chapter 31, Petition for Certification of Representatives, Case 2-R-6396, March 25, 1946, Formal and Informal Unfair Labor Practice and Representation Case Files, 1946, NLRB; Raimist to NLRB Region 2, March 28, 1946, Folder 7, Box 13, AFAE 66; NLRB,

Agreement for Consent Election, Case 2-R-6396, April 3, 1946, Formal and Informal Case Files, 1946, NLRB; NLRB Region 2, Tally of Ballots, Case 2-R-6396, April 9, 1946, Formal and Informal Case Files, 1946, NLRB; "FAECT—UOPWA Merger Completed, New Technical Division Set Up," *OPN*, April 1946, 2; "Design Office Organized," *OPN*, May 1946, 6.

112. "Ebasco Negotiations," *TT*, June 1946, 5; "15 percent Wage Increase Won at Ebasco; Strike Vote Forces Negotiations," *TT*, August 1946, 1, 3; "CTAL Support Aids Ebasco Drive," *TT*, August 1946, 2; "Ebasco Contract Signed," *TT*, October 1946, 1–2; "CTAL Official Helps," *TT*, October 1946, 2; "Costa Ricans Trounce U.S. Bond and Share, *Ebasco Unit*, November 1946, 3, Folder 75, Box 9, AFAE 66; "Review Wins New Raises at Ebasco," *TT*, January 1947, 1; "Organization Notes: Architects and Designers," *TT*, June 1946, 6; "Drive Starts in Design Offices," *TT*, August 1946, 1–2; "Union Victory Points the Way for All Technical Men," *TT*, October 1946, 2; "Start Negotiation at Four Architectural Firms," *TT*, October 1946, 1, 6; "Contract Won at Architect's Office," *TT*, February 1947, 1; "Contract at P. Copeland," *TT*, February 1947, 3.

113. Ad Guild pamphlet, 1946, Folder 10, Box 11, CLA-CRF; American Business Consultants, "Memo Re: United Office and Professional Workers Union," August 30, 1946, Folder 10, Box 11, CLA-CRF.

114. On the surveillance and infiltration of the Ad Guild, see all memoranda from informants "No. 64" and "No. 65" in Folder 11, Box 11, CLA-CRF; and T. C. Kirkpatrick, "Subject: Advertising Guild—UOPWA," September 29, 1947, Folder 13, Box 11, CLA-CRF. Also see "Pact at Ad Firm," *OPN*, January 1946, 3; and "Ad Agency Organized," *OPN*, August 1946, 2.

115. On the political dynamic in 1946, see Fraser, *Labor Will Rule*, 567–72; Zieger, *CIO*, 241–45; Lichtenstein, *Walter Reuther*, 254–57; Cohen, *Consumers'* Republic, 100–109; and Jacobs, *Pocketbook Politics*, 221–31.

116. ICCASP, "Report from Washington" newsletter, April 1946, Folder 6, Box 5, CLA-CRF; "Save Price Control: Consumers Appeal to the Senate," *B&B*, May 4, 1946, 1–2; "OPA Action," *BCAW*, June 24, 1946, 4; "Inflation is Here," *OPN*, September 1946, 1; "Unconditional Surrender on Meat: The Collapse of Price Control," *B&B*, October 26, 1946, 1–2.

117. "Prices and Cost of Living: Prices in the Second Quarter of 1946," *MLR* 63 (September 1946): 409–23; Sidney Margolius, "Dollar Worth 63 Cents and Still Falling," *PM*, February 28, 1947, 3; "Prices in the Fourth Quarter and Year 1946," *MLR* 64 (March 1947): 378–96.

118. "U.S. Big Business Boasts It Corrupts Public Opinion Through Press, Radio, School, Church," *IF*, November 19, 1945, 1–4. For a survey of the public relations efforts of business in the aftermath of the war and the 1945–1946 strike wave, see Elizabeth Fones-Wolf, *Selling Free Enterprise: The Business Assault on Labor and Liberalism, 1945–60* (Urbana: University of Illinois Press, 1994), 33–44.

119. "'Stay-at-Home' Folks Elected that 80th Congress," *CION*, July 26, 1948, 2.

120. Peter Lyon et al. to Dear Member, June 28, 1946, Folder 6, Box 5, CLA-CRF.

121. NCPAC, *A Report to America on Radio Broadcasting*, October 1945, Folder 5, Box 474, JBM; Federal Communications Commission, *Public Service Responsibility of Broadcast Licensees* (Washington, DC: G.P.O., 1946); "FCC Report Has NAB Mad," *Billboard*, March 16, 1946, 5, 12; John McManus, "Labor's Best Bet Is Its Own Outlet," *PM*, February 18, 1947, 15; Konecky, *American Communications Conspiracy*, 19–65. Also see Barnouw, *Golden Web*, 227–36; Newman, *Radio Active*, 166–91; Fones-Wolf, *Waves of Opposition*, 134–36, 140–48; Stamm, *Sound Business*, 152–58, 171–80; and Pickard, *America's Battle for Media Democracy*, 62–97.

122. Renee Shapiro to Rockwell Kent, November 11, 1946, Frame 598, Reel 5222, RK; PRF, flyer for December 13, 1946 performances, Frame 602, Reel 5222, RK; PRF, flyer for "Columbus Discovers Tennessee" performance, Folder 11, Box 7, CLA-CRF; Konecky, *American Communications Conspiracy*, 107–109. Also see Stamm, *Sound Business*, 160–61.

123. Corliss Lamont to Rockwell Kent, January 10, 1945, Frame 503, Reel 5222, RK; Kent to Lamont, January 14, 1945, Frame 505, Reel 5222; "Reports Communists Behind Plea for New FM Station," *PM*, March 12, 1947, 19; "FCC Approved FM, Television Pleas," *NYT*, April 16, 1947, 34; Joseph Brodsky to the Directors of the Peoples Radio Foundation, May 23, 1947, Frame 613, Reel 5222, RK; Konecky, *American Communications Conspiracy*, 105–106. Also see Fones-Wolf, *Waves of Opposition*, 152–60; and Stamm, *Sound Business*, 161–64, 181.

124. Konecky, *American Communications Conspiracy*, 109–10.

CHAPTER 6

1. Radio Writers Guild Fact-Finding Committee on Blacklisting, Notes Re: Case Number Four, December 12, 1952, Folder 6, Box 60, RWG; Minutes of the Fact-Finding Committee on Blacklisting, May 27, 1952, Folder 6, Box 60, RWG; Minutes of the Fact-Finding Committee, June 24, 1952, Folder 6, Box 60, RWG.

2. Jack Gould, "C.B.S. Dismisses a Girl Office Employee for Refusal to Sign Its Loyalty Statement," *NYT*, January 26, 1951, 15.

3. See, among numerous examples, Dalton Trumbo, *The Time of the Toad: A Study of Inquisition in America by One of the Hollywood Ten* (Hollywood, CA: Hollywood Ten, 1949); Daniel Gilmor, *Fear, the Accuser* (New York: Abelard-Schuman, 1954); Lillian Hellman, *Scoundrel Time* (Boston: Little, Brown, 1976); and Walter Bernstein, *Inside Out: A Memoir of the Blacklist* (New York: Knopf, 1996).

4. See, for example, Merle Miller, *The Judges and the Judged: A Report for the American Civil Liberties Union* (New York: Doubleday, 1952); John Cogley, *Report on Blacklisting: Volume Two, Radio and Television* (New York: Fund for the Republic, 1956); Navasky, *Naming Names*; and Patrick McGilligan and Paul Buhle, eds., *Tender Comrades: A Backstory of the Hollywood Blacklist* (New York: St. Martin's Press, 1997).

5. See, for instance, Ted Morgan, *Reds: McCarthyism in Twentieth-Century America* (New York: Random House, 2003); and David Everitt, *A Shadow of Red: Communism and the Blacklist in Radio and Television* (Chicago: Ivan R. Dee, 2007).

6. Bernard Prockter to Radio Writers Guild, October 20, 1948, Folder 36, Box 39, RWG; "Television-Radio Reviews: *Treasury Men in Action*," *Billboard*, April 11, 1951, 8; Bernard Prockter to Arnold Perl, May 15, 1951, Folder 70, Box 32, RWG; "'Police Story' to Go on CBS-TV Sked," *Billboard*, February 23, 1952, 8.

7. Minutes of the Fact-Finding Committee on Blacklisting, May 27, 1952; Radio Writers Guild Fact-Finding Committee on Blacklisting, Notes Re: Case Number Four, December 12, 1952; May Bolhower to Prockter Productions, December 15, 1952, Folder 10, Box 32, RWG.

8. See Harris, *Right to Manage*, 118–27; Jacoby, *Modern Manors*, 195–203; and Ruth O'Brien, "Taking the Conservative State Seriously: Statebuilding and Restrictive Labor Practices in Postwar America," *Labor Studies Journal* 21 (Winter 1997): 33–63.

9. See George Lipsitz, *Rainbow at Midnight: Labor and Culture in the 1940s* (Urbana: University of Illinois Press, 1994), 172–73, 177–78; and Lichtenstein, *Walter Reuther*, 261–70.

10. See Vinel, *Employee*, 150–67.

11. See, for example, Tami Friedman, "Exploiting the North-South Differential: Corporate Power, Southern Politics, and the Decline of Organized Labor after World War Two," *JAH* 95 (September 2008): 323–48.

12. For an overview of the official anticommunist measures directed at unions, see Ellen Schrecker, "McCarthyism and the Labor Movement: The Role of the State," in *The CIO's Left-Led Unions*, ed. Steve Rosswurm (New Brunswick: Rutgers University Press, 1992), 139–57.

13. "Un-American Committee Plan to Work on Commentators," *Billboard*, October 20, 1945, 6; "Wood Committee Denies Attempt at Witch Hunt," *Billboard*, October 27, 1945, 12; "Un-Amer. Comm. Gets Works," *Billboard*, November 3, 1945, 10, 32; "House Group Sifts Talks of 7 on Radio," *NYT*, November 7, 1945, 25. Also see Fones-Wolf, *Waves of Opposition*, 131–33.

14. Albert Kahn, *Treason in Congress: The Record of the House Un-American Activities Committee* (New York: Progressive Citizens of America, 1948); *Counterattack*, June 23, 1948, 1; C. P. Trussell, "Red Underground in Federal Posts Alleged by Editor in New Deal Era," *NYT*, August 4, 1948, 1, 3; Trussell, "Hiss and Chambers Meet Face to Face," *NYT*, August 26, 1948, 1–2; Chambers, *Witness*, 529–784. Also see Caute, *The Great Fear*, 58–62, 88–103; Schrecker, *Many Are the Crimes*, 174–75; and Jason Roberts, "New Evidence in the Hiss Case: From the HUAC Files and the Hiss Grand Jury," *ACH* 1, no. 2 (2002): 143–62.

15. "Radio, Television, and Floodlights Will Open Red Film Inquiry Today," *NYT*, October 19, 1947, 14; "Film Men Admit Activity by Reds; Hold It Is Foiled," *NYT*, October 21, 1947, 1, 3; Samuel Tower, "Hollywood Communists 'Militant,' but Small in Number, Stars Testify," *NYT*, October 24, 1947, 1, 12; "Editorial: The

Thomas Circus," *Billboard,* November 1, 1947, 3; "Film Men Ask Ban on Contempt Move," *NYT,* November 2, 1947, 20. Also see Caute, *Great Fear,* 491–500; Navasky, *Naming Names,* 78–96; and Lary May, "Movie Star Politics: The Screen Actors' Guild, Cultural Conversion, and the Hollywood Red Scare," in *Recasting America: Culture and Politics in the Age of Cold War,* ed. May (Chicago: University of Chicago Press, 1989), 125–53. Bertolt Brecht was in fact an eleventh procommunist witness subpoenaed by HUAC, although his deliberately obfuscating testimony did not result in a contempt citation, and he repatriated to Germany shortly after his appearance.

16. Robert Kenny, "Loyalty Order Spearheads Drive on Civil Liberties," *PC,* May 1947, 1, 4; *Counterattack,* July 30, 1948, 9–10. Also see Caute, *Great Fear,* 169–80; Landon Storrs, "Red Scare Politics and the Suppression of Popular Front Feminism: The Loyalty Investigation of Mary Dublin Keyserling," *JAH* 90, no. 2 (2003): 491–524; Robert Goldstein, *American Blacklist: The Attorney General's List of Subversive Organizations* (Lawrence: University of Kansas Press, 2008); and Elaine Tyler May, "Security Against Democracy: The Legacy of the Cold War at Home," *JAH* 97, no. 4 (2011): 939–57.

17. *Counterattack,* July 23, 1948, 1–2. Also see Caute, *Great Fear,* 187–99; and Schrecker, *Many Are the Crimes,* 97–98, 145.

18. Max Lerner, "The Long March: An Appraisal of the New Liberal Movements," *PM,* January 9, 1947, 2–3; "PCA Opens Drive for 100,000 Here," *PM,* February 5, 1947; "Action Keynotes PCA Debut," *PC,* February 1947, 1, 3; Jo Davidson to Dear Member, February 14, 1947, Folder 7, Box 5, CLA-CRF; PCA, "Stop Reaction's Advance" pamphlet, 1947, Folder 7, Box 5, CLA-CRF.

19. Seymour Peck, "New Group to Battle for Liberals in Radio," *PM,* March 3, 1947, 19; "Ether Experts to Probe Airwave Bias and Abuse," *PC,* March 1947, 1; Peck, "Famous People Fight to Keep Shirer on the Air," *PM,* March 25, 1947, 19; PCA Radio Division, Program for April 19, 1947 Radio Conference, Folder 7, Box 5, CLA-CRF; Memorandum on "Crisis in Radio Conference," April 24, 1947, Folder 7, Box 5, CLA-CRF; John McManus, "Stars, Commentators Rally for Air Freedom," *PM,* May 6, 1947, 19; Miller, *Judges and the Judged,* 170–71.

20. John T. Hawkes, "Lewis in My Coffee!" *VOF,* December 1947, 2, Folder 37, Box 8, CLA-CRF; "Who's Telling You What to Think," *VOF,* December 1947, 2, Folder 37, Box 8, CLA-CRF. Also see Fones-Wolf, *Waves of Opposition,* 137, 149–50, 155.

21. "Wallace Candidacy Gives Voters Choice in November," *PC,* January 1948, 1, 7; "Statement of UOPWA Officers: The Wallace Candidacy," *OPN,* January 1948, 5; Henry Wallace, "The Progressive Party Is Here to Stay," *Uncensored,* September 1948, 1–2, Frames 1184–85, Reel 5224, RK. Also see Thomas Devine, *Henry Wallace's 1948 Presidential Campaign and the Future of Postwar Liberalism* (Chapel Hill: University of North Carolina Press, 2013), 1–70.

22. American Business Consultants, *Objective Study of United Office and Professional Workers of America, C.I.O. (Special Report No. 1)* (New York: Counterattack, 1947);

and American Business Consultants, *Red Channels: The Report of the Communist Influence in Radio and Television* (New York: Counterattack, 1950); "The Truth about *Red Channels*: Part Two," *Sponsor,* October 22, 1951, 30–31, 76–86; Miller, *Judges and the Judged,* 61–97. Also see Schrecker, *Many Are the Crimes,* 67, 218; and Robert Lichtman, "J. B. Matthews and the 'Counter-Subversives': Names as a Political and Financial Resource in the McCarthy Era," *ACH* 5, no. 1 (2006): 1–36.

23. See Michael Harrington, "Catholics in the Labor Movement: A Case History," *LH* 1, no. 3 (1960): 231–63; Steve Rosswurm, "The Catholic Church and the Left-Led Unions: Labor Priests, Labor Schools, and the ACTU," in *CIO's Left-Led Unions,* ed. Rosswurm, 119–37; and Schrecker, *Many Are the Crimes,* 72–75.

24. "Legion Fights Liberalism, Socialism, PAC, Trade Unionism in 'Isms' War; Omits Fascism," *IF,* December 30, 1946, 1–3; "American Legion's New Bedfellows," *IF,* February 21, 1950, 3–4; Louis Budenz, "How the Reds Invaded Radio," *American Legion Magazine,* December 1950, Folder 5, Box 128, JBM; Miller, *Judges and the Judged,* 157–61; Cogley, *Report on Blacklisting: Volume Two, Radio and Television,* 110–14. Also see Schrecker, *Many Are the Crimes,* 61–64, 217.

25. Quoted in Oliver Pilat, "Blacklist: The Veto Power in TV-Radio," *NYP,* January 27, 1953, 4, 14. Also see Cogley, *Report on Blacklisting: Volume Two, Radio and Television,* 54–56, 100–109.

26. "PCA Demands Public Ownership of Coal Mines, Railroads and Power," *PC,* July 1947, 1, 3; Henry Wallace, "Why I Choose to Run" brochure, 1947, Frames 1124–31, Reel 5224, RK; "PCA's Program for Congress," *PC,* February 1948, 7; New York State Art Division, National Council of Arts, Sciences, and Professions, "A Platform for Artists" brochure, 1948, Frames 1138–42, Reel 5224, RK. Also see White and Maze, *Henry A. Wallace,* 241–82; Patricia Sullivan, *Days of Hope: Race and Democracy in the New Deal Era* (Chapel Hill: University of North Carolina Press, 1996), 243–73; and Devine, *Henry Wallace's 1948 Presidential Campaign,* 71–155.

27. See James T. Patterson, *Grand Expectations: The United States, 1945–1974* (New York: Oxford University Press, 1996), 148–61; Jonathan Bell, *The Liberal State on Trial: The Cold War and American Politics in the Truman Years* (New York: Columbia University Press, 2004), 121–59; Simon Topping, "'Never Argue with the Gallup Poll': Thomas Dewey, Civil Rights, and the Election of 1948," *JAS* 38, no. 2 (2004): 179–98; Richard Fried, "'Operation Polecat': Thomas E. Dewey, the 1948 Election, and the Origins of McCarthyism," *JPH* 22, no. 1 (2010): 1–22.

28. "Communists Plan to Use Wallace," *NYT,* July 17, 1948, 6; "Here's Proof of Communist Control of New 'Progressive' Party," *Counterattack,* July 30, 1948, 1–8; Arthur Krock, "Truman Leads Wallace in Early Returns: Forecasts Upset," *NYT,* November 3, 1948, 1, 3; James Hagerty, "Dewey Wins State," *NYT,* November 3, 1948, 1, 11. Also see White and Maze, *Henry A. Wallace,* 283–88; Patterson, *Grand Expectations,* 161–63; and Devine, *Henry Wallace's 1948 Presidential Campaign,* 269–85.

29. On the stifling of the "Fair Deal" agenda, see Alonzo Hamby, "The Vital Center, the Fair Deal, and the Quest for a Liberal Political Economy," *AHR* 77, no. 3 (1972): 653–78; Patterson, *Grand Expectations,* 165–69; and Arnold Hirsch, "Less than *Plessy:* The Inner City, Suburbs, and State-Sanctioned Residential Segregation in the Age of *Brown,*" in *The New Suburban History,* ed. Kevin Kruse and Thomas Sugrue (Chicago: University of Chicago Press, 2006), 33–56.

30. A. H. Raskin, "Left-Wing CIO Office Union to 'Discipline' Communists," *NYT,* December 17, 1946, 1–2; "C.I.O. Left Wing Under Fire," *BW,* December 28, 1946, 64, 66; Nelson Frank, "Office Workers Divided on Reds," *NYW-T,* January 24, 1947; *Counterattack,* July 18, 1947, 1; and C. Wright Mills, *The New Men of Power: America's Labor Leaders* (New York: Harcourt, Brace and Co., 1948), 191.

31. Lewis Merrill to Rockwell Kent, April 1, 1947, Frame 1400, Reel 5211, RK; Kent to Merrill, April 3, 1947, Frames 1401–102, Reel 5211, RK; Harold Stevens to Merrill, June 3, 1947, Folder 5, Box 16, CIO-C; Merrill to UOPWA General Executive Board, June 5, 1947, Folder 5, Box 16, CIO-C; "Merrill Resigns as CIO Union Head," *NYT,* June 8, 1947, 42; "Office Union Picks Durkin," *NYT,* June 30, 1947, 20; "Durkin Elected New President," *OPN,* July 1947, 1, 3.

32. "Our Answer to Taft, Hartley, and Co.—We Have Just Begun to Fight," *OPN,* July 1947, 1, 4; Martin Cooper, "Union Will Fight Slave Law," *TT,* July 1947, 1–2; "FAECT Strikes at Ebasco," *TT,* September 1947, 1; "400 Strike Over Pay in Engineers' Office," *NYT,* September 6, 1947, 3.

33. George Curran to All State Federations of Labor, Central Trades and Labor Councils, Joint Councils, and Local Unions, American Federation of Labor, September 12, 1947, Folder 70, Box 9, AFAE 66; Martin Cooper to George Dietz, September 14, 1947, Folder 70, Box 9, AFAE 66; Dietz to Cooper, September 16, 1947, Folder 70, Box 9, AFAE 66; "Designers Down Drawing Boards, Strike Ebasco," *OPN,* October 1947, 1, 4; "Job Shops," *TT,* October 1947, 2; GNYIUC Minutes, October 2, 1947, Folder 16, Box 9, NGNY; "Topics of the Day in Wall Street," *NYT,* October 8, 1947, 35; "Confer on Ebasco Strike," *NYT,* October 15, 1947, 30.

34. "Job Shops Picketed," *TT,* November 1947, 1; "Strike Solid at Ebasco," *TT,* November 1947, 1, 4; Robert N. Denham et al., Memorandum of Points and Authorities upon Issues and Procedures Arising Pursuant to Petition for Injunction under Section 10 (1) of the National Labor Relations Act, as Amended, November 1947, Folder 7, Box 106, RBSKL; "Taft Law Invoked in Picketing Case," *NYT,* December 3, 1947, 19; FAECT Local 231, "Injunction!" flyer, December 1948, Folder 75, Box 9, AFAE 66; GNYIUC Minutes, December 18, 1947, Folder 16, Box 9, NGNY.

35. "Ebasco Strikers Fight Taft-Hartley Injunction with Support of CIO," *OPN,* January 1948, 2; "Ebasco Strike Passes 100th Day; Local Pledges Increased Support," *TT,* January 1948, 1–2; "Writ Denied NLRB in 'Boycott' Case," *NYT,* January 27, 1948, 21; "Ebasco Strike Terminated," *TT,* February 1948, 1, 4; "Pushing Forty: The Following Letter Tells a Story," *TT,* April 1948, 2.

36. "Screen Local Acts to Stop Union-Busting Witch-hunt," *OPN*, January 1948, 4; "Un-American Com. Threatens Free Publishing, Says Book Guild," *OPN*, January 1948, 4; "Anti-Reds Retreat from Union Test," *NYT*, March 2, 1948, 18; "CIO Leftists Win in Office Union," *NYT*, March 4, 1948, 19; GNYIUC, "Memorandum on Coordination of Wage and Strike Struggles," May 13, 1948, Folder 17, Box 9, NGNY.

37. Jack Turcott, "25,000 Swap Unions in Red Protest," *NYP*, June 3, 1948; UOPWA, "Leaders' Bulletin," July 1, 1948, Folder 18, Box 11, CLA-CRF; "Statement of the General Executive Board of the United Office and Professional Workers of America on the Taft-Hartley Issue," July 11, 1948, Folder 18, Box 11, CLA-CRF; John Stanley to All Local Unions, and All Office and Chapter Chairmen, July 13, 1948, Folder 18, Box 11, CLA-CRF; Stanley to Members of All Local Unions Under Suspension, July 14, 1948, Folder 18, Box 11, CLA-CRF; "Rules in Conducting Referendum," *OPN*, August 1948, 2.

38. Nelson Frank, "Union Fight on in Film Offices Here," *NYW-T*, May 25, 1948; "Screen Workers Plan All-Out Fight to Lick Industry–IATSE Gang-Up," *OPN*, June 1948, 5; Sidney Young to All Film Industry Members, June 15, 1948, Folder 13, Box 11, CLA-CRF; "Screen Workers Prime for Biggest Bargaining Battle," *OPN*, July 1948, 3, 5; SOPEG, "We Are Eating Less" flyer, 1948, Folder 13, Box 11, CLA-CRF; Honore Armstrong to Thomas J. Murphy, September 7, 1948, Folder 21, Box 24, NGNY; Barry Balaban to Young, September 23, 1948, Folder 16, Box 11, CLA-CRF; James Rogers to T. C. Kirkpatrick, September 30, 1948, Folder 16, Box 11, CLA-CRF; *Counterattack*, October 8, 1948, 2–3.

39. "Wallace 3rd Party Maps '48 Race," *CION*, January 5, 1948, 12; "CIO Opposes 3rd Party; Sets Legislative Agenda," *CION*, January 28, 1948; Allan Swim, "Hank May Have Meant Well But—He Caused Trouble," *CION*, February 16, 1948, 4. Also see Lichtenstein, *Walter Reuther*, 304–306; Ziegler, *The CIO*, 266–77.

40. "Unions Here Defy CIO on Wallace," *NYT*, March 19, 1948, 46; "'Right Wing' in CIO Sets up PAC Here," *NYT*, March 24, 1948, 22; "CIO Council Here Loses PAC Rights," *NYT*, April 22, 1948, 18.

41. *New York Tenant News*, Septmeber 20, 1948 issue located in Folder 3, Box 8, CLA-CRF.

42. Fiorello LaGuardia, "Don't Fall for a 10-Cent Fare," *PM*, February 9, 1947, 3–4; GNYIUC Minutes, January 8, 1948, Folder 17, Box 9, NGNY; "CIO Council Opposes 8-Cent Transit Fare," *NYT*, January 9, 1948, 9; "CIO Unit Accepts Quill Resignation," *NYT*, April 2, 1948, 3; "Quill Heads Drive on Leftists in CIO," *NYT*, May 25, 1948, 22; Joshua Freeman, *In Transit: The Transport Workers Union in New York City, 1933–1966* (New York: Oxford University Press, 1989), 282–314.

43. "The Facts About the Picketing at Gimbels Last Night" (advertisement), *NYW-T*, July 16, 1948, 5; "C.I.O. Council is Assailed for Store Picketing," *NYHT*, July 17, 1948; "Picketing of Store Forbidden by CIO," *NYT*, July 24, 1948, 7; Freeman,

Working-Class New York, 78; Opler, *For All White-Collar Workers,* 163–74; Phillips, *Renegade Union,* 100–13.

44. GNYIUC Minutes, October 7, 1948, Folder 17, Box 9, NGNY; David McConnell, "Fist Fight Halts CIO's Inquiry of N.Y. Council," *NYHT,* October 15, 1948; CIO Executive Board Committee, "Report, Findings, and Recommendations," Folder 50, Box 11, CLA-CRF; Freeman, *Working-Class New York,* 79.

45. James Durkin to All Local Unions, November 7, 1948, Folder 16, Box 11, CLA-CRF; *Counterattack,* November 12, 1948, 1; Howard Coughlin, OEIU Local 153 Organization Report, June 21, 1949, Reel 1, OEIU 153 Minutes; Minutes of Membership Meeting, March 21, 1950, Reel 1, OEIU 153 Minutes; "Pickets Press Film Fight," *Career,* April 15, 1949, 1, 4; "A.F.L. Union Wins Poll of Insurance Men," *NYHT,* July 28, 1949; "Security—the Stake in Met, Pru Polls," *Career,* July 1, 1949, 1.

46. Allan Swim, "Give the Commies the Boot! Must be Prevented from Using Trade Unions to Carry out Red Policies," *CION,* December 6, 1948, 4; "Office Union Plans Organizing Drive," *NYT,* December 28, 1948, 40; "Office Union Asks for 'Fighting Fund,'" *NYT,* January 10, 1949, 14; Allan Haywood to All CIO Regional and Sub-Regional Directors, January 19, 1949, Folder 8, Box 112, Part I, CIO-ST; "Lefties Say They'll Fight to Stay in CIO," *CION,* September 5, 1949, 11.

47. Charles Owen Rice to Members of the UOPWA, December 1948, Folder 16, Box 11, CLA-CRF; Rice to James Durkin, December 31, 1948, Folder 15, Box 11, CLA-CRF; Freeman, *Working-Class New York,* 83–84.

48. UOPWA, "Leaders' Bulletin," August 4, 1949, Folder 12, Box 11, CLA-CRF; James Durkin to All Local Unions, October 14, 1949, Folder 7, Box 112, Part I, CIO-ST; Allan Swim, "Convention Action Won't End Battle," *CION,* October 31, 1949, 4; "CIO Starts Purge of Leftist Officers," *NYT,* November 5, 1949, 1; Bernard Mooney to James Carey, January 30, 1950, Folder 7, Box 112, Part I, CIO-ST; "4 CP-Dominated Unions Expelled," *CION,* February 20, 1950, 6–7; Mooney to Carey, March 1, 1950, Folder 7, Box 112, Part I, CIO-ST; Carey to Mooney, March 17, 1950, Folder 7, Box 112, Part I, CIO-ST; Tom Harris to Allan Haywood, March 10, 1950, Folder 23, Box 3, CIO. For examples of anticommunist dissidence in the UOPWA, see the many letters from members in CIO-ST, Part I, Box 112, Folders 7 and 8. Also see Davis, *Prisoners of the American Dream,* 91–100; and Zieger, *The CIO,* 287–94.

49. "Office Workers Win CBS Pay Increase," *Billboard,* November 27, 1948, 10; "CBS Demands White Collars' Recertification," *Billboard,* October 15, 1949, 14; "CBS, Radio Guild Negotiations Are Resumed," *Broadcasting,* October 24, 1949, 37; "Election at CBS," *Broadcasting,* December 19, 1949, 70; "Union to Rep CBS White Collar Crew," *Billboard,* January 28, 1950, 9; "Operation Picketline Tonight," *Sights and Sounds* (UOPWA Radio Guild newsletter), May 3, 1950, Folder 18, Box 11, CLA-CRF; Radio Guild Local 50, "Remember?" flyer, 1950, Folder 19, Box 103, District 65.

50. James Durkin, "United Labor Action Becomes More Urgent," *Champion*, August 1950, 2; *Counterattack*, August 18, 1950, 2–3; "GEB Recommends Merger, Puts Vote to Members," *Champion*, September 7, 1950, 1, 5; "3 Left-Wing Unions Approve Merger," *NYT*, October 9, 1950, 14; Robert Freeman, General Office Division Report on Unification, February 15, 1951, Folder 73, Box 16, District 65; Anne Berenholz, Report on Screen Executive Board, November 14, 1950, Folder 20, Box 16, District 65. Also see Phillips, *Renegade Union*, 114–16.

51. Anne Berenholz, Report on Screen Executive Board, November 14, 1950; Radio Guild Executive Board Minutes, January 24, 1951, Folder 77, Box 16, District 65; Irving Albert to Alfred A. Knopf Inc., March 9, 1951, Folder 6, Box 102, District 65; Sterns and Reubens to Albert, March 13, 1951, Folder 6, Box 102, District 65; Morris Rosenzweig to Knopf Inc., April 9, 1951, Folder 6, Box 102, District 65; Pearl Fishman, "Random House" memo, November 1950, Folder 11, Box 125, District 65; "Re: Random House Meeting on Premises After Work," December 8, 1950, Folder 8, Box 125, District 65; Book and Magazine Guild Executive Board Minutes, April 24, 1951, Folder 76, Box 16, District 65; Robert K. Haas to Book and Magazine Guild, May 16, 1951, Folder 11, Box 125, District 65; Nelson Frank, "Jury Trial to Decide if Leftist Book Union Is a 'Paper Organization,'" *NYW-T*, June 1, 1951, 13.

52. John Horn to CBS Employees, February 15, 1951, Folder 2, Box 172, NGNY; "C.B.S. Office Help Will Vote on Union," *NYT*, February 16, 1951, 27; Arthur Goldberg to Newspaper Guild of New York, February 26, 1951, Folder 2, Box 172, NGNY; "The End of Confusion," *Sight and Sound* (CBS Newspaper Guild shop paper), February 28, 1951, Folder 2, Box 172, NGNY; "Election Special," *Sight and Sound*, March 9, 1951, Folder 2, Box 172, NGNY; Radio Guild Executive Board Minutes, March 29, 1951, Folder 77, Box 16, District 65; "Columbia Broadcasting System, Appendix A," 1951, Folder 2, Box 172, NGNY; "When Is a Job a Job?" *Sight and Sound*, April 2, 1951, Folder 2, Box 172, NGNY; Thomas Murphy to Frank Stanton, April 12, 1951, Folder 2, Box 172, NGNY; "Guild Files Objection to CBS Vote," *Frontpage*, April 20, 1951, 1, 8.

53. Sidney Cahn to All Members of the CU Staff, January 10, 1951, Folder 24, Box 82, District 65; "NLRB Vote at CU Plant," *Frontpage*, January 19, 1951, 4; "10 percent Initial Wage Increase Won at Consumers Union," *Frontpage*, April 3, 1951; William South to Peter Flynn, November 21, 1951, Folder 14, Box 174, NGNY; "Saturday Review NLRB Vote Due," *Frontpage*, February 2, 1951, 5; "Sat. Review Contract Set," *Frontpage*, January 11, 1952, 4.

54. Book and General Office Stewards Minutes, October 4, 1951, Folder 76, Box 16, District 65; DPOWA Executive Board Minutes, October 23–25, 1951, Box 1, NA; "Distributive Unit Gains in Shake-Up," *NYT*, November 4, 1951, 35.

55. "Two Union Officials Jailed for Contempt," *NYT*, April 2, 1952, 24; "4 Unions a Menace, U.S. Jury Asserts," *NYT*, November 26, 1952, 15; Freeman, *Working-Class New York*, 89–93; Opler, *For All White-Collar Workers*, 197–200; Phillips, *Renegade Union*, 135–44.

56. Book and General Office Minutes, May 5, 1952, Folder 45, Box 16, District 65; David Livingston, Report to the District 65 Convention, May 17, 1952, Box 1, NA; Book and General Office Minutes, June 2, 1952, Folder 45, Box 16, District 65; John Devlin, "6 Top Union Aides Balk at Red Query," *NYT*, July 7, 1953, 8; "State C.I.O. to Direct Strike at Hearns with Committee from 5 Unions in Charge," *NYT*, August 19, 1953, 44; "3 Unions Pressing Plans for Merger," *NYT*, May 21, 1954, 23. Also see Phillips, *Renegade Union*, 154–65.

57. Sig Maitles to James Carey, May 17, 1949, Folder 7, Box 112, Part I, CIO-ST; Seymour Roman to Allan Haywood, June 13, 1949, Folder 7, Box 112, Part I, CIO-ST; SPG Executive Board Minutes, May 28, 1951, Folder 68, Box 16, District 65; SPG Executive Board Minutes, September 5, 1951, Folder 68, Box 16, District 65; Screen Local Minutes, July 17, 1952, Folder 41, Box 16, District 65; Screen Local Minutes, September 23, 1952, Folder 41, Box 16, District 65; Screen Local Minutes, April 27, 1954, Folder 1, Box 26, District 65.

58. George Nelson, Report to SPG Membership, April 27, 1954, Folder 1, Box 26, District 65; "Of Local Origin," *NYT*, October 18, 1957, 19; "Film Publicists Sign 2 Pacts," *NYT*, April 12, 1960. This George Nelson (of the SPG) was not the renown architect, designer, and writer George Nelson discussed elsewhere in this book.

59. Albert A. Blum, *Management and the White-Collar Union* (New York: American Management Association, 1964), 5, 14.

60. AFL-CIO Industrial Union Department, *Labor Looks at the White-Collar Worker: Proceedings of Conference on the Problems of the White-Collar Worker* (Washington, DC: AFL-CIO, 1957), 3–4; "Nonproduction Workers in Factories, 1919–56," *MLR* 80 (1957): 435–40; John Pastin, *White Collar Organization in Industrial Unions* (Pittsburgh: United Steelworkers of America, 1958); and Everett Kassalow, "Organization of White-Collar Workers," *MLR* 84 (1961): 234–38.

61. Blum, *Management and the White-Collar Union*, 5, 14, 21–22, 25, 49; Carol Barry, "White-Collar Employment: I—Trends and Structure," *MLR* 84 (1961): 11–18; Bernard Goldstein and Bernard Indik, "Unionism as a Social Choice: The Engineers' Case," *MLR* 86 (1963): 365–69.

62. "Murray and Rodgers War on Reds in Guild," *E&P*, February 22, 1947, 10; "Guild Here Red-Run, Says National Head," *NYT*, March 16, 1947, 35; "N.Y. Delegates Back Ryan, Boo Murray," *E&P*, March 22, 1947, 11; "Milton Murray Censured by National Guild Board," *Frontpage*, April 1947, 11; John McManus, "The Choice Before Us," *Frontpage*, June 1947, 3; "Murray Withdraws in News Guild Race," *NYT*, June 28, 1947, 6; John McManus to Thomas Murphy, October 1, 1947, Folder 28, Box 58, NGNY; "News Guild to Qualify," *NYT*, November 4, 1947, 28.

63. Committee for Guild Unity, "Here is Your Team," *Frontpage*, December 1947, 6; "The United Guild Committee Asks You to Elect These Leaders," *Frontpage*, December 1947, 7; "New Slate Elected by Newspaper Guild," *NYT*, December 21, 1947, 42; "Holmes, Murphy, Deegan Elected as N.Y. Vote Sets Record," *Frontpage*, January 1948, 3.

64. "Left-Wing Slate Wins," *NYT*, January 16, 1948, 15; "Frontpage Forum," *Frontpage*, February 1948, 7; "6 N.Y. Guild Officers Lose ANG Appeal," *Frontpage*, March 1948, 4; Thomas Murphy to Saul Mills, July 9, 1948, Folder 17, Box 9, NGNY; Newspaper Guild of New York Press Release, July 11, 1948, Folder 15, Box 7, NGNY; Mills to Murphy, July 12, 1948, Folder 17, Box 9, NGNY; "A Statement of Policy on Executive Committee," *Frontpage*, July 1948, 4; "Resignations Accepted: Representative Assembly Acts on Left-Wing News Guilders," *NYT*, July 15, 1948, 24; "Guild Officers Answer Eight Who Resigned," *Frontpage*, August 1948, 4; Digest of NGNY Executive Committee Meeting, January 10, 1949, Folder 16, Box 7, NGNY.

65. "Uniform Contracts Sought by Guild," *Frontpage*, March 1947, 7; "Memorandum on the 25 Percent Wage Demand of the Newspaper Guild of New York," February 5, 1948, Folder 1, Box 7, NGNY.

66. Minutes of *PM* Negotiations, February 19, 1947, Folder 36, Box 54, NGNY; Lawrence Resner, "Field to Give up Newspaper *PM*—Sale Rests on Guild Concessions," *NYT*, March 13, 1948, 1, 10; Newspaper Guild of New York press release, March 15, 1948, Folder 29, Box 54, NGNY.

67. "This Is the Story of the Deal for *PM*: The Guild's Fight to Save 162 Jobs," *Frontpage*, April 1948, 4–5; "*PM* Gets Another Stay," *NYT*, April 14, 1948, 29; Statement of the *PM* Unit of the Newspaper Guild, April 28, 1948, Folder 28, Box 54, NGNY; "*PM* Control Sold to Crum, Barnes," *NYT*, April 29, 1948, 25; "If Anyone Should Ask You What's Happening at *PM*," *Frontpage*, June 1948, 4; "Axe Falls on 30 Guildsmen at the *Star*," *Frontpage*, August 1948, 6; Milkman, *PM*, 145, 201–10.

68. "New AM Tab Begins Hiring Staff," *Frontpage*, May 6, 1949, 1, 7.

69. "City-Wide Conference to Discuss Wage Deadlock," *Frontpage*, September 16, 1949, 1, 4; "City-Wide Meeting Sets Bargaining Floors," *Frontpage*, September 30, 1949, 1, 3; "Trib Unit Votes Strike," *Frontpage*, October 16, 1949, 1, 3.

70. "Combined Papers Make Appearance," *NYT*, January 6, 1950, 23; Robert U. Brown, "*Sun* Bondholders Get Paid in Sale to *World-Telegram*," *E&P*, January 7, 1950, 5, 6; "N.Y. *World-Telegram and Sun* Stopped by Guild Strike," *E&P*, June 17, 1950, 5, 6; "Telegram, Guild Sign Peace Terms," *NYT*, August 24, 1950, 22; "Strike Settled, *W-T&S* Publishes Again Monday," *E&P*, August 26, 1950, 5, 6; "Unionists Hail United Front in Guild Strike," *E&P*, September 16, 1950; "Publishers Face New Trend in United Labor Front," *Frontpage*, October 6, 1950, 2; "W-T-S Strike Broke Publishers Bloc," *Frontpage*, January 5, 1951, 1, 4; ANG, "Collective Bargaining Manual—Reporter and Photographer Top Minimums in 129 Guild Contracts as of June 15, 1953," Folder 12, Box 78, NGNY.

71. "*Brooklyn Eagle* Set to Close in Strike," *NYT*, January 26, 1955, 16; "Walkout Is Begun at *Eagle* by Guild," *NYT*, January 29, 1955, 30; NGNY Executive Board Minutes, February 16, 1955, Folder 10, Box 148, NGNY; "Guild Set for Long Strike," *Frontpage*, February 16, 1955, 1, 3; "'No More Eagle'—Schroth; But Guild

Strike Goes On," *Frontpage,* March 18, 1955, 1, 3; NGNY Executive Board Minutes, July 25, 1955, Folder 10, Box 148, NGNY.

72. Margaret March to Jack Ryan, May 26, 1947, Folder 32, Box 24, NGNY; Barbara Thorndike to Mort Stone, August 14, 1947, Folder 27, Box 58, NGNY; Transcript of Time Inc. Negotiations, January 13, 1947, 10–12, 16–19, Folder 16, Box 60, NGNY; Transcript of Time Inc. Negotiations, October 31, 1947, 1–24, Folder 19, Box 60, NGNY; Transcript of Time Inc. Negotiations, November 30, 1947, 1–14, Folder 19, Box 60, NGNY; "Shop Stuff," *Frontpage,* January 1948, 4; Transcript of Time Inc. Negotiations, April 22, 1948, 1–7, Folder 22, Box 60, NGNY "The Man Gratz," *Frontpage,* August 1948, 7.

73. Transcript of Time Negotiations, October 2, 1947, 11–12, Folder 19, Box 60; Transcript of Time Inc. Negotiations, April 7, 1947, 43, Folder 18, Box 60, NGNY; Time Inc. Guild Unit, Petition to Management, October 31, 1947, Folder 14, Box 60, NGNY; "Guild Wage Survey," January 1948, Folder 14, Box 60, NGNY; Minutes of Time Inc. Unit Meeting, July 28, 1949, Folder 4, Box 58, NGNY.

74. "Guild Wage Survey," January 1948; Time Management, "Time Inc. Policy on Writing and Speaking," May 2, 1947, Folder 25, Box 61, NGNY; Time Management, "Policy on the Use and Taking of Pictures Outside of Time Inc.," May 2, 1947, Folder 25, Box 61, NGNY.

75. John Hersey, *A Bell for Adano* (New York: Knopf, 1944); Hersey, "Hiroshima," *NYer,* August 31, 1946; John Hersey to Roger Butterfield c/o Irving Gilman, May 11, 1946, Folder 25, Box 58, NGNY. Also see Susan Carruthers, "'Produce More Joppolos': John Hersey's *A Bell for Adano* and the Making of the 'Good Occupation,'" *JAH* 100, no. 4 (2014): 1086–1113.

76. James Agee and Walker Evans, *Let Us Now Praise Famous Men* (Boston: Houghton Mifflin, 1941). Also see Pells, *Radical Visions,* 246–51; and Paula Rabinowitz, "Voyeurism and Class Consciousness: James Agee and Walker Evans' *Let Us Now Praise Famous Men,*" *Cultural Critique* no. 21 (Spring 1992): 143–70.

77. Time Management, "Time Inc. Policy on Writing and Speaking."

78. Jeanne Curtis to Irving Gilman, May 9, 1947, Folder 25, Box 61, NGNY; Margaret March to Jack Ryan, June 9, 1947, Folder 32, Box 24, NGNY; Statement by Newspaper Guild of New York on Time Inc. Editorial Policy, August 1947, Folder 46, Box 60, NGNY.

79. "Fight for Freedom and Honesty of Press Highlights Guild Conference," *Frontpage,* March 1947, 1, 3; Roy Larsen to The Staff, August 29, 1947, Folder 28, Box 58, NGNY; Cedric Belfrage, "A Cuckoo in Henry Luce's Nest," *Frontpage,* September 1947, 5; *Guild Shop News,* September 5, 1947, Folder 37, Box 61, NGNY; Irving Gilman, "Summary of Talk with Davidson Taylor, V.P. in Charge of the News at CBS," September 13, 1947, Folder 25, Box 61, NGNY; CBS Views the Press script dated September 20, 1947, Folder 27, Box 58, NGNY; "Radio Suppression," *IF,* September 22, 1947, 1; "*On Time,*" *Frontpage,* August 1947, 7; "*On Time*: Censored," *Frontpage,* September 1948, 5.

80. Thomas Murphy to Anna DeCormis, February 11, 1949, Folder 32, Box 58, NGNY; DeCormis to Murphy, April 12, 1949, Folder 32, Box 58, NGNY; Minutes of Time Inc. Unit Meeting, February 10, 1949, Folder 4, Box 58, NGNY; Transcript of Time Inc. Negotiations, June 4, 1948, 1–17, Folder 22, Box 60, NGNY; Newspaper Guild, "Time Inc. Contract Demands," August 4, 1948, Folder 27, Box 60, NGNY; Transcript of Time Inc. Negotiations, September 30, 1948, 23–35, Folder 24, Box 60, NGNY; Minutes of Time Inc. Unit Meeting, January 13, 1949, Folder 4, Box 58, NGNY; Hilde Adelsberger and Jean Davidson to Fellow Guildmember, January 26, 1949, Folder 27, Box 58, NGNY; Minutes of Time Inc. Unit Meeting, May 9, 1949, Folder 4, Box 58, NGNY.

81. Minutes of Time Inc. Unit Meeting, February 19, 1948, Folder 4, Box 58, NGNY; Minutes of Time Inc. Unit Meeting, May 16, 1949, Folder 4, Box 58, NGNY; Time Inc. Unit, "Summary Comparison of Management Offer and Guild Demands," June 29, 1949, Folder 32, Box 58, NGNY; Minutes of Time Inc. Unit Meeting, July 7, 1949, Folder 4, Box 58, NGNY; Minutes of Time Inc. Unit Meeting, July 28, 1949, Folder 4, Box 58, NGNY; Minutes of Time Inc. Unit Meeting, September 8, 1949, Folder 4, Box 58, NGNY; Time Inc. Unit, "Progress but No Settlement," September 27, 1949, Folder 32, Box 58, NGNY; Minutes of Time Inc. Unit Meeting, October 6, 1949, Folder 4, Box 58, NGNY.

82. "Business and Finance," *On Time,* November 15, 1949, Folder 38, Box 61, NGNY; Lolita Brown to New York Local, June 16, 1950, Folder 33, Box 58, NGNY; Transcript of Time Inc. Negotiations, September 21, 1950, 1–10, Folder 7, Box 61, NGNY.

83. "Contract Push on at Time," *Frontpage,* September 21, 1951, 1; "Contract Okayed," *Frontpage,* October 24, 1951, 1; Thomas Murphy to Eva Jollos, Septmeber 4, 1953, Folder 12, Box 78, NGNY; Murphy to Jollos, Septmeber 9, 1953, Folder 12, Box 78, NGNY; "Time Inc. Unit Presses for Improved Contract," *Frontpage,* October 23, 1953, 1; "Guild Facing Stiff Battle on Time Inc. Contract," *Frontpage,* November 6, 1953, 1, 3; Executive Board Minutes, April 4, 1956, Folder 10, Box 148, NGNY; "Win $10 Raise, $165 Minimum at Time Inc.," *Frontpage,* December 18, 1956, 4; "$3 to $7.50 Raises Won at Time Inc.," *Frontpage,* January 13, 1961, 3.

84. "High of $154 Won in Newsweek Pact," *Frontpage,* August 18, 1952, 1; Amendment to Editorial Department Contract, Weekly Publications and Newspaper Guild of New York, March 1, 1953, Folder 12, Box 78, NGNY; "$163.50 Set at *Newsweek,*" *Frontpage,* July 26, 1954, 1; "$13 Top Raise at *Newsweek,*" *Frontpage,* December 18, 1958, 1, 4; "$200 Minimum for Writers Won in *Newsweek* Contract," *Frontpage*, January 13, 1961, 3.

85. "Macfadden Unit Started," *Frontpage,* March 16, 1951, 1; "Macfadden Publications Employees Select Guild," *Frontpage,* May 25, 1951, 8; Meyer Dworkin to John Deegan, June 1, 1951, Folder 1, Box 211, NGNY; Dworkin to Deegan, September 12, 1951, Folder 2, Box 211, NGNY; Thomas Murphy to Frank Brown, November 29, 1951, Folder 2, Box 211, NGNY; "N.Y. Guild Files NLRB Petition for Fairchild

Employees," *Frontpage,* April 25, 1952, 1; "Stalling Action by Fairchild Delays Vote," *Frontpage,* May 12, 1952, 1, 3; "NLRB Vote at Fairchild Will Be Held June 11," *Frontpage,* May 23, 1952, 1; "Guild Loses at Fairchild by a 3–2 Margin," *Frontpage,* June 13, 1952, 1, 3; H. E. Knowlton to Macfadden Publications, September 24, 1952, Folder 1, Box 211, NGNY.

86. Jack Gould, "Panel Talks over Wechsler Ousting," *NYT,* August 8, 1952, 15; "Excerpts from Testimony of Wechsler Before McCarthy Inquiry," *NYT,* May 8, 1953, 14; "Wechsler Implores ASNE to Speak out Eloquently," *E&P,* May 9, 1953, 7–8; "Winchell Quips Curbed by Court," *NYT,* April 13, 1954, 45; Navasky, *Naming Names,* 45–69; Nissenson, *Lady Upstairs,* 154–65.

87. "News Guild Plans Tighter Red Curb," *NYT,* August 3, 1954, 7; "ANG Policy on Communists," *Frontpage,* August 20, 1954, 1; "Ask Views on Draft Red Ban," *Frontpage,* March 18, 1955, 1, 8; Jerry Walker, "Guild Won't Fight Firing of Commies," *E&P,* July 2, 1955, 7, 10.

88. "CBS Newsman Names Commies Formerly with *Brooklyn Eagle,*" *E&P,* July 2, 1955, 8, 58; Cogley, *Report on Blacklisting: Volume Two, Radio and Television,* 126–27; Caute, *Great Fear,* 451–53; Edward Alwood, *Dark Days in the Newsroom: McCarthyism Aimed at the Press* (Philadelphia: Temple University Press, 2007), 80–94.

89. Allen Drury, "2 Newspaper Men Balk at Red Inquiry," *NYT,* July 14, 1955, 1, 10; "Guild Fights *Times, News* '5th' Firings," *Frontpage,* July 15, 1955, 1, 7; "N.Y. *Times* Discharges 5th Amendment Pleader," *E&P,* July 16, 1955, 11, 57; NGNY Executive Board Minutes, July 25, 1955, Folder 10, Box 148, NGNY; NGNY Executive Board Minutes, October 14, 1955, Folder 10, Box 148, NGNY; "Send '5th' Firings to Arbitrator," *Frontpage,* October 18, 1955, 1, 3; "Arbitration Debated in '5th' Case Firing," *E&P,* November 26, 1955, 10; "Pros and Cons on Referendum," *Frontpage,* December 9, 1955, 4; "Guild Not to Defend Each Balky Witness," *NYT,* December 17, 1955, 12; "Referendum Vote, 3 to 2, Sets Policy," *Frontpage,* January 16, 1956, 1, 3. Also see Tifft and Jones, *The Trust,* 266–71; and Alwood, *Dark Days in the Newsroom,* 95–107.

90. "6 Ousted from Newsroom Jobs by Eastland Committee Quiz," *E&P,* January 14, 1956, 11, 80; "3 More Fired in Red Probe," *Frontpage,* January 16, 1956, 1, 3; NGNY Executive Board Minutes, February 23, 1956, Folder 10, Box 148, NGNY; NGNY Executive Board Minutes, April 4, 1956, Folder 10, Box 148, NGNY; Luther Huston, "6 Indicted by U.S. in Senate Inquiry," *NYT,* November 27, 1956, 22. Also see Alwood, *Dark Days,* 108–21.

91. "Defiant Witness Ousted by *Mirror,*" *NYT,* January 7, 1956, 7; "Arbiter Upholds Ouster of Editor," *NYT,* June 20, 1956, 10; "*Mirror* Is Upheld in Dismissal Case," *NYT,* November 10, 1956, 31; NGNY Executive Board Minutes, November 26, 1956, Folder 10, Box 148, NGNY.

92. "*Times* Man Gets Contempt Term," *NYT,* January 26, 1957, 11; "Newsman Guilty in Contempt Case," *NYT,* April 10, 1957, 18; "Newsman Jailed in Contempt Case,"

NYT, April 13, 1957, 9; Luther Huston, "Union Aide Victor: Contempt Case Ruling Given by Warren," *NYT,* June 18, 1957, 1, 20; "Newsman Freed in Contempt Case," *NYT,* July 12, 1957, 9; Anthony Lewis, "Contempt Convictions of Six Voided by Supreme Court," *NYT,* May 22, 1962, 1, 26; Lewis, "Courts Settling 8 Contempt Cases," *NYT,* March 22, 1964, 32. Also see Alwood, *Dark Days,* 122–37.

93. "433 Million Radio's '46 Total Gross," *Billboard,* January 4, 1947, 6; Ben Atlas, "Broadcast Gross Near $1,000,000,000 Peak," *Billboard,* December 5, 1953, 1, 3.

94. "Night Radio Cheaper by 60 percent over Video," *Billboard,* December 2, 1950, 4; "TV Networks' $44 Million for 1950; AM Take Sags," *Billboard,* December 23, 1950, 3; Sam Chase, "Alas, Poor Network Radio, We Knew It Once, Says Report," *Billboard,* September 25, 1954, 1, 7–8; Leon Morse, "TV Webs' Grosses Rocket to Record $300,000,000 High," *Billboard,* December 11, 1954, 1, 3; "All-Round Record for CBS-TV in '54," *Broadcasting,* December 27, 1954, 76. Also see Barnouw, *Golden Web,* 284–303; Boddy, *Fifties Television,* 48–62, 113–31; and Baughman, *Same Time, Same Station,* 8–28.

95. "Radio Turns Air Scripters into Grub Streeters, FCC Reveals," *Billboard,* April 20, 1946, 7, 19.

96. "RWG-AAAA Meets Moving Towards Paper," *Billboard,* December 15, 1945, 8; RWG National Executive Council Minutes, September 13–15, 1946, Folder 5, Box 3, RWG; Sam Moore, "Report from the Guild President," October 9, 1946, Folder 11, Box 1, RWG; Moore to Dear Guild Member, March 10, 1947, Folder 21, Box 2, RWG.

97. Sam Moore to Peter Lyon et al., January 31, 1947, Folder 12, Box 1, RWG; Moore to Dear Guild Member, March 14, 1947, Folder 21, Box 2, RWG; Milton Merlin to Dear Member (plus attached advertisement), April 4, 1947, Folder 21, Box 2, RWG; "Writers' Strike Nearing," *NYT,* April 9, 1947, 18; "National RWG Semi-Annual Report," August 1947, Folder 12, Box 1, RWG.

98. "National RWG Semi-Annual Report," August 1947, Folder 12, Box 1, RWG; Jack Gould, "News of Radio," *NYT,* November 1, 1947, 30; "RWG Ratifies 6 ½-Year Pact With the Four Major Networks," *Broadcasting,* November 3, 1947, 20; "Writers Score Strong Gains in Script Ownership Rights under Newly Signed RWG Contract," *Billboard,* November 8, 1947, 7, 15; Peter Lyon, "A Milestone for the RWG," November 1947, Folder 7, Box 4, RWG.

99. Roy Langham to Bernard Duffy, August 7, 1947, Folder 40, Box 37, RWG; Langham to Erik Barnouw et al., May 10, 1948, Folder 13, Box 1, RWG; Langham to Barnouw et al., June 2, 1948, Folder 13, Box 1, RWG; Langham to Barnouw et al., August 27, 1948, Folder 13, Box 1, RWG.

100. Roy Langham to Erik Barnouw et al., September 1, 1948, Folder 13, Box 1, RWG; Jack Gould, "Writers for Radio Threaten a Strike," *NYT,* October 15, 1948, 12; Erik Barnouw and Roy Langham to Emerson Foote, October 24, 1948, Folder 28, Box 38, RWG; RWG Press Release, October 26, 1948, Folder 21, Box 2, RWG; Irv Marder, "RWG Strike," *Broadcasting,* November 1, 1948, 23, 61; "RWG Skeds

Picket Lines for Strike Vs. Ad Agencies," *Billboard,* November 6, 1948, 6; Marder, "RWG Truce," *Broadcasting,* November 8, 1948, 28; "RWG and Agencies Hopeful of Early Strike Settlement," *Billboard,* November 13, 1948, 6; "Settle Freelance Scripter Dispute," *Variety,* December 15, 1948, 27, 38; "RWG, Agencies in Peace Pact," *Billboard,* December 18, 1948, 5; "Freelance Contracts," *Broadcasting,* June 27, 1949, 28.

101. Erik Barnouw to Sam Moore et al., March 16, 1948, Folder 13, Box 1, RWG. Also see "RWG Will Oppose FCC Policy Change," *Broadcasting,* November 17, 1949, 101; Jack Gould, "News of Radio," *NYT,* January 28, 1948, 46. Also see Pickard, *America's Battle for Media Democracy,* 98–123.

102. Stella Holt to Roy Langham, July 20, 1949, Folder 38, Box 41, RWG; Stella Holt to Dear Friends, March 14, 1950, Folder 38, Box 41, RWG. Also see "VOF All-Out for Negro Commentator," *VOF,* January-February 1949, 1, Folder 37, Box 8, CLA-CRF; *Counterattack,* February 4, 1949, 2–3; and "Negro Commentator Campaign," *VOF,* Summer 1949, 3, Folder 37, Box 8, CLA-CRF.

103. Roy Langham to Sam Moore et al., January 5, 1949 (misdated 1948), Folder 13, Box 1, RWG; "Trust Law Breach Laid to Play Guild," *NYT,* January 5, 1949, 23; Langham to Moore et al., May 20, 1949, Folder 14, Box 1, RWG; *Ring v. Authors' League of America, Inc., et al* 186 F. 2d 637 (1951). Also see Fisk, *Writing for Hire,* 218–25.

104. Roy Langham to Mike Davidson, July 20, 1949, Folder 15, Box 1, RWG; Langham to Milton Merlin et al., August 18, 1949, Folder 15, Box 1, RWG; Langham to Erik Barnouw et al., October 3, 1949, Folder 14, Box 1, RWG; Webb Kelley to Dear Guild Member, October 28, 1949, Folder 15, Box 1, RWG; Jim Stabile to Paul Franklin et al., February 20, 1950, Folder 16, Box 1, RWG; Stabile to Luise Sillcox, May 12, 1950, Folder 4, Box 60, RWG.

105. "TV Writers Guild Gets League Okay," *Variety,* November 17, 1948, 29; "Authors' League Faces SWG Clash over TV Authority," *Billboard,* January 22, 1949, 12; Evelyn Burkey to Michael Davidson, February 2, 1949, Folder 14, Box 1, RWG; Roy Langham to Erik Barnouw et al., April 28, 1949, Folder 14, Box 1; Resolution by RWG Eastern Regions Shop Stewards, April 28, 1949, Folder 14, Box 1, RWG; Langham to RWG ALA Council Members, June 28, 1949, Folder 14, Box 1, RWG; Barnouw to Luise Sillcox, October 28, 1949, Folder 15, Box 1, RWG; "Scripters in TV Tug-of-War," *Variety,* November 23, 1949, 35, 41; "Authors' League Calls January Huddle on TV," *Billboard,* December 17, 1949, 6.

106. "NABUG Joins in Unions' Probe of Radio 'Blacklist'," *Variety,* July 20, 1949, 25, 34; *Counterattack,* July 22, 1949, 1–2; "Radio Unions Join in Probe of 'Blacklist'," *Billboard,* July 23, 1949, 7; VOF, "Blacklist" brochure (late summer 1949), Folder 36, Box 8, CLA-CRF; *Counterattack,* August 19, 1949, 1–2; Miller, *Judges and the Judged,* 170–72, 176–77; Cogley, *Report on Blacklisting: Volume Two, Radio and Television,* 24–29.

107. *Counterattack,* May 26, 1950, 2–3; Mike Davidson to Jim Stabile and Sheldon Stark, June 30, 1950, Folder 16, Box 1, RWG; *Counterattack,* July 28, 1950, 1–2.

108. "RWG Blowup Threatened in Political Show of Hands over Anti-Commie Proposal," *Variety,* August 2, 1950, 25, 32; Jim Stabile to Paul Franklin et al., August 11, 1950, Folder 16, Box 1, RWG; RWG Eastern Region Council to All Members, August 23, 1950, Folder 21, Box 2, RWG; "RWG Factions Gird for All-Out Battle," *Variety,* September 6, 1950, 27, 36; Erik Barnouw to Sheldon Stark, October 8, 1950, Folder 16, Box 1, RWG; Stark to Dear Guildmember, October 26, 1950, Folder 21, Box 2, RWG; Hector Chevigny to Dear Guildmember, October 27, 1950, Folder 21, Box 2, RWG; Stabile to National Council, November 6, 1950, Folder 16, Box 1, RWG. Also see Cogley, *Report on Blacklisting, Volume Two,* 147–51.

109. American Business Consultants, *Red Channels,* 114–15; "Jean Muir Incident," *Sponsor,* August 28, 1950, 72; "Red Problem Mounts," *Broadcasting,* September 25, 1950, 27, 93; "The Truth about *Red Channels*: Part One," *Sponsor,* October 8, 1951, 27–29, 75–81; Miller, *Judges and the Judged,* 35–44, 46; Oliver Pilat, "The Blacklist: The Panic in TV and Radio," *NYP,* January 26, 1953, 4, 14; Cogley, *Report on Blacklisting: Volume Two,* 29–30.

110. *Red Channels,* 100–101; "The Truth about *Red Channels*: Part One"; Jack Gould, "Actor Is Dropped from Video Cast," *NYT,* January 8, 1952, 29; "TvA, Equity Probe Facts on Phil Loeb," *Billboard,* January 19, 1952, 7; "Loeb Settles Contract with 'The Goldbergs,'" *Billboard,* February 2, 1952, 6; Miller, *Judges and the Judged,* 44–46; Cogley, *Report on Blacklisting: Volume Two,* 35–38.

111. *Red Channels,* 116; Bernard Prockter to Arnold Perl, May 15, 1951, Folder 70, Box 32, RWG; Grievance Report, Arnold Perl against Prockter Television, April 3, 1953, Folder 70, Box 32, RWG.

112. Radio Writers Guild Fact-Finding Committee on Blacklisting, Notes Re: Case Number Four, December 12, 1952; Pilat, "The Blacklist: The Panic in TV and Radio"; Cogley, *Report on Blacklisting, Volume Two,* 115–28. Also see Cynthia Meyers, "Inside a Broadcasting Blacklist: *Kraft Television Theater,* 1951–1955," *JAH* 105, no. 3 (2018): 589–616.

113. RWG Press Release, August 27, 1952, Folder 3, Box 61, RWG; C. P. Trussell, "McCarran Inquiry Unit Says Pro-Reds Rule Radio Guild," *NYT,* August 28, 1952, 1–2; *Counterattack,* August 29, 1952, 2; "Radio-TV Subversive Probe to Spread to Entire Industry: Closed Door Testimony Is Revealed," *Billboard,* August 30, 1952, 1, 4, 11; Earl Abrams, "Red Probings," *Broadcasting,* September 1, 1952, 27, 88; May Bolhower to Officers and Executive Board Members, September 18, 1952, Folder 18, Box 1 RWG, Folder 18; Hector Chevigny to Dear Member, October 25, 1952, Folder 21, Box 2, RWG; RWG Press Release, November 8, 1952, Folder 18, Box 1, RWG; Cogley, *Report on Blacklisting, Volume Two,* 152–54.

114. "Radio and TV Artists Vote, 982 to 514, to Condemn AWARE, Anti-Red Group," *NYT,* July 4, 1955, 23; Jack Gould, "TV: More about AWARE," *NYT,* July 11, 1955, 43; Cogley, *Report on Blacklisting, Volume Two,* 129–40, 154–58.

115. "AFTRA to Seek Pensions & Welfare," *Billboard,* August 7, 1954, 14; Val Adams, "Performers on TV Win a Pension Plan," *NYT,* November 19, 1954, 1, 32; "George Heller Is Dead at 49," *Billboard,* June 11, 1955, 4.

116. "Motions Passed at the National Executive Committee of the RWG, May 30–June 1, 1952," Folder 18, Box 1, RWG; "RWG Strikers Spend Hot 4th," *Broadcasting,* July 12, 1952, 5; "Settle Strike of Writers at Two Webs," *Billboard,* July 26, 1952, 5; May Bolhower to Mike Davidson, August 22, 1952, Folder 18, Box 1.

117. "TV Writers' Union in Parley Tonight," *NYT,* May 25, 1953, 32; "TWA Wins!" *TW,* July 1953, 1, 6; Dick Powell, "TWA Opens Second Front," *TW,* July 1953, 1, 4; Hector Chevigny, "Report of Meeting—RWG Eastern Council & RWG League Council Delegates," July 27, 1953, Folder 5, Box 3, RWG; Philo Higley and Nelson Sykes to Dear Guild Member, October 5, 1953, Folder 21, Box 2, RWG.

118. "Two Witnesses Silent," *NYT,* December 17, 1953, 34; "East Union Head Quits TV Writers," *NYT,* January 14, 1954, 22; "TWA Toppers Quit in Midst of Web Confabs," *Billboard,* January 23, 1954, 2, 8.

119. "TV Scripters Threaten Web with Walk-Out," *Billboard,* July 10, 1954, 2; "Union Shop Plans Halt TWA Talks," *Billboard,* July 17, 1954, 2; "TWA, TWG Jurisdiction May Arise," *Billboard,* July 31, 1954, 18; "Video Writers End 3-Network Strike," *NYT,* August 4, 1954, 28; "TV Union to Disband," *NYT,* September 3, 1954, 24.

120. Nelson Sykes to RWG Council Members and Officers, April 8, 1954, Folder 20, Box 2, RWG; Thomas Pryor, "Screen Writers Back New Union," *NYT,* May 21, 1954, 18; "Unions Okay Writers Guild," *Billboard,* September 4, 1954, 8; Oscar Godbout, "TV Writers Agree to Network Pact," *NYT,* June 5, 1956, 71; Murray Schumach, "Writers to Fight Coast Blacklist," *NYT,* December 22, 1959, 41.

121. *Counterattack,* January 18, 1952, 1–2; "Progressives May Get Equal Time Free," *Billboard,* August 30, 1952, 11; "Crack the Back of Counterattack" flyer, 1951, Folder 1, Box 172, JBM; *Counterattack,* April 13, 1951, 3–4; *Counterattack,* September 14, 1951, 4.

122. Interveiew of Joan LaCour Scott by Paul Buhle, in *Tender Comrades,* ed. Patrick McGillan and Paul Buhle, 585–606; David Pressman, "Directed By? A Memory from the Blacklist," *DGA Magazine,* September-October 1997, 55–56; Archive of American Television, Interview of David Pressman by Karen Herman, July 27, 2004, Parts 3 and 4 (online at http://www.emmytvlegends.org/interviews/people/david-pressman#).

123. Archive of American Television, Interview of Ernest Kinoy by Sunny Parich, October 29, 1998, Part 5 (online at http://www.emmytvlegends.org/interviews/people/ernest-kinoy#); Archive of American Television, Interview of Sidney Lumet by Ralph Engleman, October 28, 1999, Parts 3 and 4 (online at http://www.emmytvlegends.org/interviews/people/sidney-lumet#); Everitt, *Shadow of Red,* 107; *Matter of Writers Guild (Prockter Prods.)* 1 N.Y. 2d. 305 (1956).

124. Cogley, *Report on Blacklisting: Volume Two,* 89–99.

CHAPTER 7

1. Don Wallance to John Kenneth Galbraith, February 15, 1961, "Other" folder, Box 1, DW. On the actual TV debate between Galbraith and Lynes, see Jack Gould, "Federal Role in the Arts," *NYT*, February 13, 1961, 45.

2. Galbraith, *Affluent Society*, 149.

3. Ibid., 342, 345.

4. See Brick, *Transcending Capitalism*, 2,

5. See Lily Geismer, *Don't Blame Us: Suburban Liberals and the Transformation of the Democratic Party* (Princeton, NJ: Princeton University Press, 2015), 1–172.

6. "JWT: A New Approach to Creativity," *MA*, September 1966, 25.

7. Calculations by the author using 1970 data from Steven Ruggles, J. Trent Alexander, Katie Genadek, Matthew B. Schroeder, and Matthew Sobek, *Integrated Public Use Microdata Series: Version 5.0 Machine-Readable Database* (Minneapolis: University of Minnesota Press, 2010). Data based on household survey, not establishment survey. Also see Tables A.14 and A.15 in the appendix.

8. Maurine Christopher, "Gains in Hiring Minority People Seen Minimal," *AA*, January 13, 1969, 1, 82.

9. Milton Moskowitz, "As Advertising Grows, So Grows Consumers Union, Now 25 Years Old," *AA*, May 29, 1961, 72–73.

10. Arthur Kallet, "The State of the Union," *CUR*, August 1938, 12; Madeline Ross, "The State of the Union: Staff Report," *CUR*, September 1938, 17; CU Shop Committee, "Statement Prepared for the Board of Directors and Presented to the Executive Board by the Shop Committee of Consumers Union, UOPWA #1," December 3, 1945, Folder 22, Box 82, District 65; Kallet to Shop Committee, October 29, 1946, Folder 22, Box 82, District 65; CU Shop Committee to All Members of the CU Board of Directors, November 26, 1947, Folder 23, Box 82, District 65.

11. "Bread and Butter: Monopoly and the Green Light," *CUR*, July 1947, 267–69; "CU's Radio Report," *CUR*, April 1948, 187; Harold Aaron, "How Group Medicine Really Works," *CUR*, October 1948, 461–62; Aaron, "Health Insurance around the Corner," *CUR*, January 1949, 32–34; "The AMA and National Health Insurance," *CUR*, April 1949, 175–78; "Economics for Consumers," *CUR*, May 1949, 230–32.

12. On Noyes's career trajectory, see John Harwood, *The Interface: IBM and the Transformation of Corporate Design, 1945–1976* (Minneapolis: University of Minnesota Press, 2011), 18–37.

13. Eliot Noyes, "The Shape of Things," *CUR*, June 1947, 210; Noyes, "The Shape of Things: Modern Furniture," *CUR*, September 1947, 363–65; Noyes, "The Shape of Things," *CUR*, May 1948, 204–205; Noyes, "The Shape of Things," *CUR*, June 1950, 278–79.

14. Eliot Noyes, "The Shape of Things," *CUR*, July 1947, 263. Also see Noyes, "The Shape of Things," *CUR*, July 1949, 312–15; and Noyes to Don Wallance, August 10, 1949, "Correspondence: March 1949— May 1950" folder, Box 2, DW.

15. K. V. Amatneek to Betty Medinz, November 15, 1950, Folder 24, Box 82, District 65; William South to Sol Malofsky, December 26, 1950, Folder 24, Box 82, District 65; CU Board of Directors Resolution, January 4, 1951, Folder 24, Box 82, District 65; Samuel Sacher to NLRB Region 2, January 29, 1951, Folder 24, Box 82, District 65; "CU Contract Talks Start," *Frontpage*, February 2, 1951, 8; Marian Minus to Frank Meyer, February 26, 1951, Folder 20, Box 177, NGNY; Sacher to NLRB Region 2, August 21, 1951, Folder 14, Box 174, NGNY; Charles Douds to Consumers Union and Newspaper Guild of New York, August 29, 1951, Folder 14, Box 174, NGNY; South to Peter Flynn, November 21, 1951, Folder 14, Box 174, NGNY.

16. Arthur Kallet to Members of the CU Board of Directors, March 28, 1952, Folder 14, Box 174, NGNY; William South to Kallet, July 1, 1952, Folder 16, Box 177, NGNY; "Lockout at Consumers Union Continues into Fourth Week," *Frontpage*, July 28, 1952, 1, 4; Statement by Consumers Union Management, August 1, 1952, Folder 16, Box 177, NGNY; Louis Hollander and Harold Garno to All Affiliates of the State CIO Council, August 1, 1952, Folder 17, Box 177, NGNY; "Guild Scores Smashing Victory," *Frontpage*, August 18, 1952, 1, 4; "Settlements," *Newsweek*, August 25, 1952, 49–50.

17. Chester Tanaka to Members of the Management and Board of Directors of Consumers Union, February 17, 1955, Folder 14, Box 174, NGNY; Marian Minus to Michael Potoker, February 24, 1955, Folder 14, Box 174, NGNY; Bill South to Potoker, July 14, 1955, Folder 14, Box 174, NGNY; Potoker to Howard Snyder, April 30, 1956, Folder 15, Box 174, NGNY.

18. "A Letter to Readers on Honesty, Policy, and Subversiveness," *CUR*, October 1951, 434, 476; "Where Does CU Stand?" *CUR*, April 1953, 142.

19. Harold Velde to Consumers Union, February 2, 1954, Folder 14, Box 174, NGNY; "House Unit Clears Consumers Union," *NYHT*, February 7, 1954, 19; Velde to John O'Hara, March 18, 1954, Folder 13, Box 210, CR; M. C. Phillips to Lee Pennington, April 9, 1954, Folder 23, Box 199, CR; "Why the Secrecy?" *American Legion Magazine*, May 1954, 6–7. For context, see Storrs, *Second Red Scare*, 147–76.

20. CU Committee of Officers, Draft Plan of Interim Organization, May 22, 1957, Folder 15, Box 174, NGNY; "Arthur Kallet," *CUR*, August 1957, 354; "Personnel: Consumer's Report," *Time*, August 12, 1957, 80; "Marian Minus, Long a Guild Leader, Now *Consumer Reports* Executive," *Frontpage*, October 20, 1958, 2; NGNY Executive Board Minutes, October 29, 1958, Folder 11, Box 148, NGNY.

21. John Finney, "Scientists Term Fall-Out Monitoring Inadequate," *NYT*, June 6, 1962, 7: Walter Sullivan, "Chemists Debate Pesticides Book," *NYT*, September 13, 1962, 34; CU display ad, *NYT*, September 22, 1962, 8; CU display ad, *NYT*, September 8, 1963, BR27; Ruth and Edward Brecher, "How to Give up Smoking—Maybe," *NYT*, January 26, 1964, SM16, SM66–68; David Jones, "U.S. Agency Spurs Car Safety Drive," *NYT*, January 27, 1965, 1, 15; "Credit Sales Held Dealers' Bonanza," *NYT*, May 21, 1965, 16; Jack Gould, "TV: Critics on Wheels," *NYT*, June 1, 1965, 79. Also see Rachel Carson, *Silent Spring* (New York: Houghton Mifflin, 1962);

David Caplovitz, *The Poor Pay More: Consumer Practices of Low-Income Families* (Glencoe, IL: Free Press, 1963); and Ralph Nader, *Unsafe at Any Speed: The Designed-In Dangers of the American Automobile* (New York: Grossman, 1965).

22. George Seldes, "Editorial Postscript," *IF*, July 21, 1947, 4; Seldes, "Editorial: Do You Want This Work to Go On?" *IF*, May 22, 1950, 4; Seldes, "Editorial: To All Our Faithful Subscribers," *IF*, October 2, 1950, 1–3; *Counterattack*, October 6, 1950, 2–3; Seldes, *Tell the Truth*, 263–69; Seldes, *Never Tire of Protesting*, 53–57.

23. D. D. Gutenplan, *American Radical: The Life and Times of I. F. Stone* (Evanston: Northwestern University Press, 2012), 382.

24. John McManus to Dear Friend, December 17, 1949, Folder 19, Box 410, JBM; Special Statement of Ownership, Management, and Circulation, *National Guardian*, October 1956, 9. Also see Cedric Belfrage and James Aronson, *Something to Guard: The Stormy Life of the* National Guardian, *1948–1967* (New York: Columbia University Press, 1978), 1–193; and Maurice Isserman, *If I Had a Hammer: The Death of the Old Left and the Birth of the New Left* (New York: Basic Books, 1987), 1–34.

25. Fones-Wolf, *Waves of Opposition*, 184–201. Also see Kevin Boyle, *The UAW and the Heyday of American Liberalism, 1945–1968* (Ithaca, NY: Cornell University Press, 1995), 61–106; and Lichtenstein, *Walter Reuther*, 271–326.

26. See Anna McCarthy, *The Citizen Machine: Governing by Television in 1950s America* (New York: New Press, 2010), 205–40.

27. "News Guild Acts to Found Papers," *NYT*, July 1, 1950, 25; ANG International Executive Board, "Project X" pamphlet, 1950, Folder 6, Box 4, NGNY; Michael Potoker to Unit Chairmen, August 18, 1950, Folder 6, Box 4, NGNY; ANG Official Referendum Return for Newspaper Guild of New York, September 19, 1950, Folder 6, Box 4, NGNY.

28. Albert Maltz, "What Shall We Ask of Writers?" *NM*, February 12, 1946, 19–22; Isidor Schneider, "Background to Error," *NM*, February 12, 1946, 23–25; Howard Fast, "Art and Politics," *NM*, February 26, 1946, 6–8; Joseph North, "No Retreat for the Writer," *NM*, February 26, 1946, 8–10; Alvah Bessie, "What Is Freedom for Writers?" *NM*, March 12, 1946, 8–10; John Howard Lawson, "Art Is a Weapon," *NM*, March 19, 1946, 18–20; Maltz, "Moving Forward," *NM*, April 9, 1946, 8–10, 21–22. Also see Navasky, *Naming Names*, 285–302; Hemingway, *Artists on the Left*, 195–99, 207–24, 279–82; John Sbardellati, "'The Maltz Affair' Revisited: How the American Communist Party Relinquished Its Cultural Influence at the Dawn of the Cold War," *Cold War History* 9, no. 4 (2009): 489–500; and Alan Wald, *American Night: The Literary Left in the Era of the Cold War* (Chapel Hill: University of North Carolina Press, 2012), 1–21, 49–83.

29. *Counterattack*, June 23, 1950, 1–2.

30. Reeves quoted in Martin Mayer, *Madison Avenue, U.S.A.* (New York: Harper and Brothers, 1958), 49. Also see Mayer, *Madison Avenue*, 47–53, 293–97; Frank, *Conquest of Cool*, 38–47; and Daniel Horowitz, "The Émigré as Celebrant of

American Consumer Culture: George Katona and Ernest Dichter," in *Getting and Spending: European and American Consumer Societies in the Twentieth Century*, ed. Susan Strasser, Charles McGovern, and Matthias Judt (New York: Cambridge University Press, 1998), 149–66.

31. Henry Lee, "Ted Bates' Rosser Reeves," *MA*, April 1965, 32–34, 38, 62.

32. Dwight Macdonald, "A Theory of Mass Culture" (1953), in *Mass Culture: The Popular Arts in America*, ed. Bernard Rosenberg and David Manning White (Glencoe, IL: Free Press, 1957), 59–60, 65, 70. Also see Pells, *Liberal Mind*, 216–32; Wreszin, *Rebel in Defense of Tradition*, 285–89, 325–26, 336–40; and Horowitz, *Consuming Pleasures*, 19–44.

33. T. W. Adorno, "Television and the Patterns of Mass Culture" (1954), in *Mass Culture*, ed. Rosenberg and White, 474, 482.

34. On the persistence and evolution of theories of culture that stressed the work involved in the reception and interpretation of cultural forms, the complexity of these processes, the agency of consumers, and the role of contingency, see Denning, *Cultural Front*, 123–36, 151–59, 423–62; and Horowitz, *Consuming Pleasures*, 1–18, 45–121, 163–305.

35. Griffith, "The Selling of America"; and Fones-Wolf, *Selling Free Enterprise*, 32–63.

36. Mayer, *Madison Avenue*, 29.

37. Seymour Banks, Ronald Reisman, and Charles Yang, "Ad Volume Rises 5.6 percent to $18.3 Billion in 1968 as U.S. Economy Flourishes, Advertising Age's Yang Estimates Show," *AA*, March 3, 1969, 45–46, 48.

38. Erik Barnouw, *The Image Empire: A History of Broadcasting in the United States since 1953* (New York: Oxford University Press, 1970), 150.

39. For background on JWT in this period, see Mayer, *Madison Avenue, U.S.A.*, 72–76; and Henry Lee, "J. Walter Thompson's Dan Seymour," *MA*, November 1964, 24–30, 39.

40. JWT Research Department, "Number of Employees in J. Walter Thompson Company Branch Offices," June 12, 1940, "Domestic-NYO-Staff, 1931–1979" folder, Box 15, JWT-IC; JWT, "J. Walter Thompson Staff Members as of December 31, 1959," "Domestic-NYO-Staff, 1931–1979" folder, Box 15, JWT-IC.

41. JWT Television Department, "Television, Radio and Motion Pictures," April 2, 1956, "Administrative—Department Organization, 1955–1960 and Undated (1 of 3) folder, Box 1, JWT-JD; William Whited to John Devine, June 25, 1958, "Programming—New York Office TV Workshop, 1955–1960 and Undated (3 of 3)" folder, Box 19, JWT-JD; Whited to Devine, February 13, 1959, "Programming—New York Office TV Workshop, 1955–1960 and Undated (3 of 3)" folder, Box 19, JWT-JD; Evelyn Peirce to Whited, September 26, 1961, "Programming—New York Office TV Workshop, 1955–1960 and Undated (3 of 3)" folder, Box 19, JWT-JD. Also see Mayer, *Madison Avenue, U.S.A.*, 86–87; and Lawrence Samuel, *Brought to You By: Postwar Television Advertising and the American Dream* (Austin: University of Texas Press, 2001), 55–58.

42. Howard Kohl to Account Representatives, March 8, 1957, "Domestic-NYO-Representatives, 1946–1976" folder, Box 15, JWT-IC; JWT, "Facts You Will Want to Know about the J. Walter Thompson Company," August 1, 1957, "Domestic—NYO—Fact Books, 1957–1967" folder, Box 11, JWT-IC.

43. J. Walter Thompson Company, "How Research Can Improve Advertising for J. Walter Thompson Clients," June 11, 1959, "Domestic-NYO-Consumer Behavior 1929, 1959–1963, 1969–1970, 1977" folder, Box 11, JWT-IC. Also see Mayer, *Madison Avenue, U.S.A.*, 87–89, 280–90.

44. JWT, "J. Walter Thompson Staff Members as of December 31, 1959"; JWT, "Women's Copy Group" copywriting assignments, November 15, 1960, "Domestic—NYO—Creative Department—Creative Assignments, 1960–1976" folder, Box 11, JWT-IC; JWT, "Women's Editorial" copywriting assignments, October 1, 1963, "Domestic—NYO—Creative Department—Creative Assignments, 1960–1976" folder, Box 11, JWT-IC; JWT, "Facts You Will Want to Know about the J. Walter Thompson Company"; and "It's a Woman's World Too! *Madison Avenue* Looks at Women in Advertising," *MA*, February 1963, 42–49.

45. Calculations by the author using data from *Integrated Public Use Microdata Series: Version 5.0 Machine-Readable Database*. Figures based on professional and technical employees who earned salary income and worked 30 or more hours a week at the time they were surveyed for the 1960 US Census, and who reported three or more weeks of unemployment in the previous year.

46. Jerry Fields, "Salaries in Advertising," *MA*, February 1962, 30–31; "I'm Going Broke on $25,000 a Year," *MA*, October 1962, 48–50.

47. Jerry Della Femina with Charles Sopkin, *From Those Wonderful Folks Who Gave You Pearl Harbor: Front-Line Dispatches from the Advertising War* (New York: Simon and Schuster, 1970), 48–65.

48. Jerry Fields, "Where Do Old Admen Go?" *MA*, September 1963, 26, 55.

49. Unsigned to "Chief of Guild Membership Recruitment," October 2, 1960, Folder 27, Box 123, NGNY.

50. Peter Bart, "Advertising: New Billings for Papert, Koenig," *NYT*, October 16, 1961, 42; George Lois with Bill Pitts, *George, Be Careful* (New York: Saturday Review Press, 1972), 65–69.

51. Mayer, *Madison Avenue, U.S.A.*, 65–68. Also see Victor Navasky, "Advertising Is a Science? An Art? A Business?" *NYT*, November 20, 1966, 52, 162, 164, 167, 169–70, 172, 174, 176; "Doyle Dane Bernbach," *MA*, February 1968, 13–18, 32; Don Grant, "DDB Bosses Distribute Advice as Agency Marks Its 20th Birthday," *AA*, June 9, 1969, 52, 54; and Frank, *Conquest of Cool*, 52–73.

52. Peter Bart, "Advertising: Papert, Koenig May 'Go Public,'" *NYT*, May 10, 1962, 59; Bart, "Advertising: Pros and Cons of Going Public," *NYT*, May 13, 1962, F14; William Smith, "Advertising: Papert, Koenig Splits Its Stock," *NYT*, September 29, 1964, 60; Lois, *George, Be Careful*, 65–69, 118–20.

53. Peter Bart, "Advertising: Function of Agency is Debated," *NYT*, November 11, 1962, 186; Bart, "Advertising: Does It Have a Role in Politics?" *NYT*, October 27, 1963, 152; Lois, *George, Be Careful*, 75–76, 79–80, 103–12. Also see Frank, *Conquest of Cool*, 80–86.

54. Philip Dougherty, "Advertising: Lois to Create His Own Shop," *NYT*, September 15, 1967, 60; "The Three Musketeers," *MA*, January 1968, 12–18; "How Are the New Agencies Really Doing?" *MA*, September 1968, 12–17; James O'Gara, "$8.4 Billion Billed by 600 Agencies in Record 1968," *AA*, February 24, 1969, 1, 3B; Lois, *George, Be Careful*, 158–88, 195–234.

55. Bart, "Advertising: New Billings for Papert, Koenig."

56. "Agency Open a Month Lands Volvo," *NYT*, June 2, 1967, F65; Philip Dougherty, "Advertising: Car Campaigns Getting Tough," *NYT*, September 13, 1967, 58. "The Paper Car!" advertisement, *Life*, October 6, 1967, R8–R9.

57. "Ally 1968," *MA*, May 1968, 32–37; "The Protest Workshop," *MA*, January 1969, 10–13.

58. Philip Dougherty, "Advertising: The Message Is 'Give a Damn,'" *NYT*, May 16, 1968, 76; Dougherty, "Advertising: Tackling the Problem of Slums," *NYT*, June 25, 1968, 63; "Y&R Leads Clio Awards; BBDO, DDB Follow," *AA*, May 19, 1969, 3, 24; Dougherty, "A Most Honored Drive—Against Poverty," *NYT*, June 8, 1969, F16; "'Incredibly Honest' Ads Won for Lindsay: Frankfurt," *AA*, November 10, 1969, 2, 8; Dougherty, "Advertising: The 2d Toughest Campaign," *NYT*, November 11, 1969, 73. On Lindsay and the 1969 mayoral race, see Freeman, *Working-Class New York*, 233–37; and Lizabeth Cohen and Brian Goldstein, "Governing at the Tipping Point: Shaping the City's Role in Economic Development," in *Summer in the City: John Lindsay, New York, and the American Dream*, ed. Joseph Viteritti (Baltimore: Johns Hopkins University Press, 2014), 163–92.

59. "It's a Woman's World Too!"; "What's Up with Jack Tinker and Partners," *MA*, August 1965, 12–18, 51; Navasky, "Advertising Is a Science? An Art? A Business?"; "What's with Jack Tinker and Partners," *MA*, January 1967, 22–25; "Woman in the Corner Office," *MA*, September 1967, 38–42; "The Wondrous World of WRG (Revisited)," *MA*, December 1967, 14–19; "How Are the New Agencies Really Doing?"; "$8.4 Billion Billed by 600 Agencies in Record 1968"; "Mrs. Lawrence Signs WRG Pact," *AA*, April 28, 1969, 3, 8; and Mary Wells Lawrence, *A Big Life in Advertising* (New York: Knopf, 2002), 5–126. Also see Frank, *Conquest of Cool*, 123–30.

60. James O'Gara, "663 U.S. Agencies Increase Billings 11 Percent to Record $9.9 Billion in 1969," *AA*, February 23, 1970, 1, 184.

61. Maxwell Dane, "15 Percent—Fact or Fiction," *MA*, May 1966, 28–29, 42, 48; Walter Carlson, "Advertising: Interpublic is Growing Again," *NYT*, September 30, 1966, 61; Navasky, "Advertising Is a Science? An Art? A Business?"; Philip Dougherty, "Advertising: The Push for New Products," *NYT*, April 2, 1967, 146; Dougherty, "Advertising: Interpublic Trimming Its Sails," *NYT*, November 27,

1967, 89; Dougherty, "Advertising: Another Interpublic Venture," *NYT*, March 18, 1968, 72; Henry Bernstein, "Interpublic Prospectus Is Stormy Chronicle," *AA*, May 18, 1970, 1, 16.

62. "BBDO's Communication Design Center," *MA*, January 1965, 34–38.

63. "Automated Advertising," *MA*, April 1962, 20–22; "The New York Media Department," *MA*, September 1962, 18–23; "The Complex World of Media at Ted Bates," *MA*, November 1966, 28–35, 50; Jackie DaCosta, "Computers at the Advertising Agency: A Basic Review," *MA*, January 1969, 6–7; Herbert Maneloveg, "Don't Sneer at Computers," *AA*, April 28, 1969, 65–66, 68.

64. "What's Up with Jack Tinker and Partners"; "JWT: A New Approach to Creativity," *MA*, September 1966, 24–32, 64; Della Femina, *From the Wonderful Folks*, 102–103.

65. Philip Dougherty, "Advertising: Xerox and P.K.L. Agency Part," *NYT*, March 6, 1968, 72; "PKL, Electronics Company Agree to Terms of Merger," *AA*, March 24, 1969, 2; "PKL 'in Black' Despite National's Shift to Free," *AA*, May 19, 1969, 1, 143; Dougherty, "Advertising: Transfusion Time at Papert?" *NYT*, October 3, 1969, 74; "3 Ex-Tinkerites Join Papert Shop" *AA*, October 6, 1969, 1, 91; "Billings of 66 Agencies in the $10,000,000 to $25,000,000 Range," *AA*, February 23, 1970, 42; Dougherty, "Julian Koenig Resigns from PKL Companies," *NYT*, April 10, 1970, 68; "Papert to Leave Agency Work but Keep PKL Ties," *AA*, May 11, 1970, 23.

66. Bart, "Advertising: Pros and Cons of Going Public"; Herbert Strauss, "The Case for Going Public," *MA*, December 1968, 12–13.

67. Strauss, "The Case for Going Public"; James O'Gara, "JWT Takes New Stand; World's No. 1 Shop to Go Public with 27 percent of Stock," *AA*, March 31, 1969, 1, 127; Kathryn Sederberg, "Some Agency Stocks Display Resiliency in Slumping Market," *AA*, May 18, 1970, 1, 10; Leonard Sloane, "Ad Agency Stocks on Upswing," *NYT*, June 13, 1976, III, 14.

68. Mary Wells Lawrence, "Madison Ave.: On Going Public," *NYT*, October 4, 1970, 147.

69. "Survey Shows Ad Spending Off," *NYT*, February 20, 1974, 56.

70. Philip Dougherty, "Class of '67: Where Are They?" *NYT*, September 12, 1971, F19.

71. Calculations by the author using data from Steven Ruggles, J. Trent Alexander, Katie Genadek, Matthew B. Schroeder, and Matthew Sobek, *Integrated Public Use Microdata Series: Version 5.0 Machine-Readable Database* (Minneapolis: University of Minnesota Press, 2010).

72. Interview with William Friedman by Mary McChesney, 2; Alexandra Winton, "'A Man's House is His Art': The Walker Art Center's Idea House Project and the Marketing of Domestic Design, 1941–1947," *JDH* 17, no. 4 (2004): 377–96.

73. "The Gallery of Everyday Art," *EAQ* no. 1 (Summer 1946): 1.

74. Hilde Reiss to Elizabeth McCausland, October 25, 1945, Folder 39, Box 25, EM; McCausland, "The Everyday Art Gallery of the Walker Art Center," February 20, 1946, Folder 40, Box 25, EM; "Ideas for Better Living," *EAQ* no. 1 (Summer

1946): 5–7; "News Report: *Everyday Art Quarterly*," *College Art Journal* 6 (Autumn 1946): 69–70; Pulos, *American Design Adventure*, 62, 71.

75. D. S. Defenbacher, "A Man's House is His Art," *EAQ* no. 5 (Fall 1947): 1–2; William Friedman and Hilde Reiss, "Floorplan for Idea House II," *EAQ* no. 5 (Fall 1947): 3; "The Idea of the House," *EAQ* no. 5 (Fall 1947): 4–5; Winton, "'A Man's House is His Art.'" Also see Pulos, *American Design Adventure*, 62–64.

76. See, for example, William Friedman to Elizabeth McCausland, January 21, 1946, Folder 39, Box 25, EM; McCausland to Friedman, January 21, 1946, Folder 39, Box 25, EM; Paul Triling to McCausland, January 20, 1947, Folder 34, Box 3, EM; Minutes of ICCASP Art Division Executive Council Meeting, January 22, 1947, Folder 34, Box 3, EM.

77. Eva Zeisel, "Registering a New Trend," *EAQ* no. 2 (Fall 1946).

78. Donald Wallance, "Design in Plastics," *EAQ* no. 6 (Winter 1947/48): 3–4. Also see Betty Pepis, "For the Home: 'Good Design' Is International," *NYT*, January 16, 1951, 36.

79. Stanley Abercrombie, *George Nelson: The Design of Modern Design* (Cambridge, MA: MIT Press, 1994), 1–21.

80. George Nelson, "Mechanizing the Architect," *TA*, April 1938, 3–4.

81. George Nelson, "Storagewall," *ArchFor*, November 1944; George Nelson, "Furniture Industry," *Fortune*, January 1947, 106–11; "George Nelson Starts Furniture Row," *ArchFor*, February 1947, 12; Abercrombie, *George Nelson*, 68–72, 83–101.

82. See Donald Wallance, *Shaping America's Products* (New York: Reinhold, 1956), 108–13; Pulos, *American Design Adventure*, 78–107; Pat Kirkham, "Humanizing Modernism: The Crafts, 'Functioning Decoration,' and the Eameses," *JDH* 11, no. 1 (1998): 15–27; and Alexandra Lange, "This Year's Model: Representing Modernism to the Post-war American Corporation," *JDH* 19, no. 3 (2006): 233–48.

83. Galbraith, *Affluent Society*, 334. Also see Shelley Nickles, "More Is Better: Mass Consumption, Gender, and Postwar America," *AQ* 54, no. 4 (2002): 581–622.

84. "Up from the Egg," *Time*, October 31, 1949, 68–74; Donald Wallance, "Case Study 36-A" memo, July 11, 1950, "Case Study (36-A) Raymond Loewy Associates" folder, Box 4, DW; Wallance, *Shaping America's Products*, 48; Elizabeth Reese, "Design and the American Dream: Associates of Loewy," in *Raymond Loewy: Pioneer of American Industrial Design*, ed. Schönberger, 39–49.

85. "Up from the Egg"; Raymond Loewy Associates, *Supermarkets of the Sixties* (Chicago: Super Market Institute, 1960); Edward Carpenter, "Statement: New Directions for Industrial Design," *ID*, August 1964, 62–64; William Snaith, "The Consumer Observed," *ID*, April 1966, 46–48; and >Raymond Loewy/William Snaith Inc. *The Motivations Toward Homes and Housing* (New York: The Project Home Committee, 1967).

86. Paul Makovsky, "Being Irving Harper," *Metropolis*, June 2001; and Irving Harper interview with the author, Rye, NY, March 16, 2004.

87. Mary Roche, "19 Architects Get Prizes for Houses: Win $10,800 in Bloomingdale Contest for Contemporary and Traditional Designs," *NYT*, April 11, 1946, 32; Makovsky, "Being Irving Harper"; and Harper interview.

88. George Nelson to Don Wallance, August 19, 1949, "Research/Design, Craftsmanship I: Correspondence, 1949–50" folder, Box 2, DW.

89. Makovsky, "Being Irving Harper"; Harper interview; and Guy Trebay, "Undercover Icon," *NYT: T Style* (magazine supplement), May 2, 2010, M2, 46. Catherine Fisk utilizes the comparable contrast between the anonymity of advertising copywriters and the creative credit conspicuously assigned to Hollywood screenwriters as one of the central organizing principles of *Writing for Hire*.

90. "General Motors Opens First Completed Buildings of Technical Center," *ArchRec*, October 1951, 12; "General Motors Technical Center," *ArchFor*, November 1951, 111–23; "General Motors Technical Center," *ProgArch*, February 1955, 94–103; "Architecture for the Future: GM Constructs a Versailles for Industry," *Life*, May 21, 1956, 102–107; "Production Model of GM's Versailles: Fisher Body and Chevrolet Buildings; Warren, Michigan," *ArchFor*, December 1956, 136–41.

91. "The Role of the Corporate Industrial Designer: General Motors," *ID*, September 1965, 120–26. Also see "The Role of the Corporate Industrial Designer: Ford," *ID*, September 1965, 72–75; Pulos, *American Design Adventure*, 362–93; and Gartman, *Auto Opium*, 141–203.

92. Donald Wallance, "Confidential Case Study 14-A" memo, December 16, 1949, "Case Study (14-A) General Electric Co." folder, Box 4, DW; A. N. BecVar to Wallance, September 30, 1952, "Case Study (14-A) General Electric Co." folder, Box 4, DW. On postwar labor relations at GE, see Kim Phillips-Fein, *Invisible Hands: The Making of the Conservative Movement from the New Deal to Reagan* (New York: Norton, 2009), 87–114.

93. Arthur N. BecVar, "The Corporation Designer and the Consultant Designer," Society of Industrial Designers Annual Meeting, October 1953, "Research/Company Designer—Consultant Designer" folder, Box 2, DW.

94. Pulos, *American Design Adventure*, 129; Abercrombie, *George Nelson*, 72–74.

95. Wallance, *Shaping America's Products*, 65–75; "The Role of the Corporate Industrial Designer: General Electric," *ID*, September 1965, 104–113.

96. Don Wallance to William Friedman, March 28, 1949, "Correspondence: March 1949—May 1950" folder, Box 2, DW; "Report by D. A. Wallance of Activity to July 1, 1949," "General/Activity Reports, 1949–50" folder, Box 2, DW; Wallance to Hilde Reiss, November 11, 1949, "Correspondence: March 1949—May 1950" folder, Box 2, DW; "Report by D. A. Wallance of Activity from Feb. 25 to April 25, 1950," "General/Activity Reports, 1949–50" folder, Box 2, DW; D. S. Defenbacher, "A Study of Design and Craftsmanship in Today's Products" memo, September 14, 1950, "General/Activity Reports, 1949–50" folder, Box 2, DW; Wallance, *Shaping America's Products*, iii.

97. Wallance, *Shaping America's Products*, 2–3. On discourses of taste in postwar America, see Jackson Lears, "A Matter of Taste: Corporate Cultural Hegemony in a Mass-Consumption Society," in *Recasting America*, ed. May, 38–57.

98. Wallance, *Shaping America's Products*, 3, 9.

99. Ibid, 15–19.

100. On the annual International Design Conference and related cultural and intellectual programming in Aspen during the 1950s and 1960s, see Allen, *Romance of Commerce and Culture*, 201–81.

101. C. Wright Mills, "The Man in the Middle: The Designer," *ID*, November 1958, 70–75.

102. Ibid.

103. Scott Kelly, "Curator of Corporate Character: Eliot Noyes and Associates," *ID*, June 1966, 38, 40, 43.

104. C. F. Graser and Walter F. Kraus, "Developing the Product 6: International Business Machine's System/360," *ID*, August 1964, 34–38; Harwood, *Interface*, 87–99. Also see Patricia Dreyfus, "CRT Display Terminals," *ID*, April 1971, 32–34.

105. Kelly, "Curator of Corporate Character," 43.

106. Edward Carpenter, "Partitioning the Office," *ID*, February 1964, 26–33; Abercrombie, *George Nelson*, 216–24.

107. Mina Hamilton, "Office Desks," *ID*, February 1964, 34–39; Abercrombie, *George Nelson*, 211–16.

108. "Nixon and Khrushchev Argue in Public as U.S. Exhibit Opens," *NYT*, July 25, 1959, 1; "In Sokolniki Park: Assembling the U.S. Exhibition in Moscow," *Interiors*, September 1959, 154–57; and "Designing the Moscow Exhibit: Architects of Permanent Structures, W. Beckert and Associates; Design of Interior and Exterior Exhibits, George Nelson and Co.," *ArchRec*, November 1959, 169–76. Also see Pulos, *American Design Adventure*, 236–65; Abercrombie, *George Nelson*, 159–76; and Robert Haddow, *Pavilions of Plenty: Exhibiting American Culture Abroad in the 1950s* (Washington, DC: Smithsonian Institution Press, 1997).

109. Victor Gruen Associates, *Shopping Centers of Tomorrow* (n.p.: American Federation of Arts, 1954); "Northland: A New Yardstick for Shopping Center Planning," *ArchFor*, June 1954, 102–19; "Typical Downtown Transformed," *ArchFor*, May 1956, 145–55; Victor Gruen, "The Emerging Urban Pattern," *ProgArch*, July 1959, 116–62; Edward Carpenter, "Brave New Town," *ID*, March 1964, 62–67. Also see Jeffrey Hardwick, *Mall Maker: Victor Gruen, Architect of an American Dream* (Philadelphia: University of Pennsylvania Press, 2001), 91–209.

110. On modernist logos and corporate identity in the postwar era, see Pulos, *American Design Adventure*, 271–79; Paul Rand, *From Lascaux to Brooklyn* (New Haven, CT: Yale University Press, 1996), 79–94; and Harwood, *Interface*, 38–43, 49–54.

111. Peter Blake, *God's Own Junkyard: The Planned Deterioration of America's Landscape* (New York: Holt, Rinehart and Winston, 1964).

112. "The Aspen Papers," *ID*, August 1964, 58–61.

113. Mary MacNeil, "Design Lag in the Radio and Television Industry," *ID*, July 1965, 70–71.

114. Ann Ferebee, "Progress Report on the New York World's Fair," *ID*, May 1963, 78–80; Mary MacNeil, "All's Fair," *ID*, March 1964, 46–49; Vincent Scully, "If This Is Architecture, God Help Us," *Life*, July 31, 1964, 9; Abercrombie, *George Nelson*, 176–79; Harwood, *Interface*, 182–95.

115. Scully, "If This Is Architecture, God Help Us"; Judith Miller, "Goodbye to All That," *ID*, November 1965, 25.

116. Robert Venturi and Denise Scott Brown, with Steve Izenour, *Learning from Las Vegas* (Cambridge, MA: MIT Press, 1972), 6, 153–54. Also see Horowitz, *Consuming Pleasures*, 344–59.

117. Vance Packard, *The Waste Makers* (New York: David McKay, 1960), vii–viii, 5–6, 37, 204. Also see Daniel Horowitz, *Vance Packard and American Social Criticism* (Chapel Hill: University of North Carolina Press, 1994), 102–205.

118. "A Solution for Pollution," *ID*, April 1970, 62–66.

119. See Felicity Scott, *Architecture or Techno-Utopianism: Politics after Modernism* (Cambridge, MA: MIT Press, 2007).

120. Richard Branham, "The Case for Computerized Design," *ID*, March 1970, 22–29.

121. See, for instance, "Meet Japan's Designers," *ID*, March 1964, 28–31.

122. Wallance, *Shaping America's Products*, 118–22; Wallance, "The Formative Years of United States Industrial Design, 1927–1953, Questionnaire for Industrial Design Society of America," January 30, 1978, "Biographical Statements, Questionnaires, and Related Materials" folder, Box 1, DW. Also see Raymond Spillman to Wallance, November 7, 1977, "Biographical Statements, Questionnaires, and Related Materials" folder, Box 1, DW.

CHAPTER 8

1. John K. Jessup, "A Crucial New *Life* Series: 'The National Purpose,'" *Life*, May 23, 1960, 22–41. Also see Curtis Prendergast with Geoffrey Colvin, *The World of Time Inc. The Intimate History of a Changing Enterprise, Volume Three: 1960–1980* (New York: Athenaeum, 1986), 37–53; and Brinkley, *The Publisher*, 390–428.

2. "Frigidaire Stereo-Cooling Room Air Conditioners" advertisement, *Life*, May 23, 1960, 42.

3. "A Preference for Nixon," *Life*, October 25, 1968, 42; "Life Magazine Endorses Nixon," *NYT*, October 20, 1968, 75; "The Case for Four More Years," *Life*, October 27, 1972, 12; "The Massacre at Mylai," *Life*, December 5, 1969, 36–44. For context, see James Baughman, *The Republic of Mass Culture: Journalism, Filmmaking, and Broadcasting in America since 1941*, 2nd ed. (Baltimore: Johns Hopkins University Press, 1997), 59–90, 117–42.

4. "*Life's* HCL," *Broadcasting*, July 10, 1950, 34; "*Life* Ad Figures," *Broadcasting*, July 30, 1951, 24; "It's CBS-TV, NBC-TV and *Life*—In That Order," *Broadcasting*,

December 27, 1954, 51; *Life* trade advertisement in the February 1962 issue of *MA*; "Time, Inc., Reports Best Year; Revenues, Net Both Rose 11 Percent," *NYT*, February 17, 1967, 76. Also see Prendergast, *World of Time Inc., Volume Three*, 53–64.

5. "Ailing *Saturday Evening Post* Will Reduce Subscription List," *NYT*, May 4, 1968, 34; Robert E. Bedingfield, "Curtis Publishing to Show Big Loss for '68," *NYT*, August 22, 1968, 55; Herbert Maneloveg, "*Post* Gives Lesson in How Not to Market a Magazine," *AA*, February 10, 1969, 56; Chris Welles, "*Post*-Mortem," *NYMag*, February 10, 1969, 32–36; Philip Dougherty, "Postmortem on *Saturday Evening Post*," *NYT*, March 30, 1969, F16. Also see Otto Friedrich, *Decline and Fall: The Struggle for Power at a Great American Magazine,* The Saturday Evening Post (New York: Harper & Row, 1970), 269–490.

6. Philip Dougherty, "Selling *Life* to Public and Madison Ave.," *NYT*, January 11, 1970, 134; "*Life*, Pares Base, Rates; Drops 2 Editions," *AA*, October 5, 1970, 2, 60; John Revett, "*Life, Look* Cuts in Circulation Might Bolster Both Books," *AA*, October 12, 1970, 1, 72; Dougherty, "*Life* to Cut Its Circulation and Seek Rate Increases," *NYT*, November 25, 1971, 61. Also see Prendergast, *World of Time Inc., Volume Three*, 276–86.

7. Edwin Diamond, "Why the Power Vacuum at Time Inc. Continues," *NYMag*, October 23, 1972, 84–98; Philip Dougherty, "*Life-Look* Battle Ends, but War Goes on," *NYT*, May 10, 1970, 141; Chris Welles, "Another One Drowns in Red Ink," *NYT*, September 19, 1971, E4; NGNY Executive Committee Minutes, September 21, 1971, Folder 6, Box 150, NGNY; "*Life* Magazine is Eliminating 80 to 90 Jobs," *NYT*, December 2, 1971, 43. Also see Prendergast, *World of Time Inc., Volume Three*, 294–96.

8. Philip Dougherty, "Dated Publishing Strategy Linked to Downfall of *Life*," *NYT*, December 9, 1972, 16; Deirdre Carmody, "Tears and Reminiscing Meet News of Closing," *NYT*, December 9, 1972, 1, 16; NGNY Executive Committee Minutes, December 19, 1972, Folder 8, Box 150, NGNY; Hedley Donovan, "*Life's* Last Issue: A Message to Our Readers," *Life*, December 29, 1972, 1. Also see Prendergast, *World of Time Inc., Volume Three*, 305–11.

9. "Jobs Sought for 325 Employees of *Life*," *NYT*, December 10, 1972, 42; Eric Pace, "Heavy Losses Doom Publication That Started in '36," *NYT*, December 9, 1972, 1, 16.

10. Calculations by the author using data from Steven Ruggles, J. Trent Alexander, Katie Genadek, Matthew B. Schroeder, and Matthew Sobek, *Integrated Public Use Microdata Series: Version 5.0 Machine-Readable Database* (Minneapolis: University of Minnesota Press, 2010). Data based on household survey, not establishment survey. See Tables A.14 and A.15 in the Appendix.

11. Joseph Fried, "Job Market for the College Graduate Projected as Tighter Through 1970s," *NYT*, September 25, 1972, 1, 32.

12. Calculations by the author using data from Steven Ruggles, J. Trent Alexander, Katie Genadek, Matthew B. Schroeder, and Matthew Sobek, *Integrated Public Use*

Microdata Series: Version 5.0 Machine-Readable Database (Minneapolis: University of Minnesota Press, 2010). Data based on household survey, not establishment survey. See Table A.13 in the appendix.

13. Calculations by the author using data from Steven Ruggles, J. Trent Alexander, Katie Genadek, Matthew B. Schroeder, and Matthew Sobek, *Integrated Public Use Microdata Series: Version 5.0 Machine-Readable Database* (Minneapolis: University of Minnesota Press, 2010). Data based on household survey, not establishment survey. See Tables A.14 and A.15 in the appendix.

14. Peter Kihss, "Employment of Negroes in News Media Put at 4.2 percent," *NYT*, December 8, 1968, 65.

15. "DuMont Live TV Headed for Pasture," *Broadcasting*, May 16, 1955, 127–28. Also see David Weinstein, *The Forgotten Network: DuMont and the Birth of American Television* (Philadelphia: Temple University Press, 2004).

16. For an overview of the evolution of network procurement practices during the 1950s and early 1960s, see Barnouw, *Image Empire*, 25–40, 61–65, 80–84, 147–54; Boddy, *Fifties Television*, 132–84; and Baughman, *Same Time, Same Station*, 153–218, 257–95.

17. See Barnouw, *Image Empire*, 70–74; Ledbetter, *Made Possible By*, 29–33, 38–57; and McCarthy, *Citizen Machine*, 119–203.

18. Thomas Brady, "TV in Hollywood," *NYT*, June 4, 1950, X9; Brady, "California Made," *NYT*, October 3, 1954, X13.

19. CBS, "Miracles Made Easy" advertisement, *Billboard*, November 15, 1952, 5.

20. Thomas Pryor, "Filming for Video Making Big Gains," *NYT*, November 13, 1954, 13; Leo Kovner, "TV Film Employment," *Broadcasting*, December 13, 1954, 44, 48.

21. See Timothy White, *Blue-Collar Broadway: The Craft and Industry of American Theater* (Philadelphia: University of Pennsylvania Press, 2015), 76–83, 90–99.

22. "New TV Studio," *Broadcasting*, January 7, 1952, 64; Roma Lipsky, "Then and Now: Old Vitagraph's Lot, a Silent Movie Cradle, Today Is Swaddling TV in Color," *NYT*, September 12, 1954, SM18; NBC-TV Dedicates New Color Studio," *Broadcasting*, September 13, 1954, 88; "NBC Accelerates Its Color Expansion," *Broadcasting*, August 20, 1956, 90; "NBC's Got a Real Estate Problem; *Home* Studio, Colonial Theatre Idle," *Variety*, July 31, 1957, 25; "NBC's Stake In '30 Rock' for Next Quarter of a Century," *Variety*, September 10, 1958, 32, 34; "Strike Cued Tint Lopoff at NBC, Studios Closed," *Variety*, May 20, 1959, 22; "NBC to Abandon the Ziegfeld Theatre, One Legiter Left," *Variety*, November 8, 1961, 39.

23. "Filmways Starts N.Y. Pix Production Push," *Billboard*, January 23, 1954, 5; Bernard Stengren, "TV Commercial Shop: Filmways Uses Large Staff to Produce Variety of Advertising Messages," *NYT*, September 17, 1961, X21.

24. Gene Plotnik, "N.Y. Video Center: All Talk, No Action," *Billboard*, July 10, 1954, 1, 12; "West Side 'TV City' Proposed by Stark," *NYT*, April 24, 1956, 63. Also see Robert Caro, *The Power Broker: Robert Moses and the Fall of New York* (New York: Knopf, 1974), 961–83, 1005–25, 1040–66; Joel Schwartz, *The New York*

Approach: Robert Moses, Urban Liberals, and the Redevelopment of the Inner City (Columbus: Ohio State University Press, 1993), 229–60; and Freeman, *Working-Class New York*, 143–51.

25. Oliver Treyz, "Target for Television: New Advertising Money," *Broadcasting*, January 2, 1956, 56–57; JWT Media Research, "Report on Television as an Advertising Medium," March 1959, 124, Folder 64D, Box 24, JWT-IC; Federal Communications Commission, Office of Network Study, *Second Interim Report: Television Network Program Procurement, Part II* (Washington, DC: G.P.O., 1965), 44.

26. On the dynamic relationship by which television shaped postwar suburban consumer culture, see Lynn Spiegel, *Make Room for TV: Television and the Family Ideal in Postwar America* (Chicago: University of Chicago Press, 1992), 36–72, 99–180.

27. "70 percent of Net Shows to Come from Hwd.," *Billboard*, June 17, 1957, 3; Jack Gould, "End of an Era?" *NYT*, December 22, 1957, 57; Gould, "Hollywood Assembly Line," *NYT*, December 29, 1957, 63. Also see Boddy, *Fifties Television*, 187–213.

28. David Susskind to Paddy Chayefsky, June 16, 1958, "General Business Correspondence, 1957–1963" Folder, Box 42, DS.

29. "Major Talents Band Together in a Big Push to 'Save N.Y. TV,'" *Variety*, June 18, 1958, 39; Jack Gould, "TV Under Assault," *NYT*, June 22, 1958, X11; "Open Drive to Improve TV," *Billboard*, June 23, 1958, 7; "TAC's Riddle: Why Are Webs against Gotham 'TV City'?" *Variety*, July 2, 1958, 23.

30. Macdonald, "Theory of Mass Culture," 63–64.

31. George McNickle, "The Quickest Sell: Film Commercials Are Bread, Butter for Some Actors, Gravy for Others," *NYT*, July 5, 1959, X9; Art Woodstone, "'Gotham Ghost' Alerts Labor: Unions to Aid in N.Y. TV Buildup," *Variety*, September 14, 1960, 27.

32. "Minow Lays It on the Line: Demands Better Programming in Public Interest, Warns Nothing Sacred about License," *Variety*, May 10, 1961, 25, 72; "Excerpts from Speech by Minow," *NYT*, May 10, 1961, 91; Jack Gould, "TV: At the Wailing Wall," *NYT*, May 11, 1961, 75. Also see Barnouw, *Image Empire*, 196–98; Boddy, *Fifties Television*, 233–55; and Baughman, *Same Time, Same Station*, 296–301.

33. Richard Shepard, "TV Artists to Give FCC Their Views," *NYT*, June 17, 1961, 49.

34. FCC, *Second Interim Report: Television Network Program Procurement, Part II*, 549, 569–70, 580.

35. Ibid., 627, 630–31, 633–34.

36. Murray Horowitz, "Tony Miner on *Play of the Week*'s Success: 'You Gotta Stimulate 'Em,'" *Variety*, January 11, 1961, 23, 44; "Ely Landau's Bid to Buy WNTA-TV, but Educ'l Interests Also Want It," *Variety*, February 22, 1961, 29; "Who's Gonna Get WNTA-TV? It's a Cliff-Hanger," *Variety*, March 8, 1961, 27, 46.

37. Jack Gould, "Citizens' Group Is Likely to Buy Channel 13 for Educational TV," *NYT*, April 16, 1961, 84; "NTA Sells off WNTA-TV to ETV Citizens Group

for $6,200,000," *Variety*, July 5, 1961, 26; Anthony Lewis, "F.C.C. Spurred Sale of WNTA By Pressure Behind the Scenes," *NYT*, December 11, 1961, 1, 39; Gould, "TV: A Big Challenge," *NYT*, December 23, 1961, 41; "WNTA-TV Finally Goes Educational," *Variety*, December 27, 1961, 22; "The 'Big Time' For Educ'l TV?" *Variety*, July 4, 1962, 67, 83; Gould, "Union Halts School TV Station in a Bid to Represent Teachers," *NYT*, September 6, 1962, 1, 63; Richard Shepard, "Dispute at WNDT Finally Settled," *NYT*, September 29, 1962, 22; Gould, "New Look on Channel 13," *NYT*, October 7, 1962, X19.

38. On independent producers in the 1960s, see Mark Alvey, "The Independents: Rethinking the Television Studio System," in *The Revolution Wasn't Televised*, ed. Spiegel and Curtin, 139–58. On *The Defenders* and *The Nurses*, see Paul Buhle and Dave Wagner, *Hide in Plain Sight: The Hollywood Blacklistees in Film and Television, 1950–2002* (New York: Palgrave, 2003), 49, 53–55; and Jon Kraszewski, *The New Entrepreneurs: An Institutional History of Television Anthology Writers* (Middletown, CT: Wesleyan University Press, 2010), 118–38.

39. Val Adams, "Blacklist a Topic for *Defenders*," *NYT*, November 6, 1963, 67; Ernest Kinoy, "Television's 'Blacklist' and the Social Conscience," *NYT*, January 12, 1964, X19; Jack Gould, "TV: Drama about Modern Witch Hunt," *NYT*, January 20, 1964, 87.

40. Robert Alan Aurthur, "Outline of Pilot for Social Worker Series: 1st Draft," n.d., "*East Side/West Side* General" folder, Box 16, DS; "CBS-TV Pacts for Susskind Hr. Pilot," *Variety*, November 28, 1962, 20; David Susskind to Michael Dann, November 29, 1962, "*East Side/West Side* General" folder, Box 16, DS. Also see Stephen Bowie, "*East Side/West Side*," *Television Chronicles* 9 (1997): 17–32.

41. Robert Jelinek to David Susskind, December 26, 1962, "*East Side/West Side* General" folder, Box 16, DS; Joel Glickman, *East Side/West Side* pilot budget, January 3, 1963, "*East Side/West Side* General" folder, Box 16, DS; "CBS' Hurry-Up Job on *East Side/West Side* All Around the Town," *Variety*, January 16, 1963, 27.

42. Staff of *East Side/West Side* Memo to Writers, n.d., 1, 9–10, Folder 8, Box 68, DS.

43. Arnold Perl to Larry White, August 21, 1963, Folder 1, Box 67, DS; "Arnold Perl: End of an Era," *Variety*, September 4, 1963, 22; Perl to George Scott et al., October 14, 1963, Folder 1, Box 67, DS; George Litto to Dan Melnick, October 16, 1963, Folder 1, Box 67, DS. Also see Buhle and Wagner, *Hide in Plain Sight*, 49–52.

44. Michael DiSilvestro to David Susskind, January 24, 1963, Folder 18, Box 66, DS; Martin Schneider to George White, February 1, 1963, Folder 18, Box 66, DS.

45. Don Kranze to Larry Arrick, November 1, 1963, Folder 17, Box 66, DS; Harold Stern to David Susskind and Dan Melnick, December 11, 1963, Folder 1, Box 67, DS; Vincent Canby, "N.Y. Pix Need Room to Boom," *Variety*, January 1, 1964, 1, 54.

46. Willard Levitas to Crew, May 20, 1963, Folder 5, Box 68, DS; David Susskind to Jacob Javits, October 29, 1963, Folder 1, Box 67, DS. For ratings reports and summaries, see the contents of Folder 1, Box 68, DS.

47. "Southern Stations Bump *East Side/West Side* Seg," *Variety*, November 6, 1963, 24; "Lotsa Sponsor Support on *East Side/West Side* despite Its Iffy Status," *Variety*, January 15, 1964, 25; David Golden to Cast and Crew, January 27, 1964, Folder 3, Box 67, DS; Jack Gould, "Miseries Galore," *NYT*, February 23, 1964, X19.

48. Art Woodstone, "Brodkin, Others 'Disgusted' with N.Y. Vidfilm Curbs, Itch for Coast," *Variety*, February 6, 1963, 26; Canby, "N.Y. Pix Need Room to Boom"; Val Adams, "TV Film Artists End Strike Here," *NYT*, May 16, 1964, 51; Adams, "Production of TV Shows Shifts More and More to Hollywood," *NYT*, March 30, 1965, 95.

49. See the itemized production budgets for each episode that are in Folder 18, Box 66, DS. On writers' salaries, see Richard Wincor to Audrey Mass, et al., March 12, 1963, Folder 8, Box 68, DS.

50. Don Silverman to Arnold Perl, September 14, 1966, Folder 13, Box 96, DS; "Susskind Gets Access to N.Y. Police Files for ABC-TV Spec (& Pilot)," *Variety*, November 30, 1966, 24; "New York Continues Backslide as Production Centre for Nighttime TV," *Variety*, February 22, 1967, 30; Talent Associates contract with American Broadcasting Company, March 1, 1967, Folder 1, Box 97, DS; "ABC Sets *N.Y.P.D.*" *Variety*, March 1, 1967, 25; Richard Wincor to David Susskind, March 10, 1967, Folder 13, Box 96, DS; Leonard Goldberg to Sam Northcross, May 24, 1967, Folder 1, Box 97, DS; "*NYPD*'s No. 1 Fan—The Mayor," *Variety*, September 27, 1967, 30.

51. Rex Reed, "Are You Ready for Cops-and-Robbers a la Alain Resnais?" *NYT*, July 23, 1967, 79; "Producers Giving All-16m of *NYPD* a Private Eyebrow," *Variety*, October 25, 1967, 27; "*NYPD* Saved from Gallows," *Variety*, May 1, 1968, 31; George Gent, "A.B.C. Plans to Replace 12 TV Programs in Fall," *NYT*, March 1, 1969, 63.

52. Steve Toy, "AFTRA Training Its Members for 'Civilian' Work to Narrow Job Gap," *Variety*, September 27, 1972, 28; "AFTRA Beefs at Fall in N.Y. Prod," *Variety*, December 4, 1974, 2.

53. JWT Media Research, "Report on Newspapers as an Advertising Medium," March 1959, 7, 38, Folder 64A, Box 23, JWT-IC; JWT Media Research, "Report on Magazines as an Advertising Medium," March 1959, 14, 18, 68, 72, Folder 64B, Box 24, JWT-IC; Philip Dougherty, "What Future for Magazines?" *NYT*, April 27, 1969, F1, F13.

54. *Herald Tribune* Promotions Research, "Circulation Averages for New York Daily Newspapers, 1931–1959," Folder 15, Box 78, NGNY. Also see Kluger, *The Paper*, 520–646.

55. Eva Jollos to Thomas J. Murphy, September 24, 1953, Folder 12, Box 78, NGNY; John Barry, "American Newspaper Guild Collective Bargaining Manual," December 1, 1953, Folder 12, Box 78, NGNY; "Report on Meeting of Editorial Staff of Proposed Paper," October 30, 1956, Folder 13, Box 78, NGNY; "All Units Alerted—Strike on One Paper Expected at Midnight," *Citywide Bulletin*, October 31, 1960, Folder 15,

Box 78, NGNY; "Why We Want What We Want," *The News Shop Paper*, October 2, 1962, Folder 16, Box 78, NGNY.

56. NYT Members telegram to Thomas J. Murphy, November 4, 1958, Folder 5, Box 78, NGNY; Murphy to Anthony Stella, November 6, 1958, Folder 5, Box 78, NGNY.

57. "Guild Strike at the *News*," *Citywide Bulletin*, November 1, 1962, Folder 16, Box 78, NGNY; *The News Shop Paper*, November 2, 1962, Folder 16, Box 78, NGNY; "The Strike Goes On," *Citywide Bulletin*, November 3, 1962, Folder 16, Box 78, NGNY; "N.Y. *News* Struck; Guild Spurns $7.25," *E&P*, November 3, 1962, 10; "Best Contract Ends 8-Day *News* Strike," *Citywide Bulletin*, November 9, 1962, Folder 16, Box 78, NGNY.

58. "Strike Vote Close, Contract Is Signed," *E&P*, September 23, 1961, 14; "New York Contract Negotiations Go On," *E&P*, November 17, 1962, 64; Peter Kihss, "N.L.R.B. Upholds Publishers Pact," *NYT*, November 22, 1962, 21; "NLRB Unanimous: Defensive Shutdown Agreement Is Legal," *E&P*, November 24, 1962, 10; "N.Y. Publishers, ITU Deadlocked," *E&P*, December 15, 1962, 9, 11, 12; NGNY Executive Board Minutes, December 17, 1962, Folder 2, Box 149, NGNY; "Publishers Say They're Negotiating for Survival," *E&P*, December 22, 1962, 9, 49; A. H. Raskin, "The Strike: A Step-by-Step Account," *NYT*, April 1, 1963, 1, 22–24; "Unions Are Militant for Job Protection," *E&P*, April 27, 1963, 72, 74. Also see Kluger, *The Paper*, 646–55; and Tifft and Jones, *The Trust*, 354–63.

59. "Strike!" *MA*, January 1963, 26–28, 49; "Retailer Analyzes Effect of Shutdown," *E&P*, January 12, 1963, 17; "N.Y.C. Stores Feel Pinch of Strike in January Sales," *E&P*, January 26, 1963, 19; "New York's Temporary Tabloid," *MA*, March 1963, 56–57; Peter Kihss, "Strike's Impact Was Widely Felt," *NYT*, April 1, 1963, 21; "114-Day Blackout Put a Damper on the Arts, Amusements and Other Phases of City's Cultural Life," *NYT*, April 1, 1963, 21; Thomas Ronan, "Sales Tax Yield up Despite Strike," *NYT*, April 3, 1963, 38; Dennis Duggan, "Papers' Blackout Cut Realty Sales," *NYT*, April 7, 1963, R1.

60. "*New York Post* Resumes With 600,000 Daily Run," *E&P*, March 9, 1963, 9, 10, 71; Raskin, "The Strike: A Step-by-Step Account." Also see Nissenson, *Lady Upstairs*, 275–82.

61. M. Michael Potoker to Charles Perlik, February 14, 1963, Folder 2, Box 149, NGNY; NGNY Executive Board Minutes, February 19, 1963, Folder 2, Box 149, NGNY; "What Happened Before Big 6 Voted to Stay Out on Strike," *E&P*, March 23, 1963, 19, 49; "Engravers' Rebellious Veto Throws Acid on N.Y. Papers," *E&P*, March 30, 1963, 10, 11; Raskin, "The Strike: A Step-by-Step Account"; "N.Y. Newspapers Back Exultant, Exuberant," *E&P*, April 6, 1963, 10, 11, 79; NGNY Executive Board Minutes., June 12, 1963, Folder 2, Box 149, NGNY.

62. *Citywide Bulletin*, October 16, 1963, Folder 15, Box 184, NGNY; Gay Talese, "Forlorn Staff Stands by as *Mirror* Shuts Down," *NYT*, October 16, 1963, 31; Peter Kihss, "*Mirror's* Close Laid in Part to Type of Circulation," *NYT*, October 17, 1963,

30; "Short, Quick, Snappy: *Mirror* Here 39 Years," *E&P*, October 19, 1963, 10; NGNY Executive Board Minutes, October 29, 1963, Folder 3, Box 149, NGNY.

63. NGNY Executive Board Minutes, October 29, 1963; Partial List of Ex-*Mirror* Guild Members Available for Work, December 2, 1963, NGNY, Box 184, Folder 15; NGNY Executive Board Minutes, January 15, 1964, NGNY, Box 149, Folder 4.

64. "Federal Inquiry Sought by Guild," *NYT*, October 16, 1963, 31; NGNY Executive Board Minutes, October 29, 1963.

65. "Collective Bargaining Program Recommendations to the Citywide Conference," December 7, 1964, Folder 2, Box 79, NGNY; NGNY Executive Board Minutes, February 17, 1965, Folder 5, Box 149, NGNY; "New York Newspapers at the Brink—Again," *Fortune*, March 1965, 231–32, 234; NGNY Executive Board Minutes, March 16, 1965, Folder 5, Box 149, NGNY; A. H. Raskin, "The Great Manhattan Newspaper Duel," *Saturday Review*, May 8, 1965, 58–60, 69–72.

66. NGNY Executive Board Minutes, June 23, 1965, Folder 5, Box 149, NGNY; "There's Only One Way to Get a Contract," *New Lead* (*Herald Tribune* shop paper), August 11, 1965, Folder 2, Box 79, NGNY; "Important Issues," *New Lead*, August 20, 1965, Folder 2, Box 79, NGNY; *Times* Negotiating Committee (Management), "Newspaper Guild Negotiations Report #25," September 14, 1965, Folder 2, Box 79, NGNY; "We Want It in Writing!" *Guild Telegram*, November 1, 1965, Folder 2, Box 79, NGNY; "What Will it Be? Agreement or a Strike?" *Overset* (*Journal-American* shop paper), November 9, 1965, Folder 2, Box 79, NGNY; Martin Tolchin, "Talks Bog Down on a Guild Pact," *NYT*, December 11, 1965, 27.

67. Damon Stetson, "World-Telegram President to Head Company Operating Merged Papers," *NYT*, March 29, 1966, 21; NGNY Executive Board Minutes, April 18, 1966, Folder 6, Box 149, NGNY; "U.S. Clears Merger," *NYT*, April 21, 1966, 36. On the *Herald Tribune*, its launching of *New York* magazine, and its relationship to the "New Journalism," see Kluger, *The Paper*, 671–736; and Marc Weingarten, *The Gang that Wouldn't Write Straight: Wolfe, Thompson, and the New Journalism Revolution* (New York: Crown, 2005), 67–96.

68. *Merger Strike Bulletin*, April 25, 1966, Folder 1, Box 134, NGNY; NGNY Executive Board Minutes, May 11, 1966, Folder 6, Box 149, NGNY; Stetson, "News Guild Split Threatens Talks," *NYT*, June 1, 1966, 44; Emanuel Perlmutter, "300 Offer to Quit in Paper Merger," *NYT*, June 5, 1966, 67; NGNY Executive Board Minutes, June 27, 1966, Folder 6, Box 149, NGNY; Stetson, "Tribune's Closing Could Reopen All Union Talks," *NYT*, August 14, 1965, 29; Murray Schumach, "Final Period: A Long, Losing Battle for Survival," *NYT*, August 16, 1966, 27; NGNY Executive Board Minutes, September 19, 1966, Folder 6, Box 149, NGNY.

69. Jimmy Breslin, "A Struck Paper, Famous and Needed, Goes Down," *Life*, August 26, 1966, 27–29.

70. NGNY Executive Board Minutes, September 19, 1966; McCandlish Phillips, "A Paper's Death Evokes Silence, Then Banter," *NYT*, May 6, 1967, 14; Sylvan Fox, "Paper Got Alarmingly Thin After Painful Birth Last Fall," *NYT*, May 6, 1967, 15;

NGNY Executive Board Minutes, May 15, 1967, NGNY, Box 149, Folder 6; A. H. Raskin, "What's Wrong with American Newspapers?" *NYT*, June 11, 1967, 249.

71. NGNY Executive Board Minutes, November 28, 1966, Folder 6, Box 149, NGNY; NGNY Executive Board Minutes, January 16, 1967, Folder 6, Box 149, NGNY; Emanuel Perlmutter, "Strike at Time, Inc., Averted by Pact," *NYT*, February 12, 1967, 37; NGNY Executive Board Minutes, February 20, 1967, Folder 6, Box 149, NGNY; NGNY Executive Board Minutes, April 22, 1967, Folder 6, Box 149, NGNY; NGNY Executive Board Minutes, September 25, 1967, Folder 6, Box 149, NGNY; NGNY Executive Board Minutes, April 22, 1968, Folder 6, Box 149, NGNY.

72. Magazine Council Minutes, May 21, 1968, Folder 3, Box 112, NGNY; Magazine Council Minutes, June 17, 1968, Folder 3, Box 112, NGNY; NGNY Executive Board Minutes, November 7, 1968, Folder 7, Box 149, NGNY; NGNY Executive Board Minutes, June 4, 1970, Folder 3, Box 150, NGNY; NGNY Executive Board Minutes, November 19, 1970, Folder 3, Box 150, NGNY.

73. Tom Murphy to Moe Potoker, August 7, 1963, Folder 2, Box 149, NGNY; NGNY Executive Board Minutes, March 16, 1965; NGNY Executive Board Minutes, April 22, 1968; NGNY Executive Board Minutes, November 20, 1969, Folder 2, Box 150, NGNY; NGNY Executive Board Minutes, May 21, 1970, Folder 3, Box 150, NGNY.

74. John Deegan to Albert Shanker, September 14, 1967, Folder 2, Box 134, NGNY; Thomas Murphy to Dorothy Schiff, September 14, 1967, Folder 2, Box 134, NGNY; NGNY Executive Board Minutes, September 25, 1967; NGNY Executive Board Minutes, September 25, 1967; Deegan to Leonard Arnold, September 28, 1967, Folder 2, Box 134, NGNY; A. H. Raskin, "Labor: Teachers' Strike—Impact on City and Law," *NYT*, October 1, 1967, 183.

75. NGNY Executive Board Minutes, September 24, 1968, Folder 6, Box 149, NGNY; "Negro Unionists Back Ocean Hill," *NYT*, October 26, 1968, 24; John Deegan to All Guildmembers, November 22, 1968, Folder 3, Box 134, NGNY; NGNY Executive Board Minutes, April 10, 1969, Folder 7, Box 149, NGNY; NGNY Executive Board Minutes, July 24, 1969, Folder 1, Box 150, NGNY. Also see Jim Sleeper, *The Closest of Strangers: Liberalism and the Politics of Race in New York* (New York: Norton, 1990), 98–103; Freeman, *Working-Class New York*, 213–27; and Ferguson, *Top Down*, 130–66.

76. NGNY Executive Board Minutes, September 17, 1970, Folder 3, Box 150, NGNY.

77. Neil Sheehan, "News Guild Aided by Groups Linked to CIA Conduits," *NYT*, February 17, 1967, 1, 14; Pete Hamill, "The Guild," *NYP*, February 21, 1967, 49; NGNY Executive Board Minutes, February 20, 1967.

78. Time, Inc. Guild Unit Council Resolution, May 13, 1970, Folder 5, Box 134, NGNY; John Deegan to Wilton Woods, May 15, 1970, Folder 3, Box 150, NGNY; NGNY Executive Board Minutes, May 21, 1970. Also see Freeman, *Working-Class New York*, 228–55.

79. NGNY Executive Committee Minutes, February 16, 1971, Folder 6, Box 150, NGNY.

80. On the flourishing of radical feminist organizing between 1968 and 1970, see Echols, *Daring to Be Bad*, 51–202.

81. Bryna Taubman, "The Great *Post* Backfire," *WM*, October 1969, 1, 4; "Action Project Needs You," *WM*, November 1969, 4; "*Women's Monthly* Hits the Movement Right on Time," *NNY*, November 1969, 5; "This Ad Insults Women," *NNY*, April 1970, 4; Susan Brownmiller, *In Our Time: A Memoir of a Revolution* (New York: Dial Press, 1999), 82–84.

82. "American Civil Liberties Union Women's Rights Project," *NNY*, January 1970, 3; Henry Raymont, "As *Newsweek* Says, Women Are in Revolt, Even on *Newsweek*," *NYT*, March 17, 1970, 30; NGNY Executive Board Minutes, March 19, 1970, Folder 2, Box 150, NGNY; Media Women's Association, *Rooms with No View: A Woman's Guide to the Man's World of the Media*, ed. Ethel Strainchamps (New York: Harper and Row, 1974), 56–60; Lynn Povich, *The Good Girls Revolt: How the Women of* Newsweek *Sued Their Bosses and Changed the Workplace* (New York: Public Affairs, 2012), 51–109.

83. "Time Inc. Accused of Bias by Women," *NYT*, May 4, 1970, 11; NGNY Executive Board Minutes, May 21, 1970; "Time Inc. and State Agree on Job Policy for Women," *NYT*, February 7, 1971, 33; Media Women, *Rooms with No View*, 34–41, 75–87.

84. Susan Brownmiller, "'Sisterhood Is Powerful': A Member of the Women's Liberation Movement Explains What It's All About," *NYT*, March 15, 1970, SM27, 128–36, 140; Grace Lichtenstein, "Feminists Demand 'Liberation' in *Ladies' Home Journal* Sit-In," *NYT*, March 19, 1970, 51; Brownmiller, *In Our Time*, 84–94. Also see Dow, *Watching Women's Liberation*, 95–119.

85. Susan Vanucci, Rita Mae Brown, and Michela Griffo, "1970," *NNY*, January 1970, 9–13; Media Women, *Rooms with No View*, 45–48; Brownmiller, *In Our Time*, 94–101. Also see Echols, *Daring to Be Bad*, 204–10.

86. Lilla Lyon, "The March of *Time's* Women," *NYmag*, February 22, 1971, 26–30; Povich, *Good Girls Revolt*, 89.

87. Elinor Ferry to Thomas J. Murphy, February 27, 1970, Folder 2, Box 150, NGNY; NGNY Executive Board Minutes, March 19, 1970; NGNY Executive Board Minutes, November 19, 1970; *Equality Now! A Report to the 1970 ANG Conference on Sex Discrimination and Women's Rights in the Industry* (Washington, DC: American Newspaper Guild, 1970), Folder 22, Box 75, NGNY; NGNY Executive Committee Minutes, June 22, 1971, Folder 6, Box 150, NGNY.

88. Midge Kovacs, "NOW Takes on 'The Good Grey Times,'" *NYW*, July 1972, 1; NGNY Executive Committee Minutes, December 19, 1972, Folder 8, Box 150, NGNY; Nan Robertson, *The Girls in the Balcony: Women, Men, and* The New York Times (New York: Random House, 1992), 140–59.

89. "*Newsweek* Agrees to Speed Promotion of Women," *NYT*, August 27, 1970, 30; "*Newsweek* Charged with Sex Bias by 50," *NYT*, May 17, 1972, 34; NGNY Executive Committee Minutes, May 23, 1972, Folder 8, Box 150, NGNY; Murray Illson, "*Newsweek* Signs Pact with Union," *NYT*, June 29, 1973, 57; NGNY Executive Committee Minutes, February 19, 1974, Folder 10, Box 150, NGNY; Media Women, *Rooms with No View*, 284–98; Povich, *Good Girls Revolt*, 111–54.

90. "Monitor Sexist Media," *NNY*, October 1970, 6; "Television Monitoring Project of N.O.W./N.Y. Image Committee," *NNY*, January 1971, 3; "Forms for Femmes, Etc., Now Required by FCC," *Variety*, December 22, 1971, 48.

91. On Sanders's role at ABC, see Dow, *Watching Women's Liberation*, 120–43.

92. George Gent, "Women's Group Challenges WABC-TV's Renewal," *NYT*, May 2, 1972, 87; "Citizens Groups Ganging up on N.Y. Vidstations at License Time," *Variety*, May 10, 1972, 1, 84; Judith Alder Hennessee and Joan Nicholson, "NOW Says: TV Commercials Insult Women," *NYT*, May 28, 1972, SM12–13, 48–51; Maria Lanteri, "NOW Challenges Male-Dominated WABC-TV," *New York Woman*, June 1972, 2.

93. NOW, "Proposed Agreement between WABC-TV and New York National Organization for Women," July 18, 1972, Folder 9, Box 12, NOW-NYC, 1–11.

94. Ibid.

95. Ibid., 12–34.

96. WABC-TV to Janice Goodman, New York Chapter NOW, undated [summer 1972], Folder 9, Box 12, NOW-NYC.

97. "Court to FCC: Action on NOW's Bias Beefs," *Variety*, January 29, 1975, 47; "NOW Challenges Vs. Network O&O's Rejected by FCC," *Variety*, March 26, 1975, 39.

98. Media Women, *Rooms with No View*, xxv-xxvi.

99. Ibid., 153–57. Also see Eric Pace, "Harper & Row Employees Set to Strike," *NYT*, June 16, 1974, 20; and Pace, "Harper Employees End 17-Day Strike," *NYT*, July 4, 1974, 17.

100. Judith Cummings, "Women in Media Hold Parley Here," *NYT*, December 8, 1974, 64; "Sanders Says Male Views of Femmes Hog TV Programs," *Variety*, December 11, 1974, 30, 41.

101. Cummings, "Women in Media Hold Parely Here." Also see Marylin Bender, "Macmillan Under the Gun," *NYT*, December 1, 1974, III, 1, 8.

102. Betsy Wade to Yetta Riesel, December 13, 1974, Folder 31, Box 1, BW-NG. Also see Robertson, *Girls in the Balcony*, 93–95, 137–40, 166–69.

103. Wade used her married name for the lawsuit, which was filed as *Elizabeth Boynton vs. The New York Times Company*. Robertson, *Girls in the Balcony*, 168–69.

104. Betsy Wade memo, August 3, 1976, Folder 31, Box 1, BW-NG. Also see Wade's reminiscences on her stint as president of the Women's Media Group in 1985 at http://www.womensmediagroup.org/our-history (Accessed August 8, 2017).

105. Lenora Williamson, "*N.Y. Times*, Women Staffers Settle Out of Court," *E&P*, October 21, 1978, 16, 39; Robertson, *Girls in the Balcony*, 199–212.

106. John Consoli, "Guild Grabs the Spotlight in N.Y. Newspaper Talks," *E&P*, April 8, 1978, 18, 66; "Violence Mars Strike by N.Y. News Guild," *E&P*, June 17, 1978, 8, 14; "Guild Ratifies 3-Year Pact at *New York News*," *E&P*, June 24, 1978, 42; Michael Murphy, "Lengthy New York Strike Predicted," *E&P*, August 19, 1978, 9, 12; "Strike Continues in New York," *E&P*, August 26, 1978, 9, 14.

107. "Murdoch Pulls Out of Joint Talks," *E&P*, September 30, 1978, 12; "Murdoch Makes Union Deal so *N.Y. Post* Can Publish," *E&P*, October 7, 1978, 10; John Consoli, "Murdoch: 'They Made a Complete Fool out of Me'," *E&P*, October 14, 1978, 13; "Tentative Long Term Pact Reached with N.Y. Pressmen," *E&P*, November 4, 1978, 12; Consoli, "*Times* and *Daily News* Publish Again in N.Y.," *E&P*, November 11, 1978, 12, 31.

108. Committee for the Responsibility Slate, "Responsibility Slate: New Guild Slate Fights to Return Union to Members," November 27, 1978, Folder 6, Box 2, BW-NG; Committee for the Responsibility Slate, "Q&A," 1978, Folder 6, Box 2, BW-NG.

109. On the impact of race-based affirmative action in American manufacturing, see Judith Stein, *Running Steel, Running America: Race, Economic Policy, and the Decline of American Liberalism* (Chapel Hill: University of North Carolina Press, 1998), 89–195. On labor activism by women and minorities more generally in the 1970s context of economic dislocation and diminished employment opportunities, see Lane Windham, *Knocking on Labor's Door: Union Organizing in the 1970s and the Roots of a New Economic Divide* (Chapel Hill: University of North Carolina Press, 2017), 1–81.

EPILOGUE

1. On the economic, political, and social impact of the energy crisis of the 1970s, see Meg Jacobs, *Panic at the Pump: The Energy Crisis and the Transformation of American Politics in the 1970s* (New York: Hill and Wang, 2016).

2. Annual data on income and wealth distribution in the United States is available through the World Wealth and Income Database at http://wid.world/country/usa/ (Accessed January 24, 2018).

3. Quarterly data on real gross domestic product per capita since 1947 is available through the Federal Reserve Economic Data (FRED) project of the Federal Reserve Bank of St. Louis at https://fred.stlouisfed.org/series/A939RX0Q048SBEA (Accessed January 24, 2018).

4. For an example of the pursuit of niche marketing segments, see, for instance, Karen Stabiner, "Tapping the Homosexual Market," *NYT*, May 2, 1982, SM34–36, SM74–81.

5. On postwar trends in manufacturing wages in New York City, see A. H. Raskin, "Wages Here Rank Lowest in Study of 18 Cities in U.S.," *NYT*, June 11, 1961, 1, 70;

Raskin, "Low Pay Called Pattern in City," *NYT*, June 26, 1961, 32; and Peter Kihss, "Planners Say Region Lost Population and Is Lagging in Economic Recovery," *NYT*, November 28, 1977, 35.

6. On New York City's fiscal crisis, and the way in which its resolution served as a model for neoliberal governance in the United States and abroad since the 1970s, see Freeman, *Working-Class New York*, 256–87; Jonathan Soffer, *Ed Koch and the Rebuilding of New York City* (New York: Columbia University Press, 2010), 105–20; Charles Morris, "Of Budgets, Taxes, and the Rise of a New Plutocracy," in *Summer in the City*, ed. Viteritti, 81–105; and Kim Phillips-Fein, *Fear City: New York's Fiscal Crisis and the Rise of Austerity Politics* (New York: Metropolitan Books, 2017).

7. Kihss, "Planners Say Region Lost Population and Is Lagging in Economic Recovery"; and Lee Daniels, "An Industry Poll Finds Landlords Expect 'Wave' of Abandonments," *NYT*, April 30, 1981, B3.

8. Midge Decter, "Looting and Liberal Racism," *Commentary*, September 1977, 48–54.

9. On Carter's visit, see Joseph Fried, "The South Bronx, U.S.A.," *NYT*, October 7, 1977, 27; and Fred Ferretti, "After 70 Years, South Bronx Street Is at a Dead End," *NYT*, October 21, 1977, 29. On the idea of a "culture of poverty," see Michael Harrington, *The Other America: Poverty in the United States* (New York: Macmillan, 1962), 14–18, 121–38; Alice O'Connor, *Poverty Knowledge: Social Science, Social Policy, and the Poor in Twentieth-Century U.S. History* (Princeton, NJ: Princeton University Press, 2001), 99–123; and Daniel Geary, *Beyond Civil Rights: The Moynihan Report and Its Legacy* (Philadelphia: University of Pennsylvania Press, 2015), 7, 32–41, 55–72, 186–93, 207–12.

10. See Alfred D. Chandler Jr., "The Competitive Performance of U.S. Industrial Enterprises since the Second World War," *BHR* 68, no. 1 (1994): 1–72; and Louis Hyman, "Rethinking the Postwar Corporation: Management, Monopolies, and Markets," in *What's Good for Business: Business and American Politics since World War Two*, ed. Kim Phillips-Fein and Julian Zelizer (New York: Oxford University Press, 2012), 195–211.

11. For a survey of some of the impediments faced by the supporters of organized labor more generally during the 1970s and early 1980s, see Jefferson Cowie, *Stayin' Alive: The 1970s and the Last Days of the Working Class* (New York: New Press, 2010), 23–74, 213–312.

12. Blake Fleetwood, "The New Elite and an Urban Renaissance," *NYT*, January 14, 1979, SM16–20, SM22, SM26, SM34–35. Also see Soffer, *Ed Koch*, 256–59; and Suleiman Osman, *Inventing Brownstone Brooklyn: Gentrification and the Search for Authenticity in Postwar New York* (New York: Oxford University Press, 2011), 270–80.

13. Boston Consulting Group, "The Media and Entertainment Industry in NYC: Trends and Recommendations for the Future," October 2015. Accessed on December 27, 2017 at http://www1.nyc.gov/assets/mome/pdf/bcg-report-10.15.pdf.

14. Jeff Greenfield, "TV Producers Are Nibbling at the Big Apple," *NYT*, July 31, 1977, X 1, 21.

15. Doug Hill, "TV Producers Have Their Eye on the Big Apple," *NYT*, August 16, 1981, D1, D21. Also see Dee Wedemeyer, "TV a Medium in Need of Space," *NYT*, March 26, 1978, R1, R6; "Astoria Studio Pushed," *NYT*, April 14, 1978, C22; and Lawrence Van Gelder, "East Side, West Side, the Cameras Are Rolling All Around the Town," *NYT*, April 13, 1980, D1, D10.

16. "Various Govt. and Other Monies Assure Re-Structure at Astoria," *Variety*, October 8, 1980, 5; "Showbiz Angels Up Astoria Studio Coin," *Variety*, November 25, 1981, 3; "Public, Private Elements Unite to Modernize the Astoria Studios," *Variety*, February 24, 1982, 4, 42; and Jim Robbins, "N.Y. Studio Facilities Prepare for '84 after Up & Down Year," *Variety*, Wednesday, January 11, 1984, 11, 80.

17. Shawn Kennedy, "A Film and TV Base Is Growing in Long Island City," *NYT*, November 23, 1983, B6. Also see "1st Silvercup Studio Claims Quick Sellout," *Variety*, August 17, 1983, 5, 33; and Robbins, "N.Y. Studio Facilities Prepare for '84 after Up & Down Year," *Variety*, Wednesday, January 11, 1984, 11, 80.

18. Helen Dudar, "Why 'Literary' Is a Dirty Word at Simon & Schuster," *NYmag*, January 16, 1978, 36–40. Also see Ann Crittenden, "Merger Fever in Publishing," *NYT*, October 23, 1977, F1, F9.

19. Thomas Whiteside, *The Blockbuster Complex: Conglomerates, Show Business, and Book Publishing* (Middletown, CT: Wesleyan University Press, 1981), 98.

20. "Authors League Glad McGraw Bd. Rebukes Am. Exp.," *Variety*, February 7, 1979, 3, 41; Edwin McDowell, "A Data Conglomerate: McGraw-Hill Takes Over the Numbers," *NYT*, September 9, 1979, F1, F9; Karen De Witt, "Authors Assail Publishers' Takeovers," *NYT*, March 14, 1980, C23; N. R. Kleinfield, "The Publishers' Year: Problems and a Few Solutions," *NYT*, December 28, 1980, BR3, BR14; and Whiteside, *Blockbuster Complex*, 123–38.

21. Edwin McDowell, "Angry Writers Talk of Forming a Union," *NYT*, May 27, 1982, C22; and McDowell, "Writers Union Meeting Criticizes Publishers," *NYT*, October 22, 1984, C19.

22. Philip Dougherty, "Advertising," *NYT*, December 4, 1978, D8; Dougherty, "Advertising," *NYT*, July 25, 1979, D13.

23. Philip Dougherty, "Lorimar Buying K&E," *NYT*, March 23, 1983, D19.

24. Sandra Salmans, "Saatchi & Saatchi's Buying Binge," *NYT*, July 14, 1985, F1, F21; Philip Dougherty, "Bates Said to Accept Saatchi Bid," *NYT*, May 12, 1986, D1; and Art Kleiner, "Bare Knuckles on Madison Avenue," *NYT*, November 8, 1987, SM34–39, SM95, SM102, SM112–13. Also see D. A. Leslie, "Global Scan: The Globalization of Advertising Agencies, Concepts, and Campaigns," *Economic Geography* 71 (1995): 402–26.

25. Eileen Prescott, "How Don Johnston Lost JWT," *NYT*, August 9, 1987, F1, F10; Randall Rothberg, "Brits Buy up the Ad Business," *NYT*, July 2, 1989, SM14–19, SM26, SM29, SM38.

26. Kleiner, "Bare Knuckles on Madison Avenue"; Philip Dougherty, "Celebrations Mask Fear at Agencies," *NYT*, December 24, 1987, D14; John Philip Jones, "The Advertising Slump: Cure the Industry with More Creativity," *NYT*, September 10, 1989, F3; and Aimee Stern, "Selling Yourself on Madison Avenue," *NYT*, October 1, 1989, F4.

27. See Thomas Kiernan, *Citizen Murdoch* (New York: Dodd, Mead & Co., 1986), 198–222; Nissenson, *Lady Upstairs*, 338–413; and Soffer, *Ed Koch*, 131.

28. "Guild Objects to Staff Cuts at N.Y. *Post*," *E&P*, April 15, 1978, 12; "Texans Train for New York *Post*," *NYT*, April 15, 1978, 16; Peter Kihss, "*Post* Notifies Guild It Is Dismissing 18," *NYT*, May 24, 1978, B2; and "N.Y. *Post* Dismisses 18 Guild Employees," *E&P*, May 27, 1970, 54.

29. NGNY Executive Committee Minutes, May 18, 1976, 4, Folder 2, Box 151, NGNY; "Time Inc. Is Threatened with Strike on Wednesday," *NYT*, May 27, 1976, 28; NGNY Executive Committee Minutes, June 15, 1976, 4–6, Folder 2, Box 151, NGNY.

30. "Time's Magazines Called On Schedule Despite the Strike," *NYT*, June 4, 1976, 31; "*Time* Publishes Issue; Labor Talks Slated Today," *NYT*, June 8, 1976, 29; NGNY Executive Committee Minutes, June 15, 1976, 4–6; Emanuel Perlmutter, "Guild Ends *Time* Strike; Pact Is Like June 2 Offer," *NYT*, June 22, 1976, 51; NGNY Executive Committee Minutes, September 21, 1976, 7–8, Folder 2, Box 151, NGNY; "On Time" unit newsletter, December 1, 1976, Folder 17, Box 166, NGNY; "On Time" unit newsletter, December 21, 1976, Folder 17, Box 166, NGNY

31. Daniel Menaker, "The Committee," *n + 1* no. 21 (Winter 2015): 19–40.

32. Rose Mary Mechem to Members of the Open Shop/Magazines Committee, January 30, 1979, Folder 19, Box 3, BW-NG; Harry Fisdell to Dear Fellow Guild Member, June 6, 1980, Folder 1, Box 2, BW-NG; David Kirkpatrick and Rose Mary Mechem to Guild Members, June 30, 1980, Folder 1, Box 2, BW-NG.

33. See, for instance, Betsy Wade to Thomas Bieluczyk and Bill Leukhardt, December 7, 1980, Folder 7, Box 2, BW-NG; *Backpage* (Membership Slate organ), December 10, 1980, Folder 7, Box 2, BW-NG; Joan Cook to Barry Lipton, April 30, 1982, Folder 3, Box 2, BW-NG; *Post* Unit Officers to Ed Egan and Barry Lipton, June 7, 1982, Folder 3, Box 2, BW-NG.

34. "*New York Times* Minorities Class Action Suit—Summary of Settlement," September 25, 1980, Folder 28, Box 4, BW-NG; Joy Cook to Ed Egan and Jim Orcutt, December 15, 1981, Folder 5, Box 3, BW-NG; David Hardy to Peter McLaughlin, January 15, 1986, Folder 12, Box 3, BW-NG.

35. Chris Welles, "The Bad News in Store for *The New York Times*," *NYmag*, April 12, 1976, 49–55; Edwin Egan to Hugh Carey, January 22, 1982, Folder 3, Box 2, BW-NG; Egan to George McDonald, February 1, 1982, Folder 3, Box 2, BW-NG: New York *News* Inc. Proposal to Newspaper Guild of New York, June 18, 1982, Folder 14, Box 1, BW-NG; *Talk of 42nd Street* (*News* unit shop paper), July 1982, Folder 14, Box 1, BW-NG.

36. "Newspaper Guild Conference: Health Protection for Operators of VDT's/ CRT's," flyer, May 1980, Folder 1, Box 2, BW-NG; *Backpage* (Membership Slate organ), December 3, 1980, Folder 7, Box 2, BW-NG.

37. Betsy Wade to Ellis Baker and Jim Cesnik, March 15, 1981, Folder 2, Box 2, BW-NG; James Orcuft to Joe Knowles, April 7, 1981, Folder 2, Box 2, BW-NG.

38. *Backpage* (Membership Slate organ), January 15, 1981, Folder 7, Box 2, BW-NG; Membership Slate, "Executive Committee Rescinds Action on Rerunning Election" flyer, September 18, 1981, Folder 7, Box 2, BW-NG; *Backpage* (Membership Slate organ), March 17, 1982, Folder 8, Box 2, BW-NG; Betsy Wade to Edwin Egan, May 20, 1982, Folder 3, Box 2, BW-NG.

39. *Backpage* (Membership Slate organ), September 2, 1982, Folder 8, Box 2, BW-NG. For their opponents' views, see the "Democratic Slate" campaign ephemera also in Folder 8, Box 2, BW-NG.

40. *Guild Strike News*, October 27, 1990, Folder 17, Box 1, BW-NG; Alessandra Stanley, "Some Guild Workers Rush to Picket, Others Mourn," *NYT*, October 27, 1990, 26; *Guild Strike News*, October 29, 1990, Folder 17, Box 1, BW-NG; *Guild Strike News*, October 30, 1990, Folder 17, Box 1, BW-NG; *Guild Strike News*, November 12, 1990, Folder 17, Box 1, BW-NG; *Guild Strike News*, November 27, 1990, Folder 17, Box 1, BW-NG; *Guild Strike News*, December 8, 1990, Folder 17, Box 1, BW-NG; *Guild Strike News*, December 22, 1990, Folder 17, Box 1, BW-NG; *Guild Strike News*, January 2, 1991, Folder 17, Box 1, BW-NG; *Guild Strike News*, January 8, 1991, Folder 17, Box 1, BW-NG; Alex Jones, "Saving *The News* Is Complicated by the Preparations for Its Demise," *NYT*, February 22, 1991, B3; *Guild Strike News*, February 27, 1991, Folder 17, Box 1, BW-NG; Jones, "Account of Failure: Talks at *The* News," *NYT*, March 3, 1991, 39; Alan Finder, "3 Unions at *The News* Would Bear Brunt of Job Cuts, Leaders Say," *NYT*, March 10, 1991, 30; *Guild Strike News*, March 12, 1991, Folder 17, Box 1, BW-NG; Jones, "Guild Fights Zuckerman Plan," *NYT*, June 26, 1992, B3; Jones, "What's Good for *Daily News* Means Different Things for Other Papers," *NYT*, September 20, 1992, 44; William Glaberson, "Zuckerman and Guild Battle as Sale of *The News* Nears," *NYT*, December 2, 1992, B3; Glaberson, "Seeds of a Newspaper Struggle," *NYT*, December 8, 1992, B3; Robert McFadden, "Taking Reins, Zuckerman Faces Union Challenge," *NYT*, January 9, 1993, 26; McFadden, "A Harsh Start to a New Beginning for Winnowed *Daily News*," *NYT*, January 10, 1993, 28; and NGNY, "Mort Massacres 180 Jobs!" pamphlet, 1993, Folder 19, Box 1, BW-NG.

41. Michel Marriott, "On Return, *Post* Employees Join in Ritual of Relief," *NYT*, February 22, 1988, B2; "Alex Jones, "*Post* Survives as Last Union Accepts Pact," *NYT*, September 18, 1990, B1–2; Jones, "*New York Post* Workers Are Offered Reassurances," *NYT*, August 21, 1991, D6; Steven Meyers, "From Defiance to Defeat: Union's Struggle Ends in Bitterness," *NYT*, October 3, 1993, 38; William Glaberson, "Waiting for the *Post* to Call," *NYT*, November 14, 1993, 40; and Don Bacheller memo, 1994, Folder 9, Box 1, BW-NG.

42. For an excellent analysis of one of the epic labor struggles in the newspaper industry outside of New York during the 1990s, see Chris Rhomberg, *The Broken Table: The Detroit Newspaper Strike and the State of American Labor* (New York: Russell Sage Foundation, 2012).

43. On the precarity of culture workers representing other forms of precarious labor, see Richard Wells, "The Labor of Reality TV: The Case of *The Deadliest Catch*," *Labor* 12, no. 4 (2015): 33–49. On conditions of culture workers more generally, see the essays in Michael Curtain and Kevin Sanson, eds., *Precarious Creativity: Global Media, Local Labor* (Oakland: University of California, 2016).

Bibliography

PRIMARY SOURCES

Manuscript Sources and Archives

American Catholic History Research Center and University Archives, Mullen Library, Catholic University of America, Washington, DC
  Congress of Industrial Organizations Central Office Records
Archives of American Art, Smithsonian Institution, Washington, DC and New York
  Elizabeth McCausland Papers
  Federal Art Project Records
  Francis V. O'Connor Papers
  Holger Cahill Papers
  Irene Rice Pereira Papers
  Rockwell Kent Papers
Archives of Labor and Urban Affairs, Walter P. Reuther Library, Wayne State University, Detroit
  Congress of Industrial Organizations, Office of the Secretary-Treasurer Records
  Donald Montgomery Papers
Billy Rose Theater Division, New York Public Library
Radio Writers Guild Records
Cooper Hewitt National Design Museum, Smithsonian Institution, New York
  Donald Wallance Collection
David M. Rubenstein Rare Book and Manuscript Library, Duke University, Durham, NC
  J. B. Matthews Research Collection
  J. Walter Thompson Company Collections
National Archives and Records Administration, College Park, MD
  National Labor Relations Board Records (Records Group 25)
Rare Book and Manuscript Library, Columbia University, New York
  Lewis Corey Papers

Schlesinger Manuscript Library, Radcliffe Institute, Harvard University, Cambridge, MA
Clara Savage Littledale Papers
Frances Ullman D'Armand Papers
Special Collections, Alexander Library, Rutgers University, New Brunswick, NJ
Consumers' Research Collection
Tamiment Library and Robert F. Wagner Labor Archives, New York University, New York
American Business Consultants' *Counterattack* Research Files
Betsy Wade's Newspaper Guild of New York Files
Clarina Michelson Papers
Congress of Industrial Organizations Files of John L. Lewis
Greater New York Industrial Union Council Minutes
National Organization for Women, New York City Chapter Records
New Yorkers at Work Oral History Collection
Newspaper Guild of New York Records
Norma Aronson Papers
Office Employees International Union Local 153 Minutes
Oral History of the American Left Collection
Peter Hawley and Jane Benedict Papers
Rabinowitz, Boudin, Standard, Krinsky, and Lieberman Legal Files
United Automobile, Aircraft, and Vehicle Workers of America, District 65 Records
United Scenic Artists Records
Wisconsin Center for Film and Theater Research, Wisconsin Historical Society, Madison
David Susskind Papers

Periodicals

Advertising Age
Advertising and Selling
American Federationist (AFL organ)
Architectural Forum
Architectural Record
Art Front (Artists' Union organ)
Arts and Decoration
Billboard
Bread and Butter (Consumers Union organ)
Broadcasting
Bulletin of the Congress of American Women
Bulletin of the Museum of Modern Art

Business Week
Career (UOPWA organ after *Office and Professional News*)
The Champion (UOPWA organ)
CIO News
Consumers' Research Bulletin
Consumers Union Reports (*Consumer Reports* after 1942)
Counterattack
Designing Engineer (Society of Designing Engineers organ)
Decisions of the National Labor Relations Board
Direction
Editor and Publisher
Everyday Art Quarterly
Fortune
Friday
Frontpage (Newspaper Guild of New York organ)
Guild News (Book and Magazine Guild organ)
Guild Reporter (American Newspaper Guild organ)
In Fact
Industrial Design
The Ledger (UOPWA organ prior to *Office and Professional News*)
Life
Madison Avenue
Magazine of Art
Metropolis
Monthly Labor Review
The Nation
National Guardian
New Masses
New Republic
New York Daily News
New York Guild News (Newspaper Guild of New York organ prior to *Frontpage*)
New York Herald Tribune
New York (Magazine)
New York Post
New York Times
New York Woman (NOW New York Chapter organ)
New York World-Telegram
The New Yorker
Newsweek
NOW New York (NOW New York Chapter organ)
Office and Professional News (UOPWA organ)
The Office Worker (BS&AU Local 12646 organ)

The Office Worker (OWU organ)
Parents
Pencil Points
PM
politics
Printer's Ink
Progressive Architecture
Progressive Citizen (PCA organ)
Publishers' Weekly
Reader's Scope
Saturday Evening Post
Space and Time
Sponsor
Sales Management
Tech Talk (FAECT organ)
Technical America (FAECT organ)
Tide
Time
The TV Writer (TWA organ)
Variety
Working Woman (CPUSA organ)

Books

AFL-CIO Industrial Union Department. *Labor Looks at the White-Collar Worker: Proceedings of Conference on the Problems of the White-Collar Worker.* Washington, DC: AFL-CIO, 1957.

Agee, James, and Walker Evans, *Let Us Now Praise Famous Men.* Boston: Houghton Mifflin, 1941.American Business Consultants. *Objective Study of United Office and Professional Workers of America, C.I.O. (Special Report No. 1).* New York: Counterattack, 1947.

American Business Consultants. *Red Channels: The Report of the Communist Influence in Radio and Television.* New York: Counterattack, 1950.American Woman's Association. *The Trained Woman and the Economic Crisis: Employment and Unemployment Among a Selected Group of Business and Professional Women in New York City.* New York: American Woman's Association, 1931.

American Woman's Association. *Women Workers Through the Depression: A Study of White Collar Employment Made by the American Woman's Association.* New York: Macmillan, 1934.

Aronovici, Carol, ed. *America Can't Have Housing.* New York: Committee on the Housing Exhibition by the Museum of Modern Art, 1934.

Belfrage, Cedric, and James Aronson. *Something to Guard: The Stormy Life of the National Guardian, 1948–1967*. New York: Columbia University Press, 1978

Bel Geddes, Norman. *Horizons*. Boston: Little and Brown, 1932.

Bell, Daniel. *The Coming of Post-Industrial Society: A Venture in Social Forecasting*. New York: Basic Books, 1973.

Bell, Daniel. *Work and Its Discontents: The Cult of Efficiency in America*. Boston: Beacon Press, 1956.

Bernstein, Walter. *Inside Out: A Memoir of the Blacklist*. New York: Knopf, 1996.

Bingham, Alfred. *Insurgent America: The Revolt of the Middle Classes*. New York: Harper, 1935.

Blake, Peter. *God's Own Junkyard: The Planned Deterioration of America's Landscape*. New York: Holt, Rinehart and Winston, 1964.

Blum, Albert A. *Management and the White-Collar Union*. New York: American Management Association, 1964.

Bollens, Leo. *White-Collar or Noose? The Occupation of Millions*. New York: North River Press, 1947.

Brownmiller, Susan. *In Our Time: A Memoir of a Revolution*. New York: Dial Press, 1999.

Caplovitz, David. *The Poor Pay More: Consumer Practices of Low-Income Families*. Glencoe, IL: Free Press, 1963.

Carson, Rachel. *Silent Spring*. New York: Houghton Mifflin, 1962.

Chambers, Whittaker. *Witness*. New York: Random House, 1952.

Chase, Stuart. *The Tragedy of Waste*. New York: Macmillan, 1925.

Chase, Stuart, and F. J. Schlink. *Your Money's Worth: A Study in the Waste of the Consumer's Dollar*. New York: Macmillan, 1927.

Cogley, John. *Report on Blacklisting: Volume Two, Radio and Television*. New York: Fund for the Republic, 1956.

Corey, Lewis. *The Crisis of the Middle Class*. New York: Covici, Friede, 1935.

Della Femina, Jerry, with Charles Sopkin. *From Those Wonderful Folks Who Gave You Pearl Harbor: Front-Line Dispatches from the Advertising War*. New York: Simon and Schuster, 1970.

Department of Labor. *The Termination Report of the National War Labor Board: Industrial Disputes and Wage Stabilization in Wartime*. 3 vols. Washington, DC: G.P.O., 1947.

Federal Communications Commission. *Public Service Responsibility of Broadcast Licensees*. Washington, DC: G.P.O., 1946.

Federal Communications Commission, Office of Network Study. *Second Interim Report: Television Network Program Procurement, Part II*. Washington, DC: G.P.O., 1965.

Friedrich, Otto. *Decline and Fall: The Struggle for Power at a Great American Magazine, The Saturday Evening Post*. New York: Harper & Row, 1970.

Galbraith, John Kenneth. *The Affluent Society*. Boston: Houghton Mifflin, 1958.

Gilmor, Daniel. *Fear, the Accuser*. New York: Abelard-Schuman, 1954.

Harrington, Michael. *The Other America: Poverty in the United States.* New York: Macmillan, 1962.

Hawes, Elizabeth. *Hurry Up Please, It's Time.* New York: Reynal and Hitchcock, 1946.

Hawes, Elizabeth. *Why Women Cry? Or, Wenches with Wrenches.* New York: Reynal and Hitchcock, 1943.Hellman, Lillian. *Scoundrel Time.* Boston: Little, Brown, 1976.

Hersey, John. *A Bell for Adano.* New York: Knopf, 1944.

Hitchcock, Henry-Russell Jr., and Philip Johnson. *The International Style: Architecture Since 1922.* New York: Norton, 1932.

Hofstadter, Richard. *The Age of Reform: From Bryan to F.D.R.* New York: Vintage, 1955.

Horowitz, Irving, ed. *Power, Politics, and People: The Collected Essays of C. Wright Mills.* New York: Oxford University Press, 1963.

Ingersoll, Ralph. *Point of Departure: An Adventure in Autobiography.* New York: Harcourt and Brace, 1961.

Kahn, Albert. *Treason in Congress: The Record of the House Un-American Activities Committee.* New York: Progressive Citizens of America, 1948.

Kallet, Arthur. *Counterfeit: Not Your Money but What It Buys.* New York: Vanguard Press, 1935.

Konecky, Eugene. *The American Communications Conspiracy.* New York: People's Radio Foundation, 1948.

Lathrop, Milo. *Home Front: A Victory Program for Trade Union Consumers.* New York: Consumers Union, 1942.

Lawrence, Mary Wells. *A Big Life in Advertising.* New York: Knopf, 2002.

League of Professional Groups for Foster and Ford. *Culture and the Crisis: An Open Letter to the Writers, Artists, Teachers, Physicians, Engineers, Scientists, and other Professional Workers of America.* New York: n.p., 1932.

Loewy, Raymond. *Industrial Design.* Woodstock: Overlook Press, 1979.

Loewy, Raymond. *Never Leave Well Enough Alone.* New York: Simon and Schuster, 1951.

Lois, George, with Bill Pitts. *George, Be Careful.* New York: Saturday Review Press, 1972.

Lundberg, Ferdinand, and Marynia Farnham. *Modern Woman: The Lost Sex.* New York: Harper and Bros., 1947.

Lynd, Robert, and Helen Lynd. *Middletown: A Study in Modern American Culture.* New York: Harcourt and Brace, 1929.

Marot, Helen. *American Labor Unions.* New York: Henry Holt, 1914.

Matthews, J. B., and R. E. Shallcross. *Partners in Plunder: The Cost of Business Dictatorship.* New York: Covici, Friede, 1935.

Mayer, Martin. *Madison Avenue, U.S.A.* New York: Harper and Brothers, 1958.

McGilligan, Patrick, and Paul Buhle, eds. *Tender Comrades: A Backstory of the Hollywood Blacklist.* New York: St. Martin's Press, 1997.

Media Women's Association. *Rooms with No View: A Woman's Guide to the Man's World of the Media*, ed. Ethel Strainchamps. New York: Harper and Row, 1974.

Miller, Merle. *The Judges and the Judged: A Report for the American Civil Liberties Union.* New York: Doubleday, 1952.

Mills, C. Wright. *White Collar: The American Middle Classes.* New York: Oxford University Press, 1951.

Mills, C. Wright. *The New Men of Power: America's Labor Leaders.* New York: Harcourt, Brace and Co., 1948.

Mitchell, Wesley, ed. *Recent Social Trends in the United States.* New York: McGraw-Hill, 1932.

Mumford, Lewis. *Technics and Civilization.* New York: Harcourt, Brace and Co., 1934.

Nader, Ralph. *Unsafe at Any Speed: The Designed-In Dangers of the American Automobile.* New York: Grossman, 1965.

National Industrial Conference Board. *Clerical Salaries in the United States.* New York: National Industrial Conference Board, 1926.

National War Labor Board. *Directive Orders and Opinions of the National War Labor Board in the "Little Steel" Case.* Washington, DC: G.P.O., 1942.

Packard, Vance. *The Waste Makers.* New York: David McKay, 1960.

Pastin, John. *White Collar Organization in Industrial Unions.* Pittsburgh: United Steelworkers of America, 1958.

Phillips, M. C. *Skin Deep: The Truth about Beauty Aids.* New York: Vanguard Press, 1934.

Povich, Lynn. *The Good Girls Revolt: How the Women of* Newsweek *Sued Their Bosses and Changed the Workplace.* New York: Public Affairs, 2012.

Rand, Paul. *From Lascaux to Brooklyn.* New Haven, CT: Yale University Press, 1996.

Raymond Loewy Associates. *Supermarkets of the Sixties.* Chicago: Super Market Institute, 1960.

Raymond Loewy/William Snaith Inc. *The Motivations Toward Homes and Housing.* New York: The Project Home Committee, 1967.

Riesman, David, with Nathan Glazer and Reuel Denney. *The Lonely Crowd: The Changing American Social Character.* New Haven, CT: Yale University Press, 1950.

Robertson, Nan. *The Girls in the Balcony: Women, Men, and* The New York Times. New York: Random House, 1992.

Rorty, James. *Our Master's Voice: Advertising.* New York: John Day Co., 1934.

Rorty, James. *Where Life Is Better: An Unsentimental American Journey.* New York: Reynal and Hitchcock, 1936. Rosenberg, Bernard, and David Manning White, eds. *Mass Culture: The Popular Arts in America.* Glencoe, IL: Free Press, 1957.

Schlink, F. J. *Eat, Drink, and Be Wary.* New York: Covici, Friede, 1935.

Schlink, F. J., and Arthur Kallet. *100,000,000 Guinea Pigs: Dangers in Everyday Food, Drugs and Cosmetics.* New York: Vanguard Press, 1932.

Seldes, George. *Freedom of the Press.* New York: Harper, 1935.

Seldes, George. *Lords of the Press.* New York: Julian Messner, 1938.

Seldes, George. *Never Tire of Protesting.* New York: Lyle Stuart, 1968. Seldes, George. *Sawdust Caesar: The Untold History of Mussolini and Fascism.* New York: Harper, 1935.

Seldes, George. *Tell the Truth and Run.* New York: Greenberg, 1953.

Seldes, George. *You Can't Print That: The Truth behind the News.* Garden City: Garden City, 1927.

Seldes, Gilbert. *The Seven Lively Arts.* New York: Harper, 1924.

Steward, Paul, J. Frederic Dewhurst, and Louise Field. *Does Distribution Cost Too Much? A Review of the Costs Involved in Current Marketing Methods and a Program for Improvement.* New York: Twentieth Century Fund, 1939.

Trumbo, Dalton. *The Time of the Toad: A Study of Inquisition in America by One of the Hollywood Ten.* Hollywood, CA: Hollywood Ten, 1949.

United Office and Professional Workers of America. *Officers' Report to the Seventh Constitutional Convention of the United Office and Professional Workers of America, CIO.* New York: United Office and Professional Workers of America, 1948.

United Office and Professional Workers of America. *Report of the General Executive Board to the Fifth Constitutional Convention of the United Office and Professional Workers of America, CIO.* New York: United Office and Professional Workers of America, 1944.United States Senate, Committee on Education and Labor. *Fixed Incomes in the War Economy: Hearings before the Subcommittee on Wartime Health and Education of the Committee on Education and Labor,* United States Senate, 78th Congress, 2nd Session, Part 3. Washington, DC: G.P.O., 1944.

Veblen, Thorstein. *Absentee Ownership and Business Enterprise in Recent Times.* New York: B. W. Hubesch, 1923.

Veblen, Thorstein. *The Theory of Business Enterprise.* New York: Scribner and Sons, 1904.

Veblen, Thorstein. *The Theory of the Leisure Class.* New York: Macmillan, 1899.

Venturi, Robert, and Denise Scott Brown, with Steve Izenour. *Learning from Las Vegas.* Cambridge, MA: MIT Press, 1972.

Victor Gruen Associates. *Shopping Centers of Tomorrow.* New York: American Federation of Arts, 1954.

Wallance, Donald. *Shaping America's Products.* New York: Reinhold, 1956.

Whiteside, Thomas. *The Blockbuster Complex: Conglomerates, Show Business, and Book Publishing.* Middletown, CT: Wesleyan University Press, 1981.

Whyte, William H. Jr. *The Organization Man.* New York: Simon and Schuster, 1956.

SECONDARY SOURCES

Abercrombie, Stanley. *George Nelson: The Design of Modern Design.* Cambridge, MA: MIT Press, 1994.

Agnew, Jean-Christophe. "A Touch of Class." *democracy* 3, no. 2 (1983): 59–72.

Allen, James Sloan. *The Romance of Commerce and Culture: Capitalism, Modernism, and the Chicago-Aspen Crusade for Cultural Reform.* Chicago: University of Chicago Press, 1983.

Altenbaugh, Richard. *Education for Struggle: The American Labor Colleges of the 1920s and 1930s.* Philadelphia: Temple University Press, 1990.

Alvey, Mark. "The Independents: Rethinking the Television Studio System." In *The Revolution Wasn't Televised: Sixties Television and Social Conflict*, edited by Lynn Spiegel and Michael Curtin, 139–58. New York: Routledge, 1997.

Alwood, Edward. *Dark Days in the Newsroom: McCarthyism Aimed at the Press*. Philadelphia: Temple University Press, 2007.

Baldasty, Gerald. *E. W. Scripps and the Business of Newspapers*. Urbana: University of Illinois Press, 1999.

Banta, Martha. *Taylored Lives: Narrative Productions in the Age of Taylor, Veblen, and Ford*. Chicago: University of Chicago Press, 1993.

Barnouw, Erik. *The Golden Web: A History of Broadcasting in the United States, 1933–1953*. New York: Oxford University Press, 1968.

Barnouw, Erik. *The Image Empire: A History of Broadcasting in the United States, Volume III—from 1953*. New York: Oxford University Press, 1970.

Barnouw, Erik. *A Tower in Babel: A History of American Broadcasting to 1933*. New York: Oxford University Press, 1966.

Baughman, James. *The Republic of Mass Culture: Journalism, Filmmaking, and Broadcasting in American since 1941*. 2nd ed. Baltimore: Johns Hopkins University Press, 1997.

Baughman, James. *Same Time, Same Station: Creating American Television, 1948–1961*. Baltimore: Johns Hopkins University Press, 2007.

Bayley, Stephen. *Harley Earl and the Dream Machine*. New York: Knopf, 1983.

Bearor, Karen A. "The Design Laboratory: New Deal Experiment in Self-Conscious Vanguardism." *Southeastern College Art Conference Review* 13, no. 1 (1996): 14–31.

Becker, Craig. "A Wide View of the Wagner Act at Eighty." *Labor* 14, no. 3 (Summer 2017): 49–53.

Bell, Jonathan. *The Liberal State on Trial: The Cold War and American Politics in the Truman Years*. New York: Columbia University Press, 2004.

Bentley, Joanne. *Hallie Flanagan: A Life in the American Theater*. New York: Knopf, 1988.

Binkiewicz, Donna. *Federalizing the Muse: United States Art Policy and the National Endowment for the Arts, 1965–1980*. Chapel Hill: University of North Carolina Press, 2004.

Birch, Bettina. *Radical by Design: The Life and Style of Elizabeth Hawes*. New York: Dutton, 1988.

Black, Cheryl. "'New Negro' Performance in Art and Life: Fredi Washington and the Theatrical Columns of the *People's Voice*, 1943–47," *Theater History Studies* 24 (June 2004): 57–72.

Blake, Casey. *Beloved Community: The Cultural Criticism of Randolph Bourne, Van Wyck Brooks, Waldo Frank, and Lewis Mumford*. Chapel Hill: University of North Carolina Press, 1990.

Bledstein, Burton. *The Culture of Professionalism: The Middle Class and the Development of Higher Education in America*. New York: Norton, 1978.

Blum, John Morton. *V Was for Victory: Politics and American Culture During World War II*. New York: Harcourt Brace Jovanovich, 1976.

Boddy, William. *Fifties Television: The Industry and Its Critics*. Urbana: University of Illinois Press, 1992.

Boddy, William. *New Media and Popular Imagination: Launching Radio, Television, and Digital Media in the United States*. New York: Oxford University Press, 2004.

Bogart, Michele. *Artists, Advertising, and the Borders of Art*. Chicago: University of Chicago Press, 1995.

Boris, Eileen. *Art and Labor: Ruskin, Morris, and the Craftsman Ideal in America*. Philadelphia: Temple University Press, 1986.

Boyle, Kevin. *The UAW and the Heyday of American Liberalism, 1945–1968*. Ithaca, NY: Cornell University Press, 1995.

Brandt, Nat. *Harlem at War: The Black Experience in WWII*. Syracuse: Syracuse University Press, 1996.

Brenson, Michael. *Visionaries and Outcasts: The NEA, Congress, and the Place of the Visual Artist in America*. New York: New Press, 2001.Brick, Howard. *The Age of Contradiction: American Thought and Culture during the Sixties*. Ithaca, NY: Cornell University Press, 2000.

Brick, Howard. *Daniel Bell and the Decline of Intellectual Radicalism*. Madison: University of Wisconsin Press, 1986.

Brick, Howard. *Transcending Capitalism: Visions of a New Society in Modern American Thought*. Cornell: Cornell University Press, 2006.Brinkley, Alan. *The End of Reform: New Deal Liberalism in Recession and War*. New York: Knopf, 1995.

Brinkley, Alan. *The Publisher: Henry Luce and His American Century*. New York: Knopf, 2010.

Brinkley, Alan. "Richard Hofstadter's *The Age of Reform:* A Reconsideration." *Reviews in American History* 13, no. 3 (1985): 462–80.

Brown, David. *Richard Hofstadter: An Intellectual Biography*. Chicago: University of Chicago Press, 2006.

Bryan-Wilson, Julia. *Art Workers: Radical Practice in the Vietnam War Era*. Berkeley: University of California Press, 2009.

Buhle, Paul. *A Dreamer's Paradise Lost: Louis C. Fraina/Lewis Corey (1892–1953) and the Decline of Radicalism in the United States*. Atlantic Highlands, NJ: Humanities Press, 1995.

Buhle, Paul, and Dave Wagner. *Hide in Plain Sight: The Hollywood Blacklistees in Film and Television, 1950–2002*. New York: Palgrave, 2003.

Caro, Robert. *The Power Broker: Robert Moses and the Fall of New York*. New York: Knopf, 1974.

Carruthers, Susan. "'Produce More Joppolos': John Hersey's *A Bell for Adano* and the Making of the 'Good Occupation.'" *Journal of American History* 100, no. 4 (2014): 1086–113.

Caute, David. *The Great Fear: The Anti-Communist Purge under Truman and Eisenhower*. New York: Simon and Schuster, 1978.

Chandler, Alfred D. Jr. "The Competitive Performance of U.S. Industrial Enterprises since the Second World War." *Business History Review* 68, no. 1 (1994): 1–72.

Chandler, Alfred D. Jr. *The Visible Hand: The Managerial Revolution in American Business*. Cambridge, MA: Belknap Press, 1977.

Clayton, Virginia Tuttle. "Picturing a 'Usable Past.'" In *Drawing on America's Past: Folk Art, Modernism, and the Index of American* Design, edited by Virginia Tuttle Clayton, Elisabeth Stillinger, Erika Doss, and Deborah Chotner, 1–43. Washington, DC and Chapel Hill: National Gallery of Art/University of North Carolina Press, 2002.

Cobble, Dorothy Sue. *The Other Women's Movement: Workplace Justice and Social Rights in Modern America*. Princeton, NJ: Princeton University Press, 2004.

Cobble, Dorothy Sue. "A Wagner Act for Today: Save the Preamble but Not the Rest?" *Labor* 14, no. 3 (Summer 2017): 43–47.

Cogdell, Christina. "The Futurama Recontextualized: Norman Bel Geddes' Eugenic 'World of Tomorrow.'" *American Quarterly* 52 (June 2000): 193–245.

Cohen, Lizabeth. *A Consumers' Republic: The Politics of Mass Consumption in Postwar America*. New York: Knopf, 2003.

Cohen, Lizabeth. *Making a New Deal: Industrial Workers in Chicago, 1919–1939*. New York: Cambridge University Press, 1990.

Cohen, Lizabeth, and Brian Goldstein. "Governing at the Tipping Point: Shaping the City's Role in Economic Development." In *Summer in the City: John Lindsay, New York, and the American Dream*, edited by Joseph Viteritti, 163–92. Baltimore: Johns Hopkins University Press, 2014.

Cowie, Jefferson. *Stayin' Alive: The 1970s and the Last Days of the Working Class*. New York: New Press, 2010.

Curtain, Michael, and Kevin Sanson, eds. *Precarious Creativity: Global Media, Local Labor*. Oakland: University of California Press, 2016.

Davis, Clark. *Company Men: White-Collar Life and Corporate Cultures in Los Angeles, 1892–1941*. Baltimore: Johns Hopkins University Press, 2001.

Davis, Mike. *Prisoners of the American Dream: Politics and Economy in the History of the U.S. Working Class*. New York: Verso, 1987.

Davis, Natalie Zemon. "Toward Mixtures and Margins." *American Historical Review* 97, no. 5 (1992): 1409–16.

Denenberg, Thomas. *Wallace Nutting and the Invention of Old America*. New Haven, CT: Yale University Press, 2003.

Denning, Michael. *The Cultural Front: The Laboring of American Culture in the Twentieth Century*. New York: Verso, 1996.

DeVault, Ileen. *Sons and Daughters of Labor: Class and Clerical Work in Turn-of-the-Century Pittsburgh*. Ithaca, NY: Cornell University Press, 1990.

Devine, Thomas. *Henry Wallace's 1948 Presidential Campaign and the Future of Postwar Liberalism*. Chapel Hill: University of North Carolina Press, 2013.

Devlin, Rachel. *Relative Intimacy: Fathers, Adolescent Daughters, and Postwar American Culture*. Chapel Hill: University of North Carolina Press, 2005.

Doss, Erika. "American Folk Art's 'Distinctive Character': The Index of American Design and New Deal Notions of Cultural Nationalism." In *Drawing on America's Past: Folk Art, Modernism, and the Index of American Design*, edited by Virginia Tuttle Clayton, Elisabeth Stillinger, Erika Doss, and Deborah Chotner, 61–73. Washington, DC and Chapel Hill: National Gallery of Art/University of North Carolina Press, 2002.

Douglas, Susan. *Inventing American Broadcasting, 1899–1922*. Baltimore: Johns Hopkins University Press, 1987.

Douglas, Susan. *Listening In: Radio and the American Imagination*. Minneapolis: University of Minnesota Press, 2004.

Dow, Bonnie. *Watching Women's Liberation, 1970: Feminism's Pivotal Year on the Network News*. Urbana: University of Illinois Press, 2014.

DuBois, Ellen. "Eleanor Flexner and the History of American Feminism," *Gender and Society* 3, no. 1 (1991): 81–90.

Echols, Alice. *Daring to Be Bad: Radical Feminism in America, 1967–1975*. Minneapolis: University of Minnesota Press, 1989.

Ehrenreich, Barbara, and John Ehrenreich, "The Professional-Managerial Class." *Radical America* 11, no. 2 (March–April 1977): 7–31.

Ermann, M. David. "The Operative Goals of Corporate Philanthropy: Contributions to the Public Broadcasting Service, 1972–1976." *Social Problems* 25, no. 5 (1978): 504–14.

Everitt, David. *A Shadow of Red: Communism and the Blacklist in Radio and Television*. Chicago: Ivan R. Dee, 2007.

Ferguson, Karen. *Top Down: The Ford Foundation, Black Power, and the Reinvention of Racial Liberalism*. Philadelphia: University of Pennsylvania Press, 2013.

Fine, Gary. "The Social Construction of Style: Thorstein Veblen's *The Theory of the Leisure Class* as Contested Text." *Sociological Quarterly* 35, no. 3 (1994): 457–72.

Finley, Joseph. *White-Collar Union: The Story of the OPEIU and Its People*. New York: Octagon Books, 1975.

Fisk, Catherine. *Writing for Hire: Unions, Hollywood, and Madison Avenue*. Cambridge, MA: Harvard University Press, 2016.

Flink, James. *The Automobile Age*. Cambridge, MA: MIT Press, 1988.

Florida, Richard. *The Rise of the Creative Class*. New York: Basic Books, 2002.

Fones-Wolf, Elizabeth. *Selling Free Enterprise: The Business Assault on Labor and Liberalism, 1945–60*. Urbana: University of Illinois Press, 1994.

Fones-Wolf, Elizabeth. *Waves of Opposition: Labor and the Struggle for Democratic Radio*. Urbana: University of Illinois Press, 2006.

Forty, Adrian. *Objects of Desire*. New York: Pantheon, 1986.

Fox, Richard. "Epitaph for *Middletown:* Robert S. Lynd and the Analysis of Consumer Culture." In *The Culture of Consumption: Critical Essays in American History, 1880– 1980,* edited by Richard Fox and Jackson Lears, 101–41. New York: Pantheon, 1983.

Frank, Dana. *Purchasing Power: Consumer Organizing, Gender, and the Seattle Labor Movement, 1919–1929.* New York: Cambridge University Press, 1994.

Frank, Thomas. *The Conquest of Cool: Business Culture, Counterculture, and the Rise of Hip Consumerism.* Chicago: University of Chicago Press, 1997.

Fraser, Steven. *Labor Will Rule: Sidney Hillman and the Rise of American Labor.* New York: Free Press, 1991.

Freeman, Joshua. *In Transit: The Transport Workers Union in New York City, 1933–1966.* New York: Oxford University Press, 1989.

Freeman, Joshua. *Working-Class New York: Life and Labor since World War Two.* New York: New Press, 2001.

Fried, Richard. "'Operation Polecat': Thomas E. Dewey, the 1948 Election, and the Origins of McCarthyism." *Journal of Policy History* 22, no. 1 (2010): 1–22.

Friedman, Walter. *Birth of a Salesman: The Transformation of Selling in America.* Cambridge, MA: Harvard University Press, 2004.

Friedman, Tami. "Exploiting the North-South Differential: Corporate Power, Southern Politics, and the Decline of Organized Labor after World War Two." *Journal of American History* 95 (September 2008): 323–48.

Gabin, Nancy. *Feminism in the Labor Movement: Women and the United Auto Workers, 1935–1975.* Ithaca, NY: Cornell University Press, 1990.

Gartman, David. *Auto Opium: A Social History of Automobile Design.* New York: Routledge, 1994.

Geary, Daniel. *Beyond Civil Rights: The Moynihan Report and Its Legacy.* Philadelphia: University of Pennsylvania Press, 2015.

Geary, Daniel. *Radical Ambition: C. Wright Mills, the Left, and American Social Thought.* Berkeley: University of California Press, 2009.

Geary, Daniel. "The 'Union of the Power and the Intellect': C. Wright Mills and the Labor Movement." *Labor History* 42, no. 4 (2001): 327–45.

Geismer, Lily. *Don't Blame Us: Suburban Liberals and the Transformation of the Democratic Party.* Princeton, NJ: Princeton University Press, 2015.

Gellman, Erik. *Death Blow to Jim Crow: The National Negro Congress and the Rise of Militant Civil Rights.* Chapel Hill: University of North Carolina Press, 2012.

Genter, Robert. *Late Modernism: Art, Culture, and Politics in Cold War America.* Philadelphia: University of Pennsylvania Press, 2010.

Georgakas, Dan and Marvin Surkin. *Detroit: I Do Mind Dying: A Study in Urban Revolution* (1975), rev. 3rd ed. Chicago: Haymarket Books, 2012.

Glickman, Lawrence. *Free Enterprise: An American History.* New Haven, CT: Yale University Press, 2019.

Glickman, Lawrence. *A Living Wage: American Workers and the Making of Consumer Society.* Ithaca, NY: Cornell University Press, 1997.

Glickman, Lawrence. "The Strike in the Temple of Consumption: Consumer Activism and Twentieth-Century American Political Culture." *Journal of American History* 88 (June 2001): 99–128.

Godfried, Nathan. "Struggling over Politics and Culture: Organized Labor and Radio Station WEVD during the 1930s." *Labor History* 42, no. 4 (2001): 347–69.

Godfried, Nathan. *WCFL: Chicago's Voice of Labor, 1926–78.* Urbana: University of Illinois Press, 1997.

Goldin, Claudia. "America's Graduation from High School: The Evolution and Spread of Secondary Schooling in the Twentieth Century." *Journal of Economic History* 58 (June 1998): 345–74.

Goldin, Claudia. "Egalitarianism and the Returns to Education during the Great Transformation of American Education." *Journal of Political Economy* 107 (December 1999): S65–S94.

Goldin, Claudia, and Robert Margo. "The Great Compression: The Wage Structure in the United States at Mid-Century." *Quarterly Journal of Economics* 107 (February 1992): 1–34.

Goldstein, Robert. *American Blacklist: The Attorney General's List of Subversive Organizations.* Lawrence: University of Kansas Press, 2008.

Golia, Julia. "Courting Women, Courting Advertisers: The Woman's Page and the Transformation of the American Newspaper, 1895–1935." *Journal of American History* 103 (2016): 606–28.

Gonzáles, Juan and Joseph Torres, *News for All the People: The Epic Story of Race and the American Media.* New York: Verso, 2011.

Gordon, Colin. *New Deals: Business, Labor, and Politics in America, 1920–1935.* New York: Cambridge University Press, 1994.

Green, Martin. *New York, 1913: The Armory Show and the Paterson Strike Pageant.* New York: Scribner, 1988.

Greenberg, Cheryl. "The Politics of Disorder: Reexamining Harlem's Riots of 1935 and 1943," *Journal of Urban History* 18, no. 4 (1992): 395–441.

Griffith, Robert. "The Selling of America: The Advertising Council and American Politics, 1942–1960." *Business History Review* 57, no. 3 (1983): 388–412.

Guarneri, Julia. *Newsprint Metropolis: City Papers and the Making of Modern Americans.* Chicago: University of Chicago Press, 2017.

Gutenplan, D. D. *American Radical: The Life and Times of I. F. Stone.* Evanston: Northwestern University Press, 2012.

Haddow, Robert. *Pavilions of Plenty: Exhibiting American Culture Abroad in the 1950s.* Washington, DC: Smithsonian Institution Press, 1997.

Hamby, Alonzo. "The Vital Center, the Fair Deal, and the Quest for a Liberal Political Economy." *American Historical Review* 77, no. 3 (1972): 653–78.

Hardwick, Jeffrey. *Mall Maker: Victor Gruen, Architect of an American Dream.* Philadelphia: University of Pennsylvania Press, 2001.

Harrington, Michael. "Catholics in the Labor Movement: A Case History." *Labor History* 1, no. 3 (1960): 231–63.

Harris, Howell John. *The Right to Manage: Industrial Relations Policies of American Business in the 1940s.* Madison: University of Wisconsin Press, 1982.

Hartman, Susan M. "Women's Employment and the Domestic Ideal in the Early Cold War Years." In *Not June Cleaver: Women and Gender in Postwar America, 1945–1960,* edited by Joanne Meyerowitz, 84–100. Philadelphia: Temple University Press, 1994.

Harvey, David. *A Brief History of Neoliberalism.* New York: Oxford University Press, 2005.

Harvey, David. *The Condition of Postmodernity.* New York: Basil Blackwell, 1993.

Harwood, John. *The Interface: IBM and the Transformation of Corporate Design, 1945–1976.* Minneapolis: University of Minnesota Press, 2011.

Hawley, Ellis. *The New Deal and the Problem of Monopoly: A Study in Economic Ambivalence.* Princeton, NJ: Princeton University Press, 1966.

Haynes, John Earl and Harvey Klehr. *Venona: Decoding Soviet Espionage in America.* New Haven, CT: Yale University Press, 1999.

Helfand, Jessica. *Paul Rand: American Modernist.* New York: William Drenttel, 1998.

Heller, Steven. *Paul Rand.* New York: Phaidon, 2000.Hemingway, Andrew. *Artists on the Left: American Artists and the Communist Movement, 1926–1956.* New Haven, CT: Yale University Press, 2002.

Hemingway, Andrew. "Cultural Democracy by Default: The Politics of the New Deal Art Programmes." *Oxford Art Journal* 30, no. 2 (2007): 271–87.

Hills, Patricia. "1936: Meyer Schapiro, *Art Front*, and the Popular Front." *Oxford Art Journal* 17, no. 1 (1994): 30–41.

Hirsch, Arnold. "Less than *Plessy:* The Inner City, Suburbs, and State-Sanctioned Residential Segregation in the Age of *Brown.*" In *The New Suburban History*, edited by Kevin Kruse and Thomas Sugrue, 33–56. Chicago: University of Chicago Press, 2006.

Hirsch, Jerrold. *Portrait of America: A Cultural History of the Federal Writers' Project.* Chapel Hill: University of North Carolina Press, 2003.

Hoopes, Roy. *Ralph Ingersoll: A Biography.* New York: Athaeneum, 1985.

Hornstein, Jeffrey. *A Nation of Realtors: A Cultural History of the Twentieth-Century American Middle Class.* Durham, NC: Duke University Press, 2006.

Horowitz, Daniel. *Betty Friedan and the Making of* the Feminine Mystique: *The American Left, the Cold War, and Modern Feminism.* Amherst: University of Massachusetts Press, 1998.

Horowitz, Daniel. *Consuming Pleasures: Intellectuals and Popular Culture in the Postwar World.* Philadelphia: University of Pennsylvania Press, 2012.

Horowitz, Daniel. "The Émigré as Celebrant of American Consumer Culture: George Katona and Ernest Dichter." In *Getting and Spending: European and American Consumer Societies in the Twentieth Century*, edited by Susan Strasser, Charles McGovern, and Matthias Judt, 149–66. New York: Cambridge University Press, 1998.

Horowitz, Daniel. "Feminism, Women's History, and American Social Thought at Midcentury." In *American Capitalism: Social Thought and Political Economy in the Twentieth Century*, edited by Nelson Lichtenstein, 191–209. Philadelphia: University of Pennsylvania Press, 2004.

Horowitz, Daniel. *The Morality of Spending: Attitudes Towards the Consumer Society in America*. Baltimore: Johns Hopkins University Press, 1985. Horowitz, Daniel. *Vance Packard and American Social Criticism*. Chapel Hill: University of North Carolina Press, 1994.

Horowitz, Irving Louis. *C. Wright Mills: An American Utopian*. New York: Free Press, 1983.

Hounshell, David. *From the American System to Mass Production, 1800–1932*. Baltimore: Johns Hopkins University Press, 1984.

Hyman, Louis. "Rethinking the Postwar Corporation: Management, Monopolies, and Markets." In *What's Good for Business: Business and American Politics since World War Two*, edited by Kim Phillips-Fein and Julian Zelizer, 195–211. New York: Oxford University Press, 2012.

Igo, Sarah. *The Averaged American: Surveys, Citizens, and the Making of a Mass Public*. Cambridge, MA: Harvard University Press, 2007.

International Typographical Union. *A Study of the History of the International Typographical Union*. Colorado Springs: ITU Executive Council, 1964.

Isserman, Maurice. *If I Had a Hammer: The Death of the Old Left and the Birth of the New Left*. New York: Basic Books, 1987.

Jacobs, Meg. *Panic at the Pump: The Energy Crisis and the Transformation of American Politics in the 1970s*. New York: Hill and Wang, 2016.

Jacobs, Meg. *Pocketbook Politics: Economic Citizenship in Twentieth-Century America*. Princeton, NJ: Princeton University Press, 2004.

Jacoby, Sanford. *Modern Manors: Welfare Capitalism since the New Deal*. Princeton, NJ: Princeton University Press, 1997.

Jeffers, Wendy. "Holger Cahill and American Art." *Archives of American Art Journal* 31, no. 4 (1991): 2–11.

Jodard, Paul. *Raymond Loewy*. London: Trefoil, 1992.

Johanningsmeier, Edward. "The Trade Union Unity League: American Communists and the Transition to Industrial Unionism, 1928–1934." *Labor History* 42 (May 2001): 159–77.

Johnston, Robert D. "Historians and the American Middle Class." In *The Middling Sorts: Explorations in the History of the American Middle Class*, edited by Burton J. Bledstein and Robert D. Johnston, 296–306. New York: Routledge, 2001.

Jordan, John. *Machine-Age Ideology: Social Engineering and American Liberalism, 1911–1939*. Chapel Hill: University of North Carolina Press, 1994.

Kammen, Michael. *The Lively Arts: Gilbert Seldes and the Transformation of Cultural Criticism in the United States*. New York: Oxford University Press, 1996.

Kantor, Sybil Gordon. *Alfred H. Barr and the Intellectual Origins of the Museum of Modern Art*. Cambridge, MA: MIT Press, 2002.

Kassalow, Everett M. "White-Collar Unionism in the United States." In *White-Collar Trade Unions: Contemporary Developments in Industrialized Societies*, edited by Adolf Strurmthal, 305–64. Urbana: University of Illinois Press, 1967.

Katznelson, Ira. *Fear Itself: The New Deal and the Origins of Our Time*. New York: Norton, 2013.

Kelley, Robin. "Notes on Deconstructing 'The Folk.'" *American Historical Review* 97, no. 5 (1992): 1400–108.

Kempton, Murray. *Part of Our Time: Some Ruins and Monuments of the Thirties*. New York: Simon and Schuster, 1955.

Kennedy, David. *Freedom from Fear: The American People in Depression and War, 1929–1945*. New York: Oxford University Press, 1999.

Kentgens-Craig, Margaret. *The Bauhaus and America: First Contacts, 1919–1936*. Cambridge, MA: MIT Press, 1999.

Kessler-Harris, Alice. *In Pursuit of Equity: Women, Men, and the Quest for Economic Citizenship in Twentieth-Century America*. New York: Oxford University Press, 2001.

Kiernan, Thomas. *Citizen Murdoch*. New York: Dodd, Mead & Co., 1986.

Kinter, Charles. "The Changing Pattern of the Newspaper Publishing Industry." *American Journal of Economics and Sociology* 5, no. 1 (1945): 43–63.

Kirkham, Pat. "Humanizing Modernism: The Crafts, 'Functioning Decoration,' and the Eameses." *Journal of Design History* 11, no. 1 (1998): 15–27.

Klehr, Harvey. *The Heyday of American Communism: The Depression Decade*. New York: Basic Books, 1984.

Klehr, Harvey, John Earl Haynes, and Kyrill Anderson. *The Soviet World of American Communism*. New Haven, CT: Yale University Press, 1998.

Klein, Jennifer. *For All These Rights: Business, Labor, and the Shaping of America's Public-Private Welfare State*. Princeton, NJ: Princeton University Press, 2003.

Kluger, Richard. *The Paper: The Life and Death of the* New York Herald Tribune. New York: Knopf, 1986.

Kocka, Jürgen. *White-Collar Workers in America, 1890–1940: A Social-Political History in International Perspective*. Translated by Maura Kealey. Beverly Hills, CA: Sage Publications, 1980.

Kopczuk, Wojciech, Emmanuel Saez, and Jae Song. "Earnings Inequality and Mobility in the United States: Evidence From Social Security Since 1937." *Quarterly Journal of Economics* 125 (February 2010): 91–128.

Korstad, Robert, and Nelson Lichtenstein. "Opportunities Found and Lost: Labor, Radicals, and the Early Civil Rights Movement." *Journal of American History* 75, no. 3 (1988): 786–811.

Kraszewski, Jon. *The New Entrepreneurs: An Institutional History of Television Anthology Writers*. Middletown, CT: Wesleyan University Press, 2010.

Kritzberg, Barry. "An Unfinished Chapter in White-Collar Unionism: The Formative Years of the Chicago Newspaper Guild, Local 71, American Newspaper Guild, A.F.L.-C.I.O." *Labor History* 14 (Summer 1973): 397–413.

Lang, Clarence. *Grassroots at the Gateway: Class Politics and Black Freedom Struggle in St. Louis, 1936–75*. Ann Arbor: University of Michigan Press, 2009.

Langa, Helen. "Elizabeth Olds: Gender Difference and Indifference." *Woman's Art Journal* 22, no. 2 (Fall 2001/Winter 2002): 5–11.

Lange, Alexandra. "This Year's Model: Representing Modernism to the Post-war American Corporation." *Journal of Design History* 19, no. 3 (2006): 233–48.

Leab, Daniel. *A Union of Individuals: The Formation of the American Newspaper Guild, 1933–1936*. New York: Columbia University Press, 1970.

Leach, William. *Land of Desire: Merchants, Power, and the Rise of a New American Culture*. New York: Vintage, 1993.

Lears, Jackson. *Fables of Abundance: A Cultural History of Advertising*. New York: Random House, 1994.

Lears, Jackson. "Making Fun of Popular Culture." *American Historical Review* 97, no. 5 (1992): 1417–26.

Lears, Jackson. "A Matter of Taste: Corporate Cultural Hegemony in a Mass-Consumption Society." In *Recasting America: Culture and Politics in the Age of Cold War*, edited by Lary May, 38–57. Chicago: University of Chicago Press, 1989.

Leberstein, Stephen. "Purging the Profs: The Rapp-Coudert Committee in New York, 1940–1942." In *New Studies in the Politics and Culture of U.S. Communism*, edited by Michael Brown, Randy Martin, Frank Rosengarten, and George Snedeker, 91–122. New York: Monthly Review Press, 1993.

Ledbetter, James. *Made Possible By: The Death of Public Broadcasting in the United States*. New York: Verso, 1997.

Leff, Mark. "The Politics of Sacrifice on the American Home Front in World War II." *Journal of American History* 77, no. 4 (1991): 1296–318.

Lenthall, Bruce. *Radio's America: The Great Depression and the Rise of Modern Mass Culture*. Chicago: University of Chicago Press, 2007.

Leuchtenberg, William. "Art in the Great Depression," in Townsend Ludington, ed., *A Modern Mosaic: Art and Modernism in the United States*. Chapel Hill: University of North Carolina Press, 1999, 227–55.

Levine, Lawrence. "The Folklore of Industrial Society: Popular Culture and Its Audiences." *American Historical Review* 97, no. 5 (1992): 1369–99.

Lichtenstein, Nelson. *Labor's War at Home: The CIO in World War II*. New York: Cambridge University Press, 1982.

Lichtenstein, Nelson. *Walter Reuther: The Most Dangerous Man in Detroit*. Urbana: University of Illinois Press, 1997.

Lichtman, Robert. "J. B. Matthews and the 'Counter-Subversives': Names as a Political and Financial Resource in the McCarthy Era." *American Communist History* 5, no. 1 (2006): 1–36.

Lipsitz, George. *Rainbow at Midnight: Labor and Culture in the 1940s*. Urbana: University of Illinois Press, 1994.

Loughery, John. *John Sloan: Painter and Rebel*. New York: Henry Holt, 1995.

Lynes, Russell. *The Good Old Modern: An Intimate Portrait of the Museum of Modern Art*. New York: Athenaeum, 1973.

MacLean, Nancy. *Freedom Is Not Enough: The Opening of the American Workplace*. Cambridge, MA: Harvard University Press/Russell Sage Foundation, 2006.

Marchand, Roland. *Advertising the American Dream: Making Way for Modernity, 1920–1940*. Berkeley: University of California Press, 1985.

Marchand, Roland. *Creating the Corporate Soul: The Rise of Public Relations and Corporate Imagery in American Big Business*. Berkeley: University of California Press, 1998.

Marchand, Roland. "The Designers Go to the Fair II: Norman Bel Geddes, The General Motors' 'Futurama,' and the Visit to the Factory Transformed." *Design Issues* 8 (Spring 1992): 23–40.

Margo, Robert. "Employment and Unemployment in the 1930s." *Journal of Economic Perspectives* 7, no. 2 (1993): 41–59.

Margo, Robert. "The Microeconomics of Depression Unemployment." *Journal of Economic History* 51, no. 2 (1991): 333–41.

Marquardt, Virginia. "The American Artists School: Radical Heritage and Social Content Art." *Archives of American Art Journal* 26, no. 4 (1986): 17–23.

Marshall, Jennifer. "In Form We Trust: Neoplatonism, the Gold Standard, and the *Machine Art* Show, 1934." *Art Bulletin* 90 (December 2008): 597–615.

Mathews, Jane De Hart. "Arts and the People: The New Deal Quest for Cultural Democracy." *Journal of American History* 62, no. 2 (1975): 316–39.

Matthews, Glenna. *"Just a Housewife": The Rise and Fall of Domesticity in America*. New York: Oxford University Press, 1987.

Matthews, Henry. "The Promotion of Modern Architecture by the Museum of Modern Art in the 1930s." *Journal of Design History* 7, no. 1 (1994): 43–59.

Mattson, Kevin. "John Kenneth Galbraith: Liberalism and the Politics of Cultural Critique." In *American Capitalism: Social Thought and Political Economy in the Twentieth Century*, edited by Nelson Lichtenstein, 88–108. Philadelphia: University of Pennsylvania Press, 2004.

May, Elaine Tyler. *Homeward Bound: American Families in the Cold War Era*. New York: Basic Books, 1988.

May, Elaine Tyler. "Security Against Democracy: The Legacy of the Cold War at Home." *Journal of American History* 97, no. 4 (2011): 939–57.

May, Lary. "Movie Star Politics: The Screen Actors' Guild, Cultural Conversion, and the Hollywood Red Scare." In *Recasting America: Culture and Politics in the Age of Cold War*, edited by Lary May, 125–53. Chicago: University of Chicago Press, 1989.

May, Lary. *Screening Out the Past: The Birth of Mass Culture and the Motion Picture Industry*. New York: Oxford University Press, 1980.

McCarthy, Anna. *The Citizen Machine: Governing by Television in 1950s America*. New York: New Press, 2010.

McCartin, Joseph. "'As Long as There Survives': Contemplating the Wagner Act After Eighty Years." *Labor* 14, no. 3 (Summer 2017): 21–42.

McChesney, Robert. *Telecommunications, Mass Media, and Democracy: The Battle for Control of U.S. Broadcasting, 1928–1935.* New York: Oxford University Press, 1993.

McClay, Wilfred. *The Masterless: Self and Society in Modern America.* Chapel Hill: University of North Carolina Press, 1994.

McColloch, Mark. *White-Collar Labor in Transition: The Boom Years, 1940–1970.* Westport, CT: Greenwood Press, 1983.

McComb, Mary C. *The Great Depression and the Middle Class: Experts, Collegiate Youth, and Business Ideology, 1929–1941.* New York: Routledge, 2006.

McCoy, Garnett. "The Rise and Fall of the American Artists' Congress." *Prospects* 13 (October 1988): 325–40.

McGovern, Charles. *Sold American: Consumption and Citizenship, 1890–1945.* Chapel Hill: University of North Carolina Press, 2006.

McKellar, Susie. "'The Beauty of Stark Utility': Rational Consumption in America—*Consumer Reports*, 1936–1954." In *Utility Reassessed: The Role of Ethics in the Practice of Design*, edited by Judy Attfield, 73–90. Manchester: Manchester University Press, 1999.

McKinzie, Richard. *The New Deal for Artists.* Princeton, NJ: Princeton University Press, 1973.

McMillan, John. *Smoking Typewriters: The Sixties Underground Press and the Rise of Alternative Media in America.* New York: Oxford University Press, 2011.

Meikle, Jeffrey. *Twentieth-Century Limited: Industrial Design in America, 1925–1939.* Philadelphia: Temple University Press, 1979.

Meyers, Cynthia. "Inside a Broadcasting Blacklist: *Kraft Television Theater*, 1951–1955." *Journal of American History* 105, no. 3 (2018): 589–16.

Meyerowitz, Joanne. "Beyond the Feminine Mystique: A Reassessment of Postwar Mass Culture, 1946–1958." *Journal of American History* 79, no. 4 (1993): 1455–82.

Milkman, Paul. PM: *A New Deal in Journalism.* New Brunswick, NJ: Rutgers University Press, 1997.

Milkman, Ruth. *Gender at Work: The Dynamics of Job Segregation by Sex during World War II.* Urbana: University of Illinois Press, 1987.

Monroe, Gerald. "Artists on the Barricades: The Militant Artists Union Treats with the New Deal." *Archives of American Art Journal* 18, no. 3 (1978): 20–23.

Montgomery, David. *The Fall of the House of Labor: Workers, Employers, and the State, 1865–1925.* New York: Cambridge University Press, 1987.

Moody, Kim. *An Injury to All: The Decline of American Unionism.* New York: Verso, 1988.

Morgan, Ted. *Reds: McCarthyism in Twentieth-Century America.* New York: Random House, 2003.

Morris, Charles. "Of Budgets, Taxes, and the Rise of a New Plutocracy." In *Summer in the City: John Lindsay, New York, and the American Dream*, edited by Joseph Viteritti, 81–105. Baltimore: Johns Hopkins University Press, 2014.

Moskowitz, Marina. *Standard of Living: The Measure of the Middle Class in Modern America*. Baltimore: Johns Hopkins University Press, 2004.

Mott, Frank Luther. *American Journalism: A History, 1690–1960*. New York: Macmillan, 1962.

Musher, Sharon. *Democratic Art: The New Deal's Influence on American Culture*. Chicago: University of Chicago Press, 2015.

Nasaw, David. *The Chief: The Life of William Randolph Hearst*. New York: Mariner, 2001.

Navasky, Victor. *Naming Names*. New York: Viking Press, 1980.

Newman, Kathy. *Radio Active: Advertising and Consumer Activism, 1935–1947*. Berkeley: University of California Press, 2004.

Nickles, Shelley. "More Is Better: Mass Consumption, Gender, and Postwar America." *American Quarterly* 54, no. 4 (2002): 581–622.

Nickles, Shelley. "'Preserving Women': Refrigerator Design as a Social Process in the 1930s." *Technology and Culture* 43, no. 4 (2002): 693–727.

Nissenson, Marilyn. *The Lady Upstairs: Dorothy Schiff and the* New York Post. New York: St. Martins, 2007.

Noble, David F. *America by Design: Science, Technology, and the Rise of Corporate Capitalism*. New York: Knopf, 1977.

Nye, David. *American Technological Sublime*. Cambridge, MA: MIT Press, 1994.

Nye, David. *Electrifying America: Social Meanings of a New Technology, 1890–1940*. Cambridge, MA: MIT Press, 1990.

O'Brien, Ruth. "Taking the Conservative State Seriously: Statebuilding and Restrictive Labor Practices in Postwar America." *Labor Studies Journal* 21 (Winter 1997): 33–63.

O'Connor, Alice. *Poverty Knowledge: Social Science, Social Policy, and the Poor in Twentieth-Century U.S. History*. Princeton, NJ: Princeton University Press, 2001.

Olney, Martha L. *Buy Now, Pay Later: Advertising, Credit, and Consumer Durables in the 1920s*. Chapel Hill: University of North Carolina Press, 1991.

Opler, Daniel. *For All White-Collar Workers: The Possibilities of Radicalism in New York City's Department Store Unions, 1934–1953*. Columbus: Ohio State University Press, 2007.

Orvell, Miles. *The Real Thing: Imitation and Authenticity in American Culture, 1880–1940*. Chapel Hill: University of North Carolina Press, 1989.

Osman, Suleiman. *Inventing Brownstone Brooklyn: Gentrification and the Search for Authenticity in Postwar New York*. New York: Oxford University Press, 2011.

Patterson, James T. *Grand Expectations: The United States, 1945–1974*. New York: Oxford University Press, 1996.

Pells, Richard. *The Liberal Mind in a Conservative Age: American Intellectuals in the 1940s and 1950s*. New York: Vintage, 1985.

Pells, Richard. *Radical Visions and American Dreams: Culture and Social Thought in the Depression Years*. New York: Harper and Row, 1973.

Phillips, Lisa. *A Renegade Union: Interracial Organizing and Radical Unionism*. Urbana: University of Illinois Press, 2012.

Phillips-Fein, Kim. *Fear City: New York's Fiscal Crisis and the Rise of Austerity Politics.* New York: Metropolitan Books, 2017.

Phillips-Fein, Kim. *Invisible Hands: The Making of the Conservative Movement from the New Deal to Reagan.* New York: Norton, 2009.

Pickard, Victor. *America's Battle for Media Democracy: The Triumph of Corporate Libertarianism and the Future of Media Reform.* New York: Cambridge University Press, 2015.

Piketty, Thomas, and Emanuel Saez. "The Evolution of Top Incomes: A Historical and International Perspective," *American Economic Review* 96 (2006): 200–205.

Piketty, Thomas, and Emanuel Saez. "Income Inequality in the United States, 1913–1998," *Quarterly Journal of Economics* 118 (February 2003): 1–39.

Platt, Susan. *Art and Politics in the 1930s: Modernism, Marxism, Americanism.* New York: Midmarch Arts Press, 1999.

Pommer, Richard. "The Architecture of Urban Housing in the United States during the Early 1930s." *Journal of the Society of Architectural Historians* 37 (December 1978): 235–64.

Pope, Daniel. "His Master's Voice: James Rorty and the Critique of Advertising." *Maryland History* 19 (Spring/Summer 1988): 5–16.

Pope, Daniel. *The Making of Modern Advertising.* New York: Basic Books, 1983.

Porter, Glenn. *Raymond Loewy: Design for a Consumer Culture.* Wilmington: Hagley Museum and Library, 2002.

Prendergast, Curtis, with Geoffrey Colvin. *The World of Time Inc. The Intimate History of a Changing Enterprise, Volume Three: 1960–1980.* New York: Athenaeum, 1986.

Pulos, Arthur J. *American Design Adventure, 1940–1975.* Cambridge, MA: MIT Press, 1988.

Pulos, Arthur J. *American Design Ethic: A History of Industrial Design to 1940.* Cambridge, MA: MIT Press, 1983.

Pulos, Arthur J. "Nothing Succeeds Like Success: Raymond Loewy: The Thirties and Forties." In *Raymond Loewy: Pioneer of American Industrial Design*, edited by Angela Schönberger, 75–86. Munich: Prestel-Verlag, 1990.

Quirke, Carol. *Eyes on Labor: News Photography and America's Working Class.* New York: Oxford University Press, 2012.

Rabinowitz, Paula. "Voyeurism and Class Consciousness: James Agee and Walker Evans' *Let Us Now Praise Famous Men.*" *Cultural Critique* no. 21 (Spring 1992): 143–70.

Radford, Gail. *Modern Housing in America, Policy Struggles in the New Deal Era.* Chicago: University of Chicago Press, 1996.

Radway, Janice. *Reading the Romance: Women, Patriarchy, and Popular Literature.* Rev ed. Chapel Hill: University of North Carolina Press, 1991.

Razlogova, Elena. *The Listener's Voice: Early Radio and the American Public.* Philadelphia: University of Pennsylvania Press, 2011.

Reese, Elizabeth. "Design and the American Dream: Associates of Loewy." In *Raymond Loewy: Pioneer of American Industrial Design*, edited by Angela Schönberger, 39–49. Munich: Prestel-Verlag, 1990.

Rhomberg, Chris. *The Broken Table: The Detroit Newspaper Strike and the State of American Labor*. New York: Russell Sage Foundation, 2012.

Roberts, Jason. "New Evidence in the Hiss Case: From the HUAC Files and the Hiss Grand Jury." *American Communist History* 1, no. 2 (2002): 143–62.

Rogin, Michael. "How the Working Class Saved Capitalism: The New Labor History and *The Devil and Miss Jones*." *Journal of American History* 89 (June 2002): 87–114.

Ross, Andrew. "The Mental Labor Problem." *Social Text* 18 (Summer 2000): 1–31.

Ross, Dorothy. *The Origins of American Social Science*. New York: Cambridge University Press, 1991.

Ross, Phyllis. "Merchandising the Modern: Gilbert Rohde at Herman Miller." *Journal of Design History* 17, no. 4 (2004): 359–76.

Rosswurm, Steve. "The Catholic Church and the Left-Led Unions: Labor Priests, Labor Schools, and the ACTU." In *The CIO's Left-Led Unions*, edited by Steve Rosswurm, 119–37. New Brunswick, NJ: Rutgers University Press, 1992.

Rybczynski, Witold. *Home: A Short History of an Idea*. New York: Penguin, 1987.

Saab, A. Joan. *For the Millions: American Art and Culture Between the Wars*. Philadelphia: University of Pennsylvania Press, 2004.

Saab, A. Joan. "Historical Amnesia: New Urbanism and the City of Tomorrow." *Journal of Planning History* 6 (August 2007): 191–213.

Samuel, Lawrence. *Brought to You By: Postwar Television Advertising and the American Dream*. Austin: University of Texas Press, 2001.

Sbardellati, John. "'The Maltz Affair' Revisited: How the American Communist Party Relinquished Its Cultural Influence at the Dawn of the Cold War." *Cold War History* 9, no. 4 (2009): 489–500.

Schneirov, Matthew. *The Dream of a New Social Order: Popular Magazines in America, 1893–1914*. New York: Columbia University Press, 1994.

Schrecker, Ellen. *Many Were the Crimes: McCarthyism in America*. Princeton, NJ: Princeton University Press, 1998.

Schrecker, Ellen. "McCarthyism and the Labor Movement: The Role of the State." In *The CIO's Left-Led Unions*, edited by Steve Rosswurm, 139–57. New Brunswick, NJ: Rutgers University Press, 1992.

Schudson, Michael. *Discovering the News: A Social History of American Newspapers*. New York: Basic Books, 1978.

Schwartz, Joel. *The New York Approach: Robert Moses, Urban Liberals, and the Redevelopment of the Inner City*. Columbus: Ohio State University Press, 1993.

Scott, Felicity. *Architecture or Techno-Utopianism: Politics after Modernism*. Cambridge, MA: MIT Press, 2007.

Scott, William, and Peter Rutkoff. *New York Modern: The Arts and the City*. Baltimore: Johns Hopkins University Press, 1999.

Seltzer, George. *Music Matters: The Performer and the American Federation of Musicians*. Metuchen, NJ: Scarecrow Press, 1989.

Sklar, Martin. *The Corporate Reconstruction of American Capitalism, 1890–1916: The Market, the Law, and Politics.* New York: Cambridge University Press, 1988.

Sleeper, Jim. *The Closest of Strangers: Liberalism and the Politics of Race in New York.* New York: Norton, 1990.

Smith, Terry. *Making the Modern: Industry, Art, and Design in America.* Chicago: University of Chicago Press, 1993.

Snyder, Carl. *White-Collar Workers and the UAW.* Urbana: University of Illinois Press, 1973.

Sobek, Matthew. "New Statistics on the U.S. Labor Force, 1850–1990." *Historical Methods* 34, no. 2 (Spring 2001): 71–87.

Sobek, Matthew. "Work, Status, and Income: Men in the American Occupational Structure since the Late Nineteenth Century." *Social Science History* 20, no. 2 (1996): 169–207.

Soffer, Jonathan. *Ed Koch and the Rebuilding of New York City.* New York: Columbia University Press, 2010.

Sparrow, James. *Warfare State: World War II Americans and the Age of Big Government.* New York: Oxford University Press, 2011.

Spiegel, Lynn. *Make Room for TV: Television and the Family Ideal in Postwar America.* Chicago: University of Chicago Press, 1992.

Stamm, Michael. *Dead Tree Media: Manufacturing the Newspaper in Twentieth-Century North America.* Baltimore: Johns Hopkins University Press, 2018.

Stamm, Michael. *Sound Business: Newspapers, Radio, and the Politics of New Media.* Philadelphia: University of Pennsylvania Press, 2011.

Staniszewski, Barbara. *The Power of Display: A History of Exhibition Installations at the Museum of Modern Art.* Cambridge, MA: MIT Press, 1998.

Stein, Judith. *Pivotal Decade: How the United States Traded Factories for Finance in the 1970s.* New Haven, CT: Yale University Press, 2010.

Stein, Judith. *Running Steel, Running America: Race, Economic Policy, and the Decline of American Liberalism.* Chapel Hill: University of North Carolina Press, 1998.

Sterling, Christopher H. and Michael C. Keith, *Sounds of Change: A History of FM Broadcasting.* Chapel Hill: University of North Carolina Press, 2008.

Stock, Catherine McNicol. *Main Street in Crisis: The Great Depression and the Old Middle Class on the Northern Plains.* Chapel Hill: University of North Carolina Press, 1992.

Stole, Inger. *Advertising on Trial: Consumer Activism and Corporate Public Relations in the 1930s.* Urbana: University of Illinois Press, 2006.

Stoltzfus, Duane. *Freedom from Advertising: E. W. Scripps's Chicago Experiment.* Urbana: University of Illinois Press, 2007.

Stone, Katherine Van Wezel. "Imagining a New Labor Law for a New Era of Work." *Labor* 14, no. 3 (Summer 2017): 55–59.

Stone, Katherine Van Wezel. "The Legacy of Industrial Pluralism: The Tension between Individual Employment Rights and the New Deal Collective Bargaining System." *University of Chicago Law Review* 59, no. 2 (1992): 575–644.

Stone, Katherine Van Wezel. "The Post-War Paradigm in American Labor Law." *Yale Law Journal* 90, no. 7 (1981): 1509–80.

Strom, Sharon Hartman. *Beyond the Typewriter: Gender, Class, and the Origins of Modern American Office Work, 1900–1930*. Urbana: University of Illinois Press, 1992.

Strom, Sharon Hartman. "'We're No Kitty Foyles': Organizing Office Workers for the Congress of Industrial Organizations, 1937–1950." In *Women, Work and Protest: A Century of Women's Labor History*, edited by Ruth Milkman, 211–26. Boston: Routledge, 1985.

Storrs, Landon. "Red Scare Politics and the Suppression of Popular Front Feminism: The Loyalty Investigation of Mary Dublin Keyserling." *Journal of American History* 90, no. 2 (2003): 491–524.

Storrs, Landon. *The Second Red Scare and the Unmaking of the New Deal Left*. Princeton, NJ: Princeton University Press, 2013.

Sugrue, Thomas. *Origins of the Urban Crisis: Race and Inequality in Postwar Detroit*. Princeton, NJ: Princeton University Press, 1996.

Suisman, David. *Selling Sounds: The Commercial Revolution in American Music*. Cambridge, MA: Harvard University Press, 2009.

Sullivan, Patricia. *Days of Hope: Race and Democracy in the New Deal Era*. Chapel Hill: University of North Carolina Press, 1996.

Sumner, Gregory. *Dwight Macdonald and the politics Circle: The Challenge of Cosmopolitan Democracy*. Ithaca, NY: Cornell University Press, 1996.

Swerdlow, Amy. "The Congress of American Women: Left-Feminist Peace Politics in the Cold War." In *U.S. History as Women's History: New Feminist Essays*, edited by Linda Kerber, Alice Kessler-Harris, and Kathryn Kish Sklar, 296–312. Chapel Hill: University of North Carolina Press, 1995.

Taft, Maggie. "Better Than Before: László Moholy-Nagy and the New Bauhaus in Chicago." In *Chicago Makes Modern: How Creative Minds Changed Society*, edited by Mary Jane Jacobs and Jacquelynn Baas, 31–43. Chicago: University of Chicago Press, 2012.

Tedlow, Richard. *New and Improved: The Story of Mass Marketing in America*. New York: Basic Books, 1990.

Tifft, Susan, and Alex Jones. *The Trust: The Private and Powerful Family behind* The New York Times. New York: Back Bay/Hachette, 1999.

Tomlins, Christopher. "The New Deal, Collective Bargaining, and the Triumph of Industrial Pluralism." *Industrial and Labor Relations Review* 39, no. 1 (1985): 19–34.

Topping, Simon. "'Never Argue with the Gallup Poll': Thomas Dewey, Civil Rights, and the Election of 1948." *Journal of American Studies* 38, no. 2 (2004): 179–98.

Turk, Katherine. *Equality on Trial: Gender and Rights in the Modern American Workplace*. Philadelphia: University of Pennsylvania Press, 2016.

Vanderlan, Robert. *Intellectuals Incorporated: Politics, Art, and Ideas inside Henry Luce's Media Empire*. Philadelphia: University of Pennsylvania Press, 2010.

Vinel, Jean-Christian. *The Employee: A Political History*. Philadelphia: University of Pennsylvania Press, 2013.

Wald, Alan. *American Night: The Literary Left in the Era of the Cold War*. Chapel Hill: University of North Carolina Press, 2012.

Weigand, Kate. *Red Feminism: American Communism and the Making of Women's Liberation*. Baltimore: Johns Hopkins University Press, 2001.

Weingarten, Marc. *The Gang that Wouldn't Write Straight: Wolfe, Thompson, and the New Journalism Revolution*. New York: Crown, 2005.

Weinstein, David. *The Forgotten Network: DuMont and the Birth of American Television*. Philadelphia: Temple University Press, 2004.

Wells, Richard. "The Labor of Reality TV: The Case of *The Deadliest Catch*." *Labor* 12, no. 4 (2015): 33–49.

Westbrook, Robert. "'I Want a Girl, Just Like the Girl that Married Harry James': American Women and the Problem of Political Obligation in World War II," *American Quarterly* 42, no. 4 (1990): 587–614.

Westbrook, Robert. "Tribune of the Technostructure: The Popular Economics of Stuart Chase." *American Quarterly* 32, no. 4 (1980): 387–408.

White, Graham, and John Maze. *Henry A. Wallace: His Search for a New World Order*. Chapel Hill: University of North Carolina Press, 1995.

White, Timothy. *Blue-Collar Broadway: The Craft and Industry of American Theater*. Philadelphia: University of Pennsylvania Press, 2015.

Williams, Raymond. *Culture and Materialism: Selected Essays*. London: Verso, 1980.

Williams, Raymond. *Marxism and Literature*. Oxford: Oxford University Press, 1977.

Williams, Raymond. *Television: Technology and Cultural Form*. New York: Schocken, 1975.

Windham, Lane. *Knocking on Labor's Door: Union Organizing in the 1970s and the Roots of a New Economic Divide*. Chapel Hill: University of North Carolina Press, 2017.

Winton, Alexandra. "'A Man's House is His Art': The Walker Art Center's Idea House Project and the Marketing of Domestic Design, 1941–1947." *Journal of Design History* 17 (2004): 377–96.

Witwer, David. "Westbrook Pegler and the Anti-Union Movement," *Journal of American History* 92, no. 2 (2005): 527–52.

Woloch, Nancy. *A Class by Herself: Protective Laws for Women Workers, 1890s-1990s*. New York: Oxford University Press, 2015.

Workman, Andrew. "Creating the National War Labor Board: Franklin Roosevelt and the Politics of State Building in the Early 1940s." *Journal of Policy History* 12, no. 2 (2000): 233–64.

Wreszin, Michael. *A Rebel in Defense of Tradition: The Life and* politics *of Dwight Macdonald*. New York: Basic Books, 1994.

Wright, Bradford. *Comic Book Nation: The Transformation of Youth Culture in America*. Baltimore: Johns Hopkins University Press, 2003.

Wright, Gwendolyn. *Moralism and the Model Home: Domestic Architecture and Cultural Conflict in Chicago, 1873–1913*. Chicago: University of Chicago Press, 1980.

Ziegler, Robert. *The CIO, 1935–1955*. Chapel Hill: University of North Carolina Press, 1995.

Zunz, Olivier. *Making America Corporate, 1870–1920*. Chicago: University of Chicago Press, 1990.

Index

For the benefit of digital users, indexed terms that span two pages (e.g., 52–53) may, on occasion, appear on only one of those pages.